The Rough Guide to

Crete

written and researched by

John Fisher and Geoff Garvey

ROUGH
GUIDES

NEW YORK • LONDON • DELHI

www.roughguides.com

△ Orthodox chapel

Introduction to

Crete

Crete is a great deal more than just another Greek island. Much of the time, especially in the cities or along the developed north coast, it doesn't feel like an island at all, but a substantial land in its own right. Which of course it is – a mountainous, wealthy and at times surprisingly cosmopolitan one with a tremendous and unique history. There are two big cities, Iráklion and Haniá, a host of sizeable, historic towns, and an island culture which is uniquely Cretan: the Turks were in occupation little over a hundred years ago, and the Greek flag raised for the first time only in 1913.

Long before, Crete was distinguished as the home of Europe's earliest civilization. It was only at the beginning of the twentieth century that the legends of King Minos, and of a Cretan society that ruled the Greek world in prehistory, were confirmed by excavations at Knossós and Festós. Yet **the Minoans** had a remarkably advanced and cultured society, at the centre of a substantial maritime trading empire, as early as 2000 BC. The artworks produced on Crete at this time are unsurpassed anywhere in the ancient world, and it seems clear, wandering through the Minoan palaces and towns, that life on Crete in those days was good. The apparently peaceful Minoan culture survived a number of major disasters, following each of which the palaces were rebuilt on an even grander scale. It is only after a third catastrophe that significant numbers of weapons start to appear in the ruins, probably because Mycenaean Greeks had taken control of the island. Nevertheless, for nearly five hundred years,

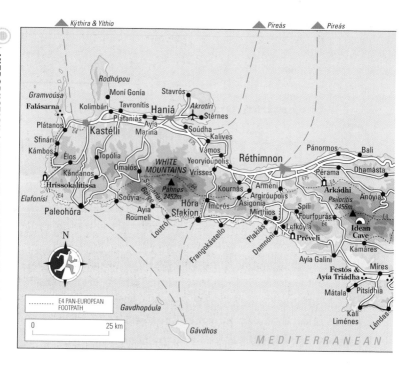

by far the longest period of peace the island has seen, Crete was home to a civilization well ahead of its time.

The Minoans are believed to have come originally from Anatolia, and the island's position as meeting point – and strategic fulcrum – between

▽ Cretan door sign

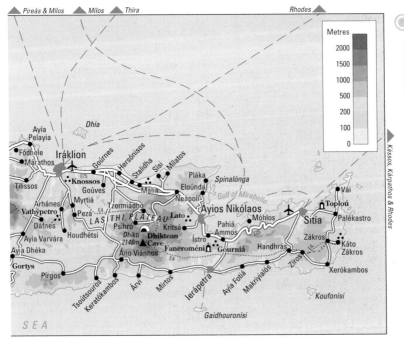

east and west has played a crucial role in its **subsequent history**. Control passed from Greeks to Romans to Saracens, through the Byzantine Empire to Venice, and finally to Turkey for two hundred years. During World War II Crete was occupied by the Germans, and gained the dubious distinction of being the first place to be successfully invaded by parachute. Each one of these diverse rulers has left some mark, and more importantly they have moulded the islanders and forged for the land a personality toughened by endless struggles for independence.

Today, with a flourishing agricultural economy, Crete is one of the few Greek islands that could support itself without tourists. Nevertheless, tourism is heavily promoted, and is rapidly taking over parts of the island altogether. Along the populous **north coast**, Crete can be as sophisticated as you want it, and the northeast, in particular, can be depressingly overdeveloped. In the less known coastal reaches of the **south** it's still possible to find yourself alone, but even here places which have not yet been reached are getting harder and

> Crete's mystery is extremely deep. Whoever sets foot on this island senses a mysterious force branching warmly and beneficently through his veins, senses his soul begin to grow.
>
> Níkos Kazantzákis, *Report to Greco*

v

Fact file

- Some 260km long and ranging between 15km and 60km in breadth, Crete is the largest of the Greek islands and the fifth largest in the Mediterranean, with a **land area** of 8300 square kilometres and a population of 550,000.

- Crete is one of Greece's ten administrative regions returning sixteen members to the Greek national parliament. The island is made up of **four provinces** or nomes, with its **capital** at the north-coast seaport of **Iráklion** (pop. 130,000). The island's other three provincial capitals – Haniá (pop. 60,000), Réthimnon (pop. 20,000) and Áyios Nikólaos (pop. 7000) – are the focus for local government and cultural activities.

- Agriculture and tourism are the mainstays of the Cretan economy. Half the island's territory is devoted to agriculture, with olives, grapes and citrus fruit the main crops, whilst over two million visitors take holidays here each year.

- Crete has attracted **invaders** throughout its history. Europe's first civilization, the Minoans, were the earliest known colonizers, but Dorian Greeks, Romans, Arabs, Byzantines, Venetians, Turks and the Germans in World War II all conquered the island in their turn.

- Crete's dominant **religion** is the Greek Orthodox creed.

harder to find. By contrast, the high mountains of the interior are barely touched, and one of the best things to do on Crete is to hire a vehicle and head for remoter villages, often only a few kilometres off some heavily beaten track.

The **mountains**, which dominate the view as you approach and make all but the shortest journey inland an expedition, are perhaps the most rewarding aspect of Crete. In the west, the White Mountains are snowcapped right into June, Psilorítis (Mount Ida) in the centre is higher still, and in the east the heights continue through the Dhíkti and Sitía ranges to form a continuous chain from one end of the island to the other. They make a relatively small place feel much larger: there are still many places where the roads cannot reach.

▽ Lighthouse at Haniá

Cretan goats

Goats have been around a long time in Crete and Greece and have even lent their name (*tragos* in ancient Greek) to one of the major forms of drama. This came about because of the ancient Greek ritual of sacrificing a goat to the god of wine, Dionysos, to thank him for the vintage – the goat died because it was the enemy of the vine, and was apt to eat and destroy it. Whatever the ancients thought of them, the goats carried on regardless, and unruly flocks still roam across Cretan hillsides voraciously devouring any green leaf or shoot they find. Long ago, the mountains and hills of Crete were thickly forested with trees that attracted rainfall and held the soil. Erosion caused by centuries of cutting back the woodland, particularly in the Venetian period, has been compounded by the seedling-hungry domestic goat, whose insatiable appetite has turned vast tracts of Crete and Greece into the barren deserts of bare rock they are today – a tragedy indeed.

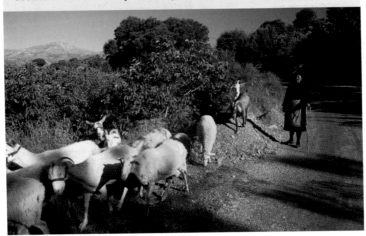

Where to go

Every part of Crete has its loyal devotees and it's hard to pick out highlights. On the whole, if you want to get away from it all you should head for the ends of the island – west, towards **Haniá** and the smaller, less well-connected places along the south and west coasts, or east to **Sitía**. Wherever you're staying though, you don't have to go far inland to escape the crowds.

Whatever you do, your first objective will probably be to leave behind the sprawling city of **Iráklion** (Heraklion) – having paid the obligatory, and rewarding, visits to the **archeological museum** and nearby

Knossós. The **Minoan sites** are of course one of the major attractions of Crete: as well as Knossós itself there are many other grand remains scattered around the centre of the island – **Festós** and **Ayía Triádha** in the south (with Roman **Górtys** to provide contrast) and **Mália** on the north coast. Almost wherever you go though, you'll find some kind of reminder of this history – the Minoan town of **Gourniá** and the Dorian Greek sites of **Drirós** and **Lató** near the tourist enticements of **Áyios Nikólaos**, the palace of **Zákros** over in the far east or Roman **Áptera** and a host of lesser sites scattered around the west.

For many people, unexpected highlights also turn out to be Crete's **Venetian forts** and defensive **walls and bastions** – dominant at **Réthimnon**, **Iráklion** and **Haniá**, magnificent at **Frangokástello**, and found in various stages of ruin around most of the island. **Byzantine**

churches and remote **monasteries**, many containing stunning medieval **wall paintings**, are Crete's other glories; the most famous frescoes are at **Kritsá** but, again, they can be discovered almost anywhere, with fine clusters in the south and west of Haniá province. The smaller Cretan **towns**,

▽ Village street

supply centres for the island's farmers, are always worth visiting for their vibrant markets, shops and tavernas, whilst larger conurbations like **Réthimnon** and **Haniá** are atmospheric, cluttered old places with mysterious corners full of Venetian and Turkish relics.

The mountains and valleys of the interior also deserve far more attention than they get. Only the **Lasíthi** plateau in the east and the **Samariá Gorge** in the west really see large numbers of visitors, but almost anywhere you can turn off the main roads and find agricultural villages going about their daily life, and often astonishingly beautiful scenery. This is especially true in the west, where the Lefká Óri – the **White Mountains** – dramatically dominate every view, and numerous lesser gorges run parallel to the Samariá one down to the Libyan Sea. But there's lovely country behind Iráklion too, in the foothills of the Psilorítis range, and especially on the other side of these mountains in the **Amári valley**, easily reached from Réthimnon. The east also has its moments, in the **Dhíkti range**, the spectacular cliff-top drive from Áyios Nikólaos to Sitía and the isolated stretch of picturesque coastline lapped by a turquoise sea, to the south of Zákros. Things have been improved for **walkers** in these zones by the upgrading and waymarking of the **E4 Pan-European Footpath** (see map), which crosses the island from east to west, taking in some of its most stunning scenery.

As for **beaches**, you'll find great ones almost anywhere on the north coast. From Iráklion to Áyios Nikólaos there's very heavy development, and most package tourists are aiming for the resort hotels here. These places can be fun if nightlife and crowds are what you're after – especially the biggest of them, like **Mália**, **Hersónisos** and **Áyios Nikólaos**, which have the added advantage of being large enough to have plenty of cheap food and accommodation, plus good transport links. Mália and Hersónisos also have sand as good as any on the island (if you can find it

Village Crete

Despite the rapid urban growth in the last fifty years of towns like Haniá, Réthimnon and particularly Iráklion, Crete remains a land rooted in its villages. These villages are the island's pulse, each with its own character and traditions where the pace of the year is determined by the agricultural calendar. In the villages you can still find everyday life lived as it has been for centuries, where potters spin clay into ewers and jars, weavers make rugs in traditional patterns and farmers cart their olives to the local press. At the end of a day the men unwind with a relaxing *raki* at the local *kafenío* whilst the women prepare the evening meal.

through the crowds), but Áyios Nikólaos really doesn't have much of a beach of its own. Further east things get quieter: **Sitía** is a place of real character, and beyond it on the east coast are a number of beautifully tranquil places – especially **Zákros** and **Kserókambos** – although in high

summer the beautiful palm beach at **Vái** gets incredibly crowded with day-trippers. To the west there's another tranche of development around **Réthimnon**, but the town itself is relatively unscathed, and a rather lesser cluster of apartments and smaller hotels near **Haniá**, the most attractive of the bigger towns. Other places at this end of the island tend to be on a smaller scale.

Along the **south coast**, resorts are far more scattered, and the

mountains come straight down to the sea much of the way along. Only a handful of places are really developed – **Ierápetra**, **Ayía Galíni**, **Mátala**, **Paleohóra** – and a few more, like **Plakiás** and **Makriyialós**, on their way. But lesser spots in between, not always easy to get to, are some of the most attractive in Crete.

When to go

As the southernmost of all Greek islands, Crete has by far the longest summers: you can get a decent tan here right into October and swim at least from April until early November. **Spring** is the prime time to come: in April and May the island is relatively empty of visitors, the weather clear and not overpoweringly hot, and every scene is brightened by a profusion of wildflowers.

By mid-June the rush is beginning. **July** and **August** are not only the hottest, the most crowded and most expensive months, they are also intermittently blighted by fierce winds and accompanying high seas, which make boat trips very uncomfortable, and at their worst can mean staying indoors for a day or more at a time. The south coast is particularly prone to these. In September the crowds gradually begin to thin out, and **autumn** can again be a great time to visit – but now the landscape looks parched and tired, and there's a feeling of things gradually winding down.

△ Lakki

Winters are mild, but also vaguely depressing: many things are shut, it can rain sporadically, sometimes for days, and there's far less life in the streets. In the mountains it snows, even to the extent where villages can be cut off; on the south coast it's generally warmer, soothed by a breeze from Africa. You may get a week or more of really fine weather in the middle of winter, but equally you can have sudden viciously cold snaps right through into March.

Crete's weather

	Jan	Feb	Mar	Apr	May	Jun	Jul	Aug	Sep	Oct	Nov	Dec
Average daytime temperature												
°C	12	12	14	17	21	23	25	26	25	21	18	14
°F	52	52	57	62	70	74	77	79	77	70	64	57
Average water temperature												
°C	15	15	16	17	20	23	24	25	24	23	19	17
°F	59	59	61	62	68	74	75	77	75	74	66	62
Average rainy days												
	14	11	8	6	3	1	0	0	2	6	8	12

things not to miss

It's not possible to see everything that Crete has to offer in one trip – and we don't suggest you try. What follows is a selective and subjective taste of the island's highlights, from world-famous archeological sites to stunning mountains and gorges, lively resorts and great beaches. They're arranged in five colour-coded categories to help you find the very best things to see, do and experience. All entries have a page reference to take you straight into the Guide, where you can find out more.

01 Haniá Page **309** • Wander the streets of Haniá's old town, to discover its beautiful harbour and haunting vestiges of the Venetian and Ottoman past.

02 Loutró Page **355** • Reachable only by boat or on foot, this tiny idyllic retreat on the edge of its own bay is the perfect place to get away from it all.

04 Archeological Museum, Iráklion Page **87** • A visit to Crete's major museum reveals the world's finest collection of Minoan frescoes, jewellery, ceramics and sculpture.

03 Margarítes potters' village Page **262** • Carrying on an island tradition thousands of years old, the potters of Margarítes turn out a variety of ceramic wares, including giant *píthoi*.

05 **Spinalónga** Page **186** • A visit to the forbidding islet of Spinalónga makes for a memorable excursion – once an impregnable Venetian fortress, it later served as a leper colony, the last of its kind in Europe.

06 **Knossós** Page **101** • Crete's biggest attraction, this remarkable 3500-year-old Minoan palace is a sprawling maze of royal chambers, grand staircases, storerooms, workshops and the oldest throne room in Europe.

07 **Górtys** Page **138** • The enormous basilica of Ayíos Títos stands at the centre of the island's most extensive Greco-Roman city.

08 **Vái beach**
Page **209** • This shimmering white-sand beach is fringed with exotic palm trees, claimed to be Europe's only wild date-palm grove.

09 **Markets** Page **315** • The colourful markets of Haniá and Iráklion sell everything from Cretan cheese and herbs to baskets, bags and traditional leather boots.

11 Samariá Gorge Page **348** • Europe's longest gorge is both a spectacular natural wonder and a magnet for hikers.

10 Lyra music Page **458** • The three stringed *lyra* is Crete's "national" instrument – no baptism party, wedding feast or celebration is complete without its accompaniment.

12 Áyios Nikólaos Page **177** • Overlooking twin harbours from its hillside setting, this is one of the island's most picturesque towns.

13 Réthimnon Page **241** • Fanning out around its Venetian harbour, and lit by terraces of fish tavernas at night, elegant Réthimnon has museums, Venetian and Turkish monuments, and a fine beach.

14 Mátala Page **149** • Explore ancient burial caves cut into the cliffs overlooking Mátala's fabulous beach, also famed for its spectacular crimson sunsets.

xx

15 **Kalathás, Akrotíri** Page **321** • Explore the ruggedly beautiful Akrotíri peninsula, with its superb beaches and ancient monasteries – it's also where *Zorba the Greek* was filmed.

16 Moní Arkádhi Page **252** • Crete's most celebrated monastery with its fine Venetian church is an emblem of the island's struggle for independence.

17 Byzantine frescoes Page **187** • Some of the finest Byzantine frescoes in Greece are found in Crete's country churches, the most famous of which is the Panayía Kirá in Kritsá.

18 Birds of prey Page **443** • Griffon vultures are just one of the large and dramatic birds of prey that are a common sight in the mountains of Crete.

19 **Kouremenos beach** Page **211**
At the island's eastern tip, this is Crete's major windsurfing location.

20 **Windmills** Page **172** •
Traditional windmills are a feature of rural Crete – on the Lasíthi plateau they are still used to raise water for irrigation.

21 **Country churches** Page **115** • Ancient chapels and churches in stunning locations are a Cretan speciality: the Church of the Panayía at Fódhele is a fine example.

22 **Iraklion** Page **73** •
Crete's capital offers a host of monuments, museums and churches, and its harbour is over-looked by a magnificent Venetian fortress.

23 **Paleohóra** Page **385** • The major resort of southwest Crete, Paleohóra has fine beaches and bags of laid-back charm.

24 **Wine and raki** Page **47** • Wine has been made on Crete for thousands of years and *raki* spirit – made from the pips and stalks left behind – is the most popular icebreaker.

25 **The kafeníon** Page **47** • A focal point of Cretan life, the *kafeníon* is a great place to discuss or play *távli* (backgammon) whilst downing a coffee, ouzo or a fiery *raki*.

26 **Elafonísi** Page **382** • A turquoise sea, rose-tinted sands and shallow, warm waters make this coral reef lagoon one of Crete's most exotic locations.

27 **Fish and seafood**
Page **46** • Crete is a wonderful place for dining on fish and seafood, freshly landed from the hundreds of fishing boats that bring in the catch.

28 **Sitía** Page **200** • Set around a beautiful bay, one of the island's most easy-going towns is an excellent base for touring the east.

Contents

Using this Rough Guide

We've tried to make this Rough Guide a good read and easy to use. The book is divided into six main sections, and you should be able to find whatever you want in one of them.

Colour section

The front colour section offers a quick tour of Crete. The **introduction** aims to give you a feel for the island, with suggestions on where to go. We also tell you what the weather is like and include a basic fact file. Next, our authors round up their favourite aspects of Crete in the **things not to miss** section – whether it's world-famous archeological sites, great beaches, stunning mountain scenery or atmospheric old towns. Right after this comes a full **contents** list.

Basics

The Basics section covers all the **pre-departure** nitty-gritty to help you plan your trip. This is where to find out how to get to your destination, what paperwork you'll need, what to do about money and insurance, about Internet access, food, security, public transport, car rental – in fact just about every piece of **general practical information** you might need.

Guide

This is the heart of the Rough Guide, divided into user-friendly chapters, each of which covers a specific province. Every chapter starts with a list of **highlights** and an **introduction** that helps you to decide where to go, depending on your time and budget. Likewise, introductions to the various towns and smaller regions

within each chapter should help you plan your itinerary. We start most town accounts with information on arrival and accommodation, followed by a tour of the sights, and finally reviews of places to eat and drink, and details of nightlife. Longer accounts also have a directory of practical listings. Each chapter concludes with **public transport** details for that region.

Contexts

Read Contexts to get a deeper understanding of what makes Crete tick. We include a brief history, articles about archeology, Crete in myth, wildlife, Cretan music and a detailed further reading section that reviews dozens of **books** relating to the island.

Language

The **language** section gives useful guidance for speaking Greek and pulls together all the vocabulary you might need on your trip, including a comprehensive menu reader.

Index + small print

Apart from a **full index**, which includes maps as well as places, this section covers publishing information, credits and acknowledgements, and also has our contact details in case you want to send in updates and corrections to the book – or suggestions as to how we might improve it.

Chapter list and map

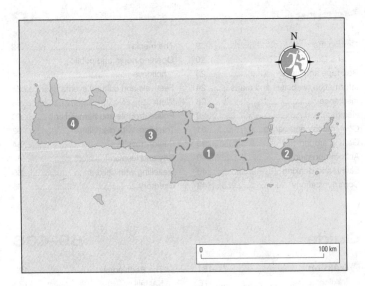

Contents

Contexts

Language

Small print and Index

Basics

Basics

Getting there

It's no surprise that by far the easiest way to get to Crete is to fly. There are no direct, scheduled international flights to the island, and the vast majority of visitors are Northern Europeans on a package tour that includes a charter flight direct to Crete.

Even if your starting point is North America, Australia or New Zealand, the most cost-effective way to reach Crete may well be to get to London – or Amsterdam or many other Northern European cities – and pick up a charter from there. The chief disadvantage of charters is their lack of flexibility – usually they go once a week with a maximum stay of three weeks. Anyone planning a longer visit will have to fly to Athens and take a domestic flight or the ferry from there; see p.19 for details of connections.

Airfares depend on the season, with the highest – especially for charters and packages – in July, August and Easter week. May, June and September are also popular: you'll get the best prices on flights to Athens during the low season, November to March (excluding Christmas and New Year weeks, when prices are hiked up and seats are at a premium). Few charters operate through the winter, though.

There are two main **airports** on Crete, at Iráklion (Heraklion) for the centre and east of the island, and at Haniá (Chania) for the west. Both have regular charters from across Europe, and several daily flights from Athens. Charters to Haniá tend to be harder to come by and slightly more expensive, but it's normally a slightly less chaotic arrival point. Sitía in the east has also had its airport upgraded in the hope of encouraging direct charters, and flying there direct may be a possibility by the time you read this. There are regular flights to Sitía from Athens.

You can often cut costs by going through a **specialist flight agent** – either a consolidator, who buys up blocks of tickets from the airlines and sells them at a discount, or a **discount agent**, who in addition to dealing with discounted flights may also offer special student and youth fares and a range of other travel-related services such as travel insurance, rail passes, car rentals, tours and the like. Be aware too that a **package deal**, with accommodation included, can sometimes be as cheap (especially from the UK) as a flight alone: tour operators offering these are listed on p.13. If you are under 26, or a full-time student, or over 60, you may well be eligible for special **student/youth or senior fares**, so it's worth asking about these.

Overland alternatives from the UK or Northern Europe involve three to four days of non-stop travel. If you want to take your time over the journey, then driving or taking the train can be enjoyable, although invariably more expensive than flying. Once in Greece, of course, you still have to negotiate the crossing to Crete (see p.19 for details).

Booking online

Many airlines and discount travel **websites** allow you to book tickets, hotels and holiday packages online, cutting out the costs of agents and middlemen. There are some bargains to be had on auction sites too, if you're prepared to bid keenly and don't mind the inflexibility of nonrefundable, nonchangeable deals. Look out too for obscure flight routings: some sites will sell you direct charters to Crete or straightforward fares via Athens, but because of the lack of scheduled flights others may try to offer a flight involving several stops in Eastern Europe en route. If you are simply looking for a flight to Athens, life will be much simpler. All the airlines that fly direct to Greece also have their own websites, offering tickets that are sometimes just as cheap and often more flexible. Good general travel websites are listed below; it's also worth checking with the **specialist operators** (see p.13), many of whom are online.

Online booking agents and general travel sites

ⓦ www.cheapflights.co.uk (bookings from UK & Ireland; from the US ⓦ www.cheapflights.com; from Canada ⓦ www.cheapflights.ca; from Australia & New Zealand ⓦ www.cheapflights .com.au). Flight deals, travel agents, plus links to other travel sites.

ⓦ www.cheaptickets.com Discount flight specialists (US only).

ⓦ www.ebookers.com Efficient, easy to use flight finder, with competitive fares.

ⓦ www.expedia.co.uk (bookings from UK & Ireland; from the US ⓦ www.expedia.com; from Canada ⓦ www.expedia.ca). Discount airfares, all-airline search engine and daily deals.

ⓦ www.geocities.com/thavery2000 An extensive list of airline websites and US toll-free numbers.

ⓦ www.kelkoo.co.uk Useful UK-only price-comparison site, checking several sources of low-cost flights (and other goods and services) according to specific criteria.

ⓦ www.lastminute.com (bookings from UK & Ireland; from Australia ⓦ www.lastminute.com.au; from New Zealand ⓦ www.lastminute.co.nz). Good holiday-package and flight-only deals available at very short notice.

ⓦ www.opodo.co.uk Popular and reliable source of cheap UK airfares. Owned by, and run in conjunction with, nine major European airlines.

ⓦ www.priceline.com (US). Name-your-own-price auction website that has deals at around forty percent off standard fares.

ⓦ www.skyauction.com Bookings from the US only. Auctions tickets and travel packages to destinations worldwide.

ⓦ www.travel.com.au (bookings from Australia; from New Zealand ⓦ www.travel.co.nz). Comprehensive online travel sites, with discounted fares.

ⓦ www.travelocity.co.uk (bookings from UK & Ireland; from the US ⓦ www.travelocity.com; from Canada ⓦ www.travelocity.ca; from Australia ⓦ www.zuji.com.au). Destination guides, hot web fares and deals for car rental, accommodation and lodging as well as fares.

ⓦ www.travelshop.com.au Australian website offering discounted flights, packages, insurance and online bookings.

ⓦ travel.yahoo.com Incorporates some Rough Guides material in its coverage of destination countries and cities across the world, with information about places to eat and sleep.

Flights from the UK and Ireland

In the age of the low-cost airline, flights to Crete can be pricey: even charters rarely cost much less than £180 return, and can be over £300 in high season. Most of the cheaper flights from Britain and Ireland are **charters**, sold either with a package holiday or (less commonly) as a flight-only option. The flights have fixed and unchangeable outward and return dates, and usually a maximum stay of three or, at the outside, four weeks.

For longer stays or more flexibility, or if you're travelling out of season (when few charters are available), you'll need a **scheduled flight** via Athens (occasionally also routed via Thessaloníki). Only Olympic has both domestic and international flights, though other airlines may be able to offer the Athens to Crete connection with either Olympic or their domestic rival Aegean. The cheapest way to get to Crete is usually to fly to Athens and take the ferry from there. As with charters, fares vary widely, and are often sold off at a discount by agents – check the weekend travel sections of newspapers like *The Independent*, *The Guardian*, *The Observer*, *The Telegraph* and *The Sunday Times*, as well as weekly listings magazines such as *Time Out*. So far the only **no-frills** airline serving Athens is easyJet; they can be very cheap if you're flexible about times and book in advance, though at peak times fares can be higher than on the regular airlines.

Charter flights

Travel agents throughout Britain sell **charter flights** to Crete, which usually operate from late April or early May to late October, often with late-night departures and early-morning arrivals. Flight time is around three-and-a-half hours from London, four from Manchester. Even the high-street chains frequently promote "flight-only" deals or discount all-inclusive holidays. The main charter airlines which offer flight-only to Crete are Excel, Monarch, TUI (Thomson/Britannia) and Thomas Cook, though flight-only deals are rare at peak season; flight-only tickets are also sold occasionally by specialist Crete operators such as Simply Crete (p.13). Round-trip purchases are usually mandatory, often with a maximum period away of three or four weeks.

Most of the **flights** go from London Gatwick and Manchester. There are summer departures from other **regional airports**, but choice is far more limited and prices likely to be higher. Off-season **fares** start at under £200 for a Gatwick–Iráklion flight, up to around £250 for regional departures and flights into Haniá, £220–£320 in high season. Similarly, **from Dublin** you'll find a limited number of direct summer charters, at significantly higher prices: rarely less than €400.

Charter airlines

Britannia Airways ☏0870 607 6757, ⓦ www.britanniaairways.com.
Excel Airways ☏0870 998 9898, ⓦ www.excelairways.com.
Monarch Airlines ☏0870 040 5040, ⓦ www.monarchairlines.com.
Thomas Cook ☏0870 750 5711, ⓦ www.thomascook.com.
Thomson ☏0800 000 747, ⓦ www.thomson-holidays.com.

Scheduled flights

The theoretical advantages of **scheduled flights** is that they can be booked well in advance, tickets are valid longer (up to a year), there are fewer restrictions, and they leave at more convenient hours. In practice, however, many of the cheaper fares have all sorts of restrictions, and are on flights that arrive at Athens at 4am – plus you then have to get a connecting flight or a ferry to Crete (see p.19). As with charters, discount fares on scheduled flights are available from high-street travel agents and specialist flight and student/youth agencies, though it's also worth contacting the airlines direct (see p.12). Most airlines offer discounts of £5–10 for booking return journeys on their website, with e-confirmation and e-ticketing to the fax or email address of your choice.

The national carrier **Olympic Airways**, notorious as the least punctual airline in the skies, has two daily services (noon and late afternoon) from London Heathrow to Athens, as well as two weekly red-eye flights to Athens from Manchester, and four to five weekly evening departures from London Gatwick to Thessaloníki. **British Airways** offers three daily flights from Heathrow to Athens (morning, noon and evening), as well as one morning flight from Gatwick in summer. Both airlines have a range of fares, and even in July and August, discount flight agents or websites can come up with deals, valid for sixty days away, for as low as £170 return, including tax; more realistically, you'll pay around £220 return during high season from London, £300 from Manchester. In the spring (except around Easter) or autumn, return fares to Athens run to about £150 including taxes, and in winter dip to about £125. **Onward connections** to Crete typically add around £100 to these prices: the one big advantage of Olympic is that you stick with the one airline all the way through, and when you arrive late they should ensure that you get on a flight to Crete.

You'll also find that while most websites work fine for London–Athens flights, few can cope properly with connections to Crete or from regional airports; for those you're better off speaking to someone. Flights from British regional airports route through Heathrow, involving a further supplement of £70–80. Olympic has a code-sharing partnership with bmi, which should ease the pain (and possibly the cost) of connections from Scotland and the north of England in particular.

Two relative newcomers, easyJet and Hellas Jet, are usually cheaper from London to Athens. **easyJet**, with several flights daily out of Luton and Gatwick to Athens has fares from £29 to £159 one way, tax included. The price depends on the season, how far in advance you book and availability – a last-minute booking for three weeks from the end of August will probably result in a combined return fare of £210, over Christmas/New Year's £290. Departures also vary with time of year, but typically there are two a day from Luton, in the early afternoon and late in the evening, and at least one from Gatwick in the early morning, with an additional early evening flight April to October. You can change your ticket after booking for a small fee, provided space is available. While there's no on-board meal service, you can buy drinks and snacks.

The newest airline on the scene is **Hellas Jet**, a subsidiary of Cyprus Airways which began operations in 2003 and quickly garnered a reputation for decent service and competitive fares. They offer a daily overnight service from Heathrow to Athens, as well as a very convenient daily late-morning service from Gatwick. Fares run from £95–120 in low season to £210 in high season.

Irish travellers will find year-round scheduled services with **Aer Lingus** and **British Airways** operating from both Dublin and Belfast via Heathrow or Manchester to Athens, or from Dublin via Heathrow on bmibaby and Olympic. All are pricey compared to charters. Travelling to London and buying a separate ticket when you get there is an alternative if direct flights from Ireland are in short supply, and may sometimes save you a little money, but on the whole it's rarely worth the time and effort. Budget flights to London from Ireland are offered by bmibaby, Aer Lingus and Ryanair.

Scheduled Airlines

Aer Lingus UK ℡ 0845 084 4444, Republic of Ireland ℡ 0818 365 000, ⓦ www.aerlingus.com.
bmi ℡ 0870 607 0555, ⓦ www.flybmi.com.
bmibaby UK ℡ 0870 264 2229, Republic of Ireland ℡ 01/435 0011, ⓦ www.bmibaby.com.
British Airways UK ℡ 0870 850 9850, Republic of Ireland ℡ 1800 626 747, ⓦ www.ba.com.
easyJet ℡ 0870 000 000, ⓦ www.easyjet.com.
Hellas Jet ℡ 0870 751 7222, ⓦ www.hellas-jet.com.
Olympic Airways ℡ 0870 606 0460, ⓦ www.olympicairlines.com.
Ryanair UK ℡ 0871 246 0000, Republic of Ireland ℡ 0818 303 030, ⓦ www.ryanair.com.

Flight and travel agents

Aran Travel International Galway ℡ 091/562595. Good-value flights to all parts of the world.
Argo ℡ 0870 460 7000, ⓦ www.argo-holidays.com. Long-established Greek specialist with holidays and flight-onlys from the UK and Ireland, and good deals on scheduled flights.
Avro ℡ 0870 458 2841, ⓦ www.avro.co.uk. Seat-only flight sales from most UK airports.
Greece & Cyprus Travel Centre ℡ 0121/355 6955, ⓦ www.greece-cyprus.co.uk. Competent flight consolidator for Olympic and Hellas Jet in

particular, with fares to suit every need, including one-ways.
Joe Walsh Tours Dublin ℡ 01/676 0991, ⓦ www.joewalshtours.ie. General budget fares agent.
McCarthys Travel Republic of Ireland ℡ 021/427 0127, ⓦ www.mccarthystravel.ie. General flight agent; no online booking.
North South Travel ℡ 01245/608291, ⓦ www.northsouthtravel.co.uk. Friendly, competitive flight agency, offering discounted fares worldwide – profits are used to support projects in the developing world, especially the promotion of sustainable tourism.
Rosetta Travel Belfast ℡ 028/9064 4996, ⓦ www.rosettatravel.com. Flight and holiday agent, specializing in deals direct from Belfast.
STA Travel ℡ 0870 160 0599, ⓦ www.statravel.co.uk. Worldwide specialists in low-cost flights and tours for students and under-26s. A dozen branches across England, especially on or near university campuses.
Thomas Cook ℡ 0870 750 0316, ⓦ www.thomascook.com. Good selection of packages and flight-onlys.
Thomson ℡ 0870 165 0079, ⓦ www.thomson-holidays.com. Now part of TUI; flight-onlys and packages.
Trailfinders UK ℡ 020/7938 3939, ⓦ www.trailfinders.com, Republic of Ireland ℡ 01/677 7888, ⓦ www.trailfinders.ie. One of the best-informed and most efficient agents for independent travellers; branches in all the UK's largest cities, plus Dublin.

Packages and tours

Virtually every major British **tour operator** includes Crete in its programme, though with many of the larger, cheap-and-cheerful outfits you'll find choices are limited to the established resorts, mainly in the northeast. If you buy one of these at a last-minute discount, especially in spring or autumn, you may find it costs little more than a flight – and you can use the accommodation included as much or as little as you want.

For a more low-key and genuinely local resort, however, it's better to book your holiday through one of the **specialist agencies** listed opposite. Most of these are fairly small-scale operations, providing competitively priced packages and often more traditional village-based accommodation. They also make an effort to get to out-of-the-way places. Such agencies tend to divide into two types: those which, like the major chains, contract a block of accommodation and flight seats (or even their own plane) for a full season, and an increasing number of bespoke agencies which tailor holidays at your request, making all transport and accommodation arrangements on the spot. These can work out somewhat more expensive, but the quality of flights and lodging is often correspondingly higher.

There are also a number of specialist operators offering **walking** or **nature** holidays – usually small groups of ten to fifteen people plus an experienced guide, sometimes following a self-guided itinerary with arranged accommodation each day – or other special interests such as **photography** or **yoga**.

Hotel, villa or village accommodation holidays

Cachet Travel ☎020/8847 3847, @www.cachet-travel.co.uk. Attractive range of villas and apartments, mainly in the south and west.

CV Travel ☎0870 787 9712, @www.cvtravel.co.uk. Quality villas.

Direct Greece ☎0870 516 8683, @www.direct-greece.co.uk. Moderately priced villas and apartments.

Filoxenia ☎01422/375999, @www.escapepackages.com. High-quality tailor-made itineraries and fly-drives as well as special-interest holidays including walking and diving.

Freelance Holidays ☎0870 442 2658, @www.freelance-holidays.co.uk. Good-value apartment and villa holidays across Crete, mostly in the west.

Hidden Greece ☎020/7839 2553, @www.hidden-greece.co.uk. Specialist agent putting together tailor-made packages at reasonable prices; mostly small hotels in the west.

Planet Holidays ☎0870 066 0909, @www.planet-holidays.net. Specialises in four- and five-star hotels.

Pure Crete ☎020/8760 0879, @www.pure-crete.com. Characterful, converted cottages and farmhouses in western Crete.

Simply Crete ☎020/8541 2201, @www.simply-travel.com. Although now part of the vast TUI organisation, Simply Crete still manages a personal touch, and has plenty of excellent, upmarket accommodation across the island.

Smart Holidays ☎01789/267623 @www.smart-holidays.co.uk. Wide range of apartments and villas right across Crete, including plenty of budget options: this is the British agent for a consortium of Cretan travel operators.

Sunvil Holidays ☎020/8568 4499, @www.sunvil.co.uk/greece. High-quality outfit specializing in upmarket hotels and villas.

Travel Club of Upminster ☎01708/225000, @www.travelclub.org.uk. Relatively small operator with a long history in Crete and an excellent reputation. Apartment and hotel holidays in the west.

Walking, nature and special interest holidays

ATG Oxford ☎01865/315678, @www.atg-oxford.co.uk. Somewhat pricey but high-standard guided walks in the far west.

Exodus ☎0870 240 5550, @www.exodus.co.uk. One-week treks through the White Mountains.

Explore Worldwide ☎01252/760 000, @www.exploreworldwide.com. Walking trips, including an option to return round the island by boat.

Footloose Adventure Travel ☎01943/604030, @www.footlooseadventure.co.uk. Week-long courses in yoga and holistic therapies in West Crete. Also independent accommodation for walking and touring.

Jonathan's Tours @www.jonathanstours.com. Family-run walking holidays with a very experienced guide.

Marengo Guided Walks ☎01485/532710, @www.marengowalks.com. Easy walks guided by botanist Lance Chilton, an expert on Crete who returns only once every eighteen months to two years.

Naturetrek ☎01962/733051, @www.naturetrek.co.uk. Botanical and bird-watching tours.

Ramblers Holidays ☎01707/331133, @www.ramblersholidays.co.uk. Big, specialist walking-holiday company with week-long holidays in the west; Manchester and Gatwick departures.

Sherpa Expeditions ☎020/8577 2717, @www.sherpa-walking-holidays.co.uk. Week-long self-guided walking itineraries in the west.

The Travelling Naturalist ☎01305/267994, @www.naturalist.co.uk. Wildflie holiday company that runs an excellent annual bird-watching trip to Crete.

Yoga Plus ☎01273/276175, @www.yogaplus.co.uk. Yoga courses in a remote part of the south. Accommodation is included, but transport is not.

By rail from the UK, Ireland and the rest of Europe

Travelling **by train** from Britain or Ireland to Crete takes three to four days, and works out vastly more expensive than flights. The train will only take you as far as mainland Greece, from where you'll have to continue your journey by plane or ferry (see p.19), and once you reach Crete there are no trains at all. However, an ordinary ticket does give you the chance to stop over on the way – in France, Switzerland and Italy – while with an InterRail or Eurail pass you can take in Greece as part of a wider rail trip around Europe.

The most practical **route** from Britain crosses France and Italy before embarking on the ferry from Bari or Brindisi to Pátra (Patras). Book seats well in advance, especially in summer (for ferry information, see the box on p.16).

Until 1990, the all-overland route through **former Yugoslavia** was the most popular; for obvious reasons this is a nonstarter for the foreseeable future. A more roundabout alternative from Budapest runs via **Bucharest** and **Sofia** to **Thessaloníki**, from where Athens is a further six to seven hours.

It's not possible to buy a through train ticket from Britain to Greece, and if you attempt to piece together the various sectors (London–Paris, Paris–Italy, Italy–Greece) the outbound journey alone exceeds £300. It's much cheaper to cross Europe on an InterRail pass (see below), and to buy another InterRail pass in Greece to come home.

Rail passes

An **InterRail pass** offers unlimited travel (except for express-train supplements and reservation fees) on a zonal basis with 28 European rail networks. These passes are only available to **European residents**, and come in over-26 and (cheaper) under-26 versions.

To reach Greece via Italy you'll need a **one-month pass** valid for at least two zones, G and E. For the route via central Europe you have to buy an all-zone pass. InterRail passes do not allow free travel between Britain and the continent, although they do make you eligible for discounts on rail travel in Britain and Northern Ireland, on cross-Channel ferries, and the London–Paris Eurostar service.

For **North Americans, Australians, New Zealanders** and other non-Europeans, a **Eurail Pass** will not pay for itself except as part of a bigger trip. This pass, which must be purchased before arrival in Europe, allows unlimited free first-class train travel in Greece and sixteen other countries, and is

available in increments of fifteen days, 21 days, one month, two months and three months. If you're under 26, you can save money with a Eurail Youthpass, which is valid for second-class travel or, if you're travelling with one to four other companions, a joint Eurail Saverpass. A Eurail Flexipass may offer better value, and is good for ten or fifteen days' travel within a two-month period. This, too, comes in first-class, under-26/second-class (Eurorail Youth Flexipass) and group (Eurail Saver Flexipass) versions.

Rail contacts

UK and Ireland

The Man in Seat 61 ⓦwww.seat61.com. Expert advice for planning a train journey; you can't buy tickets here, but all the necessary links are provided.
Rail Europe UK ⓣ0870 584 8848, ⓦwww.raileurope.co.uk. Discounted rail fares for under-26s on a variety of European routes; also agents for InterRail and Eurostar.

North America

DER Travel ⓣ1-888 337-7350, ⓦwww.dertravel.com/rail. Eurail, Europass and many individual country passes.
European Rail Services Canada ⓣ1-800 205-5800 or 416/695-1211, ⓦwww.europeanrailservices.com. Eurail, Europass and many individual country passes.
Europrail International Inc Canada ⓣ1-888 667-9734, ⓦwww.europrail.net. Eurail, Europass and many individual country passes.
Rail Europe US ⓣ1-877 257-2887, Canada ⓣ1-800 361-RAIL, ⓦwww.raileurope.com. Official North American Eurail Pass agent; also sells most single-country passes.

Australia and New Zealand

CIT World Travel Australia ⓣ02/9267 1255 or 03/9650 5510, ⓦwww.cittravel.com.au. Eurail and Europass rail passes.
Rail Plus Australia ⓣ1300 555 003 or 03/9642 8644, ⓦwww.railplus.com.au. Sells Eurail passes.
Trailfinders Australia ⓣ02/9247 7666, ⓦwww.trailfinder.com.au. All European passes.

By car from the UK and Ireland

If you have the time and inclination, **driving to Crete** can be a pleasant proposition.

Realistically, though, it's only worth considering if you are going to stay for an extended period – a month at the very least – or want to take advantage of various stopovers en route. The most popular **route** is down through France and Italy to catch one of the Adriatic ferries. A much longer alternative through Eastern Europe (Hungary, Romania and Bulgaria) is just about feasible, but only makes sense if you want to explore the rest of Greece on the way.

The fastest way to get across **to the continent** is the **Eurotunnel** (bookings and information ℡0870 535 3535, ⓦwww.eurotunnel.com), which operates shuttle trains 24 hours a day, for cars, motorcycles, buses and their passengers. There are also **ferry or high-speed catamaran** links between Dover and Calais or Boulogne (the quickest and cheapest routes) or Newhaven and Dieppe. Longer routes head from the southwest of England to Le Havre, Cherbourg, St-Malo or Caen, while Irish drivers can bypass Britain altogether, sailing direct to Le Havre, Roscoff or Cherbourg.

Ferry and shuttle **prices** vary according to the time of year and, for motorists, the size of your car. The short Channel crossing to Calais or Boulogne, for example, starts at about £245–340 open return for a car with up to five passengers, though this range can nearly double in peak season. Book well in advance for the best fares.

Channel and Irish Sea crossings

Brittany Ferries UK ℡0870 366 5333, ⓦwww.brittanyferries.co.uk, Republic of Ireland ℡021/427 7801, ⓦwww.brittanyferries.ie. Portsmouth to Caen, St Malo or Cherbourg; Poole to Cherbourg; Plymouth to Roscoff; Cork to Roscoff.
Eurotunnel ℡0870 535 3535, ⓦwww.eurotunnel.com.
Hoverspeed UK ℡0870 240 8070, ⓦwww.hoverspeed.co.uk. High-speed services. Dover to Calais; Newhaven to Dieppe.
Irish Ferries Britain ℡0870 517 1717, Northern Ireland ℡0800 018 2211, Republic of Ireland ℡1890 313 131, ⓦwww.irishferries.com. Dublin to Holyhead; Rosslare to Pembroke, Cherbourg and Roscoff.
P&O Ferries UK ℡0870 520 2020, ⓦwww.poferries.com. Dover to Calais; Hull to Zeebrugge (Belgium); Portsmouth to Cherbourg; Portsmouth to Le Havre.
P&O Irish Sea UK ℡0870 242 4777, Republic of Ireland ℡1800 409 049, ⓦwww.poirishsea.com. Larne to Cairnryan; Larne to Troon; Larne to Fleetwood; Dublin to Liverpool; Dublin to Mostyn; Dublin to Cherbourg; Rosslare to Cherbourg.
P&O Stena Line ℡0870 600 0600, ⓦwww.posl.com. Dover to Calais.
Sea France ℡0870 571 1711, ⓦwww.seafrance.com. Dover to Calais.
Stena Line ℡0870 570 7070, Republic of Ireland ℡01/204 7777, ⓦwww.stenaline.co.uk. Rosslare to Fishguard; Dun Laoghaire or Dublin to Holyhead; Belfast to Stranraer.

Via Italy

The route **via Italy** – with a ferry across to Greece – is the obvious route to Crete. Initial routes down to Italy through **France** and **Switzerland** are very much a question of personal taste. One of the most direct is Calais–Reims–Geneva–Milan and then down the Adriatic coast to the Italian port of your choice. Even on the quickest autoroutes (with their accompanying tolls), the journey will involve two overnight stops.

Once in **Italy**, you've a choice of five **ports**. Regular car and passenger ferries link **Ancona**, **Bari** and **Brindisi** with **Igoumenítsa** (the port of Epirus in western Greece) and/or **Pátra** (at the northwest tip of the Peloponnese and the handiest port for Crete). Generally, these ferries run year-round, but services are reduced December to April. Ferries also sail less regularly from **Venice** and **Trieste** to Pátra via Igoumenítsa/Corfu. High- season prices to **Pátra from Brindisi** start at around €50 per person deck class, plus €55 for a small car: the longer routes are more expensive, but the extra cost almost exactly matches what you'll pay in Italian motorway tolls and fuel to get to Brindisi. For direct access to Crete head for Pátra, from where you can cut across country to Pireás for daily ferries to the major cities, or head down through the Peloponnese to Yíthio, from where there are two to three sailings a week to Kastélli in western Crete. For details of Greece to Crete ferries, see p.19.

In summer (especially July–Aug) it's essential to **book tickets** a few weeks ahead. During the winter you can usually just turn up at the main ports (Brindisi and Ancona

Italy–Greece ferries

The following companies operate ferries from Italy to Greece: these are their local Italian agents, and their websites, most of which have full route, fare and booking details. Viamare Travel Ltd (☎020/7431 4560, ⓦwww.viamare.com) is the UK agent for most of these companies, and there are also links and booking for all of them at ⓦwww.ferries.gr. The dialling code for Italy is ☎39; when ringing from overseas you must include the initial "0" of the local area code.

Agoudimos Brindisi: c/o Hellas Ferry Lines, ☎0831/548044, ⓦwww.agoudimos-lines.com.

ANEK Ancona: Stazione Marittima ☎071/207 2275; Trieste: Via Rossini 2 ☎040/322 0561, ⓦwww.anek.gr.

Blue Star Brindisi: ☎0831/548 115; Ancona: Stazione Marittima ☎ & ⓕ071/207 0218; Venice: Stazione Marittima 123 ☎041/277 0559, ⓦwww .bluestarferries.com.

Fragline Brindisi: Costa Morena ☎0831/548 318, ⓦwww.fragline.gr.

Med Link Lines Brindisi: c/o Discovery Shipping, Costa Morena ☎0831/548 116, ⓦwww.mll.gr.

Minoan Lines Ancona: Via Astagno 3 ☎071/201 708, ⓕ201 933; Bari: c/o P. Santelia, Via Latilla 15 ☎080/521 0266; Venice: Stazione Marittima 123 ☎041/2407177, ⓦwww.minoan.gr.

Superfast Ferries Ancona: Via XXIX Settembre 2/0 ☎071/202 033; Bari: Corso A. de Tullio 6 ☎080/521 1416, ⓦwww.superfast.com.

Ventouris Bari: c/o P. Lorusso & Co, Stazione Marittima Booths 18–20 ☎080/5217609, ⓦwww.ventouris.gr.

have the most reliable departures at that time of year), but it's still wise to book a few days in advance if you're taking a car or want a cabin. A few phone calls or Internet searches before leaving home are in any case advisable, as the range of fares is considerable. If you do just turn up at the port, it's worth shopping around the agencies.

Via Hungary, Romania and Bulgaria

Avoiding former Yugoslavia involves a substantial diversion through Hungary, Romania and Bulgaria. Too exhausting and too problematic at the best of times, this is not a drive to contemplate unless you actively want to see the countries en route, plus the whole of Greece on your way down to Crete. However, it is at least simpler than it was, with visas easier to obtain at the borders if you haven't fixed them in advance.

From **Budapest**, the quickest route **through Romania** is via Timişoara, then on towards Sofia in Bulgaria and across the Rila Mountains to the border at Kulata. Once at the Greek border, you have a ninety-minute drive to Thessaloníki. Bear in mind that road conditions are often poor and border

formalities extensive. Contact the relevant embassies and the AA for more advice.

Flights from North America

The Greek national airline, Olympic Airways, flies to Athens out of New York (JFK), Montréal and Toronto. The airline – and also its domestic competitor Aegean – can offer reasonably priced add-on flights to Crete. Delta is the only North American carrier currently offering any direct service to Athens, though American Airlines, Air Canada and US Airways have code-sharing agreements with Olympic, and thus quote through-fares to/from Boston, Chicago, Dallas/Fort Worth, Denver, Los Angeles, Miami, San Francisco, Tampa, Vancouver and Washington, DC.

Another option is picking up any suitable flight to Europe and making your way to Crete on a charter flight or by rail from there: see the preceding sections for details.

Nonstop flights **to Athens out of New York-JFK** on Olympic (5–7 weekly) start at around US$600 round trip in winter, rising to around $1100 in summer for a maximum thirty-day stay. Delta has several weekly summertime direct services from New York-

JFK to Athens, but even discount fares are pricey at around $1450. Sometimes one-stop flights are cheaper; winter flights on BA via London can be around $550. Travelling during the May and October "shoulder seasons" will also yield significant savings.

Common-rating (ie price-fixing) agreements between different airlines means that fares to **Athens from the Midwest, Deep South or the West Coast** don't vary much; from Chicago, Miami, Denver or Los Angeles you're looking at $1200–1500 high season, $650–820 in winter, something in between at shoulder season. These tickets typically involve the use of American Airlines, US Airways, United, Air France, Alitalia, Iberia and Swiss, via their European gateway cities. With little to distinguish these itineraries price-wise, you might examine the stopover time at their respective European hubs, as these often differ by several hours. You may be better off getting a domestic add-on to New York and heading directly to Athens from there.

As with the US, airfares **from Canada to Athens** vary depending on where you start your journey, and whether you take a direct service. Olympic flies out of Toronto, with a stop in Montréal, three to four times weekly for return fares of just under Can$1400 in winter, climbing to nearly Can$2500 in summer. Indirect flights from Montréal on Lufthansa via a German hub can cost about the same in summer, but much more during low season. From Calgary or Vancouver, there are no direct flights; expect to pay Can$2050–3000 during low/high seasons respectively, on such combinations as Air Canada/Lufthansa via Germany or Air Canada/Olympic via London.

For all of the above, a **connecting flight to Crete** will add $75–150 (Can$100–200), depending on season and the airline.

Airlines

Air Canada ☏1-888 247-2262, ⊛www.aircanada.com.
Air France ☏1-800 237-2747, Canada ☏1-800/667-2747, ⊛www.airfrance.com.
Alitalia ☏1-800 223-5730, Canada ☏1-800 361-8336, ⊛www.alitalia.com.
American Airlines ☏1-800 433-7300, ⊛www.aa.com.
British Airways ☏1-800 AIRWAYS, ⊛www.ba.com.

Delta Air Lines ☏1-800 241-4141, ⊛www.delta.com.
Iberia ☏1-800 772-4642, ⊛www.iberia.com.
KLM/Northwest US ☏1-800 447-4747, ⊛www.klm.com.
Lufthansa US ☏1-800 645-3880, Canada ☏1-800/563-5954, ⊛www.lufthansa.com.
Olympic Airways ☏1-800 223-1226 or 718/896-7393, ⊛www.olympic-airways.gr.
Swiss ☏1-877 FLY-SWISS, ⊛www.swiss.com.
United Airlines ☏1-800 538-2929, ⊛www.united.com.
US Airways ☏1-800 622-1015, ⊛www.usair.com.
Virgin Atlantic Airways ☏1-800 862-8621, ⊛www.virgin-atlantic.com.

Travel companies

Air Brokers International ☏1-800 883-3273 or 415/397-1383, ⊛www.airbrokers.com. Consolidator and specialist in RTW tickets.
Airtech ☏212/219-7000, ⊛www.airtech.com. Standby seat broker; also deals in consolidator fares and courier flights.
Educational Travel Center ☏1-800 747-5551 or 608/256-5551, ⊛www.edtrav.com. Low-cost fares worldwide, student/youth discount offers, Eurail passes.
Flightcentre US ☏1-866 WORLD-51, ⊛www.flightcentre.us, Canada ☏1-888 WORLD-55, ⊛www.flightcentre.ca. Rock-bottom fares worldwide.
New Frontiers US ☏1-800 677-0720 or 212/986-6006, ⊛www.newfrontiers.com. Discount firm, specializing in travel from the US to Europe.
STA Travel US ☏1-800 329-9537, Canada ☏1-888/427-5639, ⊛www.statravel.com. Worldwide specialists in independent travel; also student IDs, travel insurance, car rental, rail passes, etc.
Student Flights ☏1-800 255-8000 or 480/951-1177, ⊛www.isecard.com/studentflights. Student/youth fares, plus student IDs and European rail and bus passes.
TFI Tours ☏1-800 745-8000 or 212/736-1140, ⊛www.lowestairprice.com. Consolidator with global fares.
Travel Avenue ☏1-800 333-3335, ⊛www.travelavenue.com. Full-service travel agent that offers discounts in the form of rebates.
Travel Cuts US ☏1-800 592-CUTS, Canada ☏1-888 246-9762, ⊛www.travelcuts.com. Popular, long-established student-travel organization, with worldwide offers.
Travelers Advantage ☏1-877 259-2691, ⊛www.travelersadvantage.com. Discount travel club, with cashback deals and discounted car rental. Membership required ($1 for 3 months' trial).

Travelosophy US ☎1-800 332-2687, ⊛www.itravelosophy.com. Good range of discounted and student fares worldwide.

Specialist tour operators

Astra ☎303/321-5403, ⊛www.astragreece.com. Very personal, idiosyncratic, two-week tours led by veteran Hellenophile Thordis Simonsen.

Classic Adventures ☎1-800/777-8090, ⊛www.classicadventures.com. Ten- and twelve-day hiking and biking tours.

Hellenic Adventures ☎1-800 851-6349 or 612/827-0937, ⊛www.hellenicadventures.com. Tailor-made itineraries plus small-group tours that include Crete along with other parts of Greece.

Homeric Tours ☎1-800/223-5570, ⊛www.homerictours.com. Arranges hotel packages, individual tours, escorted group tours (though none exclusively to Crete), and fly/drive deals. Good source of inexpensive flights.

Northwest Passage ☎1-800/RECREATE, ⊛www.nwpassage.com. Excellent cycling, sea-kayaking and hiking "inn-to-inn" tours of Crete, as well as one trip combining yoga, kayaking and walking.

Tourlite Zeus ☎1-800/272-7600, ⊛www.tourlite.com. Specialists in Greek travel, can arrange tailor-made or package vacations in Crete.

Flights from Australia and New Zealand

With the huge Greek-emigrant community in Australia, it's absolutely staggering that Olympic suspended all direct air links to Greece in October 2002 – a measure of its woes. Neither are there any direct flights from New Zealand – you'll have to get yourself to Southeast Asia or a North American hub for onward travel. Tickets purchased direct from the airlines tend to be expensive; travel agents or Australia-based websites offer much better deals on fares and have the latest information on limited specials and stopovers.

If Greece is only one stop on a longer journey, you might consider buying a **Round-the-World** (RTW) fare. At present only the more expensive, fifteen-stop "Global Explorer" (roughly A$3400) offered by the One World airline group includes Athens. RTW fares from any point in Australia are usually common-rated, ie the price is the same from whichever Australian airport you commence travel. From New Zealand, allow almost NZ$4000 for the same itinerary.

For a **simple return fare to Athens**, you may have to buy an add-on internal flight to reach the international gateways of Sydney or Melbourne. Tickets are **valid for one year**; at the time of writing, **high-season** departures could be had for A$2270–2500 on such airlines as Lufthansa, Singapore Airlines, Thai Airways, Gulf Air or Austrian Airlines plus Lauda Air, for multi-stop itineraries via Southeast Asia, the Middle East and a European hub. For $A2270, you could fly eastbound via North America on a combination of United Airlines, Air Canada and Lufthansa. Leaving at **low season** means fares of A$1547–1736 on Singapore Airlines, Thai Airways, Lufthansa or Qantas plus Royal Jordanian.

From New Zealand, the usual routes to Athens are either westbound several times weekly via Bangkok, Sydney or Singapore, or eastbound almost daily via Los Angeles with Air New Zealand on the first leg. At **high season** count on paying NZ$2449–2729 on Singapore Airlines, Emirates, Thai Airways or (for an eastbound itinerary) Air New Zealand plus Lufthansa. During **low season** prices aren't much different: NZ$2199–2349 for travel on Thai Airways, Emirates or (again going east) Air New Zealand plus Lufthansa.

You should be able to add a **connecting flight from Athens to Crete** with Olympic or Aegean for around A$100–200, NZ$115–230.

Airlines

Aeroflot ☎02/9262 2233, ⊛www.aeroflot.com.au.

Air New Zealand Australia ☎13 24 76, ⊛www.airnz.com.au, New Zealand ☎0800 737 000, ⊛www.airnz.co.nz.

Alitalia Australia ☎02/9244 2445, New Zealand ☎09/308 3357, ⊛www.alitalia.com.

British Airways Australia ☎1300 767 177, New Zealand ☎0800 274 847, ⊛www.ba.com.

Egyptair Australia ☎02/9241 5696, ⊛www.egyptair.com.eg.

Emirates Australia ☎1300 303 777 or 02/9290 9700, New Zealand ☎09/377 6004, ⊛www.emirates.com.

Gulf Air Australia ☎02/9244 2199, New Zealand ☎09/308 3366, ⊛www.gulfairco.com.

Lufthansa Australia ☎1300 655 727, New Zealand ☎0800 945 220, ⊛www.lufthansa.com.

Qantas Australia ☎13 13 13, New Zealand ☎0800 808 767 or 09/357 8900, ⓦwww.qantas.com.

Royal Jordanian Australia ☎02/9244 2701, New Zealand ☎03/365 3910, ⓦwww.rja.com.jo.

Singapore Airlines Australia ☎13 10 11, New Zealand ☎0800 808 909, ⓦwww.singaporeair.com.

Thai Airways Australia ☎1300 651 960, New Zealand ☎09/377 3886, ⓦwww.thaiair.com.

Travel agents

Flight Centre Australia ☎13 31 33, ⓦwww.flightcentre.com.au, New Zealand ☎0800 243 544, ⓦwww.flightcentre.co.nz.

Grecian Tours Australia ☎03/9663 3711, ⓦwww.greciantours.com.au. A variety of accommodation and sightseeing tours, plus flights.

House of Holidays Australia ☎1800 335 084, ⓦwww.houseofholidays.com.au. Plenty of Greek tours, though only a few include Crete.

STA Travel Australia ☎1300 733 035, New Zealand ☎0508/782 872, ⓦwww.statravel.com.

Student Uni Travel Australia ☎02/9232 8444, ⓦwww.sut.com.au, New Zealand ☎09/379 4224, ⓦwww.sut.co.nz.

Sun Island Tours Australia ☎02/9283 3840, ⓦwww.sunislandtours.com.au. Good choice of hotel-based package holidays.

Trailfinders Australia ☎02/9247 7666, ⓦwww.trailfinders.com.au.

Flights from Athens and Greece

Flying to Crete from Greece doesn't necessarily mean going via Athens, although the vast majority of people do. There are also daily direct flights with both Aegean and Olympic from Thessaloníki, and in summer from the island of Rhodes, as well as connections from every other regional Greek airport. **From Athens**, however, Olympic and Aegean between them operate at least fifteen flights a day to Iráklion in peak season, and seven or eight daily to Haniá, plus three a week on Olympic to Sitía. Journey time is less than an hour. This may seem plenty of flights, but in summer they are all booked well in advance. If time is your main consideration, flying is good value when weighed against a twelve-hour (or five-and-a-half hour superfast) ferry trip: one-way prices are around €85.

Whether flights are fully booked or not, it can be worth trying for a **stand-by** ticket, especially if you arrive at Athens airport in the middle of the night and can be first in the queue next morning. You have to purchase a ticket (by credit card will do) in order to get on the stand-by list: if, in the end, you don't manage to fly they should give you a full refund. Once you're on the list the system works pretty well, despite appearances – just make sure you are by the departure gate when they call out the names of the lucky few for each flight.

Domestic airlines

Aegean Vouliagménis 572 ☎210 99 88 300, reservations ☎801 11 20 000, airport ☎ 210 35 30 101.

Olympic Fillelínon 15 ☎210 92 67 663, reservations ☎96 66 666, airport ☎210 93 68 424.

Ferries from Pireás and elsewhere

The vast majority of ferry traffic to Crete goes from **Pireás** (the port of Athens), leaving in the evening and arriving the following morning, or, in the case of the new fast ferries, departing in the late afternoon. There are also services from the Peloponnese (handy if you're coming overland via Italy) and from many of the Cycladic and Dodecanese islands.

You can buy ferry and catamaran **tickets** from dozens of agencies at the harbour in Pireás, or in central Athens, as well as from booths on the docks near the boats. If you're taking a car or want a cabin it's worth booking ahead, but deck-class tickets are almost always available on the spot. Itineraries, tickets and office addresses are available on the ferry-line websites (see p.22).

The cheapest tickets are in deck class, which gives you the run of almost the entire boat, excluding the cabins and the upper-class restaurant and bar. Most of the ferries serving Crete are modern and reasonably luxurious, with plenty of café and "pullman seating" areas inside, though often without a huge amount of deck space. If you are travelling deck class, it's worth getting on board reasonably early (perhaps an hour before departure) to claim a good space. Cabins are also available, ranging from four-berth, shared cabins inside (all en-suite and perfectly adequate) through various grades up to deluxe suites with huge picture windows.

Travelling to Crete **via Athens** provides a great opportunity to explore the Greek capital. Transformed by its pre-Olympic make-over, Athens is worth a day or two of anyone's time, with some magnificent ancient sites and buzzing nightlife. A couple of nights' stopover will allow you to take in the Acropolis, ancient Agora and major museums, wander the old quarter of Pláka and the bazaar area, and sample some of Greece's best restaurants and clubs. But even an early morning flight into Athens gives plenty of time to take a look at the Acropolis and Pláka, before heading down to Pireás to catch one of the early evening ferries on to Crete.

Arrival, transport and information

Athens' new **airport** is some 26km east of the city centre. By mid-2004, a **light-rail line** should whisk you from the airport to Dhoukíssis Plakentías station, where you can pick up the metro (eventually trains should run straight through to the centre). Alternatively, take the #E94 express **bus** (every 15–30min, 6am–midnight) from outside arrivals to metro station Ethnikí Ámyna and then continue by metro, or the #E95 all the way to central Sýndagma Square (every 25–35min around the clock). For **Pireás**, you can take the metro via the centre, but the most direct route is the #E96 express bus (every 20–40min, about 1hr 20min), going via the beach suburbs. All these services cost €2.90 (with a one-day travelcard valid on all Athens public transport included in the price).

A **taxi** to Athens or Pireás should cost no more than €20 – the journey should take less than an hour. Make sure the meter is working, but be warned that various legitimate surcharges will be added, including a €2 airport surcharge and €0.20 for each item of luggage.

From the centre of Athens to **Pireás** a **taxi** can take you straight to your ferry (if you don't already have a ticket, most will happily take you to an agent and wait while you get one). A taxi should cost around €5–7, depending on your start-point and how many bags you have. You may have fellow passengers in the cab: this is permitted, and each drop-off will pay the full fare. Otherwise, Line 1 of the **metro** terminates by the harbour, a five- to ten-minute walk from most of the Crete ferries (the Blue Star boat is further round, but there should be a bus to take you there).

The **Greek National Tourist Office** (EOT) has a branch at the airport as well as a central office at Amalías 26, just off Sýndagma Square.

Accommodation

Finding **accommodation** in Athens is usually not a problem except during midsummer – though it's always best to phone ahead. The places listed below range from hostels to fairly comfortable hotels. For a quick stay, **Pláka**, the oldest quarter of the city, and neighbouring **Monastiráki** are the obvious choices: central, within easy walking range of the Acropolis and most other major sites, and with lots of outdoor restaurants and cafés. It's possible to stay in Pireás, too, though with ferries leaving in the evening there's no real need.

Acropole Goúnari 7, Pireás ☎210 41 73 313. ⑤
Acropolis House Kódrou 6–8 ☎210 32 22 344. ⑤
Adonis Kódrou 3 ☎210 32 49 737. ⑥
John's Place Patróöu 5 ☎210 32 29 719. ②
Kouros Kódrou 11 ☎210 32 27 431. ⑥
Nefeli Iperídhou 16, Pláka ☎210 32 28 044. ⑦
Phaedra Herefóndos 16 ☎210 32 27 795. ⑤
Student's Inn Kydhathinéon 16 ☎210 32 44 808. ⑤, dorm €24
Tempi Eólou 29 ☎210 32 13 175. ⑤
Thisseus Inn Thisséos 10 ☎210 32 45 960. ③
Thission Apostólou Pávlou 25 ☎210 34 67 634. ⑥

YHA Victor Hugo 16 ⌖210 52 34 170. Metro Metaxouryío. Further from the action, but cheap dorm beds from €8.

Eating

Pláka and Monastiráki are bursting with touristy **restaurants**, most of them poor value. Three with nice sites *and* good, inexpensive food are *Iy Ipiros*, on Platía Ayíou Filíppou in the Monastiráki flea market, *O Thanasis* at Mitropóleos 69 and *Baïraktaris*, nearby at the corner of Platía Monastirakíou, both of which have dynamite *souvláki* and kebabs. For a bit more atmosphere try *Nefeli*, Pános 24 (eves only), high up in Pláka with fine views, or head for the nightlife and packed tavernas of the Psyrrí area.

The city and sights

Central Athens is compact and easily walkable. Its hub is **Sýndagma Square** (Platía Syndágmatos), flanked by the Parliament building, banks and major hotels. Pretty much everything you'll want to see in a fleeting visit – the Acropolis, Pláka, the major museums – lies within thirty minutes' walk of here. Just east of the square are the **National Gardens**, the nicest spot in town for a siesta or picnic.

Head first for Pláka, the surviving area of the nineteenth-century, pre-Independence village. Largely pedestrianized, it is a delightful area just to wander around – and it is the approach to the Acropolis. For a bit of focus to your walk, take in the fourth-century BC **Monument of Lysikratos**, to the east, and the Roman-era **Tower of the Winds** in the **Roman Forum** site (April–Sept daily 8am–7pm; Oct–March Tues–Sun 8.30am–3pm; €2) to the west. Climb south from the Roman Forum and you reach the eclectic **Kanellopoulou Museum** (Tues–Sun 8am–3pm; €2), beyond which paths lead to the Acropolis and Ancient Agora.

Head north from the Roman Forum, along Athinás or Eólou streets, and you come to an equally characterful part of the city – the **bazaar** area of Monastiráki, which shows Athens in its Near Eastern lights. On **Platía Monastirakíou**, as well as a handy metro station, one of the few surviving Ottoman mosques is now a museum of ceramics. On Sundays a genuine **flea market** sprawls to the west of the square, out beyond the tourist shops promoted as "Monastiráki Flea Market".

Even with a few hours to spare between flight and ferry, you can squeeze in a visit to the **Acropolis** (daily: April–Sept 8am–7pm; Oct–March 8am–4.30pm; site and museum €12). The complex of temples, rebuilt by Pericles in the "Golden Age" of the fifth century BC, is focused on the famed Parthenon. This, and the smaller Athena Nike and Erechtheion temples are given context by a small museum housing some of the original artworks left behind by Lord Elgin.

If you have more time, make your way down to the **Theatre of Dionysos**, on the south slope (daily: summer 8am–7pm; winter 8.30am–3pm; €2 or joint Acropolis ticket), and/or to the **Ancient Agora** (southeastern entrance down the path from the Areopagus; northern entrance on Adhrianoú; daily: summer 8am–7pm; winter 8.30am–3pm; €4 or joint Acropolis ticket), presided over by the Doric **Hephasteion**, or Temple of Hephaestus.

Athens' major museum is the **National Archeological Museum** on Patissíon 28, due to reopen summer 2004 after a lengthy refit. Its highlights include the Mycenaean (*Odyssey*-era) treasures, Classical sculpture and, upstairs, the brilliant Minoan frescoes from Santoríni (Thíra).

Two other superb museums are the **Benáki** (Mon, Wed, Fri & Sat 9am–5pm, Thurs 9am–midnight, Sun 9am–3pm; €6, temporary exhibitions €3), a fascinating personal collection of ancient and folk treasures, and the **Goulandhris Museum of Cycladic and Ancient Greek Art** (Mon & Wed–Fri 10am–4pm, Sat 10am–3pm; €3.50), with its wonderful display of figurines from the Cycladic island civilization of the third millennium BC.

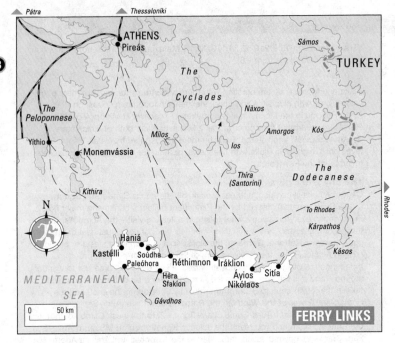

▲ Pátra   ▲ Thessaloníki

ATHENS
Pireás
Sámos
TURKEY

The
C y c l a d e s

The
Peloponnese

Nàxos
Amorgos   Kós

Yíthio
Mílos
Ios
Monemvássia

Thíra
(Santorini)
The
D o d e c a n e s e

Kithira

Rhodes

N

To Rhodes
Kárpathos

Haniá
Kástélli   Soúdha   Réthimnon   Iráklion
Paleóhora   Héra   Áyios   Sitía
Sfakíon   Nikólaos

M E D I T E R R A N E A N
S E A

Gávdhos
Kásos

0   50 km

FERRY LINKS

Ferries from Pireás are operated by ANEK (to Iráklion, Haniá and Réthimnon), Minoan (regular and high speed to Iráklion), Blue Star (high speed to Haniá) and LANE (to Áyios Nikólaos and Sitía). Beware of tickets offered on any other line – these will almost certainly involve a roundabout route through the Cyclades and take twice as long.

For Iráklion there are two daily **departures** between 8.30 and 10pm, arriving between 5.30 and 7am, while the fast ferry runs daily at around 4pm, arriving at 10pm. Haniá schedules are identical, but there's usually just one overnight ferry; for Réthimnon there's a daily departure at 8pm. For Áyios Nikólaos and Sitía there's a departure five days a week (not Tues or Sat) at 7pm.

Prices to Iráklion range from around €25 deck class to €50 for a berth in a basic cabin to €85 per person in a luxurious double, while cars go for €70–€80 and motorbikes for around €20: the older, slower ferries are generally slightly cheaper than the more luxurious, faster ones; fares to Haniá are also marginally lower.

Much the most useful of the other ferry services is that from the **Peloponnese**, on the *Mirtidiotissa*, a boat operated by ANEN Lines. On its high summer schedule (July and Aug) it runs from Yíthio to Kastélli Kissámou three times a week (Mon at 8pm, Tues and Wed at 4pm, arriving about eight hours later). Departure days and times change outside the high summer period, and at any time this service is subject to delays as the ferry follows its convoluted schedule.

Ferry companies

ANEK Lines Kapodístriou 2 and Aktí Possídonos, Pireás ☎210 41 97 420, ⓦwww.anek.gr.
Blue Star Aktí Possídonos 26, Pireás ☎210 89 19 800, ⓦwww.bluestarferries.gr.
Minoan Lines Aktí Possídonos 26, Pireás ☎210 41 45 700, ⓦwww.minoan.gr.
LANE Lines Loudovíko 2, Pireás ☎210 42 74 011, ⓦwww.lane.gr.
ANEN Lines Aktí Possídonos and Leohárous, Pireás ☎210 41 97 420, ⓦwww.anen.gr.

Red tape and visas

UK and all other EU nationals (plus those of Norway, Switzerland and Iceland) need only a valid passport for entry to Greece. You are no longer stamped in on arrival or out upon departure, and (in theory at least) EU nationals enjoy uniform civil rights with Greek citizens. US, Australian, New Zealand, Canadian and most non-EU Europeans receive mandatory entry and exit stamps in their passports and can stay as tourists for ninety days (cumulative) in any six-month period. Note that such nationals arriving by flight or boat from another EU state not party to the Schengen Agreement (see below) may not be stamped in routinely at minor Greek ports, so it's best to ensure this is done to avoid problems on exit. Note also that all passports must be valid for at least three months after your arrival date.

If you are planning to **travel overland** to Greece you should check current visa requirements for Hungary, Romania and Bulgaria at their closest consulates; transit visas for most of these territories are at present issued at the borders, though at a higher price than if obtained in advance at a local consulate.

Greek immigration officials have become much stricter lately, and visitors from **non-EU** countries, unless of Greek descent, are currently not being given extensions to tourist visas by the various Aliens' Bureaux in Greece, though in theory these are available for the hefty sum of €450. You must leave not just Greece but the entire Schengen Group – essentially the entire EU as it was before the Eastern European expansion of May 2004, minus Britain and Ireland, plus Norway and Iceland – and stay out until the maximum-90-days-in-180 rule is satisfied. If you **overstay** your time and then leave of your own volition – ie are not deported – you'll be hit with a hefty spot fine upon departure, probably in the region of €450, and possibly be banned from re-entering for a period of time.

By EU law, EU nationals are allowed to stay indefinitely in any EU state, but to be sure of avoiding any problems, it's best to get a five-year **residence permit** (ádhia

paramonís) and (if appropriate) a work permit – for both, see "Work", p.59. If you're not employed (self- or otherwise), you will be required to prove that you have sufficient resources to support yourself, and health insurance.

Residence/work permits for non-EU nationals can now only be obtained on application to a Greek embassy or consulate outside of Greece; you have a much better chance of securing one if you are married to a Greek, or have permanent-resident status in another EU state, but even then there will be wrangles and delays.

Greek embassies abroad

Australia 9 Turrana St, Yarralumla, Canberra, ACT 2600 ☎02/6273 3011.

UK 1A Holland Park, London W11 3TP ☎020/7221 6467, ⓦwww.greekembassy.org.uk.

Canada 80 Maclaren St, Ottawa, ON K2P 0K6 ☎613/238-6271.

Ireland 1 Upper Pembroke St, Dublin 2 ☎01/676 7254.

New Zealand 5–7 Willeston St, Wellington ☎04/473 7775.

USA 2221 Massachusetts Ave NW, Washington, DC 20008 ☎202/939-5800, ⓦwww.greekembassy.org.

Information, websites and maps

The obvious first stop for information on Crete is the Greek National Tourist Organization (Ellinikós Organismós Tourismóu, or EOT; GNTO abroad, ⓦwww.gnto.gr), even though few of their glossy pamphlets apply exclusively to the island. When visiting any EOT office (particularly abroad) it helps to go armed with specific questions, or you'll simply be given the general leaflet on Crete, which has plenty of pictures, a very small-scale map, and hardly any hard information at all. On Crete, the offices in major towns should stock up-to-date bus and ferry timetables and prices.

The National Tourist Organization maintains offices in most European capitals (though not Dublin), Australia and North America; see below for addresses.

Tourist information

On the island, there are **EOT** (or partly funded by EOT) **offices** in Iráklion (see p.82), Haniá (see p.307) and Réthimnon (see p.242). Where there is no EOT office, you can get information (and often a range of leaflets) from **municipal tourist offices** or sometimes from the **tourist police**. The latter comprise a branch (or often just a single delegate) of the local police, and deal with complaints about restaurants, taxis, hotels and all things tourist-related; call ☎171 for information and help, and see individual towns for local addresses. They can occasionally provide you with lists of rooms to rent, which they regulate. In addition, local **travel agencies** are always helpful and many voluntarily act as improvised tourist offices, often making a pretty good job of it, too; we've listed many of these throughout the guide.

Greek tourist offices abroad

If your home country isn't listed here, apply to the embassy. Note that there are no Greek tourist offices in Ireland, New Zealand or South Africa.

Australia 51 Pitt St, Sydney, NSW 2000 ☎02/9241 1663.
Britain 4 Conduit St, London W1R 0DJ ☎020/7734 5997, ⓦwww.gnto.co.uk.
Canada 91 Scollard St, 2nd Floor, Toronto, ON M5R 1GR ☎416/968-2220; 1223 rue de la

Montagne, QCH 3G, Montréal ☎514/871-1535.
Denmark Vester Farimagsgade 1,2 DK-1606 Kobenhavn V ☎325-332.
Netherlands Kerkstraat 61, 1017 GC Amsterdam ☎20/6254212, ⓦwww.grieksverkeersbureau.nl.
Norway Ovre Slottsgate 15B, 0157 Oslo 1 ☎02/426-501.
Sweden Apelbergsgatan 36, PO Box 3377, 10367 Stockholm ☎08/679 6580, ⓦwww.travelgate.net/greecegate.
USA 645 Fifth Ave, New York, NY 10022 ☎212/421-5777, ⓦwww.greektourism.com; 168 N Michigan Ave, Chicago, IL 60601 ☎312/782-1084; 611 W 6th St, Los Angeles, CA 90017 ☎213/626-6696.

Crete on the Internet

Crete is strongly represented on the Internet with many bilingual English–Greek websites offering information on nearly every conceivable subject. Some of the more informative ones are listed below and many of these have links to myriad other sites. To read Greek characters on a website, you may have to select "Unicode" in "Character set" under the "View" pull-down menu in Internet Explorer – selecting "Greek" shows accented vowels as a "?" character.

Tourist information

ⓦ**www.bsa.gla.ac.uk/knossos/index.html** Information on Knossós, with photos and 3D download of the site.
ⓦ**www.cretanvista.gr** Guide to the Rodhópou Peninsula in Haniá, with lots of info and links.
ⓦ**www.dilos.com/region/crete** Travel operator with substantial site, general and cultural information and photos.

ⓦ www.explorecrete.com Comprehensive travel operator's site, with ideas of things to do on the island plus general and cultural information and images.

ⓦ www.infocrete.com Miscellaneous site with lots of interesting Crete-related businesses and links.

ⓦ www.interkriti.gr Extraordinarily comprehensive site, including maps, superb images, aerial photography, lists of hotels, local travel agents and car rental outlets, as well as details of all the major towns, sites, museums and personalities of the island, and even Cretan recipes.

ⓦ www.odysseas.com General interest site with brief tourist guides to most places of interest and some accommodation and other practical information.

ⓦ www.ourcrete.co.uk Idiosyncratic site run by two anglo Cretaphiles, with personal impressions, information on the island and some good images.

ⓦ www.plata.gr General site dealing with Haniá and Réthimnon provinces.

ⓦ www.sfakia-crete.com Potpourri site dealing with the Sfakiá area of the south coast, with everything from useful ferry timetables (including those to Gávdhos) and articles on Sfakiá's history to images of the fish you're likely to encounter on your taverna plate.

ⓦ www.west-crete.com Cretophiles' website which, despite its name, is not restricted to the west of the island. It covers travel and cultural topics (including trekking and naturist beaches) and has links to helpful businesses.

Telephone directory

ⓦ www.ote.gr Online telephone directory with anglicized section dealing with Crete.

Transport and accommodation

ⓦ www.crete-direct.com Site for viewing and booking villas and country houses.

ⓦ www.ferries.gr The site of the Paleologos Shipping agency, with excellent information on domestic and international ferry schedules.

ⓦ www.forthnet.gr/internetcity Forthnet is a Greek server that hosts a number of Crete-related sites. The intercity section has information on transport and accommodation in all the main towns (especially in Lasíthi) together with lots of links.

ⓦ www.greekhotel.com A site with links to fairly upmarket Greek and Cretan hotels, with images of many in this guide.

ⓦ www.greekislands.gr Good source for routes, timetables and fares for Greek ferries connecting with Crete and elsewhere, including the routes to Italy.

ⓦ www.gtp.gr The website of *Greek Travel Pages* (the fat printed manual on every Greek travel agent's desk). Mostly used for its ferry schedules (also kept on a separate site, ⓦ www.gtpweb.com) and despite a recent revamp is still not completely reliable.

ⓦ www.ktel.org The Cretan bus network's comprehensive website, giving details of seasonal timetables and fares.

ⓦ www.travelling.gr/camping/Crete A list of all the campsites on the island, with addresses and opening dates but no information on facilities.

ⓦ www.villasincrete.com Villa holidays site where you can view the property and book online.

ⓦ www.west-crete-rooms.com Site run by the Haniá Rental Accommmodation Union, with extensive listings of rooms places and small hotels throughout Haniá province. Online booking for most.

News and weather

ⓦ www.athensnews.gr The online edition of the *Athens News*, Greece's longest-running quality English-language newspaper.

ⓦ www.ekathimerini.com The online edition of the abridged English translation of *Kathimerini*, one of Greece's most respected dailies. It's fully archived for years back and has an excellent search facility.

ⓦ http://forecast.uoa.gr A good one-stop weather site maintained by the University of Athens physics faculty. To get the forecast for Crete you click on a thumbnail image of the entire country which must be enlarged to read conditions at specific places.

ⓦ www.georgioupoli.net Site of Local Explorer magazine, an English- and German-language publication, with news about the Apókoronas area centred on Yeoryioúpolis.

ⓦ www.hellas.com General Greek site with useful info and plenty of links to Greek news, sports, weather and traffic sites (in English) as well as Internet radio broadcasts.

ⓦ www.poseidon.ncmr.gr A Greek oceanographer's site maintained by the National Centre for Marine Research, which profiles Aegean weather meticulously, including groovy graphics of sea currents and surface winds, based on satellite imaging.

ⓦ www.stigmes.gr Excellent online version of Crete's leading monthly current affairs and style magazine; has a variety of stuff in English including cartoons and interesting articles on Cretan topics, as well as useful links to an online bookstore and other sites.

ⓦ www.usatoday.com/weather/basemaps /nw167540.htm Five-day Iráklion forecast.

Archeology and architecture

ⓦ www.uch.gr/crete/archaio/venetian.html A list of all the Venetian edifices surviving on the island.

ⓦ www.culture.gr The Greek Ministry of Culture's website. Good alphabetical gazetteer to monuments, archeological sites and museums.

Music and entertainment

ⓦ www.cretan-music.com An interesting website with useful background on Cretan traditional music, instruments and festivals.

ⓦ www.media.net.gr Complete listings and frequencies for Greek radio and TV stations; the Cretan sections are broken down into regions.

ⓦ http://stigmes.gr/br Informative site produced by Crete's leading monthly magazine which, in addition to background on Crete generally, has a section covering the history of Cretan folk music, particularly lyra.

Books and souvenirs

ⓦ www.cretashop.gr Online shop selling all kinds of Cretan products including herbs, wines, clothes, herbs, CDs and books.

ⓦ www.hellenicbookservice.com Website of major UK stockist of Greek- and Crete-related books complete with opinionated reviews of its stock and an online purchasing facility.

Work

ⓦ www.skywalker.gr Useful site for seeking employment in Greece and Crete with job postings and links to Greek newspaper job ads. Mainly aimed at professionals.

Maps

Island **maps** are available locally, but you'll almost certainly find a better one at home. Due to the reasons outlined below all maps suffer from lapses in accuracy, especially when it comes to minor roads and footpaths. The best for **driving** and **general use** are the Harms-Verlag, Road Editions and the *Rough Guide Crete* map. The Nelles and Freytag & Berndt (the latter published in Crete under the Efstathiadis Group imprint) maps are also satisfactory.

The best available maps are the Harms-Verlag (ⓦ www.harms-ic-verlag.de) two-map edition (*Crete Touring Map*) covering the eastern and western sectors at 1:100,000. Despite a relatively large scale the maps include many footpaths and topographical features missing from other publications. The two-map set is available from bookshops in Iráklion, Réthimnon and Haniá, as well as by mail order from specialist suppliers like Stanfords in London (see opposite).

Slightly more accurate for details – though in a busier and less easy on the eye format – are three maps by the Greek company Road Editions (ⓦ www.road.gr): a 1:200,000 map of the whole island as well as two 1:100,000 maps covering the western and eastern halves of Crete. The 1:140,000 *Rough Guide Crete* (ⓦ www.roughguides.com) map is also good, has been cross-checked by the authors and highlights many locations mentioned in the *Guide*.

Due to Greece's (and Crete's) geographical position, flanked by Turkey to the east and its Balkan neighbours to the north, government paranoia about maps falling into the wrong hands (usually Turkish ones) severely restricts the accuracy of what can be published. This particularly affects the more detailed **hiking or topographical maps**, making life in Crete often a trial for walkers and climbers.

A Cretan publication, the 1:100,000 *Crete Trekking and Road Map*, produced by Iráklion publisher **Petrákis**, is a worthy attempt to improve the situation for walkers. The island is covered in four provincial maps, and it's the first series to contain most of the walking trails, tracks and walkable gorges on the island (including the E4 European Footpath). Another decent map for walkers is the *Crete Map & Guide* pack produced by **Freytag & Berndt**; the 1:50,000 map is very clear, detailing twenty walks across the island described in the accompanying guide. The Haniá branch of the **Greek Mountaineering Club** also produce a guide with maps to the Haniá province section of the E4, and is stocked by the Haniá tourist office. Most of the maps mentioned here should be available from the map outlets in your own country (see opposite); Greek-produced maps, particularly the Petrákis editions, tend to be sold only on Crete and are available from bookshops on the island or by post from Planet International Bookstore, Hándhakos and Kidonias, in Iráklion (☎2810 289605, ℮pirgos@otenet.gr).

Finally, some parts of the island are covered by maps and guidelets produced by foreign ramblers, especially the areas around Yeoryioúpolis and Plakiás – these are mentioned in the relevant sections of the *Guide*, as well as the "Books" section of Contexts.

Map outlets

In the UK and Ireland

Stanfords 12–14 Long Acre, London WC2E 9LP ☎020/7836 1321, ⊛www.stanfords.co.uk. Also at 39 Spring Gardens, Manchester ☎0161/831 0250, and 29 Corn St, Bristol ☎0117/929 9966.

Blackwell's Map Centre 50 Broad St, Oxford OX1 3BQ ☎01865/793 550, ⊛maps.blackwell .co.uk. Branches in Bristol, Cambridge, Cardiff, Leeds, Liverpool, Newcastle, Reading and Sheffield.

Easons Bookshop 40–42 Lower O'Connell St, Dublin 1 ☎01/858 3881, ⊛www.eason.ie.

Heffers Map and Travel 20 Trinity St, Cambridge CB2 1TJ ☎01223/586 586, ⊛www.heffers.co.uk.

Hodges Figgis 56–58 Dawson St, Dublin 2 ☎01/677 4752, ⊛www.hodgesfiggis.com.

The Map Shop 30a Belvoir St, Leicester LE1 6QH ☎0116/247 1400, ⊛www.mapshopleicester.co.uk.

National Map Centre 22–24 Caxton St, London SW1H 0QU ☎020/7222 2466, ⊛www.mapsnmc.co.uk.

National Map Centre Ireland 34 Aungier St, Dublin ☎01/476 0471, ⊛www.mapcentre.ie.

Newcastle Map Centre 55 Grey St, Newcastle, NE1 6EF ☎0191/261 5622, ⊛www.newtraveller.com.

John Smith and Sons 26 Colquhoun Ave, Glasgow G52 4PJ ☎0141/221 7472, ⊛www.johnsmith.co.uk.

James Thin Melven's Bookshop 29 Union St, Inverness IV1 1QA ☎01463/233500, ⊛www.jthin.co.uk.

The Travel Bookshop 13–15 Blenheim Crescent, London W11 2EE ☎020/7229 5260, ⊛www.thetravelbookshop.co.uk.

Traveller 55 Grey St, Newcastle-upon-Tyne NE1 6EF ☎0191/261 5622, ⊛www.newtraveller.com.

In the US and Canada

110 North Latitude US ☎336/369-4171, ⊛www.110nlatitude.com.

Book Passage 51 Tamal Vista Blvd, Corte Madera, CA 94925 and in the historic San Francisco Ferry Building ☎1-800/999-7909 or ☎415/927-0960, ⊛www.bookpassage.com.

Distant Lands 56 S Raymond Ave, Pasadena, CA 91105 ☎1-800/310-3220, ⊛www.distantlands.com.

Globe Corner Bookstore 28 Church St, Cambridge, MA 02138 ☎1-800/358-6013, ⊛www.globecorner.com.

Longitude Books 115 W 30th St #1206, New York, NY 10001 ☎1-800/342-2164, ⊛www.longitudebooks.com.

Map Town 400 5 Ave SW #100, Calgary, AB T2P 0L6 ☎1-877/921-6277 or ☎403/266-2241, ⊛www.maptown.com.

Travel Bug Bookstore 3065 W Broadway, Vancouver, BC V6K 2G9 ☎604/737-1122, ⊛www.travelbugbooks.ca.

World of Maps 1235 Wellington St, Ottawa, ON K1Y 3A3 ☎1-800/214-8524 or ☎613/724-6776, ⊛www.worldofmaps.com.

In Australia and New Zealand

Map Centre ⊛www.mapcentre.co.nz.

Mapland (Australia) 372 Little Bourke St, Melbourne ☎03/9670 4383, ⊛www.mapland.com.au.

Map Shop (Australia) 6–10 Peel St, Adelaide ☎08/8231 2033, ⊛www.mapshop.net.au.

Map World (Australia) 371 Pitt St, Sydney ☎02/9261 3601, ⊛www.mapworld.net.au. Also at 900 Hay St, Perth ☎08/9322 5733, Jolimont Centre, Canberra ☎02/6230 4097 and 1981 Logan Rd, Brisbane ☎07/3349 6633.

Map World (New Zealand) 173 Gloucester St, Christchurch ☎0800/627 967, ⊛www.mapworld.co.nz.

Insurance

Even though basic EU health care privileges apply in Greece (see opposite for details), you'd do well to take out an insurance policy before travelling to cover against theft, loss, illness or injury. Before paying for a whole new policy, however, it's worth checking whether you are already covered: some all-risks homeowners' or renters' insurance policies *may* cover your possessions when overseas, and many private medical schemes (such as BUPA or WPA in the UK) offer coverage extensions for abroad.

In Canada, provincial health plans usually provide partial cover for medical mishaps overseas, while holders of official student/teacher/youth cards in Canada and the US are entitled to meagre accident coverage and hospital inpatient benefits. **Students** will often find that their student health coverage extends during the vacations and for one term beyond the date of last enrolment. Most **credit-card issuers** also offer some sort of vacation insurance, which is often automatic if you pay for the holiday with their card; however, it's vital to check just what these policies cover.

After exhausting the possibilities above, you might want to contact a **specialist travel insurance** company, or consider the travel insurance deal we offer (see box below). A typical travel insurance policy usually provides cover for the **loss** of baggage, tickets and – up to a certain limit – cash,

cards or cheques, as well as **cancellation** or curtailment of your journey. Most of them exclude so-called **dangerous sports** unless an extra premium is paid: in Crete this includes horse-riding, windsurfing, trekking, mountaineering and motorbiking. Many policies can be chopped and changed to exclude coverage you don't need – for example, sickness and accident benefits can often be excluded or included at will. If you do take medical coverage, ascertain whether benefits will be paid as treatment proceeds or only after return home, whether there is a **24-hour medical emergency number**, and how much the deductible is (sometimes negotiable). When securing baggage cover, make sure that the **per-article limit** – typically well under £500 in the UK – will cover your most valuable possession. Travel agents and tour operators in the UK are likely to **require travel insurance** when

Rough Guide travel insurance

Rough Guides Ltd offers a low-cost travel insurance policy, especially customized for our statistically low-risk readers by a leading British broker, provided by the American International Group (AIG) and registered with the British regulatory body, GISC (the General Insurance Standards Council). There are five main Rough Guides insurance plans: No Frills for the bare minimum for secure travel; Essential, which provides decent all-round cover; Premier for comprehensive cover with a wide range of benefits; Extended Stay for cover lasting four months to a year; and Annual multi-trip, a cost-effective way of getting Premier cover if you travel more than once a year. Premier, Annual Multi-Trip and Extended Stay policies can be supplemented by a "Hazardous Pursuits Extension" if you plan to indulge in sports considered dangerous, such as scuba-diving or trekking. For a policy quote, call the Rough Guide Insurance Line: toll-free in the UK ☎0800 015 0906 or ☎+44 1392 314665 from elsewhere. Alternatively, get an online quote at ⊛www.roughguides.com/insurance.

you book a package holiday, though they can no longer insist that you buy their own – however, you may be required to sign a declaration saying that you have a policy with a particular company.

If you need to make a **medical claim**, you should keep receipts for medicines and treatment, and in the event you have anything stolen or lost, you must obtain an **official statement** from the police or the airline which lost your bags. In the wake of growing numbers of fraudulent claims, most insurers won't even entertain one unless you have a police report. This can occasionally be a tricky business in Greece, since many officials simply won't accept that anything could be stolen on their turf, or at least don't want to take responsibility for it. Be persistent, and if necessary enlist the support of the local tourist police or tourist office. Bear in mind also that there's usually a **time limit** for submitting claims after the end of your journey.

Health

No inoculations are required for Greece, though it's wise to have a typhoid-cholera booster, and to ensure that you are up-to-date on tetanus and polio. Don't forget to take out travel insurance (see p.28), so that you're covered in case of serious illness or accidents.

The **water** is safe pretty much everywhere, and especially refreshing when it pours straight from a mountain spring. Despite this, in places like restaurants everyone drinks the bottled stuff instead. Crete has few of the water shortages which bedevil smaller islands – it's only in isolated villages or resorts that have grown faster than the plumbing can cope with that you're likely to have a problem.

Medical attention

For **minor complaints** it's enough to go to the local *farmakío*. Greek **pharmacists** are highly trained and dispense a number of medicines which in other countries can only be prescribed by a doctor. In the larger towns there'll usually be one pharmacist who speaks good English. If you regularly use any **prescription drug** you should bring along a copy of the prescription together with the generic name of the drug – this will help if you need to replace it and also avoid possible problems with customs officials. **Codeine** is banned in Greece, and if you import any you might find yourself in serious trouble – it's often found in common headache drugs such as Panadeine, Veganin, Solpadeine, Codis and Empirin Codeine, so check labels carefully.

Homeopathic and **herbal** remedies are also widely available: there are homeopathic pharmacies in Iráklion and Haniá and some larger towns; all homeopathic pharmacies are identified by the characteristic green cross.

Doctors and hospitals

For serious medical attention you'll find English-speaking **doctors** in any of the bigger towns or resorts: the tourist police or your consulate should be able to come up with some names if you have any difficulty.

EU nationals are officially entitled to **free medical care** in Greece, by virtue of the E111 form (see box, p.30) – but "free" means admittance to only the lowest grade of **state hospital** (known as a *yenikó nosokomeío*). In practice, hospital staff tend to greet E111s with uncomprehending looks, and you may have to request

The E111 form

At the time of writing, the E111 is available as a paper form – you can get one from post offices throughout the UK, or download it from the UK Department of Health website (⬤www.dh.gov.uk). However, the paper form is due to be replaced by a **European Health Insurance card** by December 2005; details will appear on the Department of Health website. For general information on the E111, obtain a copy of the excellent *Health Advice for Travellers* leaflet, published in the UK by the Department of Health and available free from post offices, doctors' surgeries and some travel agents.

reimbursement by the NHS upon your return (so get **receipts** for all drugs and treatments paid for). Basic treatment for cuts, broken bones and emergencies is given, but extended care and nursing are virtually non-existent; Greek families take food and bedding into hospitals for relatives, so as a tourist you'll face difficulties.

Rather better are the ordinary **state out-patient clinics** (*yatría*) attached to most hospitals and also found in rural locales. These operate on a first-come-first-served basis, so go early – usual hours are 8am–noon. Again, EU citizens are eligible for free treatment; if you don't have an E111, outpatient clinics make a small charge.

Specific health problems

The main health problems experienced by most visitors result from overexposure to the sun, and the odd nasty creature from the sea. To combat the former, wear a hat and drink plenty of fluids in the hot months to avoid any danger of **sunstroke**, and don't underestimate the power of even a hazy sun to burn. **Hayfever** sufferers should be prepared for an earlier season than at home. Remedies are available at most pharmacies but can work out expensive, so it's better to come prepared. On beaches a pair of goggles for swimming and footwear for walking over wet rocks are useful.

Hazards of the sea

You may have the bad luck to meet an armada of **jellyfish** (*tsoúkhtres*), especially in late summer; they come in various colours and sizes ranging from purple "pizzas" to invisible, minute creatures. Various over-the-counter remedies are sold in resort pharmacies to combat the sting, and baking soda or diluted ammonia also help to lessen the effects. The welts and burning usually subside of their own accord within a few hours; there are no deadly species in the waters around Crete.

Less vicious but more common are spiny **sea urchins**, which infest rocky shorelines year-round. If you're unlucky enough to step on, or graze against one, an effective way to remove the spines is with a needle (you can crudely sterilize it with heat from a cigarette lighter) and olive oil. If you don't remove the spines, they'll fester. You can take your revenge by eating the roe of the reddish-purple urchins, served as a delicacy (*achinósalata*) in many seafood restaurants.

The worst maritime danger – fortunately very rare – seems to be the **weever fish** (*dhrakéna*), which buries itself in tidal zone sand with just its highly poisonous dorsal and gill spines protruding. If you tread on one the pain is excruciating, and the consequences can range up to permanent paralysis of the affected area. The imperative first aid is to immerse your foot in water as hot as you can stand, which degrades the toxin and relieves the swelling of joints and attendant pain; however, you should also seek medical attention as soon as possible.

Another more common hazard are **stingrays** (Greek names include *platí*, *selakhí*, *vátos* or *trígona*), which mainly frequent bays with sandy bottoms where they can camouflage themselves. Though shy, they can give you a nasty lash with their tail if trodden on, so shuffle your feet a bit when entering the water. When snorkelling in deeper waters around the island, you may happen upon a brightly coloured

moray eel (*smérna*) sliding back and forth out of its rocky lair. Keep a respectful distance – their slightly comical air and clown-colours belie an irritable temper and the ability to inflict nasty bites or even sever fingers.

Mosquitoes and sandflies

While Cretan **mosquitoes** (*kounóupia*) don't carry anything worse than a vicious bite, they can be infuriating. The best solution is to burn pyrethrum incense coils (*spíres* or *fidhákia* in Greek), widely and cheaply available. If you're going to be staying in hotels you can also use an electrical device, called by the trade names Vape-Nat or Bay-Vap in Greece, which vaporizes an odourless insecticide tablet. These are often sold in pharmacies, for much less than they cost at home. A refinement of this contraption, Baygon, uses a 40-day fluid cartridge rather than tablets. Whilst eating or drinking outdoors, a rub-on stick such as Autan is equally effective.

If you are sleeping on or near a beach, it's wise to use an insect repellent, either lotion or wrist/ankle bands, and/or a tent with a screen to guard against **sandflies**. Their bites are potentially dangerous, carrying visceral leishmaniasis, a rare parasitic infection characterized by chronic fever, listlessness and weight loss.

Scorpions, snakes and insects

Adders (*ohiés*) and **scorpions** (*scorpií*) are found throughout the island. Both creatures are shy, but take care when climbing over dry stone walls where snakes like to sun themselves, and – particularly when camping – don't put hands or feet in places, like shoes, where you haven't looked first.

Snakebite causes very few deaths in Europe. Many snakes will bite if threatened, whether they are venomous or not. If a bite injects venom, then swelling will normally occur within thirty minutes. If this happens, get medical attention; keep the bitten part still, and make sure all body movements are as gentle as possible. If no medical attention is available then bind the limb firmly to slow the blood circulation, but not so tightly as to stop the blood flow. Like snakes, many reptiles – especially **tortoises** – can harbour salmonella bacteria, so avoid handling them.

Finally, in addition to munching its way through a fair amount of Greece's surviving pine forests, the **pine processionary caterpillar** – which takes its name from the long, nose-to-tail convoys which individuals form at certain points in their lifecycle – sports highly irritating hairs, with a poison worse than a scorpion's. If you touch one, or even a tree-trunk they've been on recently, you'll know all about it for a week, and the welts may require antihistamine to heal.

Costs, money and banks

Although prices have risen in recent years Crete is still inexpensive when compared with almost anywhere else in Europe. Travelling around is reasonably affordable, as are the costs of restaurant meals, accommodation and public transport, and if you're willing to cut a few corners and avoid the more overtly developed areas, you can still get by on relatively little.

Average costs

Prices tend to depend on where and when you go. The cities and tourist resorts are usually more expensive, and costs increase in July, August and at Easter. **Solo travellers**, of course, invariably spend more than if they were sharing food and rooms.

In most places, by keeping costs to the bare minimum, it should be possible to manage on a **daily budget** of around €25–30, assuming you're prepared to camp out and rough it a little – which probably means staying away from bars and tavernas and preparing your own meals. On €30–40 a day you can start to enjoy some comfort, providing you're sharing room costs. A budget of €40–50 will get you a share of a double room with bath or shower, breakfast, a picnic or simple taverna lunch, bus ride, museum tickets, a couple of beers and a restaurant evening meal. On €50–60 a day you could live quite well and even run to sharing a motorbike or small car.

Buses on Crete are still fairly inexpensive, although fares are rising. Iráklion to Haniá (about 140km) currently costs €10.50 one way whilst travelling almost the length of the island, from Haniá to Sitía (about 270km), costs around €21 one way. A basic one way **ferry** ticket to Athens will cost around €23 for deck class but frills such as aircraft seats, cabins or using a fast ferry will all add to the price.

For **accommodation**, you should always be able to find a basic room for two for around €20–30 a night and often cheaper in out-of-the-way mountain villages. However, although popular tourist venues like Áyios Nikólaos or Haniá and major towns like Iráklion are more expensive in high season, the coast is generally pricier than the inland areas, and the mountains and the south coast tend to be less expensive than the north. **Single accommodation** is rare, and much poorer value – you'll often have to pay the full double-room price in the resorts or haggle for around a third off. **Campsites** cost about €4 a person (plus about €4 for a tent and about €5 for a car) – and most campsites have tents or caravans to rent, usually much cheaper than rooms. With discretion, you can camp on your own near the beaches for free, although you should be sensitive to increasing local concerns about squalor and rubbish.

A solid **taverna meal**, even with considerable quantities of local wine, rarely works out much above €10–15 a head, although

adding a better bottle of wine, going for a classier place with an "international" menu or eating seafood in a touristy place could easily mean you'll pay more than double that. Sharing seafood and *mezédhes* (Greece's version of Spanish tapas) with salads and dips as sideplates is a good way to keep costs down, even in the pricier places.

Youth and student discounts

Various official and quasi-official **youth/student ID cards** soon pay for themselves in savings. Full-time students are eligible for the International Student ID Card (ISIC; Ⓦ www.isiccard.com), which entitles the bearer to special air and ferry fares and discounts at museums, theatres and other attractions. For Americans there's also a health benefit, providing token medical coverage and a per-day stipend for hospital stays up to two months. The card costs $22 for Americans, Can$16 for Canadians, A$16.50 for Australians, NZ$21 for New Zealanders, £6 in the UK, and €12.70 in the Republic of Ireland.

You only have to be 26 or younger to qualify for the **International Youth Travel Card**, which costs US$22/£7 and carries the same benefits. Teachers qualify for the **International Teacher Identity Card (ITIC)**, offering similar discounts and costing US$22, Can$16, A$16.50, NZ$21, and £6 in the UK. All these cards are available in the US from STA and Travel CUTS and, in Canada, Hostelling International; in the UK, Australia and New Zealand from STA.

Several other travel organizations and accommodation groups also sell their own cards, good for various discounts. A university photo ID might open some doors, but is not as easily recognizable as the ISIC cards, although the latter are often not accepted as valid proof of age.

Note that teachers, journalists and senior travellers also get discounts at sites and museums.

Money

Greece is one of twelve European Union countries that have changed over to a single currency, the **euro** (€). All prices in this book are given in euros and are correct at the time of going to press. Since the introduction of the new currency there have been many complaints in Greece (along with several other euro nations) about unjustified price increases and the practice of "rounding up" prices when converted from the old currency, the drachma.

The euro is a decimal currency comprised of 100 cents. Euro **coins** are issued in **denominations** of 1, 2, 5, 10, 20 and 50 cents and 1 and 2 euro; euro **notes** come in denominations of 5, 10, 20, 50, 100, 200 and 500 euro. The latter two high-value notes are rarely seen, and many shops, restaurants and other businesses refuse to accept them, fearing the risk of currency fraud.

At the time of writing the **exchange rate** for the euro was around €1.49 to the pound sterling (or £0.66 to one euro) and €1.25 to the dollar (€0.80 to one dollar). For the most up-to-date **exchange rates** of the US dollar or the pound sterling against the euro, consult the very useful currency speculators' website ⓦwww.oanda.com or ⓦwww.xe.com.

Banks and exchange

The airports at Haniá and Iráklion should always have an **exchange desk** operating for passengers on incoming international flights – but at peak periods there's often a queue and it's well worth taking some local currency to tide you over the first few hours.

Banks on Crete are normally open Mon–Thurs 8.30am–2pm, Fri 8.30am–1.30pm. Certain branches in the tourist centres open extra hours in the evenings and Saturday mornings to change money, while outside these hours larger hotels, travel agencies and even tourist information offices can often change money, albeit sometimes with hefty commissions. When using a bank, always take your passport with you as proof of identity and be prepared for at least one long queue – often you have to line up once to have the transaction approved and again to pick up the cash. **Commissions** vary considerably (€1.50–€2.50 per transaction is typical), even between branches of the same bank, so ask first.

There are a few alternatives to banks. **Travel agents** often serve as general purpose information centres in smaller resorts and will change travellers' cheques and bank notes. Although they're likely to be trustworthy, you should have a rough idea of what the official exchange rate is before you begin. Both commission and rate will usually (though not always) be worse than the banks'. The major tourist centres in the north of the island have a number of authorized **change bureaux** for exchanging foreign cash and travellers' cheques. When changing small amounts, choose those that charge a percentage commission (usually one percent) rather than a high flat minimum. Government and local government **tourist offices** offer exchange facilities at a rate similar to (and sometimes better than) the banks – they're in most of the major centres, and usually stay open until quite late in the evening. There are also a small number of 24-hour automatic **note-changing machines** in major towns on the north coast, but again a high minimum commission tends to be deducted.

Travellers' cheques

Travellers' cheques are the safest and easiest way to carry money, and are obtainable from banks (even if you don't have an account) or from offices of Thomas Cook or American Express. You'll pay a commission of between one and two percent, though enquire about any special commission-free deals from your travel agent or your home bank. They're accepted at all banks and also at quite a number of hotels, agencies and tourist stores. If you intend to spend much time away from the bigger centres in Crete, though, you should plan to have a fair amount of currency to hand.

Credit cards and ATMs

Major **credit cards** are widely accepted, but only by the more expensive stores, hotels and restaurants: they're useful for renting cars, for example, but no good in the cheaper tavernas or rooms places. If you run short of money, you can also get a **cash advance** on a credit card; however, there's a minimum limit of around €50. However, there is usually a two percent credit-card charge, often unfavourable rates and always interminable delays while transaction approval is sought by telex. Some private exchange places and even the odd hotel or travel agency also give advances on credit cards – there's a lower minimum, but they may charge more.

It's much easier to use the small but growing network of 24-hour **ATMs** (cash dispensers), although these are presently confined to the major towns along the north coast and Ierápetra, Plakiás and Paleohóra in the south. Due to frequent power and computer failures and eccentric machines telling you to come back later, you'd be wise not to rely solely on this means of getting hold of cash. Check in advance with your bank whether your card offers this facility (for which you will need a PIN number). It's much cheaper to use an ATM for transactions linked to a current (checking) account via the Plus/Cirrus systems, with charges of 2.25 percent on the sterling/dollar transaction value making them the **least expensive** way to get money in Greece as long as you withdraw more than €100. On the other hand, using credit cards at an ATM is one of the **most expensive** ways of obtaining cash: a cash advance per-transaction fee of £2 minimum typically applies in the UK, plus a foreign transaction surcharge of up to 2.75 percent on the total, depending on the card issuer; the "tourist" (not the more favourable "interbank") exchange rate will also be applied.

Wiring money

In an emergency you can have substantial amounts of **money wired** from your home bank, to a bank in Crete. Receiving funds by SWIFT transfer takes between two and ten working days. From the UK, a bank charge of 0.03 percent, with a minimum of £17, maximum £35, is typically levied for two-day service; some building societies charge a £20 flat fee irrespective of the amount. If you choose this route, your home bank will need the address and (ideally) the branch number of the bank where you want to pick up the money. It's unwise to transfer more than the equivalent of €10,000; above that limit, as part of measures to combat money-laundering, the receiving bank will begin asking awkward questions and imposing punitive commissions.

Having money wired from home using one of the **companies** listed below is never convenient; local affiliate offices other than the post offices are thin on the ground in Crete and it's also more expensive than using a bank. However, the funds should be available for collection at Amex's, Thomas Cook's or Western Union's local representative office within hours, sometimes minutes, of being sent.

Money-wiring companies

Thomas Cook US ☎1-800 287-7362, Canada ☎1-888 823-4732, Britain ☎01733/318 922, Northern Ireland ☎028/9055 0030, Republic of Ireland ☎01/677 1721, ⓦwww.thomascook.com. **Travelers Express MoneyGram** US ☎1-800 955-7777, Canada ☎1-800 933-3278, UK ☎0800 018 0104, Republic of Ireland ☎1850 205 800, Australia ☎1800 230 100, New Zealand ☎0800 262 263, ⓦwww.moneygram.com. **Western Union** US and Canada ☎1-800 325-6000, Australia ☎1800 501 500, New Zealand ☎0800 270 000, UK ☎0800 833 833, Republic of Ireland ☎1800 395 395, ⓦwww.westernunion.com.

Getting around

By Greek standards Crete is pretty well served for roads and transport. The main towns and resorts along the north coast are linked by an excellent road and a fast and frequent bus service. However, if you're keen to escape the crowds and experience some of Crete's remoter beaches and spectacular mountain scenery, you'll need to get off the main roads; for at least some of your time it's worth considering renting some transport or, better still, setting out on foot.

The main public transport **routes** and **timings** are detailed at the end of each chapter in "Travel details".

Buses

The only form of public transport on Crete, **buses** cover the island remarkably comprehensively. Modern, fast and efficient buses run along the main north-coast road every hour or so, while off the major routes services vary. The ones used primarily by tourists (to Omalós and Hóra Sfakíon for the Samariá gorge, or Festós and Mátala) tend also to be modern and convenient. Those that cater mainly for locals are generally older vehicles which run once-daily as transport to market or school – into the provincial capital very early in the morning and back out to the village around lunchtime, which means they're of little use for day-trips. There are few places not accessible by bus, but if you combine buses with some walking you'll get about extremely cheaply, if not always especially quickly.

Buses on Crete are a turquoise-green colour, and are run by a consortium of companies jointly known as **KTEL** (Kratikó Tamío Ellinikón Leoforíon). That this is not one single company is most obvious in Iráklion where there are two separate termini, operated by several companies each serving different directions. On the whole, buses serving a given village run from the provincial capital – Iráklion, Réthimnon and Haniá, or in Lasíthi province from Áyios Nikólaos and Sitía. There are also a number of small-scale services which cross inter-provincial borders. A **timetable** of island-wide services is produced each year, available from bus stations and tourist offices. You can also look up

KTEL's website (ⓦ www.ktel.org) which details current timetables and fares.

Taxis and tours

Local **taxis** are exceptionally good value, at least as long as the meter is running or you've fixed a price in advance. Much of their business is long-distance, taking people to and from the villages around the main towns (at some city taxi ranks and all major airports, there's a printed list of prices to the most common destinations). If you want to visit somewhere where there's only one bus, or spend some time hiking and get a ride back, it's well worth arranging for a taxi to pick you up: four people together in a taxi will pay little more per person than on the bus.

It's also quite easy to negotiate a day's or half-day's **sightseeing** trip by taxi, although this requires some Greek, and over long distances can become expensive.

A simpler alternative for a one-off visit is to take a **bus tour**. Travel agents everywhere offer the obvious ones – the Samariá gorge, Vái beach, and a local "Cretan night". A few offer much more adventurous alternatives – some of the best of these are detailed in the *Guide*. They're worth at least considering as a relatively inexpensive and easy way to see things you might otherwise be unable to get to, and you can always escape from the rest of the group once there.

Driving

While cars have obvious advantages for getting to the more inaccessible areas, Greece is one of the more expensive countries in Europe to **rent a car**, although prices have been coming down in recent years as competition has got fiercer. If you drive **your own vehicle** to and through Greece (not really an option on a short visit to Crete) via EU member states, you no longer require a Green Card. In accordance with EU directives, insurance contracted in any EU member state is valid in any other, but in many cases this is only third-party cover – the statutory legal minimum. Competition in the insurance industry is so intense however, that many UK insurers will throw in full pan-European cover for free or for a nominal sum, up to sixty days.

Upon arrival with EU number plates, your passport should no longer get a carnet stamp, and the car is, in theory, free to circulate in the country until its road tax or insurance expires. Beware, however, that the rules governing **car import** are in a constant state of flux, and there are reports of people being only allowed to use their cars for six-month periods each year (you choose the time period). Other nationalities will get a non-EU car entered in their passport; the **carnet** normally allows you to keep a vehicle in Greece for up to six months, exempt from road tax. It's difficult, though not impossible, to leave the country without the vehicle; the nearest customs post will seal it for you (while you fly back home for a family emergency, for example) but you must find a Greek national to act as your guarantor, and possibly pay storage. This person will assume ownership of the car should you ultimately abandon it.

Car rental

Car rental in Crete starts at €150 a week in high season for the smallest model (such as a Fiat Panda or Fiat 500), including unlimited mileage, tax and insurance. However, if you hire from a major international company like Hertz or Budget you pay at least 25 percent more than this. But **prices** vary wildly, so it's worth shopping around if you are looking to rent a car on the island; however, don't be fooled by the headline low prices offered by many renters who omit basic insurance protection in their rates. Outside peak season, at the smaller local outfits, you can sometimes get terms of about €30 per day, all inclusive, but three days is the preferred

minimum duration. The increasingly popular open jeeps begin at about €45 per day, rising to around €55 in high season. You may get a better price from one of the **foreign companies** such as Autos Abroad, Suncars or Holiday Autos (see box opposite) that deal with local firms than if you negotiate for rental in Crete itself. However, this is not always the case, particularly in low season, when if you have time to tour the local dealers and are willing to haggle you can often pick up a real bargain. Most **travel agents** can also offer car rental in Greece, though their rates are generally higher than the specialist rental agents.

In Crete, Clubcars, Reliable and Motor Club are dependable medium-sized companies with branches in many towns; all are considerably cheaper than (and just as reputable as) the biggest international operators. Throughout the *Guide* we have also listed a number of reliable local single-branch dealers in towns and resorts. Avoid renting a car on impulse from offices at the airport – you'll pay a premium for picking up your vehicle there, and rates are always higher than normal, often considerably so.

All agencies require either a credit card or a large cash **deposit** up front. Minimum age requirements vary from 21 to 25; in theory an **International Driving Licence** is also needed for non-EU drivers, but in practice European, Australasian and North American licences are honoured.

Note that initial rental prices quoted in Greece almost never include tax, **collision damage waiver** fees or personal insurance. All three are essential; the coverage included by law in the basic rental fee is generally inadequate, and failure to cover yourself properly could land you with a huge bill, often up to the total value of the vehicle if you seriously damage it or write it off. Expect to pay around €10 per day extra to cover yourself on the most basic model – and make sure you check the **small print** dealing with this in the leaflets given out by the rental companies or stated on your contract. Also, be careful of the hammering that cars get on minor roads and tracks; tyres and the underside of the vehicle are often excluded from insurance policies, especially when rented locally.

In terms of **available models**, the more competitive companies on the island tend to offer the Subaru Vivio, the Fiat Cinquecento and Panda and Seat Marbella as A-group cars, and Opel (Vauxhall) Corsa, Nissan Micra, Renault Clio and Fiat Uno/Punto in the B-group. The Seat Marbella should be avoided unless you're sticking to the coast – it's just not built for the Cretan terrain. Many dealers now offer more cars with air conditioning and radio-cassette; in slack periods companies will often rent you a car with these features for the same price as a model without.

Car rental agencies

In Britain

Avis ☎0870/606 0100, ⓦwww.avis.co.uk.
Budget ☎01442/276 266,
ⓦwww.budget.co.uk.
Europcar ☎0870/607 5000,
ⓦwww.europcar.co.uk.
National ☎0870/536 5365,
ⓦwww.nationalcar.co.uk.
Hertz ☎0870/844 8844, ⓦwww.hertz.co.uk.
Holiday Autos ☎0870/400 0099,
ⓦwww.holidayautos.co.uk.
Suncars ☎0870/500 5566, ⓦwww.suncars.com.
Thrifty ☎01494/751 600, ⓦwww.thrifty.co.uk.

In Ireland

Avis Northern Ireland ☎028/9024 0404, Republic of Ireland ☎021/428 1111, ⓦwww.avis.ie.
Budget Republic of Ireland ☎09/0662 7711,
ⓦwww.budget.ie.
Europcar Northern Ireland ☎028/9442 3444,
Republic of Ireland ☎01/614 2888,
ⓦwww.europcar.ie.
Hertz Republic of Ireland ☎01/676 7476,
ⓦwww.hertz.ie.
Holiday Autos Republic of Ireland ☎01/872 9366, ⓦwww.holidayautos.ie.

In North America

Alamo US ☎1-800462-5266, ⓦwww.alamo.com.
Auto Europe US and Canada ☎1-888223-5555,
ⓦwww.autoeurope.com.
Avis US ☎1-800230-4898, Canada
☎1-800272-5871, ⓦwww.avis.com.
Budget US ☎1-800527-0700, Canada
☎1-800472-3325, ⓦwww.budget.com.
Dollar US ☎1-800800-3665, ⓦwww.dollar.com.
Enterprise Rent-a-Car US ☎1-800726-8222,
ⓦwww.enterprise.com.

Europcar US & Canada ☎1-877/940 6900,
ⓦwww.europcar.com.
Europe by Car US ☎1-800223-1516,
ⓦwww.europebycar.com.
Hertz US ☎1-800654-3131, Canada
☎1-800263-0600, ⓦwww.hertz.com.
National ☎1-800962-7070,
ⓦwww.nationalcar.com.
Thrifty US and Canada ☎1-800847-4389,
ⓦwww.thrifty.com.

In Australia

Avis ☎13 63 33 or 02/9353 9000,
ⓦwww.avis.com.au.
Budget ☎1300/362 848, ⓦwww.budget.com.au.
Europcar ☎1300/131 390,
ⓦwww.deltaeuropcar.com.au.
Hertz ☎13 30 39 or 03/9698 2555,
ⓦwww.hertz.com.au.
Holiday Autos ☎1300/554 432,
ⓦwww.holidayautos.com.au.
National ☎13 10 45, ⓦwww.nationalcar.com.au.
Thrifty ☎1300/367 227, ⓦwww.thrifty.com.au.

In New Zealand

Apex ☎0800/93 95 97 or 03/379 6897,
ⓦwww.apexrentals.co.nz.
Avis ☎09/526 2847 or 0800/655 111,
ⓦwww.avis.co.nz.
Budget ☎09/976 2222 or ☎0800/652-227,
ⓦwww.budget.co.nz.
Hertz ☎0800/654 321, ⓦwww.hertz.co.nz.
Holiday Autos ☎0800/144 040,
ⓦwww.holidayautos.co.nz.
National ☎0800/800 115 or ☎03/366-5574,
ⓦwww.nationalcar.co.nz.
Thrifty ☎09/309 0111, ⓦwww.thrifty.co.nz.

In Crete

Blue Sea Iráklion ☎2810 221215,
ⓦwww.interkriti.gr/tour/bluesea.
Clubcars Áyios Nikólaos and other locations
☎28410 25868, ⓦwww.clubcars.net.
El Greco Cars Haniá ☎28210 90432.
Ellotia Tours Réthimnon ☎28310 51981,
ⓦwww.forthnet.gr/elotia.
Hermes Haniá ☎28210 54418.
Ilias Áyios Nikólaos ☎28410 28339.
Kosmos Iráklion; ☎2810 245345,
ⓦwww.cosmos-sa.gr.
Motor Club Iráklion and other locations ☎2810 222408, ⓦwww.motorclub.gr.
Reliable Iráklion ☎2810 344212.
Ritz Iráklion ☎2810 223638.
Tellus Haniá ☎28210 73788.

Driving in Greece

Greece has the highest **accident rate** in Europe after Portugal, and many of the roads can be quite perilous, particularly Crete's main highway, the E75 (see p.114). On other roads deep potholes can do serious damage to your axles, and an asphalted road can suddenly turn into a dirt track without warning on the smaller routes.

Regardless of traffic regulations, Greek drivers tend to insist on their **right of way** as when approaching a one-lane bridge – **headlights flashed** at you mean the opposite of what they mean in the UK or North America, signifying that the driver is coming through. On highways this signal is also used to alert fellow drivers coming in the opposite direction that there is a police speed trap or drink-driving control ahead – Greek drivers generally tend to regard authority as an unwarranted check on their freedom. In line with other European countries, children under ten are not allowed to sit in the front seats, and wearing a **seatbelt** is compulsory. However, most Greek drivers regard this as a ridiculous imposition from the EU headquarters in Brussels, and many still drive without a seatbelt. Greek and Cretan motorists also tend to **drink and drive** much more frequently than their European counterparts – bear this in mind, particularly when driving at night.

If you are involved in any kind of **accident** it's illegal to drive away, and you can be held at a police station for up to 24 hours. If this happens, ring your consulate immediately to get a lawyer (you have this right). Don't make a statement to anyone who doesn't speak, and write, very good English.

On the spot fines for minor traffic infringements such as speeding or crossing a central double white line are now common. You'll be issued with a ticket by a police officer, describing the infraction (in Greek) plus the amount of the fine, which varies from between €40 and €200 depending on the gravity of the offence. The address on the ticket will detail the office in the nearest town to which you should go to pay the fine. If you're in a hire car don't be tempted to discard the ticket: the system sends a fax within hours to the car rental office with details of the offence and the fine, which will be added to your hire charge. If you wish to contest the ticket go to the nearest police station in the town where you pay the fine. There's usually someone who speaks passable English and you should ask to speak to a senior officer; these characters have real pull, and if you manage to convince them your case is valid they have the power to reduce the fine, often by as much as half.

Tourists with proof of membership of official motoring associations such as AA, RAC and AAA are given free **road assistance** from **ELPA**, the Greek equivalent, which runs breakdown services – there's an office based in Crete (the information number is ☎174). In an **emergency** ring their road assistance service on ☎104, from anywhere in the country. Many car rental companies have an agreement with ELPA's competitors, Hellas Service and Express Service, but they're prohibitively expensive to summon on your own – over €140 to enrol as an "instant member" for a year.

Petrol/gasoline currently costs around €0.76 a litre for unleaded (*amólivdhi*) or super and €0.69 a litre for diesel (the same in Greek). It's easy to run out of fuel after dark or at weekends, especially in the extreme east and west of the island; most rural stations close at 7 or 8pm and some shut at weekends. When touring in these areas it's wise to maintain a full tank, especially when a weekend or national holiday is approaching. Also it's worth knowing that frequent power cuts also affect filling station pumps, which work on electricity. Filling stations normally take credit cards, although some of the more rural places may not have the facilities.

Bikes, mopeds, scooters and cycles

Motorbikes, mopeds and **Vespas** are also widely available to rent in Crete, at prices starting at around €18 a day (€90 a week) for a 50cc moped, and €25 a day (€140 a week) for a 175cc trail bike. Reputable establishments demand a full motorcycle driving licence for any engine over 90cc (the law actually stipulates "over 50cc"), and you will usually have to leave your passport (sometimes a valid credit card is acceptable) as security. For smaller models any driving licence will do.

The smaller bikes and scooters – known in Greek as **papákia** (little ducks) after their characteristic noise – are ideal for pottering around for a day or two, but don't regard them as serious transport: Crete is very mountainous and the mopeds simply won't go up some of the steeper hills, even carrying only one person. Be sure not to run beyond the range of your petrol tank either, as they're not designed for long-distance travel and there are few filling stations outside the towns. For serious exploration, or to venture into the mountains, you really need a motorbike or a powerful Vespa – the latter is cheaper but much more dangerous.

Whatever you rent, make sure you check it thoroughly before riding off, since many are only cosmetically repaired. If you break down it's often your responsibility to return the machine, so always take the phone number of the rental company.

Although motorbikes are enormous fun to ride around, you need to take more than usual care: there's an alarming number of **accidents** each year (many fatal) among visitors and locals because basic safety procedures are not followed. It's only too easy to come to grief on a potholed road or steep dirt track, especially at night. You should never rent a bike which you feel you can't handle, and always use a **helmet** (the latter is required by Greek law, which after years of laxity is now being more strictly enforced). All operators should have helmets (*kránio*), but you'll probably have to ask for one; for reasons of comfort and hygiene some people now bring their own helmet with them. Quite apart from any injuries, you're likely to be charged a criminally high price for any repairs needed for the bike, so make sure that you are adequately **insured**, both in the rental agreement (which you should read carefully) and by your own travel insurance (see p.28). Note that many of these schemes specifically exclude injuries sustained while riding/driving a rented vehicle.

If you are thinking of touring Crete by motorbike, it's worth getting hold of a copy of *Unexplored Crete* (see p.456), which covers the island from a biker's viewpoint with suggested itineraries and details of many off-road tracks, along with helpful hints.

Cycling

Cycling isn't greatly popular in Crete – not surprising, perhaps, in view of the mountainous terrain and fierce summer heat. Even so, riding a bike offers an incomparable view of the island and – if you're reasonably fit – guarantees contact with locals whom the average visitor could never meet. You can bring your own bike by plane (it's normally free within your ordinary baggage allowance) or by sea if you're coming from Italy or Athens (in which case it should go free on the ferry). On the island you may have difficulty with bus conductors – always protective of their luggage compartments – and cycle repair shops are hard to find outside the major towns of Iráklion, Réthimnon and Haniá, so bring as many spares as you think you'll need. The popularity of **mountain bikes** has resulted in a proliferation of rental outlets in all the major tourist centres.

Walking and hitching

The idea of **walking** for pleasure has yet to catch on widely in Crete. However, if you have the time and stamina it's probably the single best way to see the island. There are suggestions for hikes – from easy strolls to serious climbing – throughout the *Guide*, and further tips for hikers in Contexts. *Landscapes of Eastern Crete* and *Landscapes of Western Crete* (see "Books", p.456) make excellent further reading; for details of walkers' **maps** of Crete, see p.26.

If you're planning some serious walking – such as any of the various gorges – stout shoes or trainers are essential and **walking boots** with firm ankle support recommended, along with protection against the sun and adequate water supplies. Crete also offers some exciting possibilities for **climbers**: contacts for the local mountaineering clubs (EOS) in Iráklion, Réthimnon and Haniá are given in their respective listings.

When you get tired of walking, or you're stuck in a place after the last bus back has gone, **hitching** is an option – although this is potentially dangerous, and is certainly inadvisable for women travelling alone. Attendant risks aside, it can also be a wonderful way to get to know the island and to pick up some Greek. Your luck hitching in Crete very much depends on where you are. The main road along the north coast is very fast if you want to travel some distance in a hurry, though drivers are less inclined to stop. In rural areas, hitching can be great as long as you're not too pushed for time – most people will stop (the more obscure the road, the better your chance), but there may be little traffic and locals are rarely going further than the next village.

Ferries

Around the island numerous **local ferry services** run to offshore islets and isolated beaches; these are detailed throughout the *Guide*. Where there is no ferry service you can often arrange a trip by **kaïki** (small boat) with local fishermen. An enquiry at the bar in the nearest fishing village will usually turn up someone willing to make the trip – it's always worth trying to knock a bit off the first price quoted. To give some idea of prices, a *kaïki* from Móhlos, near Áyios Nikólaos, to Psíra would cost about €40 return, which includes a couple of hours on the island.

Accommodation

There are vast numbers of beds available for tourists in Crete, and most of the year you can rely on turning up pretty much anywhere and finding something. In July and August, however, you can run into problems unless you've booked in advance, especially in the bigger resorts and the towns of Iráklion, Haniá and Áyios Nikólaos. The best solution is to ring ahead (just after noon is a good time, which is when rooms have to be vacated) or to turn up at each new place early in the day and take whatever is on offer in the hope that you'll be able to exchange it for something better later.

Hotels and rooms

Hotels are categorized by the tourist police from "Luxury" down to the almost extinct "E" class, and all except the top category have to keep within set price limits. Letter ratings are supposed to correspond to facilities available, though in practice categorization can depend on such factors as location within a resort and "influence" with tourism authorities. "D"-class places usually come with en-suite bath and WC, whilst in "C" class this is mandatory, along with a bar or breakfast area. Having a pool and/or tennis court means a B-class rating, while A-class hotels must have a bar, restaurant, lifts and extensive common areas. Away from the cities, often they and the deluxe outfits (essentially

self-contained complexes) back onto a beach. C- and D-class places tend to be very reasonably priced, costing €45–75 for a double room with bath and €30–60 for (rare) single rooms. More luxurious establishments and quite a few of the more "charming" smaller hotels, except perhaps in the centres of larger towns, are often fully booked in advance by foreign tour operators.

If you're on a limited budget, for much of the time you'll be staying in "**rooms**" (*dhomátia* – but usually spotted by a "Rooms for Rent" or "*Zimmer Frei*" sign), which again are officially controlled and classed "A" to "C". Many of these establishments are generally cleaner and much more congenial than lower-category hotels of a similar price. Most rooms places are in new

Accommodation price codes

Throughout the book we've categorized accommodation according to the following **price codes**, which denote the cheapest available double room in high season. For rented apartments and villas, the price code refers to the price of the whole apartment, not just to a double room within the apartment. Out of season, room rates can drop by up to fifty percent, especially if you negotiate rates for a stay of three or more nights. Single rooms, where available, cost around seventy percent of the price of a double. **Breakfast** is often included in the room price, and we've indicated where this is so. Note also that prices tend to be higher in the main towns and coastal resorts than in the less touristy places inland.

❶ up to €20	❹ €40–49	❼ €80–99
❷ €20–29	❺ €50–59	❽ €100–130
❸ €30–39	❻ €60–79	❾ €130 upwards

purpose-built apartment buildings, but some are literally rooms in people's homes, where you'll often be treated with disarming hospitality. The most basic rooms – now becoming rare – might consist of a bare concrete space with a bed and a hook on the back of the door, and toilet facilities (cold water only) outside in the courtyard; at the fanciest end are fully furnished places with en-suite marble bathrooms. Between these extremes you'll probably find a choice of rooms at various prices – they'll always offer you the most expensive first. Price and quality are not necessarily directly linked, so always ask to see the room first. A double room without its own bath or shower could cost anything from €20 for a very basic place out of season, to €50–plus for high-season luxury in a resort. Note that rooms are not generally available from late October through to the beginning of April, when only hotels tend to remain open.

Many rooms (sometimes described as "**studios**") have a small **kitchenette** – usually a fridge, sink and a couple of hotplates in the room itself, with pans, cutlery and crockery normally provided.

Finding a room is usually simple, and owners frequently descend on ferry or bus arrivals in order to fill any space they have. In smaller places, just ask in a taverna or *kafeníon*: even if there are no official places around, there's often someone prepared to earn extra money from putting you up. In larger places the tourist police now post signs warning against going with people who offer rooms. Some caution is sensible – make sure that you at least know where you're being taken. It's also wise to be aware of the "airport taxi scam" when you pick up a cab at Iráklion or Haniá airports: drivers frequently attempt to persuade you to go to a "good" hotel or rooms establishment (perhaps after rubbishing the one you have in mind) with which, of course, he has an arrangement.

Rooms proprietors usually ask to keep your **passport**: ostensibly "for the tourist police", but in reality to prevent you leaving with an unpaid bill. Some may be satisfied with just taking down the details, as in hotels, and they'll almost always return the documents once you get to know them, or if you need them for changing money. In the larger resorts the only way to keep hold of your passport may be to pay in advance.

Prices for rooms and hotels should be displayed on the back of the door (often referred to as the "door price"): if you feel you're being overcharged at an officially registered place, threaten to go to the tourist police (who are very helpful in such cases), although small amounts over the odds may be legitimately explained by tax or out-of-date forms. In recent years there has been more bed capacity than visitors, which has led to proprietors vigorously undercutting their competitors. Away from the coast you'll often pay less than the official door price – occasionally in the towns, too, if you arrive well out of season or bargain hard. It's worth remembering that Greeks and Cretans are

Hot water

Rooftop **solar units** (*iliaká*), with their non-existent running costs, are more popular in hotels and rooms than electric **immersion heaters** (*thermosífona*). Under typical high-season demand, however, solar-powered tanks tend to run out of hot water with the post-beach shower crunch around 6–7pm, with no more available until the next day. A heater, either as a backup or primary source, is more reliable; proprietors may either jealously guard the **boiler controls** or entrust you with its workings, which involves either a circuit breaker or rotary switch turned to "I" for fifteen minutes. Never shower with a *thermosífina* powered up (look for the glow-lamp indicator on the tank) – besides the risk of electric shock from badly earthed plumbing, you're likely to empty a smaller tank and burn out the heating element.

born traders, so haggling for a better price is quite acceptable, providing you're not seen as being unreasonable.

Apartments and villas

Although one of the great traditions of Greek travel is finding that perfect coastal **villa** and renting it for virtually nothing for a whole month, these days this is almost impossible, certainly at the height of the Cretan summer. All the best seaside villas are contracted out to agents and let through foreign operators. Even if you do find one empty for a week or two, renting it in Crete costs far more than it would have done to arrange from home (to arrange this, see the specialist operators on p.13).

Having said that, if you arrive and decide you want to drop roots for a while, you can still strike lucky if you don't mind avoiding the coast altogether. Pick an untouristed inland village – in the Amári valley, for example, up behind Paleohóra or inland from Réthimnon or Haniá – get yourself known and ask about; you might still pick up a wonderful deal. Out of season your chances are much better – even in touristy areas, between October and March (sometimes as late as April and May) you can bargain a very good rate, especially for stays of a month or more. Travel agents are another good source of information on what's available locally, and many rooms places have an apartment on the side or know someone with one to rent. Likely villa-renting possibilities are suggested throughout the *Guide*.

Another alternative is to rent an **apartment** in one of the larger towns. Most proprietors hope for longer-term tenants, but you might be able to strike a deal: look for a sign

"*Enoikhiázete*" or check classified ads in the local papers.

Youth hostels

Even cheaper than rooms, there are four official and semi-official **youth hostels** (*ksenón neótitas*) on Crete, all of which must be among the least strictly run in the world. However the official hostel movement in Greece is in a state of upheaval, largely due to funding problems; as a result many hostels on the island have closed down and others have been left to fend for themselves. This has raised prices, and whilst the better establishments are still good places to meet people, you may well pay as much as the cheaper rooms places. Crete's surviving hostels are in Iráklion, Hersónisos, Réthimnon and Plakiás; the last two are particularly good. Facilities are basic – you pay around €7–10 a night for a dormitory bed on which to spread your sleeping bag – but they usually offer cheap meals and/or kitchen facilities, a good social life and an excellent grapevine for finding work or travelling companions. They rarely ask to see a membership card, though if you want to be on the safe side, join your home country's hostelling association before you go.

A few of the downmarket hotels, especially in Iráklion and Haniá, are run on similar lines as unofficial hostels: here or from a sympathetic rooms or taverna proprietor, you may be able to negotiate **roof space**. Sleeping on the tiles is better than it sounds – most Cretan buildings have flat concrete roofs on which will be provided a mattress on which to lay your sleeping bag; there's also often an awning for shade. The nights are generally warm and the stars are stunning, though as this practice is now officially illegal and proprietors face losing their licence, it's becoming increasingly rare.

Camping

Official **campsites** in Crete are surprisingly rare. On the whole they're not very good, tending to be either very large and elaborate or else nothing more than a staked-out field. Although prices start at around €4 a night per person at the latter (and rise to at least double this at the more upmarket places), they mount up once you've added a charge for a tent (about €3 for a two-person model or €5 for something larger), and the same again for a vehicle and for everyone in your group – a basic room may represent better value, unless of course you're hankering for the great outdoors. A leaflet detailing Crete's seventeen official campsites and seven mountain refuges is widely available from tourist offices on the island.

"**Freelance camping**" outside authorized campsites has always been the cheapest and in many ways most pleasant means of travel around the Greek islands. In Crete, however, it's a dying tradition. For a start, it's illegal, and once in a while the law on this

gets enforced. Also, the best sites are gradually being developed, which inevitably means turfing off the "undesirables" (and irresponsible campers have sometimes left otherwise scenic sites filthy). Nevertheless, with discretion and sensitivity it can still be done, and just occasionally you may find yourself with nowhere to sleep but the beach. Obviously the police crack down on people camping rough on (and littering) popular mainstream tourist beaches, especially when a large community of campers is developing; elsewhere, though, nobody is really bothered. The best plan is to find a sympathetic taverna near which to camp: if you eat there regularly they'll often be prepared to guard your gear during the day and let you take showers. If you do camp like this, however, take your rubbish away with you.

From May until early September it's warm enough to sleep out in just a lightweight sleeping bag (though the nights can be chilly in mountainous zones), so you don't even need to drag round a tent. A waterproof bag (available from camping shops) or groundsheet is useful to keep out the late summer damp, and a foam pad lets you sleep in relative comfort almost anywhere.

Eating and drinking

Greeks spend a lot of time socializing outside their homes, and sharing a meal is one of the chief ways of doing it. The atmosphere is almost invariably relaxed and informal, and expense-account prices are rare. Greeks are not prodigious drinkers – tippling is traditionally meant to accompany food – though there are plenty of bars and pubs in the tourist resorts, while you can always get a beer, a glass of wine or an ouzo at a café.

While **Greek food** is not generally regarded as one of the world's great cuisines, at its best it can be delicious – fresh, simple and flavoured with the herbs that scent the countryside. The most common complaint is that

food is often lukewarm and always oily. Both are deliberate, and any local will be happy to lecture you on the dangers of consuming too-hot food and on the life-enhancing properties of good olive oil. To get your food hot ask that it be served "*zestó*", and to get it with little or no oil stress "*horís ládhi*", although the fact remains that many foods are cooked in olive oil.

This oil obsession has some justification, as the island's extremely **healthy diet**, based on wheat, olive and grapes (the so-called Mediterranean diet) has led to its having one of the longest-lived and least diseased populations in the world. In the countryside, and in the better town tavernas, the food may be plain, but its ingredients will be fresh and local and often naturally organic; most Cretans have access to a smallholding of some kind, or if not, to local markets where the island's excellent agricultural produce is sold.

Breakfast, fast food and snacks

In common with their classical forebears, Greeks generally don't eat much in the way of **breakfast** – hence this is not a meal normally served in regular Cretan bars and restaurants. Don't despair though – if your hotel doesn't offer it, all the major resorts have plenty of places offering a choice of English or Continental starts to your day. For something more authentic and better value, search out instead a **galaktopoleío** (milk bar), which serve puddings and yoghurt (many *kafenía* also serve yoghurt with honey), or a **zaharoplastío** (patisserie) for gorgeously sweet and syrupy cakes and pastries. A combination **galaktozaharopolío** (quite a mouthful in every sense) is not uncommon.

At **bakeries**, you'll find oven-warm flaky pies filled with feta cheese (*tirópita*), with spinach or wild greens (*spanakópita* or *hortópita*), sausage (*louhanikópita*) or, better still, *bougátsa*, filled with creamy cheese and sprinkled with sugar. In the tourist areas many of the bakeries now cater for northern European palates by turning out croissants, doughnuts and even wholemeal (*olikís*) and rye (*sikalísio*) breads. *Kafenía* normally make no objections if you eat these at an outdoor table, but politeness demands that you order at least a coffee.

Ubiquitous **fast-food** snacks include **souvláki** – small kebabs most commonly in the form of the doner-kebab type **yíros píta** or chunks of *píta-souvláki*, stuffed into a doughy bread (more like Indian naan than

pita bread) along with salad and yoghurt, and quite superb. These are all inexpensive, and are at their best and most varied in the larger towns. You'll also find places serving **pizza** – usually excellent at specialist places and awful in tavernas – and **tost** – bland ham-and-cheese toasties; but avoid Cretan hamburgers at all costs.

For a food and drink glossary, see p.469.

Tavernas and restaurants

Most Cretan restaurants describe themselves as **tavernas**, though you can also get a meal at an *estiatório* or a *psistariá* as well as in *ouzerís* and many others. **Estiatória** are very similar to tavernas but tend to be simpler and less expensive, perhaps more traditionally Greek. **Psistariés** are restaurants that specialize in fresh prepared plates – predominantly grilled meat but often good vegetables too. A **psarótaverna** is a taverna which specializes in fish. **Ouzerí** (the same in the Greek plural – we've added "s" for clarity) are bars specialising in ouzo and *mezedhés*. They are well worth trying for the marvellous variety of **mezedhés** (small plates of food) they serve, although the most authentic are to be found in the larger towns and resorts where there's a large enough customer base to keep them on their toes. At the better places several plates of *mezedhés* will effectively substitute for a meal at a taverna (though it may not work out any cheaper if you have a healthy appetite; and *mezedhés* are also served at many tavernas). Wherever you eat, chic appearance is not always a good guide to quality; often the most basic place will turn out to be the best, and in swankier restaurants you may well be paying for the linen and stemmed wine glasses.

Often at traditional tavernas and *estiatória* there are no menus and you're taken into the **kitchen** to inspect what's on offer: uncooked cuts of meat and fish, simmering pots of stew or vegetables, trays of baked foods. Even where there is a **menu** (usually in English as well as Greek) it's often a standard printed form that bears little relation to what is actually on offer: again, check the kitchen or display case.

If you're unsure about the **price** of something, ask before ordering since it always

Crete's top ten tavernas

There are some great restaurants and tavernas across the island and, regrettably, quite a few that could do better. We've found those below (ranked in no particular order) to be outstanding in terms of quality, value, ambience and welcome.

El Greco Lendas (p.155)
Creta Giannis Hersónisos (p.123)
Pagopoleion Iráklion (p.96)
Pelagos Áyios Nikólaos (p.182)
Aiolus Pahiá Ámmos (p.194)

Porfira Makryialós (p.224)
To Pigadi Réthimnon (p.249)
Akrogiali Haniá (p.316)
Karnáyio Haniá (p.316)
Caravella Paleohóra (p.389)

seems to turn out more expensive if you wait until after you've eaten. Fish is almost always priced by weight, and is usually very expensive. All restaurants and tavernas must by law display a written menu with prices, taxes and service charges (if any). At the end of the meal you are entitled by law to a **bill** (check), and cash register receipts are now required in all establishments, but these often only state the grand total and don't always itemize the individual dishes. There's always a small **cover charge**, which includes the bread you'll inevitably be given. You can always ask for an itemized bill, but as this will often be scribbled in totally illegible Greek script, it may not be much help. Though most places in Crete are honest, if you think you're being hoodwinked get the waiter or manager to explain in detail what you are being asked to pay for. If you're still not satisfied the local tourist office will often be willing to take up your claim, or you could try the tourist police who are usually sympathetic. Taxes and service are normally included in the prices of the dishes in most restaurants and tavernas so, unless you're feeling overwhelmingly expansive, a **tip** of five percent will suffice.

Cretans generally eat late: **lunch** is served at 2–3pm, **dinner** at 9–11pm. You can eat earlier than this, but you're likely to get indifferent service at a tourist establishment or find yourself eating alone everywhere else. If you find that you can't wait that long, do what the locals do: take an aperitif along with a few *mezédhes*.

Greek dishes and Cretan specialities

As Cretan restaurants increasingly adapt themselves to tourists, you'll find that some of the advice below on traditional Greek foods and restaurants no longer applies in the resorts, where you're more likely to get western European–style service (places much patronised by the French, for example, offer fixed-price set menus. On the other hand, the better tavernas have started to recognize the value of their culture and serve more consciously **traditional foods** in traditional ways – usually excellent.

A typical Greek **meal** consists of appetizers and main course (only the tourist restaurants serve desserts though there's often fruit or fresh yoghurt) – the Greek practice is to visit a *zaharoplastío* for pastries, coffee and liqueurs once the main course is over.

The most interesting starters are also often served as **mezédhes** from which you can make up a meal. They include tzatziki (yoghurt, garlic and cucumber dip), *melitzanosaláta* (aubergine/eggplant dip), *kolokythákia tiganitá* (courgette/zucchini slices fried in batter) or *melitzánes tiganités* (aubergine/eggplant slices fried in batter), *yígandes* (white haricot beans in tomato sauce), *tyropitákia* or *spanakópites* (small cheese and spinach pies), *revythókeftedhes* or *pittaroúdhia* (chickpea patties similar to falafel), *okhtapódhi* (octopus) and *mavromátika* (black-eyed peas).

In tavernas, courses are often served at the same time – if you want the main course later, stagger your ordering. The **main course** of meat or fish comes on its own except for maybe a piece of lemon or half a dozen chips (fries); lamb, where available, is usually the best meat, local and excellent, if a little pricier than the alternatives. Salads and **vegetables** are served as separate dishes and usually shared. Vegetable dishes (usually cooked in a tomato sauce) are often very good in themselves and, if you order a

Vegetarians

If you're vegetarian, the news from Crete is nowadays far better than it used to be. Quite apart from the fact that meals based on pizza are always available, as are traditional snacks like *tirópita*, the increased interest in local cuisine, as well as pressure from tourists, has seen far more vegetable dishes appear on local menus. Many *mezédhes* like tzatziki and *yígandes* are naturally meat free; you'll find excellent salads everywhere, and there are frequently vegetable baked dishes like *briam*, *imam bayaldi* or *bouréki*.

few between several people, can make a satisfying meal. Check out the kitchen for **oven-baked casserole dishes** such as *moussakas* or *pastítsio* (macaroni and minced meat), meat or game **stews** like *kokinistó*, *stifádho* or simply *arní me patátes* (lamb with potatoes), and *yemistá* (stuffed tomatoes or peppers), which are generally delicious and less expensive than straight meat or fish dishes.

In season, **fish** is varied and delicious, but in summer visitors get a relatively poor choice: most of what is on offer is frozen, farmed or imported from Egypt and North Africa. Dragnet trawling is prohibited from the end of May until the beginning of October, when only lamp-lure, trident and multi-hook line methods are allowed. During these warmer months, such few fish as are caught tend to be smaller and dry-tasting. Taverna owners often comply only minimally with the requirement to indicate when seafood is frozen (look for the abbreviation "*kat*" on the Greek-language side of the menu), so don't look too disparagingly at the solitary seafront taverna that tells the truth: the others may prefer to leave you in ignorance. All that said, there are quite a few excellent fish tavernas across the island, and although seafood can be relatively expensive it's still a bargain compared with typical northern European restaurant prices. And if the prices on the menu seem phenomenally high, that's generally because they are **per kilo**; most tavernas will encourage you to go into the kitchen to see what's available and when you've selected your fish they'll weigh it to determine the actual price (don't leave it to the waiter, or you'll get the biggest). An average portion of whitefish should weigh in the region of 200–300g. Some Cretan favourites are *sargós* (white bream), *skorpídi* (scorpion fish), *barbounía* (red mullet), *fangrí* (common

sea bream) and *skáros* (parrotfish), a tasty white fish which is eaten whole. The least expensive consistently available fish are *gopés* (bogue), *atherína* (sand smelts) and *maridhés* (picarel), eaten head and all, best rolled in salt and sprinkled with lemon juice. The island's *kakaviá*, a fish soup flavoured with lemon, wild onions and herbs can be a fabulous treat.

Traditional **Cretan specialities** increasingly find their way onto menus too: some of the more common among dozens of typical dishes are snails (*tsalingária*) and rabbit (*kounéli*), both often served as a *stifádho* (stewed with onions). Look out too for *kalitsounia* (savoury stuffed pastries). Another speciality you also shouldn't miss if you get a chance is *hórta* – the wild greens that grow in abundance on the Cretan hills. These are gathered and boiled to be served up luke-warm (or sometimes cold), dressed with olive oil and vinegar, and can be delicious – or at the very least good for you. Although you can eat them all year round, spring and autumn are the best times, when they grow vigorously in the damper climate.

Self-catering

Stores and markets open very early and yoghurt, bread, eggs or fruit, as well as picnic foods like cheese, salami, olives and tomatoes are always easy to buy. Remember that Greek **cheese** isn't all feta (salty white sheep's cheese) and, if you ask, there are some remarkably tasty local Cretan varieties: try *mitizíthra*, *káskavali*, *kritiƙo* or *graviéra*, the last a peppery, mature, full-fat sheep's cheese. Unfortunately, they're all surprisingly expensive. Beach picnics can be further supplemented by tinned foods such as stuffed vine leaves (*dolmádhes*) or baby squid (*kalamarákia*).

Fruit is wonderful, and seasonal fruits are exceptionally inexpensive – look out for what's on offer in the markets or by the roadside: cherries in spring; melons, watermelons, plums and apricots in summer; pears and apples in autumn; oranges and grapes most of the time. They even grow small bananas in the area around Mália – an endeavour heavily subsidized by the EU.

Drinking

For ordinary drinking you go to a **kafeníon** – a simple Greek coffee shop or café usually filled with old men arguing and playing *távli* or backgammon, a national obsession (most places will lend you a set). They start the day selling coffee (*kafé*) until this is gradually replaced by ouzo (an aniseed-flavoured spirit, drunk neat or mixed with water). Later still, brandy is served (usually Metaxa or Botrys, graded with three, five or seven stars – you'll be hard pressed to tell the difference) or *raki*, a burningly strong, flavourless spirit also known in Crete as *tsípouro* or *tsikoudhiá*. *Raki* is also Greece's great ice-breaker and the symbol of the hand of friendship being extended: wherever you're offered one you're being honoured, so it's polite to accept even if you have to force it down. Outside the major towns, most *raki* will be home-made – stills are everywhere in the countryside, especially the mountains. Cretans pride themselves on being able to detect the most subtle distinctions in taste and quality of one brew against another. Commercial brands on the market are usually viewed with contempt, and everyone thinks his own concoction to be the nectar of the gods.

The miniature Greek **coffee** is what most Westerners would call "Turkish". It makes a great start to the day or a pick-me-up later – once you've acquired the taste and learned to leave the grounds behind in the cup. Most Cretans drink it medium-sweet or *métrio*; if you want no sugar at all, ask for *skéto*, while *glikó* is sickeningly sweet. If you like Greek coffee, ask for a *kafé ellinikós* – many Cretan *kafeníon* proprietors assume foreigners dislike their native brew, so by choosing it you'll rise greatly in their estimation. Ordinary coffee is also usually available – ask for "Nescafé", which is what it generally is (*Nes*

me gála is Nescafé with milk); refreshing iced coffee is known as *frappé*. Ouzo and other drinks are traditionally served with small snacks – **mezédhes** (see p.44) – nowadays you generally have to order and pay for these, though in country districts you may be pleasantly surprised at the generosity of many *kafenía*.

Tea (*tsá*), is often available too, usually served black with a tin of milk to add, although it can taste better with lemon instead (*me lemóni*). In the towns, many of the new-style *kafenía* now serve a whole range of herbal teas, including Cretan **dittany** (*díktamos*), an infusion made from the leaves of a plant unique to the island and used by the ancients as a medicinal panacea.

Real **bars** are rare in traditional Crete, though occasionally you'll find an *ouzerí*, which differs little from a *kafeníon*. Bars for the younger set now proliferate in the major towns and cities, mostly following northern European design with stylish décor, fancy drinks and prices to match. Tourist bars in the resorts tend to be either staid affairs where you can sit outside in cushioned armchairs sipping exotic, expensive cocktails, or hectic, crowded disco-bars serving less exotic but even more expensive concoctions.

Cretan wine

Wherever you can eat in Crete you can invariably drink, and **wine** is the usual accompaniment to most meals, especially in restaurants and tavernas. Whilst Cretans are happy to drink their home-made brews, many visitors now require a more polished product and in recent years Hellenic wines have vastly improved to cater to this demand.

The island's wines come in many varieties; the hot, dry summers are more suited to producing dry red wines – dark and powerful – than whites. Using the six grape varieties predominant on the island – *kotsifáli*, *thrapsathíri*, *liátiko*, *mandilariá*, *roméiko* and *vilána* – there are four appellation wine-growing areas: Pezá, Dafnés, Sitía and Arhánes, the last still using vineyards cultivated by the Minoans almost four thousand years ago. The house wine offered in most tavernas is normally the brown and cloudy rosé-style

Cretan **kókkino** (red), especially good around Kastélli in the west or Sitía in the east, or the white which often has a sherry tang. These locally made brews can vary enormously in quality due to the vagaries of production. If you want to test one before committing yourself to a *karáfa* (which come in kilo or half-kilo measures), most places will be happy to let you try a glass first.

Although **retsína** is not as popular here as on the mainland (it was largely unknown in Crete before World War II), it's now produced on the island. It usually comes in half-litre bottles: you may also find it served from the barrel in quarter, half or kilo metal mugs. This resinated wine is an acquired taste, but some varieties are extremely good. It's also exceptionally cheap: a litre can cost under €1.50, often less than a litre of beer. The *retsína* produced by the Central Union of Haniá Wine Producers is recommended, but stay well clear of the same co-operative's red variety, which is quite awful.

Cretan **bottled wine** is rather more expensive – Pezá brands like *Minos* red and white, which you can get everywhere, are palatable if rather boring, although the more mature vintages such as *Minos Sant Antonio* and *Palace VDQS* (red and white) are getting much better. *Minoiko* and *Mantiko*, also from the Pezá district (located to the south of Iráklion) are full-bodied reds with a bit more character, whilst *Logado* is another safe, if unexciting red. The Arhánes wine region (to the west of Pezá and based on the town of the same name) also produces some pretty good red and white vintages, most notably by a co-operative which sells its wines under the *Arhánes* brand name. The Sitian wines *Topiko* (medium-dry with a hint of sherry) and *Myrtos* are both good everyday whites to drink with seafood. In the west, *Kissamos* red is another good bet.

One of the great marketing successes of recent years has been the widely available *Vin de Crete*, a blended French-style wine using Cretan grapes (produced by the Kourtakis company from the mainland). However, while it's popular in northern Europe, it is rather bland. Some of the island's smaller producers now make excellent wines, especially Lyrarakis from the Pezá region, whose Kotsifáli and Syrah red

compares with some of the best in Europe; its Dafni dry white is also distinguished. Keep an eye out too for the wines of Santorini (Thíra), the volcanic island to the north, which are becoming noted; any of the Santos vineyard's output are worth a try, particularly the white *Asyrtiko*.

Whichever wines you try, irregular production processes often lead to wines of the same vintage tasting quite different from each other (even when the bottle label is identical), and duff bottles are common. If you suspect any wine, call the waiter for a second opinion; you'll usually get another bottle and an apology.

Mainland wines

Many of Greece's better known **mainland wines** are widely available on the island and are worth looking out for. Some of the best are produced by major winemaker Boutari – especially their *Lac des Roches* and *Rotonda* whites and the justifiably famous *Naoussa* red from the Macedonian region in the north. Another Naoussa producer is Tsantalis whose own *Naoussa* red (at its best between five and ten years old) is worth looking out for. In nearby Thrace the Chateau Lazaridis is turning out some fine wines including the stunning *Magic Mountain* white and fine *Merlot Lazaridi* red. In addition to the Naoussa region, Greece's other great wine area is Nemea in the north-eastern Peloponnese; here the Gaia vineyard produces an outstanding *Gaia Estate* red and a fruity *Notios* white, although in Crete you're more likely to come across the less inspiring *Boutari Nemea*. In the western Peloponnese the Mercouri estate turns out the delicious *Foloi Fumé* white and an equally elegant *Ktima Mercouri* red. Other fine red wines from northern Greece are *Porto Carras* by the Halkidikí producer Carras, and Tsantalis's *Tsantsali Rapsani* from Thessaly. Of the brands which appear most frequently on taverna wine lists, *Marko*, *Cambas* (now owned by Boutari) and the superior *Afelia* red are all drinkable, if unremarkable.

An affordable classic is the sweet Muscat of the island of Samos (the best is produced by the island's co-operative, EOSS) which compares with fine French dessert wines. For special occasions, CAIR (Agricultural and Industrial Company of Rhodes) produces its own widely available **"champagne"** in both brut and demi-sec versions. It's hardly Moët & Chandon, but at around €6 a bottle in supermarkets you can't complain.

Unfortunately, many restaurants and tavernas offer a poor choice in their wine lists. The better restaurants do tend to try harder and some of the very best places (we've highlighted these in the *Guide*) go out of their way to find excellent bottles from smaller growers. A useful wine guide is *Greek Wines* by Geoff Adams (see p.457).

Beer

Beer comes as standard European lager served in half-litre bottles or smaller cans. The locally brewed Amstel and Henninger are fairly tame versions of their north European counterparts, and imported Heineken (known locally as *prásino* – the green one, after its green bottle) and Lowenbräu are worth the extra few eurocents. Two domestic labels, the outstanding Mythos and the less exceptional Alpha, compare favourably with the foreign competition. Beware of exotic brands or gold-trimmed bottles served by bars in tourist areas (especially if you leave it to the waiter) – the mark-up on these is usually outrageous.

Communications

The Greek postal system is adequate, especially for outgoing mail. Service provided by OTE (Organismós Tiliepikinoníon Elládhos, the state-run telecom company) has improved drastically since the 1990s, under the twin threats of privatization and competition from thriving mobile networks. Mobile phone users are well looked after with a reliable service covering most parts of Crete, while Internet facilities are widely available at cafés in the major towns and resorts.

Post

Local **post offices** are open from about 7.30am to 2pm, Monday to Friday; in big towns and important tourist centres, hours may extend into the evening and include Saturday morning.

Airmail letters take three to six days to reach the rest of Europe, five to twelve days to get to North America, and a bit more for Australia and New Zealand. **Aerograms** are faster and surer, but **postcards** can be inexplicably slow, although things are gradually improving: up to ten days for Europe, three weeks to the Americas or the Pacific. For a modest fee (about €2) you can use the **express service** (*katepígonda*), which cuts letter delivery

time to two days for the UK and three days for the Americas.

For a simple letter or card, **stamps** (*grammatósima*) can also be purchased at a *períptero* (corner kiosk). However, kiosk proprietors are entitled to a ten percent commission and are unlikely to know the current international rates. Ordinary **post boxes** are bright yellow, express boxes are red. However, it's best to use only those by the door of an actual post office if possible, since days may pass between collections at other street-corner or wall-mounted boxes. If you are confronted by two slots, use the one marked "*Esoterikó*" for Greek mail and "*Exoterikó*" for international.

Parcels should only be handled in sizeable towns, preferably a provincial capital, so your package will be in Athens and on an international flight within a day or two. **Registered** (*sistiméno*) delivery is available but extremely slow, unless coupled with express service.

Receiving mail

For receiving mail, the *poste restante* (general delivery) system is reasonably efficient, especially at the big town post offices. Mail should be clearly addressed and marked "*poste restante*", with your surname capitalized and underlined, to the main post office of whichever town you choose. It will be held for a month and you'll need your passport to collect it. Alternatively, **American Express** cheque- or card-holders can use the office in Iráklion as a mail drop: c/o Creta Travel Bureau, Epimenídhou 20–22, Iráklion (℡2810 227002).

Phones

Making a call in Crete is relatively straightforward. In recent years services have improved and rates have dropped; all land-line exchanges are now digital, and you should have few problems reaching any number from either overseas or on the island.

Call boxes, invariably sited at the noisiest street corner or where there is zero shade, are now all **cardphones** taking no coins at all and functioning only with **phone cards** (*tiliekarta*) sold in €3 and €10 versions. The more expensive card offers better value per unit. They can be bought from kiosks, OTE offices and newsstands. The call-box phones are equipped to give instructions in a number of languages: press the "i" on the dialling panel to get the one you want. Many hotel lobbies and cafés have **counter coin-op phones**, taking five, ten, twenty and fifty cent euro coins; unlike the street phone boxes, they can receive incoming calls. Most of them are made in northern Europe and bear instructions in English.

If you won't be around long enough to use up a phone card, it's probably easier to make local calls from a *periptero* (**street kiosk**). Here the phone is metered, and you pay after you have made the call. Local calls cost around €0.15 for three minutes, but **long-distance** ones carry some of the most expensive rates in Europe, so you'd do better to use a phone card. Another option for calls – and possibly the only one in remoter areas – is from a **kafeníon** or bar, but make sure the phones are metered: look for a sign "*Tiléfono me metrití*". Avoid making long-distance calls from a **hotel**, as they slap a fifty percent surcharge onto the already exorbitant rates. If you have access to a **private phone** you can dial the international operator on ℡161 to get a reverse-charge call put through, or dial direct (see box).

For **international** (*exoterikó*) calls, it's again best to use on-street card phones. You can no longer make metered calls from Greek telecoms offices (the OTE) themselves – most keep daytime hours only and offer at most a quieter cardphone or two. Like BT Phoneshops in the UK, they are mainly places to get Greece-based service (including OTE's own mobile network Cosmote), pay your bills, and buy one of an array of phones and fax machines for sale. **Faxes** are best sent from post offices and some travel agencies – at a price; receiving a fax may also incur a small charge.

Overseas phone calls with a phone card cost approximately €0.40 per minute to EU countries and much of the rest of central Europe, North America and Australia – versus €0.28 per minute on a private subscriber line. There is no particular cheap rate for overseas calls to these destinations, and dialling countries with problematic phone systems like Russia, Israel or Egypt is obviously rather more. **Within Greece**, undiscounted rates are €0.16 per minute on a subscriber line, more from a cardphone; a twenty-percent discounted rate applies daily from 10pm to 8am, and from 10pm Saturday until 8am Monday.

Credit-card call services from Greece back to the home country are provided in the UK by British Telecom (℡0800 345144, ⓦ www.chargecard.bt.com) and NTL (℡0500 100505); in North America, Canada Direct, AT&T (℡0800 890011, then 888/641 when you hear the AT&T prompt to be transferred to the 24-hr Florida Call Centre), MCI and Sprint; in Australia, Optus (℡1300 300 937) or Telstra (℡1800 038 000), and in New Zealand Telecom NZ (℡04/801 9000).

British Telecom, as well as North American long-distance companies such as AT&T, MCI and Sprint all allow their customers to make long distance **credit-card calls** from Greece, as do Telstra or Optus in Australia and Telecom NZ in New Zealand, but only back to the home country. There are now a few local-dial numbers with some providers, which enable you to connect to the international network for the price of a one-unit call, and then charge the call to your home number – usually cheaper than the alternatives.

Mobile phones

Mobile phones are an essential fashion accessory in Greece, with the highest per capita usage in Europe outside Italy. There are four networks at present: Panafon-Vodafon, Telestet, Cosmote and newcomer Q-Telecom. Calling any of them from Britain, you will find that costs are exactly the same as calling a fixed phone – so you won't need to worry about ringing them when given as alternative numbers for accommodation – though of course such numbers are pricey when rung locally.

Coverage on Crete is fairly good, though there are a few "dead" zones in the shadows of mountains or on remote islets. **Pay-as-you-go** contract-free plans are heavily promoted in Greece (such as Telestet B-free and Panafon-Vodafon A La Carte), and if you're going to be around for a while – for example, studying, or working for a season in the tourist industry – an outlay of €90 or less will see you to a decent apparatus and your first calling card. This lasts up to a year – even if you use up your talk time you'll still have an incoming number, along with a voice-mail service. Top-up calling cards – starting from denominations of €8–9 depending on the network – are available at all *períptera* (street kiosks).

If you want to use your **home-based mobile abroad**, check with your provider whether it will work. North American users will only be able to use tri-band rigs in Greece. Any GSM mobile from the UK, Australia or New Zealand should work fine in Greece.

In the UK you'll have to inform your service network before going abroad to get international access ("roaming") switched on. You may get charged extra for this, depending on the terms of your package and where

---

Useful phone codes and numbers

Phoning Greece from abroad
Dial your international access code (given below), then 30 (country code for Greece), then the area code, then the number.

Australia	☏0011	New Zealand	☏00
Canada	☏011	UK	☏00
Ireland	☏010	USA	☏011

Phoning abroad from Greece
Dial the country code below, then the area code (minus its initial zero, except in Canada and the US), and then the number.

Australia	☏0061	New Zealand	☏0064
Canada	☏001	UK	☏0044
Ireland	☏00353	USA	☏001

Useful Greek phone numbers

Operator (domestic)	☏132	Fire service (urban)	☏199
Operator (international)	☏139	Forest fire reporting	☏191
Medical emergencies	☏166	ELPA breakdown	☏104
Police/emergency	☏100	assistance	
Tourist police	☏210	Speaking clock	☏141

you are travelling to. You'll also be charged extra to have **incoming calls** forwarded abroad, as the people calling you will be paying the usual rate; discount plans are available with most providers to reduce the cost of forwarding the call to you overseas by as much as seventy percent. If you want to **retrieve messages** while you're away, you'll probably have to ask your provider for a special access number, as your one-stroke "mail" key may not always work abroad.

Experience has shown that the Greek network selected out of the four existing ones for roaming purposes makes little difference in terms of **call charges**: depending on the length of chat, these can equal £0.70 VAT exclusive per minute, whether to Greek numbers or back to Britain (including voice-mail retrieval). To get round this you can buy a Greek-based pay-as-you-go **SIM** upon arrival (roughly €15–20), and substitute it for the UK-based SIM in your phone. UK providers may tell you that this can't be done, but you are legally entitled to the phone-unblock code from the manufacturer after (usually) six months of use. Otherwise, a phone shop in Greece can free up the phone with a simple five-minute computer procedure.

Email and the Internet

Email and Internet use in Greece and Crete has now caught on in a big way; electronic addresses or websites are given in the *Guide* for the growing number of travel companies, hotels and businesses that have them. For your own email needs Internet cafés are mushrooming across the island, particularly in the major towns and resorts; rates tend to be around €4.50 per hour, often less.

Ideally you should sign up for a free **Internet email address** that can be accessed from anywhere, for example YahooMail or Hotmail – accessible through ⓦwww.yahoo.com and ⓦwww.hotmail.com. Once you've set up an account, you can use these sites to pick up and send mail from any Internet café, or hotel with Internet access.

If you are carrying your own **laptop**, you will need about two metres of North American–standard cable (UK cables will not work), lightweight and easily purchasable in Crete, with RJ-11 male terminals at each end. The Greek **dial tone** is discontinuous and thus not recognized by most modems – instruct it to "ignore dial tone". Many newer hotel rooms have RJ-11 **sockets**, but some older ones still have their phones hard-wired into the wall. You can often get around this problem with a female **adaptor**, either RJ-11 or 6P6C-configured, available at better electrical retailers. They weigh and cost next to nothing, so carry both (one is sure to work) for making a splice between your cable and the RJ-11 end of the cable between the wall and phone (which you simply unplug). You will usually have to dial an initial "9" or "0" to get around the hotel's central switchboard for a proper external dial tone.

The media

Greeks and Cretans are great devourers of newsprint – although few would describe Greek media as a paradigm of responsible or objective journalism. Papers are almost uniformly sensational, whilst state-run TV and radio are often biased in favour of whichever major party happens to be in government.

Newspapers

British newspapers are fairly widely available in Crete for €2–2.50, or €3–4 for Sunday editions. You'll find day-old copies of the *Independent* and the *Guardian*'s European Edition in all the resorts as well as in Haniá and Iráklion. **American** and international papers are represented by USA Today as well as Time and Newsweek. The more readable International Herald Tribune has the free bonus of an abridged English edition of the same day's Kathimerini (online at Ⓦ www.eKathimerini.com), a respected Greek daily, thus allowing you to keep up with Greek and Cretan news too.

The daily Athens News (Ⓦ www .athensnews.gr) and weekly Kriti News are less pricey and more up-to-date, though heavily biased in favour of US press-agency reports. They're on sale anywhere there might be a market for them, and publish selections from the Greek press. This Month Crete is a monthly bilingual English-German publication which, as well as printing feature articles on Crete, also carries useful information on food and entertainment. It's free, and available from hotels, tourist shops and bars in all the major towns.

Much of the **Greek national press** is tied to (and partly funded by) political groups, which tends to decrease the already low quality of Greek dailies. Among these, only the centrist Kathimerini approaches the standards of a major European newspaper. Eleftherotypia, once a PASOK mouthpiece, now aspires to more independence and has links with the UK's Guardian. To Pondiki (The Mouse) is a satirical weekly review in the same vein as Britain's Private Eye; its famous covers are spot-on and accessible to anyone with minimal Greek.

Crete's main newspapers are, like much else on the island, divided along regional lines. Iráklion's main dailies are the socialist-slanted Tólmi, the ND-supporting Messóghios and the centrist Patrís, the latter (part of the Ta Nea group) with the biggest circulation due to its small ads. A new arrival is Nea Kriti (owned by the Kriti TV group below), which has swiftly built up its readership and now holds second place in sales behind Patrís. In the east, Lasíthi's Anatoli is a politically neutral organ with another good small-ads section. Réthimnon's Rethemiotika Nea is one more paper which gets its sales from small ads, easily beating the PASOK-supporting daily Kritiki Epitheorisi into second place. Haniotika Nea, with more classifieds, is the main Haniá paper, followed by Kiryx, owned by the prominent Néa Dhimokratía politician and ex-Greek premier Constantine Mitsotákis. Gnomi is a new, PASOK-supporting arrival.

Radio

The BBC World Service (broadcasting in Greece on 6.18, 9.41, 15.07 and 12.09 MHz short-wave) is a standby for international news but its shortwave services are being phased out in many parts of the world. Consult Ⓦ www.bbc.co.uk/world-service for current frequencies. There are also regular news bulletins and tourist information in English on local Greek stations. The Voice of America, with its transmitters on Rhodes, can be picked up at the eastern end of the island on medium wave, while in the extreme east around Zákros you can often receive crystal-clear BBC domestic radio programmes on FM, disseminated from the British base on Cyprus.

As regards the **Greek stations**, Greek music programmes are always accessible (if variable in quality), despite the language barrier. Regional stations have mushroomed, and in some places the airwaves are now positively cluttered, as every town sets up its own studio and transmitter. Crete's stations are particularly good for traditional music, particularly lyra; try Cretorama (97.9FM) or Kritikos (88.5FM). Radio Kriti (101.5FM) is the island's favourite station with a mix of news and popular (Cretan and Greek) music.

TV

Greece's centralized, government-controlled **TV stations**, ET1, NET and ET3, lose out in the ratings war with a clutch of private, decidedly right-wing channels – Mega, Antenna, Star, Skaï and Seven-X. On NET, news summaries in English are broadcast daily at 6pm. The main Cretan TV stations are Kriti TV and Creta Channel in Iráklion, and Kydon and Kriti One, both based in Haniá. Programming on all stations tends to be a mix of soaps (especially Italian, Spanish and Latin American), game shows, westerns, B-movies and sports. All foreign films and serials are broadcast in their original language with Greek subtitles. Numerous **cable** and **satellite channels** are received, including Sky, CNN, MTV, Filmnet, Euronews (in English), Super Channel, and French TV5 and Italian Rai Due. The range largely depends on which hotel you stay in, although in most Cretan budget hotels you'll be lucky to have a TV at all.

Opening hours and public holidays

It's virtually impossible to generalize about Cretan opening hours, except to say that they change constantly. The traditional timetable starts early – stores open at 7 or 8am – and runs through until lunchtime, when there is a long break for the hottest part of the day; things may then reopen in the mid- to late afternoon. In tourist areas, though, stores and offices may stay open right through the day – certainly the most important archeological sites and museums do so.

Matters are further confused by Crete's **public holidays**, during which almost everything will be closed; there's a list of the most important ones in the box opposite. It's worth bearing in mind, too, that many public buildings and banks tend to close either side of major festivals (see p.56) – keep an eye on the calendar and plan accordingly.

Businesses and shops

Most **government agencies** are open to the public on weekdays from 8am to 2pm. In general, however, you'd be optimistic to show up after 1pm expecting to be served the same day, as queues can be long. Private businesses, or anyone providing a service, especially to tourists, frequently operate a straight 9am–5/6pm schedule. Many shops, though, do still follow a split shift as detailed below.

Shopping hours during the hottest months are theoretically Monday, Wednesday and Saturday from approximately 9am to 2.30pm, and Tuesday, Thursday and Friday from 8.30am to 2pm and 6 to 9pm. During the cooler months the morning schedule shifts slightly forward, the evening session a half or even a full hour back. There are so many exceptions to the rule though, by virtue of holidays and professional idiosyncrasy, that you can't count on getting anything done, except from Monday to Friday between 9.30am and 1pm or so. Closed pharmacies are supposed to have a sign on their door referring you to the nearest open one.

Museums and archeological sites

Museums tend to close on Mondays, except for certain major ones such as the

Entrance fees

Entry charges for archeological sites and museums vary from €2 to around €6 for an important site such as Knossós. Most of them offer **substantial reductions** for senior citizens, students, teachers and journalists with proper identification. In addition, entrance to all state-run sites and museums is **free** on Sundays and public holidays outside of the peak season (theoretically, this only applies to EU citizens).

Public holidays

January 1
January 6
March 25
First Monday of Lent (Feb/March; see below)
Easter weekend (April/May, according to the Orthodox calendar; see below)
May 1
Pentecost or Whit Monday (fifty days after Easter; see below)
August 15
October 28
December 25 and 26

Variable religious feasts

Lenten Monday	Easter Sunday		Whit Monday	
March 14	2005	May 1	2005	June 20
March 6	2006	April 23	2006	June 12

archeological museum in Iráklion, where the hours will usually be curtailed. Opening hours vary between **archeological sites**; as far as possible, individual times are quoted in the *Guide*, but these change with exasperating frequency and, at smaller sites, can be subject to the whim of a local keeper who may decide to close early, or even leave the gate open after the official closing time or on the official closing day (usually Mon). A list of current opening hours is available from tourist offices. Smaller archeological sites generally close for a long lunch and siesta (even where they're not meant to), as do **monasteries**. Most monasteries are fairly strict on dress, too, especially for women: they don't like shorts and often expect women to cover their arms and wear skirts. They are generally open from about 9am to 1pm and 5 to 7pm.

Festivals and cultural events

Most of the big Greek popular festivals have a religious basis, so they're observed in accordance with the Orthodox calendar: this means that Easter, for example, can fall as much as three weeks to either side of the Western festival.

On top of the main religious festivals, there are scores of local festivals, or **paniyíria**, celebrating the patron saint of the village church. With some 330-odd possible saints' days you're unlikely to travel round for long without stumbling on something. Local tourist offices should be able to fill you in on events in their area.

Easter

Easter is by far the most important festival of the Greek year – much more so than Christmas – and taken way more seriously than anywhere in the West apart from, perhaps, southern Spain. From Wednesday of Holy Week, the radio and TV networks are given over solely to

The festival year

Epiphany (Jan 6). The hobgoblins who run riot on earth during the twelve days of Christmas are rebanished to the nether world by various rites of the Church. Most important of these is the blessing of baptismal fonts and all outdoor bodies of water. At lake or seashore locales the priests cast a crucifix into the deep to be recovered by crowds of young men. There used to be a substantial cash prize for the winner, but this has mostly been replaced by lesser value victory tokens owing to serious violence between contenders.

Pre-Lenten carnivals. These span three weeks, climaxing over the seventh weekend before Easter.

Clean Monday (Kathará Dheftéra). The beginning of Lent, a traditional time to fly kites and to feast on all the things which will be forbidden over the coming weeks.

Independence Day and the **Feast of The Annunciation (March 25)**. Parades and dancing to celebrate the beginning of the revolt against Turkish rule in 1821 combined with church services to honour the news being given to Mary that she was to become the mother of Christ. There are special celebrations in Paleohóra.

The Feast of St George (April 23). Áyios Yeóryios is the patron saint of shepherds, and big rural celebrations are held throughout Crete with much feasting and dancing. There's a major celebration in Asigoniá (near Réthimnon).

May Day. The great urban holiday – most people make for the countryside to picnic. In the towns demonstrations by the left claim the day, *Ergatikí Protomayiá* (Working-Class First of May), as their own.

Battle of Crete (May 20–27). The anniversary of the battle is celebrated in Haniá and a different local village each year, with veterans' ceremonies, sporting events and folk dancing.

Áyios Konstandínos (May 21). The feast of St Constantine (the first Byzantine Orthodox ruler) and his mother, Ayía Eléni (St Helena), with services and celebrations at churches and monasteries named after the saint, especially Arkádhi.

Summer Solstice/John the Baptist (June 24). Bonfires and widespread celebrations.

Naval Week (late June). Naval celebrations culminate in fireworks – especially big at Soúdha.

Réthimnon Wine Festival (July). A week of wine tasting and traditional dancing.

Iráklion Festival (July & Aug). A wide variety of cultural events from drama and film to traditional dance and jazz, at scattered sites through most of the summer.

Metamórfosi/Transfiguration (Aug 6). Another excuse for feasting. Specially celebrated in Voukoliés (Haniá), Máles (Ierápetra) and Zákros.

---

religious programmes until the following Monday. It is an excellent time to be in Crete, both for the beautiful and moving religious ceremonies and for the days of feasting and celebration which follow. If you make for a smallish village, you may well find yourself an honorary member for the period of the festival.

The first great ceremony takes place on **Good Friday** evening as the Descent from the Cross is lamented in church. At dusk, the *Epitáfios*, Christ's funeral bier, lavishly decorated by the women of the parish, leaves the sanctuary and is paraded solemnly through the streets. Late **Saturday** evening sees the climax in a majestic mass to celebrate Christ's triumphant return. At the stroke of midnight all lights in each crowded church are extinguished and the congregation plunged into the darkness which envelops Christ as He passes through the underworld. Then there's a faint glimmer of light behind the altar screen before the priest appears, holding aloft a lighted taper and chanting "*Avtó to fos...*" (This is the Light of the World). Stepping

Áyios Matthaíos (Aug 12). The feast of St Matthew, with special celebrations in Kastélli Kissámou.

Sitía Sultana Festival (mid-Aug). An enjoyable, week-long celebration of the local harvest, with plenty of wine.

Assumption of the Virgin (Aug 15). Celebrated in towns and villages throughout Crete, the great feast of the *Apokímisis tís Panayías* is a day when people traditionally return to their home village, often creating problems for unsuspecting visitors who find there's no accommodation left. Services in churches begin at dawn, but latecomers usually arrive for the *psomí*, *arní*, and *krasí* (bread, lamb and wine), served in the churchyard at the end of the service around lunchtime. Neápoli is a main centre for this feast, though the great event is the pilgrimage to the island of Tínos.

Áyios Eftíhios (Aug 24). Celebrations of this saint's day are especially fervent in the southwest corner of the island, where many infants are given his name; there are special festivities at Kambanós near Soúyia (Haniá).

Áyios Títos (Aug 25). The patron saint of Crete – celebrated all across the island and with a big procession in Iráklion.

Cretan Wedding (late Aug). A "traditional" wedding laid on in Kritsá for the tourists – quite a spectacle nonetheless.

Áyios Ioánnis (Aug 29). A massive name-day pilgrimage to the church of Áyios Ioánnis Giónis on the Rodhópou peninsula in Haniá.

Áyios Stavrós/Holy Cross (Sept 14). Special festivities at Tzermiádho and Kalamáfka.

Mihaíl Arhángelos (Oct 11). The feast of the archangel is especially popular at Potamiés (Lasíthi).

Chestnut Festival (mid-Oct). Celebrated in Élos and other villages of the southwest where chestnuts are grown.

Óhi Day (Oct 28). Lively national holiday, with parades and folk dancing, commemorating Prime Minister Metaxas' one-word reply ("No") to Mussolini's ultimatum in 1940.

Arkádhi (Nov 7–9). One of Crete's biggest gatherings celebrates the anniversary of the explosion at the monastery of Arkádhi.

Áyios Nikólaos (Dec 6). The feast of the patron saint of seafarers. Many chapels are dedicated to him around the island's coastline, including the one at the resort named after him, where processions and festivities mark the day.

down to the level of the parishioners he touches his flame to the unlit candle of the nearest worshipper, intoning "*Devthe, levethe fos*" (Come take the light) – to be greeted by the response "*Hristós Anésti*" (Christ is risen). And so it goes round, this affirmation of the miracle, until the entire church is ablaze with burning candles. Later, as the church bells ring, the celebrations begin with fireworks and the burning of effigies of Judas.

Even atheists are likely to find this moving, as worshippers leave the church carefully attempting to preserve their flickering candles alight, to symbolically carry the "Light of the World" into their own homes. The successful achievement of this is regarded as a sign of good fortune and the sign of the cross is made on the lintel with the flame, leaving a black smudge, visible for the rest of the year. The traditional greeting, as firecrackers explode all around you in the streets, is "*Hristós Anésti*" and the reply "*Alithos Anésti*" (He is risen indeed). In the week leading up to Easter Sunday, you should wish acquaintances "*Kaló Páskha*"

(Happy Easter); on or after the day, you say "Khrónia Pollá" (Many Happy Returns). The Lenten **fast** is traditionally broken early Sunday morning with a meal of *mayirítsa* (a soup based on lamb tripe, rice and lemon); later the rest of the lamb will be roasted.

The Greek equivalent of **Easter eggs** are hard-boiled eggs (painted red on Holy Thursday and signifying the rebirth and blood of Christ), which are baked into twisted, sweet bread-loaves (*tsouréki* or *lambrópsomo*) or distributed on **Easter Sunday**. People rap their eggs against their friends' eggs, and the owner of the last uncracked egg is considered lucky.

Local entertainments

The events of the various festivals aside (and Iráklion's lasts for much of the summer), organized entertainment on the island is limited. **Dancing** is of course a tradition here as throughout Greece; the stuff put on for tourists is enjoyable, but may not be entirely authentic. For the real thing you have to go to a *paniyíri*, or else be exceptionally lucky in falling into the right company which may just get you an invite to a wedding feast – an event unlikely to be soon forgotten. With regard to **music**, keep an eye out in the villages for posters advertising *lyra* and *laoúto* (lute or Cretan *bouzoúki*) concerts. The *lyra* is Crete's "national" instrument: a three-stringed violin made from mulberry or maple which is propped on the knee and played with a small bow. These events can be highly entertaining, and you'll often be the only foreigner present, thus ensuring a warm Cretan welcome.

For more on Cretan music, see p.458.

Work

Greek membership of the EU means that a citizen of any EU state has (in theory) the right to work in Crete. In practice, however, there are a number of bureaucratic hurdles to overcome. Teaching English, for example, is now subject to severe restrictions for non-Greeks, while that other long-standing fallback of long-haul backpackers, picking fruit or greenhouse vegetables, is now dominated by Eastern European and Albanian immigrants. The best chance is probably finding something in the commercial or tourist field.

EU membership notwithstanding, **short-term work** is almost always on an unofficial basis. For this reason it will generally be where you can't be seen by the police, or you're badly paid – or often both. Since 1990, the influx of around a million (estimates vary) immigrants to Greece has resulted in a surplus of unskilled labour and severely depressed wages. Crete is perhaps less affected than much of the country, but you'll still struggle. The necessary documents for **long-term employment**, which will almost certainly mean self-employment or being recruited from abroad for your particular skills by a Greek company, are set out below.

Non-EU nationals who wish to work in Crete mostly do so surreptitiously, with the ever-present risk of denunciation to the police and instant deportation. Greek immigration authorities are keen to be seen to be active, and have been cracking down hard on any suitable targets, be they Albanian, African, Swiss or North American.

If, on the other hand, you are a non-EU foreign national of **Greek descent** you are termed *omólogos* (returned Greek diaspora member) and in fact have tremendous privileges relating to employment, taxation and residence rights – for example, you can open your very own language school without any qualifications.

Tourism-related work

Most women working casually in Crete find jobs in **bars** or **restaurants** around the main resorts. Men, unless they are trained chefs, will probably find it much harder to find any work, even washing up.

If you're waiting or serving, most of your **wages** will probably have to come from tips, but you may well be able to get a deal that includes free food and lodging; evening-only hours can be a good shift, leaving you a lot of free time. The main drawback may be the machismo and/or chauvinist attitudes of your employer. This is perhaps especially true in Haniá, where the proximity of large NATO bases has traditionally meant bars hire young women to lure men in and persuade them to drink: ads in the local press for "girl bar staff" should be treated with great caution. Ideally, start looking around April or May; you'll get better rates at this time if you're taken on for a season.

On a similar, unofficial level you might be able to get a sales job in a **tourist shop**, or (if you've the expertise) helping out at a watersports centre or the like. Perhaps the best type of tourism-related work, however, is that of courier/greeter/group coordinator for a **package holiday company**. All you need is EU nationality and language proficiency compatible with the clientele, though knowledge of Greek is a big plus. Some of the big villa companies, or hotels with an English-speaking clientele may also be a possibility on the spot for odd jobs like portering or pool cleaning, too.

Many such staff are recruited through ads in newspapers issued outside Greece, but it's also possible to be hired on the spot in April or May. You're usually guaranteed about six months of steady work, often with use of a car thrown in, and if things work out you may be re-employed the following season with an explicit contract and better wages.

Selling and busking

You may do better by working for yourself. Travellers report rich pickings during the tourist season from **selling jewellery** on beaches or on the street – craftware from Asia is especially popular with Greeks. Once you've managed to get the stuff past the customs officials (who will be sceptical, for instance, that all those trinkets are presents for friends), there rarely seem to be problems with the local police, though it probably pays to be discreet. **Busking** can also be quite lucrative.

Agriculture

As already noted, agricultural work is largely taken over by immigrants, and it's poorly paid and easily abused by employers. However, at **harvest** time there is some chance of work, especially during the very busy olive harvest, between October and December. The citrus harvest lasts through the winter, from October to February, or later, concentrated in the plains behind Haniá, especially around Alikianós.

Teaching English

There were never a huge number of language schools in Crete, and with tighter regulation you're now very unlikely to find a position. The few jobs going are available only to TEFL certificate-holders – preferably Greeks, non-EU nationals of Greek descent and EU nationals in that order.

Documentation for long-term employment

If you plan to work professionally for someone else, you first visit the nearest Department of Employment and collect two forms: one an **employment application** which you fill in, the other for the formal offer of work by your prospective employer. Once these are vetted, and revenue stamps (*hartósima*, purchased at kiosks) applied, you take them to the Aliens' Bureau (*Ypiresía Allodhapón*) or, in its absence, the central police station, to support your application for a **residence permit** (*ádhia paramonís*). For this, you will also need to bring your passport, six photographs, more *hartósima* and a stable address (not a hotel). Permits are given for terms of five years.

Allow four to six weeks for all the formalities to be completed; the bottleneck is usually the required **health examination** at the nearest public hospital and its subsequent endorsement by the local **public health office**, who have to issue a certificate of approval. Finally you take this to the local police or **Aliens' Bureau**, which should have your permit ready, free of charge other than for a few more *hartósima*, within three working days.

Self-employment

As a **self-employed professional**, you must satisfy the requirements of the Greek state with equivalent qualifications to native Greeks plying the same trade. You should also befriend a good accountant, who will advise you on which of the several varieties of incorporation are to your advantage. You will need to sign on with **TEBE**, the Greek National Insurance scheme for self-employed people. If you are continuing to contribute to a social insurance scheme in a country that has reciprocal agreements with Greece (all EU states do), this must be proved in writing – a tedious and protracted process.

Once you're square with TEBE, visit the tax office or *eforía* to be issued a **tax number**, which must be cited in all transactions. To be issued with one you need to bring a birth certificate showing the full unmarried names of both your parents. You will be required to prepare receipt and invoice books with your tax number professionally printed on them, or have a rubber stamp made up for applying that number to every sheet. The tax office will also determine which rate of **VAT** you should pay for each kind of transaction; VAT returns must be filed every two months, which is where a friendly accountant comes in handy again.

Police, trouble and harassment

Crete, along with Greece as a whole, remains one of Europe's safest regions, with a low crime rate and a deserved reputation for honesty. If you leave a bag or wallet at a café, you'll most likely find it scrupulously looked after, pending your return. Similarly, Greeks are relaxed about leaving possessions unlocked or unattended on the beach, in rooms or on campsites.

However, in recent years there has been an increase in **thefts** and **crimes** on the mainland, mainly in cities and resorts. Whilst Crete is still generally unaffected by this, it would be wise not to take chances and to make sure to lock your car, cycle or other property. You should also beware of **counterfeit euro notes** (particularly €100 and €200). The currency changeover has been a bonanza for forgers, leading to the introduction of bill scanners in many shops, bars and tavernas, many of which refuse to accept higher denomination notes (especially €200s and the rarely seen €500 bills). The best test with the naked eye is to examine the bill's face and ensure notes have a hologram strip or (for €50 and over) a hologram patch at the right end; there should also be a watermark at the other end and a security thread embedded slightly left of centre. If you end up being given a forged note, you're advised to bite the bullet: if you unwittingly or otherwise try to pass it on, or report it in good faith to the police, you'll still be assumed party to the scam, and face a session of interrogation at the very least.

The island's **police** tend to be laid back in the extreme (policewomen are often seen wearing high heels and make-up). The most common causes of a brush with authority for visitors are nude bathing or sunbathing, camping outside an authorized site – all of these technically illegal – and (a major crime in the Greek book) taking or possessing drugs.

Below are a few pointers to offences that might get you into trouble locally, and some advice on **sexual harassment** – all too much a fact of life given the classically Mediterranean machismo culture.

Specific offences

Nudity is currently legal on only a very few beaches, and is deeply offensive to many more traditional Cretans; you need to exercise considerable sensitivity to local attitudes. As a general rule, stay away from families with children, the main entrance of a beach and any tavernas – it's also considered very bad etiquette to swim or sunbathe nude within sight of a church. If a beach has become fairly established for nudity, or is secluded, it's highly unlikely that the police are going to come charging in. Where they do get bothered is if they feel a place is turning into a "hippy beach" or if nudity is getting too overt on mainstream tourist stretches. But there are no hard-and-fast rules; it all depends on the local cops. Mostly the only action would be a warning, but you can officially be arrested straight off – facing three days in jail and a stiff fine. Toplessness for women is now technically legal nationwide, but specific locales often opt out of the "liberation" by posting signs to that effect, which should be heeded.

Similar guidelines exist for **camping rough** (see p.43); you'll probably incur no more than a warning to move on – which you should comply with or risk arrest and a brief spell in the cells.

Drug offences, however, are treated as major crimes, particularly with a growing local problem of abuse and addiction. The maximum penalty for "causing the use of drugs by someone under 18", for example, is life imprisonment and an astronomical fine. Theory is by no means practice, but foreigners caught in possession of quite small amounts of cannabis do get jail sentences of up to a year – much more if there's any suggestion that they're supplying others. Greek prisons are not to be recommended.

If you get arrested for any offence you have an automatic right to contact your country's **consul**, who will arrange a lawyer for your defence. Beyond this, there's little they can or will do.

Sexual harassment

Many women travel about Greece on their own without feeling intimidated or **harassed** – but some undoubtedly are. This often has little to do with the way individuals look or behave and only indirectly relates to the way Greek women themselves are treated. What is important is that different assumptions are made about you as a foreign woman depending on where you are.

In most **rural areas** you'll be treated first and foremost as a *ksénos* – a word which means both stranger and guest – in much the same way as a foreign man. You can sit and drink ouzo in the exclusively male *kafenía* (there's often nowhere else) without always suspecting the hospitality and friendliness that's offered. In the large **resorts** and **towns**, however, where tourism has for a long time determined the local culture, things can be very different. Here the myths and fantasies of the "liberated" and "available" woman are widespread; not perhaps to the extent of other Mediterranean countries but oppressive nonetheless. The Greek version of **machismo** is strong; most of the hassle you are likely to get is from Greek *kamákia* ("fish harpoons" or barflies) who migrate to the main resorts and towns in summer in pursuit of foreign females. The locals, who become increasingly protective of you as you become more of a fixture, treat these outsiders (particularly if they're Athenians) with contempt. Their obvious stake-outs are beach bars and discos. Without a good control of the language it can be hard to deal with; words worth remembering as an unambiguous response are "*stamáta*" or "*pápsteh*" (stop it), "*afisteme*" (leave me alone) and "*fíyete*" (go

Consumer protection on holiday

In a tourist industry as developed as Greece's there are inevitably a number of cowboys and shady characters amongst the taxi-drivers, hoteliers and car rental agencies. **EKPIZO**, the **Greek Consumers' Association**, has established a "Legal Information and Assistance for Tourists" programme, to be run yearly from June to September. Their main branch is in Athens (☎010 330 4444), but there is also an office in Iráklion at Milatou 1 (☎28102 40666), slightly east of Platía Venizélou ("Fountain Square"). EKPIZO issues a pamphlet about holidaymakers' rights, available in airports and tourist offices. They are always prepared to pursue serious cases, by friendly persuasion, or by court action if necessary.

away), the latter intensified by *"dhrómo"* (road, as in "Hit the road!").

Hitching in Crete is not advisable for lone women travellers. **Camping** is generally not a problem, though away from recognized sites it's often wise to attach yourself to a local family by making arrangements to use nearby private land. In the more remote areas you may feel more uncomfortable about travelling alone. The intensely traditional Greeks may have trouble understanding why you are unaccompanied, and might not welcome your presence in their exclusively male *kafenía* – often the only place where you can get a drink. Travelling with a man, you're more likely to be treated as a *ksénos*.

Travellers with disabilities

It is all too easy to wax lyrical over the attractions of Crete – the stepped, narrow alleys, the ease of travel by bus and ferry, the thrill of clambering around the great archeological sites. Travellers who use a wheelchair or have limited mobility or vision may not be so impressed. There will always be real problems with uneven pavements, with steep streets, and with lack of facilities in ancient towns. But new hotels and apartments are increasingly taking people with disabilities into account in their design, and it's possible to enjoy an inexpensive and trauma-free holiday in Crete with a little forward planning.

Much existing or readily available information is out of date, so you should always double-check; a number of addresses of contact organisations are detailed opposite. The **Greek National Tourist Office** is also a good first step as long as you have specific questions to put to them; they publish a useful questionnaire which you could send to hotels or owners of apartment/villa accommodation.

Contacts for travellers with disabilities

UK and Ireland

Holiday Care 7th Floor, Sunley House, 4 Bedford Park, Croydon, Surrey CRO 2AP ☎0845 124 9971, ⓦwww.holidaycare.org.uk. Provides lists of accessible accommodation abroad, and information on financial help for holidays.

Irish Wheelchair Association Blackheath Drive, Clontarf, Dublin 3 ☏01/833 8241, ⓦwww.iwa.ie. Useful information provided on travelling abroad with a wheelchair.

Opus 23 Sourdock Hill, Barkisland, Halifax, West Yorkshire HX4 0AG ☏01422/371796, ⓦwww.escape-packages.com. Associated with recommended tour operator Filoxenia, this organisation has holidays in a fully accessible apartment in Crete, plus many other options if you're travelling with a carer.

Tripscope The Vassall Centre, Gill Avenue, Bristol BS16 2QQ ☏0845 758 5641, ⓦwww.tripscope.org.uk. This registered charity provides a national telephone information service offering free advice on UK and international transport for those with a mobility problem.

US and Canada

Access-Able ⓦwww.access-able.com. Online resource for travellers with disabilities.

Directions Unlimited 123 Green Lane, Bedford Hills, NY 10507 ☏1-800 533-5343 or 914/241-1700. Tour operator specializing in custom tours for people with disabilities.

Mobility International USA 451 Broadway, Eugene, OR 97401; Voice and TDD ☏541/343-1284, ⓦwww.miusa.org. Information and referral services, access guides, tours and exchange programmes. Annual membership $35, including a quarterly newsletter.

Society for the Advancement of Travelers with Handicaps (SATH) 347 5th Ave, New York, NY 10016 ☏212/447-7284, ⓦwww.sath.org. A nonprofit educational organization that has actively represented travellers with disabilities since 1976.

Wheels Up! ☏1-888 389-4335, ⓦwww.wheelsup.com. Provides discounted airfare, tour and cruise prices for disabled travellers, also publishes a free monthly newsletter and has a comprehensive website.

Australia and New Zealand

ACROD (Australian Council for Rehabilitation of the Disabled) PO Box 60, Curtin ACT 2605 ☏02/6283 3200, TTY 02/6282 4333, ⓦwww.acrod.org.au. Provides lists of travel agencies and tour operators for people with disabilities.

Disabled Persons Assembly 4/173–175 Victoria St, Wellington, New Zealand ☏04/801 9100 (also TTY), ⓦwww.dpa.org.nz. Resource centre with lists of travel agencies and tour operators for people with disabilities.

Planning a holiday

There are **organized tours** and **holidays** specifically for people with disabilities; many companies in Britain will advise on the suitability of holidays or villas advertised in their brochures.

It might be useful to make a list of all the facilities that will make your life easier while you are away so that you can fully brief travel agencies, insurance companies, airlines and other travel operators of your **needs**. If you use a wheelchair, it's advisable to have it serviced before you go, and carry a repair kit. Before purchasing **travel insurance**, ensure that people with a pre-existing medical condition are not excluded. A **medical certificate** of your fitness to travel, provided by your doctor, is also extremely useful; some airlines or insurance companies may insist on it.

You should also carry extra supplies of any required **drugs** and a prescription including the generic name in case of emergency. It's probably best to assume that any special equipment, drugs or clothing you may require is unavailable in Crete and will need to be brought with you.

Senior travellers

Travellers over sixty are accorded every respect in Crete and are entitled to discounts at state-run attractions of 25 to thirty percent. Some archeological sites and museums are even free. Olympic Airways (and some other airlines) also offer discounts on full fares on domestic flights, and you may also get cut-rates on buses and ferries. For any of these, you'll need to have proof of age to hand – the easiest way to do this is by carrying your passport with you.

Contacts for senior travellers

UK

Saga Holidays ☎0800 096 0074, ⓦwww.saga.co.uk. The country's biggest and most established specialist in tours and holidays aimed at older people.

US

American Association of Retired Persons 601 E St NW, Washington, DC 20049 ☎1-800 424-3410, ⓦwww.aarp.org. Can provide discounts on accommodation and vehicle rental. Membership open to US and Canadian residents aged 50 or over for an annual fee of US$12.50.
Elderhostel 75 Federal St, Boston, MA 02110 ☎1-877426-8056, ⓦwww.elderhostel.com. Runs a worldwide network of educational and activity programmes, cruises and homestays for people over 60 (companions may be younger). Several tours include Crete.
Saga Holidays 222 Berkeley St, Boston, MA 02116 ☎1-800 343-0273, ⓦwww.sagaholidays.com. Specializes in worldwide group travel for seniors.
Vantage Travel ☎1-800 322-6677, ⓦwww.vantagetravel.com. Specializes in worldwide group travel for seniors.

Gay and lesbian travellers

In modern Crete overtly gay behaviour in public remains largely taboo, though attitudes towards foreign same-sex couples are generally pretty relaxed. There are no specifically gay resorts on Crete, and few gay holidays offered by tour operators.

Homosexuality is **legal** over the age of 17, and (male) bisexual behaviour common but rarely admitted; the law code itself, however, still contains pejorative references to passive partners. Greek men are terrible flirts, but cruising them is a semiotic minefield and definitely at your own risk – references in gay guides to "known" male cruising grounds should be treated sceptically. "Out" gay Greeks are rare, and "out" local lesbians rarer still; foreign same-sex couples will generally be regarded with some bemusement but accorded the standard courtesy as foreigners.

Contacts for gay and lesbian travellers

In the UK

ⓦwww.gaytravel.co.uk Online gay and lesbian travel resource, offering good deals and links to all types of holiday. Also lists gay- and lesbian-friendly hotels around the world.

Madison Travel 118 Western Rd, Hove, East Sussex BN3 1DB ☎01273/202532, ⓦwww .madisontravel.co.uk. Established travel agents specializing in packages to gay- and lesbian-friendly mainstream destinations, and also to gay/lesbian destinations. They do offer Crete, but not as part of a specifically gay package.

In the US and Canada

Damron Company PO Box 422458, San Francisco, CA 94142 ☎1-800 462-6654 or 415/255-0404, ⓦwww.damron.com. Publisher of the *Men's Travel Guide*, a pocket-sized yearbook full of listings of hotels, bars, clubs and resources for gay men; the *Women's Traveler*, which provides similar listings for lesbians; and *Damron Accommodations*, which provides detailed listings of over 1000 accommodations for gays and lesbians worldwide. All of these titles are offered at a discount on the website. ⓦwww.gaytravel.com ☎1-800 GAY-TRAVEL. The premier site for trip planning, bookings, and general information about international gay and lesbian travel.

International Gay & Lesbian Travel Association 4331 N Federal Hwy, Suite 304, Ft Lauderdale, FL 33308 ☎1-800 448-8550, ⓦwww.iglta.org. Trade group that can provide a list of gay- and lesbian-owned or -friendly travel agents, accommodation and other travel businesses.

In Australia and New Zealand

Gay and Lesbian Travel Australia ⓦwww.galta.com.au. Directory and links for gay and lesbian travel in Australia and worldwide.

Parkside Travel ☎08/8274 1222, Ⓔparkside@herveyworld.com.au. Gay travel agent associated with local branch of Hervey World Travel; all aspects of gay and lesbian travel worldwide.

Silke's Travel ☎1800 807 860 or 02/8347 2000, ⓦwww.silkes.com.au. Long-established gay and lesbian specialist, with the emphasis on women's travel.

Tearaway Travel ☎1800 664 440 or 03/9510 6644, ⓦwww.tearaway.com. Gay-specific business dealing with international and domestic travel.

Travelling with children

Children are worshipped and indulged in Greece, arguably to excess, and travelling with them presents few problems – wherever you go, your kids will be welcome. As elsewhere in the Mediterranean, children are not segregated from adults at mealtimes, and early on in life are inducted into the typical late-night routine – you'll see plenty of kids at tavernas, expected to eat (and up to their capabilities, talk) like adults.

While there's not much in the way of specifically child-oriented holidays to Crete – no club hotels or the like – many hotels and newer apartment complexes have children's pools and small playgrounds, and most tour operators will be able to book you something suitable. Almost all hotels and rooms places will have three- and four-bed rooms, and often interconnecting or adjoining ones; and many places have apartments with fridges and simple cooking facilities, which can make life easier. For older kids there are

a few water parks dotted around the island, and activities like gorge-hiking or boat trips can become real adventures (though don't be overambitious, they can also be really gruelling in the heat). The worst of your problems are likely to be excessive exposure to heat and sun.

Baby foods and **nappies** (diapers) are readily available and reasonably priced; private rooms establishments and luxury hotels are more likely to offer some kind of **babysitting** service than the mid-range, C-class hotels.

Contacts for travellers with children

UK and Ireland

Simply Crete ☎020/8541 2201, ⓦwww.simply-travel.com. Can usually provide qualified, English-speaking nannies to come to your villa and look after the children (as can some other villa companies).

US

Travel With Your Children 40 5th Ave, New York, NY 10011 ☎212/477 5524 or 1-888 822-4388. Publish a regular newsletter, *Family Travel Times*, ⓦwww.familytraveltimes.com, as well as a series of books on travel with children including *Great Adventure Vacations With Your Kids*.

In Australia and New Zealand

Family Travel ☎09/839 0371 or 520 5710, ⓦwww.familytravel.co.nz. Travel agency devoted to travel with kids both at home and abroad, from cruises to city breaks.

Holidays With Kids ⓦwww.holidayswithkids .com.au. The website of the popular *Holidays With Kids* magazine, this site lists kid-friendly destinations and accommodation worldwide as well as providing advice to frazzled parents. You can book tours and holidays here too.

Directory

Addresses in Greek are usually written with just the street name followed by the number (eg Sífaka 11); numbers outside the city centres usually represent a whole block so you may get an individual building number added in brackets. *Odhós* means street; *leofóros*, avenue; *platía*, square. In a multistorey building, the ground floor is the *isóyeio*; there may be a mezzanine (*imiórofos*) before the first upper floor (*prótos órofos*).

Admission charges All the major ancient sites are now fenced off and, like museums, most charge admission. This ranges from a token €1 to a hefty €6 at the five-star sites such as Knossós, but with an ISIC youth card you can get up to fifty percent reductions or even free admission, so it's always worth asking. Current students of archeology, classics or history of art qualify for a free admission permit – write well in advance to the Ministry of Science and Culture (Museums Section), Aristídhou 14, Athens. Those over sixty can also get a small reduction. Entrance to all state-run sites and museums is free to EU nationals on Sundays and public holidays outside the peak season (Oct–Mar).

Bargaining is not a regular feature of life, though you'll find it possible with "rooms" and some off-season hotels. It's worth offering to use your sleeping bag, saving the washing of the sheets. Similarly, you should be able to negotiate discounted rates for vehicle, motorbike and scooter rental, especially in low season or when you are renting for longer periods.

Cinema You're unlikely to see any very inspiring films in a Cretan cinema, but most English-language titles are subtitled rather than dubbed, and the open-air screens which can be found in all the major towns in summer are wonderful.

Contraceptives Condoms (*kapótes*) are available from city kiosks or *farmakía*; the pill, too, can be obtained from a *farmakío* – you shouldn't need a prescription.

Electricity is 220 volt AC (British appliances should work, US ones need a transformer). Plugs are usually the standard European variety of two round pins and you should pick up an adapter before you leave home, as they can be difficult to find locally. Power cuts are a common feature in Crete, particularly in summer, when generating capacity is stretched to breaking point. Hassles which affect visitors include bank computers and ATMs going down, non-functioning fuel pumps at garages and warm beer and wine in restaurants; many places (especially cinemas) have their own back-up generators.

Greek language courses Many places offering Greek courses to foreigners are to be found in the major towns along the north coast. One language centre in Haniá with a good reputation is Lexis, Dhaskaloyiánnis 48 (☎ & ☎28210 55673, ⓔelexis-glacc @cha.forthnet.gr). In Réthimnon the University of Crete runs four-week summer courses during July (☎28310 077278, ⓔmoderngreek@phl.uoc.gr).

Laundries These are rare, with service laundries (about €6 for a big wash and dry) more common in the big towns; they appear in the relevant "Listings" and "Practicalities" sections of the *Guide*. Off the beaten track, hotels and rooms places almost always have somewhere to wash your own clothes. Ask to use the laundry trough (*skáfi*) rather than risk destroying your room's plumbing.

Name days In common with other parts of the Mediterranean, Greeks get two birthdays a year – one is the anniversary of their actual birth whilst the other (and more important one) celebrates the feast day of the saint he or she is named after; it is unusual for any Greek not to be named after a saint. Popular names on Crete such as Ioánnis and Yeóryios mean that the celebrations on these saints' days make for an island-wide holiday.

Períptero A *períptero* is a street-corner kiosk. They sell everything – pens, combs, phone cards, razors, stationery, postcards, soap, sweets, nuts, condoms, *komboloi* ("worry" beads) – double as phone booths, and stay open long after everything else has closed.

Skiing Believe it or not, it is possible to ski in Crete in winter, and there's even a tiny ski lift on the Nídha Plain above Anóyia, while the *Kalleryi Lodge* in the White Mountains may also open for ski parties. Don't come specially.

Spectator sports Soccer and basketball are Crete's major sports. OFI, from Iráklion, is Crete's leading first-division football team and, in season (Sept–June), matches – normally played on Sundays – against many of the mainland's other major sides are easy enough to catch at their ground, Demotikou, in the west of he city. Warm-up games for the new season in late August often feature visits by foreign teams.

Time As throughout the EU, Greek summer time begins at 2am on the last Sunday in March, when the clocks go forward one hour, and ends at 2am on the last Sunday in October when clocks fall back one hour. Be alert to this, as scores of visitors miss planes and ferries every year; the changeover is not well publicized. Greek time is thus two hours ahead of the UK, and three hours when the respective changes to summer time fail to coincide. For North America, the standard time difference is seven hours ahead of Eastern Standard Time, ten hours ahead of Pacific Standard Time, with again an extra hour for those weeks in April and October when one place is on daylight saving and the other isn't. A recorded time message (in distinctly slow Greek) is available by dialling ☎141.

Toilets Public toilets, generally foul, are usually in parks or squares, often subterranean. Otherwise try a bus station. Throughout Greece (and to the horror of most first-time visitors) you're urged to toss paper in adjacent wastebaskets, not in the bowl: learn this habit, or you'll block the pipes. It's worth carrying toilet paper with you – though it's provided by the attendants at public facilities, there may be none in tavernas or cafés.

Useful items It's worth bringing an alarm clock for early buses and ferries, as well as a torch for camping out, coping with power cuts, visiting caves and churches or finding your way to a midnight swim. A pair of binoculars will enhance enjoyment of the plentiful birdlife, and a pocket knife (Swiss Army type or similar), with tweezers, mini screwdriver and other similar accessories comes in handy for everything from cutting up fruit or cheese to extracting sea urchin spines.

Guide

Guide

Iráklion

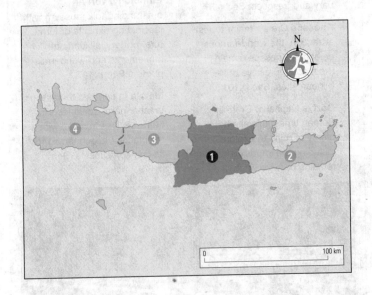

CHAPTER 1 # Highlights

✳ **Iráklion** The bustling capital city of Iráklion boasts good restaurants and cafés, a vibrant market and an impressive harbour fortress. See p.76

✳ **Archeological Museum, Iráklion** The world's most important museum of Minoan civilization, with a fabulous array of jewellery, vases, statuary and frescoes. See p.87

✳ **Knossós** Crete's major tourist attraction, the world-famous palace of Knossós remains the most impressive of the Minoan sites. See p.101

✳ **Górtys** Capital of Crete in Roman times, this site has plenty of ruins to explore, including the imposing remains of Áyios Títos, the

island's first Christian church. See p.138

✳ **Festós and Mália palaces** These two outstanding ancient sites in picturesque locations are superb examples of Minoan architecture. See p.142 & p.126

✳ **Museum of Cretan Ethnology, Vori** An outstanding folk museum with fascinating exhibits of furniture, pottery, all kinds of implements and wonderful photos. See p.147

✳ **Mátala** In contrast to Iráklion's brasher north coast resorts, Mátala is less frenetic, with a spectacular beach famed for its crimson sunsets. See p.149

△ Venetian fortress, Iráklion harbour

Iráklion

The province of **Iráklion** sees more tourists than any other in Crete. They come for two simple reasons: the string of big resorts which lies to the east of the city, only an hour or so from the airport, and the great Minoan sites, almost all of which are concentrated in the centre of the island. **Knossós**, **Mália** and **Festós** are in easy reach of almost anywhere in the province, and there are excellent beaches all along the north coast. The price you pay is crowds: **Iráklion** is a big, boisterous city with a population of around 130,000, the development to the east is continuous and huge, and in summer, the great sites are constantly packed with people.

There seems little here of the old Crete, ramshackle and rural, and yet, by taking the less obvious turn, it is still possible to escape. West and south of Iráklion, the beaches are smaller and the coastline is less amenable to hotel builders. The south coast in particular is far less peopled: beaches are accessible only in a handful of places (of which only **Mátala** is at all exploited), whilst the interior remains traditional farming country, the Crete of shepherds and flocks, simple hamlets and ancient churches.

Iráklion and the north coast

Iráklion itself can at first sight seem an unattractive traffic-clogged metropolis, particularly if you arrive expecting a quaint little island town. You find yourself instead in the fifth largest city in Greece: strident and modern, a maelstrom of crowded thoroughfares, building work and dust. Penetrate behind this facade, however, and you can discover a vibrant working city with a myriad of attractive features which do much to temper initial impressions. Stay long enough and you can begin to like the place – after all, there is plenty to see and do here. But if you've come to escape the urban grind you're perhaps better off taking the city for what it has: the major Minoan palace of Knossós and an outstanding Archeological Museum most famously, but also snatched

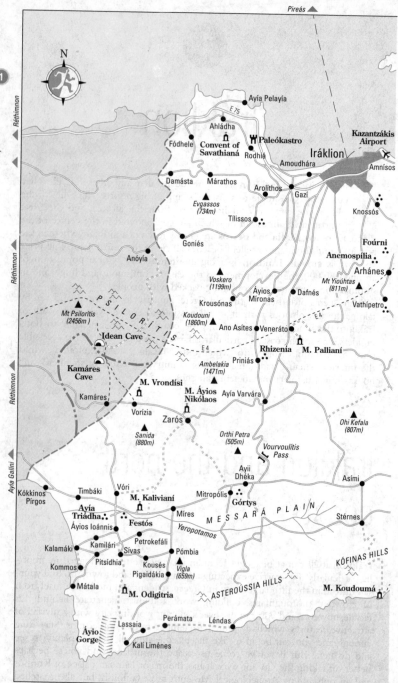

Áyios Nikólaos, Rhodes, Cyprus & Israel

Dhía

Lasíthi Plateau

Ierápetra

Mírtos & Ierápetra

Tombrouk

Kátó Goúves
Goúrnes
Háni Kokkíni
Finikas
E 75
Cave of Eileíthyia
Goúves
BYPASS
Skotinó Cave

Old Hersónisos
Hersónisos (Límin Hersonísou)
Piskopianó
Stalidha
Koutoulafari
Mália
Palace of Mália
BYPASS (OPEN 2004)

Potamiés
Mohós
Krási
Panayía Kardhiótissa

Episkopí
Avdhoú
Goníes

Mirtiá
Apóstoli
Piyí
Kastélli
Ayios Pandeleímon
Lyttos
Ksidhás

Pezá
Ayía Paraskiés
Thrapsanó
Kastamonitsa

Houdétsi
Geraki
Mathiá
Afendis (1578m)
D H Í K T I

Arkalohóri
Panayía
E 4
Afendis Hristos (2141m)
Káto Síni

Mártha
Áno Viánnos
Amirás
Kalámi

Teféli
Skiniás
Hóndhros
Akrotíri Sidonía
Árvi

Kastilianá
Kastrí
Keratókambos

Protória
Mesohório
Tsoútsouros

Pírgos
Kotási

Ethiá

MEDITERRANEAN SEA

0   10 km

visions of another city of magnificent fortifications, a wonderful market, the occasional ancient alley and curious smaller museums – and then move on to more immediately inviting places.

Knossós apart, the immediate surrounds of Iráklion offer little compensation. If you are based in the city with time on your hands, then the Minoan remains at **Arhánes** or the views from **Mount Yioúhtas** are worth taking in and, due to the crowds that rush to escape the city in summer, transport to local beaches is excellent.

East of Iráklion, the startling pace of tourist development is all too plain to see. The merest hint of a beach is an excuse to build at least one hotel, and these are outnumbered by the concrete shells of rivals-to-be. It can be hard to find a room in the peak season in this monument to the package tour, and expensive if you do. Some of the resorts, most notably **Mália** and **Hersónisos**, do at least have good beaches and lively nightlife. They wouldn't be at all bad if you were on a package deal – providing you don't mind crowds, noise and commercialism. But turn up hoping to find somewhere to stay on the off-chance and you won't regard them as the most welcoming of places. As a general rule, the further you go, the better things get: even where the road veers briefly inland, a more appealing Crete – of olive groves, tidy villages and picturesque mountain vistas – reveals itself.

West of Iráklion, there's much less to detain you, with mountains which drop virtually straight to the sea. There is just one small, classy resort – in the bay at **Ayía Pelayía** – a few isolated hotels and, in the hills behind, a number of interesting old villages: **Fódhele** is the possible birthplace of El Greco, and **Tílissos** has a famous Minoan villa.

Iráklion

The best way to arrive in **IRÁKLION** is from the sea, the traditional approach and still the one which shows the city in its best light, with Mount Yioúhtas rising behind, the heights of the Psilorítis range to the west and, as you get closer, the city walls encircling and dominating the oldest part of town. As you sail in, you run the gauntlet of the great fortress guarding the harbour entrance. Less romantically, the old harbour can't handle ships of ferry size, and the ferries actually dock at giant concrete wharves alongside. What little remains of the old city has been heavily restored, often from the bottom up, but the slick renovations often look fake, pristine and polished alongside the grime which coats even the most recent buildings – a juxtaposition which seems to neatly sum up much about modern Iráklion.

Iráklion's name is of Roman origin (Heraclium), taken from a port which stood hereabouts and readopted at the beginning of the twentieth century. The present city was founded by the **Saracens**, who held Crete from 827 to 961. In those days, it was known as **El Khandak**, after the great ditch that surrounded it, later corrupted by the Venetians to **Candia** or Candy as Shakespeare titled it, a name also applied to the island as a whole. This Venetian capital was, in its day, one of the strongest and most spectacular cities in Europe – a trading centre, a staging-point for the Crusades and, as time wore on, itself the front line of Christendom. The **Turks** finally conquered the city after 21 years of war, which culminated in a bitter siege from May 1667 to September 1669.

Under its new Turkish rulers, the city's importance declined in relation to Haniá's, but it remained a major port and the second city in Crete. It was here,

Street of the August Martyrs

Properly named **Odhós Martírion 25-Avgoústo** (the 25th of August Martyrs), the name of the city's major thoroughfare derives from one of the final acts in the ending of Turkish domination of the island at the end of the nineteenth century. In 1898 under the aegis of the great powers of post-Napoleonic Europe (France, Italy, Russia and Britain), an autonomous Cretan state with an Executive Council was formed under Turkish sovereignty, regarded by most Cretans as a prelude to union with Greece. On August 25th a detachment of British soldiers was escorting Council officials along this street from the harbour when they were attacked by a violent mob of Turkish Cretans, smarting at what they saw as the betrayal of their birthright. In the bloody riot that ensued, hundreds of Christian Cretans lost their lives as well as seventeen British soldiers and the British Honorary Consul. This stirred the British to take reprisals and, on the principle of an eye for an eye, they rounded up and hanged seventeen of the Turkish Cretan ringleaders and slapped many more in prison. Shortly after this, the British navy sailed into the harbour and the city was cleared of Turkish troops. The following November the last Turkish military forces left the island they had controlled for 230 years.

too, that the incident occurred which finally put an end to Turkish occupation of the island (see the box above). Finally united with **Greece**, Iráklion's future prosperity was assured by its central position. Almost all that you see, though, dates only from the last few decades, partly through the reconstruction following the heavy bombing it suffered during World War II but also through a boom in agriculture, industry and tourism – the city is now the wealthiest in Greece per head of population. In 1971, Iráklion regained the official title of island **capital**. Its growth continues, as you'll see if you venture to the fringes of town, where the concrete spreads inexorably, but it can hardly be said to add to the attraction. In recent years, Iráklion's administrators have been giving belated attention to dealing with some of the city's image problems, and large tracts of the walled city have undergone costly landscaping and refurbishment schemes designed to present a less daunting prospect to the visitor. Whilst Iráklion will never be one of the jewels of the Mediterranean, the ebullient friendliness of its people and an infectious cosmopolitan atmosphere may well tempt you into giving it more than the customary one-night transit.

Orientation, arrival and information

Virtually everything you're likely to want to see in Iráklion lies within the walled city, with the majority of the interest falling into the relatively small sector of the northeastern corner. The most vital thoroughfare, **Odhós 25-Avgoústou**, links the harbour with the commercial city centre (see the box above). At the bottom it's lined with shipping and travel agencies, car and motorbike rental outfits, but as you climb, these give way to banks, restaurants and city-centre shops. **Platía Venizélou** (Fountain Square), off to the right, is thronged with cafés and restaurants favoured by Iráklion's younger set; behind Venizélou is the small **El Greco Park**, with the OTE office and more bars, which, with nearby Hándhakos to the west and Korai to the east, comprises one of the town's main nightlife zones. On the opposite side of 25-Avgoústou from the park are some of the more interesting of Iráklion's older buildings, including the church of **Áyios Títos** and the Venetian Loggia.

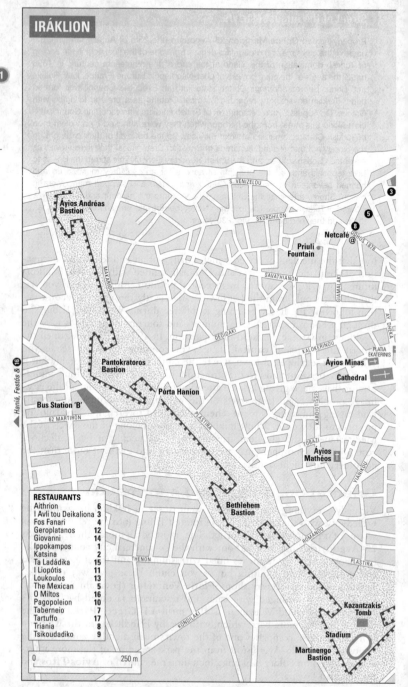

Haniá, Festos & ⑩

RESTAURANTS
Aithrion	6
I Avlí tou Deikaliona	3
Fos Fanari	4
Geroplatanos	12
Giovanni	14
Ippokampos	1
Katsina	2
Ta Ladádika	15
I Liopótis	11
Loukoulos	13
The Mexican	5
O Miltos	16
Pagopoleion	10
Taberneio	7
Tartuffo	17
Triania	8
Tsikoudadiko	9

0   250 m

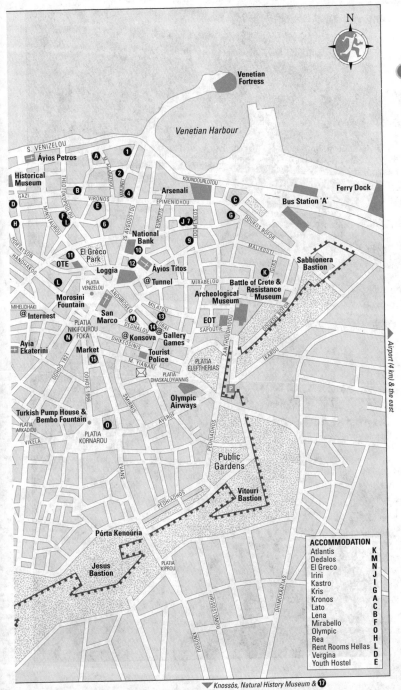

N

Venetian Fortress

Venetian Harbour

S. VENIZELOU

Áyios Petros

Historical Museum

GAZI

Arsenali

KOUNDOUROTOU

EPIMENIDHOU

Ferry Dock

Bus Station 'A'

DOUKOS BOFOR

VIRONOS

25 AVGOUSTOU

EUROPIS

DOMENEHOS

National Bank

MALIKOUTI

El Gréco Park

OTE

Loggia

Áyios Títos

@ Tunnel

MIRABELOU

Sabbionera Bastion

Morosini Fountain

PLATIA VENIZELOU

ANDHROYEO

MILATOU

Battle of Crete & Resistance Museum

Archeological Museum

IGIAS

DOUKOS BOFOR

@ Internest

San Marco

DEDHALOU

IDAI

EOT

SAPOUTIE

ZANTHOUDHIDHOU

IKAROU

MIHELIDHAKI

PLATIA NIKIFOROU FOKA

Ayia Ekaterini

DHIKEOSINIS

@ Konsova Gallery Games

Tourist Police

PLATIA ELEFTHERIAS

Market

M. YIANARI

PLATIA DHASKALOYIANNIS

ODHOS 1821

ODHOS 1866

SMIRNIS

P

Olympic Airways

Turkish Pump House & Bembo Fountain

PLATIA ARKADIOU

VIKELA

PLATIA KORNAROU

AVEROF

PEDHIADHOS

EVANS

PEDHIADHOS

Public Gardens

Vitouri Bastion

Pórta Kenoúria

PLATIA KIPROU

DHIMOKRATIAS

Jesus Bastion

HRISOSTOMOU

KNOSSOU

Airport (4 km) & the east

Knossós, Natural History Museum & ⑰

△ Church interior, Iráklion

At its southern end, 25-Avgoústou meets **Platía Nikifourou Foka**, which forms a junction for central Iráklion's other main arteries; **Kalokerinoú** heads westwards down to the Pórta Haníon and out of the city, straight ahead, Odhós 1821 – a fashionable shopping street – heads off southwest towards the obscure Platía Arkadiou, while the adjacent 1866 is given over to the animated **market**, one of the best on the island. To the east of the junction, another major shopping street, **Dhikeosínis**, leads to the recently revamped **Platía Eleftherías** (Liberty Square), also linked to Platía Venizélou by the pedestrianized alley **Dedhálou**, which runs parallel to Dhikeosínis and is the venue for many of Iráklion's top designer clothing stores. Eleftherías is very much the traditional centre of the city, both for traffic, now routed around the edge of a refurbished pedestrian area, and for life in general; it is ringed by upmarket cafés and bar terraces, and in the evening comes alive with strolling locals.

Arrival

Iráklion **airport**, 4km east of the city, lies right on the coast – you come in to land low over some of the better local beaches. Bus #1 leaves for Platía Eleftherías every few minutes from the car park in front of the terminal; buy your ticket (€0.70) at the booth before boarding. There are also plenty of taxis outside (which you'll need to use if you miss the last bus at 11pm) and prices to major destinations are posted; it's €6–€8 to the centre of town, depending on traffic. Get an agreement on the fare before taking the cab and beware if the driver extols the virtues of a particular hotel – he may be motivated by the prospect of a kickback from the proprietors, rather than your best interests. If you haven't already lined up a place to stay, the central Platía Eleftherías is a good destination to quote to the driver; from here, many of the accommodation options are within easy walking distance.

From the wharves where the **ferries** dock, the city rises directly ahead in steep tiers. If you're heading for the centre on foot, for the Archeological Museum or the tourist office, cut straight up the stepped alleys behind the bus station (from where there are buses to the centre) onto Doúkos Bófor and to Platía Eleftherías (about a 15min walk). For accommodation, though, and to get a better idea of the layout of Iráklion's main attractions, it's simpler to follow the main roads: head west along the coast, past the major eastbound bus station and on by the Venetian harbour before cutting left towards the centre on Odhós 25-Avgoústou.

Arriving in town **by car**, you'll face the problems of parking that now bedevil most large Greek cities. Rather than spend valuable time searching for a space, you'd be best advised to use one of the signposted city-centre car parks, which are reasonably priced (around €3 for a full day). One of the best is the large Museum car park on Doúkos Bófor, 70m downhill from the Archeological Museum, which uses space below the city walls and has the bonus of plenty of shade.

There are two main bus stations (often titled A and B on maps). **Bus station A** is sited on both sides of the main road (Koundouriotou) between the ferry dock and the Venetian harbour. Buses run from here west to Réthimnon and Haniá and east along the coastal highway to Hersónisos, Mália, Áyios Nikólaos, and Sitía, as well as southeast to Ierápetra and points en route. Local bus #2 to Knossós also leaves from here. Buses for the southwest (Festós, Mátala and Ayía Galíni) and along the inland roads west (Tílissos, Anóyia and Fódhele) operate out of **bus station B** just outside Pórta Haníon, a very long walk from the centre up Kalokerinoú (or jump on any city bus heading up this street).

Information

Iráklion's **tourist office** (Mon–Fri 9am–2.30pm; ☎28102 28225, ⓦwww.heraklion-city.gr) is just below Platía Eleftherías, opposite the Archeological Museum at Zanthoudhídhou 1. There is also a tourist office at the **airport** (April–Sept daily 9am–9pm). The **tourist police** (☎28102 83190; 7am–11pm) – more helpful than most – are on Dhikeosínis, halfway between Platía Eleftherías and the market.

Accommodation

Iráklion has a distinct lack of decent, reasonably priced **accommodation**, especially in the height of summer. If possible, arrive early in the day; roll up after 8pm or so without a reservation and you'll be lucky to find anything at all (though the hostels are always worth a try). In August, on national holidays and around Easter you'd be advised to take any rooms available – you can always set out early next day to find something better. Noise can be a problem wherever you stay; we've indicated some of the more tranquil locations.

There's a good selection of mid-range **hotels** conveniently located in the areas to the east and west of Odhós 25-Avgoústou. For hotels of C class and above (see p.40), it's usually simplest to approach the tourist office first – they should know where there are available rooms and if they're not too harassed can phone for you. At quieter times it's worth trying your luck at some of the B and C class hotels – during slack periods they sometimes reduce prices by fifty percent or more.

The greatest concentration of **inexpensive rooms** is to be found near Platía Venizélou, around Hándhakos, in the vicinity of the "A" bus station and near the Venetian Harbour. There are a few central, but rather noisy and marginally more expensive places around El Greco Park and by the bottom of the market, and another small enclave of generally less pleasant places clustered towards the bottom of Kalokerinoú, near the Pórta Hanión. Few of the downmarket places offer private bathrooms, but they should all be clean and have (some) hot water.

There are no **campsites** within striking distance of Iráklion. The nearest sites are both to the east of the city – *Camping Creta* (☎28970 41400) at Káto Goúves, 16km east, and *Caravan Camping* (☎28970 22901) at Hersónisos, 28km east.

El Greco Park area

Kastro Theotokopoúlou 22 ☎28102 85052, ⓦwww.kastro-hotel.gr. Refurbished three-star hotel offering a/c rooms with satellite TV, strong-box, and balcony or terrace. ❻

Kronos Agarathou 2, west of 25-Avgoústou ☎28102 82240, ⒻP28102 85853. Pleasant, modern hotel where en-suite rooms come with sea-view balconies and TV. ❺

Lena Lahana 10 ☎28102 23280, Ⓕ28102 42826. This quiet and efficient small hotel has a/c rooms with and without bath, and some with TV; the second floor is airier. ❹

Mirabello Theotokopoúlou 20 ☎28102 85052, ⓦwww.mirabello-hotel.gr. Good-value family-run hotel just north of El Greco Park in a peaceful street. Pleasant balcony rooms with and without bath, most with a/c and TV. ❹–❺

Rea Kalimeráki 1 ☎28102 23638, Ⓕ28102 42189. A friendly, comfortable and clean pension in a quiet street. Some rooms with washbasin, others with own shower. Guests can claim a thirty percent discount on cars hired with Ritz, the pension's own car hire firm (see p.98). ❷–❸

Rent Rooms Hellas Hándhakos 24 ☎28102 88851, Ⓕ28102 84442. Occupies the small but spruced-up original youth hostel building, and has dorm beds for €7 per person; facilities include roof garden and snack bar. Also has some private rooms. ❶

Vergina Hortátson 32 ☎28102 42739. Basic but pleasant rooms with washbasins and shared baths, set around a courtyard that boasts an enormous banana tree. ❷

Youth Hostel Vironos 5 ☎28102 86281, Ⓔheraklioyouthhostel@yahoo.com. The former official youth hostel, now privately operated, this is a good place to stay, with friendly and helpful proprietors. It has plenty of space and some beds (albeit illegal) on the roof, if you fancy sleeping out under the stars. Private rooms as well as dorms (€10 per bed); hot showers, breakfast and other meals available. ❶–❷

The Port and Venetian Harbour area

Atlantis Igias 2 ☎ 28102 29103, ⓦ www.grecotel.gr. Iráklion's premier five-star luxury hotel is aimed at the business market and hosts many conferences. It has all the usual room facilities for this category, and its public areas include a roof garden and pool. The cheapest double in high season is €160. ❾

Irini Idomeneos 4 ☎ 28102 29703, ⓕ 28102 26407. Central hotel offering decent rooms with TV, a/c, fridge and spacious balconies. ❻

Kris Doúkos Bófor 2 ☎ 28102 23211. Attractive studio rooms with kitchenette, fridge and balconies overlooking the harbour. Very friendly. ❺

Lato Epimenidou 15 ☎ 28102 28103, ⓦ www.lato.gr. Stylish and luxurious hotel where a/c rooms come with minibar, TV and fine balcony views over the old Venetian port (suites 3, 4 and 5 have the best). There's also a *hammam* (Turkish bath) and gym, making this easily the best of the upmarket places. Breakfast included. ❽

Around Platía Eleftherías

Dedalos Dedhálou 15 ☎ 28102 44812, ⓔ daedalos@internet.gr. Recently refurbished hotel with balcony rooms overlooking this pedestrianized shopping street which is quiet at night. All rooms are en suite and equipped with TV, and three have a/c (€4 surcharge); fans available for the rest on request. ❹

El Greco Odhós-1821 4 ☎ & ⓕ 28102 81071, ⓔ elgrecohotel@her.forthnet.gr. One of Iráklion's best-known hotels, but with little to distinguish it from any of the others in its price range. Supplement (€7) charged for a/c rooms. Breakfast included. ❻

Olympic Platía Kornárou ☎ 28102 88861, ⓔ irolymp@otenet.gr. Recently modernised 1960s hotel with double-glazed windows overlooking a busy (and sometimes noisy) square and the famous Bembo and Turkish fountains. Rooms come with a/c, minibar, TV and strongbox. Breakfast included. ❽

The City

Despite Iráklion's rather cheerless reputation, parts of the old town can be genuinely picturesque. By far the most striking aspect of the city is its harbour **fortress** and massive **Venetian walls** framing the old quarters where most of the sights are located. Focal to this area are the **Venizélou** and **Eleftherías** squares, and most of the churches, museums and other monuments are never more than a few minutes' walk from either. The **Archeological Museum**, holding the world's foremost collection of Minoan antiquities, lies just off Platía Eleftherías and should not be missed. Other sights include the impressive **Museum of Religious Art**, a superb collection of **icons** housed in the church of Ayía Ekaterini and an important **Natural History Museum**, the island's first.

The Venetian fortress and the Arsenali

The obvious starting point for your explorations is the **Venetian fortress** (Tues–Sun 8.30am–3pm; €2), which stands guard over the harbour. Built between 1523 and 1540, the fortress was known to the Venetians as the Rocca al Mare, to the Turks as Koule. Painstakingly refurbished, it now often houses temporary exhibitions which may disrupt the standard opening hours. Taken simply as a structure, it is undeniably impressive: massively sturdy walls command superb views over harbour and town, and protect a series of chambers (many still piled with cannonballs) in which the defenders must have enjoyed an overwhelming sense of security. It is easy to see here how Venetian Iráklion managed to resist the Turks for so long. On the other hand, there is something unsatisfying about the way the edifice has been so thoroughly scrubbed, polished and cosseted, losing any hint of atmosphere in the process.

While you may know that this stronghold is the genuine sixteenth-century article from the lions of St Mark adorning the exterior and the simple solidity of the stone, it feels as if it were built yesterday for some swashbuckling Hollywood production. At night, when the fortress is floodlit, the causeway leading to it is the haunt of courting couples, while the niches in the walls provide temporary accommodation for people awaiting ferries or for fishermen: it's a fine place to watch the ships coming and going.

The only other survivors of the Venetian harbour installations are the vaulted **Arsenali** on the harbour's southern flank. Now lost in a sea of traffic scooting hither and thither along the harbour road, here ships were built or dragged ashore to be overhauled and repaired – close up, you may still find bits of broken boat lying about.

The City walls

The **walls** themselves – though well preserved and restored in parts – are rather harder to penetrate and access is often difficult. The easiest approach is to follow Odhós Pedhiádhos south from the back of Platía Eleftherías and find your way up one of the dusty tracks which lead to the top of the rampart. With luck and a little scrambling, you can walk all the way around from here, clockwise, to the Áyios Andréas Bastion overlooking the sea in the west. There are some curious views as you walk around, often looking down onto the rooftops, but the fabric of the walls themselves is rarely visible – it's simply like walking on a dusty path raised above the level of its surrounds. A word of warning, though: usually completely safe in daytime, the walls tend to attract less desirable types from dusk onwards.

On the Martinengo Bastion, facing south, is the **tomb of Níkos Kazantzákis**, Crete's greatest writer (see p.108). Despite his works being banned for their unorthodox views, Kazantzákis' burial rites were performed at Áyios Mínos Cathedral, although no priests officially escorted his body up here. His simple grave is adorned only with an inscription from his own writings: "I hope for nothing, I fear nothing, I am free". At the weekend, Iráklians gather to pay their respects – and to enjoy a free, grandstand view of the matches played by the city's once proud, but now second-string football team Ergotelis (see p.99) in the stadium below.

For more impressive views of the defences, from the outside, stroll out through one of the elaborate gates – the **Pórta Haníon** at the bottom of Kalokerinoú or the **Pórta Kenoúria** at the top of Odhós Evans. Both of these date from the second half of the sixteenth century, when the majority of the surviving defences were completed. Originally thrown up in the fifteenth century, the walls were constantly improved thereafter as Crete became increasingly isolated in the path of Turkish westward expansion: their final shape owes much to Michele Sanmicheli, who arrived here in 1538 having previously designed the fortifications of Padua and Verona. In its day, this was the strongest bastion in the Mediterranean, as evidenced at the Pórta Kenoúria, where the walls are over forty metres thick. The road heading south from this gate (Odhós Knosoú) leads to the Natural History Museum (see p.87).

If you want to follow the city walls in the other direction, from the sea up, simply head west a couple of kilometres along the coastal road from the harbour until you reach them.

The Historical Museum

About 300m from the harbour is the **Historical Museum** (Mon & Wed–Fri 9am–5pm, Tues & Sat 9am–2pm; €3; Ⓦ www.historical-museum.gr). The collection does help fill the gap which, for most people, yawns between Knossós and the present day, and since it's always virtually deserted, wandering around is a pleasure. The **ground floor**, if you're working chronologically, is the place to start; it contains sculptures and architectural fragments from the Byzantine, Venetian and Turkish periods. There are some beautiful pieces, most especially a fifteenth- or sixteenth-century tiered fountain from a Venetian palace. The **first floor** has religious art, wall paintings and documents from the same periods, a reconstruction of a typically domed Cretan church and a rather unusual work by the Cretan artist **El Greco** – a view of Mount Sinai painted around 1570. Upper floors bring things to the present with reconstructions of the studies of Níkos Kazantzákis and of the Cretan statesman (and Greek prime minister) Emanuel Tsouderós; photos and documents relating to the occupation of Crete by the Germans, plus the odd helmet and parachute harness; and a substantial selection of folk art – particularly textiles. The recent extension has also given the museum the space to re-create the interior of a Cretan farmhouse. When you exit, take a look behind the museum at the charming Venetian **fountain of Idomeneus** (mentioned by Kazantzákis in his novel *Freedom or Death* (see p.108), partly obscured by bushes in the daytime, added to in the evening by diners on the terrace of a nearby taverna.

Odhós 25-Avgoústou and Platía Venizélou

Heading inland from the harbour, Odhós 25-Avgoústou offers a less strenuous walk past more obvious attractions. On the left as you approach Platía Venizélou, the church of **Áyios Títos** commands a lovely little plaza. Originally Byzantine, but wholly rebuilt by the Venetians in the sixteenth century, it was adapted by the Turks as a mosque and rebuilt by them after a major earthquake in 1856. The Orthodox Church renovated the building after the Turkish population left Iráklion, and it was reconsecrated in 1925. A reliquary inside contains the skull of Áyios Títos (St Titus; see p.416). Originally brought to Iráklion from his tomb in Górtys – the rest of the body was never found – the skull was later taken to Venice, where it stayed from the time of the Turkish invasion until 1966. In the Middle Ages, it was regularly and ceremonially exhibited to the people of Iráklion.

On the top side of this square, abutting 25-Avgoústou, stands the Venetian City Hall with its famous **loggia**, reconstructed after the work of earthquakes was compounded by the rigours of World War II. Just past here on the left is **San Marco**, a church very much in the Venetian style which, following its own restoration, is used for exhibitions and occasional lectures or meetings. Under the Venetians it was the cathedral, and under the Turks a mosque: nowadays, the church steps make a handy overflow for the cafés in **Platía Venizélou**. In the square, the **Morosini Fountain** (hence the popular name "Fountain Square") dates from the final years of Venetian rule. On first sight, it's a rather disappointing little monument especially as it's rarely working. However, a recent cleaning and restoration job now enables the fine marine decoration on the basins to be appreciated close up; the lions on guard, which replaced an original statue of Neptune and are two to three hundred years older than the rest of the structure, are wonderful.

Odhós 1866 and Platía Kornárou

Straight across the main crossroads, Odhós 1866 is packed throughout the day with the stalls and customers of Iráklion's **market**. This is one of the few living reminders of an older city, with an atmosphere reminiscent of an eastern bazaar. There are luscious fruit and vegetables, as well as butchers' and fishmongers' stalls and others selling a bewildering variety of herbs and spices, cheese and yoghurt, leather and plastic goods, souvenirs, an amazing array of cheap kitchen utensils, pocket knives and just about anything else you might conceivably need – including a shop halfway down with a fine selection of straw and cotton sun hats. At the far end, you emerge in a quiet square, **Platía Kornárou**, the focal point of which is a beautiful **Turkish pumphouse**. Heavily restored, this hexagonal building houses a welcome café which serves as a lively meeting place for the male octogenarians of this quarter, who converse at the tables under the trees. Standing beside the café, a small sixteenth-century Venetian drinking fountain – the **Bembo Fountain** (named after its designer Zuanne Bembo) – incorporates a headless Roman torso imported from Ierápetra. Incidentally, this was the first fountain to supply the town with running water.

Cathedral and Museum of Religious Art

Turning right before the market leads you down Kalokerinoú towards the Pórta Haníon and the main road west. Veer left after about 100m, up Áyii Dhéka or one of the streets immediately after, and you'll reach a large open space beside the **Cathedral of Áyios Mínas**. The cathedral, a rather undistinguished nineteenth-century building, is notable mainly for its size. Just in front, however, stands the tiny original medieval church of Áyios Mínas: the interior is worth a look and contains some interesting icons (if it's closed, ask at the cathedral).

Far more worthwhile, and just at the bottom of the same square, is the sixteenth-century church of **Ayía Ekateríni** (Mon–Sat 8.30am–1.30pm, plus Tues, Thurs & Fri 5–7pm; €2), which houses a **Museum of Religious Art**, the finest collection of **Cretan icons** anywhere. Built in the fifteenth century, the church was part of a monastic school which, up to the end of Venetian rule, was one of the centres of the Cretan Renaissance, a last flourish of Eastern Christian art following the fall of Byzantium. Among the school's students were Vitzéntzos Kornáros, author of the Cretan classic *Erotókritos*, and many leading Orthodox theologians; most importantly, however, it served as an art school where Byzantine tradition came face to face with the influences of the Venetian Renaissance. Among the greatest of the pupils was the late sixteenth-century painter **Mihaílis Dhamaskinós**, and six of his works – including the *Adoration of the Magi*, the *Last Supper* and *Christ Appearing to the Holy Women* – form the centre of the collection. It was the much-imitated Dhamaskinós who introduced perspective and depth to Byzantine art, while never straying far from the strict traditions of icon painting; in his later works he reverts to a much purer, archaic style. The most famous Cretan painter of them all, **El Greco**, took the opposite course – wholeheartedly embracing Italian styles, to which he brought the influence of his Byzantine training. Although there is little evidence, it's generally accepted that these two – Dhamaskinós and El Greco – were near contemporaries at the school. Two further icons now attributed to Dhamaskinós are in the fourteenth-century church of **Áyios Mathéos**, now sitting below street level on Odhós Taxiárhou Markopoúlou as it leads southwest from the cathedral. Alongside Ayía Ekateríni is the church of **Áyii Dhéka**, a seventeenth-century building that acted as a chapel to the larger church. The square facing Ayía Ekateríni, Platía Ekaterinis, is a pleasant oasis away from the bustle of the town centre and has a few inviting cafés with tables under the trees.

Platía Eleftherías and around

Turning left from the cathedral before the market brings you quickly up to the recently face-lifted **Platía Eleftherías**, where a line of pricey pavement cafés face a concourse dotted with gumtrees and benches which have replaced the formerly whirling traffic. After years of construction work to effect the transformation, the square has once again become the city's most popular venue for walking, talking and sitting out. There's a small bust of Níkos Kazantzákis and a larger-than-life statue of Elefthteríos Venizélos (the leading figure in the struggle for union with Greece), staring out over the harbour from the ramparts and looking remarkably like Lenin. Beyond the statue, you reach the entrance to the **Public Gardens**, as often as not half taken over by a funfair, but otherwise relatively peaceful. Above all, however, Platía Elefthterías offers access to the **Archeological Museum** (see below) off its northeast corner, as well as the **Battle of Crete and Resistance Museum** (Mon–Fri 9am–2.30pm; free) on the corner of Doúkos Bófor and Hatzidaki which uses photos as well as military equipment and uniforms to tell the story of this critical period in the island's modern history.

The Natural History Museum

Two kilometres south of the Pórta Kenoúria (and well signed) along the road to Knossós is Iráklion and Crete's first **Natural History Museum** (July–Aug daily 9am–8pm; Sept–June Mon–Fri 9am–3pm, Sun 9am–5pm; €4.50; Ⓦ www.nhmc.uoc.gr), administered by the University of Crete. You can reach the museum on the same bus that goes to Knossós (#2 from Platía Elefthterías; ask for the "Pagritio School" stop) or take a taxi (around €3) from the centre; many bus and taxi drivers are not yet familiar with the museum – should you have problems ask for the *Mouseio Fisikis Istorias Kritis*.

Despite a steep admission charge, it's a splendid addition to the city's museums. Set out on three floors, the exhibits detail the island's geological evolution, the arrival of man, and the environment as it would have appeared to the Minoans. Other sections deal with fossils, rocks, minerals and caves, and a series of dioramas illustrates the flora and fauna of Crete today. The museum is now teaching new generations of Cretans to appreciate, respect and care for their environment, a factor that hasn't featured greatly in the Greek education system thus far. A **botanical garden** at the rear of the museum has living examples of the island's aromatic shrubs and coastal plants; it's also the location for a pleasant **café** terrace.

The Archeological Museum

Iráklion's **Archeological Museum** (April–Sept Mon 12–7pm, Tues–Sun 8am–7pm; Oct–March daily 8am–5pm; €6, free Sun Nov–May) on Zanthoudhídhou, just off Platía Elefthterías, is one of the major reasons to visit the city. The museum houses far and away the most important collection of **Minoan art** and artefacts anywhere in the world, and a visit to Knossós or the other sites will be greatly enhanced if you've been here first. That said, many visitors are disappointed by the museum's dreary nineteenth-century style of presentation and sparsely labelled exhibits – most of the innovations in museum design over the past few decades have had little impact here. However, a major **renovation** of the building and reorganization of the collection is now planned, which should improve things dramatically over the next few years (see the box on p.88).

The museum is almost always crowded (at least in summer) and at times becomes quite overwhelmed by coach parties, with an endless procession of guided tours in all languages monopolizing the major exhibits. It's best to try and see it early, late, or during everyone else's lunch break. The collection is

The Archeological Museum's renovation

A long-overdue **renovation** of the Archeological Museum is planned to begin in 2004 which, once completed, should place it at the forefront of museum presentation in Greece. New buildings are projected to house the administration offices, freeing up more space for exhibits, and a new subterranean floor is to be excavated beneath the museum to stage special exhibitions.

Preliminary soundings for this latter section have uncovered the remains of a **Roman Villa**, a **Venetian aqueduct**, vestiges of the **Turkish town** as well as the remnants of a **Franciscan monastery**, all of which previously occupied the site at different times. These will need to be properly investigated before any work can begin, thus making any completion date for the project difficult to forecast. Once work is under way there will inevitably be some frustration for visitors as rooms are closed and items moved around in years to come. All this means that our account may not be entirely accurate, but it should still be possible to identify the major items in the collection without too much difficulty. The **Yiamalakis Collection** (see p.94) may also not be on view, but will return when the reorganization is complete.

large and will prove a lot more rewarding in small doses: take in the highlights first time around and go back later for whatever you feel you've missed – tickets are valid for re-entry the same day. Several good **museum guides** are on sale at the bookstore in the entrance foyer: the best are probably the glossy guides by J.A. Sakellarakis and the more recent publication (with better images) by Andonis Vasilakis; either would make an excellent reference work to take home. However, neither is essential, and the following account should give you some idea of what to expect. Basically, the galleries on the ground floor, which you have little choice but to walk through in order, follow a chronological pattern: they run from the Neolithic era right through to Roman times, with the more important Minoan periods also divided according to where the items on display were discovered. Upstairs, larger rooms show the fabulous Minoan frescoes.

Prehistory to the early Minoans

Room I covers the earliest signs of human settlement (around 6000 BC) to the beginnings of Minoan civilization in the Pre-Palatial period. There's a bit of everything here, of interest mainly because it is so very old: statuettes, including a Neolithic "fertility goddess"; pottery, among which the blotchy **Vasilikí ware** (Case 6) with elegant elongated spouts points to the great things to come; and stone jars from the island of Móhlos (Case 7), displaying an early mastery of the lapidary's craft. Among the miniature sculpture, don't miss a **clay bull** (Case 15) with tiny acrobats clinging to its horns: an early sign of the popularity of bull sports. In the central cases, and typical of what is to be seen later in the museum, is a display of sophisticated early **jewellery** alongside some intricately engraved **seal stones** – among the latter, one from ancient Mesopotamia (no. 1098), suggesting early contact between the island and its Near Eastern neighbours.

Room II contains objects from the earliest period of occupation of Knossós and Mália (2000–1700 BC), along with items found in various peak sanctuaries of the same era. Archeologically most significant is the **Kamáres ware** pottery, with often elaborate white and red decoration on a dark ground. For casual visitors, however, the miniature figures are of far more immediate interest, in particular the famous "**Town Mosaic**" from Knossós in Case 25. This consists of a series of glazed plaques depicting multistorey Minoan houses, beautiful pieces which probably fitted together to form a decorative scene. There are also some lovely figurines and tiny animals, mostly offerings found in the peak sanctuaries: look out for the three-columned shrine with a dove perched on the top of each column, thought to represent the epiphany, or a manifestation, of the goddess worshipped there. Finally, note the **clay statuettes** (Cases 21 and 24) of sanctuary worshippers – their arms crossed or placed on the chest in reverential attitudes – as well as the *taxímata* (ex votos) representing parts of the human body the deity was requested to heal, a custom still followed in churches all over Greece today.

Room III is devoted to the same period at Festós. Here, the **Kamáres ware** is even more elaborate, and it was at Festós that this art reached its peak – exemplified by a magnificent vase with sculpted white flowers in high relief. In Case 30 you'll find the original pieces, retrieved from the cave at Kamáres, which gave the style its name. Nearby in Case 33a, there is a unique portrayal of lively dolphins plunging among cockles and seaweed. The celebrated **Festós Disc** (Case 41) is a circular slab of clay upon which hieroglyphic characters have been inscribed in a spiral pattern. The disc is frequently described as the earliest-known example of printing, since the impressions of hieroglyphs were made with stamps before it was fired. The various signs are divided up into groups, believed to be words; some are repeated, leading scholars to suggest that what is represented on the disc may be some form of prayer or hymn. Despite a plethora of theories – and claims in several books on sale around the island to "reveal the secret" of the disc – this earliest Minoan script remains undeciphered.

New Palace period

Room IV represents the New Palace period (1700–1450 BC) in which the great sites reached their peak of creativity, rebuilt after the first destruction. Kamáres pottery is now replaced by new styles with patterns painted in dark colours on a light background, and themes drawn from nature (in particular marine life) rather than abstract patterns. The **Jug of Reeds** in Case 49 is a brilliant example of this stylistic development. Other objects are more immediately striking: above all, in Case 51 the renowned **bull's head rhyton**, a sacred vessel used in religious ceremonies and found in the Little Palace at Knossós. Carved from black stone (steatite) with inlaid eyes and nostrils (the wooden horns are new), the bull is magnificently naturalistic. There are other animal heads here too, including another rhyton in the form of a lioness's head crafted from white limestone, and the stunning leopard's-head axe (Case 47) from Mália. In Case 46 are a number of vessels connected with the snake cult; some of them may have been snake containers. These are pertinent to Case 50, where two representations of the **snake goddess** – both wearing tight-waisted, breast-baring dresses and decorated aprons, each with snakes coiling around their hands – may equally be priestesses engaged in sacred rituals. A delicate ivory acrobat (Case 56), generally accepted to be a bull-leaper, and a faïence relief of a *kri-kri*, or wild goat, suckling her kid (Case 55), also stand out. The **gaming board** in Case 57, from the Corridor of the Draughtsboard at Knossós, is beautiful too – made of ivory, blue paste, crystal, and gold and silver leaf, with ivory pieces – and a further reminder of the luxurious life which some Minoans at least could enjoy. Room IV also contains a collection of tools and weapons (especially, a giant sword from Mália), almost all bronze with decorative work in ivory, gold and semiprecious stones. Finally, in Case 44, two small clay cups may hold important clues to the history of Minoan writing, of which so little survives. These vessels bear inscriptions written in

Linear A script – developed from the cumbersome hieroglyphic – using cuttlefish ink. This use of ink suggests the existence of other suitable writing materials (possibly imported papyrus or even domestically produced palm-leaf paper) that have since perished in the Cretan climate.

Room V is devoted to the last period of the palace culture (1450–1400 BC), mainly at Knossós; the objects are considerably less exciting. In pottery, similar decorative themes continue to be used, but with a new formalism and on new types of vessel, which has been taken as a sign that Mycenaean influences were beginning to take hold – such similarities in style are clear on the giant amphorae which stand against the walls. The numerous **Egyptian objects** found at Knossós are interesting too, providing important evidence of the extent of trade between the two civilizations and, for archeologists, vital ammunition in the war over dates. In Case 70a is a clay model of a modest **Minoan dwelling** from Arhánes: with small rooms and tiny windows to keep out the bright Cretan sun and fierce winds, it has a small court in one corner which must have served to let in light. The roof terrace above, with typical tapered columns, is similar to those seen on village houses throughout Crete today. Side by side in Case 69, you can also see examples of both Linear A and Linear B scripts. A recent addition here is a fine "marine style" vase found in a tomb at Poros, near Iráklion.

Room VI covers finds from cemeteries at Knossós, Festós and Arhánes of approximately the same period. First are some small groups of **clay figures** from a tomb near Festós, in particular one of a ritual dance inside a circle decorated with horns of consecration – very crude work but wonderfully effective and reminiscent of the *pentozalis* danced by Cretan men today. In Case 75a (against the wall) is the curious horse burial found in a fourteenth-century *thólos* tomb at Arhánes, and now believed to be a sacrifice in honour of the possibly royal personage buried in the same tomb. After slaughter, the beast had been systematically dismembered and its parts carefully placed in the position in which they are now displayed. In the centre of the room is some of the museum's finest **jewellery**: gold signet rings, necklaces of gold and beads, and other gold work demonstrating the subtle granulation typical of Minoan style. The martial arts are represented by some fine gold sword hilts and two fabulous **helmets**, one of boar's tusks (reconstructed), the other of bronze with long cheekpieces. The boar's tusk helmet also makes an appearance on a ceramic amphora in Case 82. Taken with the other weapons displayed here, these items can be seen as further proof of the subordination of Minoan culture to the more warlike Mycenaean in this period.

Minor sites and jewellery

Room VII backtracks slightly in time to include objects from minor sites – mostly small villas and sacred caves, but also incorporating the larger complex of Ayía Triádha – throughout the main palace period and beyond (1700–1300 BC). As you enter, you'll see great bronze double axes, erected on wooden poles, stone horns of consecration and bronze cauldrons set about the room. In the cases themselves are some very famous pieces, in particular the three **stone** (steatite) **vases** from Ayía Triádha and the **gold jewellery** from a grave near Mália. The "Harvesters Vase" is the finest of the three vases, depicting with vivid realism a procession returning home from the fields; the harvesters are led by a strangely dressed character with long hair and a big stick, possibly a priest, and accompanied by musicians, one of whom is waving a *sistrum* (a percussion instrument which sounds rather like a maraca). The other two show scenes from boxing and wrestling matches and a chieftain receiving a report from an official.

The Málía jewellery is to be found in a single case (101) in the centre of the room – worth seeing above all is the stunningly intricate **pendant of two bees** around a golden disc (the latter supposedly a drop of honey which they are storing in a comb). Beside it are a number of other gold animal pendants, as well as necklaces and rings. Some **bronze figurines** in Case 89 depict worshippers making the ritual "salute" gesture to the deity whilst leaning backwards, and there's also a rare depiction of an older man released from the constriction of the customary tight belt, demonstrating that not all Minoans had such sylph-like figures as their art would lead you to believe. The enormous bronze cauldrons are worth a closer look: superbly crafted from sheets of metal riveted with nails, their discovery at Tílissos led to the excavation of the villas there. More mundane items in Case 99 include large copper ingots, almost certainly used as a form of currency.

Zákros and the eastern sites

Room VIII is given over to finds from the palace at Zákros (1700–1450 BC) and again includes several superlative items. There's a magnificent **rhyton of rock crystal** with a handle of beads and a collar that hides a join between two pieces encased in gold (Case 109). Its beauty aside, this exhibit is always singled out by guides as an example of the painstaking reconstruction undertaken by the museum – when discovered, it was broken into more than three hundred fragments. Also striking, in Case 111, is the **Peak Sanctuary Rhyton**, a green stone vessel on which a low-relief scene depicts a mountain shrine with horns of consecration decorated with birds and wild goats. Originally covered in gold leaf, this discovery provided valuable information on Minoan religion. In the case parallel to this is a bull's head rhyton, smaller than but otherwise similar to that in Room IV. Room VIII also has a fine display of pottery from both palace and town, mostly from the zenith of the **marine and floral periods**. Finally, there are some outstanding stone and ceramic miniatures – shells and a butterfly in particular – and an assortment of the craftsmen's raw materials: a giant elephant's tusk, burnt in the fire which destroyed the palace, and unused ingots of bronze from the storerooms.

Room IX contains discoveries of the same period from lesser sites in the east. As usual, there is an assortment of pottery and everyday objects, the most important of which are a series of **terracotta figurines** from a peak sanctuary at Piskoképhalo (Case 123). These naturalistic figures are fascinating in that they show what ordinary Minoans must have looked like and how they dressed – albeit for worship. Beside them are some charming miniature animals and models of sanctuaries. In Case 127 you can see a collection of bronze tools and weapons from the workers' village at Gourniá: hammers, picks, cutters and even "razor blades". Also in this room (Case 128) is the museum's largest collection of **seal stones**. Two things stand out about these. First, the intricacy of the carving, superbly executed in tiny detail on the hardest of stones, and second, the abundance of different themes (for obvious reasons, no two seals are the same) relating to almost every aspect of Minoan life, from rare portraits of individuals to religious ceremonies, hunting scenes and, most commonly, scenes from nature. The seals were used to fasten parcels or clay amphorae and for signing correspondence – a number of impressions of seals in clay have survived from Minoan times, mostly baked hard in accidental fires. Some of the larger seals, especially those in precious stones or with non-natural designs, may also have seen use as charms or amulets.

The post-Minoan age

Room X begins the museum's post-Minoan collection, covering a period (1400–1100 BC) when Crete was dominated by Mycenaean influences. The stylization and repetition of the themes employed in pottery decoration, coupled with a near-abandonment of the highly skilled craft of stoneworking, are obvious indications of artistic decline. Figurines from the sanctuaries are also far less naturalistically executed; there are many examples of a stereotyped goddess, both hands raised, perhaps, in blessing. However, an evocative clay sculpture of a **dancing group** with a lyre player from Palékastro (Case 132) does seem to echo past achievements, but even here the permeation of Mycenaean design is apparent.

Room XI continues the theme into the period of the arrival of Dorian Greeks (1100–900 BC). Among the Minoans, the goddess with raised hands remained important. The anguished features of the example from Mount Karfi (Case 148) – a remote mountain above the Lasíthi Plateau to where many Minoans fled from the vulnerable coastal areas – seem to foreshadow the end. The newcomers introduced stylistic changes: the **clay cart** drawn by curiously portrayed bodyless oxen is a new form of ritual vessel. The passing of the Bronze Age is reflected in Case 153: the metal of the new age was iron, which came to be used for the vast majority of weapons and tools. But some Minoan beliefs and traditions survived, such as worship at the cave sanctuary of the Minoan goddess of childbirth, Eileíthyia, to the east of Iráklion; Cases 149 and 158 display votive offerings from the cave dating from Hellenistic and Roman times. Some clay figurines portray couples engaged in sexual intercourse, pregnant women or women giving birth – leaving the goddess in little doubt as to what was required of her.

Room XII takes the collection up to about 650 BC. The early part of the period simply shows a development of the art of the previous era; later exhibits betray eastern, notably Egyptian, influences. This is most evident in the pottery, which is decorated with griffins, and with figures which would look at home in Tutankhamun's tomb. An interesting jug in Case 163 is typical of this era: on the vessel's neck two lovers – thought by some to be Theseus and Ariadne – embrace fondly. There are also some fine pottery and bronze figures, and a small treasure of gold jewellery.

Cases 160 and 161 display figurines and artefacts found at the remote mountain shrine of **Káto Sími** near Ano Viannos in the south, east of Iráklion province (see p.161). As the objects on view from the Minoan, Greek and Roman periods demonstrate, this is one of the few shrines in Crete where worship continued without interruption from pre-historical times to the end of antiquity. Notable pieces include bronze figurines of worshippers and ivory-handled swords from the Minoan age, and a figurine of Hermes playing a lyre from the Hellenistic period (the Greeks dedicated Káto Sími to this deity). On the right-hand wall, an inscription to Hermes Dendrites affirms the Greek god's patronage of the shrine.

Room XIII may well come as a relief, simply because there is nothing tiny or intricate to look at. Instead, it contains a collection of **lárnakes** (clay coffins) from various periods, their painted decoration reflecting the prevailing pottery style. The Minoan burial position of knees drawn up to the chest explains the small size of the coffins – and also suggests that the bodies would have been placed in them soon after death, before the onset of rigor mortis. They come in two basic shapes: chests with lids and "bathtubs" (which may well have been used as such during their owners' lifetimes). From here, stairs lead to the rooms on the second floor.

The palace frescoes

Upstairs, **Room XIV**, the **Hall of the Frescoes**, is perhaps the most exciting in the museum – and warrants another visit if, by now, you're too weary to appreciate it. Only tiny fragments of actual frescoes survived, but they have been almost miraculously reconstituted, and mounted on backgrounds which continue the design to give as true an impression of the entire fresco as possible. Frescoes are among the greatest achievements of Minoan art: they were originally painted directly onto wet plaster, using mostly plant dyes but also colours from mineral sources and even shellfish – a technique which has ensured their relatively unfaded survival. The job of the restorers was helped to an extent by knowledge of the various conventions, which matched Egyptian practice: men's skin, for example, was red, women's white; gold is shown as yellow, silver as blue and bronze, red.

Most of the frescoes shown in the museum come originally from Knossós, and date from the New Palace period (1700–1450 BC). Along the left-hand wall are four large panels from the enormous fresco which led all the way along the Corridor of the Procession at Knossós; an artist's impression shows how the whole might originally have looked. Two groups of youths are shown processing towards a female figure, presumably a priestess or goddess. Between the doors there's the **fresco of griffins** from the Throne Room at Knossós, and then, on the far side, a series from the villa at Ayía Triádha, some blackened by fire. Among these, the animation of the wild cat is especially striking; a floor painting of a seascape is also shown here. The opposite wall signals a return to Knossós, with some of the most famous of the works found there: the shields which adorned the Grand Staircase; the elegant **priest-king**, or Lily Prince; the great relief of a bull's head; a heavily restored fresco depicting elegantly attired ladies of the court; a beautifully simple fresco of dolphins from the queen's apartment; and the famous depiction of athletes leaping over a bull. Finally, there are two simple pictures of lilies from the walls of a villa at Amnísos (see p.100).

In some ways more striking than the frescoes themselves – because nothing has been restored or reconstructed – is the **Ayía Triádha sarcophagus**, decorated in the same manner, which stands in the centre of the room. The only stone sarcophagus to be found in Crete, its unique and elaborate painted-plaster ornamentation has led archeologists to assume that it was made originally for a royal burial and later reused. On one side is an animal sacrifice, with a bull already dead on the altar and two goats tied up awaiting their fates. On the other are two scenes, perhaps of relatives making offerings for the safe passage of the deceased. The ends feature a scene of goddesses riding in a chariot drawn by griffins, and of two women in a chariot pulled by goats above a procession of men. Also in this room is a wonderful wooden model of the **Palace of Knossós**.

Rooms XV and XVI have more **frescoes** of the same period. The most famous of them is **"La Parisienne"**, so dubbed for her bright red lips, huge eyes, long hair and fancy dress, but in reality almost certainly a priestess or a goddess if her twin image on the next panel has been interpreted correctly. Among other fresco fragments here, the most interesting is the **"Saffron Gatherer"**. Originally reconstructed as a boy, it has since been decided that this in fact represented a blue monkey; the two versions are shown side by side. Nearby is the **"Captain of the Blacks"**, a work from the troubled end of the New Palace period. It apparently shows a Minoan officer leading a troop of African soldiers, probably Sudanese mercenaries – a sign of the period's increasing militarism.

Rooms XVII–XVIII are now in a state of some confusion until the scheduled refurbishment (see box on p.88) is complete. At the time of writing, Room XVII houses the "Ring of Minos" exhibition focused on the so-called **ring of King Minos** found seventy years ago close to the Knossós palace. After disappearing whilst in the possession of a local priest, the solid gold ring emerged again when one of the priest's descendants sold it to the museum. Highly important for its depiction of Minoan religion, the ring is engraved with a scene showing a goddess with worshippers as well as a sailing boat.

The Yiamalakis Collection which formerly occupied this room and the Archaic and Roman Crete collection (formerly in Room XVIII) will probably not be on view again until renovation work is finished. In anticipation of this, we have included a description of the most important pieces in these collections.

The next two sections of the museum break off from the chronological approach to display the accumulations of an Iráklion doctor and antiquities collector, the **Yiamalakis Collection**, which was purchased by the museum in 1962. This covers the entire remit of the museum in a single room, and it has some very fine pieces indeed. Of particular note is a steatopygous ("fat-buttocked" in plain English) **Neolithic figurine** – perhaps a fertility goddess – from near Ierápetra. There are also stunning gold jewels, especially the bull's head and two other pieces of the "Zákros Treasure"; some fine miniatures, bronze and ceramic; and from later periods, huge Roman figures and a mosaic relaid on the floor. The following section continues the chronological collection right through from the Archaic period to the division of the Roman empire (c.650 BC–400 AD). There are an enormous variety of styles and objects here, including a collection of Roman **oil lamps** upon which – if you strain your eyes — are featured some fairly saucy erotic images. Among the larger items, a striking terracotta figurine of a spear-bearing Athena and a sensitively worked bronze of a youth in toga and sandals from Roman Ierápetra stand out – but the period was not one of Crete's artistic high points.

The collection continues **downstairs**, with **Room XIX** backtracking a little to display larger pieces from the early years of this final period, the Archaic (650–500 BC), in particular three large **bronze figurines** of Apollo and Artemis with their mother, Leto, from the early sanctuary of Apollo Delphinios at Dréros. These are impressive in their simplicity, and significant as early examples of works made from sheets of hammered bronze, riveted together.

Room XX is devoted to Classical Greek and Greco-Roman sculpture which, as happens frequently in Crete, is not given the attention it deserves due to the overwhelming interest in Minoan civilization (indeed, when there are staff shortages, this room is often closed). Most of the items on view – some of them extremely fine and which would stand out in any other museum – do not carry any provenance or details, which lessens their impact. That said, look out for a magnificent **statue of Apollo** (or Athena) plus a superbly carved second-century AD Roman sarcophagus found at Mália, as well as a number of other outstanding examples of the sculptor's craft. There are also a few good Roman copies of Greek Classical works, and some stern portrait busts of members of Rome's imperial families, all deserving of a better standard of presentation.

Shopping

The market is best for food as well as for cheap practical goods, leatherware and most standard tourist items. **Herbs** make an unusual souvenir from Crete – one of the best places to buy is at the stall belonging to Kostas Stathakis along Odhós 1866, about 50m from the junction with Dhikeosínis, on the right. Sweet-smelling dried Cretan thyme is like no other, and red saffron is a real bargain here, but get the fine strands and not the powdered stuff. More upmarket shops – jewellery, clothes and fabrics especially – can be found down Dedhálou. Everyday shops and **embroidered textiles** are down Kalokerinoú, and clothes and shoe-shops around Averof are good value in the late-July sales. Small minimarkets in tourist areas are open every day, and out towards Amoudhára is a Continent hypermarket. CDs and cassettes of Cretan and Greek music including *lyra* and *rembétika* can be purchased at Aerakis, Dedhálou 35, or Bardoulakis, Platía Nikifourou Foka 1, by the entrance to the market at the start of Odhós 1866.

Eating

Big city as it is, in the main visitor areas Iráklion disappoints when it comes to **eating** – and even more so when it comes to going out after you've had a meal. The cafés and tavernas of the main squares – **Venizélou** and **Eleftherías** – are quintessential places to sit and watch the world pass by, but their food is on the whole expensive and mediocre. The cafés and tavernas on and around **Dedhálou**, the pedestrianized street linking the two main squares, are popular with tourists too, but again are not particularly good value. For better quality and reasonably priced food, you need to get away from the more obvious tourist haunts; a more atmospheric option is to head for the little alley **Fotiou Theodosaki**, which runs through from the market to Odhós Evans, and is entirely lined with the tables of rival taverna owners, who cater for market traders and their customers as well as tourists.

At the basic end of the scale, **takeaways** are widely available. There's a whole group of *souvláki* stalls, for instance, clustering around 25-Avgoústou at the entrance to El Greco Park; the park itself is handy if you need somewhere to sit and eat. For *tyropíta* and *spanakópita* (cheese or spinach pies) and other pastries, sweet or savoury, there's no shortage of *zakharoplasteía*; try *Everest*, just north of the Morosini fountain, which does takeaways of these, as well as a whole bunch of other savouries.

Restaurants

There are good **restaurants** scattered across town. Just off Eleftherías at **Platía Dhaskaloyiánnis** (where the post office is) are some inexpensive, if not exceptional, tavernas. The platía is a good place to break your tour of the nearby Archeological Museum; close at hand are a couple of authentic *ouzerí* (try *Ta Asteria* or *40 Kymata*) serving up tasty *mezédhes*. Nearer **Venizélou**, you could explore some of the backstreets to the east, off Dedhálou and behind the *loggia*. Down around the **harbour**, you'll find a number of slightly more expensive restaurants, many specializing in fish. Far more promising just to the south is a line of *ouzerí*, plying fish *mezédhes*, along the narrow **Marineli** (a passage leading into Platía Áyios Dimítrios, with a pint-sized church of the same name). On the unpromising coastal outskirts west of town is a trio of fish tavernas worth seeking out.

Aithrion Junction of Arkoleontos & Almirou, near El Greco Park. Reasonably priced restaurant with linen tablecloths and an attractive leafy terrace; well-prepared fish and meat dishes, with a decent selection of wines.

I Avli tou Deikaliona Kalokairinoú 8, at the rear of the Historical Museum ☏ 28102 44215. Popular new taverna with a great little terrace fronting the Idomeneus fountain, serving up meat and fish dishes. In high summer, you may need to book to ensure an outdoor table.

Fos Fanari Marineli 1, opposite the tiny church of Ay. Dimítrios. The first in a row of *ouzerí*s that line this alley off Vironos, sloping down to the harbour. Good fish dishes and *mezédhes*.

Geroplatanos In the square fronting the church of Ay. Títos. Taking its name from the great old plane tree beneath which its tables are set out, this is one of the most tranquil lunch spots in town and provides the usual taverna staples.

Giovanni On the alley Koraí, parallel to Dedhálou ☏ 28103 46338. Similar in style to its neighbour *Loukoulos* (see below), this upmarket and over-expensive taverna offers sleek service and an Italian-slanted menu aimed more at Iráklion's smart set than the casual tourist.

Ippokampos Sófokli Venizélou, west of 25-Avgoústou, close to the *Kronos* hotel. The best and least expensive fish to be had in Iráklion, served in unpretentious surroundings. Deservedly popular with locals, this place is often crowded late into the evening, and you may have to queue or turn up earlier than the Greeks eat. Even if you don't see a space, it's worth asking, as the owner may suddenly disappear inside the taverna and emerge with yet another table to carry further down the pavement.

Katsina Marineli 12. A simple and friendly *ouzerí* serving tasty and economical seafood *mezédhes* at outdoor tables.

Ta Ladádika Tzikritzi 5, near the market. Welcoming little *ouzerí* in small pedestrianized street with outdoor tables. Excellent *mezédhés* – try their *dolmadhákia* (stuffed vine leaves).

I Liopótis Kronaki (aka Paleologou) 14, the continuation of Minotaurou. Another good little

ouzerí-taverna with outdoor terrace offering a variety of grilled fish and meat dishes.

Loukoulos On the alley Koraí, parallel to Dedhálou ☏ 28102 24435. Rather snooty garden restaurant with an Italian slant to its international menu; diners come here to be pampered by over-fussy service and prices to match.

The Mexican Hándhakos 71. Inexpensive Mexican tacos and beers, complimented by salads and bean dishes.

O Miltos Linoperamata, 5km west of the centre ☏ 28108 21584. Excellent, friendly fish taverna with a terrace overlooking the sea. This is one of a cluster of economical fish tavernas owned by three competing brothers. *Taverna Delfini*, which has the best reputation, and *I Kalouba* are the others here, but unlike *O Miltos*, are open eves only. You'll need your own transport or a taxi to get here; they are located on the sea 1km west of the city's power station, with its distinctive red and white chimney stacks, and close to the Aget Iraklis cement factory – but don't let that put you off.

Pagopoleion Platía Áyios Títos. Iráklion's most original bar (see p.98) has now added a mid-priced restaurant serving Cretan and international dishes to a high standard; the wine list includes interesting bottles from little-known but excellent small vineyards around the island. There's also a recommended *mezedhákia* buffet (Sat & Sun 1–4pm) that enables you to fill a plate for €5.

Taberneio Idomeneos 4, near the Arsenali. Good little neighbourhood taverna offering a wide selection of *mezédhes* and traditional meat-based dishes, plus some more adventurous Indian and Chinese dishes.

Tartuffo Dhimokratías 83, near the *Galaxy* hotel. The ten-minute walk south along the road to Knossós is worth it for excellent and inexpensive pizzas.

Triania Odhós-1878, west of the centre. Excellent, unpretentious *mezédhes* place offering a variety of fish and vegetable choices, with a small street terrace.

Tsikoudadiko Idomeneos 10a. Very pleasant little *ouzerí* that specializes in seafood and salads, tucked away in a backstreet with a charming patio terrace. Try their *kokloí boubouristoí* (fried snails).

Cafés

Several **cafés** in Venizélou and at the top of Dhikeosínis specialize in luscious pastries to accompany a strong mid-morning coffee; local treats include *bougátsa* and *loukoumades*.

Aktarika N. Foká 5, the alleyway between Dhikeosínis and Dedhálou, near the entrance to the market. This café specializes in *loukoumades*:

you can watch the yeasty dough bubbling away before it is dropped into hot oil to cook, then served with honey syrup, sesame seeds and crushed nuts. These confections are traditionally taken with a glass of cold water.

Bougátsa Kirkor Facing the Morosini fountain in Venizélou. The place to sample authentic *bougátsa*, a creamy cheese pie served warm and sprinkled with sugar and cinnamon.

Ta Leontaria Next door to *Bougátsa Kirkor* (above). Another classic *bougátsa* place, with tables on the square.

Sinaïtiko Platía Ayía Ekateríni, near the cathedral. One of a number of relaxing cafés on this pleasant square with tables under the trees.

Street Cafe Kandanoléon 2. A good breakfast place on the southwestern side of El Greco Park which offers a wide range of cakes and pastries as well as the usual standards, such as *tirópita* and *spanakópita*.

Drinking and entertainment

As for **nightlife**, Iráklion is a bit of a damp squib when compared to many other towns on the island. Much of what happens takes place in the suburbs or out along the hotel strip to the west at Amoudhára. If you're determined, however, there are a couple of city-centre possibilities, and plenty of options if all you want to do is sit and drink. Indeed, there's a new breed of **kafeníon** emerging in Iráklion, aimed at a younger crowd: the drinks are cocktails rather than *raki*, the music is modern Greek or Western, and there are prices to match.

There are also a number of **cinemas** scattered about: check the posters at the tourist police office for programme details. Whilst the Teatro Níkos Kazantzákis at the Jesus Bastion doubles up as an open-air cinema when it's not being used for staging the city's summer arts and music festival, perhaps the most enjoyable venue is the open-air cinema on the beach to the west of the city.

Bars

Bars congregate in the same areas as the restaurants. Perhaps the most animated are in Platía Koraí, a quiet square behind Dedhálou, while slightly more touristy alternatives are centred around Platía Venizélou and on the fringes of El Greco Park. After ten at night, a lively bar scene also fans out into the streets around **Hándhakos** – just follow the crowds.

Aiesy Platía Dhaskaloyiánnis. This laid-back café-bar casts off its daytime serenity after 10pm, when locals gather to sink into the canvas chairs on the square, listen to soft rock and sip long drinks.

To Avgo Platía Koraí. Trendy little bar frequented by students, on a pleasant square just to the north of Dedhálou.

Casino Sofokles Venizélou, at the bottom of Hándhakos near the sea. Stylish bar which also has live satellite TV broadcasts of English football games (remember to allow for the time difference).

Flash Platía Koraí. This bar has outdoor tables and serves a wide variety of exotic (and expensive) beers and cocktails – those on a tight budget can nurse a *frappé* for hours.

Idaean Andron Perdhíkari 1, just east of Platía Venizélou. A good example of the new-style *kafeníon*, with an amiable, easy atmosphere.

Imperial Café Platía Venizélou. Pleasant rooftop bar above *Bougátsa Kirkor* (see above), with a terrace overlooking the square and Morosini fountain.

Jasmin Ayiostefanitón 6, tucked in an alley on the left midway down Hándhakos. One of several similar bars on this street, *Jasmin* is another good nighttime rendezvous, with jazz, soul and Latin music, and an outdoor terrace. Also serves 45 different types of tea, including herbal varieties.

Korais On the alley Koraí, parallel to Dedhálou. Glitzy open-air café with spacious plant-festooned terraces, overhead movie screens and music – highly popular with Iráklion's stylish set.

Mayo Milatou 11, just north of Koraí. This new nighttime extravaganza of a bar with spotlights, screens and music under a big canopy terrace is the latest place to be seen for Iráklion's student crowd. Its arrival has spawned a whole new set of bars and cafés along the same street.

To Mílon tis Eridos Platía Koraí, facing *Flash*. This café-bar serves everything from twelve types of coffee to cocktails and herbal teas, including *diktamo* (Cretan dittany).

Orionas Psaromíligon 15. Lively music and drinks bar on two floors with a stylish terrace upstairs; has a varied programme of live music at weekends in summer, with alternating jazz, blues, reggae and rock acts.

Pagopoleion (Ice Factory), Platía Áyios Títos. Stunningly stylish bar created by photographic artist Chryssy Karelli inside Iráklion's former ice factory. She has preserved much of the old building including a lift for hauling the ice from the basement freezer and a fascistic call to duty in German Gothic script on one wall – a remnant of Nazi occupation of the factory in World War II. The toilets are in an artistic league of their own.

Rebels Perdhíkari 3. A trendy bar which has cloned numerous similar places nearby. On weekends in summer, this whole zone is *the* place to be if you're under 30.

Clubs and discos

Intown **clubs** and **discos** are largely unexciting, with a playlist dominated by techno interspersed with Greek music – for livelier nightlife you're better off heading to the nearby resorts. **Nightclubs** are clustered in two areas around twenty minutes' walk apart: down around the harbour, and (in winter) on Ikarou, downhill from Platía Eleftherías.

Aman Junction of Odhós Ay. Títos and Idomeneos, slightly east of Áyios Títos church. Three bars and cinema screens around the dance floor project films and video clips. Other places nearby include *Hijaz*, *Blue Iguana* and *Kathodon*, all lively music bars.

Envy Foot of Doúkos Bófor, close to the *Privilege Club*. Popular dancing place with a terrace at the back overlooking the harbour.

Privilege Club The most popular of the clubs down towards the harbour at the bottom of Doúkos Bófor, below the Archeological Museum.

Listings

Airlines Olympic, Platía Eleftherías (☎28102 29191, @www.Olympic-airways.gr) and Aegean, Dhimokratias 11 (☎28103 44394, @www.aegeanair.com) are the main scheduled airlines with connecting flights to Athens and other parts of Greece. Charter airlines flying into Iráklion mostly use local travel agents as their representatives.

Airport information ☎28102 28402. Bus #1 runs from Platía Eleftherías to the airport every few minutes; buy a ticket (€80) from the booth on the square first.

Banks The main branches are on 25-Avgoústou, many of which have 24hr ATMs; there are more machines at banks along Dhikeosínis.

Bike and car rental 25-Avgoústou is lined with rental companies, but you'll often find less expensive rates on the backstreets; it's always worth asking for discounts, especially during low season or slack periods. Good places include Blue Sea, Kosma Zotou 7 off the west side of 25-Avgoústou (☎28102 41097) for cars and bikes; Kosmos, 25-Avgoústou 15 (☎28102 41357); Reliable, 25-Epimenidou 8 off the east side of the same street (☎28103 44212); Caravel, 25-Avgoústou 39 (☎28103 00150); Ritz in the *Hotel Rea*, Kalimeráki 1 (☎28102 23638) and Sun Rise, 25-Avgoústou 46 (☎28102 21609). All offer free delivery to hotels and the airport.

Buses See p.81 for locations of bus stations, and p.163 for destination details.

Festivals The Iráklion Summer Festival runs from July to mid-September. Held at the Teatro Níkos Kazantzákis at the Jesus Bastion, it includes exhibitions, concerts and plays by groups from around the world, some of which are top-notch; details and a free brochure listing all the events are available from the tourist office. August 25 (St Titus' Day) is marked by a major procession from the church of Áyios Títos.

Football OFI Crete is Iráklion's and Crete's major team playing in the Greek first division. Their matches take place at the Demótikou stadium, Platía Ayía Varvára in the Kaminia district on the west side of town (☎28102 83920). The city's other team, Ergotelis, play at the stadium below the Martinengo Bastion.

Hospitals There are three hospitals; the one on Apollónion (☎28102 29713, southwest of Platía Kornárou, between Alber and Moussoúrou, is reasonably central. The others are out of town, including a modern one at Voutes, Periferiako Panenistemiako Veniko Nosokomeio Irakleio (PAYNE; ☎28102 69111) – not one to get your lips around when you're feeling under the weather.

Internet Iráklion now has a number of Internet cafés in and around the city centre. A good option is Netcafé, Odhós-1878 4 (@www.the-netcafe.net; daily 10am–2am; €2.40 per hr, or €0.60 for 15min), near the sea to the west of the Historical Museum. Other central places with similar charges and hours are Internest, Mihelidhaki 23; Gallery Games, Korai 14; Tunnel, junction of Áyios Títos & Milatou; and Konsova, Dhikeosínis 25. See city map for locations.

Laundry Washsalon, Hándhakos 18 ☎ 28102 80858 (daily 8.30am–9pm; €6 for 6kg) is reliable and will wash, dry and fold. Laundry Perfect, at the junction of Idoméneos and Malikoúti to the east of Áyios Títos church, is another good place (daily 9am–9pm; €5.80 for 6kg).

Left luggage There's a left luggage office in the eastbound and southwest bus stations (bus station A on city map; daily 6.30am–8pm; €1 per bag, per day) but not at the westbound one. There's also a commercial agency at Hándhakos 18 (daily 24hr; €1.50 per large locker, per day). You can also leave bags at the youth hostel, even if you don't stay there, for €1.50 per bag, per day. If you want to leave your bag while you go off on a bike for a day or two, the company from which you rent the bike should be prepared to store it.

Mountaineering The local EOS is at Dhikeosínis 53 ☎ 28102 27609.

Newspapers and books English-language and other foreign newspapers are sold throughout the city centre – the most central is Bibliopoleio, almost opposite the Morosini fountain on Platía Venizélou. The best selection of English-language titles, including a wide range of books and maps on Crete and Greece, is at the excellent Planet International Bookstore at the corner of Hándhakos and Kidonias ☎ 28102 89605, behind Platía Venizélou.

Pharmacies Plentiful on the main shopping streets. At least one will be open 24hrs on a rota basis; check the list on the door of any pharmacy for the nearest 24hr one. There are also traditional herbalists in the market.

Post office Main office in Platía Dhaskaloyiánnis, off Eleftherías (Mon–Fri 7.30am–8pm).

Taxis Major taxi stands are in Platía Eleftherías, Platía Venizélou and El Greco Park; or call ☎ 28102 10102 or ☎ 10168. Prices displayed on boards at the taxi stands.

Telephones The OTE head office is in El Greco Park, with long queues but an efficient 24hr service. Most destinations abroad can now be phoned from street booths by using a phonecard obtainable from a *períptero* (street kiosk).

Toilets In El Greco Park and the Public Gardens and near the cathedral, at the bus stations and the Archeological Museum (no need to pay entrance charge to use them).

Travel agencies 25-Avgoústou is crammed with shipping and general travel agents. Discount/student specialists include the extremely helpful Blavakis Travel, Platía Kallergon 8, just off 25-Avgoústou by the entrance to El Greco Park (☎ 28102 82541); and Prince Travel, 25-Avgoústou 30 (☎ 28102 82706). Ferry tickets and information are also available from Paleologus Travel, 25-Avgoústou 5 ☎ 28103 46185, ⓦ www.ferries.gr; ⓦ www.greekislands.gr; Minoan Lines, 25-Avgoústou 78 ☎ 28102 29646, ⓦ www.minoan.gr; and Anek Lines, 25-Avgoústou 33 ☎ 28102 22481. For excursions around the island, villa rentals and so on, the bigger operators are probably easier: try Creta Travel Bureau, Epiménidhou 20–22 (☎ 28102 27002) or Adamis Tours, 25-Avgoústou 23 (☎ 28103 46202). The latter is the local American Express agent.

Beaches near Iráklion

If all you want to do is escape Iráklion to lie on a **beach** for a few hours, the simplest course is to head **east**, beyond the airport, to the municipal beach **Amnísos** or to the marginally quieter **Tobróuk** beach. Beaches to the **west** are less prone to aircraft noise but are also more commercialized. All are easily reached by public transport.

Beaches to the east: Amnísos and around

Bus #7 heads eastwards every fifteen minutes or so from the tree-shaded stop opposite the *Hotel Astoria* in Platía Eleftherías. Leaving the city through its sprawling eastern suburbs and the town of Néa Alikarnassós into which they merge, the bus follows the old road as it skirts around the airport. Even in spring, this manages to be a wasted and dusty-looking landscape – an impression not helped by the ill-camouflaged bunkers of the Greek air force base which shares the runway. Once past the airport, however, the road swings down to the coast and a narrow patch of level ground between the sea and the hills. First stop is at the **municipal beach** – fenced off (you pay to get in) and provided with showers and changing rooms. There seems little point in paying, however, unless you want to study the undercarriages of incoming planes in intimate detail – this beach tends to be crowded and only marginally cleaner than the free sections.

The next halt is **Amnísos**, where there are a couple of tavernas and food stalls immediately behind the beach, and even a huddle of hotels. Although you're unlikely to want to stay here, it's not a bad beach to find so close to the city. The main drawback is the stream of planes coming in to land: on peak weekends there seems to be one every few minutes, while during the week quiet periods are enlivened by fighters on low-level runs.

The last of these beaches, **Tombróuk**, is perhaps the best, with more tavernas and drink stalls, slightly fewer people, and relative peace to be found if you walk a little way along the sand.

Amnísos and the Cave of Eileíthyia

Amnísos is also a famous name in Minoan archeology, although today the site is not particularly impressive, and the remains by the road down to Amnísos beach, on the low hill to the left, can only be glimpsed through a fence. There was a small settlement here, apparently a port for Knossós, from which the Cretan forces engaged in the **Trojan War** are said to have set sail, and it was in a villa here that the unusual **Fresco of the Lilies** was found – now on display in the Iráklion Archeological Museum (see p.93). The site is also noted for Marinatos' excavations in the 1930s, when the archeologist's discovery of pumice fragments amongst the ruins prompted him to develop his theory attributing the destruction of Minoan palaces to an eruption of the volcanic island of Thíra (see p.413). The scorch marks on many of the remaining stones testify to the intense fire which destroyed the villa during this period. On the west side of the rocky outcrop behind the villa, new excavations have unearthed the remains of a harbour, possibly verifying the link with the world of Homer.

On the eastern edge of Amnísos, a sign points inland from the main road towards the hills (the turn-off to Episkopí) indicating another significant ancient site, the **Cave of Eileíthyia**, which gets a mention in the *Odyssey* as one of Odysseus's stopovers on his way home from Troy. Just over 1km up the steep road from the junction, the cave's entrance is signed on the left and lies below the road, next to a fig tree. Eileíthyia was a goddess, primarily of childbirth, of very ancient origin and this cave was a cult centre from Neolithic times. Inside are two large walled stalagmites, which were almost certainly regarded as fertility totems. One of these has been worn smooth by the touch of countless worshippers who conducted rituals here until the fifth century AD. The cave itself is now fenced and locked, and if you are intent on making a survey (it's about 50m deep), you'll need to get a key from the guardian 7km away at Nírou Háni (see p.119).

Beaches to the west

The **beaches** to the west of the city are less noisy but also less atmospheric and more developed than the eastern ones. Bus #6 heads from in front of the *Hotel Astoria* in Platía Eleftherías out through the Pórta Haníon (Haniá Gate) and into Iráklion's more prosperous western extremities. Eventually, you'll end up on the road which runs behind the hotel strip, past the Continent hypermarket and finally to the luxury *Creta Beach* hotel complex, unappealingly sited immediately before the power station and cement works (see p.96 for some excellent fish tavernas here). You can get off almost anywhere in this area and attempt to get to **Amoudhára Beach**, though this is not always easy; the beach is open to the public, but there are very few access roads to it, and the hotels and campsite try hard to prevent any non-residents walking through their grounds.

Knossós

. . . a dancing place
All full of turnings, that was like the admirable maze
For fair hair'd Ariadne made, by cunning Daedalus

Homer, *The Odyssey*

The archeological site of **KNOSSÓS** (April–Sept daily 8am–7pm; Oct–March daily 8.30am–3pm; €6) lies some 5km south of Iráklion on a low, largely artificial hill. By far the largest of the **Minoan palaces**, it thrived over three-and-a-half thousand years ago at the heart of a highly sophisticated island-wide civilization. Long after Minoan culture had collapsed, a town on this site remained powerful, rivalling Górtys on into the Roman era. No matter when you come, you won't get the place to yourself, but there's still the opportunity to appreciate individual parts of the palace during the brief lulls between groups. The best time of day to avoid the crowds in summer is two hours before closing time, which also has the advantage of being cooler. If you get the opportunity to come back a second time, it will all begin to make a great deal more sense. Although only the palace itself is much visited, the surrounding hills are rich in lesser remains dating from the twentieth century BC through to the second or third century AD.

Less than a hundred years ago, Knossós was a place thought to have existed only in mythology. Here, legend has it that **King Minos** ruled and that his wife, Pasiphae, bore the **Minotaur** – a creature that was half-bull, half-man. On this site, the **labyrinth** was constructed by Daedalus to contain the monster, and youths were brought from Athens as human sacrifice, until finally **Theseus** arrived to slay the beast and, with Ariadne's help, escape its lair. Imprisoned in his own maze, Daedalus later constructed the wings that bore him away to safety – and his son **Icarus** to his untimely death.

The excavation of the palace, and the subsequent clothing of these legends with fact, is among the most amazing tales of modern archeology. Today's Knossós, whose fame rivals any such site in the world, is primarily associated with **Sir Arthur Evans**, who excavated the palace at the turn of the twentieth century and whose bust is one of the first things to greet you at the site. The autocratic control he exerted, his working standards and procedures, and, above all, the restorations he claimed were necessary to preserve the building have been a source of furious controversy among archeologists ever since. It has become clear that much of Evans's upper level, the *Piano Nobile*, is pure conjecture. Even so, his guess as to what the palace might have looked like is certainly as good as anyone else's, and it makes the other sites infinitely more meaningful if you have seen Knossós first. Without the restorations, it would be hard to visualize the ceremonial stairways, strange top-heavy pillars and brightly frescoed walls that distinguish Knossós – and almost impossible to imagine the grandeur of the multistorey palace. To get an idea of the size and complexity of the palace in its original state, take a look at the cutaway drawings on sale outside; they may seem somewhat fantastic, but are probably not too far from reality.

Transport and orientation

Getting to Knossós from Iráklion could hardly be easier. **Buses** #2 and #4 set out every ten minutes from the city bus stands adjacent to the eastbound bus station, then proceed up 25-Avgoústou (with a stop just below Platía Venizélou) and out of town on Odhós 1821 and Evans. If you're **driving**, you can take this route through Evans Gate, or follow the signs from Platía Eleftherías; from anywhere other than Iráklion, turn directly off the bypass onto the badly signed Knossós road. **Taxis** from the city cost about €5 to the site entrance.

On arrival, you're confronted first by a string of rather pricey tavernas and tacky souvenir stands. There are several **rooms** places here too, and if you're really into Minoan culture there's a lot to be said for staying out this way to steal an early start. Be warned, though, that the site area is expensive and unashamedly commercial. At the end of all the development, on the left approaching from town and immediately before the site entrance with a tav- erna on the corner, is the free official **car park** – although it tends to be inad- equate at peak times. Beware of the numerous unofficial car parks on the last stretch of road before the site, where you'll be charged exorbitant amounts to park your vehicle. Arriving by scooter, you have the bonus of being able to park beneath the canopy at the entrance, a mere twenty metres from the ticket booth. This area is also where the bus drops you, and it's alongside the coach park that you **enter** the site proper, having first run the gauntlet of map sales- men and tour guides on the way to purchasing your ticket. To catch the bus back to Iráklion, you'll have to walk a short way back up the road; a ruse no doubt designed to force you once again past all those souvenir shops.

The site

When you enter the **Palace of Knossós** through its West Court – the ancient ceremonial entrance – you soon discover how the legends of the labyrinth grew up around it. Sadly, you are no longer able to freely wander through the complex, as Knossós has finally succumbed to the abuse and damage caused by hundreds of thousands of feet annually treading its stairways, stones and courts. A series of **timber walkways** now channels visitors around the site, severely restricting the scope for independent exploration. This is particularly true of the Royal Apartments, where access to many rooms is now denied or reduced to partial views from behind glass screens. Another disadvantage of the new arrangement is that it becomes ever more difficult to avoid the guided tours that congregate at every point of significance en route. However, if you're wor- ried about missing the highlights, you can always tag onto one of these tours for a while, catch the patter and then hang back to take in the detail when the crowd has moved on.

The remains you see are mostly those of the **second palace**, rebuilt after the destruction of around 1700 BC (see p.411) and occupied – with increas- ing Mycenaean influence – through to about 1450 BC. At the time, it was

The British School at Athens has a useful website (Ⓦ www.bsa.gla.ac .uk/knossos) dedicated to Knossós with details on the history of the site and excavations, in addition to a virtual tour.

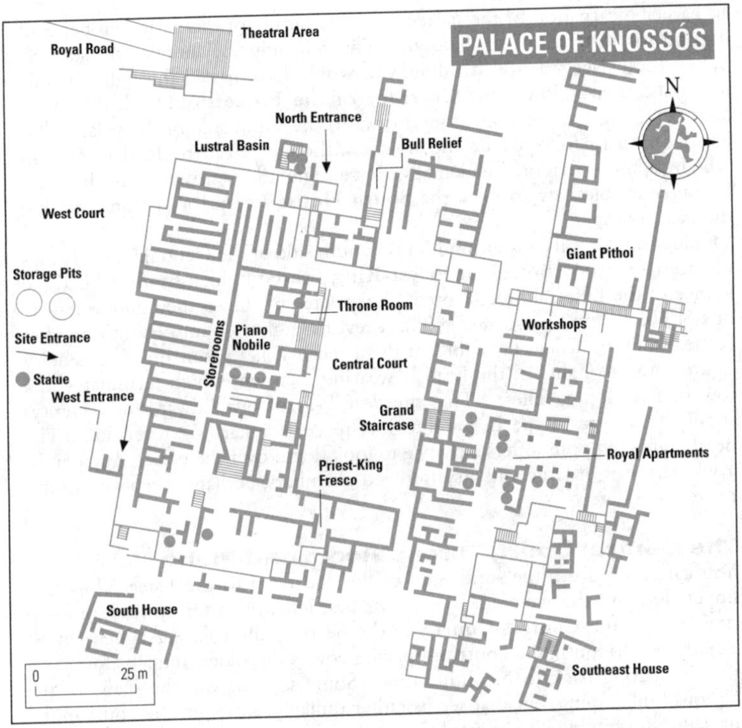
PALACE OF KNOSSÓS
Theatral Area
Royal Road
N
North Entrance
Lustral Basin
Bull Relief
West Court
Giant Pithoi
Storage Pits
Throne Room
Workshops
Site Entrance
Piano Nobile
Storerooms
Central Court
Statue
West Entrance
Grand Staircase
Royal Apartments
Priest-King Fresco
South House
Southeast House
0
25 m

surrounded by a town of considerable size. The palace itself, though, must have looked almost as much of a mess then as it does now – a vast bulk, with more than a thousand rooms on five floors, which had spread across the hill more as an organic growth than a planned building, incorporating or burying earlier structures as it went. In this, the palace simply followed the pattern of Minoan architecture generally, with extra rooms being added as the need arose. It is the style of building still most common on Crete, where finished buildings are far outnumbered by those waiting to have an extra floor or room added when need and finance dictate.

The West Court and first frescoes

The **West Court**, across which you approach the palace, was perhaps a marketplace or, at any rate, the scene of public meetings. Across it run slightly raised walkways, leading from the palace's West Entrance to the Theatral Area, and once presumably onto the Royal Road. There are also three large **circular pits**, originally grain silos or perhaps depositories for sacred offerings, but used as rubbish tips by the end of the Minoan era. When these were excavated, remains of early dwellings – visible in the central pit, dating from around 2000 BC and thus preceding the first palace – were revealed. The walls and floor surfaces were found to have been coated with red plaster, and these are among the earliest-known remains on the site. Following the walkway towards the West Entrance nowadays, you arrive at a typically muddled part of the palace, not at all easy to interpret. First, there's a line of stones marking the original wall of an earlier incarnation of the palace, then the facade of the palace proper, and beyond that a series of small rooms of which only the foundations survive. When the palace was still standing, you would have passed through a guard-room and then followed the **Corridor of the Procession**, flanked by fres-coes depicting a procession, around towards the south side of the palace. This is still the path followed by the walkway, though it can be hard to fathom which is the corridor. Incidentally, descending the stairway near the West Entrance enables you to view the **South House** (see p.106) before entering the palace proper.

Following the walkway around on the south side of the Central Court brings you to the reproduction of the **Priest-King Fresco** (which Evans dubbed the Prince of the Lilies, although some scholars are convinced the figure is female or not even a royal personage at all). A revealing glimpse into Evans's mindset comes from an article he wrote in the *London Times* when this fragmentary figure came to light: "…the head is wearing a crown, which terminates in a row of five sloping lilies… That the *fleur-de-lis* of our Edwards and Henrys should find a prototype in prehistoric Greece is a startling revelation". The nearby viewing point offers a chance to look down over the palace. Apparently, a whole series of large and airy frescoed chambers, perhaps reception rooms, once stood here.

The Central Court, Throne Room and Piano Nobile

You can climb from the south side of the courtyard to the *Piano Nobile*, the upper floor on the west side, but this is best left until later. Instead, proceed straight into the **Central Court** and the heart of the palace. Aligned almost exactly north–south, the courtyard paving covers the oldest remains found on the site, dating back to Neolithic times. Some say this was the scene of the famous bull-leaping, but that seems rather unlikely: although the court meas-ures almost 60m by 30m, it would hardly be spacious enough to accommodate the sort of intricate acrobatics shown in surviving pictures, let alone for an audience to watch as well. In Minoan times, the courtyard, with high walls hemming it in on every side, would have had a very different atmosphere from the open, shadeless space which survives.

The entrance to one of Knossós's most atmospheric survivals, the **Throne Room**, is in the northwestern corner of the courtyard. Here, a worn stone throne sits against the wall of a surprisingly small chamber; along the walls around it are ranged stone benches and, behind, there's a copy of a fresco depicting two griffins. In all probability, this was the seat of a priestess rather than a ruler – there's nothing like it in any other Minoan palace – but it may just have been an innovation wrought by the Mycenaeans, since it appears that this room dates only from the final period of the palace's occupation. Overexposure has meant that the Throne Room itself is now closed off with a wooden gate, but you can lean over this for a good view, and in the **antechamber** there's a wooden copy of the throne on which everyone used to perch to have their photo taken, but this too now lies off limits. Opposite the real throne, steps lead down to a lustral basin – a sunken "bath", probably for ritual purification rather than actual bathing, with no drain.

Alongside the Throne Room, a stairway climbs to the first floor and Evans's reconstructed **Piano Nobile**. One of the most interesting features of this part of the palace is the view it offers of the palace storerooms, with their rows of *píthoi* (storage jars) often still in place. There's an amazing amount of storage space here, in the jars – which would mostly have held oil or wine – and in sections sunk into the ground for other goods. The rooms of the *Piano Nobile* itself are again rather confusing, though you should be able to pick out the Sanctuary Hall from stumps that remain of its six large columns. Opposite this is a small concrete room (complete with roof), which Evans "reconstructed" directly above the Throne Room. It feels entirely out of place; inside, there's a small display on the restoration of the frescoes, and through the other side you get another good view over the Central Court. Returning through this room, you could climb down the very narrow staircase on your right to arrive at the entrance to the corridor of storerooms (now fenced off) or head back to the left towards the area where you entered the palace.

The Royal Apartments

Returning to the courtyard allows you to cross to the east side, where the **Grand Staircase** (now closed to public access) leads into the **Royal Apartments**, clearly the finest of the rooms at Knossós. Timber walkways now guide you to the rooms described below. The staircase itself (which can be viewed from above) is an architectural masterpiece, not only a fitting approach to these sumptuously appointed chambers, but also an integral part of the whole design, its large well allowing light into the lower storeys. Light wells such as these, usually with a courtyard at the bottom, are a common feature of Knossós and a reminder of just how important creature comforts were to the Minoans, and how skilled they were at providing them.

For more evidence of this luxurious lifestyle, you need look no further than the **Queen's Suite** (viewed behind a glass screen), off the grand **Hall of the Colonnades** at the bottom of the staircase. The main living room is decorated with the celebrated dolphin fresco and with running friezes of flowers and (earlier) spirals. On two sides, it opens to courtyards that let in light and air; the smaller one would probably have been planted with flowers. In use, the room would probably have been scattered with cushions and hung with rich drapes, while curtains perhaps placed between the pillars allowed for privacy, and for cool shade in the heat of the day. Plausible as it all is, this is largely speculation – and some of it pure con. The dolphin fresco, for example, was found in the courtyard, not the room itself, and would have been viewed from inside as a sort of *trompe l'oeil*, like looking out of a glass-bottomed boat. There are also some who argue, convincingly, that grand as these rooms are, they are not really large or fine enough to have been royal quarters. Those would more likely have been in the lighter and airier rooms that must have existed in the upper reaches of the palace, while these lower apartments were inhabited by resident nobles or priests.

Whether or not you accept Evans's names and attributions, the rooms remain an impressive example of the sophistication of Minoan architecture – all the more so when you follow the dark passage round to the **Queen's Bathroom**, its clay tub protected behind a low wall (and probably screened by curtains when in use), and to the famous "flushing" lavatory (a hole in the ground with drains to take the waste away – it was flushed by a bucket of water). Again, this area can only be partially glimpsed behind the screens.

On the floor above the queen's domain, the Grand Staircase passes through a set of rooms which are generally described as the **King's Quarters** (currently not on view). These are chambers in a considerably sterner vein. The staircase opens into a grandiose reception area known as the **Hall of the Royal Guard**, its walls decorated in repeated shield motifs. Opening off it is the ruler's personal chamber, the **Hall of the Double Axes** (visible behind glass screens) – a room which could be divided to allow for privacy while audiences were held in the more public section, or the whole opened out for larger functions. Its name comes from the double-axe symbol, so common throughout Knossós, which here is carved into every block of masonry.

The palace fringes

From the back of the queen's chambers, you can emerge into the fringes of the palace where it spreads down the lower slopes of the hill. This is a good point at which to consider the famous **drainage system** at Knossós, some of the most complete sections of which are visible under grilles. The snugly interconnecting terracotta pipes ran underneath most of the palace (here, they have come more or less direct from the Queen's Bathroom), and site guides never fail to point them out as evidence of the advanced state of Minoan civilization. They are indeed quite an achievement – in particular, the system of baffles and overflows (most clearly seen down by the external walls), designed to slow down the run-off and avoid flooding. Just how much running water there would have been, however, is another matter: the water supply is at the bottom of the hill, and even the combined efforts of rainwater catchment and water physically carried up to the palace can hardly have been sufficient to supply the needs of more than a small elite. However, the discovery of remnants of an aqueduct system carrying water to the palace from springs on Mount Yioúhtas suggests that this was not the only water supply.

From the bottom of the slope, you get a fine impression of the scale of the whole palace complex and can circle around towards the north, climbing back inside the palace limits to see the area known as the **Palace Workshops**. Here, potters, lapidaries and smiths appear to have plied their trades, and this area is also home to the spectacular **giant píthoi**; people queue to have their photograph taken with the jars towering over them. There's also a good view of the bull-relief fresco set up by the north entrance.

Outside the main palace, just beyond the North Entrance, is the **Theatral Area**, one of the more important enigmas of this and other Minoan palaces. An open space resembling a stepped amphitheatre, it may have been used for ritual performances or dances, but there's no real evidence of this, and again there would have been very little room for an audience if that was its function.

Beyond it, the **Royal Road** sets out: originally this ran to the Little Palace (see p.107), and beyond that, probably on across the island, but nowadays it ends after about 100m at a brick wall beneath the modern road. Alongside are assorted structures variously interpreted as stores, workshops or grandstands for viewing parades, all of them covered in undergrowth. Back down the Royal Road, you can re-enter the palace by its **North Entrance**. Beside the entry is a well-preserved **lustral basin**, and beyond that, a guardroom. Heading back to the central courtyard, a flight of stairs doubles back to allow you to examine the copy of the **Bull Relief** close up.

Of the lesser structures which crowd around the palace, a number of houses on the south side are particularly worth noting, although they aren't open to the public. The one known simply as the **South House**, reconstructed to its original three floors, seems amazingly modern, but actually dates from the late Minoan period (ca.1550 BC). The dwelling is believed to have belonged to an important official or noble, since it encroaches on the palace domain. In the **Southeast House**, of the same period, a cult room with a sacred pillar was discovered, as well as stands for double axes and a libation table. Across a little valley from here, outside the fenced site, was the **Caravanserai** where travellers would rest and water their animals; the restored building contains two elegant rooms, as well as a large stone footbath still running with water from an ancient spring.

Among the other important outlying buildings are the **Little Palace**, on a site which also contains a mansion and many Roman remains (just up the narrow alley which veers off to the left as you head back towards Iráklion), and the **Royal Villa**, facing the palace from the slope to the northeast. Both are occasionally open for special visits.

About 100m along the road to Iráklion from the site entrance lies the **Villa Ariadne**, an Edwardian villa constructed by Evans and where he lived while conducting excavations. Later, the house served as a military hospital during the German siege of Iráklion and, following the city's fall, as the residence of the German commander of Crete. It was where General Kreipe was based when he was kidnapped by Patrick Leigh Fermor and others (see p.422). The villa's dining room was also where the German army signed the surrender on May 9, 1945. Although not open to the public, nobody seems to mind if you walk up the drive past the gatehouse to have a look at the house's exterior and gardens.

Some two hundred metres further north along the same road on the left lies the Roman **Villa Dionysos**. Currently not open to the public, this second-century building was near the centre of the Roman city of Cnossus founded following the Roman conquest of the island in 67 BC. The villa has extremely fine polychrome mosaics, and once restoration work is complete it is planned to open it up to the public as the focus of an archeological park. Details on the progress of this should be available from the Knossós ticket office or the Iráklion tourist office.

South to Mount Yioúhtas

The countryside south of Knossós is dominated by the bulk of **Mount Yioúhtas** (811m), which rises alone from a landscape otherwise characterized by gently undulating agricultural country. Seen from the north, and especially the northwest, the mountain has an unmistakeably human profile, and was identified with Zeus in the post-Minoan period. The ancient Cretans claimed that Zeus lay buried underneath the mountain: given that the god is immortal, this furnished proof for other Greeks of the assertion that "All Cretans are liars" – it may even have been the original basis of this reputation.

To the east of Mount Yioúhtas are two of Crete's main **wine-growing areas**, Pezá and Arhánes, once cultivated by the Minoans, offering the chance to visit one of the island's leading winemakers. Nearby at **Vathípetro**, it's possible to view the remarkable remains of a Minoan vineyard, while the village of Mirtiá has a museum devoted to Crete's most famous literary name, **Níkos Kazantzákis**. The nearby village of **Houdétsi** has an interesting music school and museum displaying a wide variety of string and percussion instruments from all over the world. Add a fine **archeological museum** in the town of Arhánes and three fascinating **Minoan sites** at Foúrni, Anemospília and the summit of Mount **Yioúhtas** itself, and you have easily enough to fill a whole day's sightseeing.

Mirtiá and Pezá

Beyond Knossós, the nature of the journey south is transformed almost immediately: the road gradually empties and the country becomes greener. Almost any of these roads makes a beautiful drive, past vineyards draped across low hills and through flourishing farming communities. Just a couple of kilometres from the archeological site, at the head of the valley, there's an extraordinary aqueduct arching along beside the road. This looks medieval and was built on the line of an earlier Roman aqueduct, but is in fact barely 150 years old, having been constructed during the brief period of Egyptian rule (1832–40) to provide Iráklion with water. It has now been taken over by a colony of noisy jackdaws. Just beyond the aqueduct are a couple of tavernas/cafés beside the road – a convenient escape from the Knossós crowds – and a little further on is a turning on the left, clearly signposted to Mirtiá.

The main reason to visit **MIRTIÁ** is for the Kazantzákis Museum in the village, but you don't need to be a fan of the writer to find the trip worthwhile. Only enthusiasts are likely to spend long over the exhibits, but it's an enjoyable collection to look over quickly and a lovely drive there on almost deserted roads. Mirtiá itself is larger than you'd expect – as indeed are many of these villages – and bright with flowers planted in old olive-oil cans. On the central *platía*, well beyond the multicoloured, multilingual signs on the main street at either end of the village, is the **Kazantzákis Museum** (March–Oct daily 9am–7pm; Nov–Feb Sunday only 10am–3pm; €3, students €1). Occupying a fine bourgeois mansion where Kazantzákis's parents once lived, the collection includes a vast quantity of ephemera relating to the great author: diaries, photos, manuscripts, first editions, translations into every conceivable language, playbills, stills from films of his works, costumes and more. There's also a video documentary in Greek. On the same *platía* are three pleasant *kafenía* where you can stop for a drink.

From Mirtiá, continue south through the village of Ayía Paraskies then turn right (west) to reach **Pezá**, the main centre of Iráklion province's wine

Níkos Kazantzákis

Níkos Kazantzákis was born in Iráklion in 1883 in the street now named after him. His early life was shadowed by the struggle against the Turks and for union with Greece. Educated in Athens and Paris, Kazantzákis travelled widely throughout his life, working for the Greek government on more than one occasion (serving briefly as minister for education in 1945) and for UNESCO, but above all writing. He produced a vast range of works, including philosophical essays, epic poetry, travel books, translations of classics such as Dante's *Divine Comedy* into Greek and, of course, the novels on which his fame in the West mostly rests. **Zorba the Greek** (1946) was his first and most celebrated novel, but his output remained prolific to the end of his life. Particularly relevant to Cretan travels are *Freedom or Death* (1950), set amid the struggle against the Turks, and the autobiographical *Report to Greco*, published posthumously in 1961 (Kazantzákis died in Freiburg, West Germany, in 1957 after contracting hepatitis from an unsterilized vaccination needle during a visit to China).

Kazantzákis is widely accepted as the leading Greek writer of the century, and Cretans are extremely proud of him, despite the fact that most of his later life was spent abroad, that he was banned from entering Greece for long periods, and that he was excommunicated by the Orthodox Church for his vigorously expressed doubts about Christianity. This last detail gained him more recent notoriety when his *The Last Temptation of Christ* was filmed by Martin Scorsese, amid much controversy. The church was also instrumental in working behind the scenes to deny him the Nobel Prize, which he lost by one vote to Albert Camus in 1957. Many critics now regard his writing as overblown and pretentious, but even they admit that the best parts are where the Cretan in Kazantzákis shows through, in the tremendous gusto and vitality of books like *Zorba* and *Freedom or Death*. Kazantzákis himself was always conscious, and proud, of his Cretan heritage.

production. The major vineyard here is **Minos** (April–Oct Mon–Fri 9am–4pm; €3; Sat 9am–1pm, tasting and buying only; ⓦ www.minoswines.gr) on the main street as you pass through, whose various wines are the top sellers on the island. They do tours of the winemaking plant, show you a video about the history of wine production on the island and allow you to taste and buy the house brands at their shop. To continue from Pezá to Arhánes, head north to Kounávi then turn left along a back road through Katálagari.

Arhánes and its Minoan sites

From the turning off to Mirtiá, it's a further 2km on the main road through vineyards to the junction where you turn right for Arhánes (taking the left fork would take you to Pezá, above). It was here, at what seems a singularly unthreatening spot, that General Kreipe was kidnapped on April 26, 1944 (see p.422). The site is now marked by a lofty modern monument but the information given on a plaque is in Greek only.

A little along the road to Arhánes from here, you'll pass on the right the new **Cretan Historical and Folklore Museum** (daily 9am–5pm; €3; ⓦ www.psaltakismuseum.com), a private venture stuffed with a fascinating collection of artefacts from diverse periods in the island's history. There's the usual collection of antique farming implements, pots and *raki* stills from Crete's agricultural past but also a section on World War II, which has photos of the occupation as well as a collection of personal effects belonging to General Kreipe, who ruled Crete from the German army's island command centre in Arhánes. Outside beneath a canopy are a collection of guns and transport vehicles from the same period.

A further 2km through Patsídhes and Káto Arhánes is the large and prosperous agricultural centre of **ARHÁNES**, a town substantial enough to have a one-way traffic system and be served by hourly buses from Iráklion but not to warrant a hotel or any other place to stay. The centre, with its small square consisting of a restored church, a couple of large, dozy *kafenía* and a few decent tavernas (try *To Spitikos*), is on the northbound side: drive through and double back. The church has an incongruous whitewashed clock tower and a fine collection of icons; elsewhere, there are Byzantine frescoes in the church of Ayía Triádha on the fringes of town and, much more importantly, at the church of **Asómatos** to the east, where the superb fourteenth-century works include a horrific *Crucifixion* and a depiction of the fall of Jericho with Joshua in full medieval armour. Before setting out, you'll need to get the key from the *Miriófiton Snack Bar* on the square, leaving a passport with them as a deposit. To get there follow the road through the town, and then the signs east for a couple of kilometres.

Arhánes was a sizeable centre of **Minoan civilization**, and there are a number of sites round about. All of them are relatively recent discoveries, having been excavated over the last few decades, and not all of the excavations have been fully published. Consequently, these sites are neither particularly famous nor especially welcoming to visitors, but many of the finds are nonetheless important. The largest of the structures is the **Palace**, in reality more likely a large villa, which lies right in the heart of modern Arhánes, signed just off the main road. Through the chain-link fence, you can see evidence of a substantial walled mansion, representing only a small part of what once stood here. Piecemeal excavation is still going on at other sites in the centre too, but much is hidden beneath more modern buildings. The Archeological Museum (see p.110) will direct you to where these excavations can be viewed.

The Archeological Museum

Arhánes has an excellent **Archeological Museum** (Tues–Sun 8.30am–3pm; free), founded by Yiannis and Effie Sakellarakis, the excavators of Anemospília (see p.111), displaying finds from the town and the sites surrounding it. To get there, follow the Vathípetro road from the main square for 100m; the museum is signed up a narrow street on the left.

Imaginatively laid out in a single room, the museum gives you an idea of how much more stimulating Iráklion's museum could be if the same principles were applied. Near the entrance are some well-preserved Minoan **larnakes** (clay coffins) from **Foúrni** dating from around 1800 BC, suggesting (because the knees needed to be drawn up to the chest to squeeze the corpses in) that the deceased would have been placed into these before the onset of *rigor mortis*. Case 4 has an interesting and unique **sistrum** (currently replaced by a copy) found in the same cemetery at Foúrni. Dating from around 2000 BC, and probably borrowed from Egypt, this musical instrument was used much like a tambourine, emitting a maraca-type sound when the clay discs suspended on wooden rods were vigorously rattled; it may well be the oldest surviving musical instrument in Europe. There's a photo nearby of the famous "Harvesters Vase" in the Iráklion museum, depicting a *sistrum* in use.

Case 7 has fascinating finds from **Anemospília** (see p.111), where human sacrifices appear to have taken place in the temple there. The **dagger** (a copy of the original in the Iráklion museum) found lying on the sacrificial victim is displayed here, with its curious motif of a hybrid animal – resembling a deformed boar – carved on the blade. There's also a copy of the seal stone (also in Iráklion) which the priest was wearing on his left wrist as well as the terracotta feet of a wooden statue which was destroyed in a fire caused by the many oil lamps used to light the shrine. Further evidence of the fire comes from two giant *píthoi*, the smaller of which was deformed by the intense blaze which consumed the temple. On the top of nearby Case 19 can be seen the terracotta "horns of consecration" also found in the shrine. Case 9 displays small terracotta cups which contained ochres used to paint the frescoes on the walls in the palaces and villas, whilst an imaginative display of **pottery shards** (Case 13) evidences five thousand years of human occupation in this town: crude works of the third millennium BC are succeeded by the various Minoan periods, then Greek, Roman, Byzantine, Venetian and Turkish pieces, down to broken pots of the present day. Case 16 has fragments of Minoan wall painting which underline their mastery of this medium and convey some idea of how brilliant the colours must have been when newly painted.

Foúrni

The second of Arhánes's sites is **Foúrni** (daily 8.30am–3pm; free), off to the right as you enter the town (immediately before the school) and about ten minutes' walk up a steep, very rocky trail. The size of Foúrni is evidence of the scale of the Minoan community that once thrived around Arhánes; what has been unearthed here is a **burial ground** used throughout the Minoan period, with its earliest tombs dating from around 2500 BC (before the construction of the great palaces), and the latest from the very end of the Minoan era. The structures include a number of early *thólos* tombs – round, stone buildings reminiscent of beehives – each of which contained multiple burials in sarcophagi and *píthoi*. Since many simpler graves and a circle of seven Mycenaean-style shaft graves were also revealed at Foúrni, it is by far the most extensive Minoan cemetery known. Its significance was increased by some of the finds made here – most importantly within "Thólos A", where a side-chamber was found which revealed the undisturbed tomb of a woman who, judging by the jewellery and other goods buried with her, was of royal descent and perhaps a priestess. Another recent suggestion is that she was a princess buried here shortly before the final destruction of Knossós Palace. Her jewellery is now on display at the Iráklion Archeological Museum, as is the skeleton of a horse apparently sacrificed in her honour.

Anemospília

Anemospília, 2km northwest of Arhánes, is considerably more worthwhile than other sites in the vicinity, enlivened by a spectacular setting and a controversial story. The approach road heads north from Arhánes: coming from Iráklion, you enter the one-way street and almost immediately turn sharp right, back on yourself, just past a small chapel. Following the road leading northwest out of the town, you begin to climb across the northern face of Mount Yioúhtas, winding around craggy rocks weirdly carved by the wind (Anemospília means "Caves of the Wind") until you reach the fenced site held in a steep curve of the road.

What stood here was a **temple**, and its interpretation has been the source of outraged controversy among Minoan scholars since its excavation at the beginning of the 1980s. The building is a simple one, consisting of three rooms connected by a north-facing portico, but its contents are not so easily described. The temple was apparently destroyed by an earthquake, which struck during a ceremony that appears to have involved **human sacrifice** – the only evidence of such a ritual found in Minoan Crete. This came as a severe shock to those who liked to portray the Minoans as the perfect peaceable society, but the evidence is hard to refute. Three skeletons were found in the western room: one had rich jewellery, indicative of a priest; another was a woman, presumably a priestess or assistant; the third was curled up on an altar-like structure, and, according to scientists, was already dead when the building collapsed and killed the others. A large bronze knife lay on top of this third skeleton. Outside the western room, another man was crushed in the corridor, apparently carrying some kind of ritual vase. These events have been dated to around 1700 BC, roughly the time of the earthquakes that destroyed the first palaces and, in the circumstances, it seems easy to believe that the priests might have resorted to desperate measures in a final attempt to appease the gods who were destroying their civilization.

The summit of Mount Yioúhtas and Vathípetro

Continuing beyond Arhánes you'll see a sign after a couple of kilometres for the summit of **Mount Yioúhtas**, up a track which is a relatively easy drive. You can also climb to the top in little over an hour from Arhánes along the same route, but it seems rather unsatisfying to do this only to discover other people rolling up on their motorbikes or in taxis. The **panoramic views** are the main lure, back across Iráklion especially, but also west to Psilorítis and east to Dhíkti. On the summit is a small and fairly ordinary chapel, and the trappings of the annual *Paniyíri* (festival), which is celebrated on August 15 and attracts villagers from all around. The impressive remains of a **Minoan Peak sanctuary** dating from the early second millennium BC occupy the north side of the hill, partly built over by an OTE telecommunications relay station. It very likely served as a cult centre, attracting pilgrims from Arhánes and Knossós, both of which can be seen in the magnificent view from the summit. An enormous number of votive offerings, including jewellery, figurines and libations vessels, were unearthed in the excavations and are now on display in the museum at Iráklion. On the shoulders of the mountain, not easily accessible, are caves associated with the local Zeus cult.

The main road running beneath Mount Yioúhtas continues south toward **Vathípetro**, which is well signposted along the way. Here, at last, is a site which can be examined close to: a large Minoan **villa** (Tues–Sun 8.30am–3pm; free), which once controlled the rich farmland south of Arhánes. Inside, a remarkable collection of everyday items was found – equipment for making wine and oil, and other tools and simple requisites of rural life. Still surrounded by a vineyard with a valid claim to be the oldest in the world (winemaking has been carried on here since the second millennium BC), the house was originally a substantial building of several storeys, with a courtyard enclosing a shrine, and fine large rooms – especially on the east. The basement workrooms, however, were the scene of the most interesting discoveries, comprising agricultural equipment and a remarkably well-preserved **winepress**, which can still be seen *in situ*. When the doors are locked, you can see something of what remains through the barred windows – which you may end up doing anyway, as the site sometimes closes early. The house on the west side of the villa was the base used by the famous Cretan archeologist Marinatos when he excavated here in the early 1950s. It has now been restored as a **cafeteria**.

Continuing southeast for 2km soon brings you to another agricultural centre, **Houdétsi**, which now has a remarkable **Museum of Musical Instruments of the World** (daily 9am–3pm & 5.30–8.30pm; €3; Ⓦ www.labyrinthmusic.gr). Founded by Irish *lyra* player Ross Daly (see the box below), who lives in the village, the museum consists of a collection of mainly string and percussion instruments (many very rare) from across the globe. Housed in an elegant mansion, with a rare, emerald-green grass lawn, it's also used as a school for courses given by Daly and other leading musicians

The Irish lyra player

One of the more remarkable stories of Cretan music is that an Irishman, **Ross Daly**, has become one of its most famous names. Born in England of Irish parents, he grew up in Asia and North America, the family settling wherever the work of his physicist father happened to take them. Daly first visited Crete in 1971 and was strongly attracted to its traditional music, studying in that same decade under master *lyra* player Kostas Mountakis, in Haniá. Part of his early career was spent in Anóyia teaching *lyra* to local children, but once he had become a *lyra* virtuoso he was not content to stay within the confines of Cretan music and began to synthesize what he had learned in Crete and Greece with music from other cultures such as Turkey, the Balkans, India and Afghanistan.

Daly now performs worldwide with his ensemble, Labyrinth, a unit comprising Russian, Greek and Cretan musicians, but always returns to his home in Crete. In addition to the *lyra*, he now plays a variety of instruments, including the *laouto* (lute), *oud*, *rabab* (Afghan lute), *sarangi* (Turkish *bouzouki*) and a special *lyra* with twenty-one strings instead of the usual three. When not on tour (he has performed concerts throughout Europe), he runs music schools in Crete and Athens, and recently founded a museum (see above) dedicated to displaying musical instruments of the world in his home village of Houdétsi. During his musical career Daly has made more than twenty albums, the latest of which is *Iris* (Protasis, Athens), in which his ensemble joins forces with Indian and Iranian musicians as well as noted Cretan artists. Details of this and his other recordings can be found on his website Ⓦ www.rossdaly.com.

during the summer months. Concerts are also held at this time, and details can be obtained from the museum or its website. To find it, head for *Bar Paranga* at the top (or south end) of the village – the museum lies opposite. Should it not be open during the hours quoted, ring the English-speaking guardian, Eleni Arvanti, from the public phone alongside the bar, and she will open it up for you (T 28107 43634). For more on Cretan music, see p.458.

West of Iráklion

Heading west from Iráklion, the modern **E75 highway**, cut into the cliffs, is – in daytime at any rate – as fast and efficient a road as you could hope to find (at night, however, avoid the highway if you can; see the box on p.114). In simple scenic terms, it's a spectacular drive, but with very little in the way of habitation; there's only a couple of developed beach resorts and the "birth-place of El Greco" at **Fódhele** until the final, flat stretch just before Réthimnon. If you go this way, the point where you join the bypass offers perhaps the best view of Zeus's profile on Mount Yioúhtas – open mouth, prominent nose and chin.

If you're in no hurry, forget the highway and try the older roads west, curl-ing up amid stunning mountain scenery. The only specific site on these back roads is the Minoan one at **Tílissos**, but they have the advantage of taking you through archetypal rural Crete, with tracks tramped solely by herds of sheep or goats, isolated chapels or farmsteads beside the road, and occasionally a village. City buses will take you as far as the *Creta Beach* hotel (see p.100), but to travel any further west, you'll need either your own transport or a KTEL bus from the "A" westbound station near the Venetian harbour.

Along the E75 highway

Once past the western city beaches, the highway heads north, climbing into the foothills of the Psilorítis range as they plunge straight to the sea. As you ascend, keep an eye out for the immaculately crafted medieval fortress of **Paleókastro**, built into the cliff right beside the road; it's easy to miss, so com-pletely do the crumbling fortifications blend in against the rocks. Just beyond, the road crosses a bridge over the modern village of Paleókastro, nestling in a little gully which leads down to the sea: a beautiful setting, with wealthy sub-urban homes and restaurants popular for weekend outings.

Ayía Pelayía

As you round the headland, **AYÍA PELAYÍA** is laid out below, a sprinkling of white cubes around a deep blue bay, unbelievably inviting from this distance. Closer up, the attraction is slightly diminished: continuing development is rapidly outpacing the capacity of the narrow, taverna-lined beach, and is begin-ning to take its toll on the village. However, the water is clear and calm, the swimming excellent and there's a superb view, too, of all the ships which pass the end of the bay as they steam into Iráklion – spectacular at night, when the brightly lit ferries go by. Water-skiing, parasailing and motorboats are also all available if you're prepared to pay. Although the main beach (a mere twelve metres in breadth) can get very crowded with day-trippers from Iráklion at weekends, the resort clings to its exclusivity in the shape of two of the best-looking luxury hotels on the island – the top-flight *Capsis Beach* (T 28108 11212, W www.capsis.gr; cheapest double €260; ❾), on a promontory

The E75 highway

The **E75 highway** which crosses the north of the island, linking Hania in the west to Sitía in the east, is one of the most **dangerous** in Greece. The fact that it is a two-lane road with a hard shoulder has not prevented the exotic Greek driving style from turning it into an unofficial four-lane highway: slow-movers are expected to straddle the line demarcating the hard shoulder, thus allowing faster cars to overtake at will. A reluctance by some tourists to follow this unwritten rule often leads to dangerous tailgating, headlight-flashing and even horn-honking by locals until the way is cleared for the driver in a hurry. Other hazards on this road are posed by small or badly positioned **roadsigns** indicating exits, frequently posted far too late to respond to safely. And missing your exit can mean travelling a considerable distance to the next one, as they are not as frequent as you might expect. Further dangers can include unexpected traffic lights where the highway passes close to a town, and **left turns**, which can be particularly scary at night when you must deal with the dual hazards of crossing the opposite lane of traffic and the possibility of someone ploughing into your rear whilst you're waiting to do so.

The best advice is to avoid using this road at night at all, if possible. In addition to the potential perils above, in summer the large number of huge Cretan wedding feasts (many with over two thousand guests) regularly leads to hundreds of **inebriated drivers** using the E75 in the small hours to get home, and accidents are frequent.

overlooking the town, and the more modestly priced *Peninsula* (℡28108 11313, ⓦwww.peninsula.gr; cheapest double €140; ⑨), over on the headland beyond, and almost a village in itself. If you feel in need of a little more space, you can always head for the nearby beaches – **Ligaria** to the east or **Mononaftis** to the west – which are much more welcoming, with a couple of tavernas fronting each beach but with fewer facilities.

Buses run six times a day from Platía Eleftherías in Iráklion (from outside the *Astoria* hotel) to the central *Capsis Beach* hotel. If you take a long-distance bus from Iráklion that is bound for Réthimnon or Haniá, you face a steep three-kilometre descent from the drop-off point on the main road; it's even worse walking back up, although residents seem favourably disposed to giving lifts.

For **food**, the seafront tavernas are much of a muchness with one exception. The recently arrived *Caldera* (℡2810 811944), towards the western end of the main beach, is a stylish *ouzerí*, bar and mid-priced restaurant serving well-prepared Cretan and international dishes on a charming terrace. The wine list is extensive and offers some excellent lesser-known Cretan and Greek wines from small producers. For cheaper eats, you could try *Taverna El Greco* at the south end of the seafront for the usual staples and fair-priced fish, or head into the village, where there are some basic takeaways and small supermarkets for the makings of a picnic on the beach.

Accommodation tends to consist of hotels and studios or apartments with cooking facilities, rather than straightforward rooms. Out of season, these can be excellent value if you're prepared to bargain hard, but through the summer they're mostly block-booked. If you do want to stay, it's a question of wandering around asking at every door with a sign – the owners will usually know who (if anyone) has a room free. A couple of places worth a try include *Zorba's Apartments* (℡ & ℻28102 56072, Ⓔzorbas@freemail.gr; ⑤) along the nameless main street behind the beach or, on the road above it, the excellent-value *Danai Rooms* (℡28102 85936; ②); the latter has a/c en-suite rooms with kitchenette and fridge. Downhill from here, the *Creta Sun Hotel* (☎28108 11626; ◐) has pleasant studio rooms with balcony and a small pool. Otherwise, try one of the travel bureaux, such as Pangosmio (☎28108 11402, ℱ28108 11424), just past the Vasilis Supermarket on the main street behind the beach at the western end. The same agency also hires cars.

Just across from Pangosmio, *Netcafé Atlas* (daily 11am–2pm & 5–11pm; ☎28108 11074) can provide **Internet** access. For late-night **entertainment**, there are plenty of bars lining the beach, including loud disco-bars, such as *Banana*, and more subdued cocktail bars like the nautically themed *Bloom*. Up the hill heading out of town, *Mythos*, *Nanu* and *Paradise* are other popular and noisy nightspots.

Fódhele

Turning inland from the main road opposite Ayía Pelayía, an old stretch of paved road runs from Ahládha to Fódhele, connected by rutted, unpaved sections with other old roads inland. Ahládha's spectacular hilltop setting serves to detract from the lack of attractions in the village itself. If you're simply heading for Fódhele, you can get there more efficiently by taking the later turn-off about 3km further along the E75, but the old, longer route is a great deal more diverting.

FÓDHELE is firmly established on the tourist circuit as the birthplace of the painter **El Greco** (1541–1614), although there's virtually no hard evidence to substantiate this and most academic opinion now believes that he was born in Iráklion. The excursion is a pleasant one, in any case: Fódhele lies in a richly fertile valley, surrounded by orange and lime groves. On the far side of the river as you drive up are a couple of small Byzantine chapels, and there's an ancient church in the village. Despite the craft and souvenir shops that line the main street, selling local embroidery, and the café tables ranged along the river bank, Fódhele most of the time is almost preternaturally sleepy – you can sit at one of these shady café tables for half-an-hour before anyone emerges to take your order, and wait as long again before your refreshment appears. Meanwhile, take a few minutes to study the plaque in the village square, made of stone from Toledo (where Domenico Theotokópoulos settled, produced the bulk of his most famous works and earned the name El Greco). The plaque was presented to Fódhele in 1934 by the University of Valladolid as an authentication of the locale's claim to fame, which must be responsible in some measure for its current prosperity, whatever the scholars may say.

To get to **El Greco's House** (May–Oct Tues–Sun 9am–5pm; €1.50), cross the bridge over the river, pass the church (which has copies of many of his works) and follow the clearly signed road (right) which heads northwards out of town among orange groves, fragrant with blossom at Eastertime. Now heavily restored, the building doesn't look old enough to have been around when the painter was; unfortunately, the selection of the artist's works in reproduction displayed within is fairly uninspiring, and there's nothing about El Greco's life and times or how the works were created. However, a **café** adjoining the house makes a pleasant place to pause for a refreshing drink.

A better reason for making the journey out here is the charming, mainly fourteenth-century **church of the Panayía Loubiniés** (Tues–Sun 9am–3.30pm; free), sited opposite the path leading to the house. This exquisite, drum-domed church was built over an eighth-century basilica – the central nave and the interesting baptismal font in the floor beside the church (deep enough for total immersion) date from the earlier building. The wonderful and recently restored thirteenth- and fourteenth-century frescoes (partially visible through windows in the apse when the church is closed), were uncovered beneath later works, but the jarring glass windows in the dome spoil the overall impression. Beneath the orange groves surrounding the church are the remains of the medieval village it once served.

A couple of **buses** a day run direct to Fódhele from the Pórta Haníon (Haniá Gate) terminal in Iráklion, but the timings aren't really conducive to a quick visit. On the other hand, it's not too far to walk back to the highway junction 3km away, so you could catch the direct afternoon bus up (currently 2.30pm; Mon–Fri only) and then try flagging down a long-distance bus on the main road. There are also occasional **tours** from Iráklion (information from the travel agents listed on p.99).

West on the old roads

Ignoring the benefits of the modern coastal highway and taking the older mountain route (which preceded the relatively modern E75) is a slower journey, but the experience of travelling through traditional Cretan countryside is a definite bonus. At first, you pass through villages such as **Gazí**, which are mostly industrial and lacklustre, but once under the raised highway, however, you immediately start to climb south into the hills. Almost straightaway, there's a right turn signed to **Rodhiá**, a sizeable village looking back down over the city. This is the quieter way to Ayía Pelayía and Fódhele, but to get there, you face more than 9km of atrocious road between here and Ahládha.

From Rodhiá, a signed detour climbs 5km northwest into the hills to the famous **convent of Savathianá** (daily 8am–1pm & 4–7pm), set in a rock cleft and surrounded by lofty cypresses. Founded in the Venetian period, the settlement has been transformed by its diligent nuns into a flower-festooned oasis. A quince orchard behind the convent is the source of home-made jams sold to visitors. The convent gained further celebrity in 1991 when an eighteenth-century icon entitled *Lord Thou Art Great*, and identical to the one at Tóplou (see p.208), was discovered; both were painted by Ioánnis Kornáros.

If you choose not to take the turning to Rodhiá, continuing southwest along the road signed for Márathos and Tílissos soon brings you to **Arolíthos**, an artificial "traditional village", which represents a surprisingly successful attempt to create the atmosphere of rural Crete in a tourist development. There are crafts workers – potters, weavers, artists, a smith – who use traditional methods, stores where you can buy their products, a restaurant with wood-fired ovens, and events such as Greek dancing evenings. There are also some upmarket rooms, though no very good reason to stay. For the moment, the place seems half-empty except when a bus tour calls by, but it's worth a look as you pass.

A little way beyond Arolíthos, the way divides: the road that used to be the main route from Iráklion to Réthimnon is the one which runs through **Márathos**, 9km northwest of Arolíthos. Famous for the honey that seems to be on sale at every house, Márathos is an attractive place with a couple of *kafenía* if you feel like breaking the journey (this road runs through very few other villages of any size). Not far beyond the village, it's possible to cut down by unpaved but reasonable track to Fódhele.

These days, more people travel by the furthest inland of the roads, the one that climbs southwest from Arolíthos through Tílissos and on via **Anóyia** (see p.266). It's a pleasant ride through the Malevísi, a district of fertile valleys filled with olive groves and vineyards renowned from Venetian times for the strong, sweet **Malmsey wine** much favoured in western Europe. England became a major market for the wine, and the growth of the shipping trade between

Candia (Iráklion) and English ports caused King Henry VIII to appoint the first-ever British consul to the island in 1522.

Tílissos

The big attraction of the first part of the trip along this inland route is **TÍLISSOS**, 12km southwest of Iráklion. Tílissos is a name famous in the annals of Minoan archeology as one of the first sites to be excavated. Local archeologist Hatzidákis, working at the beginning of the last century, revealed evidence of occupation from the early Pre-Palace period (ca.2000 BC), but interest focuses primarily on three large villas (known as Houses A, B and C) from the **New Palace** era, contemporary with the great periods at Knossós, Festós and elsewhere. They were probably not as isolated in the country-house sense as they seem today, but may well have been part of a thriving community, or even a staging post on the route west towards as yet undiscovered centres. The existence of a rather simpler villa at Sklavókambos, on the road halfway from here to Anóyia, may lend weight to this latter theory. Tílissos shared in the destruction of the palaces in about 1450 BC, but new buildings then arose, amongst which was the cistern in the northeast corner. Following

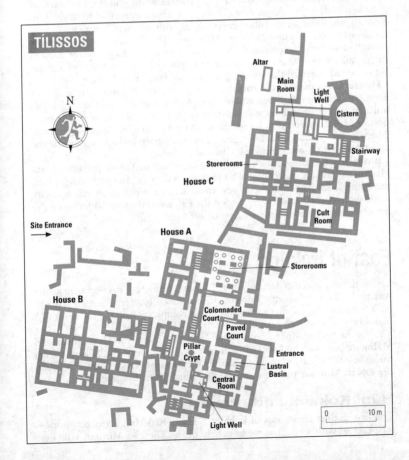

the arrival of the Dorians, Tílissos developed into a Greek city of the Classical period, issuing its own coinage. This later construction tends to make it a bit harder to get a clear picture of what's there today.

The **archeological site** (daily 8.30am–3pm; €2) is signed to the left at the foot of the main street of the modern village. While it's not always the easiest of sites to interpret, it is a lovely place to wander round, with few visitors, pine trees for shade, and some evocative remains, including staircases and walls still standing almost two metres tall – alongside some unsubtle restoration. Immediately beyond the fence, vineyards and rich agricultural land suggest a seductive, but probably illusory, continuity of rural life.

Houses A and C are of extremely fine construction and design (C is the more impressive, while little remains of House B apart from its ground plan, although it does contain some of the oldest relics here. A building of finely dressed ashlar stone, **House A** has a **colonnaded court** at its heart with a window lighting the staircase to the west side of this. In storerooms on the north side, some of the large reconstructed *píthoi* can be seen with holes near their bases for tapping the contents (probably oil). A number of Linear A tablets also came to light in this area. In the south wing, the main rooms open onto a light well, with the central room having a **lustral basin** – in this case more of a sunken bath – just off it. A stand for a double axe, similar to finds from Knossós, was found in the **pillar crypt**, along with the three enormous bronze cauldrons (now in the Iráklion Archeological Museum) that originally prompted the site's excavation. Throughout the house, fragments of painted stucco were found, leading archeologists to postulate the existence of a luxurious second storey to this dwelling, which had fallen in over time.

House C contains a **cult room** with a central pillar, storerooms and, at its northern end, the living area, where a paved main room would have been illuminated by a light well on its eastern side. At the end of one of many corridors (a Minoan speciality), a staircase would once have led to an upper floor. There is also evidence of a drainage system, while outside the house, beside the cistern, is a **stone altar** from the Classical period.

Buses run five times daily to the modern village of Tílissos from the Pórta Haníon in Iráklion, and continue towards Anóyia. It's a pleasant enough place, providing food, drink and even a few **rooms**. For a delicious Cretan omelette made with local *tirozoúli* cheese, stop at the *Estiatorio Akropolis*, 150m up on the left of the main street after the site turn-off.

East of Iráklion

East of the city beach at Amnísos there's almost continuous development all the way to Mália, as what little remains of the coastal landscape is torn apart to build yet more hotels, apartments and beach complexes flanking the main E75 highway; you'll need to turn off to reach the places below.

You're in package-tour country here and the resorts of **Hersónisos** and **Mália** are big, brash and packed with visitors all summer long. Welcome relief from the coastal hullabaloo is provided by the **Skotino Cave** near Goúves, and the superb **Minoan palace** east of Mália, which should not be missed.

Háni Kokkíni and around

The first distinct centre east of Iráklion is **Háni Kokkíni**, a grubbily nondescript resort with a long but rather pebbly beach. There's a **Minoan villa** here

(Tues–Sun 8.30am–3pm; free) – known as Nírou Háni – which must have been beautifully sited when it stood alone. With the road immediately outside and traffic roaring by, however, it is harder to appreciate. Excavations of the villa revealed the foundations of a two-storey building dating from the New Palace period (ca.1550 BC). All the usual Minoan architectural features are present – light well, storage rooms, connecting corridors, decorative paving – and the site was particularly rich in religious paraphernalia, including tripod altars and some striking bronze double axes now on display in the Iráklion Archeological Museum. These finds led the excavators to name it the "House of the High Priest". The site is now open on a regular basis, but the guardian (who also holds the key to the Cave of Eileíthyia; see p.100) is often available after hours – enquire at the nearby cafés if he's not immediately apparent.

Travelling through **Goúrnes**, the rampant commercialism gets even worse. Just west of the village, a mammoth former US air force base still dominates much of the coastline, awaiting a plan for its redevelopment. Beyond here, the beach stretches unbroken for several kilometres, but for the most part it's a narrow strip of dirty pebbles, windy and exposed. The dismal picture is completed by giant radar dishes overlooking it all from the hills. Just east of Fínikas and 18km east of Iráklion, at **Káto Goúves**, is the nearest campsite to the capital, *Camping Creta* (☏28970 41400), which shares a boundary with the former base; some shelter is provided by the small tamarisk trees. Apart from the beach, there's little here to warrant a special stop. Just before Fínikas, a **bypass** (actually the redirected E75) forks off to the right, allowing you to cut out the major traffic bottleneck of Hersónisos if you're on a journey to the east of the island. The bypass rejoins the coastal route 11km east, just before Stalídha (see p.124).

About 6km inland by car from Fínikas is the **Skotinó Cave**, one of the largest and most spectacular on the island. It's a pleasant 45-minute walk from the coast road, passing through **Goúves** village, which makes an encouragingly complete contrast to the coastal strip and which is a good stop to pick up refreshments – there are a couple of decent **tavernas** – and to check directions before continuing to the signed turn-off, on the right, for **Skotinó** (which means "dark"). It's also possible to walk from Goúves along 3km of unsigned tracks (marked on the *Harms Verlag* map). If you're driving, about a kilometre out of Skotinó village on the main road heading south, take a road signed "Cave of Ayía Paraskeví" downhill on your right after a hairpin bend marked by a taverna; the road eventually degenerates into a track, and the cave entrance is a further kilometre below a whitewashed chapel which you will see on the horizon. The cave is 160m deep and is divided into four levels with an awesomely huge main chamber. It was first investigated by Evans and more scientifically explored in the 1960s by French and Greek archeologists. A considerable number of bronze and ceramic **votive offerings** were found here (the earliest dating back to early Minoan times), suggesting that this was an important sacred shrine. The cave remained in use well into the Greek and Roman eras, when the fertility goddess Artemis was worshipped in what is thought to have been a substitution for an earlier Minoan female fertility deity, possibly Brytomartis. In the chapel above, *taxímata* (ex votos) left by pilgrims continue a tradition of supplication to the (now Christian) deity which has persisted on this same spot for well over four thousand years.

Hersónisos and around

Continuing east along the main coast road, the turning for the direct route up to the **Lasíthi Plateau** (see p.172) is signed 3km beyond the bridge over the

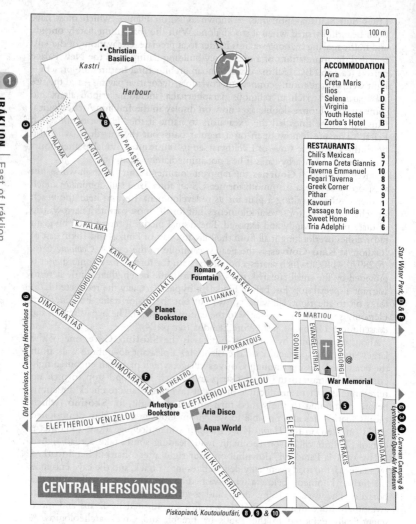

ACCOMMODATION
Avra	A
Creta Maris	C
Ilios	F
Selena	D
Virginia	E
Youth Hostel	G
Zorba's Hotel	B

RESTAURANTS
Chili's Mexican	5
Taverna Creta Giannis	7
Taverna Emmanuel	10
Fegari Taverna	8
Greek Corner	3
Pithar	9
Kavouri	1
Passage to India	2
Sweet Home	4
Tria Adelphi	6

CENTRAL HERSÓNISOS

Piskopianó, Koutouloufári, **8**, **9** & **10** ▼

Apsolémis winter torrent. Shortly after this – if you don't take the new E75 **bypass** which cuts inland – you roll into the first of the really big resorts, **HERSÓNISOS** (or, more correctly, Límin Hersonísou; Hersónisos is the village in the hills just behind). A brash, sprawling and rather seedy resort catering to mainly Dutch, Irish and Italian package tourists, Hersónisos is replete with all the trappings of mass tourism. If you're looking for tranquility and Cretan tradition, forget it; this is the world of concrete high-rise hotels, video bars, fast-food shops and Eurodisco nightlife. The town's main artery is a two-kilometre street (Odhós Elefthériou Venizélou) behind the sea, a seemingly endless ribbon of bars, travel agents, amusement arcades, beachwear shops, car and bike rental dealers, tawdry jewellery emporia and interminable traffic jams. That said, the resort has enough restaurants to keep prices down and plenty of sand to escape the crowds. The one thing you won't find in July or August is a room.

Arrival and information

Every thirty minutes from 6.30am to 10pm, **buses** run between Hersónisos and both Iráklion and Áyios Nikoláos. For shorter hops around town, **taxis** gather next to the *Aria* disco and the *Creta Maris* hotel, or can be called on ☎28970 22098. The **OTE** office (Mon–Sat 7.30am–10pm, Sun 9am–2pm & 5–10pm) is just north of Eleuthériou Venizélou (the main road through town) on the road leading up to Piskopianó, while the clearly signed **post office** (Mon–Fri 7.30am–8pm, Sat 7.30am–2pm) is nearby on Digeni Akriti. **Internet** access is available at *Café Neon*, Eleuthériou Venizélou 40, and the central *Internet Café* at Papadogiorgi 10, to the side of the church, whilst the cheapest rates are to be had at *El Greco Palace*, Eleuthériou Venizélou 109, at the eastern end of the main street. An excellent **bookshop** with a wide selection of books in English is Planet Bookstore on Sanoudhakis; also good for books with a Cretan theme is Arhetypo, at Arheo Théatro 11, near the main road at the western end of town.

Accommodation

Although you should have little problem finding somewhere to stay outside the peak season of July and August, much **accommodation** is allocated to package-tour operators and what remains is not cheap – in high season, you're unlikely to find anything less than €35 per night for a double room. Your best option is to call in at one of the travel companies on the main street, such as Zakros Tours (☎28970 22317).

Hotels in the centre are subject to a fair amount of noise both from traffic and – after dark – the vibrant nightlife. For more peaceful surroundings, it's best to head inland. If you don't mind a short taxi-ride or twenty-minute walk, the pleasant hill villages of Piskopianó or Koutouloufári (see p.122) are useful options – as is "Old" Hersónisos (see p.122), although this is not within walking distance. There are few pensions in the villages, but plenty of private rooms, studios and apartments, many of the latter taken up by the tour operators – try asking on spec or at travel agencies on the coast. A typical place in this category is *Elgoni Apartments* (☎28970 21237; ❺), high above Piskopianó with great views over the coast and a pool. Information on rooms can also be had from Supermarket Anna in Piskopianó village centre.

For **campsites**, *Caravan Camping* (☎28970 24718), by the beach at the eastern end of Hersónisos, has ample places to camp in the shade, although the pitches can be extremely close to one another. Just outside the western end of town is *Camping Hersónisos* (☎28970 22902).

Avra Beach Road ☎28970 22079. Overlooking the harbour and close to the beach, this comfortable hotel has en-suite sea-view balcony rooms and its own taverna. ❹

Creta Maris ☎28970 22115, ❺www.maris.gr. The ritziest place in the resort, with every facility you would expect from a luxury hotel; the least expensive high-season room comes in at about €150. ❾

Ilios Omirou 2, on the west edge of town just back from the main road (☎28970 22500, ℻28970 22582). Standard hotel in a relatively quiet area

with a rooftop pool and bar; extras include a/c rooms or fans. ❺

Selena Maragáki 13 ☎28970 22412. Clean, family-run establishment with a/c en-suite rooms on a quiet street and with its own taverna. ❸

Virginia Machis Critis 18 ☎ & ℻28970 22455. Friendly little place above an *ouzerí* at the quieter end of the port road. Sea-view balcony rooms with bath; also has some apartments nearby. Breakfast is included. ❹

Youth Hostel Eleuthériou Venizélou ☎28970 24567. Situated across from *Caravan Camping*, this (now private) hostel is well run by a helpful and friendly American-born Greek. Meals and laundry facilities available. ❶

Zorba's Hotel Beach Road ☎ 28970 22134,

www.hersonissos.com/zorbas. Similar in style and location to the *Avra*, the balcony rooms here are better value and come with ceiling fans and welcoming proprietors. ❸

The Town and around

Along the modern seafront, a solid line of restaurants and bars is broken only by the occasional souvenir shop. In their midst, you'll find a small and remarkable **pyramidal fountain** with broken mosaics of fishing scenes. This dates from the Roman era and is the only real relic of the ancient town of **Chersonesos**, a thriving port from Classical Greek through to Byzantine times, handling trade from Lyttos, which once lay inland near Kastélli. The **harbour** immediately to the west of the fountain is the ancient Roman one, and opposite the fountain on the water are the remains of a concrete Roman quay. Around the headland above the harbour and in odd places along the seafront, you can see more remains of Roman harbour installations, mostly submerged, and on the headland (known locally as Kastri) above the more modern church is the fenced and locked site where a very large and early Christian basilica, probably the seat of a bishop, has been excavated. On the far northern side of the same headland, you can also make out the remains of some ancient Roman fish tanks cut into the rock. But in the main, the new port covers the old.

There is little more of historic interest to keep you occupied in the town, although the entertaining **Lychnostatis Open-Air Museum** of folk culture (Sun–Fri 9.30am–2pm; €4), just past the campsite on the eastern fringes of the resort, is worth a visit, particularly if you haven't had a chance to see the "real thing" inland. A reasonably authentic-looking re-creation of a traditional Cretan village in a pleasant location next to the sea, the various exhibits relate to a way of life rapidly disappearing from the island. There are orchards and herb gardens; live displays of local crafts, such as ceramics and weaving; as well as collections of lace, embroidery and traditional costumes within the main house. Concerts of traditional music and dance are frequent, and they occasionally stage more elaborate "dance spectaculars" in the evening. At the other end of town, and up a road almost opposite the *Hard Rock Café*, **Aqua World** (April–Oct daily 10am–6pm; €5) is a small aquarium displaying many of the fish and sea creatures found off the island's coast.

A short distance inland are the three hill villages of **Koutoulafári**, **Piskopianó** and "**Old**" **Hersónisos** – all worth searching out for accommodation and for their good selection of tavernas. Despite restoration and their increasing use by tour operators, the villages still maintain a reasonably traditional atmosphere. Piskopianó has a **Museum of Rural Life** (daily 9am–1pm & 4–8.30pm; €1.50), situated in one of the narrow streets leading off the main thoroughfare, which makes for a welcome break from the hustle and bustle of Hersónisos below. There is an interesting photo-essay on oil manufacture and the olive press, and the *raki* still in the courtyard outside act as reminders to search out the village *kafenion* afterwards.

If you have kids in tow or are looking for fun and games, you might want to try the **Star Water Park** (daily: April & May 10am–6pm; June–Sept 10am–7pm; €15 for a full day, or €10 for a half-day) on the beach to the eastern side of the resort. In addition to all the usual water features, there's a range of watersports on offer, including **scuba-diving** lessons – which are also available at the PADI-certificated *Scubakreta* at the nearby *Nana Beach Hotel* (☎28970 24076).

Hersónisos' other water park is **Aqua Splash**, with similar features and prices to Star Water Park, 3km inland on the route to the Lasíthi Plateau.

Eating

Despite the abundance of **places to eat**, with a couple of notable exceptions there are few worth recommending in town itself, and the tavernas down on the harbour front are generally best avoided. A greater selection and a more relaxed atmosphere is to be found out of town in the hill villages – but even these are now succumbing to the hype and prices of the coast below. Restaurants also cluster around the main square of "Old" Hersónisos, while Piskopianó has a good *kafeníon* and a number of tavernas.

In town

Chili's Mexican Petrakis, close to the *Passage to India*. Entertaining and popular Mexican-style restaurant serving up tacos, tostadas and enchiladas.

Taverna Creta Giannis Kaniadáki 4, off the south side of Venizélou slightly east of the church. Modest little taverna producing outstanding Cretan dishes which you select from the kitchen; *koklíes me risi* (snails with rice) is a house speciality. Open from noon until the food runs out, which in busy periods can mean before 10pm.

Greek Corner Elefthériou Venizélou 158, at the east end of the main street. Decent garden-terrace taverna offering the usual standards and some vegetarian options.

Kavouri Arhéou Théatro, at the west end of Venizélou. A good but slightly pricey traditional taverna, whose decor boasts a diverting mural of inebriated crab, octopus and other seafood; the house speciality is lamb with garlic and lemon wrapped in paper.

Passage to India Petrakis, off the south side of Venizélou near the church. Excellent, authentic *tandoori* and other Indian dishes prepared by an emigré Asian family, and served on a stylish terrace. Recommended.

Sweet Home Elefthériou Venizélou 164. Hersónisos' best *zaharoplastío*, with a wide range of tarts and pastries and a pleasant terrace.

Out of town

Taverna Emmanuel Central square of Koutoulafári village. Pleasant and popular with reasonably authentic cooking, including lamb and potatoes baked in a traditional clay oven.

Fegari Taverna On the Piskopianó road near the junction to Koutoulafári. Friendly taverna serving good Greek food at reasonable prices. Entertainment is provided by the steady stream of clubbers heading down the hill to the bars and nightclubs of Hersónisos.

Pithari In Koutoulafári village, 150m uphill from *Taverna Emmanuel* (see above). Popular and pleasant taverna offering well-prepared Cretan dishes; a little on the expensive side.

Tria Adelphi (The Three Brothers) Just off the square in "Old" Hersónisos. This stands out as a more authentic taverna among the mass of more touristy places in the vicinity.

Nightlife

Hersónisos is renowned for its **nightlife** and there's certainly no shortage of it. A night's partying kicks off around the **bars** ringing the harbour, which is packed with strollers and the overspill from countless noisy bars from 10pm through to the early hours. Later on, the larger **disco-pubs** and **clubs** in the streets leading up to and along Elefthériou Venizélou are the places to be seen. If you fancy a quiet drink, you've come to the wrong resort, but you could seek refuge at the **open-air cinema** (showing original-version films with a new film every couple of days) attached to the *Creta Maris* hotel, or try the cocktails at the Hawaian-style *Kahlua Beach Bar*, at the east end of the port road. Amateurish sing-and-dance-along **Cretan evenings** are held in the *Dorian Garden Restaurant* in Elefthériou Venizélou, but for something closer to the real thing, enquire about the frequent performances at the **Lychnostatis Open-Air Museum** (see p.122). Travel agencies also run evening trips to "cultural" evenings in the inland villages, such as Kósari and Anópoli, where noted dancers and musicians often appear.

Arena Elefthériou Venizélou. A lively venue with mainly Europop music.

Aria On the main road at the western end of town, near the *Ilios Hotel*. Perennially popular glass-fronted disco, reputedly the biggest on Crete. The walls open to reveal more dance areas as the place fills up.

Camelot Ayía Paraskeví near the seafront. Glitzy dance club playing funk, Greek pop and techno.

Hard Rock Café At the west end of Elefthériou Venizélou. Frequent live music and the usual razzmatazz associated with this international chain.

Homus Five kilometres out of town along the road to Kastelli and next door to Aqua Splash waterpark (open July–Aug only). Claiming to have the best sound system (if not the loudest) on the island, this is a new, mega open-air dance venue employing sixty DJs and bussing in the crowds to fill it from all over the north coast. Opens at 10pm and goes on till dawn.

New York At the entrance to the harbour. This beach bar and pleasant breakfast venue metamorphoses into a deafening disco-pub by night.

Stalídha

The rapidly expanding beach resort of **Stalídha** is something of a Cinderella, sandwiched in between its louder, uglier sisters of Mália and Hersónisos, although it is rapidly growing to resemble them. It can offer the best of both worlds: a friendlier and more relaxed setting, a better beach with the usual array of watersports, and easy access to its two livelier neighbours. Don't be misled, though – Stalídha itself isn't exactly quiet and undeveloped.

Finding **accommodation** can be difficult as most rooms are block-booked by package companies. Out of season, however, you may well be able to negotiate a very reasonable price for a studio or apartment complete with pool, usually around ④–⑤; ask at the central travel agencies first as they will know what's available. **Eating** is less likely to be a problem, but don't expect anything particularly special: *Maria's, Hellas Taverna* and the more upmarket *Blue Sea Restaurant* are all at the western end of town, the area which comes closest to feeling like a resort centre. The **post office** (Mon–Sat 9am–1pm) is also here, and there are a couple of **banks** along the main beach road. Stalídha's **nightlife** is low-key – compared to its neighbours, anyway. There are a few discos, including *Bells* on the main coast road, and *Rhythm* on the beach, while *Sea Wolf Cocktail Bar* and *Akti Bar*, near each other along the beach, play music while you drink.

Mália

The E75 Hersónisos bypass (see p.114) is currently being extended to detour around Mália, and when it opens you'll need to turn off this to enter the resort proper. Large enough to be a substantial town in its own right, **MÁLIA** is undeniably commercial, and its **beach**, long and sandy as it is, becomes grotesquely crowded at times. If you're prepared to enter into the holiday spirit, however – party all night and sleep all day – it can be very enjoyable. And there's the bonus of a **Minoan palace** just down the road.

The town consists of two distinct parts, fanning out to the north and south of a T-junction where the main **bus** from Iráklion or Áyios Nikólaos drops you. The more raucous side of town lies along the **beach road**, which snakes for a good kilometre towards the sea. Here, you'll find supermarkets, souvenir shops, tour agents, cafés, restaurants, video bars and nightclubs. To walk the length of this will take you about fifteen minutes – longer if you allow yourself to be enticed by the sales patter along the way. At the end there's a car park, a small harbour and a couple of beaches to the west. The **main beach**, however, stretches away to the east; in summer, you'll need to walk through the mass of bodies for about another fifteen minutes before you find somewhere to spread out. At this eastern end of the beach is a small **church** backed by dunes and patches of marshy ground alive with frogs. For entertainment, you can swim out to a tiny **offshore islet**: the rocks here are sharp for barefoot exploring, but your efforts will be rewarded by a (perpetually locked) white chapel and rock-pools alive with crabs, shellfish and sea urchins on the islet's seaward side. To find a trace of traditional life in all of this, turn inland to the south of the main road. Here in the **old town**, with its narrow, twisting alleyways and whitewashed walls, old Mália determinedly clings to what remains of its self-respect.

Practicalities

In terms of both action and accommodation, Mália has a great deal more to offer than any of its rivals along the north coast, and practical matters are easily attended to, with a **post office** (Mon–Sat 7.30am–2pm), a couple of banks and an **OTE** right in the centre on the main street, Elefthériou Venizélou; good exchange rates can also be had at the three-storey tourist emporium called Mália Maria Market, a little way down the beach road on the left. **Internet** access is available at a number of places along here too, but easily the best is the efficient *Internet Café* (☎28970 29563) about a third of the way along the beach road on the right. For **bike rental**, Cretamotor (☎28970 31457), about 300m down the beach road, is a good bet (readers with this *Guide* can claim thirty percent discount. Also on the beach road, a reliable outlet for **car hire** is Motor Club (☎28970 32033), about halfway down. And, if you're shopping for food, look out for the tasty Cretan bananas sold at stalls throughout the centre: chances are they'll have been grown in the fields around the town.

Accommodation

As in Hersónisos, many rooms are taken up by the package industry, and in the peak season finding somewhere **to stay** is not always easy, although, unlike its near neighbours, Mália has a good range of small hotels and pensions in addition to apartment blocks and large resort hotels. Your best bet if you want any sleep is to try one of the numerous **rooms** signed in the old town; *Esperia* (☎28970 31086; ④), slightly east of the T-junction and down a right off the main road, is worth a try for en-suite balcony rooms, although it's not the cheapest. Slightly further into the old village and veering right, *Aspasia* (☎28970 31290; ②) has cheaper deals for simple rooms sharing a bath. Most of the cheaper hotels around the T-junction are invariably full. Backtracking from here along the main Iráklion road, there are a number of reasonably priced **pensions** including, on the right, *Hibiscus* (☎28970 31313, Ⓕ28970 32042; ④), which has good-value studios with kitchenette and fridge as well as four-person apartments ranged around a swimming pool. One central place if you're determined to be in the thick of the action is *Kostas* (☎28970 31101; ③), a family-run and surprisingly tranquil pension incongruously located behind the minigolf at the end of the beach road; tricky to find, you'll need to follow a small road on the right just beyond the minigolf; this winds around to the back of the course, where you should see the pension's sign. To save time, you could call in at one of the travel and tourist companies, such as Stallion Travel, Venizélou 128 (☎28970 33690), on the main road, which, in addition to giving information on bus excursions and car rental, can also give details of accommodation availability.

Eating

Restaurant owners jostle for your custom at every step in Mália, especially along the beach road; none is particularly good, but they know their clientele

– *moussaká* and pie and chips abound. Incidentally, the beach road also has a reputation for poisonous *souvláki*. One way of avoiding this would be with British-style fish and chips from *Rooneys*, about one-third of the way down towards the sea. The best places to eat, though, are in the **old town**, to the inland side of the main road: wander up to Platía Áyios Dhimítri, a pleasant square beside the church of the same name, where you can choose from a variety of welcoming tavernas in and around the square, including *Anemone*, *Kalimera*, the pricey *Cordon Bleu*, *Petros* and *Romantic Raphael* (Thai, Chinese and Indonesian dishes here), as well as the nearby and stylish *Kalesma* just off it, which is probably the best of the bunch and has a delightful terrace. A little harder to find, further to the west of the square, *Apolafsi* is a small, good-quality, family taverna which is slightly less pricey than the others and proudly proclaims that all their dishes are prepared in butter and not oil. For an aperitif, try the excellent local wine from the barrel at *Ouzerí Elisabeth*, facing the church.

Nightlife

Mália's beach road is transformed during the hours either side of midnight, when the profusion of **nightlife** joints – bars, discos and clubs – erupt into a pulsating cacophony. The aptly named *Zoo* is a popular club where, after midnight, great excitement is generated as one of the internal walls parts to reveal an even larger dance area with the club's other attraction: a rather dubious body-piercing studio which opens at 2am, presumably when the clients are sufficiently anaesthetized by alcohol. Other popular venues nearby (many British-owned and run) include *Cloud Nine*, *Cosmos*, *Midway*, *Zig-Zag*, *Apollo*, *Spice*, *Havana Club* and *Arthur's Camelot*, and, of course, plenty of "English pubs" with names like *Newcastle* and *Camden*. Unfortunately, good nights out are frequently spoilt by gangs of drunken youths pouring out of the bars: a great battle a few years back between hundreds of alcohol-fuelled English, German and Dutch revellers resulted in deaths and mayhem. To avoid the brawls, especially at night, stick to the old village.

The Palace of Mália

The **Palace of Mália** (daily 8.30am–3pm; €4, Nov–Mar free to all on Sun) lies 3km, or forty minutes' walk, east of the town, just off the main road. Much less imposing than either Knossós or Festós, Mália in some ways surpasses both. For a start, it's a great deal emptier, and you can wander among the remains in relative peace. And while no reconstruction has been attempted, the palace was never re-occupied after its second destruction, so the ground plan is virtually intact. Of the **ruins**, virtually nothing stands much more than a metre above ground level apart from the giant *píthoi* which have been pieced together and left about the palace like sentinels: the palace itself is worn and brown, blending almost imperceptibly into the landscape. With the mountains behind, it's a thoroughly atmospheric setting. It's also a great deal easier to comprehend than Knossós, and if you've already seen the reconstructions there, it's easy to envisage this seaside palace in its days of glory. Basking on the rich agricultural plain between the Lasíthi mountains and the sea, it retains a real flavour of an ancient civilization with a taste for the good life.

First discovered by Joseph Hatzidákis early in the twentieth century, the site's excavation was handed over to the French School at Athens in 1922. As at Knossós and Festós, there was an earlier palace dating from around 1900 BC, which was devastated by the earthquake of about 1700 BC. The remains you see today are those of the palace built to replace this, which functioned until

PALACE OF MÁLIA

0   25 m

about 1450 BC, when it was destroyed for the last time in the wave of violence which swept across the island (see p.413). From this site came the famous **gold pendant** of two bees which can be seen in the Iráklion Archeological Museum and on any local postcard stand. It was allegedly part of a horde which was plundered; the rest of the collection now resides (as the "Aegina Treasure") in the British Museum. The beautiful **leopard's–head axe**, also in the museum at Iráklion, was another of the treasures found at Mália.

Any **bus** bound for Áyios Nikólaos will stop at the palace. Alternatively, you could rent a **bike** for the pleasant, flat ride out to the site, which has the added possibility of a swim on the way back.

Entering the palace: the West Court

From the entrance a path leads into the **West Court**, from where you gain access to the palace proper. As at the other palaces, there are raised pathways leading across this, with the main one heading south towards the area of the eight circular **storage pits**. These probably held grain; the pillars in the middle of some would once have supported a protective roof. In the other direction, the raised walkway takes you to the building's north side, where you can pick up the more substantial paved road that apparently led to the sea.

Entering the palace itself through a "door" between two rocks and jinking right then left, you arrive in the **North Court**, by the storerooms and their elaborately decorated, much-photographed giant *píthoi*. Off to the right are the so-called Royal Apartments, on the far side of which is a well-preserved lustral basin or bath. Nearby lies the **Archive Room**, where a number of Linear A tablets were unearthed. Straight ahead is the **Pillared Hall**, which the excavators, encouraged by the discovery of some cooking pots, think may have been a kitchen (if correct, the relative location is almost exactly the same as that of the palace kitchen at Zákros). Above the hall is a grand dining room which looks out over the courtyard.

The Central Court and Royal Apartments

Mália's **Central Court**, a long, narrow area, about 48m in length by 22m wide, is only slightly smaller than the main courtyards at Knossós and Festós. Look out for the remains of the columns which once supported a portico at this northern end, and for traces of a similar portico down the eastern side. Still-visible post-holes were discovered between these columns by the excavators, suggesting that the court could be fenced in – possibly to protect the spectators during the bull-jumping games which may have been held here. Behind the eastern portico are more storerooms, now under a canopy. In the centre of the court is a shallow pit which may have been used for sacrifices; if this was indeed its purpose then, along with Anemospília, these are the only such Minoan sacrificial areas to have been discovered.

On the west side of the courtyard are the remains of two important stairways. The first led to the upper floor beside what is termed the **Royal Lodge** or Throne Room, which overlooks the courtyard. The second, in the southwest corner, comprises the bottom four steps of what was the main ceremonial stair to the first floor, still impressive in its scale. Beside this is the curious *kernos*, or **altar**. The purpose of this heavy limestone disc, with 34 hollows around its rim and a single bigger one in the centre, is disputed: one theory suggests an altar where, at harvest time, samples of the first fruits of the Cretan crops would be placed in the hollows as offerings to a fertility goddess, while other theories have it as a point for tax collecting or even an ancient gaming board.

The rooms along the west side of the court also merit exploration. Between the two staircases ran a long room which may have gone straight through to the upper floor, like a medieval banqueting hall. Behind this is the **Pillar Crypt**, where the double-axe symbol was found engraved on the two main pillars. Behind the Pillar Crypt runs yet another corridor of storerooms; only accessible through areas which had some royal or religious significance, these would doubtless have been depositories for things of value – the most secure storage at the palace.

New discoveries

The excavations at Mália are by no means complete. Inside and beyond the fenced site to the north and west, digs are still going on, as an apparently sizeable town comes slowly to light.

Beneath a canopy to the west of the northern end of the palace lies the **Hypostyle Hall**. This building consists of a number of storerooms and two interconnected halls of uncertain function. Benches run round three sides of the halls, leading some to speculate that this was some form of council chamber.

New excavations west of here (titled Quartier Mu or "M" – the site is divided up by archeologists using the letters of the Greek alphabet) have revealed another large section of the town, now protected by a canopy. A new approach operates here, as visitors are not allowed to walk among the ruins but view the site from a walkway suspended above it. Interesting new dwellings and streets have been unearthed, some up to roof level, which give a clearer idea of the considerable scale of the complex urban community that surrounded the palace. From the overhead walkway, it's also possible to see a series of what are believed to have been ritual or **cult rooms**, one containing the earliest known **lustral basin** yet discovered on the island – a deep affair of almost swimming-pool dimensions. Several of the other cult rooms yielded statuary, libation vessels and other artefacts connected with religious ceremonies. Archeologists are still trying to piece together what connection this complex had with the nearby palace. Was this possibly the "monastery" of a priesthood serving the palace but living separately from it, or could it have served as a temporary home for the whole palace elite whilst some restoration or repair was carried out to the palace proper? The interesting finds from this area are displayed in the museum at Áyios Nikólaos (see p.181).

Some 500m to the north, close to the sea, is the *Chrysolakkos* or **Golden Pit**, which appears to have been a large, multichambered mausoleum dating from the Old Palace period. Its elaborate construction suggests a royal burial-place, as does the wealth of grave goods discovered here, among them the gold honeybee pendant. The site is reached by turning right (west) on leaving the palace site, and then turning right again along a dirt track which heads north-east towards the sea. The fenced pit lies some 300m down the track, just before the islet of Ayía Varvára, visible offshore. The site is located slightly inland, opposite a headland where caves were used as ossuaries in ancient times.

On the way back from the palace site to the main road, take a look over the fence to the left at more **new excavations** (Quartier "E") which further underline the enormity of the urban area surrounding the palace. There are many substantial buildings here, including a large mansion where fragments of painted plaster were discovered, suggesting a sumptuously decorated interior.

Back to town via the beach

Leaving the site and turning immediately right, you can follow a road west to a lovely **beach** of clean sand which, if no longer the peaceful escape from Mália it used to be, is still a welcome place to bathe after a tour of the ruins. It's now filled with rented beach loungers and parasols, and camping rough is no longer tolerated. A solitary makeshift **taverna** at the back of the beach serves decent fresh fish, though meals can be a little pricey considering the rather basic facilities. **Moving on**, you can easily walk back along the shore to Mália itself, or to the main road, where buses pass every thirty minutes – either west to Iráklion or east towards Áyios Nikólaos.

Southeast of Iráklion: the Pedhiádha

The hinterland east of Iráklion and south of Hersónisos consists mainly of hilly farm country, with large, widely scattered villages. Known as the **Pedhiádha**, this region is quietly prosperous but sees few visitors. Indeed, if you're reliant on public transport there's little opportunity to take in a great deal of what the area has to offer – most villages are served only by their daily market bus. But with your own transport, it makes for enjoyably aimless touring, and certainly the inland roads are far more attractive than the coastal one.

The delights of touring this area lie as much in the verdant countryside as anything else, but possible diversions include the ancient site of **Lyttos** and some notable **frescoed churches** around **Kastélli**, as well as a number of scenic farming villages as the route ascends to the Lasíthi plateau.

Kastélli and the frescoed churches

The area's chief village, **Kastélli**, or Kastélli Pedhiádhos, is a pleasant enough place to pause for a while, and perhaps even to stop over if you've an interest in seeking out some of the many nearby churches and ancient ruins. Chiefly an agricultural centre whose prosperity derives from the olive groves and vineyards spread across the surrounding hills, the town goes its own way, largely unaffected by the tourist zone on the coast below. Still, there are some comfortable modern **rooms**, the best of which – with bath and TV – are to be had at the *Hotel Kalliopi* (℡28910 32685, Ⓦwww.kalliopi-hotel.gr; ❸), close to the central crossroads where the bus drops you. A slightly pricier alternative is *Rooms Elena* (aka *Rooms Veronica* ℡28910 31093; ❹), on the road leading out to the east in the direction of Ksidhás (Lyttos), where studio rooms come with cooker and fridge. For **eating and drinking**, there are a number of bars and *souvláki* places around the main junction, and just south of here is the town's best food option – *Irida*, an excellent local restaurant and pizzeria which uses the garden of an elegant early twentieth-century Neoclassical mansion (opposite) as its terrace. The main attraction of the place is the countryside, where winding lanes are traced by elderly oak and plane trees, and the many smaller satellite villages, often with frescoed medieval **churches** to visit. As you drive around, look out for signs to such churches, which are usually worth seeking out simply for the journey off the main routes, even if very often you can't find anyone to let you in.

One of the more famous of these churches is the fifteenth-century **Isódhia Theótokon**, with fine Byzantine frescoes, near the village of **Sklaverohóri** just a couple of kilometres west of Kastélli. The key is available from the house with a vine trellis about 50m before the church, on the right. Six kilometres further west again and down a side road beyond Apostolí, the **Moní Angaráthou** is in another pleasant location. Although the monastery's church dates from the last century, the surrounding buildings are mainly sixteenth-century and include a picturesque white-walled courtyard with palms, orange trees and cypresses. Another church is **Áyios Yeóryios** at **Ksidhás** (confusingly also known as Lyttos), about 3km east of Kastélli, which has frescoes dated by an inscription to 1321.

However, should you decide to see only one of the many churches in this area, make it **Áyios Pandeleímon**, off the road back to Hersónisos just before the village of **Piyí**. To get there, set off north for a good kilometre out of Kastélli and you'll see a sign ("Byzantine Church and Paradise Tavern") directing you onto a dirt track to the right. There are several alternative trails but, providing you don't mind bumpy driving, it doesn't seem to matter which one you take: they all seem eventually to pass the church – just stick to the side of the valley, parallel with the paved road. The way is shaded with huge old trees, and the church itself, which is surprisingly big, is set in a grove of oaks and planes around a spring which was very likely a sanctuary in ancient times. This idyllic spot shelters the small *Paradise Taverna* run by the eccentric Nikolaides family, who hold the key to the church (March–Oct; at other times you'll need to ask in Kastélli) and who feel that the effort of climbing the hill to open it obliges you to at least buy a drink from them. When you do enter the church, you'll find that the **frescoes**, although powerfully imposing, are weathered almost beyond recognition. Look out for images of the soldier saints on the north wall and an unusual scene of Ayía Ánna nursing the infant Mary. The structure of the church, probably early thirteenth century, is interesting for the way it incorporates parts of the original tenth-century basilica and uses as columns some much older fragments, probably taken from Lyttos. At the time of writing, the Byzantine section of the archeological department has withdrawn the key to the church and it cannot be visited. However, the Nikolaides family have petitioned for its return, and it may well be open again in the near future. The **aqueduct** that once transported water to the ancient city passes close by, and you may spot parts of it as you drive around looking for the church.

About 7km southwest of Kastélli is the large village of **Thrapsanó**, for centuries an important **pottery-making** centre in central Crete. Workshops still thrive in the village itself and along the roads out towards Vóni and Evangelismós, and all of them welcome visitors to admire the potters' skills, although there's not a great deal on offer to buy. There is, though, a good range of earthenware: *píthoi* are evident throughout Thrapsanó, not only in workshops but upturned in the main square and on the backs of parked pickup trucks. Both Thrapsano and Réthimnon's pottery centre, Margarítes (see p.262), have found a new export market in recent years for these giant *píthoi*. In northern Europe, they have become the latest decorative feature for the urban garden, and both centres have been stretched to keep up with demand.

Ancient Lyttos

A road climbs for 2km north of Ksidhás (see p.130) to the site of ancient **Lyttos**, a prominent city of Dorian Crete and mentioned by Homer as leading the Cretan contingent in the Trojan War. The ruins are located between the two small **stonebuilt chapels** of Tímios Stavrós and Áyios Yeóryios, which serve as useful landmarks as you approach. Occupying a magnificent position in the foothills of the Dhíkti range, Lyttos was one of the most powerful city-states of Classical Greece during the centuries prior to the Roman conquest, and was the bitter enemy of Górtys, Ierápytna (modern Ierápetra) and especially Knossós. When Lyttos engaged these three in a **war** for control of the island (221–219 BC), it overreached itself; whilst its army was launching an attack on Ierápetra, Knossós seized the opportunity to destroy the unguarded city, leaving it in ruins and taking its women and children into captivity. The historian Polybius vividly describes how, on their return to Lyttos, the troops broke down in tears at the sight, refused to enter their devastated homes and went for succour to Lappa (see p.256) near Réthimnon, one of its few allies. The city was, however, eventually rebuilt and enjoyed a small-scale renaissance under the Romans through to Byzantine times.

Sadly, what is visible above ground today in no way reflects the city's ancient status, as no systematic archeological exploration has yet taken place. However, what you can see underlines the fact that when the riches of Lyttos are finally excavated – including what was said by a Venetian antiquary to be the island's largest theatre, now lost – it will no doubt become one of the most important sites in Crete. Below the church of Tímios Stavrós, built over a large fifth-century basilica with stones from the ancient city, are the bastions and curtain of an enormous **city wall**. The church is believed to mark the centre, or agora, of Lyttos. The church of **Áyios Yeóryios** (which has fragmentary frescoes) on the southernmost peak is also constructed from stones scavenged from Lyttos: incorporated into the outer wall is a fine fragment of carved acanthus foliage. Nearby, the ancient city's **bouleterion** or council chamber has been excavated, with visible platforms and benches. Spend half-an-hour roaming through the vines and olive groves on the surrounding slopes and you'll come across partially excavated dwellings, delicately carved tombstones, half-buried pillars and the enormous foundation stones of buildings waiting to be unearthed.

Towards the Lasíthi plateau

The one inland route which visitors follow in any numbers is the drive from Iráklion up to the **Lasíthi plateau** (see p.172). Once again, the attractions are charmingly simple: scenery which becomes increasingly mountainous as you climb towards the plateau; old trees spreading beside the road, and still older churches in the villages. Starting from Iráklion, the normal route is to follow the coast road until just before the coastal resort of Hersónisos, where a road is signed on the right to the inland village (and original settlement) of Hersónisos and the plateau. By taking the Hersónisos **bypass** diverting around the resort, you can leave the road just to the south of the inland village and then head for the plateau, cutting out both conurbations. The route ascends first towards Kastélli, and then turns off east through the Aposelémis valley to Potamiés and Goniés. Before reaching the turn-off on the right for Kastélli (you continue left), look out for the ruins of the **Roman aqueduct** – visible in a ravine below the road – which carried water from springs in the hills near ancient Lyttos to its port at Hersónisos.

Approaching **POTAMIÉS** you'll see the small Byzantine frescoed chapel of **Sotíros Christós** (locked) to the left; soon after this a signed track, also on the left, heads for the tenth-century monastery of the **Panayía Gouverniótissa** (Assumption of the Virgin), one of the oldest in Crete. The track climbs through olive groves to a shaded parking space next to the deserted, partly ruined and rather eerie monastery buildings. The enormous **ovens** that once fed the brethren are still in evidence, and precarious staircases (not for the faint-hearted) climb to the dormitories above. The tiny **chapel**, which still attracts visitors and the faithful, stands close by in a peaceful garden with a shady lemon tree. Inside are restored **frescoes** dating from the fourteenth century, with a fine *Pantokrátor* in the dome. The chapel will probably be locked (key available from the *kafeníon* at the edge of the village), but a restricted view of the frescoes inside can be had through a small glassless window in the apse.

Five kilometres further on is **AVDHOÚ**, where there are more fine, if faded, frescoes from the fourteenth and fifteenth centuries in three churches: Áyios Andónios, Áyios Konstantínos and Áyios Yeóryios. The churches should be open; if not, enquiries in the village cafés should produce the necessary keys.

Mohós

Starting from Mália, or on a round trip into the hills from Áyios Nikólaos, you can take a short cut, turning inland at Stalídha and following the road signed for Mohós. This highway is soon crossed by the new E90 Mália bypass, under construction at the time of writing. This route is the most dramatic of the three approaches to the Lasíthi plateau (the third is from the other side at Neápoli; see p.170), offering spectacular views back over the coast as the road climbs dizzily above the Gulf of Mália. After crossing a pass, you arrive at the village of **MOHÓS**, which boasts a pleasant leafy square edged by tavernas and cafés, and a major – albeit rather touristy – **festival of the Panayía** (Virgin) on August 15 every year. The late Swedish prime minister Olof Palme was a regular summer visitor here, and when he was murdered in a Stockholm street in 1986, Mohós was plunged into mourning. His simple house, just behind the elegant Venetian church on the main square, has been turned into a shrine (ask to be directed to the **Villa Palme**), and the street in which it stands has been renamed Odhós Olof Palme. The mainly Swedish visitors to the house have filled several books with their heartfelt comments.

Krási and Panayía Kardhiótissa

Three kilometres beyond the point where the roads from Hersónisos and Stalídha join, a loop off the main route will bring you to the curiously named village of **KRÁSI** – curious because Krasí translates as "wine", but the village's fame is in fact based on water, in the form of a curative spring. This is situated under stone arcading in the shade of an enormous **plane tree**, which is claimed to be two thousand years old and the largest in Europe, with a girth that cannot be encircled by twelve people. Flanking the tree are a couple of **tavernas**. Krási's waters are reputed to be especially good for stomach complaints.

Not much further on, just before the village of **Kerá**, the convent of **Panayía Kardhiótissa** (Our Lady of the Heart; daily 8am–2pm & 4–8pm; €2 contribution towards restoration costs) lies immediately below the road and is one of the most important places of worship on Crete, with an annual celebration on September 8. The buildings date from the twelfth century, and though the heavily refurbished outside of the monastery looks like whitewashed concrete, the interior is undeniably spectacular, with restored **frescoes** throughout. These came to light only in the 1960s, when they were discovered beneath accumulated layers of paint. There is also a copy of a famous twelfth-century icon of the Virgin, the original of which was taken to Rome in 1498. According to legend, successive attempts to steal the icon were thwarted when it found its way back to Kerá, despite being chained to a marble pillar; the pillar is now in the monastery yard, while the chain (kept inside the church) is believed to alleviate pain when wrapped around the bodies of the afflicted. In a peaceful garden outside the church, one of the three remaining nuns will probably be on duty at the stone table in the shade of a mulberry tree or in the shop. If your Greek is up to it, you could ask the sisters to tell you how they were coerced by their families to "enter" the order at the age of ten – a story that reveals a darker side to the Orthodox Church in Greece.

The ascent to Séli Ambélou

Beyond the village of Kerá, the road winds on into the Dhiktean mountains, and the views become progressively more magnificent. To the left, **Mount Karfí** looms ominously, its summit over 1100m above sea level. This spire-like peak (karfí means "nail" in Greek) was one of the sites where the Minoan civilization made its last stand, following the collapse of the great centres after the twelfth century BC. In the face of Dorian advances, the last of the Minoans fled to remote refuges such as this, keeping alive shadowy vestiges of their culture. The solitary peak, now identified as a Minoan sanctuary, stands as a silent witness to the end of Europe's first great civilization.

The road continues to climb, passing the ludicrous **Homo Sapiens Village**, an unsightly pastiche of a Minoan palace-style taverna and a farcical open-air museum dedicated to the "history of man", all of which despoils the landscape, until, at **SÉLI AMBÉLOU**, you approach a dramatic **pass** flanked by stone windmills on the ridges above. Beyond the rocky outcrops, the Lasíthi plateau suddenly unfolds before you. Almost straight ahead, the highest peaks of the range dominate the landscape, including **Mount Dhíkti** – all 2148m of it. The *Séli* taverna here at the pass often serves barbecued roast lamb, and is a good place to stop and take in the sights – looking out to sea, on clear days you can see as far as the island of Thíra (Santoríni), over 100km distant.

On the ridge behind the car-parking area, a couple of the windmills have been restored and pressed into use as souvenir shops. There's a path from here leading to still higher viewpoints and eventually to the site of ancient **Karfí**, a five-kilometre hike away, but this is probably better approached from Tzermiádho (see p.174) on the plateau.

South of Iráklion: across the island

The southern half of the province is very different from the north: there's just one resort of any size – **Mátala** – and a day-trip route that takes in the major archeological sites of **Górtys**, **Festós** and **Ayía Triádha**. The rest is countryside with few concessions to tourism, which is not to say that the area is undeveloped: on the contrary, it represents the island's single most important location for agriculture. The **Messará plain**, in particular, has always been a vital resource, and its importance is reflected in the number of wealthy villages here.

The **south coast**, with the exception of Mátala, is relatively little visited, and a good part of it is quite inaccessible: east of **Léndas** (where there's excellent sand) lies well over 30km of shoreline, most of which can't be reached overland, although a couple of rough tracks lead to a pair of inviting bays and there's even a gorge to explore. To the southeast, the low-key resorts of **Tsoútsouros**, **Keratókambos** and **Árvi** have the only easily reachable beaches with facilities and places to stay. All three are solely accessed by sheer asphalted roads.

There are a number of roads that run from Iráklion towards the south coast, but almost all the traffic seems to follow the route which heads slightly southwest, towards Festós and Mátala. Plenty of **buses** come this way too, leaving from the Pórta Haníon (Haniá Gate) terminal and heading for Festós, Mátala, Léndas, or Ayía Galíni via Timbáki. **Míres**, in the heart of the Messará plain, is the southern junction for switching between these various routes. The only other regular bus service across the island from Iráklion runs southeast towards **Ierápetra**, via Áno Viánnos and Mírtos.

Southwest from Iráklion

Crossing the island **southwest from Iráklion** is not, on the whole, the most exciting of drives: you leave the city westwards (through the Haniá Gate) and on the outskirts, turn south under the highway, following the signs to Festós and Mires (or Moíres as the roadsigns prefer). From the beginning, the road climbs, heading up to the island's spine through thoroughly business-like countryside. This is more of what traditionally was the Malevísi, or Malmsey, **wine-producing region**: though some wine is still made, most of the grapes you'll see now are table grapes, grown for eating rather than pressing. Highlights along this route include an ancient site at **Rhizenía**, as well as picturesque medieval **monasteries** at Veneráto and Zarós, the latter a particularly pleasant hill village surrounded by fine **walking country** and with its own lake nearby.

Ano Asítes and Ancient Rhizenía

With your own transport, you can follow a **scenic detour** to Ayía Varvára (see p.136) by taking a right turn 12km south of Iráklion along the route signed for Voutés, Áyios Míronas and Pírgou. This road skirts the eastern slopes of the valley and is a wonderful undulating ride through some pleasant out-of-the-way villages, mostly prosperous farming places. At **Ano Asítes**, a little beyond Pírgou, the **E4 Pan-European walking route** crosses the south end of the village (clearly marked on the *Harms Verlag* map), heading for the Psilorítis mountains.

On a sharp hairpin bend 3km south of here and 2km north of Priniás, are a pair of remarkable **rock-cut tombs** on the right, part of the cemetery of ancient **Rhizenía** which was laid out across the flat-topped hill visible across the valley to the east. Founded at the end of the Bronze Age, possibly by Minoans fleeing the Dorian invasion of the north coast, the settlement later flourished as a Greek city and the remains of two temples have been discovered on the acropolis. To visit the site, continue beyond the hairpin to reach a patch of waste ground with the **acropolis** and landmark whitewashed chapel of Áyios Pandeleímon on its northern tip, visible above. A track from here leads up to a **car park** with a sign indicating the archeological site. Climb the steps to an open gate into the site. Although not a lot remains of the ancient town, the sheer quantity of broken shards littering the ground is evidence that this was once a substantial conurbation. Nosing around, you'll come across the footings of ancient dwellings, with steps and porches clearly identifiable. When you eventually reach the chapel, you're greeted with tremendous **views** in all directions, especially north towards Iráklion and the sea, with the island of Dia beyond.

South from here, 3km beyond **Priniás**, the road rejoins the main route at Ayía Varvára.

Moní Palianí and Ayía Varvára

If you're taking the **direct route** to Ayía Varvára, then just beyond a turn-off for **Dáfnes** – a village noted for its wine – at the twenty-kilometre marker in the village of **Veneráto**, you'll have the option of a two-kilometre detour to the **Moní Palianí**, an ancient monastic foundation and now a convent. After heading left off the road (signed), keep your eyes peeled for another sign directing you right, after which the road crosses a valley before climbing gently towards the convent gates. Founded as early as the seventh century, the place is an oasis of tranquility where the nuns' cells surround a courtyard filled with oleanders, geraniums, vines and palms, with a thirteenth-century church at its centre. Unlike many religious communities in Crete, this one is a viable concern, supporting itself through sales of lace and embroidery, which the nuns will be only too pleased to show you in their small shop.

Ayía Varvára, 8km south of Veneráto, is the main village of this area, a place known as the **omphalos** (navel) **of Crete**. The great chapel-topped rock which you see as you arrive is held to be the very point around which the island balances, its centre of being. Not that this makes for any great tourist attraction. There are plenty of cafés and shops along the main street, but they cater mostly for local farmers in search of a bag of fertilizer or a tractor part.

Zarós and around

On the southern fringe of Ayía Varvára, a turning takes off to the west, following the flank of the Psilorítis range towards Kamáres (see p.271) and eventually on to Réthimnon or down to Ayía Galíni. This is a beautiful drive on a relatively good, empty road. **Zarós**, 17km west of Ayía Varvára, is a particularly attractive village famous for its spring waters, which are now bottled and sold all over Crete (the bottling plant is at the edge of the village on the Kamáres road). Well-appointed **hotels** are rare inland, making the excellent-value *Idi Hotel* (☎28940 31302, ⓦwww.votomos.com; ❹ including breakfast) a lovely place to get away from it all. It's worth asking for a room overlooking the extensive gardens at the rear if you think you're likely to be disturbed by the roaring spring directly outside the hotel. Something of a retreat for German visitors – note the wooden bench by the swimming pool "made by German soldiers" based here during the wartime occupation – the hotel has information on several scenic walks in the Psilorítis range, and the *Votomos* taverna next door makes a speciality of the trout which splash around in the trout farm behind. The hotel lies a kilometre out of the village and is signed from the centre. Zarós village itself has more pleasant accommodation, including the very friendly *Rooms Keramos* (☎ & ☎28940 31352; ❸ including breakfast), signed off the main street just before the post office, where en-suite balcony rooms include the proprietor Katerina's "special breakfast" feast of home-made cheese, *spanakópita* and honey. She will also provide meals if required. Another option is *Rent Rooms Hariklia* (☎28940 31787; ❶), near the crossroads where you enter the village, which has simple, clean rooms sharing a bath.

Zarós has more surprises in store if you continue along the road beyond the *Votamos* taverna near the *Idi Hotel*; you will pass another *Votamos* taverna and, 1km further on, arrive at the beautiful **Lake Votamos** overlooked by rocky heights. For sheer location, the lakeside's fish taverna – this time called *Limni Votamos* – has the edge on its eponymous competition, and the evenings here can be truly magical (providing you remember to bring your mosquito repellent).

Moní Áyios Nikólaos and Moní Vrondísi

Along the road west from Zarós towards Kamáres there are a number of ancient churches and monasteries, the first being **Moní Áyios Nikólaos**, 2km up a signed track on the right slightly west of Zarós – on foot, there's a shorter route from the village (ask at the supermarket). Not as picturesque as the Moní Vrondísi (see p.137), this monastery, set around a courtyard, is nevertheless very welcoming, and the elderly monks will usually enquire as to your nationality before offering some of their delicious home-made goat's cheese and coffee. To view the fourteenth-century paintings in the nearby church, visitors wearing shorts will need to cover their legs with an apron taken from a box at the entrance. There's also a great **gorge walk** to be had starting from here which leads above the monastery to the **cave of St Euthymios**, an old hermitage. You can continue to climb, on foot, for a further 2km to the entrance to the **Gorge of Zarós**, whose three-kilometre length leads to the E4 Pan-European walking route which crosses the island east to west. The gorge is negotiated by a path, including steps and bridges for the difficult bits, which takes much of the strain and ends at the chapel of Áyios Ioánnis, where the E4 is joined. The gorge is rarely visited, and your exertions will be rewarded by spectacular views of the Psilorítis range and – depending on the time of year – plenty of bird, plant and even animal life.

The fourteenth- to seventeenth-century **Moní Vrondísi**, above the road about 3km beyond the turn-off for Moní Áyios Nikólaos, is a gloriously peaceful foundation overlooking the Koútsoulidi valley. In a tranquil courtyard surrounded by monks' cells (mostly empty, as the community is now down to two) and fronted by two fig trees, is the monastery's simple limestone **church**. When you have found the monk or one of the guardians to open it, you'll be admitted to see some fine fourteenth-century **frescoes**, including a moving depiction of the Last Supper in the apse; it is unique on the island, as this position is normally reserved for the *Pantokrátor* (Christ). Also on display is a collection of icons taken from the nearby church of Áyios Fanoúrios. Vrondísi itself has given up the finest of its artworks, including the six great panels by Dhamaskinós, to the icon gallery of Ayía Ekateríni in Iráklion (see p.86). Even without them, though, this is a wonderful setting, with its giant plane trees for shade, cool water gushing from a fifteenth-century Venetian fountain, with figures of Adam and Eve in the elaborate Italian style by the entrance, and views towards Festós and the Gulf of Messará. Most days, the guardians will sell you their delicious *thimárisio* (thyme honey) gathered from hives in the nearby hills.

Áyios Fanoúrios, all that survives of the **Moní Valsamónero**, is reached by a track from the next village, **VORÍZIA**. This church houses some of the best **frescoes** in Crete, painted in the fifteenth century by Konstantínos Ríkos and depicting scenes from the life of the *Panayía* (Virgin Mary), images of various saints and a fine *Pantokrátor*. The guardian is on-site most weekdays (official opening hours 8am–3pm), but if not he can be found in the village.

The road continues 3km west of Vorízia to reach Kamáres and a possible ascent to the Kamáres Cave (see p.271).

The Messará plain

Continuing by the main road south from Ayía Varvára the way becomes genuinely mountainous, and after 7km you cross the Vourvoulítis Pass (650m) and the watershed of the Messará. The **Messará plain**, a long strip running east from the Gulf of Messará, is the largest and most important of Crete's fertile flatlands. Bounded to the north by the Psilorítis range and the lower hills which run right across the centre of the island, to the east by the Dhiktean mountains, and to the south by the narrow strip of the Asteroússia and Kófinas hills, it is watered, somewhat erratically, by the Yeropótamos. Heavy with olives, and increasingly with the fruit and vegetable cash crops that dominate the modern agricultural economy, the plain has always been a major centre of population and a mainstay of the island's economy. There is much evidence of this, not only at the ancient sites of **Górtys**, **Festós** and **Ayía Triádha**, but at a wealth of lesser, barely explored sites; today's villages exude prosperity, too, surrounded by neat and intensive cultivation.

As you descend to the plain by a series of long, looping curves, the main road heads west through **Áyii Dhéka**. A left turn eastwards takes you across far less travelled country (see p.158) and all the way to Ierápetra.

Áyii Dhéka

ÁYII DHÉKA, served by frequent buses from Iráklion, is the first village you reach on the Messará and the most interesting. The place takes its name from ten early Christians who were martyred here around 250 AD, at the behest of the emperor Decius. The **Holy Ten** are still among the most revered of Cretan saints: regarded as martyrs for Crete as much as Christianity – the first in a heroic line of Cretans who laid down their lives to oppose tyrannical occupation. On the west side of the village are two churches associated with them: the older, originally Byzantine **church** is signed in the village to the south of the through road. Inside, there's an icon portraying the martyrdom of the saints and – preserved in a glass case beneath – the stone block on which they are supposed to have been decapitated. The more modern **chapel** is signed on the main road to the west of the village, where a lane heads south to reach it. Beneath this is a crypt, visible from the exterior, where you can see six of their tombs. Other reminders of the village's ancient past include the Roman statues, pillars and odd blocks of masonry scavenged from Górtys which are much in evidence – reused in modern houses, propping up walls or simply lying about in yards.

The village is a pleasant place to break your journey, and in the centre there are a number of roadside cafés and tavernas for **food**, plus a few signs offering **rooms** – *Dimitris Taverna* (☎28920 31560; ❶) has both, with excellent-value en-suite a/c rooms with views on the first floor and a splendid new terrace (with view) at the rear.

Górtys

The remnants of the ancient city of **GÓRTYS** (known traditionally as Gortyn or Gortyna) are scattered across a large, fragmented area, covering a great deal more than the fenced site beside the road that most people see. The Italian Archeological Institute is currently carrying out extensive excavations which it hopes will eventually link the disparate elements of the ancient city. The best way to get some idea of its scale is to follow the path through the fields from the village. This heads out more or less parallel to the road, opposite the chapel of Áyii Dhéka; it's an easy walk of less than a kilometre to the main site, and along the way you'll skirt most of the major remains.

Settled from at least Minoan times, when it was a minor subject of Festós, Górtys began its rise to prominence under the Dorians. By the eighth century BC, it had become a significant commercial power and, in the third century BC, it finally conquered its former rulers at Festós. The society was a strictly regulated one, with a citizen class (presumably Dorian) ruling over a population of serfs (presumably "Minoan" Cretans) and slaves. Even for the citizens, life was as hard and orderly as it was in Classical Sparta.

Evidence of early Górtys has survived thanks largely to the remarkable **law code** found here and to a lesser extent through treaties known to have existed between the Górtys of this era and its rivals, notably Knossós. **Hannibal** fled to Górtys, where he stayed briefly after his defeat by Rome, while later, the city also helped the **Romans** to conquer Crete. It was during the ensuing Roman era that the city reached its apogee, from 67 BC onwards: as the seat of a Roman praetor, it was capital of the province of Crete and Cyrenaica, ruling not only the rest of the island but also much of Egypt and North Africa. It was here that **Christianity** first reached Crete, when St Titus was despatched by St Paul to convert the islanders, but after the **Saracen** invasion in the ninth century, when much of the city was razed, Górtys was abruptly abandoned.

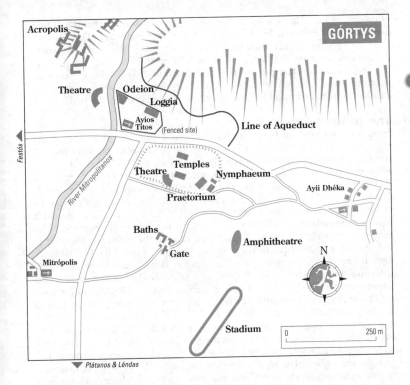

South of the road: the Roman city

In the fields en route to the site, it is the **Roman city** that dominates: this once stretched from the edges of Áyii Dhéka to the far banks of the Mitropolitanos (then known as the *Lethe*) and from the hills in the north as far south as the modern hamlet of Mitrópolis, where a small Roman basilica with good mosaics has been excavated. For most people, though, the ruins along the main path, with others seen standing in the distance, and the tantalizing prospect of what lies unexcavated beneath hummocks along the way, are quite enough. Individually, or in another setting, these might seem unimpressive, but with so many of them, abandoned as they are and all but ignored, they are amazing – you almost feel as if you've discovered them for yourself. The excavations to the south of the road are currently fenced off with no plans to allow public access, but when this happens Górtys is likely to become one of the major archeological sites on the island.

The **Praetorium** (the Roman governor's palace) has left the most extensive remains, a vast pile built originally in the second century, rebuilt in the fourth, and occupied as a monastery right up to the time of the Venetian conquest. New excavations in this area have revealed more impressive foundations, flights of steps, walls and marble columns once belonging to imposing buildings, and all indicating how much more still lies beneath the olive groves waiting to be discovered. Some trial trenches are now being opened among these groves and more ancient structures are being revealed. Within the same fenced area is a courtyard containing fountains and the **Nymphaeum**. Somewhere near here, too, was the terminus of the main aqueduct that brought water from the region of modern Zarós. About 100m to the west of the Praetorium area, you'll find the **Temple of Pythian Apollo**, which was the most important of the Roman city's temples, again later converted to a church, while the nearby **theatre**, though small, is very well preserved. Some 50m north of here are the substantial remains of the **Temple of Isis and Serapis**. If you wish to continue searching among the olive trees, you'll be able to find to the south of this zone a baths complex and traces of a yet unexcavated amphitheatre and stadium.

The fenced site

From the theatre or the Temple of Isis and Serapis, you can cut up to the road and cross to the parking area which marks the entrance to the main **fenced site** (daily 8am–7pm; €4) occupying the land to the north of the road. As you enter, it is the church of **Áyios Títos** which immediately grabs the eye, the back of its apse rising high in front of you. This is the only part of the church that has survived intact, but the shape of the whole structure is easy enough to make out. When it was built (around the end of the sixth century), it would have been the island's chief church, and it is the best remaining example of an early Christian church in the Aegean: you can see the extent to which it is still revered from the little shrine at the end of one of the aisles. The church's capitals bear the monogram of the sixth-century Byzantine emperor Justinian.

Beyond the church lies an area that was probably the ancient forum, and beyond this the most important relic of ancient Górtys, the **Odeion** (or covered theatre) and its **law code**. The law code – a series of engraved stones some 9m long and 3m high – dates from around 500 BC, but it presumably codified laws that were long established by custom and practice. It provides a fascinating insight into a period of which relatively little is otherwise known; the laws are written in a very rough Doric Cretan dialect and inscribed alternately left to right and right to left, so that the eyes can follow the writing continuously (a style known as *boustrophedon*, after the furrows of an ox plough). The code is not a complete system of law but rather a series of rulings on special cases, and reflects a strictly hierarchical society in which there were at least three distinct classes – citizens, serfs and slaves – each with quite separate rights and obligations. Five witnesses were needed to convict a free man of a crime, while one could convict a slave; the rape of a free man or woman carried a fine of a hundred *staters*, while the same offence committed against a serf was punishable by a mere five-*stater* fine. The laws also cover subjects such as property and inheritance rights, the status of children of mixed marriages (that is, between free people and serfs) and the control of trade.

The panels on which the law is inscribed are now incorporated into the round Odeion, which was erected under Trajan in around 100 AD and rebuilt in the third or fourth century (the brick terrace which protects the inscriptions from the elements is modern). The Odeion is just the latest incarnation of a series of buildings on this site in which the code has apparently always been preserved – obviously, this was a city which valued its own history. When they were discovered in the late nineteenth century, these ruins were entirely buried under eroded soil washed down from the hills behind.

In a small pavilion backing onto the site's **cafeteria** there's an impressive collection of **statuary**, demonstrating the high standard of work being achieved here during the city's halcyon days.

West of the river: the acropolis

Beside the fenced site, the **river** runs by an abandoned medieval mill and on the far bank you can see a much larger **theatre**, in rather poor repair, set against the hillside. In Roman times, the river ran through a culvert here and you could have walked straight across; nowadays, you have to go back to the road-bridge to explore this area.

The guardians at the site will provide information on exploring the outlying areas, and will give directions to the easiest path up to the **acropolis** on the hilltop above the river. Hardly anyone makes the hike up there, shying away from such a stiff climb in the heat, but the ruins are surprisingly impressive, with Roman defensive **walls** and a building known as the *kástro* (though apparently not a castle) still standing to a height of six metres in places. The lesser remains are among the earliest on the site and include scant relics of a Greek **temple** that was later converted to a church. From this hilltop vantage point, you also get a fine overview of the layout of Górtys and the ongoing excavations, and it's possible to trace the line of the aqueducts coming in from the north.

With **your own transport**, you can reach the acropolis by following the road across the river towards Míres and Festós, taking a fork on the right signed "to the Acropolis of Górtys". This road goes through the village of **Ambeloúzos**, where you should take a right turn immediately after the village sign. The route then climbs beyond and you soon need to make a right turn along a road signed to Apomarmá and Gérgeri. Soon, a sign on the right will alert you to the acropolis, visible off to the right and a five-minute walk away uphill.

Míres

MÍRES, a bustling farming town 6km west of Górtys, is the transport centre for the area. The town's lively radio station, Radio Míres, is located near the bus station, and supplies music and news to the whole of the Messará. **Buses** to Léndas and Mátala on the coast, very occasionally to Zarós and Kamáres in the mountains, to Timbáki and on to Ayía Galíni or Réthimnon, and even once a day through the Amári Valley to Réthimnon, all depart from the "bus station" on the main street, actually a rather ramshackle bar. Buses bound for Festós head directly to the site after a stop here to pick up and drop off passengers, so there's usually no need to change. Míres could hardly be described as attractive, but as a centre for local commerce as well as passing tourists it at least has plenty of life, with scores of places to eat and drink, the only bank for miles around and cheap **rooms** that are easy to find, if you happen to be stranded between buses. The *Hotel Olympic* (☎28920 22777; ❶) is characterless but clean and economical with en-suite rooms; among a few places to eat nearby there's *Pizzeria Bambola*, where the chef leaves pizzas to cook in the oven while he leaps aboard a powerful Honda to deliver telephone orders. A useful **Internet** café, *Net Escape*, is close to the bus station on the main street. On Saturday mornings, the town is enlivened by a busy **market**.

Three kilometres beyond Míres, a turning on the right leads to the **Moní Kaliviani**, an impressive monastic complex which today serves as an orphanage, boarding school and sanatorium. Inside the gates, the buildings fronting the central avenue have cascades of magenta bougainvillea in summer, and everywhere there are plants sprouting more blooms. Behind the modern church there is a tiny fourteenth-century **chapel**, dedicated to the Panayía Kalivianís, with ancient frescoes. The nuns support themselves by weaving, embroidery and making handicrafts, which they sell at their store opposite the church.

Festós

In a wonderfully scenic location on a ridge at the eastern end of the Messará plain with fine views towards the encircling mountains, the palace of **FESTÓS** (daily 8am–7pm; €4) and its neighbouring "summer palace", the charming **Ayía Triádha** (see p.145), are Minoan sites ranking second only to Knossós on the island.

Bus services to Festós are excellent, with some nine a day (fewer on Sun) from Iráklion (the last heads back there just before the site closes). Five of these continue to Mátala, and there are also services direct to Ayía Galíni. All buses stop right by the Festós parking area. If you're arriving in the afternoon, plan to visit Ayía Triádha first, as it closes early. The **Tourist Pavilion** at Festós serves drinks and food in addition to selling the usual postcards, books and souvenirs. There are **rooms** to be found in the nearby villages of Vóri and Áyios Ioánnis (see p.147), the latter also making an ideal **lunch stop** after or between sites. There are more places offering accommodation along the road towards Mátala or, alternatively, you should be able to find something in the first larger place you strike in almost any direction – Míres, Timbáki or Pitsídhia.

Some history

The palace of **Festós** was excavated by Federico Halbherr (also responsible for the early work on Górtys) at almost exactly the same time as Evans was working at Knossós. The style of the excavations, however, could hardly have been more different. Here, reconstruction has been kept to an absolute minimum, to

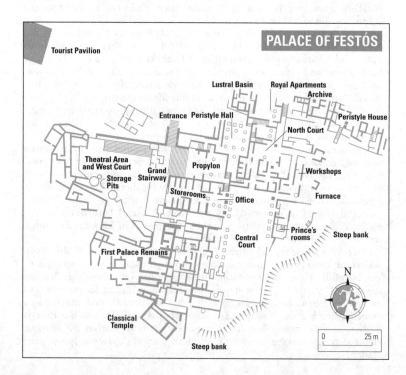

PALACE OF FESTÓS

Tourist Pavilion

Lustral Basin
Royal Apartments
Archive

Entrance Peristyle Hall
Peristyle House

North Court

Theatral Area
and West Court
Grand Stairway
Propylon
Workshops

Storage Pits

Storerooms
Office
Furnace

Central Court
Prince's rooms
Steep bank

First Palace Remains

Classical Temple

N

0   25 m

Steep bank

the approval of most traditional archeologists: it's all bare foundations, and walls that scarcely rise above ground level.

As at Knossós, most of what survives is what the excavators termed the **Second Palace**, rebuilt after its destruction around 1700 BC and occupied until ca.1450 BC. But at Festós, the first palace was used as a foundation for the second, and much of its well-preserved floor plan has been uncovered by the excavations. Fascinating as these superimposed buildings are for the experts, they make Festós extremely confusing for more casual visitors to interpret. Combined with a distinct lack of elaboration, at least in the decoration of the palace, this adds up to considerable disappointment for many. Since much of the site is also fenced off, it becomes almost impossible to get any sense of the place as it once was.

We do know, however, that only Knossós was more important, and although there are major differences between Festós and the other palaces, these are in the end outweighed by the multitude of similarities. The rooms are set about a great central courtyard, with an external court on the west side and a theatral area north of this; the domestic apartments are, as usual, slightly apart from the public and formal ones; there are the same lines of storage magazines and pits for grain; and on the east side are workshops for the palace craftsmen. While no traces of frescoes were found, this doesn't imply that the palace wasn't luxurious: the materials (marble, alabaster, gypsum) were of the highest quality, there were sophisticated drainage and bathing facilities, and remains suggest a large and airy dining hall on the upper floors overlooking the court. Bear in mind, as you explore, that part of the palace is missing: there must have been more outbuildings on the south side of the site, where erosion has worn away the edge of the ridge and a corner of the central court itself has collapsed.

Entering the site: the West Court and Grand Stairway

You enter the palace from above, down steps leading past a **Tourist Pavilion** (which has a bookshop and cafeteria) and approaching the northwest corner of the complex through the Upper Court.

Step down first into the **West Court** and integral **Theatral Area**. As at Knossós, there are raised walkways leading across the courtyard, and here one of them runs right up the steps that form the seats of the Theatral Area (accorded this title by archeologists who supposed it was used for viewing some kind of performance or spectacle). On the west side of the court are circular walled pits, probably for storing grain. The West Court itself is a rare survival from the original palace; the main walkway leads not up the stairs into the new palace but past them and into the entrance to the old palace. From there, much of the facade of the old palace can be seen as a low wall in front of the Grand Stairway which leads into the newer building. When the palace stood, of course, this would not have been apparent; then, the court was filled with rubble and levelled (though not paved) at the height of the bottom step of the stairway.

The **Grand Stairway** was a fitting approach to Festós, a superbly engineered flight of twelve shallow stone steps, 14m wide. Some of the steps are actually carved from the solid rock of the hill, and each is slightly convex in order to improve the visual impact. This remarkable architectural innovation anticipated similar subtleties of the Parthenon at Athens by twelve centuries. The entrance facade was no doubt equally impressive – you can still see the base of the pillar which supported the centre of the doorway – but it's hard to imagine from what actually survives. Once inside, the first few rooms seem somewhat cramped: this may have been deliberate, either for security purposes, to prevent a sudden rush or as a ploy to enhance the larger, lighter spaces beyond. At the end would have been a blank wall, open to the sky, and a small door to the right which led out onto stairs down towards the Central Court. Standing in the entrance area now, you can look down over the **storerooms**, and going down the stairs, you can get closer to them through a larger room that once served as an office. Exposed here is a storeroom from the old palace, with a giant jar still in place and another barred cellar to the right lined with more amphorae. At the far end, more *píthoi* stand in a room apparently used to store olive oil or other liquids; there's a stool to stand on while reaching in and a basin to catch spillage, while the whole floor slopes towards a hole in which slops would have collected.

The Central Court and Royal Apartments

From the stores "office", quite an elaborate room, you pass into the **Central Court**, which is by far the most atmospheric area of the palace. In this great paved court, with its scintillating **views**, there is a rare sense of Festós as it must have once been. Look north from here in the direction of the Psilorítis range and you can make out a black smudge to the right of a saddle between the two peaks. This marks the entrance to the Kamáres Cave (see p.271), a shrine sacred to the Minoans and the source of the great hoard of elaborate Kamáres ware pottery now in the Iráklion Archeological Museum. Even without the views – which would have been blocked by the two storeys to either side when the palace was standing – the courtyard remains impressive. Its north end, in particular, is positively and unusually grand: the doorway, flanked by half-columns and niches (possibly for sentries) covered in painted plaster, can be plainly made out. To the left as you face this are a couple of *píthoi* (left there by the excavators) and a stepped stone that some claim was an altar, or perhaps a block from which athletes would jump onto bulls. The equally unprovable counter-theory has it, more prosaically, as a base for a flowerpot.

Along each of the lengthy sides of the courtyard ran a covered **portico** or verandah, the bases of whose supports are still visible. In the southwest corner are various rooms which probably had religious functions; beyond these, and hard to distinguish from them, are parts of the old palace which are mostly fenced off. Also here, right at the edge of the site, are the remains of a **Greek temple** of the Classical era, evidence that the site was occupied long after the Minoans and the destruction of the palace.

Heading up through the grand north door – notice the holes for door pivots and the guardroom just inside – a corridor leads through the **North Court** toward the **Royal Apartments**. These have been covered and shut off to prevent damage from people walking through, and it's hard to see a great deal of the queen's rooms, or the king's rooms behind them. Above the king's quarters is a large **Peristyle Hall**, a colonnaded courtyard much like a cloister, open in the centre. On the north side, this courtyard was open to take in the view of Psilorítis: it must have been a beautiful place, and perhaps also one of some religious significance. Staircases linked the hall directly with the Royal Apartments (and the **lustral basin** on the north edge of the king's rooms); nowadays it's easier to approach from the palace entrance, turning left up the stairs from the Propylon.

Palace dependencies

Continuing past the royal quarters on the other side, you come to the dependent buildings on the northeast flank of the palace, which almost certainly predate much of the palace itself. Among the first of these is the so-called **Archive**, where the famous **Festós Disc** (see p.89) was discovered in one of a row of mudbrick boxes. A little further on is the **Peristyle House**, probably a private home, with an enclosed yard similar in design to the Peristyle Hall. From here, stairs lead back down to the level of the Central Court, into the area of the palace **workshops**. In the centre of another large courtyard are the remains of a furnace, probably used for metalworking or as a kiln. The small rooms roundabout were the workshops, perhaps even the homes, of the craftsmen. As you walk back to the central court, another suite of rooms – usually described as the **Prince's Rooms** – lies on your left, boasting its own small peristyle hall.

Ayía Triádha

AYÍA TRIÁDHA (daily May–Sept 10am–4.30pm; Oct–April 8.30am–3pm; €3) lies about 3km west of Festós on the far side of the hill, an easy drive or a walk of about 45 minutes by a well-signed road around the south slope. The site – discovered and excavated at the turn of the twentieth century by the Italian School under Federico Halbherr, who is now commemorated by a bas-relief wall plaque next to the ticket office – remains something of an enigma. Nothing exists to compare it with, in what is known of Minoan Crete, nor does it appear in any records; even the name has had to be borrowed from a nearby chapel.

AYÍA TRIÁDHA

To Tombs

Town Area

Market

Fresco Room

Stairs to Ramp

Ramp

Queen's Room

Chambers with Hall over

Courtyard

Áyios Yeóryios

Storerooms

Entrance

Shrine

N

0   25 m

In sharp contrast with unadorned Festós, however, Ayía Triádha has provided some of the most delicate Minoan **artworks** found. From this site came the three vases of carved black steatite – the "Harvesters Vase", the "Boxer Vase" and the "Chieftain Cup" – on display in the Iráklion Archeological Museum (see p.90), as well as some of the finest works in the Fresco Hall there, including the unique painted sarcophagus. Yet again, the ruins enjoy a magnificent hillside location, looking out over the Gulf of Messará. The modern view takes in the coastal plain, with Timbáki airstrip in the foreground (built by the Germans during the war, with its runways now more often used for motor races), but in Minoan times the sea would have come right up to the base of the hill. Despite this beauty and wealth, Ayía Triádha is clearly not a construction on the same scale as the great palaces: the most commonly accepted explanation is that it was some kind of royal villa or summer retreat, but it may equally have been the home of an important prince or noble, or a building of special ceremonial significance.

You approach the site from the **car park** above it. Predictably, the remains, in which buildings of several eras are jumbled, are confused and confusing. This matters much less here, however, for it is the atmosphere of Ayía Triádha that really makes the place – the absence of crowds, the beauty of the surroundings and the human scale of the villa, with its multitude of little stairways and paved corridors between rooms.

The site

To your left as you climb down are the bare ruins of a Minoan house older than most of the other remains (the villa was broadly contemporary with the new palace at Festós), and beyond them a **shrine** which contained a frescoed floor and walls now on show in the Iráklion Archeological Museum. If you keep to the higher ground here, you come into the courtyard of the villa, perhaps the best place to get an impression of its overall layout. The L-shaped building enclosed the courtyard only on its north and west sides, and the north side is further muddled by a much later hall – apparently a Mycenaean megaron – built over it. To the south of the courtyard is the early fourteenth-century chapel of **Áyios Yeóryios** (key available from the ticket office), in which there are fragments of some fine frescoes.

The **Royal Villa** now lies mostly below the level of the courtyard, but in Minoan times it would not have appeared this way: the builders made use of the natural slope to create a split-level construction, and entrances from the court would have led directly into upper levels above those you see today. The finest of the rooms were those in the corner of the "L", looking out over the sea; here, the best of the frescoes were found, including that of the famous stalking cat – now preserved in the Iráklion Archeological Museum. The quality of workmanship can still be appreciated in these chambers with their alabaster-lined walls and gypsum floors and benches. Beside them to the south is a small group of storerooms with a number of *píthoi* still in place; some bear scorch marks from the great fire which destroyed the palace about 1450 BC. From the hall and terrace out front, you can walk around the **ramp** that runs beneath the north side of the villa. The Italian excavators named this the *Rampa al Mare*, and it seems that it would have once run down to the sea.

Follow it the other way instead and you can head down to the lower part of the site, the **town area**. By far the most striking aspect of this is the **market**, a row of stores which are once again unique in Minoan architecture. The stores, identically sized and fronted by a covered portico, run in a line down the hill; in front of them is an open space and, across that, the houses of the town. There's only one problem with the easily conjured image of the Minoan populace milling around the market while their rulers looked benignly on from above: this area apparently dates only from the declining years of the Minoan culture and is contemporary not with the villa, but with the megaron erected over it. Beyond the stores (and outside the fence) lies the **Cemetery**, where remains of two *thólos* tombs and many other graves were found, including the one containing the Ayía Triádha sarcophagus.

Around Festós

Continuing **west** from Festós towards Ayía Galíni or Réthimnon, the final stretch of the Messará plain, with its acres of polythene greenhouses and burgeoning concrete sprawl, must be among the ugliest places in Crete. **Timbáki** may also be the island's drabbest town. It's a sizeable place, which means there are cafés and restaurants along the main street, stores and banks, and even a couple of hotels, but there's no reason to stay longer than you have to. Just beyond, a turning leads to **Kókkinos Pírgos** on the coast. Here, too, plastic and concrete are the overwhelming images, and the place is barely redeemed by a plentiful supply of cheap **rooms** and the lack of crowds on its none-too-beautiful beach. The more inviting beaches in this area are in and around the developed resort of **Mátala**, south of Festós (see p.149).

Inland: Vóri and the Museum of Cretan Ethnology

The road **north** from Festós confirms the rule that – as is often the way on Crete – all you have to do is turn off the main road to escape into the scenic back country away from urban (and rural) blights. **Vóri** lies only a kilometre north of the road leading to Festós and, despite being quite a big place, is a pleasant working village almost entirely off the beaten track. It even has places offering **rooms**, including the inviting *Pension Margit* (☎28920 91539; ❷), with en-suite rooms close to the pleasant village square. A couple of *kafenía* on the square itself serve up *mezedhés*. That some tourists do come here is largely due to the outstanding **Museum of Cretan Ethnology** (April–Oct daily 10am–6pm; €3), advertised by large signs along the main road. Hidden behind the church, it's worth seeking out for a comprehensive survey of traditional country life in Crete, and compares favourably with the equivalent museum in Réthimnon; the museum won a special commendation in the European Museum of the Year award in 1992. The collection itself is a miscellany of agricultural implements, building tools and materials, domestic utensils, furniture, basketware, pottery, musical instruments, weaving and embroidery, all well labelled and fascinating. There are sections on the production of olive oil, winemaking and the distillation of *raki*, as well as a display of the myriad herbs and medicinal plants sought out by Cretans since ancient times. A collection of baskets is especially interesting, with 25 different designs reflecting their various uses as beehives, eel traps, cheese-drainers, animal muzzles and snail containers. A **new section** on the first floor has artefacts illustrating more aspects of bygone Cretan daily life, including travel and transport, ceramics, and a display of photographs documenting the island's ordeal during World War II.

If you're heading for the Amári Valley and Réthimnon, you can spurn the main road and take a lovely, climbing drive on the new sealed road up through Kalohorafítis and Grigoría to **Kamáres** (see p.271).

South to Mátala

The road **south** from Festós passes the Ayía Triádha turn-off and soon approaches the village of **ÁYIOS IOÁNNIS**. Just before the village is the picturesque *Taverna Ayios Ioannis* on the main road, which serves excellent **food** on tables under a shady vine trellis; *kounéli*, the house speciality of char-coal-grilled rabbit, is recommended, and the lamb is tasty, too, but you should be aware that at busy times service tends to be slow. The taverna also has simple economical **rooms** (☎28920 42006; ❶) in a garden at the rear.

Be sure to take in the tiny, drum-domed church of **Áyios Pávlos**, 500m beyond the taverna in a walled cemetery on the left side of the road close to a junction. Encircled by cypresses, this delightful church is one of the oldest on the island with sections dating from the pre-Christian era, and perhaps part of a Roman shrine to a water deity focused on the **well** at the back of the grave-yard. The area to the rear of the church is the most ancient, with the dome probably added in the fourteenth century and the narthex, or porch – with its Venetian pointed arches – in the sixteenth. Inside (the church is normally left open), some interesting **frescoes** are dated by a frieze to 1303 and have images of the Evangelists Matthew and Luke, as well as a lurid representation of the punishments of Hell with souls being molested by serpents. This is one of the very few churches on Crete dedicated to St Paul, who was none too taken with the islanders, describing them in one of his epistles as "liars, evil beasts and lazy gluttons". To the side of the church, a charnel house contains the (visible) bones of corpses removed from the nearby tombs after a period of time to "free up" space.

The main road continues for a couple of kilometres beyond Áyios Pávlos and takes a right at a junction to bring you through Pitsídhia (see p.151) and, 7km beyond the junction, Mátala (see p.149).

Kamilári

Almost opposite the Áyios Pávlos church, a road heads west for 3km through olive groves to the attractive country hill village of **Kamilári** where, just over a kilometre beyond, you can see an early **Minoan tomb**, one of the oldest and best-preserved in Crete. To reach the tomb, just after entering the village turn right at a junction, just beyond two accommodation places. The route is indi-cated by a blue sign. Shortly after this, veer left at a fork, later turning right at another sign. A series of further signs will lead you through olive groves to the fenced hilltop site. Dating from about 1900 BC, the tomb was a circular struc-ture with a large dome, inside which communal burials took place, whilst cult rituals were carried out in adjoining rooms. The stone walls still stand two metres high in parts; important clay models depicting worship at a shrine and a circular group of dancers unearthed here are now in the Iráklion Archeological Museum. Incidentally, the design of these tombs is strikingly similar to tombs being constructed in southern Spain around the same time, but a link has not yet been proved.

There are a number of tempting **rooms** options in Kamilári, and the village would make an attractive alternative base to staying on the coast in order to explore nearby archeological sites. Near the junction as you enter the village, *Studios Pelekanos* (☎28920 42151, ✉pelekanos@pathfinder.gr; ❷) has very good-value studio rooms with a/c and kitchenette, and a little further uphill towards the upper village, the very welcoming *Apartments Ambeliotisa* (☎ & ℻ 28920 42690, ⊕www.southerncrete.gr/ambeliotisa; ❸) has superb a/c studio rooms and apartments in and around a house in its own grounds. The owner here hires out **mountain bikes**, clients have access to the **Internet** and he will collect guests from the bus stop at the Festós site (ring ahead to let him know which bus you are travelling on). In the upper village, the elegant *Pension Festias* (☎28920 42819, ⊕www.southerncrete.gr/festias; ❹) has en-suite rooms with terrace and fridge around a courtyard. The proprietor also has information on some villas to rent nearby with garden and pool. The cheapest rooms in the upper village are at *Pension Anna* (T 28920 52346; ❷), just off the main square, which has en-suite rooms with kitchenette. Also in the upper village, a decent **bar** for breakfasts, light lunches and *mezedhés* – and cocktails, as the evening progresses – is *Yassou*, close to the main square. For more elaborate **food**, the upper village has a number of tavernas, including *Acropolis*, which is a cut above the rest with a good wine list and an attractive small terrace.

The road continues west from Kamilári for 3km to Kalamáki (see p.151), another accommodation option, on the coast.

Mátala and around

MÁTALA has much the best known of the **beaches** in the south of Iráklion province, and was once one of the chief ports of Górtys. You may still meet people who will assure you that, with its cave-dwelling hippy community, this is *the* travellers' beach on Crete, but that's now history – and bears about as much relation to modern reality as Mátala's role in legend as the place where Zeus swam ashore in the guise of a bull with Europa on his back. The entry to the village should prepare you for what to expect: a couple of kilometres of new hotels, "Welcome to Mátala" signs and extensive car-parking areas line the roadsides all the way into town. It does get better, and development is still relatively small-scale, but the town never feels anything other than touristy: tour-bus arrivals in the afternoon take up every inch of sand, and prices (for rooms especially) are relatively high. On the plus side, Mátala boasts a spectacular **beach**: a curving swathe of sand tucked under the cliff in which you'll find the notorious **caves**; the crowds are relatively young, the atmosphere is boisterous and you'll never be short of somewhere to enjoy a cocktail at sunset.

The caves started it all. Nobody knows quite who started the caves, which are entirely artificial, but it seems likely that they were first hollowed out as Roman or early Christian **tombs**: they have since been so often reused and added to that it is virtually impossible to tell. The cliff in which they are carved, an outcrop of compacted sand, is soft enough to allow surprisingly elaborate decor: some caves have carved windows and doorways as well as built-in benches or beds (which may originally have been grave slabs), while others are mere scooped-out hollows. Local people inhabited the caves, on and off, for centuries, and during the war, they made a handy munitions dump, but it was in the 1960s that they really became famous, attracting a large and semi-permanent foreign community. Name a famous hippy, and there'll be someone who'll claim that they lived here, too – the most frequently mentioned are Cat Stevens, Bob Dylan and Joni Mitchell ("they're playin' that scratchy rock and roll beneath the Matala moon" crooned the latter on her 1970s album, *Blue*). It has, however, been a very long time since the caves were cleared, and nowadays they're a fenced-off **archeological site** (April–Sept daily 10am–7pm; €2), open by day to visitors but searched by the police every night.

The beach below the caves is the focus for most of the town's activity, and during the day everyone hangs out either on the sand or in the tavernas overlooking it. The swimming is great – if surprisingly rough when the wind blows – with gently shelving sand in the centre, underwater remains of the Roman port around the base of the rocks on both sides (watch out for sea urchins), and multicoloured fish everywhere. However, you should be aware that **dangerous**

currents are prevalent on this stretch of coast and red warning flags – which should be heeded – are posted when swimming is unsafe.

If the crowds on this town beach get too much, you can head south along "Hotels and Rent Rooms" street (see below) towards the hill, where a track becomes obvious; it can be quite hard going in parts, climbing over the rocks behind town, and you may end up scrambling over loose scree on the way down, but after about twenty minutes you'll reach another excellent stretch of sand known locally as **Red Beach**, which is usually half-empty. It has curious dark reddish-brown sand and wonderfully clear water. On the way, you pass more caves, many of which are inhabited through the summer; indeed, when you know where to look, it turns out that there are a number of cave dwellings around, all some way from the village, with the exact whereabouts of the better ones a closely guarded secret.

Practicalities

For all practical purposes, Mátala consists of a single street, the continuation of the main road into town as it curves round behind the beach. The market and many of the places to eat lie to the right, between the road and the beach, and the "old town", such as it is, is crammed against the rocks to the left. Almost every other practical need is easily taken care of: **car** and **bike rental** and **currency exchange** are all around the main square or up the main street, and there are also a couple of **travel agents**, among which Monza (☎28920 45757) is reliable and where you'll get a ten-percent discount on car, motorbike and scooter hire with this guide. The kiosk at the entrance to the village (to the left, opposite the turn-off for the main car park) with a blue "ELTA" sign acts as a **post office** and sells phonecards which can be used at the numerous public phone booths around the centre. A helpful source of **information** is the **bookshop** Kadianakis, near the main square, which stocks foreign newspapers and a selection of English fiction. **Internet** access is possible at *Cafe Zafiria*, next door to here, or at the nearby *Kafeneío* (see p.151). The covered **market** still has a couple of authentic stalls selling fruit and veg, but these are rapidly being displaced by souvenir stores, embroidery and beachwear stalls, and general tat. There are **boat trips** from the harbour (in addition to all the usual bus excursions on offer at the travel agents) – a taxi service to Red Beach and Kommós, and twice-weekly trips to Ayía Galíni and Préveli.

Finding a **room** should be no problem with so many alternatives, and travel agencies should be able to help if you can't face the trawl. Out of season, you may well be in a position to bargain, but Mátala does have a very long season: it's a popular Easter destination for Greek families. The most attractive place to stay is undoubtedly in the old town on one of the little backstreets, but there are very few places here. More realistic, and still right at the centre of things, is to take the little street to the left immediately after the reliable *Hotel Zafiria* (☎28920 45112, ✆info@zafiria-matala.com; ❹ including breakfast), along a road signed "Hotels and Rent Rooms", which is almost entirely lined with purpose-built accommodation places. Among the best of these is *Hotel Nikos* (☎28920 45375, ⓦwww.kreta-inside.com; ❸), with en-suite rooms (some a/c for €6 extra) around a charming plant-filled courtyard; try asking the eponymous proprietor for the cheaper rooms 25 and 26, which are furnished more simply. *Hotel Sofia* (☎28920 45134, ☎28920 45743; ❸) is also good with some a/c rooms with fridge, although rooms facing towards the town square can be very noisy. Quieter and mostly cheaper alternatives nearby include *Mátala View* (☎28920 45114, ⓦwww.c-v.net/hotel/matala/matalaview; ❷) for rooms with kitchenette, balcony and fans, as well as some larger apartments; *Iliaki* (℡28920 45110; ❷); the pleasant and modern *Fantastik* (℡28920 45362, Ⅎ28920 45492; ❷), offering balcony en-suite a/c rooms with fridge; and *Silvia* (℡28920 45127; ❷). There's a **campsite** above the beach car park, *Matala Camping* (℡28920 45340), which has shady tamarisk trees and is fine if you like camping on sand. If you don't mind being further from the beach, then *Camping Kommos* (℡28920 45596) is a better bet, with an on-site swimming pool and taverna, and a nearby stop for buses; it's located off the seaward side of the road (signed) roughly halfway between Pitsídhia and Mátala.

Eating, drinking and nightlife

Finding something to **eat** presents no difficulties at all. Tavernas with generally very similar menus fringe the bay, with sufficient competition to keep prices reasonable. The smallest and least pretentious is the *Skala* fish taverna, with sea-fresh fish and superb views across to the cliffs. It is also the furthest away, and is approached through the bar *Karnagio* – be certain of your footing across the cliffs, especially on the way back. *Kimata* and *Taverna Eleni* are other reliable possibilities near the beach. In town, *Corali* and *Antonis*, around the square, are good, while *Minos Palace* is another decent taverna, close to the *Hotel Zafiria*. Almost opposite the same hotel, *Kafeneio* is a stylish bar which makes a pleasant breakfast venue, does cocktails in the evening and offers **Internet** access in an upstairs gallery. Takeaway food and ingredients for picnics can be found in the stalls of the "market".

The chief **entertainment** in the evening is watching the invariably spectacular sunset; almost every bar and restaurant has a west-facing terrace. There's a solitary **disco**, *Kandari*, and nightlife is generally low-key. The two most popular music bars are the *Marinero* and *Tommy's Music Bar* above it, at the southern end of the bay, while *Cafe Kantari*, on the square, is another place where people gather after dark.

Around Mátala

An alternative base to Mátala, and a good way of saving some money and also enjoying rather more peace, is to stay at **Pitsídhia**, which sprawls around the main road about 5km inland. This is already a well-used option, – so don't expect an unspoilt village – and it's not quite as cheap as you might anticipate, but there are plenty of rooms, lively places to eat and an affable young international crowd.

Kalamáki, which is right on the beach about 5km west of Pitsídhia, is another possibility, best approached via the paved road from Kamilári (see p.148) – although any of the dusty tracks heading west from Pitsídhia find their way to the coast eventually. At the moment, Kalamáki seems unfinished, a dusty place caught halfway between being a beach with a few tavernas on it and a full-blown resort, but there is plenty of accommodation, as well as a "square" with a couple of **bike rental** companies, a bakery, a **minimarket** selling food items and foreign press, and a branch of Monza Travel (℡28920 45692), which does **car and scooter hire**, changes money, gives information and has a **bookshop** (stocking some English editions) attached. Add a number of places to eat, and a long, empty, windswept beach, and that's about the sum of it. Around the main square, a number of **rooms** possibilities include the good-value *Rooms Psiloritis* (℡28920 45693, Ⅎ28920 45249; ❷), a rambling place with lots of sea-view balcony rooms with bath and fridge and, around the corner on the seaward side, the pricier *Rooms Nefeli* (℡28920 45211; ❸),

△ Boats on Mátala beach

offering more sea-view a/c en-suite rooms with kitchenette. Going slightly upmarket, *Studios Dimitra* (☎28920 45510, ⓦwww.studiosdimitra.com; ❸), along the seafront, has excellent a/c studios with kitchenette, TV and sea view and, further along at the south end of the beach, the great value *Hotel Alexander* (☎28920 45195, ⓔalexander@mir.forthnet.gr; ❷) has a/c balcony rooms with fridge overlooking the beach, plus its own restaurant; it offers even cheaper off-season deals when things are slack. On the way into the village, the *Hotel Philharmonie* (☎28920 45797, ⓦwww.oleander.gr; ❸ including breakfast) is a bright new place with a/c rooms and an excellent garden pool behind. For **food**, the pick of the seafront tavernas are *Avra* at the northern end and, at the southern end, *Taverna Yiorgos Aristides*, both serving meat and fish dishes.

Kommós

At the southern end of the long beach that starts in Kalamáki lies the archeological site of ancient **Kommós** (see below for access details), a Minoan harbour town which was probably the main port for Festós and Ayía Triádha. The northwesterly winds that often lash the beach and fill the sea with white-caps here would suggest that this was not the best place for a harbour, but about 350m offshore an ancient reef (still visible on calmer days) ensured tranquil waters on its leeward side, enabling vessels to dock without problems. The sea level would also have been a couple of metres lower in Minoan times, making the reef a far more substantial bulwark. The site can also be approached from 1km west of Pitsídhia by a track signed "to *Camping Kommos*" on the right.

Sir Arthur Evans was the first to report signs of Minoan occupation here, but real excavation started only twenty years ago when Joseph Shaw began digging, funded by the American School of Classical Studies. The work carried out in the seasons since then has made it clear that Kommós is destined to become a major site of the future. Meanwhile, the excavations are fenced off and not yet officially open to visitors; the site was supposed to open to the public in 2002 (when gangways and a pay booth were put in place) but financial constraints prevented this. However, in July and August, it's possible to get the key to the site by visiting the site excavation centre in Pitsídhia (see p.151). In the centre of the village, locate the *Acropolis Taverna* and, 50m up a narrow lane opposite this, a blue gate on the right bears the sign Kommós Excavations House. The archeologists here will give you the key, a site map and a brief history of Kommós in return for the deposit of a passport. Outside this period, it is still possible to get a good look at the excavations from behind the fence.

There are three main **excavation areas**, to the north, centre and south, none of them more than a stone's throw behind the beach. It is thought that the zones surrounding the site proper will eventually yield evidence of occupation. The **northern area**, on a low hill close to the sea, contains domestic dwellings, among which is a large house (on the south side) with a paved court and a limestone winepress. The **central group** – behind a retaining wall to prevent subsidence – has houses from the New Palace era, with well-preserved walls and evidence, in the fallen limestone slabs, of the earthquake of around 1700 BC which caused much destruction here. A rich haul of intact pottery was found in this area, much of it in the brightly painted Kamáres style.

The most remarkable finds to date, however, came in the **southern sector** where what you see is partly confused by being overlaid by a Classical Greek sanctuary. Minoan remains here include a fine stretch of **limestone roadway**, 3m wide and more than 60m long, heading away inland, no doubt towards Ayía Triádha and Festós. The road is rutted from the passage of ox-drawn carts and would also have been pounded by the feet of countless Minoan mariners. Note the drainage channel on its northern side. To the south of the road, one building contains the longest stretch of **Minoan wall** on the island: over 50m of dressed stone. Some of the cut blocks in this wall (many well over three metres in length) are among the largest found in Minoan Crete. The function of this enormous building isn't known but it could conceivably have been a palace, or it may have had a storage purpose connected with the port. Some of the nearby dwellings to the north of the roadway were also of elaborate construction, and a substantial number of fresco fragments unearthed by the excavators hint at sumptuous interior decorations. Just south of here was another large building (now partly overlaid by a later Greek structure – probably a warehouse), 30m long and 35m wide, divided into five sections with its seaward end open to the sea. This was a shipshed or **dry dock** where vessels were stored out of the water during the winter (or non-sailing) season.

An interesting **temple** lies to the western side of this area, nearest the sea. Originally an early tenth-century BC Dorian temple – one of the earliest in the whole of Greece – it was replaced by a later one apparently devoted to a pillar cult similar to that of the Phoenicians, who had founded a trading empire based upon modern Lebanon. The excavators think that the Phoenicians may have erected the temple here for use by their sailors, who would have made frequent trading missions to Kommós. The other remains and altars in this area date from the Hellenistic period, when the site became a revered sanctuary. Once fully excavated and opened to the public, Kommós may well emerge as among the most important of the Minoan sites yet explored.

Léndas and Kalí Liménes

South of the Messará, two more beach resorts beckon – **Léndas** and **Kalí Liménes**. In an undeveloped way, Léndas is quite a busy place. Kalí Liménes, 20km south of Míres, is hardly visited at all, perhaps due to its role as a bunkering station for off-loading oil tankers, but it nonetheless offers plenty of scenic walks. If you have your own transport, the roads around here are all passable but mostly very slow: the Asteroússia Hills, which divide the plain from the coast, are surprisingly precipitous and even on the paved roads you have to keep a sharp eye out for sudden patches of mud, potholes and roadworks. The only halfway decent roads to the coast here are the 25-kilometre route from Górtys to Léndas via Mitrópolis, and the now sealed 22-kilometre backroad from Míres to Kalí Liménes (follow the signs carefully). Both itineraries offer great views back over the Messará plain before toiling on through a quintessentially Cretan mountain landscape, where clumps of violet-flowering wild thyme cling to the verges in early summer, and shepherds slow your progress as they herd their flocks of goats along the road at dusk.

Other than the twice-daily direct Léndas–Iráklion **buses**, public transport is very limited indeed – you'll almost always have to travel via Míres.

Léndas and around

Many travellers who arrive in **LÉNDAS** think they've come to the wrong place. The village is neat but not overly attractive, the beach is small and rocky, and the rooms are frequently all booked. Quite a few leave without ever correcting that first impression. For the real attraction of Léndas is not here at all but beyond the point to the west, a kilometre or so along the coast road, where you'll come upon an enormous kilometre-long stretch of sand named

Dytikós (or Diskós) **Beach**, where three good taverna/bars, each with a few basic rooms, overlook the beach from the roadside, and tents and makeshift shelters provide accommodation for many more down on the shore. This beach is almost entirely **nudist**, and largely caters to German tourists (all the menus are in German). Once you've discovered why Léndas is so popular, the village itself begins to look slightly more welcoming. The bus drops you off in a sandy yard which also serves as a car park for those who drive – from here, a number of cobbled paths lead down towards the beach, reached using access routes through tavernas or sometimes (should you lose the way) someone's back garden, to the outrage of a barking dog or rooting piglet.

Practicalities

The village's focus is a pleasant *platía* with an ornamental plinth built around a tamarisk tree. Most of the facilities you'll need are located here, including a couple of **supermarkets**. There's also a **phone box** and, at the *Cafe Siga*, **Internet** access. To change money and travellers' cheques, and for car hire, see *Villa Tsapakis* (see below). You'll see all the **accommodation** options pretty soon – above the village on the way in, *Studios Galini* (☎28920 95369, studiosgalini@mir.forthnet.gr; ❸) has excellent new a/c rooms with kitchenette and stunning balcony views over the bay. As you enter the village proper, *Lentas Bungalows* (☎28920 95221, ⓕ28920 95222; ❸) is relatively luxurious and good value, considering that you get a sea view, en-suite bungalow and use of a kitchen to prepare your own meals. On the square, *Rooms Evans-Dimitra* (☎28920 95205; ❷) has pleasant en-suite a/c rooms with bath and kitchenette, whilst to the east, both the *El Greco* (☎28920 95322; ❷) and *Zorbas* (☎28920 95228; ❸) tavernas have balcony en-suite rooms (and more expensive apartments) with sea views. Out at Dytikós Beach (if you're walking, you can save time by cutting across the headland), *Villa Tsapakis* (☎28920 95378, ⓦwww.villa-tsapakis.gr; ❷) has the best rooms, circling a plant-filled patio a mere 50m from the sea, and all with bath and a/c. They also do **foreign exchange**, will give money on a credit card and **rent cars** at competitive rates. *Taverna Siffis* (☎28920 95268; ❷) further west, has slightly cheaper en-suite rooms; both this taverna and the nearby *Odysseas* (connected to *Villa Tsapakis*) do decent **food**.

Worthwhile **places to eat** in or around the square in the main village include the *Akti* and *Elpida* tavernas. However, the *Taverna El Greco* (☎28920 95322), with a leafy terrace above the beach on the east side of the village, is outstanding and one of the best restaurants on the whole south coast. Run by three brothers who are dedicated to the culinary arts, the food is exceptional – try the *okhtapódhi* (octopus), *kolikithákia* (fried zucchini) or their pepper steak made with prime Messará beef. The feta cheese comes from Halkidhikí in northern Greece and the wine list has many Cretan labels rarely seen in tavernas on the island (try any of the superb Lyrarakis wines). **Nightlife** is predictably laid back and confined to a handful of bars; the *Pink Panther* pub off the square plays music and serves pizzas and cocktails, and overlooking the rocks at the beach's western end, *Why Not?* is a good place to take an aperitif or lounge over late-night drinks while watching the moon rise over the bay.

Around Léndas

If you wanted to make an attractive **walk**, you could take the dirt road left off the main road as it enters the village (signed for Loutrá, a bay 5km to the east with a decent beach and a taverna). There are more good beaches along the way, and from Loutrá, you can head inland 6km up the scenic **Trakhoúla**

gorge to Krótos, where you could meet a bus (check the times in the village before leaving) or take a taxi the ten kilometres back to Léndas. The walk is clearly marked on the *Harms Verlag Crete* (west) map (see p.26).

Slightly above the village are the hilltop remains of ancient Levín (or Leben; gate open Tues–Sun 8.30am–3pm). This was an important healing sanctuary, with an *Asklepion* sited by a spring of therapeutic waters; people were still coming here for cures until as recently as the 1960s, when the spring was diverted and the site became neglected. At its height, from the third century BC onwards, the sanctuary maintained an enormous temple and was a major centre of pilgrimage. You can still see ruins spread over an extensive area, but, sadly, little of their nature can be discerned. There's an arch through which the water once flowed, otherwise only the odd segment of broken wall survives, along with a few severed columns or statue bases, and isolated fragments of mosaic – though one fine third-century BC Hellenistic black, red and white pebble mosaic (beneath a canopy) depicting a sea-horse survived later upheavals. Much closer in, just above the main part of the village, are the more substantial remains of an early Christian basilica, with a much smaller eleventh-century chapel still standing in their midst.

Kalí Liménes and around

Leaving Léndas **to the west**, past the beach, you can follow an unpaved road along the coast to Lassaia, from where a sealed road runs for the last couple of kilometres into Kalí Liménes. It's a very bumpy drive and much easier done with a pick-up or four-wheel-drive vehicle, but it's not impossible in an ordinary car. On the way, you'll pass a number of smaller beaches. The only one of these with any sort of permanent habitation is **Platía Perámata**, a sandy little village with a couple of stores, a few basic rooms and usually the odd camper. It's really not the best of beaches, though. In both the last two bays before Kalí Liménes, small accommodation places have recently opened above little beaches. The first, **Krysóstomos**, has clean bungalow **rooms** with bath behind the *Taverna* (☎28920 97449; ❷), which has now added a swish new hotel with a/c rooms (❸) and studios with kitchenette (❹) overlooking the sea. It also has an incongruous dancing bar, *Bar Ostria*, above a pebbly beach. The second, **Lassaia**, is slightly bigger. Tumbling down a hill to a bay with a good sandy beach, this is a village of holiday homes anarchically thrown up after the Greek fashion with little regard for planning or facilities. Hence the lack of good roads, although electricity has finally arrived and the rumbling chorus of generators which used to greet the onset of dusk each evening is thankfully no more. Surprisingly, there's even a decent place **to stay** here: *Taverna Lassaia* (☎28920 97477; ❷) has spotless a/c rooms with bath, fridge, satellite TV and sea view. The taverna also does pretty good **food**, too.

KALÍ LIMÉNES, 12km west of Léndas, was an important port in Roman times, the main harbour of Górtys and the place where St Paul put in as a prisoner aboard a ship bound for Rome, in an incident described in the Bible in Acts 27. He wanted to stay the winter here, but was overruled by the captain of the ship and the centurion acting as his guard; on setting sail, they were promptly overtaken by a storm, which drove them past Clauda (the island of Gávdhos) and on, eventually, to shipwreck on Malta. Today, Kalí Liménes is once again a major port, for oil tankers this time, which has rather spoilt its chances of becoming a resort. However, it is peculiarly appealing and the constant procession of tankers gives you something to look at, as they discharge their loads into tanks on an islet just offshore. There are a/c en-suite **rooms**

with fridge and sea view on the harbour at the friendly *Taverna Panorama* (April–Nov ☎28920 97517; ❸), which is also a good place **to eat** – the fish is caught by the proprietor with his own boat. You can also camp rough along the beaches to the east and west of the village, but if you opt for this, make sure to dispose of any refuse in a responsible way. The coastline is broken up by spectacular cliffs and the beaches, lined by shacks, a couple of which serve simple food and drinks, are reasonably clean and almost totally empty. Even so, it's a long way from the picture-postcard image of Crete.

There are opportunities for some scenic **walking** around Kalí Liménes, and a little back from the village there's a dirt track heading 6km north to the **Moní Odigitria**. A wonderfully panoramic hike into the hills leads to this remote religious outpost where just two monks watch over an impressive collection of fifteenth-century icons in the fortress-like church. From here, you can either hike back to Kalí Liménes or, more adventurously, head southwest along a track leading to the **Áyio Gorge**. The gorge is walkable and marked on the *Heraklio Trekking and Road Map* produced by Petrákis (see Basics, p.26). Once on the beach (about 6km from the monastery; a three-hour walk), you'll need a boat (arranged at the harbour in advance) to get you back to Kalí Liménes, as there is no route over the cliffs. Also, make sure to take sufficient food and water, and let people know where you are heading.

North from Kalí Liménes

Heading **north** from Kalí Liménes back to the Messará plain, you're in for a stretch of mountain driving and then a total contrast once you reach the Messará on the far side. Leaving Kalí Liménes, don't attempt to drive out of the west end of the village or you'll soon grind to a halt on precipitous rocks: the road inland heads off a short way east, back towards Léndas. The road is good and climbs beyond **Pigaidákia** to the pass over Mount Vigla, from where there's a very steep hairpin descent to **Pómbia**, a large agricultural centre. The hill villages in this corner of Iráklion province are particularly attractive and worth taking the time to explore. Beyond here, you can either head straight on to Míres or take signed left turns for **Petrokefáli** and **Kousés**, where the central *Taverna Rozos* (☎28920 42348; ❶) has some excellent-value en-suite **rooms** in a restored stone-built house nearby. Touring around here, through quiet and prosperous villages surrounded by their crops of oranges, pomegranates or olives, is a wonderfully peaceful contrast to the traffic of the main road. Two kilometres west of Kousés, the village of **Sívas** is another pleasant place with more **rooms** and a couple of tavernas. The main route to Mátala (see p.149) lies a kilometre beyond Sívas.

Across the south: to Áno Viánnos and Árvi

The road **east** across the Messará, from Áyii Dhéka through Asími to Áno Viánnos in the shadow of the **Dhiktean mountains**, is paved all the way – a feat which has taken many years to complete. It is now an enjoyably solitary drive through fertile farming country and, although there's not a great deal to stop for along the way, a visit to the secluded monastic community of the **Moní Koudoumá** is an escapist's dream. Another glimpse of remote, rural Crete is available at **Ethiá**, a stone-built mountain village to the southeast of

Pírgos. If you're looking for something slightly less spartan, the low-key coastal settlements of **Keratókambos** and **Árvi** each have their attractions, while the more substantial village of **Áno Viánnos** has plenty of places for a lunch break plus a couple of churches and a folk museum to see. No buses follow this road, and, in fact, there's very little transport of any kind.

From Iráklion, the road south cuts across the centre of the island, through the featureless farming town of Arkalohóri. It joins the west–east route at Mártha, and continues through Áno Viánnos towards Ierápetra. There are a couple of daily buses on this road, but you'll still have to change buses if you hope to hit the coast before Mírtos, further east still in Lasíthi province.

The west–east coastal route

Heading **west–east** across the south of the island, access to the coast only becomes a realistic proposal beyond **Pírgos**, a sturdy farming village 10km southeast of the village of **Asími** (itself 15km east of Áyii Dhéka). However,

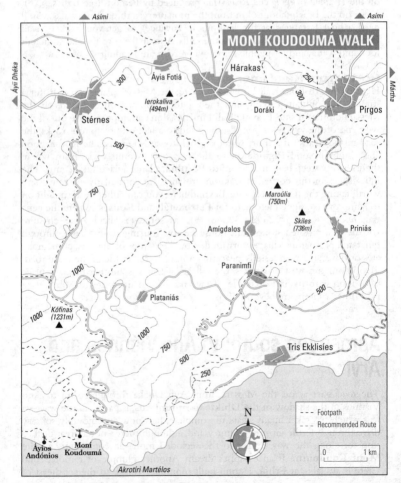

for those looking for adventure, there is a fine **walk** (see map on p.158) from Pírgos to the remote **Moní Koudoumá**, set in a spectacular seaside location.

On foot, the easiest route from Pírgos is about 20km long and should take around four to five hours. Leave the village by the Priniás road which winds down through the hamlet of Trís Ekklisíes and eventually degrades into a dirt track. **By road**, your best bet is to head west to Stérnes and then aim south along a slightly better (but still unpaved) surface. Be warned, though, that the final cliff-face section is particularly hazardous – not the kind of thing to be attempted lightly in a rented car, on a motorbike or scooter, or in bad weather. A four-wheel-drive vehicle is probably the best option or a hire car which has good clearance from the ground, taking the descent very carefully.

Should you need to spend a night in Pírgos before setting out, *Rooms Tzaridakis* (℡28930 22238; ❷), just off the main street, is pleasant enough for en-suite rooms, and just downhill, along the Prótoria–Asími road out of town, the comfortable *Hotel Arhontiko* (℡28930 23118; ❸) has the same with extras, such as a/c, TV and kitchenette. Along Pírgos's main street there are also a couple of decent **tavernas** and, at the eastern end of this thoroughfare, lies the fourteenth-century **church** of Áyios Yióryios and Áyios Konstantínos, a Byzantine edifice with some interesting faded frescoes. The key is available from the house (no. 137) to the right of the church gate.

The monastery of **Moní Koudoumá** nestles in a cove, surrounded by pinewoods, at the foot of a cliff down which descends a dizzying track of end-less switchbacks. Arriving here is a distinctly end-of-the-world experience, and the last remaining monks have only the few elderly women who inhabit the nearby dwellings for company. The monks see few visitors, but are extremely welcoming to those that do turn up, and will offer you food and a mattress (take along a sleeping bag if you think you'll be cold) in one of the dormito-ries set aside for "pilgrims". While the monks will not accept payment for their hospitality, a donation to monastery funds is unlikely to be refused. If you think the magic of the place may persuade you to prolong your stay, you should bring supplies with you. The nights here – illuminated by oil lamps in the absence of mains electricity – are exquisitely serene, broken only by the sound of the sea splashing against the rocks.

Ethiá, Tsoútsouros and Keratókambos

Heading east out of Pírgos, after 3km at Rotási a signed road climbs vertigi-nously for 10km to the semi-deserted, stone-built mountain village of **Ethiá**. A piece of living Cretan folklore, the dry-stone walls marking the fields around the village are redolent of Ireland or Scotland, and the ruined stone dwellings, with their ancient outdoor ovens and chimneys, evoke a Crete long gone. Only twenty souls live here now, most of them very old; the school has closed and the shop along with it, as the younger people have opted for an easier life in the towns and villages far below. The only hope for Ethiá's survival is the family returnees who are now restoring some of the less ruined dwellings as weekend and holiday homes. The charmingly rustic **bar** on the small main square will serve you a cool drink and, with a little Greek, you'll no doubt hear a few strange and wonderful tales about how it all used to be in the old days. Should you not wish to retrace your route from Ethiá back to Rotási, it's possible to continue through Ahendriás to rejoin the main east–west route at Mesochóri, 4km east of Rotási.

A straightforward route to the sea comes 12km east of Pírgos at Káto Kastilianá: 11km of asphalted road winding alarmingly down (and south) to **Tsoútsouros**, arching around its own bay. Formerly a simple hamlet on the sea, the village is now growing into a small resort. A line of tavernas, bars and rooms places stand behind a newly constructed harbour-marina where pleasure craft and fishing boats tie up, and to the east and west are a couple of decent, if pebbly, grey sand **beaches**. There's no bank or place to change money but there are a couple of **supermarkets**. For **accommodation**, the best deal is probably at the newly refurbished *San Georgio Hotel* (May–Sept T 28910 92322; ❷) at the eastern end of the seafront, where pleasant a/c balcony rooms come with fridge and sea view. At the extreme western end of the seafront, you could try *Rooms Lytos* (T & F 28910 92321, W www.interkriti.net/hotel/tsoutsouros/lytos; ❹), where modern rooms come with kitchenette. In the central zone between these two, *Rooms Mihalis* (T 28910 92250; ❷) has sea-view a/c balcony rooms with fridge, and the nearby *Venetia* (T 28910 92258, E aim@otenet.gr; ❸) is a new place with more en-suite a/c balcony rooms with TV, facing the sea. For **food**, there's not a lot to choose between the half-dozen or so **tavernas**, although *To Steki Tou Blami*, towards the east end of the seafront, is good for cheap *souvláki* and grilled fish, while *Inatos* and, especially, *Zorba's*, neighbours at the western end, are reliable places for the usual standards.

You may prefer, however, to hold out for **Keratókambos**, a tranquil fishing village 10km east of Tsoútsouros along a newly asphalted coastal road that has replaced the former rough dirt track. About halfway between Tsoútsouras and Keratókambos, *Apartments Kaboula* (T 28950 51407 or T 28102 25105; ❶) has four pretty and astonishingly cheap garden apartments, each with kitchen and veranda sea view. For the moment, Keratókambos remains tiny and quiet, very much a locals' resort. A single street of houses interspersed with cafés and tavernas faces a tree-lined sand and shingle beach with a shower on it. Two of the tavernas rent out a few air-conditioned **rooms** with bath: try *Morning Star* (T 28950 51209; ❷), or *Kastri Rooms* (T 28950 51231, F 28950 51456; ❸) at *Taverna Kriti* next door. Slightly west of here, pleasant studio rooms with kitchen and terrace are on offer at *Filoxenia* (T 28950 51371; ❸). More places are signed in both directions along the seafront, including *Komis Studios* (April–Nov T 28950 51390, W www.komisstudios.gr; ❼) to the east; a step up in price and quality – members of the Greek prime minister's family have been put up here - the complex consists of attractive designer studio apartments in a garden setting equipped with minibar, TV and room safe. You should bear in mind that most of the resort's rooms are booked solid during July and especially August.

For even more isolation, you could retrace your steps 2km or so to the point where the road emerges at the coast – this is **Kastrí Keratókambos** and here you'll find *Pan Apartments* (T 28950 51220, W www.pan-olivenoel.de; ❸), where splendid new studios come with kitchenette, sea view and a pretty garden. If you do stay, or you want to **camp** in isolation, you could explore better patches of deserted sand along the coast road in either direction. For **food**, both the excellent *Kriti* taverna and *Morning Star* on the central seafront, and *O Nikitas* at the eastern end, do good seafood and meat dishes. Should you wish to buy olive oil direct from the press, the proprietor of the *Kriti* taverna will sell you some of his own at a bargain price.

From Keratókambos, you have the possibility of following the coastal route along another meandering, rough but drivable track 12km east to Árvi (see p.162) that gets better the further along you go, passing beneath a great crag of rock with a ruined castle perched upon it. Alternatively, the asphalted road back up the mountain, via the highly picturesque village of Hóndhros, leads you to Áno Viánnos.

Áno Viánnos and around

The large village of **Áno Viánnos**, 9km southeast of Mártha on the main Iráklion–Ierápetra road, clings to the southern slopes of the Dhíkti range. The air is much sharper up here, even in high summer, and the cuisine more substantial than on the sweltering beaches far below. Áno (Upper) Viánnos is the traditional centre of this part of southeastern Iráklion province, but its importance has waned as the coastal settlements have grown. Nonetheless, it's still a substantial village with a couple of interesting **churches** containing well-preserved fourteenth-century frescoes: Ayía Pelayía (dating from the fourteenth century with a magnificent, if damaged, *Crucifixion* on the back wall) and Áyios Yeóryios are both located up a narrow, stepped side-street close to the enormous plane tree on the village's eastern extremity. At the opposite end of the village is an interesting **Folk Museum** (closed at time of writing) with displays of costumes, handicrafts and embroideries documenting Viánnos's social and cultural history from medieval times to World War II. A snack bar uphill from the modern church has basic **rooms** (❶), and there are a couple of places serving **food** in the centre, or you could head east along the main road for 1km to the barn-sized *Taverna O Diabatis*, which often puts on uproarious *lyra* concerts at weekends, drawing in farmers and their families from miles around for a wild night of singing and dancing.

The Ierápetra road leads east out of Áno Viánnos, skirting an alarming precipice, and continues on through **Amirás**, where you turn off south for Árvi alongside a giant memorial to the Cretans killed in World War II. From here, a paved road winds gradually down for 13km to sea level, and emerges on the coast through the gorge of a stream which waters exotic cultivated fruits.

Káto Sími

With your own transport, you can take a scenic detour to the village of **Káto Sími** and its atmospheric **ancient sanctuary** of Hermes and Aphrodite. To get there, drive for 4km beyond the war memorial at Amirás and take a signed road on the left. The docile village of Káto Sími – with a couple of bar/tavernas – is 1km beyond the turn-off. Another war memorial on the edge of the village commemorates five hundred people put to death in 1943 when Káto Sími and six other settlements were destroyed in retaliation for an attack on a German patrol. To reach the ancient site (3km above the village), from the tavernas at the centre of Káto Sími take the road north, passing a wooden hut with concrete foundations to the left. You'll soon reach a junction, where you should take the road signed in Greek for **Omalos Kristos**, a mountain chapel. A little further on, you'll come to another road leading off to the right with a spring and a ford. Ignore this and take the uphill road, signed again for Omalos Kristos. Beyond here, keep your eyes skinned for a "danger of fire" warning sign to the right depicting a lighted cigarette and flames. Alongside this is another sign in Greek announcing the site, which you should be able to spot above, behind one of the most securely built protective fences in the whole of Greece. Despite the fact that you cannot gain access to the sanctuary, the remains can easily be viewed by making a circuit of the exterior fence.

Known locally as **Kryá Vrísi** (cold spring), the site is laid out on a series of broad ledges on the mountainside where a prodigious spring gushes clear, ice-cold water all year round – certain to have been the attraction for ancient peoples. Today, rather than being used for the ablutions of pilgrims, the spring disperses down the mountainside via plastic pipes to irrigate the olive groves below. There is evidence of a **shrine** here dating back to prehistoric times, and when adopted by the **Minoans**, it became a holy place of overwhelming importance, borne out by the thousands of votive clay and bronze figurines and vases brought here by pilgrims, many of which are now on display in the Iráklion Archeological Museum. In later times, the Greeks and Romans transmuted the Minoan deities into their Hellenic equivalents, Hermes Kendrites and Aphrodite respectively, and the shrine continued to be an important centre of pilgrimage. Among the remains, it's possible to make out vestiges of temples, altars and cult rooms dating from all periods. The site is dominated by an enormous hollow plane tree on its eastern side, which certainly seems old enough to have witnessed many of the sacrifices and ceremonies that took place here in ancient times.

Árvi and around

Standing on the site of the ancient Roman town of Arvis and hemmed in by rock cliffs which trap the heat – creating a microclimate that is among the hottest in Crete – **Árvi** has, surprisingly, not been overwhelmed by development. This may have something to do with its long but pebbly beach and the villagers' greater interest in the wealth to be made from growing bananas, oranges and pineapples in this near-tropical environment. A few lean tourist years have made the village's dependence on agriculture even more critical, but it has to be said that the gauntlet of plastic greenhouses you are now forced to traverse en route to the coast has done little to add to its allure as a resort. The construction of a seafront promenade and marina-harbour (in progress at the time of writing) with grants from the EU seems a belated attempt to regenerate the seafront: it remains to be seen whether this will serve to entice back the missing tourists, though.

There are **rooms**, and there's usually no problem finding beds at any time of the year: you could try the *Hotel Ariadne* (☎28950 71300; ❸), with balcony sea views near the entrance to the village, or the slightly pricier *Gorgona* (☎28950 71353; ❸), with en-suite sea-view rooms further along the main street. Beyond the river at the east end of the beach, the *Taverna Kyma* (☎28950 71344; ❸) has very pleasant studio rooms with balcony views and kitchenette next door. The most relaxing place to stay, however, is the friendly seafront *Rent Rooms Colibi* (☎28950 71250; ❸), with a delightful garden where balcony sea-view rooms come with bath, and breakfast tables sit beneath tamarisk trees, fronting a small beach complete with showers. To get there, head west from the town for 1km until the road bends right; keep ahead here along an unpaved road running behind the beach.

Once you've settled in, there's not much to do apart from baking in the sun – something you can often do comfortably here even when the rest of the island is too cold to contemplate it. When you need shade, there are numerous stores, bars, cafés and **tavernas**: behind the beach, *Diktina* (with vegetarian options) is worth a try, as is the *Taverna Kyma* (see above). There are no places to change money and the accommodation places do not accept cards, so it would be wise to bring sufficient cash with you. The nearest ATM is in Áno Viánnos.

On the hillside overlooking the village is the picturesque nineteenth-century monastery of **Áyios Andónios**, which now has only a couple of monks in residence. To get there – and it's a pleasant fifteen-minute walk – go to the back of the village and you'll come to signposts guiding you to a track across a valley towards the monastery, on the side of a slope. It's especially tranquil here at dusk, when the monks sit out on their terrace, happy to converse with passing visitors.

Greek place names

ΑΓ ΠΕΛΑΓΙΑ	Αγ Πελαγία	Ay. Pelayía
ΑΜΝΗΣΟΣ	Αμνήσος	Amnísos
ΑΝΩ ΒΙΑΝΝΟΣ	Ανω Βιάννος	Áno Viánnos
ΑΡΒΗ	Αρβή	Árvi
ΑΡΧΑΝΕΣ	Αρχάνες	Arhánes
ΒΑΘΥΠΕΤΡΟ	Βαθύπετρο	Vathípetro
ΓΙΟΥΧΤΑΣ	Γιούχτας	Yioúhtas
ΓΟΥΡΝΕΣ	Γούρνες	Goúrnes
ΓΟΡΤΥΣ	Γόρτυς	Górtys
ΗΡΑΚΛΕΙΟ	Ηράκλειο	Iráklion
ΚΑΛΟΙ ΛΙΜΕΝΕΣ	Καλοί Λιμένες	Kalí Liménes
ΚΕΡΑΤΟΚΑΜΠΟΣ	Κερατοκάμπος	Keratókambos
ΚΝΩΣΟΣ	Κνωσός	Knossós
ΛΕΝΤΑΣ	Λέντας	Léndas
ΜΑΛΙΑ	Μάλια	Mália
ΜΑΤΑΛΑ	Μάταλα	Mátala
ΜΟΙΡΕΣ	Μοίρες	Míres
ΤΣΟΥΤΣΟΥΡΟΣ	Τσούτσουρος	Tsoútsouros
ΤΥΛΙΣΟΣ	Τύλισος	Tílissos
ΤΥΜΠΑΚΙ	Τυμπάκι	Timbáki
ΦΑΙΣΤΟΣ	Φαιστός	Festós
ΦΟΔΕΛΕ	Φόδελε	Fódhele
ΧΕΡΣΟΝΗΣΟΣ	Χερσόνησος	Hersónisos

Along a bumpy (and, with care, drivable) track **to the east** lie more isolated beaches leading eventually to the tiny coastal hamlets of Faflángos and, after 6km, the larger **Akrotíri Sidonía**, which has a good dark shingle **beach** populated mainly by Greek visitors. The centre consists of a clutch of tavernas and rooms places clustered around a main junction, from where an asphalt road heads 10km north to Kalámi, rejoining the main east–west artery. Among the **places to stay** here, *Rooms Armonia* (☎28950 61445; ❸), close to the junction, has a/c rooms with kitchenette and balcony sea views. At the eastern end of the seafront, very pleasant new sea-view rooms with balcony and kitchenette are available at *Sidonia* (☎28950 61328; ❸), above a very good taverna with the same name. It should be possible to **camp** beneath the tamarisk trees at the far eastern end of the beach, but be aware of local sensitivities: these are not developed tourist resorts but ordinary villages on the sea. Some maps don't mark the dirt track, but it continues east to Tértsa and Mírtos (see p.233), some 14km from Árvi, which makes for a pleasant coastal walk.

Travel details

Buses

Some of these services are restricted on Sundays. For the latest timetables visit KTEL's websites: ⓦwww.bus-service-crete-ktel.com, ⓦwww.crete-buses.gr and ⓦwww.ktel.org.

Iráklion to: Áno Viánnos (2 daily 6.30am & midnight; 2hr 30min–3hr); Anóyia (5 daily 6.30am–4.30pm; 1hr); Arhánes (16 daily 6.30am–8.30pm; 30min); Ay. Galíni (7 daily 6.30am–4.30pm; 2hr 15min); Ay. Nikólaos (23 daily 6.15am–10pm; 1hr 30min); Ay. Pelayía (4 daily 8.30am–5.30pm; 45min); Festós (8 daily 7.30am–4.30pm; 1hr 30min); Fódhele (2 daily 6.30am & 2.30pm; 1hr); Haniá (31 daily 5.30am–10pm; 1hr 30min–3hr); Hersónisos (every 30min 6.30am–11pm; 45min); Ierápetra (7 daily 6.15am–7.30pm, via Ay. Nikólaos; 2hr 30min); Lasíthi plateau (2 daily 9am & 2.30pm; 2hr); Léndas (1 daily; 1pm; 3hr); Mália (every 30min; 6.30am–11pm; 1hr); Milátos/Sísi (2 daily 7am & 3.15pm; 1hr 30min); Omalós (daily at 5.30am; 4hr 30min); Réthimnon/Haniá (31 daily 5.30am–10pm, a couple via the old road; 1hr 30min/3hr); Sitía (6 daily 6.30am–7pm; 3hr 15min).

Mália/Hersónisos to: Lasíthi plateau (1 daily 8.30am; 1hr 30min).

Míres to: Iráklion (13 daily 6.45am–8.30pm; 1hr 15min); Mátala (5 daily 8.40am–4.40pm; 45min); Ayía Galíni (7 daily 7.40am–5.40pm; 2hr 15min).

Domestic ferries and hydrofoils

These refer to summer timetables; schedules are severely restricted in winter. For the latest information visit ⓦ www.greekislands.gr or ⓦ www.ferries.gr.

Iráklion–The Cyclades: daily catamaran to Thíra; otherwise thrice weekly (1hr 45min or 4hr); daily catamaran or twice daily ferry to Íos (2hr 15min or 5hr) & Páros (2hr 45min–6hr), & Míkonos (3hr

30min or 7hr) & Náxos (2hr 45min or 6hr); at least 2 weekly to Tínos (8hr), & Skíros (13hr) and 1 weekly to Skíathos (14hr) & Anáfi (4hr 30min).

Iráklion–Pireás: 2 daily, at 8.30pm & 10pm (10hr). The fast-ferries *Knossós Palace* and *Festós Palace* from Minoan Lines, sail daily (11am & 10pm; 6–7hr); check ⓦ www.minoan.gr for more details.

Iráklion–Thessaloníki: Mon, Wed & Fri; times vary (22hr).

Iráklion–Thira (Santorini): Mon, Wed & Fri; times vary (2hr 30min–4hr). Daily "Flying Cat" catamaran at 9.15am (1hr 45min).

International ferries

For the latest information visit ⓦ www.greek-islands.gr or ⓦ www.ferries.gr.

Iráklion to: Limassol, Cyprus & Haífa, Israel (Fri 4pm; 28hr & 36hr).

Domestic flights

These refer to summer timetables; in winter, there are no island flights and other flights run on restricted schedules.

Iráklion to: Athens (up to 10 daily; 50min); Páros (3 weekly; 45min); Rhodes (1 daily; 40min); Thessaloníki (2 daily; 1hr 30min); Thíra/Míkonos (2 weekly; 40min/30min).

2

Lasíthi

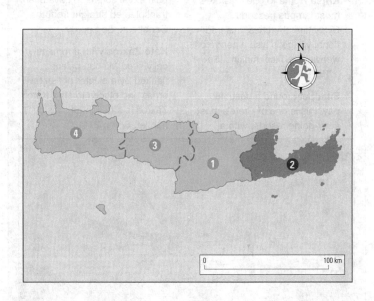

CHAPTER 2 # Highlights

✳ **Lasíthi plateau** This spectacular mountain plateau is a verdant farming area, where multicoloured wildflowers and soaring eagles compete for your attention. See p.173

✳ **Áyios Nikólaos** One of the most eye-catching towns on the island, with a good restaurant scene and buzzing nightlife. See p.177

✳ **Kritsá** Home to one of Crete's most famous frescoed Byzantine churches, this traditional village is also a centre of weaving and lacemaking. See p.189

✳ **Sitía** Set around a beautiful bay, this is one of Crete's most easy-going resorts, with a couple of interesting museums and plenty of after-dark diversions. See p.200

✳ **Monastery of Tóplou** Standing alone on a windy hilltop and built like a fortress, this is one of Crete's most atmospheric monasteries. See p.208

✳ **Vái Beach** An idyllic white-sand beach fringed by exotic palms, Vái seems to have been transplanted straight from the Caribbean. See p.209

✳ **Káto Zákros** With a romantically sited Minoan palace, flanked by a cluster of fish tavernas and places to stay, Káto Zákros is a delightful seaside hamlet. See p.214

△ Tóplou Monastery

2

Lasíthi

E astern Crete is dominated by **Áyios Nikólaos** and the mass tourism it attracts, but get beyond the town and its environs and you have the chance to experience some of the most striking highlands and wilderness coastlines on the island. Also Áyios Nikólaos is less crowded these days than it once was, and if you're looking for a place to let your hair down this is one of Crete's liveliest cosmopolitan enclaves. It's easy too, to escape from here into the surrounding hills and mountains, where the town of **Kritsá** has a famous frescoed church and the **Lasíthi plateau** – a high mountain plain with picturesque villages and abundant greenery – can be visited in a day. Follow the coast north from Áyios Nikólaos and, after the pretty resort of **Eloúnda** and its beaches, you come to the brooding islet of **Spinalónga**, once a redoubtable Venetian and Turkish fortress, later a leper colony.

Move towards the far east of the island and the pace slackens as you enter a zone which is under the sway not of Áyios Nikólaos but of **Sitía**, an attractive, traditional town where tourism has had little outward effect. The Minoan workers' village at **Gourniá** is definitely worth a stop en route whilst, at the island's eastern tip, the famed palm-studded beach at **Vái** and the Minoan palace at **Káto Zákros** are the major tourist attractions. However, for something more relaxing the isolated beaches around **Palékastro** and **Kserócambos** offer wildly contrasting escapes.

Along the south coast, there is generally far less development. **Ierápetra** is the major town in these parts, with a scenic harbour from where boats sail to the offshore desert island of **Gaidhouronísi**. In both directions from here, towards **Mírtos** and **Makriyialós**, there are a string of low-key resorts with beaches as good as any in the province.

Transport in the region is excellent, at least along the main roads. There's a constant stream of buses between Iráklion, Áyios Nikólaos, Sitía and Ierápetra stopping at major points en route, and good local services from both Áyios Nikólaos and the inland centre of Neápoli.

Mália to Áyios Nikólaos

Driving into Lasíthi from Mália, there's a choice of routes. The fast E75 highway leaves the palace at Mália behind and embarks almost immediately on the long climb inland – rising at first through the **Gorge of Selinári**, where travellers would traditionally stop at the chapel and pray to St George for safe passage. There's a truckstop here, but most traffic roars straight past and on through the tunnel blasted beneath the old pass. It's a tremendous engineering

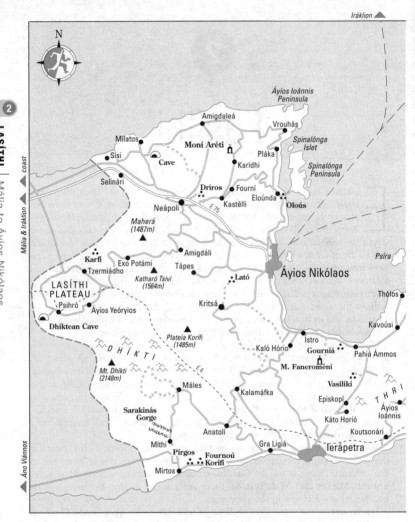

achievement, though beyond here – having bypassed **Neápoli** – there's little else to see until you emerge high above Áyios Nikólaos to spectacular views of the **Gulf of Mirabéllo**.

Sísi

The old road follows the coast for a while longer, rolling on through Sísi with a branch off to Mílatos (see p.170). **Sísi** is becoming developed, but for the moment this amounts only to scattered apartments, and the local beaches remain quiet and small-scale. **Epáno Sísi**, the inland part of the village, has one or two possibilities for rooms, but a more tempting stop is **Sísi Paralía**, 2km away on the coast. Here, a picturesque tiny harbour is overlooked by

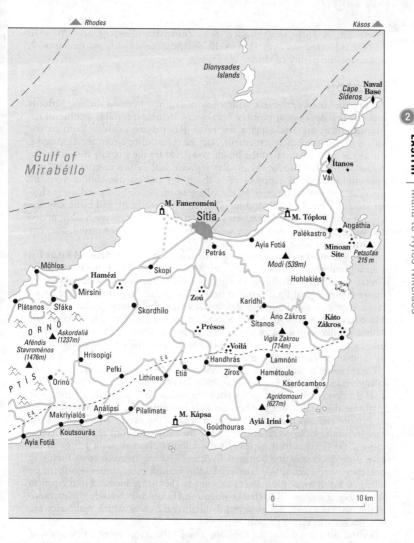

some traditional **tavernas**: try *Fisherman's Place*, *To Paradosiako* or *Angistri*, which all have harbour views and specialize in fresh fish. However, new construction has undermined the village's erstwhile tranquillity: as well as a large new holiday complex, *Kalimera Krita*, a couple of kilometres to the east, there's now also the usual array of bike rental offices, souvenir stores and even a **disco-bar**, *Faros*, close to the harbour. Scattered around Sísi Paralía are numerous **rooms**, studios and apartments, but these are usually booked up in high season; a small pension behind the harbour, *Elena* (no phone; ②), may have a room, or the *Villa Asprogas* (☎28102 85052; ④), on the outskirts as you arrive, is a charming four-person villa with pool, available for stays of three days and longer. You could also try asking at any of the tavernas near the harbour – they can usually turn up a relative with a room to rent, or even an apartment, at fairly short notice. Sísi's **campsite**, *Camping Sísi* (☎28410 71247), is located just over 1km to the west, and has its own swimming pool, restaurant and plenty of shade.

Mílatos

An unpretentious settlement with a line of tavernas fronting the sea, **Mílatos** remains less developed, possibly because of its uncomfortable pebble beach (though there are sunloungers for rent). Rooms are available both in the village and at the beach settlement 2km away, but once again during August, things can get very tight. At the beach, you could try the friendly *Rooms Taverna Sokrates* (☎28410 81375; ②) on the seafront, and in the taverna below the eponymous owner is happy to open the fridge and let you choose from the day's catch of fresh fish netted by the village boats. Nearby, cafés and stores cluster around a small church and junction on the waterfront, and more tavernas specialize in fresh fish: *Sirines*, with its own fishing boat, is reasonably priced and worth a try. Infotravel, to the west of the junction on the seafront, does **car** and **mountain bike hire**.

Although you'd never guess from what remains today, **ancient Mílatos** has a distinguished past – and even a mention in Homer's *Iliad* as one of the seven Cretan cities that sent forces to fight at Troy. In mythology – backed up by recent archeological finds – it was from Mílatos that Sarpedon (King Minos's brother, whom the king had defeated to take the throne) sailed to found Miletus, which was destined to become one of the greatest of all cities in Asia Minor. Unlike its namesake in modern Turkey, however, little has survived on the site to the east of the beach. The city faded into obscurity in antiquity and by Roman times no longer existed.

There's more recent history to be seen at the **Mílatos Cave**, 3km east of the village and signposted up a newly asphalted road. More a series of caverns than a single cave, this appears to go back for miles: with adequate lighting you might be able to discover just how far. Less adventurously, there's a small chapel to explore right at the entrance, a memorial to the events which earned the cave its notoriety. In 1823, during one of the early rebellions against the Turks, some 2700 Cretans (that, at least, is the number claimed) took refuge in the cave, were discovered and besieged. Eventually, having failed to break their way out, they were offered safe conduct by the Turkish commander – only to be killed or taken away into slavery as soon as they surrendered. From April to September, a *kantina* (cold-drinks wagon) parks up daily outside the entrance to the cave and rents out powerful flashlights (€2 each) which make viewing it a much more viable proposition.

Beyond the cave, you could continue around the Áyios Ioánnis peninsula, or across to Neápoli, by a variety of dirt roads. Back through Mílatos village, however, the scarcely used paved road to Neápoli is an equally beautiful and certainly easier way to zigzag through the mountains.

Neápoli

Despite its size, history (it's the birthplace of Pope Alexander V) and location, **Neápoli** sees virtually no tourists other than those who stop for a coffee in the square between buses or as they drive through. A charming provincial town, it was formerly the capital of Lasíthi (a role now usurped by Áyios Nikólaos) and remains the seat of the local government and of the provincial courts; it's a peaceful place for a stopover, and it is from here that one of the roads up to the Lasíthi plateau sets out.

At the south end of the main square is a mildly interesting **folklore museum** (Tues–Sun 10am–1pm & 6–9pm; €1.50). Slightly east of this, in a courtyard on the left along the road to the Lasíthi plateau, is a small archeological museum (Sun 8.30am–3pm; free) displaying finds from the surrounding area. The only **accommodation** is a superbly restored hotel, the *Neápolis* (☎28410 33967, ⓦwww.neapolis-hotel.gr; ❸), built in the Bauhaus style with fine views from some rooms; to get there, follow Odhós Ántistasis, the street facing the main square's war memorial, for 200m. Things tend to happen (or not happen) around the sleepy main square, which is lined with a few tavernas and *kafenía*, as well as a post office and a bank. At *I Driros*, the *zaharoplastío* facing the war memorial, you can try a *soumádha*, a refreshing almond drink highly popular with the locals.

Dríros

To the northeast of Neápoli, on a road off the E75 that is signed to Kouroúnes, Nofaliás and Skiniás, lies the ancient site of **DRÍROS**. The road curls steeply beyond the old and new roads (which here run almost exactly parallel) for 2km, where a signed turn-off on the right leads a further 1km to a dead end beneath a rocky hillside. The path into the unguarded site is way-marked from the parking area. Not far along this, you'll reach an arrow on the path indicating a left turn, and scrambling over piles of collapsed stones – ruins of the ancient city – will bring you to a stone-built canopy covering the eighth-century BC **Temple of Apollo Delphinios**, one of the earliest known temples in all of Greece. It was dedicated to a cult that celebrated Apollo transformed into a dolphin, a guise the god used when guiding Greek sailors. That the chief sanctuary of Miletus in Asia Minor was devoted to the same cult is further evidence of a link between this area and the founding of the colony there. In the centre of the temple can be seen the remains of a sunken hearth. Amongst the discoveries here were three hammered bronze statuettes, some of the earliest known (now in the Iráklion Archeological Museum, as well as two Eteocretan inscriptions – Greek letters used to write a Cretan, possibly Minoan, tongue. As you look around today, it's hard to believe that this temple once lay on the edge of the bustling agora, or main square. It was approached by a flight of steps – visible on the west side of the canopy, to the left of the doorway. Another flight of steps joined the temple on the east side, and to the south is a huge **cistern** constructed in the third century BC, now crammed with fig trees. The earliest remains found here date back to the eighth century BC, and the city flourished for the next seven hundred years as an important ally of Knossós, but a deadly enemy of Lyttos (see p.131). Dríros declined in importance prior to the end of the second century BC, when many of its citizens emigrated to Miletus in Asia Minor, further underlining the link between the two areas.

The path beyond the arrowed turn-off to the temple eventually guides you to a short scenic climb; collapsed stones on the hillsides all around here show how extensive this city must have been. Hopefully one day the site will be properly excavated, making the whole experience more rewarding; until then, finding anything else of note among the thorny bushes and ruined dry-stone walls is very difficult, and deciphering it once you do is virtually impossible. Nevertheless, if you make it to the top of the hill and the charming barrel-vaulted **chapel of Áyios Andónios**, the glorious views make the climb worthwhile, whilst the drab desolation of the surroundings is a startling contrast to the green country around Neápoli. The oak tree standing before the chapel – which also serves as a belfry, with the bell attached to one of its branches – provides welcome shade for a picnic.

North and east of Dríros

A drivable dirt road close to the site of Dríros heads off east through the olive groves for just over a kilometre to Kastélli, saving a journey back to the main road. To the north of Dríros, twisting roads (mostly asphalt) link a string of remote farming villages which rarely see tourists. Many of the windmills you'll see perched along the heights here are still functioning and are used to grind flour; one, at Vrouhás, actually welcomes visitors.

If you want to continue to Áyios Nikólaos by the least arduous scenic route, however, take the road east through a series of villages: Kastélli, with a **folk museum** (daily 9am–3pm; €1.50) on its eastern edge, soon followed by Fourní, where a dramatic entry road is lined with eucalyptus trees, and Pínes. From here, the route winds down to Eloúnda with yet more wonderful views of the Gulf of Mirabéllo. The characteristic landscape of this part of Crete still remains, with its stone walls and windmills which hug the steep hillsides and summits.

Worth a detour, 5km north of Fourní near the village of **Karídhi** is the impressive sixteenth-century **monastery of Aréti**, surrounded by cypresses and cedars and recently restored. In the nearby village of **Doriés**, the church of Áyios Konstantínos holds an icon of the Panayía (Virgin), the oldest known on the island, dating from the fourteenth century. The church is sited near the heart of the village, and lies down a little path off the main road (marked by a small monument in the form of a church). The cream and brown painted house next to it is that of the *papás*, who will open the church for you. For his trouble, a small donation to the church's upkeep is unlikely to be refused.

The Lasíthi plateau

Every day, scores of bus tours toil up to the **Lasíthi plateau** to view its famous sea of white cloth-sailed **windmills**. Few of the mills remain in operation though, and those that do work only for limited periods; others are found next to tavernas and used as a feature to attract custom. Nevertheless, even if you see no unfurled sails at all, the trip is still worth making for the drive alone.

From Neápoli, a long and winding road – thirty slow kilometres of it – climbs south and then west into the mountains that ring the sunken plateau. When you think you've arrived, another village appears around the corner and the road climbs again. Before you reach **Amigdháli**, there are a couple of roadside tavernas which have stunning views into the hills. If you want to break the journey up, stop off at the craftsman's house in **Zénia**, evident from the handmade spoons for sale hanging outside it, or call in at the small taverna in **Éxo Potámi**. At **Mésa Potámi**, 4km further, you are almost on the plateau, but there are more tavernas to entice you here, in addition to roadside stalls selling honey or whatever fruit is in season.

When you finally come upon the plateau laid out below you, it seems almost too perfect – a patchwork circle of tiny fields enclosed by the bare flanks of the mountains. Closer up, it's a fine example of **rural Crete** at work, with every inch given over to the cultivation of potatoes, apples, pears, cereals and almost anything else that could conceivably be grown in the cooler climate up here. The area has always been fertile, its rich alluvial soil washed down from the

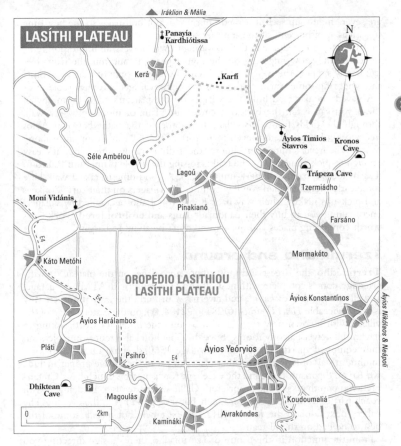

LASÍTHI PLATEAU

Panayía Kardhiótissa

Kerá

Karfí

Áyios Timios Stavros

Kronos Cave

Séle Ambélou

Lagoú

Trápeza Cave

Tzermiádho

Moní Vidánis

Pinakianó

Farsáno

Káto Metóhi

Marmakéto

**OROPÉDIO LASITHÍOU
LASÍTHI PLATEAU**

Áyios Konstantínos

Áyios Harálambos

E4

Pláti

Psihró

E4

Áyios Yeóryios

Dhiktean Cave

P

Magoulás

Koudoumaliá

Kamináki

Avrakóndes

0   2km

N

mountains and watered by the rains which collect in the natural bowl. In spring, there can be floods, which is why the villages all cluster on the higher ground around the edge of the plain, but in summer, the windmills traditionally come into use, pumping the water back up to the drying surface. Although the plateau was irrigated in Roman times – and inhabited long before that – this system was designed by the Venetians in the fifteenth century, bringing the plain back into use after nearly a century of enforced neglect (during which time, cultivation and pasture had been banned after a local rebellion). Where they survive, the windmills have barely changed, but in the past twenty years or so, most have been replaced by more dependable petrol-driven pumps. The 26 stone windmills standing guard on the ridges above the plain, also mostly ruined, were traditional grain mills. Today, only two of these are still in use.

If you **stay overnight** you'll see a good deal more than on a day-trip, as the tour parties leave and a great peace settles over the plateau. The excesses of Mália or Hersónisos seem a world away as you climb into your cot to the sound of braying donkeys and a tolling church bell outside, and wake to the cock's crow the next morning. Early in the day you'll see a diaphanous white mist floating over the plain and its windmills sparkling in the sun. The winters are severe here – up to half-a-metre of snow is not unusual – so the best time to visit is at either end of the summer season: in late spring, the pastures and orchards are almost alpine in their covering of wildflowers, an impression reinforced by the snow lingering on the higher peaks; in autumn, the fruit trees can barely support the weight of their crop. Whatever time of year you come, though, bring some warm clothing, as the nights can get extremely cold.

A paved circular road links the villages on the plateau's edge. From any of these, you can catch the **bus** as it circles the plain, or more enjoyably, walk through the fields from one village to another – the paths between Áyios Yeóryios and Káto Metóhi even form part of the E4 Pan-European walking route. Whichever route you choose, the path is rarely direct, but it's easy enough to pick your way by the trails: crossing the whole plain, from Psihró to Tzermiádho, is barely a ninety-minute walk. A good time to take a walk here is the early evening, when you'll encounter the villagers on their carts, donkeys and pick-ups making their way back home. You'll also be assailed by villagers encouraging you to buy their handmade **rugs** and **embroidered work** – it's worth comparing prices and quality, and don't be afraid to bargain.

Tzermiádho and around

Tzermiádho, the largest and most important village on the plateau's northern edge, comes complete with post office, OTE, bank (with ATM) and garage, as well as a number of *kafenía* and tavernas. Currently, the only **place to stay** is the serviceable *Hotel Kourites* (℡28440 22194; ❸), on the eastern edge of the village with its own new taverna 50m beyond the hotel; it's worth asking to stay in the newer balcony rooms above this. The hotel also rents some pleasant, fully equipped apartments in the old village (€60, sleeping up to four) for a minimum stay of two nights. Other places to eat in the village proper include *Kri Kri* on the main street, and the excellent *Kronia* nearby, which has a Cretan-French menu thanks to the proprietor's Gallic wife; it tends to be deluged with coach parties from the coast over lunch, but it's a good bet in the evening. The bakery next door to the *Kronia* sells fresh, extremely hot *tirópita*, some of the best to be had on the plateau.

From the junction in the centre of Tzermiádho, there's a sign directing you up to the **Trápeza Cave**, in which Evans and Pendlebury discovered remains and tombs dating back to Neolithic times. If you don't take up the offer from one of the many elderly "guides" who might accost you en route, you'll need to look out for a signed slope (erroneously indicating "to the Kronos Cave") on the left where the track narrows. With a new path and stone steps, it is now an easy climb to reach the narrow cave entrance. As you wander in the murky darkness (a torch is essential), it's easy to imagine that this is where Crete began: Stone Age peoples huddled around fires no doubt telling stories in the manner of surviving tribal groups today. From these modest beginnings sprang the Minoans and then, under their tutelage, the Greeks.

The ascent to Karfí

From Tzermiádho, there's also an ascent to the ancient Minoan site of **Karfí**, one of the most dramatic places in Crete, perched on the southeast slope of Mount Karfí with an opportunity to see some of the area's spectacular birds of prey. The climb takes about an hour on foot, less if you drive the first part; you'll need sturdy footwear and, in summer, plenty of water. There are a number of shady places for a picnic on the way up, or even at the site itself, but remember to take all rubbish away with you.

The start of the track up is located on Tzermiádho's western edge at the side of the district health centre, opposite a blue sign marked in English, "To the Timios Stavros church". Follow the path as it winds gently up to the **Níssimos plateau** (also accessible by car), a twenty- to thirty-minute walk offering fine views over the Lasíthi plain. Once on the plateau, you'll arrive at a fork where three dirt tracks diverge. Take the left track aiming for a small, whitewashed chapel, below a saddle between two peaks. Leave any transport near the chapel, from just to the right of which the ascent begins. You will soon spot the way-marks at the start of the climb, followed fairly soon by the name, Karfi, daubed in Greek on various rocks. It's an easy and well-marked thirty-minute ascent from here up through a rocky landscape patrolled by agile goats.

At the end of the climb, after taking in the magnificent **views** over the coast and distant Hersónisos to the north, you'll come to the **archeological site** spread across a saddle between the summit of Mount Karfi (the location of an ancient peak sanctuary) to the west and the pinnacle of Mikre Koprana (topped by a trig point) to the east. Founded in the twelfth century BC, in this enclave, Minoan refugees fleeing from the Dorian advance attempted to pre-serve vestiges of their ancestral culture. The settlement consists of a cluster of stone-built single-storey dwellings, a rather crude imitation of the site at Goúrnia. For the three thousand or so inhabitants who lived here prior to the site's peaceful evacuation around 1000 BC, life must have been a grim strug-gle, lashed by the winds and prey to the vicious winter elements. But this very inaccessibility was of great defensive value and preserved the settlement from attack, whilst the cultivation of the Níssimos plateau below provided food and pasture for livestock.

Among the ruins, excavated in the 1930s by John Pendlebury, the easiest structure to identify is what the archeologist described as the **Great House**, an important building still retaining its walls and where a number of bronze artefacts were discovered. Behind this, just to the north in an area covered with a carpet of ancient potsherds, a **shrine** was located containing remarkable, metre-high terracotta goddesses with arms raised in blessing (now in the Iráklion Archeological Museum). The remainder of this desolate village, inter-sected by a number of paved alleyways, isn't easy to make sense of, except for the dwelling thresholds and the odd evocative hand-grindstone lying among the collapsed piles of stones. Even so, this remote eyrie, with all its historical associations, remains one of the most haunting places on the island.

Whilst you're up here, there's a good chance you'll see the odd **griffon vulture** gliding majestically overhead, or maybe even the much rarer **lammergeier**, or bearded vulture, now down to a handful of isolated pairs. There are few more dramatic sights than this raptor hoisting the leg bones of its victims into the air and dashing them onto a rock below (nearly always the same one); once they are broken, the bird extracts the marrow with its specially adapted tongue.

Áyios Konstantínos and Áyios Yeóryios

Clockwise from Tzermiádho, the next village of any size is **Áyios Konstantínos**, which is where the Neápoli road emerges onto the plain. Here, too, you could find a **room** if you wanted one – tapestry seller María Vlassi has simple rooms sharing bath (☎ 28440 31048; ❶) – and because it is the first (and last) village most people visit, it is packed with souvenir stores – watch par-ticularly for a priest and his wife selling embroidered fabrics: these two could sell ice to Eskimos. You may also see a villager working her antique family "heirloom" in the doorway of her store. Natural dyes from onions, walnuts and other sources are still used here by some.

Áyios Yeóryios, 3km west and next in line, is larger and less commercial than Áyios Konstantínos. A small **Folk Museum** here (April–Oct daily 10am–4pm; €2.50) also contains a fascinating photo-biography of Crete's acclaimed writer, Níkos Kazantzákis. Just above and behind this is another **museum**, dedicated to Crete's great statesman, Eleftheríos Venizélos (April–Oct daily 10am–4pm; free), with interesting photos and news cuttings documenting the great man's life. Excellent-value simple **rooms**, food and home-made wine are to be had at the friendly *Hotel Dias* on the village's main thoroughfare (℡28440 31207; ❶), or you could try the misnamed *Hotel Rea* (℡28440 31209; ❶), further along the same street, which has more rooms with shared bath. Signs off the main street will also direct you to the friendly and bargain-priced *Hotel Maria* (℡28440 31774; ❷), offering attractive en-suite rooms; rooms with a double bed are even cheaper than those with twins. Nearby at **Magoulás**, 4km west on the road to Psihró, the roadside *Taverna Dionysos* (℡28440 31672; ❷) has rooms with bath and balcony (rooms 4 & 5 have a great view over the plain), and good food.

Psihró and around

The plateau's main destination is **PSIHRÓ**, the base for visiting Lasíthi's other chief attraction, the Dhiktean Cave, known as the birthplace of Zeus. Psihró village itself is another simple plateau community strung out along a tree-lined main street. There are a couple of **tavernas**, and **rooms** can be found at the newly rebuilt *Hotel Zeus* (℡28440 31284; ❸), a little way beyond the village towards the Dhiktean Cave. If you find everything full – as is likely during the big local festival held over the last three days in August – you may be allowed to camp at either of the two tavernas (*Antonis* or *Lassithi*) beyond the village's western edge where – not unreasonably – you'll be expected to eat at least one meal a day.

The Dhiktean Cave

The **Dhiktean Cave** (daily 8am–7pm; €4; ask for the free information leaflet on the cave) lies a kilometre southwest of Psihró, up a trail which is neither particularly long nor dauntingly steep but for which you can nonetheless hire a mule (for a hefty €10). According to legend, it was in the Dhiktean Cave that Zeus was born to Rhea. Zeus's father, Kronos, had been warned that he would be overthrown by a son, and accordingly ate all his offspring. On this occasion, however, Rhea gave Kronos a stone to eat instead and left the baby Zeus concealed within the cave, protected by the Kouretes (see p.436), who beat their shields outside to disguise his cries. From here, Zeus moved to the Idean Cave, on Psilorítis, where he spent his youth (see p.269). This, at least, is the version generally told here, and though there are scores of variations on the myth, it's undeniable that the cave was a cult centre from the Minoan period onwards, and that explorations around the turn of last century retrieved offerings to the Mother Goddess and to Zeus dating through up to Classical Greek times.

Recent alterations – including concrete steps and electric lighting – have made the cave a much safer place to visit, although some of the magic and mystery has inevitably been lost. The steps leading down into the cave now take you on a circular tour passing the bottom of the cave where you are confronted with an artificial lake. The one experience that has survived the alterations, however, is the view back from the depths of the cave towards the peephole of light at the entrance, framed in a blue haze caused by the damp atmosphere. It's not hard to believe the tales that this was the infant Zeus's first sight of the world destined to become his kingdom.

To avoid the crowds and savour the cave's mystical qualities to the full, try to arrive before noon or after 5pm. Also note that new **parking charges** at the cave car park (€2) are enforced – the money goes directly to fund local rural projects. Don't be tempted to park in the lane before the site – the parking tickets doled out here are a nice little earner for the local traffic police.

Exploring the plateau

One of the cave guardians, the genial Petros Zárvakis, takes people into the hills for **hikes** to spot wildflowers (mid-April to mid-June) and birds (April–Sept). From May to September, he also leads regular ascents to the summit of **Mount Dhíkti**, which include an overnight stay at a refuge and supper under the stars. It's not a terribly difficult climb, but you'll need stout walking boots or shoes and a sleeping bag. The cost depends on how many people there are (around €7.50 per person for a group of ten). For details, contact the polyglot Petros at the taverna facing the car park, when he's not on duty in the ticket office, or call him at his home in the village (☎28440 31600, mobile ☎6945616074).

Beyond Psihró, the road completes a circuit of the plateau via the villages of **Plati**, with more tapestry sellers, and the less exciting hamlets of Áyios Harálambos and Káto Metóhi, to meet with the road back to the coast at Pinakianó.

Áyios Nikólaos

Sited on the picturesque Gulf of Mirabéllo, "Ag Nik", as **ÁYIOS NIKÓLAOS** is known to the majority of its English-speaking visitors, was originally the ancient port for Lató, one of the dominant cities of this area in the Hellenistic era. This settlement faded in the Roman period and seems to have been abandoned in Byzantine times. The Venetians built a fortress here – of which nothing remains – and gave the surrounding gulf its name, Mirabéllo ("Lovely View"). The town came slowly back to life, and by the nineteenth century the port was again busy; following union with Greece in 1913, Áyios Nikólaos was confirmed as the **capital** of Lasíthi province.

A quiet harbour town for most of the last century, Áyios Nikólaos was discovered in the 1960s by international tourism. Its attractions are obvious: a setting on a small, hilly peninsula around a supposedly bottomless **lake** (Lake Voulisméni), now connected to the sea to form an inner harbour. It is wonderfully picturesque, and the lake, the harbour and the coast all around are fought over by restaurants, bars and hotels that charge well over the odds. Áyios Nikólaos's reputation took a nosedive some years ago when it became too crowded and too boisterous for its own good, but the town has emerged without any lasting damage. If you're looking for a decent **beach**, it's best to head a little further out – the few small patches of sand around the town are either closely guarded by expensive hotels or have standing room only by the time you've finished breakfast.

Arrival and information

You get the best impression of Áyios Nikólaos if you arrive by ferry; the dock is on a tiny peninsula, a couple of minutes' walk from the lake and the pretty

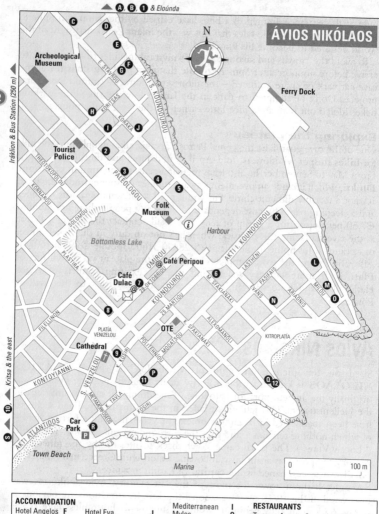

ÁYIOS NIKÓLAOS

Archeological Museum

Ferry Dock

Tourist Police

Folk Museum

Harbour

Bottomless Lake

Café Peripou

Café Dulac

OTE

PLATÍA VENIZELOU

Cathedral

Car Park

Town Beach

Marina

Iráklion & Bus Station (250 m)

& Eloúnda

Kritsa & the east

0   100 m

ACCOMMODATION						
Hotel Angelos	F	Hotel Eva	J	Mediterranean	I	
Aphrodite	H	The Green House	P	Mylos	O	
Atlantis	R	Hotel Hermes	E	Hotel Panorama	K	
Hotel Coral	A	Minos Palace Hotel	B	Hotel Pergola	L	
Hotel Creta	M	Marilena Pension	C	Perla Pension	D	
Hotel Doxa	S	Rooms Mary	N	Hotel Rea	G	
				Hotel Sgouros	Q	

RESTAURANTS			
Taverna Auoas	2	Loukakis	1
Avlí	4	Ofou To Lo	12
Du Lac	7	Pelagos	5
I Pita Tou Ríga	3	Portes	10
Itanos	9	Sarri's	11
La Strada	8	Twins	6

town centre. The **new bus station** is now at the north end of town, near the Archeological Museum. To reach the centre from here, walk uphill and turn right along Knossou and its continuation Kornarou, which brings you out above the lake; taking a left here to join Paleológou will lead you to the focal harbour zone. If you're **driving in** on the one-way system, head up the hill to Platía Venizélou, and then down into the picturesque areas past the souvenir stores which line both Koundoúrou and 28-Oktobríou. Parking places, however, are thin on the ground in the harbour area, and you're better off leaving your car in the car park near the marina or trying the less busy streets to the east of Platía Venizélou. The lake marks the centre of town in every way, and the narrow bridge over its channel is a notorious bottleneck for traffic and strolling visitors. From here, Aktí I. Koundoúrou curves around the sides of the harbour, and M. Sfakianáki strikes over a small hill to the cove of Kitroplatía. Almost all the action in Áyios Nikólaos takes place around these last two streets.

The **tourist information** office (July–Aug daily 8am–10pm, Sept–June daily 8am–9pm; T 28410 22357) is situated between the lake and the port. The tourist police are at Kontoyianni 34 (T 28410 26900), just off the bottom left corner of our town map. For departure information and details of **bike rental** and **boat trips**, see "Listings" on p.183.

Accommodation

It's become much easier to find **accommodation** in Áyios Nikólaos in recent years, though in peak season you may still struggle for choice. Nevertheless, there are literally thousands of rooms scattered all over town, and the best move is to visit the tourist information office, which normally has a couple of boards with cards and brochures about hotels and rooms. (If the prices seem very reasonable, it's probably because they're for the low season). There's no youth hostel and the nearest **campsite**, *Gournia Moon*, lies 17km southeast of the town along the coast (see p.194).

Hotel Angelos Aktí Koundoúrou 16 T 28410 23501, F 28410 23501. Welcoming small hotel offering excellent a/c balcony rooms with TV and fine views over the Gulf. ❸

Aphrodite Koritsas 27 T 28410 28058. Cheap and cheerful rooms place with lots of plants, a rooftop terrace and the use of a fridge. ❷

Atlantis Aktí Atlantidos 15 T 28410 28964, E p.mixalis@mailcity.com. Close to the town beach and the marina, this is a functional place offering balcony en-suite rooms with fridges and fans. Also has a snack bar below serving cheap breakfasts. ❷

Hotel Coral Aktí Koundoúrou, just off the top of our town map T 28410 28363, W www .hermes-hotels.gr. One of Áyios Nikólaos's leading in-town hotels (and twin of the slightly pricier *Hermes*, below) has a/c balcony rooms with sea-view, fridge and satellite TV, plus a rooftop pool and bar. When things are slack, prices can fall by up to 25 percent. Rates Include breakfast. ❼

Hotel Creta Sarolidi 22 east of the Kitroplatía T 28410 28893, W www.dantravel.biz. Very pleasant, recently modernized hotel where studio rooms come with a/c, TV, kitchenette and balcony sea-view. ❸

Hotel Doxa Idomeneos 7, close to town beach T 28410 24214, F 28410 24614. Nice, modern hotel where well-equipped, a/c balcony rooms come with TV and fridge. Open all year; rates include breakfast. ❺

Hotel Eva Stratigoú Kóraka 30 T 28410 22587. Misnamed rooms place with good en-suite balcony rooms with fans and sea view. ❷

The Green House Modatsou 15 T 28410/22025. A 1970s throwback (and little has changed here since), this is one of the cheapest places in town, popular with backpackers. It's a clean pension with shared bathrooms, a ramshackle garden, and breakfast as an optional extra. ❷

Hotel Hermes Aktí Koundoúrou on the seafront. Áyios Nikólaos's flagship hotel has similar facilities to its older sister, the *Hotel Coral*, and includes a larger rooftop pool. In slack periods, prices can fall by up to 25 percent. Rates includes breakfast. ❼

Marilena Pension Erithrou Stavrou 14 T 28410 22681, F 28410 24218. Not the bargain it once was, the Marilena is still a pleasant place to stay, with a friendly proprietor and some rooms with sea view and balcony. ❺

Rooms Mary Evans 13 near the Kitroplatía T 28410 24384. Very friendly place with en-suite, sea-view balcony rooms with fridge and use of communal kitchen. Also has some nearby and good value apartments sleeping up to four for around €50. ❷

Mediterranean S. Dhávaki 27 T 28410 23611. Clean, economical en-suite rooms with fridges and fans, and use of kitchen. ❷

Minos Palace Hotel on the promontory 1km north of the town T 28410 23801, W www .mamidakishotels.gr. The most appealing of a clutch of luxury hotels just outside town, this is a veritable village in its own right. All rooms are a/c and come with satellite TV, room safe, minibar and balcony or terrace – the pricier suites come with a private pool. Surrounding gardens have a larger pool, tennis courts and private beach. All kinds of watersports are on offer from sailing to scuba diving. The cheapest double in high season costs €202. Rates include breakfast. **9**

Mylos Sarolidi 2 ☏ 28410 23783. Sweet little pension east of the Kitroplatía, with some of the best rooms in town for the price. Spotless, en-suite balcony rooms (number 2 is a dream) with spectacular sea views over the Gulf. **3**

Hotel Panorama Sarolidi 2 ☏ 28410 28890, Ⓦ www.globtron.com/links/panorama.htm. Refurbished hotel overlooking the harbour with smart balcony, a/c rooms and an attractive roof terrace. **4**

Hotel Pergola Aktí Themistocleos ☏ 28410 28152. Very good value hotel where balcony sea-view rooms come equipped with a/c, fridge and TV. Rooms with the same facilities but with inland and side views are significantly cheaper. **2**–**3**

Pension Perla Salaminos 4 ☏ 28410 23379. Decent budget option close to the sea, on a hill to the north of the harbour. En-suite rooms come with fridge and fans, and front rooms have sea-view balconies. **2**

Hotel Rea Marathonós 1 ☏ 28410 90330, Ⓦ www.reahotel.ae.gr. Older hotel now in need of a refit, with spectacular views from balcony rooms overlooking the Mirábello Gulf. **4**

Hotel Sgouros Kitroplatía ☏ 28410 28931. Modern hotel next to one of the town's main beaches, with a/c balcony sea-view rooms with fridge and TV, and ample tavernas nearby. **4**

The Town

Things to do in town by day are pretty limited – you're not supposed to have recovered from the night before so soon. A couple of **museums** hold some interest, but for most visitors the days are taken up strolling the area around **Lake Voulisméni** (allegedly over 60m deep), nosing around in the shops, and heading for the strips of **beach** in the little cove at Kitroplatía, where there's also a rocky foreshore from which you can swim. More bathing spots lie to the north of the centre (reached along Aktí S Koundoúrou) where, by the *Dolphin* taverna, you'll find a narrow length of gritty sand, or there's a busy municipal beach (with entry fee) beyond the marina on the southwest side of town. The latter, at least, is clean and sandy, but again it's terribly crowded. Most people simply end up diving off the rocks which line the foreshore north of town, or else they get out of town altogether. There's a constant stream of people walking to the sandy beach at Almirós, 2km to the south; further in this direction by bus or bike there are good beaches around Kaló Hório, or in the other direction around Eloúnda (see following sections). The **boat trips** to beaches around the bay are also popular; see p.183 for details.

The **Folk Museum** (Mon–Fri & Sun 11am–4pm; €3) is opposite the bridge and housed on the ground floor of the harbour master's office, across from the tourist office. It has a small but interesting display of handicrafts (especially embroidery), costumes, pottery, cooking utensils and old Cretan goat-leather bagpipes. A privately run **aquarium** has opened at Aktí Koundoúrou 30, on the waterfront near the *Coral Hotel* (daily 10am–9pm; €4, children €3). Although small, the aquarium has a fascinating collection of fish, shellfish and octopuses, as well as terrapins, crabs and eels.

The Archeological Museum

There's more interest in the well-laid-out **Archeological Museum** (Tues–Sun 8.30am–3pm; €3) on Paleológou, north of the lake. A visit to the museum will mean a lot more after you've explored a few sites in the area. Things may be about to change here as a completely new museum is planned on the same site, with construction due to begin in the next two years.

Following some interesting Neolithic finds in Room 1, including a fascinating early third-millennium BC "prototype" of the Festós Disc (see p.89) from Ayía Fotiá near Sitía, Room 2 contains the museum's star exhibit, the extraordinary **Goddess of Mírtos**. This goose-necked early Minoan (ca.2500 BC) clay figurine – actually a jug – was found during the excavation of the Bronze Age settlement at Fournoú Korifí, near Mírtos. Note the pubic triangle, breasts, and the square panels thought to portray a woven garment. The beak-spouted jug she's holding (which is also the vessel's mouth) is similar to vases in the museum from the same period. These first two rooms also contain some fine examples of Vasilikí ware, named after the early Bronze Age site on the isthmus of Ierápetra where it was first discovered. The lustrous mottled finish of this pottery was achieved by uneven firing, an effect which obviously pleased its creators. Even more remarkably, these flawless artefacts – including a "teapot" and a beak-spouted ewer dating from around 2500 BC – were made not on a wheel but on the clay "turntables" exhibited in Room 2. The potter's wheel only reached Crete some six hundred years later; you can see an early example from a tomb at Kritsá in Room 5. Room 3 displays some fine Marine-style pottery which, although found in a villa near Makriyialós, is thought to have come from the Knossós workshop. There's also some interesting **jewellery**, including a beautiful gold pin bearing an intricately crafted bramble motif and a tantalizingly long inscription in the undeciphered Linear A script on the reverse. In the same room is a wonderful collection of Late Minoan **clay sarcophagi**, or *lárnakes*, decorated with birds, fish and the one-tentacled octopus which seem to have so delighted Minoan artists. Archeologists assumed, when they turned up these items, that they were all burial chests. But when they found more of these painted tubs, with clearly identifiable plug-holes in the bottom, the Minoans had the last laugh – they were obviously avid bathers.

Room 4 is devoted to finds from the Minoan Palace at Mália (see p.126), focusing on the new discoveries in the Quartier (or sector) Mu (the Greek "M"), from which exhibits of tools, altars and some delicate ceramic wares testify to the Minoans' sophistication in the plastic arts. A curious **model house** found in sector "N" of the palace has a pitched roof and chimneys – both foreign concepts in Minoan architecture. **Linear B inscriptions** found in the palace are evidence – as happened at Knossós – of a Mycenaean presence in the period 1450–1200 BC, a fact only confirmed by these recent discoveries. In the centre of the room, an exquisite **stone vase** in the form of a triton shell bears the carved relief of two genii, one pouring a libation over the outstretched hands of the other. Note that the sculptor has even included the encrustations clinging to the shell – an ingenious touch.

Room 5 contains a rare Minoan **infant burial** displayed exactly as found at its site at Kryá, near Sitía. The transfer of the whole thing, which dates from the Late Minoan period, from site to museum by Costis Davaras "without displacing a single stone" must have been some headache. Finally, Rooms 7 and 8 deal with finds from the Greco-Roman period, now reorganized with a much better standard of presentation. Here also, there's an eerie **grinning skull** from the Roman cemetery at Potamós, on the edge of Áyios Nikólaos, to send you on your way. A wreath of gold olive leaves is still in place about its crown; the bronze *aryballos* (or oil container) and strigil displayed in the same case were found at the dead man's feet. The fact that both these items were used by athletes to clean and tone the skin suggests that he was a victor in one of the important games. These men – who brought great glory upon their cities – were honoured to the end of their days by their grateful fellow citizens and were often buried in some style. The silver coin originally found in the mouth of the deceased (the traditional fare paid to the boatman Charon, who ferried the dead across the River Styx to the underworld) is now displayed separately in the case.

Eating

There are tourist-oriented **tavernas** (invariably employing overenthusiastic greeters) all round the lake and harbour, with little to choose between them apart from the different perspectives you get on the passing fashion show. Have a drink here, perhaps, or a mid-morning coffee – but choose somewhere else to eat. The places around the Kitroplatía are generally fairer value, but again you pay for the location – the best-value establishments to eat tend to be less obvious, tucked away in the backstreets behind the tourist office or close to Platía Venizélou.

Taverna Auoas Paleológou 44. On the way to the Archeological Museum, this serves very good traditional Cretan food in a plant-covered trellised courtyard. Its rather isolated position makes it sometimes a little lifeless.

Avlí Odhós P. Georgiou 12, two blocks behind the tourist office. Delightful garden *ouzeri* offering a wide *mezédhes* selection as well as more elaborate dishes. Open eves only.

Du Lac By the lake. Gets most plaudits from locals as the best on the lake for quality and service, and where the "fresh fish" usually is. The downside is that you pay through the nose for it.

Itanos Kyprou. On a side street off the east side of Platía Venizélou, this popular place serves typical – and reasonably priced – Cretan food and wine, and has a terrace across the road opposite.

Loukakis Aktí S. Koundoúrou 24. The town's oldest taverna (founded in 1952) is a good-value, traditional family-run place, a few minutes' walk away from the port along the Eloúnda road. Has a small terrace facing the sea.

Ofou To Lo Kitroplatía, last in line on the western side. The best of the tavernas fronting the beach here, offering well-cooked food, fair-priced fish

and friendly service; their *loukánika me tirí* (sausages with cheese) is a recommended starter.

Pelagos Koraka 10, behind the tourist office (℗ 28410 25737). A stylish and popular fish taverna housed in an elegant mansion. Their delightful leafy garden terrace is the best in town and complements the excellent food. Pricey, but worth it.

I Pita Tou Ríga Paleológou 24, close to the lake. Excellent Lilliputian snack-bar/restaurant serving imaginative fare – salads, filled pita breads and some Asian dishes; also has a small raised terrace up steps across the road.

Portes Anaspafseos 3, near the sports stadium. Friendly and atmospheric little neighbourhood taverna serving well-prepared taverna standards.

Sarri's Kyprou 15. Great little economical neighbourhood café-diner, especially good for breakfast and *souvláki*, served on a leafy terrace.

La Strada N. Plastira, slightly northwest of Platía Venizélou. Not bad pizzas and pretty good pasta at this popular Italian upmarket venue.

Twins Fronting the harbour. Handy pizzeria, fast-food outlet and coffee bar, open all hours. Their "small" pizzas measure 40cm in diameter.

Drinking, nightlife and entertainment

After you've eaten, you can start to get into the one thing which Áyios Nikólaos undeniably does well: **bars** and **nightlife**. Not that you really need a guide to this – the bars are hard to avoid, and you can just follow the crowds to the most popular places.

For a more relaxed drink, the *Hotel Alexandros* on Paleológou has a rooftop bar overlooking the lake which, after dark, metamorphoses into a music bar playing old hits. Even better views are to be had from the terrace bars overlooking the lake's western flank, reached by following Odhós Plastira from near Platía Venizélou – *Café Migomas* is one of a number of stylish places here; it's good for breakfast and late drinks, although their restaurant is overpriced. The pleasantly old-fashioned *Asteria* café fronting the harbour is one of the oldest, and here – unlike many places in town – you still get a bill and they trust you not to walk away without paying. A relaxed drinking scene spreads along the Aktí Koundoúrou harbourside, where a string of bars – *Café Puerto*, *Candia*, *Creta Café* and *Café Kastro* among them – play cool sounds to customers chatting on their waterside terraces. *Yiannis*, further down the harbour or, further still, *Porto*, where the ferry boats arrive, are other popular places. *Café du Lac*, 28-Oktobríou 17, near the lake is similarly stylish, serving milkshakes, icecream and cocktails, and also has **Internet** access. If you feel like a drink on the harbour itself, then head for the floating café-bar *Armida* (April–Oct), aboard a beautiful century-old wooden trading vessel, serving cocktails and simple *mezédhes*. Around midnight, when the crowds have gone, the cafés along the lakeside also make pleasant places to linger – *Zygos*, on the north side near Paleológou, is a relaxing cocktail bar with a garden.

Quiet drinking is not what it's all about in the **disco-bars**. *Lipstick*, on the Koundoúrou harbourside, is the only genuine full-blown dance club (where the foreigners rather than the locals do the dancing), and nearby *Rule Club* (above the *Creta Café*) doesn't get going until when the pubs and restaurants close. There are raucous music bars to try at the bottom of 25-Martíou (known as "Soho Street") where it heads up the hill – *Rififi*, *Royale*, *Oxygen*, *Cellar* and *Roxy* all go on into the small hours, while around the corner on K. Sfakianaki *Santa Maria* is a popular place with locals. Across the harbour, *Aquarius* and *Charlie Chan* also get lively, while *Sorrento* is another "golden oldies" music bar frequented by a north-European crowd.

Each year, Áyios Nikólaos mounts a summer-long **cultural festival**, "The Lato", which includes music, dance and theatre from Crete, Greece and other parts of Europe. Keep an eye out for posters advertising the various events, or ask at the tourist office.

Listings

Airlines Tickets and timetables for Olympic and Aegean airlines are available from Plora Travel, 28-Oktobríou 24 ☏ 28410 25868.

Banks Banks and exchange places are mostly found along Koundoúrou (where there are also ATMs) and 28-Oktobríou. The tourist office also changes money at good rates.

Boat trips Trips to points around the gulf mostly leave from the west side of the harbour, near the tourist office, and if you walk around here and along Aktí Koundoúrou northwards you'll be accosted by their operators. There are daily trips to Spinalónga (costing between €12 & €15), as well as more expensive trips with meals included. Other sailings go to Móhlos (€59 with lunch included), and there's a weekly trip to Santorini (currently sailing at 7am on Thursdays; €59 including breakfast). Other operators around the harbour also run no-frills trips, often undercutting these prices considerably.

Books and newspapers Anna Karteri, Koundoúrou 5 near Platía Venizélou, has a good selection of books in English. Quick Film at no. 44 on the same street is the best source for foreign newspapers.

Bus station For route information, call ☏ 28410 22234. Buy tickets on the bus for services to Eloúnda (€1), Kritsá (€1), Lasíthi Plateau (€3.50) and Vái (€7.70).

Car and bike rental Available from dozens of outlets, mainly in the harbour area. It's fairly expensive in high season, though outside the summer months shopping around can bring you a real bargain. For scooters and low-powered bikes, try the friendly and reliable Mike Manolis (☏ 28410 24940), who has a pitch at the junction of 25-Martíou and K. Sfakianáki near the OTE; he also rents high-quality mountain bikes. Readers with this guide will receive a twenty-percent discount. For cars, the reliable Clubcars, 28-Oktobríou 24 (☏ 28410 25868), and Ilias, Platía Venizélou (☏ 28410 28339), are worth a try.

Ferries The main agents for services to Pireás, Rhodes and the Dodecanese islands are Plora Travel at 28-Oktobríou 24 ☏ 28410 82804 and Nostos Tours, Koundoúrou 30 ☏ 28410 22819. There are many other travel agents for local tours.

Hospital The town hospital ☏ 28410 66000 is at the northern end of Paleológou, one block beyond the Archeological Museum.

Internet *Café du Lac*, 28-Oktobríou 17 (daily 9am–1am; €4.50 per hour) near the restaurant of the same name, has a couple of terminals, whilst the nearby *Internet Café Peripou*, 28-Oktobríou 25 (daily 9.30am–2am; €4.50 per hour or €1.50 for 15min) with more screens is another possibility.

Laundry To Teleio, Paleológou 13 near the junction with S. Davaki, will wash, dry and fold 5kg for around €10.50.

Left luggage Facilities are available at the bus station from 6am to 9pm, but as there is little control of who goes into and out of the area reserved, it's not really worth taking the risk.

OTE On N. Sfakianáki, just above 25-Martíou (daily: June–Oct 7am–midnight; Nov–May 7am–10.30pm; ☎28410 95513).

Post office 28-Oktobríou, above the lake (Mon–Sat 7.30am–2.30pm; ☎28410 23744).

Scuba diving The PADI-Certificated Happy

Divers are based at the *Coral Hotel* (see p.179) ☎28410 82546, ⦿www.happydivers.gr. Boats leave from the pier opposite the hotel. Courses for absolute beginners start from €50; five-day courses (beginners and advanced) cost from €325.

Shopping María Patsaki, Sfakianáki 2, sells a range of embroidery, textiles and antiques. Music Formula, Kontogianni 13 west of Platía Venizélou, has a good selection of Cretan traditional music, including songs and *lyra*. Kafekopteíon, 28-Oktobríou 3 near Platía Venizélou, has a wide range of Cretan and Greek wines, plus many different teas and coffees. Cretan Mystery, Aktí Atlantidhos 11 near the bus station, sells Cretan natural beauty products as well as herbs, spices and olive oil.

Taxis There's a rank in the main square, Platía Venizélou, and another behind the tourist office; or call ☎28410 24000.

The Gulf of Mirabéllo

North of Áyios Nikólaos, the swankier hotels are strung out along the **Gulf of Mirabéllo** coast road – top of the pile being the *Minos Palace* (see p.179), replete with bungalows, private pools and a jealously guarded beach. One reason for calling in at this upmarket oasis is to take a look at the Byzantine church of **Áyios Nikólaos**, which now lies in the hotel's grounds and from which the modern resort takes its name. To gain entry to the church (9am–6pm), you'll need to ask for the key at the hotel's reception desk, leaving your passport as deposit. The trouble is worth it in order to see some of the earliest **fresco** fragments found in Greece, dating back to the eighth or ninth century. The geometric patterns and motifs that survive are the legacy of the Iconoclastic movement, which banned the representation of divine images in religious art.

Soon after this, the road begins to climb; looking across the bay, you can make out Psíra and Móhlos against the stark wall of the Thryptís and Ornó ranges of the Sitía mountains, while nearer at hand mothballed supertankers are moored among the small islands sheltering in the lee of the peninsula. One of the largest of these islets, **Áyios Pándes**, is a refuge for the island's wild goat, the *kri-kri*. The animals have an elusive reputation and usually manage to avoid the cruise parties from Áyios Nikólaos which put in to see them.

Eloúnda and Oloús

The road drops back to sea level as it approaches the small resort of **ELOÚNDA**. Before you reach the centre of the village, there's an easy-to-miss road signed off to the east (right) leading downhill to the "sunken city" of Oloús (see p.186).

Although it has one very exclusive hotel and scores of new apartment developments, Eloúnda is low-key and slow moving – a very different proposition from Ag Nik. At its heart is an enormous square with cafés and restaurants, stores and hotels on three sides, and the seafront promenade on the fourth. This is the best place to **park** if you've driven, it's where the **bus** stops, and also where the **boats** to Spinalónga (every 30min; daily 10am–4.30pm; €7) leave from. Just about everything else in Eloúnda is in the immediate vicinity, including the **post office**, OTE (Mon–Sat 3–11pm, Sun 5–10pm), bookshop with foreign press and books, and car rental offices. Among a number of **travel agencies**, the helpful Olous Travel (ⓣ28410 41324) next to the post office doubles as a local information office, can assist with finding accommodation and apartments to rent, changes money at decent rates and also does car rental (twenty-percent discount to readers with this guide). There's also a **bank** with ATM cash dispensers and, just off to the south, an excellent bakery. **Internet** access is available at *Bar Babel* on the north side of the harbour. Courses in **scuba diving** are run by Happy Divers (ⓣ28410 41850); see p.184 for details.

Accommodation

There are several **accommodation** options around the resort, and should you have difficulty finding somewhere in high season, any of the travel agents (particularly Olous Travel) on the main square can usually come up with something satisfactory. For directions to the accommodation suggestions along the Oloús road, see the Oloús account on p.186.

Akti Olous Hotel Along the Oloús road ⓣ28410 41270, ⓦwww.greekhotels.net/aktiolous. An attractive seventy-room seafront hotel where comfortable balcony rooms come equipped with a/c, TV, fridge and room safe. Has own seashore terrace cafeteria flanked by a small beach. ❻

Christina Along the Oloús road ⓣ28410 41882. Welcoming place offering economical en-suite rooms with fridges and sea views. ❸

Elounda Beach 2km south of the village along the coast road ⓣ28410 41412, ⓦwww.eloundabeach.gr. Hidden away behind guarded security gates this is Eloúnda's luxury hotel and one of the Mediterranean's most exclusive addresses. Guests are pampered with private pools, butlers, seafront villas, sumptuous gardens and lots more. Room prices start at €350 per night and "grand suites" go for over €2200.

Milos Rooms & Delfinia Rooms Operated by the Pediaditis Bookshop (ⓣ28410 41641, ⓦwww.pediaditis.gr) on the main square, these are nearby and well-equipped rooms, studios and apartments, which come with sea views and (at the *Milos*) a pool. ❷–❹

Pension Oasis ⓣ28410 41076, ⓕ28410 41128. At the northern end of the village behind the church, this is a good and friendly budget option for comfortable en-suite rooms with fans and fridges in a garden setting. ❷

Paradisos Taverna Along the Oloús Road ⓣ28410 41631. Close to the *Christina*, this is another attractive waterfront option with balcony en-suite rooms; a/c is available for a supplementary charge. ❸

Eating and drinking

Eloúnda has a good choice of **tavernas** and **restaurants** – many of them rather pricey, particularly those along the seafront. Still, the overall standard is high and the food goes down well with the Sitían wines which seem to have cornered the market here. Good choices at the mid-to-upper end of the price scale include *Marilena*, on the harbour, which serves elaborate versions of traditional Greek dishes, and the chic and even pricier *Ferryman* (tellingly, with a menu in English only) whose earlier incarnation featured in "*Who Pays the Ferryman?*", a 1970s BBC TV drama series. *Britomartis*, noted for its fish, occupies a plum spot in the centre of the harbour, while *Poulis*, on a floating pontoon on the Oloús road, is another popular seafood place. One of the best places for good and economical fish is *Nikos*, bang in the centre of the square, but patchy service can result in yawning gaps between dishes. Other cheap options for *mezédhes* are the simple *Ouzerí Maritsa* below the church tower at the north end of the square, a small, unnamed *ouzerí* immediately left (south) of a large supermarket in the centre of the square, and the *Aligos* café and bar nearby. **Nightlife** in Eloúnda is definitely low-key, centred around café terraces and cocktail bars. The *Hellas* café, on the back road behind the beach, is a good example of the latter, and has live Greek music at weekends.

Oloús

On the southern reaches of Eloúnda, a hard-to-spot (signed) road heads east downhill to a causeway, all that remains of the sunken isthmus that once linked the peninsula of Spinalónga (often known as "big Spinalónga" to distinguish it from the more famous island of the same name) and the mainland. All around the causeway on both sides you'll find people swimming from small patches of **beach** or basking on flat rocks. Protected by it are the remains of Venetian salt pans, now fallen into disrepair, but which are worth checking for migrating birds in the spring.

The site of ancient **Oloús** lay around the far end of the causeway inland, and along the coast to the south and east where a number of structures can be made out beneath the waves. Though it is known chiefly for having been the port of Dríros, what little remains is **Roman**: there's a fenced enclosure behind the popular *Canal Bar* (good *mezédhes* and *moussaká* at lunchtime) in which you can see the floor of a fourth-century Roman **basilica** with an odd, almost patchwork-style black and white mosaic, and among the rocks a little further round (watch out for sea urchins) are the sunken traces of harbour installations now submerged due to the rise in sea level over the past couple of millennia. The site has never been excavated, however, and this is about the extent of what is visible, but the excursion is worth it for the setting – the **beaches**, causeway, "French" canal and stone windmills. On the far side of the peninsula there are better beaches still – tough to get to except by boat (enquire at any of the travel agents on the main square who may be able to put you in touch with a local fisherman).

Spinalónga and around

One of the most popular boat trips from Eloúnda is to the imposing fortress rock of **Spinalónga** at the northern end of the bay. Although the islet can be visited from Áyios Nikólaos and also Pláka, the great majority of visitors leave by boat from Eloúnda and it is certainly the most convenient way of getting there, with reasonably priced *kaïkia* (round-trip tickets €7) making the trip every half-hour or so.

Founded by the **Venetians** in 1579 to defend the approach to the gulf and the sheltered anchorages behind the peninsula of Spinalónga, the **fortress** (8am–7pm daily; €1.50) with its battlements, guard towers and seemingly impregnable walls bears all the hallmarks of the Italian republic's military architecture. Like their other island fortresses, it proved impregnable and was only handed over to the Turks by treaty in 1715, some fifty years after the rest of Crete had surrendered. The infamous part of the island's history is much more recent, however. For the first fifty years of the last century, Spinalónga was a leper colony, the last in Europe. Lepers were sent as outcasts – long after drugs to control their condition had rendered such measures entirely unnecessary – to a colony that was primitive in the extreme and administered almost as if it were a detention camp. Its jail was frequently used for lepers who dared complain about their living conditions.

Even today, there's an unnerving sense of isolation when the boat leaves you here, at a jetty from which a long tunnel leads up into the fortified centre. There are still just two easily sealed entrances: this tunnel, and a jetty on the seaward side (which you see if you approach from Áyios Nikólaos) which leads up to the old **castle gate** with its lion of St Mark. Around the base of the castle a real town grew up – Turkish buildings mostly, adapted by the lepers using whatever materials they could find. Although everything is in decay, you can still pick out a row of stores and some houses which must once have been quite grand.

Pláka

The colony's mainland supply centre was at **Pláka**, about 5km north of Eloúnda, once an isolated fishing village but now in danger of having its tranquillity shattered by the utterly misguided construction of a sprawling holiday complex which covers the side of a hill overlooking it, despoiling the view as you approach. Boats still cross to the island from the quayside behind the *Spinalonga Taverna* (April–Sept hourly 9am–6pm; €6 return). This is a good bet if you fancy having Spinalónga to yourself and don't want to share it with hundreds of others. Of the **tavernas** (each with its own fishing boat), the *Spinalonga* serves fresh fish at reasonable prices, and rents studio rooms with kitchenette and balcony sea view (℡28410 41804; ➌), while the pricier *Delfini* (℡28410 41489; ➌) also rents out **rooms** and **apartments**. For fresh fish, the latter, as well as the nearby *Gorgona*, are both worth a try. There's beautifully clear water to swim in beyond a beach on which the pebbles are rather too large for comfort. Only at weekends, when locals come to escape the crowds elsewhere, does the place lose its tranquillity – although the impact of the new hotel development may radically alter this.

On foot, you could continue north to the point of the cape in around ninety minutes, following the road which climbs almost as far as the next village, **Vrouhás**, before taking off along a track above the sea.

Kritsá and around

Aside from Spinalónga, the other popular excursion from Áyios Nikólaos is 9km inland to **Kritsá**, a "traditional" village. Despite the commercialization, this is a trip well worth making for a break from the frenetic pace of the town; buses run at least every hour from the main station. Along the way are a remarkable church, the Panayía Kirá, and an ancient site, Lató – both worthy of a visit.

Panayía Kirá

About 1km before Kritsá southwest of Áyios Nikólaos, the road runs straight past the lovely Byzantine church of **Panayía Kirá** (daily 8.30am–3pm; €3), inside which is preserved perhaps the most complete and certainly the most famous set of **Byzantine frescoes** in Crete.

Of the three naves (the buttresses and lantern are later additions), the larger, central one is the oldest, though the frescoes have all been retouched and restored to such an extent that it is impossible to say with certainty which is the most ancient. All of them originate from the fourteenth and perhaps early fifteenth centuries. Those in the **south aisle**, through which you enter, depict the life of Anne, mother of Mary – her marriage to Joachim and the birth of Mary – and the early life of the Virgin herself up to the journey to Bethlehem. In the **centre** of the church, Mary's story is continued and there are scenes from the life of Christ, including the Nativity, Herod's banquet and a superb

Last Supper. And in the **north aisle** there are vivid scenes of the Second Coming and Judgement, along with the delights of Paradise and assorted interludes from the lives of the saints (especially St Anthony). Throughout, the major scenes are interspersed with small portraits of saints and apostles.

Alongside the church are a couple of **tavernas** and a store selling excellent, but expensive, reproduction icons.

Lató

Just beyond the church, you can turn off north towards the archeological site of **Lató** (Tues–Sun 8.30am–3pm; free), about 3km up an asphalted road. At the time of writing, a new ticket office with café and toilet facilities have been constructed – this could mean that an admission charge may be levied in the future.

Although there's as much to be seen here as in many of the more celebrated sites, it's very little visited: presumably because most visitors' interests are directed to the Minoans, and this was a much later settlement, Doric in origin but flourishing through to Classical times. Even the archeologists shared this lack of curiosity, for systematic excavation of the site started only in 1967 under the French School. The city's name derives from a Cretan Doric corruption of **Leto**, the mythical mother of Artemis and Apollo. Homer relates in the *Odyssey* how Eileíthyia (the Minoan goddess of childbirth) attended Leto when she gave birth to the god Apollo on the island of Delos: it is thus fitting that Eileíthyia became the patron goddess of Lató, as coins discovered here proved. That it was an important city is clear from the sheer extent of the ruins, which spread in every direction. It is a magnificent setting – a city of sombre grey

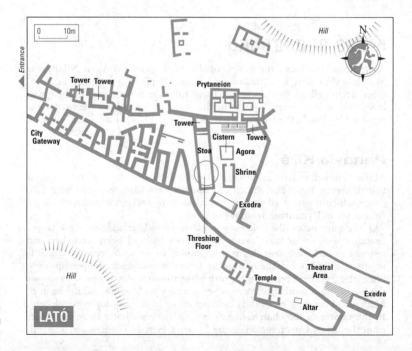

stone sprawled across the saddle between the twin peaks of a dauntingly craggy hill – and standing on the southernmost peak you can look down onto the white cluster of **Áyios Nikólaos** (Lató's ancient port), with the bay and Oloús (a major rival of Lató in its heyday) beyond, as well as inland to the valleys and climbing peaks of the Dhiktean mountains. Ruins aside, these tremendous views would be worth the effort expended in getting here. The exposed position can't have been all that practical, however, and wearing anything resembling a toga must have been a hazardous business in the fierce summer winds which gust from all directions.

You **enter** the site 200m or so below the ruins, then follow a rough path up to a rectangular area with a **gateway**, which would have been the original entrance to Lató. Continuing to climb up the street from here, you can see the stores and workshops abutting the city wall on the right, with defensive towers and gateways into the residential areas on the left. Higher up still, the open area of the **agora** is an interesting fusion of early Greek and older Minoan influences. This pentagonal space was a meeting place for citizens but also incorporates a tier of steps on its northern side, reminiscent of the theatral areas at Minoan sites such as Knossós and Festós. The steps ascend between the remains of two towers to the **prytaneion**, or town hall, with small rooms at the rear which held the city's archives. In the centre of the agora is a deep square cistern and a shrine, flanked on the western side by a colonnaded **stoa**, a shady place to shelter from the elements. The southern end of this has been cut through by a relatively modern circular threshing floor. The **exedra** nearby was a sort of public seating area, and in the southeast corner of the site is another exedra with what is termed a "theatral area" beside it – a broad flight of steps again similar to the Minoan style – which leads to a raised terrace containing a well-preserved fourth-century BC temple with a stepped altar just before it.

It's possible to retrace your steps from Lató to where the track divides, and then turn right along a newly asphalted road to head down (turning right again at the first junction) to Flamourianá on the Lakonía plain, from where there's a road – and occasional **buses** – back to Áyios Nikólaos.

Kritsá

KRITSÁ, about 10km southwest of Áyios Nikólaos, is a sizeable place known as "the largest village in Crete", but its popularity and fame as a handicrafts centre have done little to spoil it. Nowadays, it feels more like a small town, with the main street lined with tourist stores selling (mostly) leather goods or embroidery. Despite the commercialism, prices are a great deal better than in Áyios Nikólaos – though you can still pay as much as €500 and more for some of the wonderful, elaborately woven rugs – and if you manage to avoid the tour-bus crowds (early morning and mid-afternoon are the best times) the place reverts to a friendly semi-somnolence in which you're free to wander and browse under no pressure at all.

Kritsá's other chief claim to fame lies in its situation, with views back over the green valley up which you arrived and the mountains rising steeply behind. You get little impression of this at street level, other than an awareness that you are climbing quite steeply, so try to get out onto one of the balconies at the back of the cafés along the main street, where you can look back over the town and towards Áyios Nikólaos. If you arrive by car, use the signed **car park** on the way into the village, as there's no chance of finding a parking place in the narrow streets. Near the car park is a **post office,** and there's an **ATM** on the village square where the bus drops you off.

△ Textile seller, Kritsá

Staying in Kritsá is a surprisingly easy and attractive option. There are usually beds to be found – there's certainly a greater chance here than on the coast – and it's a good place to experience a genuinely Cretan atmosphere. A number of places offer **rooms**. One of the best is *Argyro*, on your way into the village (☎ & Ⓕ 28410 51174; ❷–❸), which is clean and friendly, has balcony rooms with and without private shower around a courtyard, and its own café which serves Cretan dishes. *Pension Kera* (☎ 28410 51045; ❷), up the hill from the bus stop, is a simpler, slightly cheaper and less welcoming alternative. An inviting new possibility is *The Olive Press* (☎ 28410 51296, ⓦ www .olivepress.centerall.com; ❸), a Belgian venture with two pleasant rooms in a beautifully restored, stone-built olive-oil mill. A little difficult to find, it lies at the very end of the tapestry sellers' street, close to the church of Áyios Yeóryios Harakitis. If these are all full (which is unlikely), any of the textile sellers will put you in touch with family-run rooms nearby.

For **eating** and **drinking**, there are a number of cafés in the centre of Kritsá, including *Saridhakis*, a cool place to sit out under a plane tree. Otherwise, head for the bakers for tempting *tirópita* (cheese pies) or currant breads. One of the best-situated tavernas is *Castello*, in the centre, and there are a few others near where the bus stops.

Around Kritsá

If you want to explore further, you'll find more frescoed churches here and in the immediate surroundings. **Áyios Yeóryios**, for example, is on the edge of the village, signed uphill to the left as you walk through: the frescoes here are contemporary with those at the Panayía Kirá, though in a very much worse state of preservation. Further in this same direction, **Áyios Ioánnis** lies a kilometre or so down the road to Kroústas. These churches will probably be locked, so you'll need to enquire as to accessibility from the guardian at the Panayía Kirá.

South to the isthmus

The main road south and then east from Áyios Nikólaos is not a wildly exciting one – a drive through barren hills dotted with villas above the occasional sandy cove. Beyond the reed-fringed beaches at Almirós and Amoudhára there's little temptation to stop until you reach the cluster of increasing development around **Kaló Hório**, 10km south of Áyios Nikólaos. Here, there are several tavernas and minimarkets, an OTE and mobile post office. Below them, paths wind down quite steeply to a couple of excellent small **beaches**, on the first of which is a taverna by the outflow of a small river. Immediately after is **Ístro**, a burgeoning resort in its own right, just beyond which the exclusive *Istron Bay Hotel* (☎ 28410 61303, ⓦ www.istronbay.com; ❾) hangs from the cliff above a spectacular cove with a fine sandy beach. If you walk confidently through the hotel grounds, you can get down to enjoy this and the hotel's beach bar: there's no such thing as a private beach on Crete, but seemingly nothing to prevent all the approaches to the beach being privately controlled. Unfortunately, like all the beaches in this part of the bay, much rubbish is washed up, although the hotel staff regularly clean things up.

The stretch of the E75 beyond Ístro is now undergoing major engineering works intended to bypass the archeological site of Gourniá and the coastal town of Pahía Ámmos (see p.194), making the route to Ierápetra more direct.

The long-term aim is to continue the new road east all the way to Sitía, linking up with the new airport there, but this is still some years away. Five kilometres east of Istrón, along a newly completed stretch of the E75, an exit on the left is signed for the **Moní Faneroméni**. The route soon doubles back to re-cross the E75 over a viaduct, and then heads inland. Asphalted in its early stages, the road (later a track) climbs dizzily skywards for 6km, giving spectacular views over the Gulf of Mirabéllo along the way. The **view** from the monastery itself, when you finally arrive there, must be among the finest on Crete. To get into the rather bleak-looking monastery buildings, knock loudly (and repeatedly, if necessary). When you gain entry you will be shown up to the **chapel**, built into a cave sanctuary where a sacred icon of the Virgin was miraculously discovered, the reason for the foundation of the monastery in the fifteenth century. The **frescoes**, although seventeenth century and quite late, are impressive – especially that of the Panayía Theotókou, the Mother of God. The monk who unlocks the chapel has been known to be a little mean with the time (and electric light) you need to view the artworks – a few more minutes can usually be "purchased" with a discreet contribution to monastic funds.

Gourniá

Back on the coast road, another 2km east brings you to the site of **Gourniá** (Tues–Sun 8.30am–3pm; €2), slumped in the saddle between two low peaks. A look at the map tells you much about ancient Gourniá's strategic importance, controlling, as it did, the narrow isthmus and the relatively easy communication this gave with the southern seaboard at modern Ierápetra. The overland route avoided a hazardous sea voyage around the eastern cape – a crucial factor in ancient times, especially in winter when sailing usually stopped because of rough seas.

Gourniá is the most completely preserved of the Minoan towns, and in its small scale contains important clues about the lives of ordinary people and the nature of the communities from which the palaces evolved. The desolation of the site today – you are likely to be alone save for the sleeping guard – only serves to heighten the contrast with what must have been a cramped and raucous community three-and-a-half thousand years ago.

There is evidence of occupation at Gourniá as early as the third millennium BC, but the remains you see today are those of a town of the **New Palace** period (ca.1500 BC). Around 1450 BC, as happened elsewhere, the town was destroyed by fire, possibly resulting from an earthquake or (as now seems more likely from recent evidence) warlike activity. Limited rebuilding occurred during the era of **Mycenaean** rule at Knossós – and the shrine may date from this late period – but the site was soon abandoned again and disappeared beneath the soil where it lay unsuspected until the awakening of archeological interest in the nineteenth century. Arthur Evans, as usual, was the first to scent Minoan occupation of this area, and then a young American, Harriet Boyd-Hawes, started digging in 1901. The site, a budding archeologist's dream, made her reputation.

The narrow, cobbled alleys and stairways – built for pack animals rather than carts – intersect a throng of one-roomed houses centred on a main square and the house of a local ruler or, more likely, governor. The settlement is not a large place, nor impressive by comparison with the palaces at Knossós and elsewhere, but it must have been at least as luxurious as the average Cretan mountain village of even forty years ago. Among the dwellings to the north and east of the site are some which have been clearly identified, by tools or materials discovered,

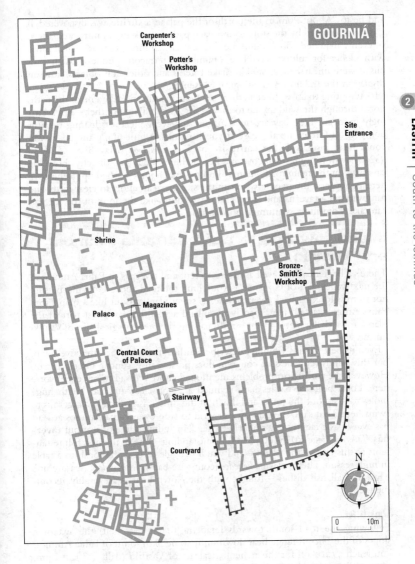

GOURNIÁ

Carpenter's Workshop

Potter's Workshop

Site Entrance

Shrine

Bronze-Smith's Workshop

Magazines

Palace

Central Court of Palace

Stairway

Courtyard

N

0   10m

as the homes of **craftspeople**: a carpenter, a smith and a potter. It's worth remembering that the rooms may not have been as small as they appear – many of these are in fact basements or semi-basements reached by stairs from the main rooms above, and the floor plans of those did not necessarily correspond with what you see today. The houses themselves were mainly built of stone on the lower courses and mud-brick above, with plaster-daubed reeds for roofing.

The **palace** (or governor's quarters) occupied the highest ground, to the north of a courtyard containing a familiar L-shaped stairway. With a smaller court at its heart, the whole is a copy in miniature of the palaces at Knossós and Festós. About 20m to the north of the palace, a **shrine** was discovered. It is easily identified by the sloping approach path paved with an intricate pattern of evenly matched cobbles, and the shrine itself, up three steps, is a small room with a ledge for cult objects. Here, a number of terracotta goddesses with arms raised were unearthed, as well as snake totems and other cult objects, now on display in the Iráklion Archeological Museum.

It's tempting to cross the road from the Gourniá site and take one of the paths north through the wild thyme to the sea for a swim. Don't bother – this seemingly innocent little bay acts as a magnet for every piece of floating detritus dumped off Crete's north coast. If you backtrack a little along the coast, you could head instead to the **campsite** of *Gournia Moon* (May–Sept; ☎28420 93243), with its own small cove and beach; there's a bus stop directly above the campsite on the main road. There's almost as much junk washed up in the cove here, but at least the people who run the site make an effort to clear it up. The campsite has a taverna and store, and if you don't like the look of the sea you can take a dip in its swimming pool instead.

Inland towards Ierápetra: Pahiá Ámmos and Vasilikí

There's a large beach, as well as rooms to rent and tavernas, at Pahiá Ámmos in the next valley east of Gourniá; as you climb the road above Gourniá, be sure not to miss looking back over the site, its street plan laid out like a map. From Pahiá Ámmos, a fast, new road heads inland across the narrowest part of the island, towards Ierápetra in the south, passing the archeological site of Vasilikí on the way.

Even its best friends wouldn't describe **Pahiá Ámmos** as an attractive town, but this windswept mess of concrete does possess an eccentric Greek charm. However, the **pollution** problems mentioned above are, sad to say, even worse here. Local political battles have stymied a grand clean-up plan (with huge moles to keep out the junk) and much of the time it is positively dangerous to swim here. That said, should you still wish to stop over, Pahiá Ámmos at least has every basic facility you're likely to need, including a line of seafront **tavernas**. *Taverna Aiolos* (☎28420 93434) is outstanding – one of the best fish restaurants at this end of the island – and you'll struggle to beat the locals to a table in high season. Their *kolokithokéftedes* (courgette balls), *achinosalata* (sea urchin's eggs) and all fish dishes – caught with their own boat – are highly recommended.

Vasilikí

Following the road south towards Ierápetra, to the east (left) the awesome slopes of the Thriptí range bear down until, some 3km south of Pahiá Ámmos, you reach a turn-off for the archeological site of **Vasilikí** (daily 8.30am–3pm; free) on the right. The site is visible from the main road, with an entrance from the side road a short distance down on the left. There is no obvious place to park off the road, and neither is the sign to the site apparent. At the time of writing, a guardian has been posted to the site but, as visitors are sparse, this may not last long. However, the gate should be left open during the above hours.

This **Pre-Palatial** settlement, dating from about 2650 to 2200 BC, may not be much to look at, but it's important for the light that it throws upon the hazy millennium preceding the Minoan great period. Remains from this period occur at Knossós and other palaces but cannot be properly excavated because of the important buildings constructed on top of them. Vasilikí was the first of these early sites to be found in a pristine condition, due to its being abandoned after a fire in about 2200 BC.

The site contains two main buildings, originally surrounded by numerous smaller (and simpler) dwellings. The remains of the edifice nearest to the entrance, on the lower slope of the hill, are slightly earlier than those on the crown. The **Red House**, as the former is named, has a number of interesting features. It's oriented with its corners towards the cardinal points of the compass, a practice normal in Mesopotamia and the Near East but alien to Egypt and the Aegean (and thus possibly a clue to Minoan origins). In the southern corner, deep basement rooms allow you to gain an idea of early Minoan building techniques: holes to support the absent wooden beams are visible as well as large patches of hard, red lime plaster, the forerunner of what later artists were to use as the ideal ground for the wonderful palace frescoes. This material gives the dwelling its modern name. The **pottery** known as Vasilikí ware – orange or red with dark, blotchy decoration – takes its name from this site, at which the fine examples on display in the archeological museums at Iráklion and Áyios Nikólaos were discovered. New excavations on the southern flank of the Red House have revealed a bath, a stretch of roadway and more dwellings.

You can continue on up the lane into the **village** of Vasilikí, where you'll find a friendly **bar** and a glimpse of traditional rural Crete well off the tourist trail.

Episkopí

The main road continues south towards the town of Ierápetra; about 7km before this, almost exactly halfway across the isthmus, it's worth turning off to visit **Episkopí**. Below the road, beside a central raised *platía* where old men play *távli* in the shade of lofty eucalyptus trees, lies a charming blue-domed **Byzantine church** with a double dedication to Áyios Yeóryios and Áyios Charálambos. The arched drum dome with elaborate blue-tile decoration, together with an unusual ground plan, make this church unique on the island. Entry to view a newly renovated interior with a late *ikonostásis* is difficult due to the frequent absences of the *papás* who apparently possesses the only key, but anyway it's the church's exterior (also restored in 2003) which gives it its standing in Byzantine architecture.

The road continues beyond Episkopí to the the town of Ierápetra, 7km further south (see p.227).

The far east

The far east of Crete marks yet another dramatic change in scenery and tempo. Although much of it is rocky, barren and desolate, it is an area of great natural beauty. With the exception of **Ierápetra**, the towns and villages are slower and quieter, with life conducted at an easier pace. **Sitía**, in particular, exudes a contented air, and is largely unperturbed by its visitors. The north coast has few beaches, and in the main the mountains drop straight to the sea (the drive towards Sitía is as dramatic as any in Crete). If you wanted a cooling dip though, there are a couple of coves which are just about accessible, and beyond Sitía, as the heights tail away, there's more opportunity for swimming. The far east is much visited only in two spots – the spectacular if rather too popular palm beach at **Vái** and the outstanding Minoan palace at **Zákros**. Away from these, it's a great area for escapists. To the south of Zákros, isolated Kserócambos has deserted beaches by the score, and along the south coast there are excellent strands at **Makriyialós**, **Ayía Fotiá**, the shoreline east of Ierápetra and at **Mírtos**.

Bus connections and main roads continue to be good: there are frequent rapid bus services from Áyios Nikólaos to Ierápetra, and good connections along the north coast to Sitía. Onwards from Sitía, it's easy enough to continue to Vái or Zákros, or to cut back south to Ierápetra; from Ierápetra, rather less readily if you're relying on public transport, you can carry on west, across the centre of Crete, to Iráklion.

The road to Sitía

Beyond the isthmus, the tawny bulk of the Ornó range of the Sitía mountains makes a formidable barrier to further progress, and the road at first is carved into the cliff face, teetering perilously above the gulf. It then climbs for six kilometres beyond Pahiá Ámmos to reach **Kavoúsi**, a pleasant enough village with its Byzantine churches and main tree-lined street of oleanders and mulberry. Should you want a **place to stay**, the *Taverna Halkidakis* (T 28420 94768; ●) has economical en-suite rooms. Many of the tempting **beaches** visible from on high are inaccessible, although **Thólos** – where there's a quiet pebble beach and chapel backed by tamarisk trees but not much else, and similar pollution problems to Pahiá Ámmos – can be reached 4km down an asphalted road on the edge of Kavoúsi. The very pleasant and good-value *Tholos Beach* taverna, with decent apartments and **rooms** (T 28420 94785, F 28420 94810; ●), lies about halfway down this stretch.

Beyond Kavoúsi, the views back across the Gulf of Mirabéllo become more expansive all the time, until at **Plátanos**, some 4km further, you reach a famous viewpoint, with a couple of tavernas – *Panorama*, and *Skinoseli* further on – where you can look down on the island of Psíra, the site of a Minoan settlement, and west across the gulf to Áyios Nikólaos to watch the sunset. After this point, the road runs further inland, emerging only occasionally to glimpses of the sea far below.

Móhlos and its islet

A more inviting coastal option than Thólos is **MÓHLOS** – though getting there involves tackling 5km or more of dusty hairpin bends. There is no bus connection down to the coast, which leaves you with the options of taking a taxi or walking from the main road. Shortest of the routes down is a road signposted soon after Plátanos at **San Pandelémas**, but you may have difficulty persuading the bus driver to stop here, and although recently sealed it's also the least attractive route, running past a large quarrying operation. There are equally obvious ways to follow down, in ninety minutes or less, from the villages of **Sfáka**, **Tourlotí** (a trail not marked on many maps) and **Mirsíni**, all of which are standard halts for the bus. The Sfáka road is also asphalted and the way to go if you have your own transport. You can also get to Móhlos **by boat** from Áyios Nikólaos – a regular trip in summer which includes a stop at Psíra: ask at the bus station in Áyios Nikólaos for details. Heading back from Móhlos to the main road involves a more serious walk, of two hours or more, which you might want to skip by taking a taxi.

Tiny and out of the way as it is, Móhlos has plenty of **tavernas**: of the four competing on the seafront, *Ta Kokília* and *To Bogázi* are the best, and the Greek-Swiss couple running the latter produce interesting "specials" and some good vegetarian dishes (try their *Creta salata*). Despite its obvious charm, Móhlos is not wholly unspoilt: rooms can be surprisingly expensive and often booked up in high season, and some of the bars and tavernas much fancier than you'd expect. Some of this may be attributed to the presence of American and Greek archeological teams still excavating on the islet offshore as well as on nearby Psíra, and they and their retinue often spend whole summers here, occupying much of the available space. Nonetheless, the atmosphere remains sleepy, there's plenty of space if you need to camp out (but be alert to local sensibilities), and plenty of rather rocky foreshore to swim off during the day. Keep an eye out for sea urchins while bathing here: they flourish in the clear, unpolluted water (the minimarket sells protective plastic shoes). In the mornings, you'll often see divers collecting them for restaurants along the coast, which serve up the roe as *achinosalata* – a much-prized delicacy.

Should you fancy a day away from the waterfront, one interesting new option is with *La Chlorophylle* (℡28430 94725, ⓦwww.chez .com/annelebrun), a small walking company run by a couple of botanists who conduct **guided walks** between the villages of this zone, pointing out flora, fauna and geological features along the way. Details are also available from the *Hotel Sofía* (see below). Just east of the *Sofía*, the **travel agent** Barbarossa Tours (℡28430 94723) rents out cars, jeeps, motorbikes, scooters and mountain bikes, and has information on boat trips and hiring boats for private excursions.

Accommodation

It's often harder to track down a room in Móhlos than its isolated location would lead you to expect – even more so when the archeological teams are in the area. Advance booking is recommended here, particularly in July and August. Some of the room options are at the back of the village and not always easy to find, especially as there are no street names – ask for directions at any of the three harbourside tavernas (English is spoken at all three).

Blue Sea ℡ & ℻28430 94237, ⓔbluesea@otenet.gr. A tempting option a kilometre or so east of the village along the Sfáka road, where welcoming proprietors offer sparkling rooms with fridge and sea-view balcony, and there's a decent taverna downstairs for taking breakfast. The same place also has some good-value apartments to let, sleeping up to four. Apartments €40–60 per night; rooms ❸

Studios Despina Hilaki ℡28430 94344. A bit further inland than most of the others (and reached by following the road inland behind the *Hotel Sofía*, this place has spacious studios with balcony, kitchenette and fans. ❹

Rooms Fragiadakis ℡28430 94020, ⓔnfragiadakis@sit.forthnet. Over the street from

Pension Hermes and run by a friendly family; good-value apartments with kitchen. ❷

Pension Hermes ℡28430 94074. Just behind the *Hotel Mochlos*, this has the village's cheapest rooms, with shared bath. ❷

Apartments Limenaria ℡ & ℻2842 27837. On a rise overlooking the bay to the west of the main waterfront, the *Limenaria* is a very pleasant and tranquil hideaway with fully equipped apartments sleeping up to three. ❹

Pension Meltemi ℡28430 94200, ℻28430 94130. Another inland possibility, offering attractive studios with kitchenette and mosquito nets. ❸

Hotel Mochlos ℡28430 94205, ⓔinc .lefteriszerbakis@yahoo.gr. Set back slightly from the centre of things, the *Mochlos* has a/c sea-view balcony rooms with fridge and kitchenette. ❸

Mochlos Mare ☎ 28430 94005, ⓦ www .forthnet.gr/internetcity/hotels/mochlosmare. Slightly before the *Blue Sea*, along the same road, this place rents attractive and economical apartments for up to four people, starting at €45. ❹–❺

Rooms Nikos ☎ 28430 94200, ⓕ 28430 94130. Slightly inland from the seafront, this is a good budget option for en-suite rooms. ❷

Hotel Sofia ☎ 28430 94738, ⓕ 28430 94238. Friendly hotel with sea-view balcony rooms above its taverna with a/c, fridge and TV; also rents apartments nearby. ❸

The islet

The **islet** looks within swimming distance – and it is when the weather is calm – but it's easier to arrange a ride there with a local fisherman. A return trip will cost around €6 for the boat; ring the chapel bell on the island when you want to return, and the boatman will come and get you. Ask at *Ta Kokilia* taverna, where many fishermen hang around after work.

Inhabited from the Pre-Palatial period, in Minoan times this barren rock was almost certainly a much less barren peninsula, and the sandy spit linking it to the mainland would have been used as a harbour (anchorages which could be approached from either side were a great advantage for boats that could sail only before the wind). You can see remains of **late Minoan houses** on the south side of the island, and there are more below the current sea level where recent excavations have also identified remnants of the ancient harbour. But the important discoveries at Móhlos were in the much more ancient **tombs** built up against the cliff. Here, very early seal stones were found (including one from Mesopotamia), as well as some spectacular gold jewellery now in the Iráklion Archeological Museum and a fine collection of marble, steatite and rock crystal vases on display in the Áyios Nikólaos and Sitía archeological museums.

Psíra

The larger island of **Psíra**, off Móhlos, was also a Minoan port, and here the remains are of a town a little like Goúrnia but built amphitheatrically around a good natural harbour. As with the islet, you should be able to arrange a ride **by boat** from Móhlos over to Psíra with a fisherman, or you could join an organized visit from Áyios Nikólaos for around €6 per person (check with the tourist office in Áyios Nikólaos for details, see p.179).

Psíra was first excavated in 1907 by an American, Richard Seager, who revealed a settlement which again was occupied from the early Minoan era. During the Neo-Palatial period, the community of merchants, sailors and fishermen shared in the general prosperity of the time. In one of a number of substantial dwellings – many containing hearths and with walls still standing up to two metres high in places – a fine relief **fresco** was found depicting female figures wearing richly embroidered dresses, the only known example outside Knossós. A long, stepped street climbs away from the harbour to the site. No palaces or obvious public buildings were discovered but the site has produced rich finds of **painted pottery**. One jar, now on display in the Iráklion Archeological Museum, is noted for its decoration of bulls' heads interspersed with the double-axe symbol. Trading with overseas areas such as Egypt and the Levant must have been necessary to import the essential requirements of life to such a parched, infertile place. The remains of what is thought to be an ancient **well** have been found, although the island is completely dry these days. The site was another of those destroyed about 1450 BC. Later, the Romans used the island for strategic and navigational purposes, and you can still make out the remains of their **lighthouse** and military settlement on the island's crown.

East to Hamézi

From Móhlos to Sitía the road, lined with a riot of pink and white oleander flowers in summer, continues to toil through villages clinging to the mountainside, now high above a deserted bay, until the final approach to the city and a descent in great loops through softer hills. As you progress, the familiar olive groves are increasingly interspersed with vineyards, and there are some fine and highly regarded local wines to be had in the village cafés, especially in **Mesa Moulianá** and its neighbour **Éxo Moulianá**. Wine, under the Agrilos label, is bottled in nearby Sitía. Most of the grapes, however, go to make sultanas: in late summer, when they are laid out to dry in the fields and on rooftops all around, the various stages of their slow change from green to gold to brown make a bizarre spectacle.

Of the villages en route, **Mirsíni** has an attractive church built around and entirely enclosing a frescoed fourteenth-century chapel – you'll need to find the priest if you want to look inside (ask at the taverna below). Apart from the church, and a small pottery and weaving workshop, the village also boasts a good **taverna**, *Kathodon* (eves only), whose terrace has stunning views across the coast below.

Hamézi and around

Near the ruined stone windmills on the final crest before the Bay of Sitía, a track on the right signed "Middle Minoan House" indicates the ancient Minoan site of **Hamézi**. Follow the drivable, winding track (about a 15min walk), keeping right at a restored windmill, which will eventually lead you, after 2km, to a Minoan edifice with a spectacular hilltop setting.

Dating from the Pre-Palatial period (ca.2000 BC), this grey stone ruin has a unique importance in Minoan archeology, for it is the only known structure to have had an **oval** ground plan, possibly dictated by the conical shape of the hill. It was thought at first to be a peak sanctuary, but the discovery of a **cistern** made a dwelling, or even a fortress, seem more likely. The ground plan sketched out by the walls – more than a metre high in places – consists of a number of rooms grouped around a central courtyard, where the cistern is located. A paved entrance is visible on the south side. Whatever the building's function, it certainly had a commanding view over the surrounding terrain. While you're taking this in, keep an eye out for the rare **Eleanora's falcon** which breeds on the offshore island of Paximádha – the valley to the east is one of its favourite hunting grounds.

Hamézi proper, a kilometre and a half further along the main Sitía highway, is a sleepy little village spreading uphill to the north of the road, where plants are festooned over buildings and down white-washed steps. The village's **folk museum** (daily 9am–1pm & 5–8pm; €1) is worth a visit – it has a collection of ancient farm implements and rooms filled with furniture and utensils from the nineteenth century. To get there, head along the main street, passing the brilliant white **church**, and turn left up a charming stepped street. The museum lies at the top of the street to the right; if it's closed, enquire at the *Bar O Antonis*, fifty metres east of the church, which should enable you to locate the key; they can also rustle up decent taverna **food**. **Rooms** are available at *To Spiti Isherwood* (☎28430 71017; ❷) near the top of the main street.

If you have the appetite for more ruins, nearby are the remains of an impressive *thólos* tomb dating from the Mycenaean period, as well as a Neo-Palatial Minoan villa. The **tomb** lies 2km to the east of the village of **Paraspóri**, up a track to the right, whilst the villa lies up another track (also on the right) 1km beyond **Ahládia**.

Moní Faneroméni

Further along the main Sitía road, just beyond the village of Skopí, you'll come to a track signed left (north) for the **Moní Faneroméni**. This partly asphalted five-kilometre track leads to a picturesque cove lapped by a turquoise sea. From here, the track climbs inland to the monastery, which can also be approached by another track 5km closer to Sitía.

The charming **monastic church** overlooks a gorge near to the sea. Standing as a metaphor for recent Cretan history, the church has been battered but still stands unbowed. In 1829, the monastery and tiny church were looted and burned by the Turks, and most of the frescoes destroyed. The beauty of what was lost is glimpsed in one scarred remaining fragment depicting a saint reading. The three indentations across his face are bullet holes, again Turkish. By the iconostasis hangs a curtain embroidered with a gold Greek cross which you may be tempted to peer behind – but the remains of the founder here are not for the squeamish. The shoals of silver *taxímata* (ex votos) hung on the icon of the Virgin to implore her miraculous intervention attest to the importance of the shrine locally today, a tradition stretching back to Minoan times and probably beyond.

From the church, there's a **footpath** which takes you to Sitía (keep left where the track forks) in two to three hours.

Sitía

After the excesses of Mália or Áyios Nikólaos, arriving in **SITÍA** can seem something of an anticlimax. But don't be fooled: the town's charms are subtle. Allow yourself to adjust to the more leisurely pace of life here and you may, like many other visitors before you, end up staying much longer than intended. **SITÍA** certainly makes an ideal base from which to visit the other attractions in the region. The town hasn't entirely escaped the tourist boom, and the increasing number of visitors attracted to the port has led to a great deal of new development at its fringes. Many of the new tourists are French or Italian, a legacy perhaps of the French troops who garrisoned the place under the Great Power protection at the end of the nineteenth century, and the Italians who occupied it during World War II.

The town is set on a hill tumbling down towards the western end of the picturesque **Bay of Sitía**. Its oldest sections, hanging steeply above the harbour, look east over the bay and the long ribbon of new development along the coast. Life concentrates on the **waterfront**, around Platía Iroon Polytehniou in the corner of the bay. North towards the port and ferry dock is a seafront promenade crowded with the outdoor tables of rival tavernas, and beyond this a newly constructed promenade leads to the ferry port. South, the main road (officially Karamanli but known as the Beach Road) runs behind the beach, flanked for miles by a rambling jumble of development.

Some history

This area was settled, as Eteia, in Classical times but may be identified with the **Minoan** *se-to-i-ja* inscribed on clay tablets found locally. That there was a substantial Minoan presence in the area is borne out by the excavations at **Petrás**,

SITÍA

Venetian Fortress

Roman Fish Tanks

ACCOMMODATION	
Apollon	F
Apostolis	E
Arhontiko	C
Elena	G
El Greco	D
Elysee	L
Flisvos Hotel	K
Itanos	J
Kazarma	A
Maria Hanilaki	H
Nora	B
Venus	I

RESTAURANTS	
The Balcony	3
Creperie Mike	5
Creta House	7
Dionysos	10
Kali Kardia	2
Mixos	1
Neromilos	11
Remezzo	4
Sitia Beach	9
To Steki	8
Zorba's	6

0   100m

Folk Museum

OTE

Internet Café Sante

Tourist Office

Wine Cooperative

Bus Station

Archeological Museum

PLATÍA IROON POLYTECHNIOU

N

B (250m), Airport (1km) & Ferry Port

Makriyiálos & Ierapetra   Vai & Zakros

the town's southern suburb, where a settlement dating to the early second millennium BC has been unearthed and where, in the later Neo-Palatial period, there was a fine town with sophisticated buildings and roads. Details concerning the subsequent Greek and Roman settlements are sketchy, although a substantial chunk of **Hellenistic Sitía** has recently been discovered on the outskirts. Apart from some tombs and fish tanks (now incorporated into an artificial pond on the harbour promenade), little tangible survives from the **Roman** town.

It was under the **Venetians** that the port really took off (they called it *La Sitia* – hence Lasíthi), as part of a conscious attempt to exploit the east of the island.

For all their efforts, the area remained cut off by land from the rest of Crete and, although what was in effect a separate fiefdom developed here, it never amounted to a great deal. Perhaps the most significant event of this era was the birth of Vitzentzos Kornáros, author of the epic Cretan poem, the *Erotókritos*. More physical remains are few, due to earthquakes and the raids of **Barbarossa**. Where once there was a walled city, now you'll find only the barest remains of a fortress. A new attempt to open up the eastern end of the island – this time to mass tourism – is materializing in the form of Sitía's **new airport**, due for completion in 2004, with new roads connecting it with the port and the route to Áyios Nikólaos.

Arrival and information

The **bus station** (☎28430 22272) lies on the southwest fringe of the centre close to the town's main **supermarket**. Although the station office has a left-luggage area of sorts, it's not entirely secure. From the station, heading north along Odhós Venizélou will bring you into the centre. **Ferry** arrivals from Áyios Nikólaos or the islands dock at the port at the northeastern end of town; it's a ten-minute walk along the new promenade (or two-minute taxi-ride) into the centre from here.

The municipal **tourist office** (Mon–Fri 9.30am–2.30pm & 5.30–9pm, Sat 10.30am–2.30pm & 5–8pm; ☎28430-28300, ⓦwww.sitia.gr) is located on the seafront along the Beach Road and can supply accommodation lists, town maps and general information on the town and province. The none-too-competent **tourist police** are at Mysonos 24 (daily 7.30am–2.30pm; ☎28430 24200).

Accommodation

Rooms are rather scattered, but except at the busiest times (usually the first half of August) you should be able to find something. Quiet and good-value places can be found in the older streets leading up the hill from the waterfront, especially behind the OTE and in the nearby streets off Kapetan Sifi. Odhós Kondhilaki, which runs down the side of the OTE, has numerous possibilities. If you are at a loss where to begin there are a number of helpful travel agencies around the centre who can suggest possible options; try Porto Belis, Karamanli 34 (☎28430 22370, ⓔpbelis@sit.forthnet.gr). The youth hostel closed in 2002 and there is little prospect of it reopening.

Apollon Kapetan Sifi 28 ☎28430 28155, ⓕ28430 22733. One of the more reasonable of Sitía's clutch of unremarkable upmarket places. Rooms come with balcony, minibar and TV. Rates include breakfast. ❹

Apostolis Kazantzákis 27 ☎28430 22993. Pleasant, friendly and central en-suite place where balcony rooms come with fridges and fans. ❷

Arhontiko Kondhilaki 16 ☎28430 28172. One of the best budget places in town, with attractive rooms and a mature orange tree in the front garden. One of the rooms is en suite. ❷

El Greco G. Arkadiou 13 ☎28430 23133, ⓕ28430 26391. Charming small hotel in the upper town, with en-suite balcony rooms with fridge, some with a/c and sea views (especially rooms 43 & 44). Also offers a/c studios and apartments sleeping up to five. Rates include breakfast. ❸–❹

Rooms Elena Kondhilaki 58 ☎28430 24844. Good budget pension, with clean rooms and friendly proprietor. ❷

Elysee Karamanli 14 ☎28430 22312, ⓦwww.elysee-hotel.gr. Attractive, small hotel on the seafront offering a/c sea-view balcony rooms with TV and fridge. ❺

Flisvos Karamanli 4 ☎ & ⓕ28430 27135. Newly refurbished hotel fronting the sea at the start of the Beach Road; a/c rooms with TV and fridge face either the sea or a patio garden behind. ❺

Itanos Platía Iroon Polytehniou ☎ 28430 22146, ⓦ www.forthnet.gr/internetcity/hotels/itanos. Smart, upper-range hotel on the town's main square with pleasant, a/c sea-view balcony rooms with TV. Rates include breakfast. ❺

Kazarma Rooms Ionias 10, near the fortress ☎ 28430 23211. Excellent en-suite studios and rooms, with use of communal kitchen. The proprietor lives off-site, so you're free to enter and choose your room; the details will be sorted later. ❷

Maria Hamilaki Kondhilaki 35 ☎ 28430 22768. Clean, simple rooms, overseen by friendly proprietress. ❷

Nora Rouselaki 31 ☎ 28430 23017, ⓔ norahotel @yahoo.gr. Near the ferry port, this is a small and friendly female-run hotel, with fine views over the harbour and bay; all rooms have a/c, TV, balcony and shower. ❸

Pension Venus Kondhilaki 60 ☎ 28430 24307. This comfortable place offers simple rooms, and has an ebullient English-speaking owner. ❷

The Town

Sitía is an absorbing place to wander around and do nothing more than enjoy the atmosphere. The narrow streets behind the seafront feature the everyday scenes of a Cretan provincial town: villagers in to stock up on news and necessities, and stores which cater to their every conceivable need, from steel drums to wooden saddles, seed to pick-up trucks. While you're people-watching, one thing not to be missed, especially on Sundays, is the **volta**, when the whole town puts on its finery to parade in front of the neighbours. To see the show, get a seat around seven in the evening at a table adjacent to the road behind the waterfront.

The summer heat will eventually draw you towards the water: the **town beach** is attractive and swimmable, and windsurfing boards can be hired along the beach road.

Aside from wandering the streets, sitting in the cafés or lying on the beach, there's a limited number of things to do. The **Folk Museum** at Kapetan Sifi 28, near the OTE (Mon–Sat 10am–1pm; €2), offers an entertaining look at traditional life, with displays of textiles, clothes and antique furniture from the region. Adam Hopkins' book *Crete* includes a wonderful section on his stay with a family in Sitía, and reveals the extent to which the old lifestyle survives to this day. On the hill above the harbour lies the restored Kazarma or **Venetian fortress**, now used as an open-air theatre. Climbing down towards the port from here, you can see the ruined remains of some **Roman fish tanks**: freshly caught fish were kept in these semicircular constructions until they were needed. The tanks have been incorporated into an artificial **pond** along the new promenade leading to the harbour, and are used as a preening perch by the pond's resident colony of swans, ducks and geese. The best view of them, however, is from the terrace of the *Di Settia* taverna which perches on the cliff above. The only other visitor attraction is the **Wine Co-operative**, Missonos 74, on the road into town from Áyios Nikólaos; visits (April–Oct Mon–Fri 9am–2.30pm; free) include a tour of the fermentation plant, a video on Cretan winemaking and a tasting session, with the possibility to buy the local brands.

The Archeological Museum

The Archeological Museum (Tues–Sun 8.30am–3pm; €2), 400m south of the centre on the Ierápetra road and sandwiched between builders' yards, contains an interesting collection of finds from the surrounding area and the palace at Zákros.

As you enter the museum, a display case holds the small **Palékastro koúros**, or male figure, discovered in the excavations at Palékastro (see p.211). Made from eight interlocking pieces of hippopotamus ivory and dating from ca.1500 BC, it is an extremely delicate work, and when complete would have been decorated with a gold Minoan belt, bracelets and shoes. Note that the left leg is placed slightly forward, following the Egyptian convention for the portrayal of this form of statue.

You veer left from here to enter the **main room** (proceeding clockwise), where finds from the early Minoan cemetery at nearby Ayía Fotiá are displayed, as well as some fine stone vases from Móhlos and its island neighbour, Psíra. A new case here contains recent finds from Petrás, Sitía's southern suburb, where important buildings from the Minoan Neo-Palatial period have been unearthed. One large building has a magazine for storing *píthoi* (the large earthenware jars), similar to that at Knossós. The archeologists are hesitant to describe it as a palace (despite this, the museum's literature does so) until more work has been done, but the early signs seem promising.

The **Zákros** section comes next: interesting exhibits here include a bronze saw, a winepress from a Minoan villa near the palace and a collection of seashells. Archeologists claim these had a sacred function, but it would be nice to think that the Minoans used them for decorative purposes as we do today.

Further on lies one of the museum's great treasures, a case full of rare **Linear A tablets**. They were discovered by archeologist Nikólaos Pláton in the archives room at the palace. Note how the Minoan characters have been delicately scratched into the soft clay. Some show evidence of being burned by the fire which destroyed the palace – in fact, it was the fire that preserved them, for as unbaked clay tablets they would have crumbled to dust. A nearby case illustrates the **domestic life** of the kitchen, the only one so far positively identified at any palace. Among the cooking pots and other utensils there's a superbly preserved terracotta grill, probably used for cooking some form of *souvláki* – a method used in the Greek world since pre-Mycenaean times and mentioned by Homer.

After the Hellenistic and Roman sections, don't miss the barnacle-encrusted tangle of **Roman pots** (probably from a wreck), preserved by placing it inside a fish tank of salinated water. This artistically stunning idea was the brainwave of the museum's founder, the eminent Cretan archeologist Níkos Papadákis, who died in 2001: his excellent guidebook to the monuments of Sitía and eastern Crete is on sale at the museum.

Eating

A line of enticing outdoor **tavernas** crowds the harbourfront, many displaying dishes and fresh fish to lure you in – though be warned that these seafront places can be very expensive. Away from the water you'll find cheaper (and often more interesting) places to dine, and there are a few good out-of-town possibilities too. If you're just looking for a **snack**, the Paradosiaka bakery at Kornárou 71, just behind the National Bank on Platía Iroon Polytechniou, sells excellent *tirópita* and *spanakópita*, whilst the nearby Picadilly (in from *Zorba's*) sells delicious chocolate cakes. Bakeries and cake stores are something of a local attraction, and there are a couple more good ones along Venizélou: try the one at no. 49. The *Café Kalambokis* has the best people-watching position on the focal Platía Iroon Polytechniou and is a good place for confectionery, fancy **breakfasts**, and cocktails or nightcaps on their nearby terrace facing the bay. Take a look at their menu, which has a charming photo-history of the town.

The Balcony Kazantzákis and Foundalídhou. Stylish new restaurant in the upper floor of an elegant town house. An eclectic menu has Mexican- and Asian-influenced dishes as well as Greek; expensive, but worth it.

Creperie Mike Venizélou 162. All kinds of crêpes, both savoury and sweet, served on a seafront terrace.

Creta House Beach Road (Karamanli). Just along from the *Hotel Itanos*, this is a reliable traditional taverna specializing in Cretan dishes, with a harbourside terrace.

Dionysos Ayía Fotiá. Located 4km east of Sitía on the edge of Ayía Fotiá, this is a good seafood taverna with a pleasant terrace near the sea; hard to miss, as it's fronted by a line of poles flying European flags.

Kali Kardia Foundalídhou 28, two blocks in from the waterfront. The popular "Good Heart" *ouzerí* lives up to its name in terms of its welcome, and is an excellent place to wash down fish, cheese and snail *mezédhes* with house retsina. You'll be mixing with the locals here, and don't be surprised if you get a few extra tit-bits on the house.

Mixos Kornárou 117. Traditional charcoal cooking on a spit in the street, served up with a very strong local wine.

Neromilos Off the road to Ayía Fotiá, 4km east of Sitía. Housed in a converted ancient watermill high above the bay, this offers magnificent views as well as a good selection of *mezédhes* and grilled meat and fish. Take a taxi, as the road down can be pretty tortuous in the dark. Nearby in Roússa Ekklisía, there's another village taverna which does great charcoal roasts and also has a superb terrace view.

Remezzo At the harbour. One of the longest established places, in business since 1941, which serves decent food at above-average prices on a terrace.

Sitia Beach Beach Road (Karamanli) 28. Decent pizzeria close to the hotel of the same name at the south end of the Beach Road.

To Steki A. Papandreou 13. Opposite Knossós bike rental, this no-frills place is popular with locals for its *souvláki* and *mezédhes*. Good value.

Zorba's At the harbour. The biggest and most popular place on the seafront, and the only restaurant in town open all year round. Good for standard dishes like swordfish.

Drinking, nightlife and entertainment

The nightlife, mostly conducted at an easy pace, centres around drinking, disco-bars and a couple of clubs. These are mainly concentrated in two zones: up at the north end of **Venizélou** towards the Roman fish tanks, and out along **Beach Road** (officially named Konstantinou Karamanli).

In the first group of **bars**, there's the *Byzantio* – on the seafront near the jetty – whose terrace has a great view over the bay, and the stylish *Nea Glyfada* nearby. Just north of here above the Roman fish tanks (but entered from Rouselaki), *Di Settia* is a laid-back taverna and music bar with a garden. Closer in along the harbour, *Skala*, *Club*, *Porto* and *Albatros* all attract big crowds on summer nights. At the southern end of town, young Sitían professionals gather at their own open-air hideaway, *Status*, on the Ierápetra road, 100m past the Archeological Museum. Here, beneath a giant palm tree – which is spotlit at night – you can sip cocktails and **dance** on a crazy-paving floor; don't arrive before 10pm. Facing the sea on the Beach Road, *Oasis* is a stylish new bar with an attractive terrace which is popular with a younger crowd. Bigger than any of these is the monster *Planitarion* **disco** a couple of kilometres beyond the ferry port (take a taxi). It's got a sliding glass roof, state-of-the-art technological gadgetry and draws in crowds from all over the east – it can hold up to a thousand people – for an eclectic mix of music including rock, jazz and Greek, all played at frightening sound levels.

Sitía's main cultural bash is the summer-long *Kornaria* **cultural festival** featuring concerts, dance and theatre by Greek and overseas participants.

Listings

Airlines Olympic are at 4-Septémbriou 5 ☎ 28430 22270, off the top end of the Beach Road, for local flights to Kásos, Kárpathos and Rhodes; there are also thrice-weekly services to Athens, Préveza (in

△ Kazarma Venetian fort, Sitía

northwest Greece) and Alexandhroúpoli (in Thrace). Information on the new airport, flights and tickets are available from Tzortzakis air and shipping agents (see "Ferries", below).

Banks and exchange There's a branch of the National Bank (Mon–Thurs 8am–2pm, Fri 8am–1.30pm) at the bottom of Odhós Sífi, facing Platía Iroon Polytechniou, with an ATM and cash-changing machines. There are also ATMs at two banks nearby: Ethniki Bank on the same *platía*; and, just south, Ionian Bank at Venizélou 47.

Bike and car rental Outlets for bikes are on Odhós A. Papandreou off the Beach Road, the best of the bunch being Petras Moto ☎28430 24849, which provides helmets. Club Cars, A. Papandreou 8 ☎28430 25104, is reliable for car rental.

Books and newspapers Arian Minimarket, Karamanli 22 (Beach Road), is currently the only place to stock foreign newspapers.

Bus station At the south end of Venizélou ☎28430 22272, near the Archeological Museum.

A range of services to Áyios Nikólaos, Iráklion, Ierápetra, Vái, Zákros and Káto Zákros.

Ferries The ferry agent (for boats to Kásos and the Dodecanese, Áyios Nikólaos and Pireás) is Tzortzakis (☎28430 25080, ✉tzortzakis@sit.forthnet.gr) Kornárou 150, behind the harbourfront down towards the dock.

Hospital Sitía's main hospital is on Herokamares, on the town's western edge ☎28430 24311.

Internet access Sante, Kornárou 15, to the south-west of Platía Iroon Polytechniou.

Laundry Sitía Launderette, Itanou 25, behind the Archeological Museum (Mon–Sat 9am–2pm & 5–8pm), will wash, dry and fold up to 7kg on the same day for €10. A little tricky to find, take the first left after the museum and it's on the left after 200m.

OTE Kapetan Sifi 22, two blocks west of Platía Iroon Polytechniou (Mon–Fri 7.30am–9.45pm).

Post office Dhimokritou 8 (Mon–Sat 8am–7.30pm).

The east: Vái and Palékastro

Vái beach, with its famous grove of palm trees and silvery sands, features alongside Knossós, the Lasíthi plateau and the Samariá gorge on almost every Cretan travel agent's list of excursions. For years, it was a popular hang-out for backpackers, but repeated fires followed by a clean-up campaign to attract a more well-heeled crowd have resulted in a ring fence around the beach with a guard to enforce the new regulations, which prohibit overnight stays. People still claim to be able to sleep there, but it hardly seems worth the hassle. If you're looking for more to do than simply sizzle on the sands, there are a number of sights within striking distance of Vái: with your own transport, the beaches and archeological sites at **Ítanos** and **Palékastro** are within reach. The scenically sited ancient monastery at **Tóplou**, just to the northwest of Palékastro, is one of the most revered on the island.

Ayía Fotiá and around

From Sitía, the road runs along the beach, and 2km out of town a signed track on the left (marked "Archeological Site") leads 100m to a farm building where you can park, beyond which lie the recently discovered remains of **Hellenistic Sitía**. Dating from the third century BC and later, the remains so far unearthed are substantial with easily identifiable ruins of dwellings, rooms and streets. The continuing excavations will no doubt add to all this in the years ahead.

The main road continues east, tracking a rocky, unexceptional coastline to the village of **Ayía Fotiá**, sited on a small cove that now supports a cluster of new development. Here, in 1971, the largest **Minoan graveyard** yet found in Crete was excavated, revealing over 250 chamber tombs from the early Pre-Palatial period. To reach the cemetery, keep your eyes peeled on the eastern edge of the village for a rough track descending sharply to the left almost opposite the *Taverna Panorama*. Alternatively, if you continue to the very end of the village, you'll come to a signed road on the left which is probably the best route to take with transport. Both routes lead, after about 200m, to the fenced-off cemetery, close to the sea. Among the outstanding finds of vases, fish hooks, daggers and stone axes (now in the Sitía and Áyios Nikólaos archeological museums) were a number of lead amulets, which suggests that these early Minoans regarded lead as a precious metal, as well as silver.

Four kilometres beyond Ayía Fotiá you pass the entrance to a nightmarish holiday development named **Village Dionysos**, with a manned guardhouse built into its entry arch. This complex of holiday villas and apartments in a hotchpotch of jarring architectural styles – stone cladding, bizarre turrets and eye-straining pastel-shaded exteriors – is quite out of keeping with the surrounding coastline. However, expansion is unlikely – the owning company have thus far found it impossible to attract buyers, and a large proportion of the villas remain unsold.

It's a relief to follow the road as it turns inland, climbing into quite deserted, gently hilly country, the slopes covered in thyme, heather and sage with the occasional cluster of strategically sited beehives. In summer, the sweet-scented, deep violet thyme flowers prove an irresistible attraction for the bees which feed on them almost exclusively and thus create the much sought-after *thimárisio* (thyme honey).

The Monastery of Tóplou

Not long after the main road leaves the coast is a side road signposted up to the **Monastery of Tóplou** (daily 9am–7pm; €2.50), which is also the short way to Vái. As you approach, the monastery looks more like a fortress, standing defiant in landscape that is empty, save for a line of intrusive wind turbines along the ridge behind. The name Tóplou is Turkish for "with a cannon" – a reference to a giant device with which the monks used to defend themselves and uphold the Cretan monastic traditions of resistance to invaders. They needed it: the monastery was sacked by pirates and destroyed in 1498, and in the 1821 rebellion it was captured by the Turks, who hanged twelve monks from the gate as an example. In World War II, it again served as a place of shelter, this time for the resistance. The opening above the main gate harks back to troubled times: the monks hurled missiles and boiling oil through it onto those attempting to gain entry.

Its forbidding exterior and grim history notwithstanding, Tóplou is startlingly beautiful within. It has a flower-decked, cloister-like **courtyard** with stairways leading up to arcaded walkways, off which are the cells. The blue-robed monks keep out of the way of visitors as far as possible, and in quieter periods their cells and refectory are left discreetly on view. And in the **church** is one of the masterpieces of Cretan art, the eighteenth-century **icon** *Lord Thou Art Great* by Ioánnis Kornáros. This is a marvellously intricate work, incorporating 61 small scenes full of amazing detail, each illustrating, and labelled with a phrase from the Orthodox prayer which begins "Lord, thou art great…" The **museum** has also been expanded, but apart from a handful of superb icons, the main addition is a collection of tedious religious engravings which fill the wall space, alongside a niche devoted to weapons and battle paraphernalia dating from the Cretan War of Independence to World War II. Outside in the shop you can buy enormously expensive reproductions of the icon, as well as postcards, books, and the monastery's own olive oil and tacky souvenirs.

As you leave the church, take a look at the **inscription** set into the exterior wall. It records an arbitration by Magnesia, a city in Asia Minor, dating from the second century BC, concerning a territorial dispute between nearby Ítanos and Ierápytna (modern Ierápetra). At this time, when the Romans held sway over Crete, these deadly rivals clashed constantly, and finally Rome, unable to placate the two, called in the Magnesians to act as honest brokers. The inscription records part of their judgement (in favour of Ítanos) and was placed in the monastery wall at the suggestion of the English traveller and antiquarian Robert Pashley, who found it being used as a gravestone in 1834.

The monastery is reputed to be incredibly wealthy – it owns most of the northeastern corner of the island and there are rumours that it is about to sell off a chunk of coastline to a property developer to build a holiday village – and this is no doubt how they can afford the endless and extensive restorations which seem set to destroy the romance of the place (the sheer weight of visitor numbers doesn't help either). Latest tasteless additions include an over-restored windmill and an ornamental garden with crazy paving and ludicrous sculpture fronting the monastery entrance, whilst more unspecified building work continues behind the monastery. Beyond Tóplou, the road descends towards Vái through the same arid, rock-strewn landscape as before. This area is another where you might catch sight of the rare **Eleonora's falcon**, which breeds on the Dionysádes islands to the north – Tóplou and Cape Síderos (a closed military zone) are regular hunting grounds.

Vái

The beach at **Vái**, famous above all for its **palm trees**, makes for a thoroughly secular contrast to the spiritual tranquillity of Tóplou – and the sudden appearance of what is claimed to be Europe's only indigenous wild date-palm grove is indeed an exotic shock. Recent scientific research on drilled-cores has revealed that the palms here are a local species present on the island for millennia and not introduced by Roman or Arab sailors, as previously thought.

As you lie on the fine sand in the early morning (especially in early spring or late autumn), the dream of Caribbean islands is hard to dismiss. During the summer months, however, the beach fills to overflowing as buses – public ones from Sitía and tours from all over the island – pour into the **car park** (€2.50); cars parking illegally along the access roads risk a ticket. On the beach itself, the boardwalks alone allow a route through the mass of baking bodies, and even the adjoining beaches get pretty crowded nowadays. You'll pay €3.50 for a sun lounger, the café and taverna are pricy once you've endured the long queues, and you'll pay again to have a shower or use the toilet. There's **no accommodation** here, as this is a protected natural park; the nearest place for a bed is Palékastro (see p.210). People still **camp rough** here, despite the signs warning that this is against the law (which for once is enforced, at least within the confines of the park which protects the palm trees). However, you can climb the steps cut into the rock behind the taverna to the less shaded cove to the south or, with rather more difficulty, clamber over the rocks to the north, and join thriving little communities at either. Having endured all this you may just, for a couple of hours at each end of the day, be able to enjoy Vái the way it ought to be. Alternatively, avoid the high season if you can.

Ítanos

The sand may not be as good, but the emptiness of the three small beaches at **Ítanos**, 1.5km north of the turning to Vái, makes them far more enjoyable, although there are no facilities, so come prepared. There's still the odd palm tree scattered around, and you can explore the remains of the **ancient city** here. Inhabited from Minoan times, Ítanos became important later, flourishing through the Classical Greek and Roman eras, when she vied with Ierápytna (modern Ierápetra) for control of eastern Crete. One twenty-year squabble between these two led to the arbitration of Magnesia in 132 BC, part of the stone record of which is preserved at Tóplou Monastery (see p.209). The settlement here remained prosperous until the medieval Byzantine era, when it was destroyed, most likely by Saracen pirates. All sorts of messy ruins strewn with potsherds survive beneath the twin acropolis, but little which retains any shape. There are two early **basilicas** you might be able to make out, as well as the beautifully cut lower courses of a **Hellenistic wall** on the western hill.

Leaving Ítanos, just south of the beach a road off to the right is signed "to the Naval Base". This is the military base which occupies the tip of **Cape Síderos**, 5km to the north. However, although the guarded base is off limits, the excellent asphalted road takes a good six kilometres getting there, crossing the scenically wild and craggy peninsula, where there are quite a few coves with tempting beaches and some likely places to snorkel. Don't use a camera in this zone – the Greeks are ultra-sensitive when it comes to military installations.

Palékastro and around

The road south from Vái towards Palékastro passes, after 2km, a turn-off on the left to **Maridati Beach**, another more tranquil, if less attractive, alternative to Vái itself. Behind the pebbly beach (1.5km down a rough track), which has a few trees for shade, there's also a **taverna**.

PALÉKASTRO, 9km south of Vái, is an attractive little farming village and a good place to stay close to the beaches, with a couple of excellent tavernas on the main square which are worth breaking your journey for if you're passing through. However, the place is now starting to realize the potential of its position, and tourism is expanding – there are even a couple of cocktail bars as well as a rather incongruous disco, *Design*, on the Vái road. The village also has a **tourist office** (April–Oct daily 9am–10pm; ☎28430 61546), on the main street 50m west of the square towards Sitía. They have information on the surrounding area, will help with finding rooms and some attractive local villas to rent, offer **exchange** facilities, and will let you make **phone calls**, send faxes and make photocopies. International **press** is available from Tsantakis, 75m downhill from the main square, along the road to the beach. They also have **Internet** access, which is also available just off the main square at the Argos Bookstore (follow the sign next to the *Hotel Hellas*). On the eastern edge of the village along the Vái road, Moto Kastri (☎28430 61477) rents out **scooters** – handy for reaching the more remote beaches.

Palékastro has an interesting **folk museum** (May–Oct Tues–Sun 8.30am–1pm & 5–8.30pm; €1.50) housed in a restored traditional cottage signed off the Sitía road a little beyond the tourist office. Inside, rooms are decorated with period furnishings, and there are the usual displays of tools and agricultural equipment.

For **accommodation**, try the *Hotel Itanos* (☎28430 61205; ❷) on the main square (ask at the restaurant below), or the better equipped *Hotel Hellas* (☎28430 61240, ✉hellas_h@otenet.gr; ❸), where a/c rooms come with balcony, TV and fridge, and there are reductions for longer stays. The *Hotel Palekastro* (☎28430 61235; ❸), 100m along the road to Sitía on the left, is another possibility; don't be misled by a drab exterior here, since the pleasant new balcony rooms with a/c and TV lie beyond a courtyard behind. There are also plenty of signs indicating **rooms**. Along the road leading to Vái, a turn-off left just out of the square leads to *Rooms Nikos* (☎28430 61123; ❸), with pleasant new balcony rooms with bath and kitchenette; apartments (⑤) for up to five persons are also available here for longer stays. A little further down and also off to the left, *Rooms Senie* (aka *Rooms Mitsakakis*; ☎28430 61414; ❸ including breakfast), with a/c en-suite rooms with fridge, is also worth a try, as is the good-value *Vai* (☎28430 61414; ❶), which has serviceable rooms with bath above a taverna at the western end of the village, on the Sitía road; they also rent some attractive apartments (❸) with TV, kitchen and garden. Slightly out of the village on the road to the beach, *Hiona Holiday Hotel* (☎28430 29623, ⓦwww.palaikastro.com/hionaholiday; ⑤) is an appealing new hotel where balcony rooms come with a/c, TV and fridge.

The best place **to eat** in Palékastro is the restaurant of the *Hotel Hellas*, which has a number of vegetarian options; the proprietor here is also a beekeeper and will sell you his excellent *thimárisio* (thyme honey) and olive oil. The *Vai*'s taverna (see above), offering many typical Cretan dishes (their *tirokeftedhes*, or cheeseballs, are recommended), is also good.

Angáthia and Palékastro's beaches

Angáthia, smaller and even quieter than its neighbour, lies a kilometre closer to the beaches. Just across the bridge leading into the village on the right, you'll find the good-value *Taverna Vaios* (☎28430 61403; ❷), which has a couple of pleasant sea-view balcony rooms with bath; they have some nearby luxury apartments too (❹), equipped with a/c, garden and balcony sea views. The taverna also makes a good lunch stop if you're at the beach. **Chiona beach**, a good stretch of EU blue-flagged pebble and sand, to the south of a flat-topped hill named **Kastrí** which dominates the coastal landscape, is a kilometre beyond Angáthia and is the beach most people visit, probably because of its car park and nearby **tavernas**, the best of which is *Taverna Batis* with a beach-front terrace, at the northern end. There is no accommodation at Chiona. South of Chiona beach along a track running beside the sea, about 200m down on the right (signed "Peak Sanctuary"), a walking track will take you to the nearby **Petsofas peak** – a pleasant three-kilometre hike. This was also the site of a Minoan peak sanctuary, and the view from the summit gives you a great overview of the ancient Minoan town and harbour.

There are some more excellent **beaches** nearby where you could easily camp out. The better sands are around the bay further to the south of Chiona, where for most of the year you can easily claim a cove to yourself. However, the best beach of all, **Kouremenos**, lies to the north of the Kastri bluff and is one of Crete's top **windsurfing** spots. At the time of writing, the windsurfing school here has closed, so to join the international windsurfing community who gather here throughout the year you'll need to bring your own rig. However, it's rumoured that a new company may be starting up the business once again, and information on this should be available at the *Marina Village Hotel* (see below). The beach's popularity has now attracted a couple of **tavernas**, including *To Botsalo*, with a pleasant terrace shaded by tamarisk trees. For **accommodation**, just behind the Kouremenos beach and surrounded by olive groves, the *Marina Village Hotel* (☎28430 61407, ⓦwww.palaikastro.com/marinavillage; ❻ including breakfast) is a peaceful haven with very nice rooms surrounded by a garden with bougainvillea and banana plants; they also have some slightly cheaper self-catering studios near the Chiona beach (❻).

Palékastro ancient site

The Minoan site of **Palékastro** lies towards the beach, about twenty minutes' walk from Palékastro village. Follow the signs to the *Marina Village Hotel* and

then towards the beach at Chíona. For archeologists, this is a very significant excavation, the largest Minoan town yet discovered and the source of much information about everyday Minoan life. It is an obvious site to settle, a broad and fertile agricultural plain set on an excellent bay beneath the protection of the high, flat-topped bluff of Kastrí – and indeed the area was extensively inhabited both before and after the Minoan era. Whilst much of the site may seem disappointing for the casual visitor when compared with the spectacular palace sites elsewhere on the island, the fact that the archeological excavations continue here means that new finds are still coming to light.

The main excavation area (known as Roussolákkos and left open) lies behind Chíona beach, which was the site of a Minoan harbour, now lost. Indeed, recent excavations on the site's northern side have revealed the road leading from the town to the harbour. Just south of here in a complex of streets, dwellings and small squares lies Building 5, where archeologists dis-covered the **Palékastro koúros**, a stunning ivory statuette now in the Sitía museum. The deep wells which dot the site would have supplied the town, and are so superbly constructed that they still contain water today. South of here again, the "main street" paved in limestone was the town's principal artery; around its main junction a number of impressive dwellings with stone walls and column bases have been revealed, and the fine, Marine-style vases found in the ruins of some of them are evidence of the status and wealth of the owners. House N, at the site's western end, is dated to the late Neo-Palatial period, and excavations revealed horns of consecration and double-axe stands which had fallen from a shrine room on an upper floor. The room at the rear produced hundreds of cups as well as jars and cooking pots, suggesting that it may have been some form of communal eating club, or perhaps an early taverna.

Beneath the olive groves on the south and west sides of the site, more of the Minoan town lies waiting to be revealed – recent geophysical surveys have indicated the existence of a very large building, maybe a palace. Excavation is due to begin in this area in the near future, and it's certain that it will continue for many years to come. Try to resist entering the excavations beyond the temporary fences erected by the archeologists, as the delicate walls and buildings are still being made safe for posterity.

Zákros and the far southeast

Palékastro is the crossroads for the road south to **Zákros**, a beautiful drive through countryside where the soil is a strange pinkish-purple colour, as if indelibly stained with grape juice (although actually it's olives which grow around here). For a fine **gorge walk**, make a stop at **Hohlakiés** (with buses to and from Áno Zákros and Palékastro), where you can follow the Hohlakiés gorge 3km to the Karoúmes Bay and beach. From here, you can either return to Hohlakiés or strike out north along the coast to Palékastro, 5km further. The route is marked on the Harms Verlag map (see p.26).

Beyond Hohlakiés, the few hamlets you pass along the way are so small that they make Zákros – or more properly Áno Zákros – seem positively urban when finally you get there. Beyond Áno Zákros lies its charming coastal offshoot **Káto Zákros**, a tiny seaside village shoehorned into the narrow space between the beach and the important **Minoan palace** behind it.

Áno Zákros

A slow-moving little country town, **ÁNO ZÁKROS** ("Upper" Zákros) boasts three or four tavernas around its central square which, throughout the summer at weekends, host numerous wedding feasts accompanied by dancing to *bouzoúki* and *lyra*; should you arrive then, you'll most likely have a glass of wine thrust into your hand by one of the multitude of smartly dressed revellers filling the square. The little trade these establishments see the rest of the time, however, is almost exclusively passing through, since Káto ("Lower") Zákros and the celebrated palace are on the coast 8km further southeast. Locally, Zákros enjoys a certain fame for its numerous **springs** which feed the lush vegetation hereabouts and which were also an attraction for the Minoans. If you follow the sign up to the right as you come into the town, or simply climb the hill from the centre, you'll reach a little **chapel** from where, in five minutes' walk, a path leads beside the stream to its source and some pleasant, shady picnic spots. Information on how to get to it or to reach the start of the "Valley of the Dead" walk (see p.214) is available from the town's small central **hotel**, the *Zakros* (T & F 28430 93379; ❷), which has some a/c rooms; those at the back have good views over the gorge behind. Guests here are entitled to free trips to Káto Zákros in the hotel's minibus; alternatively if you walk the gorge, the minibus will return you to Áno Zákros. The town has a few **tavernas**, the best of which is *Napoleon* (near the Shell petrol station on the Káto Zákros road). Nearby, *Bar Xyloporta* is a good place for breakfasts, late-night drinks and cocktails, and also has **Internet** access.

Leaving the village by the Káto Zákros and Kserócambos road, you'll soon pass the remains of a **Minoan villa** dating from the late Neo-Palatial period ca.1500 BC); here, a wine-press was discovered, which is now in the Sitía Archeological Museum. Pushing on towards the coast and passing a few **rooms** possibilities (see p.214–15), a good road winds spectacularly down to approach the small bay from the south. Although in summer a couple of daily **buses** do run all the way to Káto Zákros, most transport still stops in the upper village of Áno Zákros. You could hitch down quite easily, but it's also worth considering the walk, less than two hours to the palace via a beautiful ravine known as the **Valley of the Dead**. The easiest route traces the road for almost 2km, before turning left through a gate onto a track (curiously signposted "Dead's Gorge") which brings you out above the ravine. A path takes you to the bottom, from where the trail is easy to follow along the left-hand side of the stream bed, marked by the usual red waymarks in case of confusion. It's a solitary but magnificent walk, brightened especially in spring by plenty of plant life. High in the cliff walls you'll see the mouths of **caves**: it is these, used as tombs in Minoan times and earlier, which give the ravine its name. At the bottom you rejoin the dirt road, which runs through groves of bananas and olives and into Káto Zákros past the palace. As an alternative, you can follow the waymarked path all the way from Áno Zákros, which avoids the road altogether. To reach the path from the village square, take the road on the east side and to the right of the *Maestro Taverna* and small *kafeníon* next door, and fork right at the telegraph pole. The way descends along a path, passing beneath a stone arch. About 200m beyond this, you will come to a sign directing you to the gorge entrance. Should you experience any difficulties in finding the way, enquire at the *Hotel Zakros*.

Káto Zákros

From the first spectacular view as you approach along the clifftop road, **KÁTO ZÁKROS** is a delight. There's a pebbly sand beach, three good tavernas and a few places offering **rooms**; along with a tiny harbour with a few boats, this is about all the place amounts to. Everything you really need is here: they'll **change money** in the tavernas, and you can even make long-distance and international **phone calls** from a cardphone kiosk on the seafront, but there's absolutely nothing else, not even a store. The village does now has its first ever cocktail **bar** – the aptly named *Amnesia* on the seafront – where the clientele have even been known to dance when the mood takes them, but this hardly causes a ripple, and if it's laid-back tranquillity you're after, you've come to the right place.

Poseidon (☎28430 26896; ❷) – on a rocky outcrop with spectacular sea views – is perhaps the best **accommodation** option; it also has some more expensive rooms en suite. The *Taverna Akrogiali* (☎28430 26893, ⓔakrogiali@sit.forthnet.gr; ❷) on the harbour has rooms with and without bath plus an apartment (❹), and acts as an agent for the nearby *Athena* (❸) with a/c en-suite rooms, and *Coral* (❸), where there are more en-suite rooms. Other options are set back from the beach, among them *George Villas* (☎ & ⓕ28430 26883, ⓔgeorgevillas@sit.forthnet.gr; ❸), with a/c rooms and apartments with bath, fridge and terrace in a leafy location; follow the (drivable) track heading inland from the palace entrance for 600m. The newly opened *Stella Apartments* (☎28430 23739; ❹) next door to here has attractive and more expensive studio apartments with a/c and kitchenette. More realistic with your own transport, the friendly, family-run *Rooms Alex* (☎28430 93338; ❷) is another possibility, though it's 2km (not 500m as their publicity says) back towards Áno Zákros, close to the top of the gorge. There's also a **hiking track** with spectacular views from here to Kserókambos (see p.218), 7km south. Nearby and just opposite the top of the gorge, *Rent Rooms Faragi* (☎28430 93144; ❷) has pleasant en-suite rooms in a house surrounded by a verdant garden; breakfast is possible, and they also have apartments for longer stays. However, it's worth bearing in mind, especially if you're arriving by bus, that accommodation is severely limited due to building restrictions surrounding the archeological site, and during high season you will rarely find a room on spec; you may be able to sleep under the trees or on the beach, but the patience of the villagers is wearing thin towards people who do this.

For **eating and drinking** there are three seafront tavernas; both *Akrogiali* and its neighbour *Anesis* are good, with waterfront terraces, and the third, *Platanakis*, does tasty charcoal-grilled *kouneli* (rabbit) and (in season) game.

The Palace of Zákros

The valley behind Káto Zákros was explored by a British archeologist, David Hogarth, at much the same time as the other great Cretan palaces were being discovered, around the turn of the century. But Hogarth gave up the search, having unearthed only a couple of Minoan houses, and it was not until the 1960s that new explorations were begun by a Cretan archeologist, Nikólaos Pláton. Pláton found the palace almost immediately, just yards from where Hogarth's trenches ended. The **Palace of Zákros** (daily: July–Oct 8am–7pm; Nov–June 8am–3pm; €3) thus benefited from the most modern of techniques in its excavation and, having been forgotten even locally, it was also unlooted. The site yielded an enormous quantity of treasures and everyday items, including storerooms with all their giant *píthoi* still in place and a religious treasury full of stone vases and ritual vessels.

For the amateur, Zákros is also full of interest, and a great deal easier to understand than many of the other Minoan sites. Here, the remains are of one palace only, dating from the period between 1600 and 1450 BC. Although there is an earlier settlement at a lower level, it is unlikely ever to be excavated – mainly because this end of the island is very gradually sinking. The water table is already almost at the palace level, and anything deeper would be thoroughly submerged. Even the exposed parts of the palace are marshy and often waterlogged: there are terrapins living in the green water in the cistern. When it's really wet, you can keep your feet dry and get an excellent view of the overall plan of the palace by climbing the streets of the **town** which occupied the hill above it.

Though the palace is a small one, it can match any of the more important Minoan centres for quality of construction and materials. And it is unique in the way that so much of the town – a place very like Gourniá – can still be discerned all around. The original destruction of the palace appears to have been a very violent one, with only enough time for the inhabitants to abandon it, taking almost nothing with them. This again contributed to the enormous number of artefacts found here, but more importantly the nature of the destruction, in which the palace was flattened and burnt, is an important prop in the theory that it was the explosion of Thíra which ended the Minoan civilization. Large lumps of **pumice** found among the ruins are supposed to have been swept there by the tidal wave which followed the eruption. However, many archeologists take issue with this hypothesis and question both its chronological accuracy and the type of destruction (such as fire), seeing the palace's demise as being more consistent with human rather than natural causes.

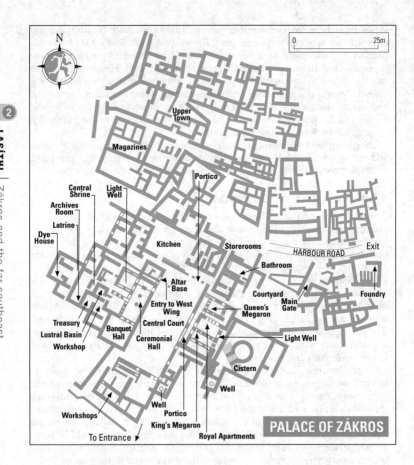

PALACE OF ZÁKROS

The entrance

A paved road led from the site to its harbour, the chief reason why a palace existed here at all. The harbour installations have disappeared beneath the sea, but two large houses excavated along the road are enough to show that this must have been a significant port, the first landfall on Crete for trade from Egypt, the Nile Delta and the Middle East. Among the ruins were found ingots of copper imported from Cyprus, elephant tusks from Syria, and gold and precious materials from Egypt.

The **entrance** has been relocated on the site's south side, and to follow our account here you will need to start from the **exit** – a white cabin visible to the far right – where you can pick up the ancient harbour road leading towards the palace. Starting from here also enables you to follow the ancient road leading directly towards the main gateway of the palace in its eastern corner.

Before entering the palace proper, you pass various dwellings to the right and left as well as the remains of a **foundry** dating from the Old Palace period, beneath a protective canopy on the left. The road (a stretch has been reconstructed) then curves round into the town, passing the palace entrance to the left. Entering the palace, the **main gate** leads to a stepped ramp, followed by a **courtyard** which may have served as a meeting place between the palace hierarchy and the townspeople. Here, in the northeast corner beneath another canopy, is a **bathroom** where visitors to the palace may have been required to wash or purify themselves before proceeding further. To the west of the courtyard lies the main or **Central Court**, a little over 30m by 12m, or about a third the size of that at Knossós. Crossing the north edge of the court, you come to an **altar base**, with the lower courses of the west-wing wall in grey ashlar stone beyond.

The west wing

The west wing (actually the northwest, as Zákros is not truly aligned north–south) is entered between two pillars and this is where, as usual, the chief ceremonial and ritual rooms were located. A **reception room** leads into a colonnaded **light well**, the hallmark of Minoan architecture. The light well's black stone crazy paving survives, as do the pillar bases and a drain in the northwest corner. It was here that the excavators unearthed what is arguably Zákros's single most important find: the **Peak Sanctuary Rhyton**, a carved stone vase depicting a peak sanctuary with wild goats, from which valuable information about Minoan religion was gleaned. The light well illuminated the **Ceremonial Hall**, beyond which lay the **Banqueting Hall**, originally a lavish room with frescoed walls and an elaborate floor. Pláton gave the room this name because of the large number of cups and drinking vessels discovered scattered about the floor.

At the heart of a complex of rooms behind the Banqueting Hall is the **Central Shrine** (with a canopy) which contains a ledge and niche, similar to the shrine at Gourniá, where idols would have been placed. Nearby is the **lustral basin**, necessary for purification before entering the shrine. Here, too, was the **Treasury**, probably the most important discovery from the excavators' viewpoint as it is the only one so far positively identified. In a number of box-like compartments (which have been partially restored), almost a hundred fine stone jars and libation vessels were discovered, including the exquisite rock-crystal rhyton – crushed into more than three hundred fragments – with its delicate crystal bead handle and collar that the Iráklion Archeological Museum is so proud of. Incidentally, the latter is used to illustrate the cover of the site information leaflet given to you on entry.

Next to the Treasury, in the **Palace Archive**, hundreds of Linear A record tablets had been stored in wooden chests. Sadly, only a handful of the top layers survived the centuries of rain and flooding; the rest had solidified into a mass of grey clay, depriving the archeologists of potentially priceless clues in their attempts at deciphering the script. On the opposite side of the treasury is a **workshop** where pieces of raw marble and steatite were found. The remaining stone slabs most likely supported a craftsman's workbench. More workshops and storerooms lay to the west of the shrine, and one of these has been identified as a **dye-house**. And if you were wondering where the occupants of this end of the palace answered the call of nature, a **lavatory** with a cesspit outside the wall was found nearby. Further west, beyond the palace confines, new excavations are still going on.

The rest of the site

On the north side of the Central Court was the palace **kitchen**, the first to be positively identified at any of the palaces. Bones, cooking pots and utensils were found strewn around the floor both here and in the storeroom or pantry next door. The south wing was devoted to **workshops**: for smiths, lapidaries, potters and even, according to Pláton, perfume-makers – possibly a borrowing from Egypt. The **well** that serviced this area still flows with drinkable water, and, close to the steps leading down into it, an offering cup was found, containing olives preserved by the waters. Pláton and his team devoured the 3500-year-old olives, which shrivelled upon contact with the air, and said that they tasted as fresh as those in the nearby tavernas.

Two large rooms regarded as **royal apartments** flank the east side of the Central Court behind a portico. The larger of the two, to the south, is called the King's Room and the smaller is claimed to be that of the queen. However, one of these may have been the throne room, and there would have been elaborate rooms on the upper floor, possibly with verandahs overlooking the courtyard below, which might more realistically have been where the rulers lived. Next to a light well in the eastern wall of the King's Room lay the colonnaded **Cistern Hall** which, with its eight steps leading down to the water contained in a plaster-lined basin, may have served as a royal aquarium or even a swimming pool (if so, the only one known). It is ingeniously designed to maintain the water at a constant level, with the excess draining into the well to the south, which lay outside the palace wall and was probably used by the townsfolk. The water from the spring was, as at Knossós, piped throughout the palace, and traces of the pipework are still to be seen around the site.

Beyond these royal apartments lay other **residential areas**, but much has been destroyed by centuries of ploughing combined with frequent waterlogging of the land here. In the steep **upper town** more survives and, close to the perimeter fence, a **narrow street** running east to west passes an impressive doorway to the left and gives you some idea of how much of the town may have looked when twin-storey buildings overlooked these narrow thoroughfares. Quite a few grindstones found in the excavations are to be seen here, and nearby there's also a charming **stone bench** which now stands exposed but would have looked into a light well. It's not hard to imagine someone sitting on it, enjoying the cool and shade of a summer evening. Near to the bench, there's a well-preserved stairway climbing a couple of metres before taking a right angle and tantalizingly continuing its climb again to the now disappeared second storey. Both the stairway and the bench are close to the perimeter fence on the eastern (or seaward) side of the upper town. The quarry from where the tufa limestone used to build the palace was taken has now been discovered at nearby Pelekita, on the coast 3km to the north.

Kserócambos and the southeast

Few tourists venture south of Zákros, and indeed there's little in the way of habitation in the whole of the southeastern corner of the island, nor any public transport whatsoever. Even the boulder-strewn dirt roads seem to be left in this condition to discourage the adventurous, but these are a bonus for the walker. With your own transport, however, a little effort is rewarded with scores of excellent **beaches** – mostly deserted. There's an inland route by which you can circle back north to Sitía, via a newly sealed road after Kserókambos, taking in an archeological site at Présos along the way.

Kserókambos and around

Leave Áno Zákros on the new road towards Káto Zákros and you'll shortly reach a track to the right (due to be asphalted in 2004), with a hand-painted sign for "Ambelos and Liviko View", next to another **Minoan villa** bisected by the road. It's not a bad surface, descending through olive groves and giant greenhouses to run along a deep ravine. After 10km, and just when you're convinced you're lost, a brilliant turquoise sea and white sandy beaches divided by rocky outcrops appear below.

Tucked in the lee of the foothills of the Sitían Mountains which rise away behind, the tiny hamlet of **Kserókambos** is as tranquil a hideaway as you could wish for. The settlement consists of one street with two tavernas, a couple of minimarkets selling basic food, and a few olive groves strung out along its length. Both tavernas will provide information and keys for **rooms** and some nice apartments (if available, which they may not be in August). Try phoning ahead to secure space at the excellent *Liviko View* (☏28430 27001, Ⓦwww.xeroscamboscreta.com; ❷), run by a couple of Greek-Australians. Rooms come with a/c and balcony sea view, and there are some more expensive apartments (❹) sleeping up to four. The cooking here – with organic ingredients grown on the family farm – is recommended, and at weekends they even put on the occasional *lyra* concert. *Asteras* (☏28430 26787; ❸), with a/c studio rooms set back from the sea, is another possibility. Alternatives for **eating and drinking** include *Taverna Kostas* (slightly before *Liviko View*) for grilled meat dishes, and the seafront *Akrogiali* for fish. **Camping** on the main beach is not allowed although you should be able to find secluded places away from here, but drinking water may be a problem.

The **main beach** – a short walk away along the beach road and one of the best on the island – is a couple of kilometres of pristine shimmering sand that hardly sees a towel or sunbed all year, and if that isn't escapist enough, to the north and especially the south are wonderful isolated coves where you might never see another soul. The crystal-clear waters here are great for **snorkelling** too – the minimarkets sell the basic equipment. Away from the sea there's little to do, but you could stretch your legs with a walk to the tiny chapel on a low hill to the south of the beach. Surrounding this are the ruins of an extensive **Minoan settlement** not yet fully explored or documented. Archeologists argue as to whether Kserókambos is the site of ancient Ambelos (in spite of a location of this name nearby), but artefacts discovered both here and at a looted peak sanctuary in the hills certainly suggest this was a settlement of some significance in ancient times, possibly connected with the Zákros palace to the north.

For a more ambitious **walk** you could follow a track (marked on the Harms Verlag map) which heads south behind the beach for 4km to the deserted village of **Ayía Iríni**, with plenty of opportunities for a dip along the way. Continuing inland from here along the same track would enable you to climb to the peak of **Agridomouri** (627m), descending to **Kaló Horió** on the other side (6km from Ayía Iríni). From Kaló Horió, you could hitch the 11km to Kserókambos via the new road.

Kserócambos has nothing at all in the way of after-dark diversions – not even a bar – but the pitch-black nights here are magical with the opportunity for beach walking, a midnight swim or simply sipping *raki* beneath a dome of stars, trying to spot the various constellations.

Back to Sitía: via Zíros, Handhrás and Etiá

An asphalt road links Kserócambos with Zíros, so it's possible to complete a circular route back to Sitía. The road zigzags upwards out of Kserócambos to finally cross the northern shoulder of Mount Agridomouri; in early summer, you'll see dense clumps of deep violet *thimári* (wild thyme) filling rock crevices and lining the roadside. This road is also populated by herds of goats who – despite the arrival of the asphalt – still regard this as their

The wind turbines of eastern Crete

The **wind turbines** that stretch across the hills and ridges of many areas of eastern Crete are a response to the acute electricity shortages the island experiences when its population doubles in the height of summer. For half the year, power demand is less than 250 megawatts, but in high summer this often leaps dramatically to almost five hundred megawatts at peak demand. The island's power station at Iráklion – with a maximum output of 450 megawatts – is often overwhelmed and unable to cope. The five turbine farms at this end of the island (of which Handhrás, with eighteen turbines, is one of the smallest) are currently capable of boosting the power supply by an additional sixty megawatts, and are seen by the authorities as the solution to inevitable power cuts. In line with the projected boosting of tourist numbers when the new Sitía airport is completed, the government in Athens recently announced a further sale of licences in Crete to allow companies to construct yet more turbines. Considering the furores in other parts of the world where these machines have been proposed, there has been little objection by phlegmatic Cretans to what elsewhere has been seen as a despoiling of the visual environment. However, if the rugged and picturesque hill country of eastern Crete is defaced by even more of these towering sentinels, visitors may well decide that they would prefer not to do their trekking in an industrial landscape.

traditional domain and are quite a hazard should you meet them while taking a bend at speed. Take care when descending too, as there are sharp curves with steep precipices and not always barriers; errors of judgement have already led to accidents.

Beyond the primitive hamlet of **Hamétoulo** – a piece of living Cretan folklore with twenty dwellings, a cobbled street and a church – all views are dominated by a giant radar dome on the mountain top, and the road itself is dotted with "No Photography" signs, alerting you that this is a military zone and the site of NATO's main command post for the eastern Mediterranean.

At the top of the climb the road levels to a plateau surrounded by rock cliffs, in the midst of which lies the fair-sized farming village of **Zíros**. Tumbling down a hillside towards a busy centre, it's a welcoming place, with a neat *platía* circled by willow and acacia trees with whitewashed trunks. There's even an occasional bus to Sitía (currently Mon–Fri at 7.15am and 2.30pm). Along the main street, and facing a couple of palm trees, *Taverna Harkiolakis* (☎28430 91266; ❷) makes an inviting stop **to eat** (the roast lamb and goat dishes are recommended), and they have now added a few en-suite **rooms**. They should also have copies of an excellent small book on the history of this area and its villages – *Ziros and Xerokampos*, by the eminent archeologist, the late Níkos Papadákis. It's produced by the local council and, amazingly, it's free. Should you come in late July, you may be lucky enough to catch the annual **festival**, when the women of the village produce huge trays of delicacies, which are laid out on tables in the square and washed down with gallons of *raki* to the accompaniment of *bouzoúki* and *lyra*. For quieter times, there are sixteenth-century frescoes to be seen in the church of **Ayía Paraskeví**, but you may prefer to soak up the atmosphere with a drink at a table in the square. In the early evening, when the rocky heights seem to crowd in on all sides, places like Zíros feel like the real heart of Crete.

Gluttons for punishment could follow a paved road south to Áyia Triáda, from where a very rough dirt road (due to be asphalted in 2004) heads down to the coast at Goúdhouras (see p.223); until the road surfacing is completed the easier way to reach the coast is via Handhrás, 4km to the west. The reasons for Zíros's size and prosperity are evident along the road out, as it cuts through olive groves and vineyards said to be among the best on the island.

Another tidy farming village, **Handhrás**, is entered past its sail-less and derelict irrigation windmills. Somewhat eerily, these have now been replaced by a surreal addition to the landscape – a phalanx of mammoth, gyrating wind turbines spaced out along the ridge above the village. The lease with the company that erected them has been signed for 99 years, so they are set to be an enduring, if hardly picturesque, feature on the landscape. There's a welcoming **taverna** here, *To Steki*, fronted by acacia trees on the main square, as well as a small **folk museum** just off this and signed.

A turning southwest out of Handhrás leads after 4km to **Etiá**, a hamlet where a ruined **Venetian mansion** stands in memorial to the glory days of the Italian city's power in Crete. Built by the Di Mezzo family (whose arms decorate the doorway) in the late fifteenth century, this once elegant edifice was badly damaged in 1828 when the local populace vented their rage on the Turks who had been using it as an administrative base; nowadays, the ground floor, with its impressive entrance hall and vaulted ceiling, is all that remains of the three-storey building. Because few country houses of the Venetian period survive on Crete, however, the mansion has been declared a national monument under the care of the Greek Archeological Service and is currently being restored. It lies 100m up a track, behind the roadside church of **Ayía Katerina**, which has an elegant carved stone tower. To the west of the church are the remains of the village of Etía that no doubt provided the labour for the mansion.

Continuing north out of Handhrás, a lane just outside the village is signed on the right for **Voilá**, a ruined medieval village that you can just see at the foot of the hill. With its Gothic arches and silent paved streets, this is a distinctly eerie place to wander round; two ornamental drinking **fountains** still function, one at each end of the village, with beautiful brass taps – a Turkish contribution to this Venetian stronghold. The twin-naved **Áyios Yeóryios** church (usually locked) has an interesting sixteenth-century gravestone fresco in an interior recess; this and a tower of the Turkish period dominate the site. You can also climb to a ruined Venetian fort on top of the hill above the village.

Ancient Présos

The archeological site of **Présos** lies close to the modern village of **Néa Présos**. This is another of those sites where what you see – in this case very little – cannot begin to match the interest and importance of the history. But even without ruins, it would be worth taking the walk around the site for the **scenery** alone. From the centre of the village, opposite a *kafeníon* with a raised terrace, a dirt road is clearly signposted downhill. After about 1.5km you'll come to a signed gate for the "First Acropolis" – this is where to leave your vehicle if you have one.

Présos first came to light in 1884, when the Italian archeologist Federico Halbherr turned up a large number of clay idols and some unusual inscriptions written in an unknown tongue – very likely the same as that of the Linear A tablets – using Greek characters. Set out with lines reading alternatively right to left and left to right, these **Eteocretan** (true Cretan) inscriptions are now believed to be evidence of the post–Bronze Age Minoans who fled the Dorian invasions to these remote fastnesses in the east of the island in an attempt to preserve their civilization. Présos seems to have been one of their principal towns, controlling the sanctuary of Dhiktean Zeus at Palékastro, probably an earlier Minoan shrine. With harbours on the north and south coasts of the island, its power eventually led to conflict with the leading Dorian city of the region, Ierápytna (modern Ierápetra). Following final victory about 155 BC, Ierápytna razed Présos to the ground and the city was never rebuilt. With this defeat, the long twilight of Minoan civilization, lasting more than a thousand years after the palaces had fallen, came to an end.

From the entrance, follow the path west to a saddle between the two hills where the ancient city lay. On the summit of the **First Acropolis** (soon signed to the right) you can make out the foundations of a temple. Further on, the path forks and to the right – on the western slope of the same hill – are the remains of a substantial **Hellenistic house** excavated by the British archeologist Bosanquet around one hundred years ago. Dating from the third century BC, the outer walls of superbly cut stone define the main living rooms at the front of the house, with workrooms at the rear. In the largest workroom, an olive press was found together with a stone tank for storing the oil. A stairway to the left of the main door led down to a cellar.

Turning left at the fork brings you – after a hundred-metre walk across the saddle – to the **Second Acropolis** where cuttings in the rock on the south side formed the foundations of dwellings; the defensive wall which encircled these two hills can still be made out in places.

From Néa Présos, it's a further 4km to the main Sitía–Ierápetra highway.

Sitía to Ierápetra

The main road across the island from Sitía to the south coast cuts between the east and west ranges of the **Sitía mountains**, giving some fine views in the hill country of the central section before descending towards the sea plain. A number of sturdy hamlets along the route, such as Áyios Yeóryios and Lithínes, make good places to stop for a snack and a beer.

South from Sitía to the coast

Just before Piskokéfalo, less than 2km out of Sitía, Minoan enthusiasts may want to pause at the remains of a **Minoan villa** (signed) cut through by the road. Dating from the late Neo-Palatial period (1550–1450 BC), it had two floors and is terraced into the hillside with the well-preserved staircase giving access to an upper floor. The villa's view would have encompassed the river valley below the road, where its farm lands were probably located.

At the entrance to Piskokéfalo itself, a dirt road is signed to the left for the village of **Zoú**, 6km further on, where there's another **Minoan villa** of the same period. Follow the road, which crosses a dry riverbed and then turns right (signed), eventually becoming asphalt as it winds up into the hills towards Zoú. The villa – not easily spotted and with no sign – lies on a high bank to the right of the road just before the village. Excavated by Nikólaos Pláton, the archeologist who unearthed the palace at Zákros, this is more a farmhouse – cultivating the land in the valley to the east – than simply a country dwelling. The rooms seem to be divided between those for domestic life and others for work and storage of farm equipment. A pottery kiln (perhaps used for making olive-oil containers) was discovered in one room, while two deep pits near the entrance probably stored grain. If you're looking for refreshment, Piskokéfalo has an excellent **taverna** on its main square, the aptly titled *I Plateía*, whose specialities include *kolokithóanthi* (stuffed courgette flowers).

Back on the main Sitía–Ierápetra road, it's a long climb to the island's spine, past Epáno Episkopí and the turning to Présos (see p.221), before the road dips towards **Lithínes**. Just after this, the islands of Koufonísi, to the east, and Gaidhouronísi, to the west, become visible beyond the coastal plain out in the Libyan Sea. You emerge, eventually, on the south coast at **Pilalímata**. For empty beaches, you should get off the bus just past here, where a road on the left is signed for the Moní Kápsa and Goúdhouras. There's a fair stretch of rather pebbly grey beach – known as **Kaló Neró**, with a couple of cafés – no more than 1km from the road. If you have transport, however, there are better strips of sand to be found scattered all along this rocky foreshore.

Moní Kápsa and Goúdhouras

Now served by an asphalt road which somewhat diminishes the sense of isolation, the **Moní Kápsa** (daily 8.30am–12.30pm & 3.30–7pm) enjoys a spectacular setting on a ledge in the cliffs just above the road and an abiding reputation for miracles. The original monastery, probably founded in the early Venetian period, was destroyed by **Turkish pirates** in 1471. It was rebuilt, but most of the present buildings were constructed in the nineteenth century, thanks to the energies of **Yerontoyiannis**, a monk who earned himself a name as a Robin Hood–style hero as well as a healer. Locally, he is revered as a saint, and although he never conducted a single service due to his illiteracy and is denied canonization by the Church, Cretans flock to leave offerings beside his silver-encased cadaver and skull in the monastery chapel. You may also visit the **cave** behind the church to where he often retreated and from where there's a fine view towards the island of Koufonísi. As you enter the monastery, pairs of baggy trousers and other battered old items of clothing are hung on pegs by the door, for use by anyone who turns up in shorts or otherwise "unsuitable" attire. At the time of writing, the clothes had disappeared, and you will need to rely on the lenience or otherwise of the monk on duty if you are wearing shorts (Greek visitors so attired seem to have no problem). Most times of the year you'll have the place to yourself, and the people around the monastery, lay workers mostly, in addition to the two remaining monks, always seem to have time to sit you down for a chat and a cold drink.

About 5km east along the same road, you come to an excellent stretch of **beach**, just before **Goúdhouras**. There should be little problem **camping** around here, taking advantage of three or four **tavernas** in the village and a fish taverna on the seafront. There are also a couple of apartment places too, but Goúdhouras itself is a particularly unattractive little place, surrounded by the dusty plastic greenhouses from which it makes its money. If you're looking for food in this area, the *Dragon's Cave Taverna*, signed off the road between Pilalímata and the Moní Kápsa, specializes in charcoal-grilled meat and has a fine view from its terrace.

Makriyialós to Ierápetra

West from Pilalímata, the route to Ierápetra passes Análipsi and **Makriyialós** (Ⓦwww.makrigialos.gr), villages which have merged into each other along the road. Makriyialós has one of the best **beaches** at this end of Crete, with taver-nas and sand that shelves so gently you begin to think you are going to walk the 320km to Africa. But while it is by no means overrun, heavy building has ensured that it's no longer exactly pretty either – and in any case, it's not some-where you're likely to find a very cheap **room**. Try *Hamlet Cottages* (☎28430 51434; ⊙), signed down a long track inland as you enter from the east, which rents stone-built cottages complete with kitchen and terrace. Up the same track and nearby is *White River Cottages* (☎28430 51120, Ⓔwrc@sit.forthnet.gr;

❺–❻), where an abandoned hamlet of traditional stone dwellings (the original Aspro Potamos or "White River") has been restored back to life as a leafy warren of charming studios and apartments with a focal pool. Back on the main road and just beyond the track leading to the above, *Villea Village* (☎28430 52232, Ⓦwww.villeavillage.com; ❻) has studio rooms in a garden setting with a full-sized pool. Cheaper but uninviting rooms line the seafront towards the middle of the town, and none are places you'd really want to put up at.

The place to go for **food** here is the outstanding *Porfira* (☎28430 52189; eves only, closed Thurs), on the main street – undoubtedly one of the best restaurants on the island. There's an attractive sea-view terrace, and the kitchen – under chef Leonidas Grammaticus – turns out Cretan traditional dishes cooked with style (try the *kotópoulo lemonato* – chicken in a clay pot), as well as many other imaginative specials, such as sea bream baked in sea salt. The lengthy wine list has some excellent bottles from Crete and Greece to complement the food and, whilst prices are above the norm, so is the quality of the fare offered – although the service is not always equal to the cooking, and delays sometimes occur. Ariston, next door to here, is a shop selling wine, honey and aromatic herbs as well as other products of the island. For a change of scene, you could also try the tavernas on the picturesque harbour at the western end of town. Here, *Faros* and *To Limani* are two of the better places for fresh fish.

As you leave Makriyialós, you pass yet another **Minoan villa** (signed only from the western approach), 200m inland from the road. Leave any transport and follow the level track starting to the west of the sign; this eventually climbs up to the site, behind a fence next to a house strewn with bougainvillea in summer. It was long suspected that such a tempting area would not have escaped the attentions of the ancient peoples, and in 1971 Costis Davaras began excavations which eventually unearthed an important villa of the late Neo-Palatial period (1550–1450 BC). As can be seen from the remains, it had strong outer walls and some fine stone-flagged floors. The ground plan is not unlike that of the palaces, with rooms situated around a **central court**, where an **altar** was also identified. The excavation also revealed that the house was destroyed by fire – yet more evidence for the endless debate over what caused the downfall of the Minoans.

Just after this, on the hill at the western end of Makriyialós, you will pass a sign to the south of the road for another archeological site. Inside a fence (the gate is left open), the remains of a neglected and extensive patrician **Roman villa** overlooking the sea are very impressive. As you stroll around you can see the remains of mosaic floors and – at the southern end – an elaborate suite of bathing rooms complete with **hypocaust** and furnace to provide underfloor heating. In other rooms, you can see traces of plasterwork on the walls and fragments of the original marble which would have no doubt covered them. On the villa's west side, an **atrium** or ornamental garden underlines the fact that this must have been the residence of a fairly important personage. Sadly, and as is so often the case with non-Minoan remains, information on the villa is very sketchy.

There's a second bay immediately beyond Makriyialós, with a smaller, emptier beach, and the road then runs along what is for the most part an exposed and rocky coast littered with ugly plastic greenhouses, and only the occasional scrubby beach. **Koutsourás**, 3km west of Makriyialós and the main village hereabouts, has little to commend it, although there are a few **rooms**. *Pension Marika* (☎28430 51214; ❷) is a reasonable seafront place for en-suite rooms, and they also rent out some seafront apartments nearby (❸). A little further east, *Pension Dassenakis* (☎28430 51203; ➋) has en-suite balcony rooms fronting the sea and is reached along a path which starts near the *Taverna Kaliotzina* (see below); they also have some attractive apartments sleeping up to five (➌–➍). On the way there, you'll pass *Taverna Robinson*, a pleasant place to eat with a wood-burning oven and offering various Cretan specials such as *misitiropita* (white cheese pie) and quite a few vegetarian options. For fish, however, the best place here is the friendly and popular *Taverna Kaliotzina* on the bend of the main road and close to the *Pension Marika* (see p.224); here, you can choose your fish from the day's catch in the refrigerator, and eat it on an attractive, tree-shaded terrace facing the sea.

Koutsourás Communal Park and Orinó

Two kilometres further west, keep an eye out on the right for a small park. A great fire here in 1993 did enormous damage to a wildlife habitat once known as Dásaki, now renamed Koutsourás Communal Park. It was not the first time that it had been devastated by fire: during World War II, it was burned by the German army in order to root out resistance forces. The latest fire reduced much of the pinewood covering the hills to a stump-strewn wasteland (although the trees are now growing back), and devastated the flora and fauna in the gorge behind, including some remarkable butterflies that were expected to return, but have not been seen since. Some believe that the fire was not the accident it appeared (see box below); many of the nearby villagers would prefer to see olives planted here or some other "sensible" use of the land.

Leave your vehicle by the café at the entrance and walk the 500m through the woods to the gorge. In late spring and summer, if they have returned, fluttering cardinal, Cleopatra and swallowtail **butterflies** drift past visitors in a

---

The fires of Crete

Recent years have seen appalling **forest fires** throughout Crete, with devastations occurring in and around the hill villages to the north of Sóuyia, at the Ayía Iríni gorge and around Kastélli Kissámou in western Crete and to the west of Ayía Galíni in the centre of the island, while terrific blazes in the hills surrounding Kalamáfka to the northwest of Ierápetra in the east also did enormous damage to the landscape.

Depressingly, these fires are not always the accidents they seem to be. Figures from the Greek Agricultural Ministry attribute no less than 57 percent of all fires to unknown causes or arson. A survey of fires throughout Greece by the *I Koinonía* newspaper showed a dramatic increase in the number of fires and highlighted further sharp escalations prior to general elections. This, of course, is when the politicians – in a desperate scramble for votes – are willing to recognize the claims to land of those who may have started the fires in the first place. Under Greek law, there is no organized system of land registry for publicly owned land, which means that if an area of woodland is burned down, the barren territory left behind becomes a no-man's-land which can be claimed under squatters' rights. Once olives or other crops have been planted, a foothold towards possession has been attained, with local politicians often smoothing over the obstacles to the ownership of the land being transferred. This callous attitude to the environment, where trees are little regarded for their beauty, has a long history. In his book *Wild Flowers of Crete*, biologist George Sfikas writes that "the Greek holds the deeply rooted view that a green wood is useless because the trees drink valuable water and don't produce anything". Until this attitude is combated and reversed, the fires will continue to transform the island from one of the most fertile in the Mediterranean into one of the most barren.

spectacular array of colour. The gorge is (or was) also a haven for blue rock thrushes, griffon vultures, crag martins and other interesting bird life, and hopefully the regenerated flora will induce their return.

The energetic may wish to walk up the gorge into the mountains of the Thriptí range, ending up at the picturesque and isolated village of **Orinó** (6km; sturdy footwear required). Alternatively, with your own transport there's a **scenic route** to Orinó, signed 2km further along the main road, which climbs steeply for 10km to reach the village surrounded by lush greenery and wildflowers. At a height of nearly 1000m, the temperature stays quite cool even in summer, and locals tend to wear jumpers for most of the year. The three rustic **bars** along the main street don't always have beer (you're really off the beaten track here) but will happily serve up their home-produced *raki*, a fairly potent brew.

Ayía Fotiá and beyond

For a few kilometres after Koutsourás there's a genuinely mountainous stretch, until the road dips down to a beach with a taverna, and in the following bay a poorly signed track leads down to **Ayía Fotiá**. Hidden from the road in a wooded valley, the tiny resort has its attractions, although an excellent small **beach** – just a couple of minutes' walk away down the stream bed – can get overcrowded, especially at weekends. There are usually enough **rooms** places to go round though, and at the upmarket end of things, the *Eden Rock Hotel* (℡28420 61370; ❼), facing the entry road down to the beach, has pricey a/c rooms with fridge and satellite TV overlooking a pool. In the beachfront hamlet below, cheaper options are available at *Markos Studios* (℡28420 26690; ❸), where studios come with a/c and kitchenette, or there are rooms with similar facilities at *Taverna Glaros* (℡28420 61288; ❸), probably the best of the **places to eat**.

Ayía Fotiá is, sadly, the final place from here until well beyond Ierápetra which could be described as inviting. The final 10km of road runs fast across a flat plain, unimaginatively developed for tourism along the coast and for hot-house agriculture inland. The next village along, Ferma, has little to offer but a kilometre or so beyond here, it's worth looking out for a sign for "Roman Fish Tanks" on the left in front of the *Kakkos Bay Hotel*. Follow a track to the left of the hotel heading towards the rocks. Keeping more or less ahead in a straight line, you'll eventually reach a remarkable **Roman fish tank** some four metres square, carved out of the rock with the sea still sloshing through an ancient sluicegate in the bottom. The carved steps leading down into the tank would have been used by the fish sellers to net the fish demanded by their customers; the pools in the surrounding rocks were no doubt used for the fish to be sold that day, whilst the smaller ones could be fattened up in the larger tank below.

The dull village of **Koutsonári**, 1km further west, is no great shakes either, despite its much vaunted "tourist village", a group of abandoned houses which have been restored to rent as holiday villas. As always though, head away from the coast and into the hills and you're back in timeless Crete. North out of Koutsonári, there's a scenic 8km drive to the hilltop hamlet of **Áyios Ioánnis**, which has four churches.

Back on the coast road and just beyond the turn-off for the centre of Koutsonári is the village's **campsite** – *Camping Koutsounari* (℡28420 61213) – which is the only campsite nearby if you want to be based at Ierápetra. It has a taverna and store, and although the campground is a bit gritty there's a good beach and plenty of shade. This is also the beginning of the aptly named **Long Beach**, a windswept line of sand (and the wind can really blow here) which stretches virtually unbroken along the final 5km of shore to Ierápetra.

Ierápetra

IERÁPETRA has various claims to fame – the largest town on the south coast of Crete, the southernmost in Europe with the most hours of sunshine – but until recently, charm was not one of them. Despite an excellent EU blue-flagged beach, it's a rather sprawling place and a major supply centre for the region's numerous and affluent farmers who have grown rich on the year-round cultivation of cucumbers, tomatoes and peppers in the plastic greenhouses which scar the landscape along this coast (see the box on p.232). The farming lobby's armlock on the town hall and its budget long stymied plans to make Ierápetra more attractive to its visitors. However, in the 1990s, under a couple of dynamic mayors, the town began to bounce back, and is now experiencing a resurgence as buildings, streets and squares are refurbished and landscaped. Ierápetra is at last starting to resemble what it actually is: one of the richest towns on the island. Regrettably, an ambitious plan to revamp the whole seafront and harbour zone with gardens and a swimming pool ran in to opposition from a stubborn car lobby which wanted to maintain the area as a car park. The dismal compromise was to leave half as a car park, while the rest has been turned into an uninspiring *platía* with strange, colonnaded walkways lacking any focus.

Some history

Although you'd hardly know it to look at the town today, Ierápetra has quite a history. Early knowledge is sketchy, but it's almost certain that there was a settlement, or at least a port, here in **Minoan** times. A look at the map suggests a link across the isthmus with Gourniá, and it was probably from Ierápetra and other south-coast harbours that the Keftiu, as the Egyptians called the Cretans, sailed for the coast of Africa.

However, it was as a **Doric** settlement that **Ierápytna**, as the place was then known, grew to real prominence. By the second century BC, it occupied more territory than any other Cretan city. Ierápytna became a bastion of the Greek Dorians against their bitter enemies the Eteocretans: the final victory over Eteocretan Présos in 155 BC ended the last Minoan presence in eastern Crete. Those Eteocretans not killed in battle or put to flight were sold into slavery, a sombre end to the last vestiges of a great civilization. Only Ítanos, near Vái, now stood between Ierápytna and the complete domination of the eastern end of the island. Prolonged wars and disputes rumbled on for almost a century, and were finally brought to an end only by Rome's ruthless conquest of the entire island. Even then, Ierápytna stubbornly resisted to the last, becoming the final city to fall to the invading legions.

When **Rome** then joined Crete to Cyrene in northern Libya, forming the province of Cyrenaica, Ierápytna embarked on a new career as an important **commercial centre** in the eastern Mediterranean, trading with Greece and Italy as well as Africa and the Near East. During this period, much impressive building took place – theatres, amphitheatres, temples – of which virtually nothing survives today, save for piles of fractured pillars and column capitals scattered in odd corners around the town.

From the Romans to the tourists is a chronicle of steady decline. The Venetians (who favoured Sitía as their administrative centre in the east) left behind a small **fortress**, now restored, defending the harbour entrance. The Turks, under whom Ierápetra languished as a backwater, are represented by a nineteenth-century **mosque** and nearby Ottoman fountain.

Arrival and information

The **bus station** is just up from Platía Plastíras on Lasthenou – the Áyios Nikólaos road – around five minutes north of the centre. It's convenient for a couple of the good budget places to stay (see p.229), though for a better impression of the town you should head down towards the water, past the souvenir stores and stalls selling foreign newspapers, to the seafront and promenade. Here, with a string of restaurants and bars stretching out in either direction – to the left behind the beach, right towards the fortress and the harbour – Ierápetra can be genuinely picturesque.

The public library (Mon–Fri 9am–2pm), to the side of the Dhimarhío (town hall) on the focal Platía Kanoupaki, can provide some **information**

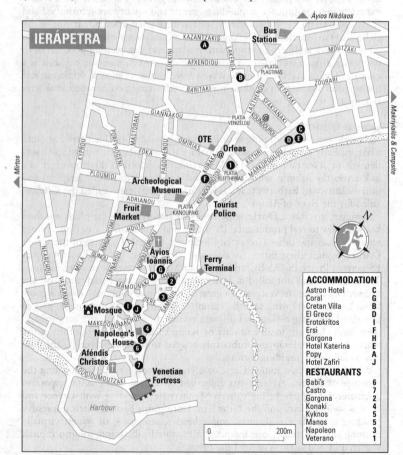

ACCOMMODATION

Astron Hotel	C
Coral	G
Cretan Villa	B
El Greco	D
Erotokritos	I
Ersi	F
Gorgona	H
Hotel Katerina	E
Popy	A
Hotel Zafiri	J

RESTAURANTS

Babi's	6
Castro	7
Gorgona	2
Konaki	4
Kyknos	5
Manos	5
Napoleon	3
Veterano	1

and will give you a town map (you can also get information on the Internet at ⓦwww.ierapetra.com, ⓦwww.ierapetra.net & ⓦwww.ierapetra.org). The **tourist police** (℡28420 22560) are located on the waterfront, across the square from the Archeological Museum, though the most you'll get from them is a few blank looks and, if you're lucky, a town map. A much better bet for all kinds of information on the town is the friendly Ierápetra Express travel agency on Platía Eleftherías (℡28420 22411, ⒠express@ier.forthnet.gr) which also rents out a number of excellent sea-side apartments for longer stays.

Accommodation

Finding accommodation is not usually a problem here. There are cheaper possibilities near the bus station and in the centre, though the hotels fronting and behind the north and easterly beach are more modern and pricey. There is no youth hostel and the nearest **campsite** is *Camping Koutsounari*, 7km east of Ieráptera on the Sitía road (see p.226). If you camp there, you'll have to come into town in the evenings for food and nightlife.

Astron Kothri 56 ℡28420 25114, ⒠htastron@otenet.gr. Ierápetra's leading hotel, where rooms come with balcony views, a/c, mini-bar, strongbox and satellite TV. Rates include breakfast. ⑥

Coral Ioannidou 12 ℡28420 22846. Located behind the beach and tavernas along Samouil, these are pleasant balcony rooms with bath and a/c (€5 extra) in a restored house in the old quarter. ②

Cretan Villa Lakerda 16 ℡28522 28522, ⓦwww.cretan-villa.com. Close to the bus station, offering sparkling en-suite, a/c rooms with satellite TV and fridge in a beautiful 190-year-old house with a delightful patio for taking breakfast. ③–④

El Greco Kothri 6 ℡28420 28471, ⒡28420 24515. Decent beachfront place with en-suite a/c (€5 supplement) rooms with balcony sea view; rooms facing inland are cheaper, and there are discounts for eating in their restaurant below. ④

Erotokritos Parados Stratigou Samouil in the old quarter ℡2842 28151. Decent, en-suite rooms – some with a/c – and apartments with kitchenette, fridges and fans. ③

Ersi Platía Eleftherías 20 ℡28420 23208. Refurbished hotel where good-value rooms come with fridge, a/c (€5 extra), bath and balcony – the higher the better for sea views. The owner here also has some apartments nearby, which come with kitchen and lounge, for the same price. ②

Pension Gorgona Katsanevaki 9 ℡28420 22573. Pleasant en-suite rooms with fans in a house in the old quarter. ③

Katerina On the seafront close to the *El Greco* ℡28420 28345, ⒡28420 28519. Good value rooms with balcony, a/c (€5 extra) and shared fridge. ②

Popy Apartments Kazantzákis 27, near the bus station ℡28420 24289, ⒡28420 27772. Good place for economical en-suite rooms; there are also two apartments with kitchen, fans and small garden. ②

Zafiri Makedonomachon, in the old quarter ℡28420 24422, ⒡28420 23339. Attractive a/c rooms with balcony, fridge and TV; guests get discounts at *Taverna Konaki* (see p.231), run by the same proprietors. Includes breakfast. ③

The Town and around

Things to do in Ierápetra by day – apart from lie on the beach – are severely limited. The **Archeological Museum**, housed in the former Turkish school, is the place most visitors head for. However, its dusty rooms (officially open Tues–Sun 8.30am–2.30pm; €2) are known to close at a moment's notice, but it's worth the effort to get in if only to see a fine Minoan terracotta **larnax**, excavated at nearby Episkopí. Dating from the very end of the Neo-Palatial period (ca.1300 BC), the *lárnax*, or clay coffin, has fascinating painted panels, one of which depicts a mare suckling her foal. Other scenes revel in the stalking of the *kri-kri*, or wild goat, by hunting dogs. If he's in the mood, the guardian (on request) will raise the *lárnax* lid to enable you to see the remains of the three corpses still inside. The Minoan cases display some interesting **Vasilikí ware** (see p.195), including typical jugs and vases as well as some potters' turntables from the Early Minoan settlement at Fournoú Korifí (see p.232). The Greek and Roman section contains a selection of statuary, mostly headless because iconoclastic Christians tended to regard the stone craniums as places where the spirit of the devil was lurking. One more recent discovery, however, managed to hang on to hers: a wonderful second-century statue of the fertility goddess **Demeter**, holding an ear of corn in her left hand. Her head is crowned by a small altar encoiled by two serpents, symbols of her divinity. Incomprehensibly, for years the staff have gone to great lengths to prevent visitors taking photographs of her, so prepare to be bawled out if you try.

Elsewhere in town, two churches which stand out from a miscellaneous collection are the twin-domed **Aféndis Christós** near the fort, a fourteenth-century building with a fine carved and painted wooden iconostasis (key held in the house to the left of the entrance), and **Áyios Ioánnis**, an equally ancient, but now restored, former mosque. The Tzami, or **Turkish Mosque**, has now been painstakingly restored and retains a substantial chunk of its minaret and – inside – the original mihrab. There's also an old house slightly northwest of the harbour in which locals claim that **Napoleon** spent the night of June 6, 1798, on his way to Egypt.

Out of town

There are a number of ways to escape the town's often stifling high summer temperatures. Simplest is the day-trip by *kaïki* to **Gaidhouronísi** (known as Chrissi or Donkey Island in much of the tourist literature), some 10km off-shore. A real desert island a little over 4km in length, with a fine cedar forest and a couple of tavernas, Gaidhouronísi has some excellent sandy **beaches** and plenty of room to escape – although you wouldn't want to miss the boat back. Should you wish to explore, there's a waymarked **walking route** around the island on which you should spot quite a few examples of the varied flora and fauna, as well as fossils and the fabulous "**Shell Beach**" covered with discarded shells from countless generations of molluscs (no souvenir-taking allowed). Boats (with an on-board bar) leave from the jetty on the seafront at 10.30am and 12.30pm, returning at 4pm and 5pm; the trip each way takes about 45min. Tickets cost €20 (children under 12 half-price) and you can either pay on the boat or get tickets in advance from the Ierápetra Express travel agency (see p.231) or World Wide Travel, Kyrba 40 behind the seafront, who can also provide a guidebook to the island.

Alternatively, there are more **beaches** along the coast a few kilometres in either direction, with good bus services along the main road behind them.

Eating and entertainment

When it comes to **eating** and **drinking**, your only problem here is sifting out the quality from the quantity. For **breakfast**, *Veterano* is a stylish terrace bar on Platía Eleftherías which has rapidly become one of the most popular venues in town. *Kafenion Takis* on Platía Kanoupaki, opposite the Archeological Museum, is another efficient bar for snacks and *mezédhes*. Along Markopoulou, the seafront promenade stretching north of the tourist police office, there's a string of restaurants with outdoor seating, but none is outstanding. Recently, quite a few of these have closed, their places taken by late-night drinking bars and the odd *zaharoplastío*. Things are better on the Samouil promenade to the south of the ferry terminal where another line of **tavernas** faces the sea. The town's best places are here: *Napoleon*, which is Ierápetra's oldest, is good for seafood and standards such as *moussaká*, whilst the nearby *Konaki*, just south, and *Gorgona*, slightly north, also do traditional dishes well. Further down towards the fortress, is newcomer *Babi's* – for seafood – and, last in line, the *Ouzeri Castro*, whose *mezédhes* are popular with locals.

The **bars** and **discos** are concentrated in the streets immediately behind the seafront, mainly along Kyrba, which is also the area to find more basic food and takeaways. Music bars abound here, with those playing Greek music to be found on the beach road, and those favouring mainstream European sounds one street inland. Along and around Kyrba, *Aglamair*, *Seven Blue Notes*, *Le Figaro* and *Saxo* are popular places. Three stylish new bars not far away which attract good crowds are *Tamam*, opposite the *Cretan Villa* pension with occasional (and restrained) live music, *Portego* on N. Fonadiakis, behind Platía Kanoupaki, and the aptly named *Odeon*, housed in a former music school – a pleasant garden bar located along Lasthenous, above Platía Venizélou on the right. One central bar with a difference is *Parados*, in the alley behind the Archeological Museum. The ambience is as laid back as the jazz – Coltrane, Davis and Monk are the proprietor's favourites; Italian-style espresso and cappuccino (try a cold cappuccino – *freddo*) are the daytime beverages of choice, whilst after dark cocktails, liqueurs and nightcaps complement the cool sounds.

On Sunday evenings in summer, free performances of Cretan **lyra** and **dance** are staged at the small open-air theatre to the left of the town hall, starting at around 10pm.

Listings

Banks The National Bank on Platía Eleftherías and the Ionian Bank on Platía Venizélou both have ATMs.

Books and newspapers Euro 2000, Koundoúriotou 13, just off Platía Eleftherías, sells foreign press and magazines, as does the Somarakis bakery, Platía Kounoupaki, opposite the Archeological Museum. The Fasma bookshop, Kothri 24, just north of Platía Eleftherías, has a good selection of maps and books on Cretan themes in English.

Bus station On Lasthenous; for information call ☎28420 28237. Services to Iráklion, Áyios Nikólaos, Sitía and Mírtos.

Hospital The main hospital is on Kalimeraki, north of the bus station ☎28420 22488.

Internet *Café Orfeas*, Koundourioútou 25, just south of Platía Venizélou, has a number of screens (€6 per hour, minimum €1 for 10min), but the best deal is at the *Internet Café* inside the *Cosmos Hotel*, Koundoúrou 16, slightly north of Platía Eleftherías (€3.60 per hour, minimum €1.80 for 30min).

Post office Kornarou 7 (Mon–Sat 7.30am–2pm).

Shopping There's an entertaining street market on Saturday mornings (until 1pm) along Psilinaki, 100m northeast of the bus station.

Telephones OTE, at Koraka 25 (Mon–Fri 7.30am–10pm).

Travel agency Ierápetra Express (☎28420 22411, ℮express@ier.forthnet.gr) on the central Platía Eleftherías is a helpful source of travel information, and also provides general information about the town and local festivals and events. It also produces a rental apartments brochure which it will send out on request.

West to Mírtos

The 13km of coastline to the west of Ierápetra offers little of interest until beyond the village of Ammoudáres, where a couple of fascinating hilltop

The plastic revolution

The plastic greenhouses that disfigure much of this stretch of coastline are a great source of wealth for the farmers of Ierápetra and its satellite villages. The system was introduced here in the 1960s by a Dutch farmer named Paul Coopers. He correctly surmised that the mild climate and fertile soil along this coast would perfectly suit greenhouse crops, which could be produced all year and sold to supermarkets in northern Europe in the depths of winter. The plastic tents were initially ridiculed, but once the canny Cretan farmers saw the size and quality of the tomatoes that emerged from them in the middle of January, the revolution began. Coopers died in a road accident in 1968 when the new system had hardly got going. However, in typically Cretan fashion, the farmers did not forget who had brought them this horn of plenty – they erected a statue to Coopers on the site of his first greenhouse.

Minoan sites are worth the climb to reach them. Slightly further west, the pleasant seaside village of **Mírtos** is another welcoming resort. Inland, detours into the hills allow visits to attractive hamlets in the foothills of the Dhiktean mountain range, with plenty of opportunities for trekking.

Inland from the coast

Heading west from Ierápetra, the first stretch of coast is grey and dusty, the road jammed with trucks and lined with drab ribbon development. Where the concrete runs out, the plastic greenhouses start, stretching almost the whole way to Mírtos.

However, if you're travelling under your own steam, there are a couple of **scenic detours** worth taking at **Gra Ligiá**, 4km west of Ierápetra. The first winds inland, upwards past a dam, followed by an unsightly quarrying operation, before climbing again – with fine views over the Libyan Sea – to the charming hamlet of **Kalamáfka**, tucked into a mountain cleft. The bars along the tiny main street provide a good excuse to stop for a while. From here, you could reach the north coast and Áyios Nikólaos via the village of **Prína** or, by taking the road to **Anatolí**, pick up the second detour. This also starts from Gra Ligiá, a hundred metres beyond the first, and is signed for Anatolí, eventually climbing to **Máles**, a village clinging to the lower slopes of the Dhíkti range. Máles would be a good starting-point if you wanted to take a **walk** through some stunning mountain terrain (the E4 Pan-European footpath passes just 3km north of here). Otherwise, the road down, signed for Míthi (where there's a great gorge walk; see p.235), has spectacular views over the Libyan Sea and eventually follows the Mírtos river valley down to Mírtos itself.

Néa Mírtos and Pírgos

Continuing west along the coast road from Gra Ligiá, it's 8km further to **Néa Mírtos**, where a Minoan site excavated in the 1960s by a British team yielded important evidence concerning early Minoan settlements. Known locally as **Fournoú Korifí** (Kiln Hill), the site is located beyond the village on the peak to your right, 500m after a church on the coastal side of the road. A roadside sign (a difficult stopping point when traffic is busy) points up a gully. Scramble up this to the top and keep ahead towards a stand of pine trees. A path just before the trees heads right across a flat expanse of brush towards a hill where the fenced site is clearly visible. The gate is left open.

The excavations – which are not always easy to make sense of – revealed not a villa but a much earlier **stone-built village** of nearly one hundred rooms, spread over the hilltop. Probably typical of numerous other settlements sited on the coast of eastern Crete during the early Pre-Palatial period (ca.2500 BC), these rooms contained stone and copper tools, carved seals and over seven hundred **pottery vessels**. Some of these were Vasilikí-type jugs with their intriguing mottled finish, and many were no doubt used to store the produce of the surrounding lands, then less arid than today – olives, vines and cereals. In a room in the southwest corner of the site was located the oldest known Minoan domestic shrine, which produced the most important of the finds: the **goddess of Mírtos**, a clay idol with a stalked neck carrying a ewer. (It's now in the Áyios Nikólaos museum, along with most of the other finds from this site and Pírgos.) Around the goddess, broken offering vessels were strewn about the floor, many of them charred by the fire which destroyed the site about 2200 BC. The riddle of the fire, which seems to have left no casualties and provoked no rebuilding, is yet another of the unresolved Minoan questions. However, the site of Pírgos may offer a few clues.

Pírgos

Pírgos, a bare kilometre further west, is considerably easier to get to and has a superb view over the coast. The sign to this Minoan villa comes immediately before a large bridge across the Mírtos river. Turn in here and follow a signed and waymarked footpath to the right, which climbs to the site.

The settlement here was inhabited at much the same time as Fournoú Korifí and was also destroyed by fire around 2200 BC. Unlike Fournoú Korifí, however, Pírgos was reoccupied and rebuilt following its destruction, when it appears to have incorporated the former's lands. By the time of the Neo-Palatial period (ca.1600 BC), the community occupying the lower slopes was dominated by a two- or three-storey country villa spread over the crown of the hill. A **stepped street** flanked by some well-cut lower courses of the villa's outer wall leads into a **courtyard**, partly paved in the purple limestone of the region. At the rear of the villa (furthest away from the sea) on the west side, it's possible to make out a **light well** floored with the same purple limestone. Many of the walls carry marks of the ferocious blaze which destroyed the villa around 1450 BC, lending credibility to the Thíra explosion theory, especially when volcanic material was discovered amidst the rubble. But it now seems that whilst the villa was burned, the surrounding settlement was untouched – another puzzle to contemplate as you savour the magnificent sea view from the courtyard.

On your way down, take a left turn at the bottom of the stepped street and follow the hill around to see the remains of an enormous plastered **cistern**, the largest found in Minoan Crete, dating from the Pre-Palatial era (ca.1900–1700 BC). When it burst over the northern side of the hill in ancient times, it was not repaired. Beyond this, a fine stretch of **paved road** survives from the early period: this led to a burial pit, now excavated.

Mírtos

Across the bridge over the River Mírtos, the main road soon turns sharply inland, while a turn-off cuts back down to the coast and **MÍRTOS**, 15km west of Ierápetra. Razed to the ground by the German army in 1943 as a punishment for resistance activities, Mírtos today is an unexpected pleasure after the drabness of what has gone before. This charming white-walled village is kept

②

clean as a whistle by its house-proud inhabitants, and most of the summer you'll find plenty of space on the long shingle beach. In August, though, the place can get pretty full, often with young travellers who sleep on the strand, to the irritation of the authorities.

A welcome new attraction in Mírtos is a village **museum** (Mon–Fri 9am–2pm; €1.50), located to the side of the church and displaying minor finds from the Minoan settlements at Néa Mírtos and Pírgos (see p.232 & p.233). It also holds a folklore section with tools, kitchen and farming implements once used by the villagers here. The collection was put together by a much-loved and respected local schoolmaster, Yiórgos Dimitrianákis, who taught most of the adults in the village prior to his death in 1994. Throughout his life, he spent much of his free time wandering the fields and hills around Mírtos collecting a wealth of finds, including ancient statuettes and vase fragments. In 1962, his discoveries came to the attention of the British School at Athens whose director, Sinclair Hood, along with two of his archeology students (the now renowned Peter Warren and Gerald Cadogan), paid a visit to the schoolmaster, who took them to the Néa Mírtos and Pírgos sites. Suspecting these sites to be of major importance, Hood requested permission from the Greek government to investigate them and excavations started in 1967. Despite the fact that Dimitrianákis wished the finds from the two sites to be kept and displayed in the village, the lack of a suitable building led to the most important artefacts being transferred to the museums in Ierápetra and Áyios Nikólaos. However, he was allowed to keep a number of items in the school, which were used in his classes with the children. These, and the household objects he collected from the villagers, now comprise the core of the collection. The museum's enthusiastic curator, Katerina Aspridaki, will be only too pleased to give you a guided tour (in English) explaining the history behind many of the items on display.

More **ancient ruins** can be seen at the eastern end of the seafront to the side of the *Big Blue* hotel (see below). A huge, brick-built circular tank construction may be a part of Roman baths, and beyond this are walls and, closer to the beach, harbour installations – all awaiting archeological investigation.

Practicalities

Most of the time there are plenty of **rooms** advertised throughout Mírtos – on every street it seems. On the main thoroughfare behind the beach there's a small and newly refurbished hotel, the *Mirtos* (☎28420 51227; ⓦwww .myrtoshotel.com; ❸), which is good value. Ask for a second-floor room with a/c, room safe, TV and balcony. Nearby, *Rooms Angelos* (☎28420 51091; ❷) offers balcony rooms with bath and kitchenette, and *Cretan House* (☎28420 51427; ⓔpgd@hol.gr; ❸) has pleasant rooms with kitchenette near the church. At the west side of the village near the beach, *Big Blue* (☎28420 51094; ⓦwww .forthnet.gr/big-blue; ❸) has sea-view balcony rooms with bath and some more expensive studios with a/c and kitchenette (❹), and there are more similar places close by. Higher still is *Villa Mare* (☎28420 51274; ❸), on the hill behind *Big Blue*, where en-suite rooms come with terrace and great views; the pricier *Panorama* (☎28420 51362; ❹) next door has similar deals. More economical options are provided by *Nikos House* in the centre (☎28420 51116, ⓦwww.nikoshouse.cz; ❷), where rooms come with fans, bath and kitchenette, and the simpler *Rooms Despina* (☎28420 51524; ❷) with good-value en-suite rooms at the back of the village, near the bus station. Just around the corner from the latter, a more upmarket place, *Kastro Apartments* (☎28420 51444; ⓔkastrohotel@in.gr; ❸–❹) has studios and apartments arranged around a garden with pool.

Information about rooms, villas for rent and lots more can also be had from the travel agency Magic Tours (☎28420 51203, ⓦwww .welcometo-magic.com), just up the street from *Hotel Mírtos*. The proprietor here also rents out **cars** (twenty-percent discount to *Rough Guide* readers with this guide), sells boat and plane tickets, **changes money** and operates a taxi service to Iráklion and Haniá airports. The village has a couple of supermarkets and bakeries to provide essentials for the growing number of visitors, and there are international **phone** and newspaper kiosks along the main street. **Internet** access is possible at *Café Edem* (see below). The **bus station** – actually a couple of rickety stands on the main road at the rear of the village – is useful for frequent buses to and from Ierápetra and less frequent services to Iráklion and Mátala. Sailing boats, kayaks and canoes can be rented from Scirocco, based on the beach, who also do sailing courses (ⓔsciroccomirtos@web.de); information is also available from the *Hotel Mírtos*.

For **eating** and **drinking**, the short promenade behind the beach is lined with bars and tavernas: *Karavostasis* at the western end and the more central *Votsalo* are good bets, while further along, *Akti* does some vegetarian dishes. In the heart of the village, the taverna of the *Hotel Mírtos* is also very good. *Katerina's*, around the corner, is the oldest-established place and has a loyal band of customers. *Café Edem* on the street between the *Hotel Mírtos* and *Katerina's* is a pleasant *zaharoplastío* coffeehouse and is a good place for **breakfast**. Once the sun goes down, there's little to do but prolong your eating and drinking into the night, although the odd bar sometimes risks breaking the late-night curfew with a blast of soft rock, and in summer there's the occasional *lyra* and *bouzoúki* concert on the beach.

Walks around Mírtos

There are more good **beaches** and a pleasant **walk** out along the dirt track which follows the coast 6km west to **Tértsa**, and then on to Árvi (see p.162). A more adventurous hike is along the scenic 150-metre-deep **Sarakinás gorge** close to the village of Míthi, some 5km north of Mírtos. To reach the start of the walk, use your own transport (or take a taxi) to Míthi and then follow the signs for the *Taverna Farangi*, where the walk begins. Incidentally, this is a good place for lamb and goat dishes, and on Friday evenings in summer they put on concerts of *lyra* and *bouzoúki*. The gorge walk begins from the taverna's terrace, and the way heads north along a concrete water channel which soon brings you into the gorge proper. Depending on the rains, the water level in the gorge may mean you'll have to do some wading in parts, so waterproof footwear, sandals or rubber shoes would be useful to bring along. It's about 2km or one hour's climb to the top of the gorge and a little less coming back down, when a meal or a beer at the *Taverna Farangi* will seem a lot more inviting. Should you not wish to repeat the scramble back down, it's possible to pick up an asphalt road back to Míthi by following the river a further 300m upstream from the top of the gorge to where it's feasible to wade across. A path heads off right from the opposite bank to meet the road.

Leaving Mírtos and moving west, the character of the main road, which heads inland towards Áno Viánnos (see p.161) and Iráklion, changes immediately as it begins to climb around the south side of the Dhíkti range, where you're back into the traditional Crete of small mountain villages and alarming precipices.

Greek place names

ΑΓΙΟΣ ΝΙΚΟΛΑΟΣ	Άγιος Νικόλαος	Áyios Nikólaos
ΑΓΙΑ ΦΩΤΙΑ	Αγία Φωτιά	Ayía Fotiá
ΒΑΙ	Βάι	Vái
ΓΟΥΡΝΙΑ	Γούρνια	Gourniá
ΕΛΟΥΝΤΑ	Ελούντα	Eloúnda
ΖΑΚΡΟΣ	Ζακρος	Zákros
ΙΕΡΑΠΕΤΡΑ	Ιεράπετρα	Ierápetra
ΚΡΙΤΣΑ	Κριτσά	Kritsá
ΛΑΣΙΘΙΟΥ	Λασίθιου	Lasíthi
ΜΑΚΡΥΓΙΑΛΟΣ	Μακρύγιαλος	Makriyialós
ΜΙΡΤΟΣ	Μίρτος	Mírtos
ΜΟΧΛΟΣ	Μόχλος	Móhlos
ΝΕΑΠΟΛΗ	Νεάπολη	Neápoli
ΠΑΛΑΙΚΑΣΤΡΟ	Παλαίκαστρο	Palékastro
ΣΗΤΕΙΑ	Σητεία	Sitía
ΣΠΗΝΑΛΟΓΚΑ	Σπηναλόγκα	Spinalónga
ΤΖΕΡΜΙΑΔΟ	Τζερμιάδο	Tzermiádho
ΨΥΧΡΟ	Ψυχρό	Psihró

Travel details

Buses

Some services are restricted on Sundays. For the latest timetables visit KTEL's websites: Ⓦ www .bus-service-crete-ktel.com, Ⓦ www .crete-buses.gr and Ⓦ www.ktel.org.

Áyios Nikólaos to: Eloúnda (20 daily; 6.15am–9pm; 20min); Ierápetra (8 daily; 6.30am–8.30pm; 1hr); Iráklion (22 daily, 6 via Iráklion airport; 6.15am–9.45pm; 1hr 30min); Kritsá (11 daily; 6am–8pm; 30min); Lasíthi plateau (1 daily; 2pm; 2hr; returning 7am); Mália (22 daily; 6am–9.45pm; 30min); Sitía (7 daily; 6.15am–8.30pm; 1hr 30min).

Ierápetra to: Áno Viánnos (Mon–Fri 2 daily; 5.50am & 5pm; 45min); Ay. Nikólaos (8 daily; 6.30am–8.30pm; 1hr); Iráklion (8 daily; 6.30am–8.30pm; 2hr 30min); Makriyialós (6 daily; 6.15am–8pm; 30min); Mírtos (6 daily; 6.30am–8pm; 30min); Sitía (6 daily; 6.15am–8pm; 1hr 30min).

Sitía to: Ay. Nikólaos (5 daily; 6.15am–5.15pm; 1hr 30min); Ierápetra (6 daily; 6.15am–8pm; 1hr 30min); Iráklion (7 daily; 6.30am–8pm; 3hr 15min); Káto Zákros (3 daily; 6am–2.30pm; 1hr); Makriyialós (6 daily; 6.15am–8pm; 1hr); Palékastro (5 daily; 9.30am–4pm; 45min); Vái (4 daily; 9.30am–4pm; 1hr).

Ferries

Services operate very infrequently in winter. For the latest domestic and international ferry timetables, visit Ⓦ www.greekislands.gr or Ⓦ www .ferries.gr.

To the Dodecanese The *Ierapetra* or *Kornaros* leaves Ay. Nikólaos on Mon, Fri & Sat for Sitía, Kásos, Kárpathos & Rhodes. There is a sailing from Sitía to Pireás via Ay. Nikólaos on Sun, Tues, Wed, Thurs & Sat, calling at Mílos on Wed, Sat & Sun.

To Kárpathos/Rhodes calling also at Kásos and Hálki: Mon, Fri & Sat at 7.30am from Ay. Nikólaos; Mon, Fri & Sat at 9.30am from Sitía (10hr/12hr).

To the Cyclades Wed, Sat & Sun: from Sitía at 3.30pm and from Ay. Nikólaos at 6pm to Anáfi, Thíra, Folégandros, Mílos, Sífnos & Pireás.

Flights

Sitía to: Athens (thrice weekly, Mon, Wed & Sat year-round); Thessaloníki (thrice weekly, Sun, Tues & Thurs year-round); Préveza (in Epirus; thrice weekly, Mon, Wed & Sat year-round); Alexandhroúpoli (in Thrace; thrice weekly, Sun, Tues & Thurs year-round); Kásos, Kárpathos & Rhodes (once weekly, summer only).

Réthimnon

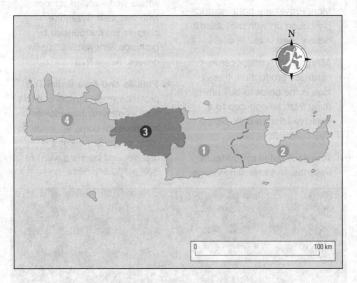

CHAPTER 3 # Highlights

✳ **Réthimnon** The provincial capital has ornate Venetian and Turkish monuments and an atmospheric old quarter, as well as good museums, restaurants and nightlife. See p.241

✳ **Moní Arkádhi & Moní Préveli** Two of Crete's most important monasteries, the imposing Moní Arkádhi and the seaside Moní Préveli are both inextricably bound up with the island's history. See p.252 & p.291

✳ **Margarítes** A major centre of ceramics production, this village is the place to buy anything from an egg-cup to a massive Minoan-style *píthos*. See p.262

✳ **Anóyia** A gateway to Mount Psilorítis, this charming village is famous for its woven rugs and tapestries. See p.266

✳ **Mount Psilorítis** Dominating the province, Crete's highest peak provides some spectacular walks to the summit chapel of the Holy Cross. See p.268

✳ **Amári valley** A delightfully scenic stretch of country, where white-walled villages with frescoed Byzantine chapels are surrounded by orchards, vineyards and olive groves. See p.276

✳ **Plakiás and Ayía Galíni** The province's twin but contrasting south-coast resorts: Plakiás has an easy-going air, while its more picturesque sister is brasher and bursting with life. See p.286 & p.281

△ Plakiás

Réthimnon

On the north coast, the provincial capital of **Réthimnon** is a relaxed university town with a reputation as the island's intellectual and cultural capital. Dominated on its western tip by one of the most imposing Venetian fortresses on the island, the town also retains a picturesque old quarter where a core of traditional urban life continues relatively unaffected. An excellent folklore museum and a fine beach are other reasons for Réthimnon's popularity.

Less desirably, the town is also at the centre of some of Crete's most drastic resort development, with hotels and apartments spreading ever eastwards along a narrow strip of plain which, worryingly, is also one of the most important nesting sites for the endangered loggerhead sea turtle. To the west, the picture is less gloomy with a sandy **coastline**, still not greatly exploited, running all the way to the borders of Haniá. Journey a little way inland from here and you're on the fringes of the White Mountains (Lefká Óri), studded with traditional hill villages such as **Argiroúpolis** and **Asigonía**, surrounded by some great **hiking** country. Heading inland from Réthimnon in the opposite direction soon brings you to the revered **Moní Arkádhi**, a beautiful ancient monastery and emblem of Crete's nineteenth-century struggle for independence against the Turks.

The **interior** of Réthimnon province – perhaps its greatest attraction – is dominated by mountains which provide many of the stunning vistas to be seen at almost every turn along the numerous winding roads. The provincial borders are defined by the island's highest peaks, in the west by the far reaches of the Lefká Óri and to the east by the looming mass of Psilorítis, Crete's highest peak. The villages ranged around the **Psilorítis massif** provide ideal bases for a series of spectacular wilderness hikes originating from them. A few days here are strongly recommended, for casual ramblers and committed hikers alike. The peaks themselves are approached most easily from **Anóyia**, a high mountain town known for its sheep-breeding, weaving and embroidery. From here, you can hike across to the south side of the mountains or down, via the summit of Psilorítis, to the pretty villages of the lushly fertile **Amári valley** – some of the least visited and most traditional places in Crete.

To the west of the valley, the attractive hill town of **Spíli** is another centre for walkers with many fine hikes in the surrounding hills and, for the more adventurous, the possibility of a longer trek down the Megapótamos river valley to **Moní Préveli**, an illustrious seaside monastery that played a pivotal role during the Battle of Crete – the monks rescued trapped Allied troops and enabled their evacuation from the nearby **Palm Beach**, one of the island's most picturesque strands.

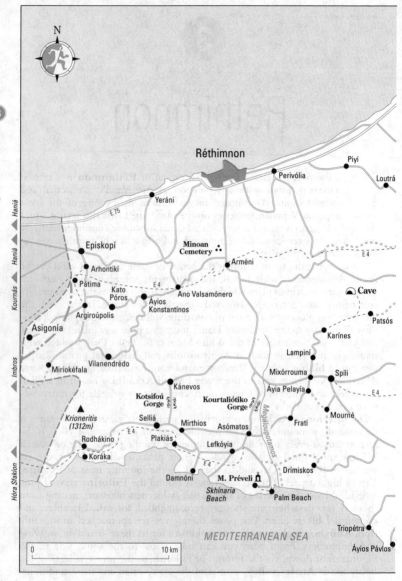

For spending time by the sea, the province's **south coast** has the most to offer with two flagship resorts, the glitzy and rumbustious **Ayía Galíni** and its rapidly emerging and more easy-going rival, **Plakiás**. Along the stretch of coast between these enclaves are a string of little-known pockets of sand – sometimes with a village attached – often hard to access but well worth it for a few lazy days.

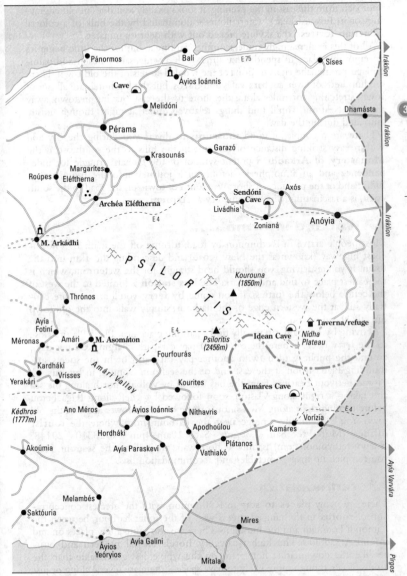

Map labels:

Pánormos
Balí
Síses
E 75
Áyios Ioánnis
Cave
Dhamásta
Melidóni
Pérama
Garazó
Krasounás
Margarítes
Roúpes
Eléftherna
Archéa Eléftherna
Sendóni Cave
Axós
Livádhia
E 4
Zonianá
Anóyia
M. Arkádhi

P S I L O R Í T I S

Kourouna (1850m)
Thrónos
Ayía Fotiní
Méronas
Amári
M. Asomáton
E 4
Psilorítis (2456m)
Idean Cave
Nídha Plateau
Taverna/refuge
Fourfourás
Kardháki
Vrísses
Yerakári
Amári Valley
Kourítes
Kamáres Cave
Kédhros (1777m)
Ano Méros
Áyios Ioánnis
Níthavris
Vorízia
E 4
Hordháki
Apodhoúlou
Kamáres
Akoúmia
Ayía Paraskeví
Vathiakó
Plátanos
Melambés
Saktoúria
Míres
Ayía Galíni
Áyios Yeóryios
Mítala

Iráklion (×4)
Ayía Varvára
Pírgos

Réthimnon and around

Although it's the third largest town in Crete, **RÉTHIMNON** never feels like a city, as Haniá and Iráklion do. Instead, it has a provincial air; it's a place that moves slowly and, for all the myriad bars springing up along the seafront, preserves much of its Venetian and Turkish appearance. Arriving, especially if you approach from the east in the evening, it looks exactly as it does in old engravings or in Edward Lear's watercolours – dominated by the bulk of a colossal **Venetian fortress**, the skyline picked out with delicate minarets.

All of this is increasingly under commercial threat, but for the time being it's an enjoyable place to spend some time, with a wide, sandy beach and palm-fringed promenade right in front of the tangled streets of the old town. There are hundreds of tavernas, bars, cafés and discos, but the big hotels are all out of town, stretching for miles along the shore to the east. Staying in town, away from the seafront, you'll find things relatively quiet at night, though noisily animated during the day.

There are a couple of good **museums** to divert you during the day and within easy striking distance of the city, in the hills to the southeast, is the **Monastery of Arkádhi**, a potent symbol of the Cretan struggle for independence and an atmospheric detour on a journey into the mountainous hinterland of the province. A short way south of town, on the road to the south coast, is a fascinating Minoan cemetery at **Arméni**.

Arrival and information

Most people arrive in Réthimnon by road, turning off the main E75 north-coast highway (known as the New Road) and descending the 1km into the town. If you're driving, you should head straight for the waterfront, which is the easiest place to find and to park. The **bus station** is located to the west of the centre below the fortress. If you come **by ferry** you'll arrive more centrally still, at the western edge of the harbour; simply walk into the old town directly ahead of you.

Arriving **by car**, you can usually find a parking place near Platía Plastíra close to the ferry dock (where there is also a pay car-park charging €2 per day), around the public garden (with another pay car-park) or in the streets surrounding Platía Iróon at the east end of the seafront. Coming in **by bus**, it's easy to get your bearings from the bus station by walking north along the sea and taking a right along Vlastou, soon followed by a left along Riga Ferou before turning right along Melissinou, or one of the narrower alleys of the old town. You'll eventually emerge near the harbour, from where the **tourist office** (Mon–Fri 8am–2.30pm, Sat 10am–4pm; ☎28310 29148, ⓦwww.rethymnon.com) is only a short walk away along the seafront. Here you can pick up maps, timetables and accommodation lists.

Accommodation

There are many **places to stay** in Réthimnon, with the greatest concentration of **rooms** in the tangled streets west of the inner harbour, between the Rimondi Fountain and the museums. There are also quite a few places on and around Arkadhíou. The higher-category **hotels** are all modern and businesslike; the downmarket hotels are, on the whole, less good value than the rooms places, though more likely to have space – there are several along or just off Arkadhíou. For central, rock-bottom budget accommodation, the only option is the **youth hostel** (see p.244). If you fancy combining the town with a beach holiday, *Apartments Lampros* (☎28310 22644, Ⓕ28310 22242; ❺) has fully equipped apartments with pool, tennis and golf facilities in the resort of **Plataniás**, 3km east of the centre.

The nearest **campsite** is *Camping Elizabeth* (☎28310 28694), a large, pleasant beach site with all facilities about 4km east of town. To get there, take the bus for the hotels (marked *Scaleta/El Greco*) from the long-distance bus station.

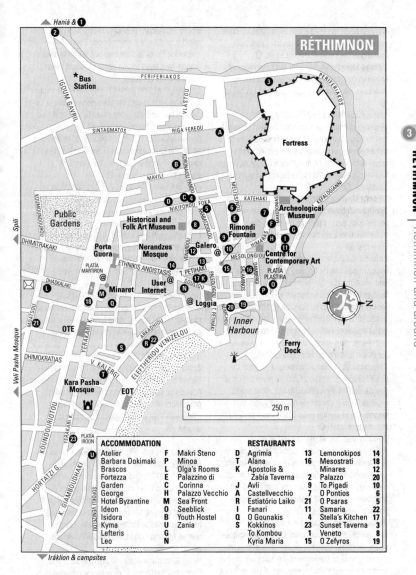

RÉTHIMNON

Haniá & ①

★ Bus Station

Fortress

Archeological Museum

Historical and Folk Art Museum

Public Gardens

Rimondi Fountain

Porta Guora

Nerandzes Mosque

Galero

Centre for Contemporary Art

Minaret

User Internet

Loggia

Inner Harbour

OTE

Kara Pasha Mosque

EOT

Ferry Dock

Veli Pasha Mosque

Spili

Iráklion & campsites

0   250 m

ACCOMMODATION						
Atelier	F	Makri Steno	D	Agrimia	13
Barbara Dokimaki	P	Minoa	T	Alana	16
Brascos	L	Olga's Rooms	K	Apostolis &	
Fortezza	E	Palazzino di		Zabía Taverna	2
Garden	C	Corinna	J	Avli	9
George	H	Palazzo Vecchio	A	Castellvecchio	7
Hotel Byzantine	M	Sea Front	R	Estiatório Laiko	21
Ideon	O	Seeblick	I	Fanari	11
Isidora	B	Youth Hostel	Q	O Gounakis	4
Kyma	U	Zania	S	Kokkinos	23
Lefteris	G			To Kombou	1
Leo	N			Kyria Maria	15

RESTAURANTS			
Lemonokipos	14		
Mesostrati	18		
Minares	12		
Palazzo	20		
To Pigadi	10		
O Pontios	6		
O Psaras	5		
Samaria	22		
Stella's Kitchen	17		
Sunset Taverna	3		
Veneto	8		
O Zefyros	19		

Around the harbour and the fortress

Atelier Himáras 32 ☎ 28310 24440, ⓔatelier@ret.forthnet.gr. Pleasant en-suite rooms with ceiling fans in a place run by a talented potter who has her studio in the basement and sells her wares in a store on the other side of the building. ②

Barbara Dokimaki Platía Plastíra 7 ☎ & ⓕ28310 24581. Strange warren of a place,

with one entrance at the above address, just off the harbourfront behind the Ideon, and another on Dambergi; ask for the better-value top-floor a/c studios with kitchenette and TV. ④

Fortezza I. Melissinou 16, near the fortress ☎28310 55551, ⓦwww.fortezza.gr. Stylish, top-of-the-range hotel with almost everything you'd expect for the price, including a/c rooms, pool and restaurant. Rates include breakfast. ⑥

243

Garden Nikiforou Foka 82 ☎ 28310 28586. Good-value rooms with bath in an ancient Venetian building in the heart of the old town. ❸

George Makedonias 32, near the Archeological Museum ☎ 28310 50965. Decent en-suite rooms with fans, and some have a fridge and kitchenette. ❷

Ideon Platía Plastíra 10 ☎ 28310 28667, ⓦ www.hotelideon.gr. Upmarket hotel in an excellent location just north of the ferry dock – try to get a balcony room with a sea view. All rooms come with a/c and TV, and there's a pool. Advance booking is essential in high season; rates include breakfast. ❻

Isidora Mavili 1 ☎ 28310 26293, ⓔ rithian@otenet.gr. Comfortable, good-value rooms with bath, fridge and kitchenette in a quiet location a couple of blocks below the Fortezza. ❷

Lefteris Kefalogianni 26 ☎ 28310 51735. Clean, pleasant pension for balcony rooms with fans, with and without bath. One-night stays allowed, but renting by the week preferred. ❸

Makri Steno Nikiforou Foka 54 ☎ 28310 55465, ⓕ 28310 50011. Another rambling but nicely renovated mansion, with light, fresh en-suite rooms with fridge, plus fans and TV (you may need to ask for these) and a huge roof terrace. ❸

Palazzino di Corinna Dambergi 7–9, near the inner harbour ☎ 28310 21205, ⓦ www.corina.gr. Sumptuous luxury suites with a/c, minibar and satellite TV in a stunningly restored Venetian palace; the charming patio has a small pool. Rates include breakfast. ❽

Palazzo Vecchio At the junction of Iróon Politehniou and I. Melissinou ☎ 28310 35351, ⓦ www.creta-info.gr/palazzovecchio. A delightful small apartment/studio hotel in a restored Venetian mansion, where beautiful rooms come with full bathroom, a/c and TV; there's also a small pool. Rates include breakfast. ❽

Seeblick Platía Plastíra 17 ☎ 28310 22478, ⓔ seeblick@rethymnon.com. On the seafront as you walk round from the inner harbour towards the outer wall of the fortress. En-suite a/c studio rooms come with kitchenette and, if you're lucky, a balcony sea view – there are cheaper rooms without views. Good value for the location, although the owners prefer to rent by the week, and won't even consider a single-night stay in August. ❹

Along and behind the beach

Kyma Platía Iróon ☎ 28310 55503, ⓕ 28310 27746. A reasonable value modern seafront hotel

where a/c balcony sea-view rooms have TV and minibar, and there's a small pool. Open all year and when space is tight they put overflow guests in their twin hotel (of the same standard) nearby. Rates include breakfast. ❻

Leo Vafe 2 ☎ 28310 26197. This hotel in another former Venetian mansion has wooden decor, a traditional feel and attractive en-suite rooms. It also has a pleasant bar downstairs. ❸

Minoa Arkadhíou 62 ☎ 28310 22508. An efficient, small and central hotel offering balconied en-suite rooms with fridges and fans; the rooms with double beds are cheaper. ❷

Olga's Rooms Souliou 57 ☎ 28310 54896, ⓕ 28310 29851. Set in a nice old building with roof garden on this touristy street, the en-suite rooms overlooking the sea are very good, with ceiling fans, fridge and TV; there are some cheaper rooms without bath. Rooms with double bed are slightly cheaper and there's a great breakfast bar below, *Stella's Kitchen* (see p.249). ❸

Sea Front Arkádhiou 159 ☎ 28310 51981, ⓔ elotia@ret.forthnet.gr. Good a/c en-suite rooms in restored old house, some have sea-view balconies (others overlook Arkadhíou), and all with fridge and TV. The owners have a number of apartments nearby. ❸

Zania Pavlou Vlastou 3 ☎ 28310 28169. A refurbished old Venetian mansion, right on the corner of Arkadhíou, run by courteous, French-speaking proprietors. The elegant high-ceilinged rooms come with their own fridge, but bathrooms are shared. ❷

Near the Public Gardens

Brascos Dhaskalaki 1, corner of Moatsou ☎ 28310 23721, ⓦ www.brascos.com. Rather bland B-class hotel which often has space when everywhere else is full and is a pretty good deal for what you get: a/c balcony rooms with fridge, hairdryer, satellite TV; extras include a roof-garden bar and Lilliputian pool. Rates include breakfast. ❹

Hotel Byzantine Vosporou 26, near the Porta Guora ☎ 28310 55609, ⓦ www.byzantineret.gr. Pleasant rooms with bath and fans in a renovated old Byzantine palace, which also has a tranquil patio bar. ❹

Youth Hostel Tombázi 41 ☎ 28310 22848, ⓦ www.yhrethymno.com. The cheapest beds in town, in dormitories or (illegally) on the roof. This hostel is large, clean, friendly and popular, and there's food, free hot showers, Internet access, clothes-washing facilities and even a library in various languages. ❶

The City

Réthimnon is a thoroughly enjoyable place to wander around. Although much of it has succumbed to fast-food outlets and supermarkets, the buildings themselves have changed little, and there's still the odd corner where English and German are not automatically spoken. You'll also find a few curious old stores, and craftsmen – often manufacturing *lyras*, the Cretan "violin" – working away in their traditional get-up of high boots, baggy trousers (*vrákes*) and black headscarves (*tsalvária*).

With the outstanding exception of the Venetian fortress, the town's monuments don't amount to a great deal, but walking between them is often every bit as interesting as what you find within. The streets are a fascinating mix of generations of **architecture**, the Venetian buildings indistinguishable most of the time from the Turkish and all of them adapted and added to by later generations. Ornate wooden doors and balconies are recurring features, ancient stonework crops up everywhere, and there are a number of elaborate **Turkish fountains** hidden in obscure corners – one by the Kara Pasha mosque, another below the south side of the fortress at the corner of Smírnis and Koronaíou, two more on Patriárhou Grigoríou leading up from here towards the Public Gardens.

The harbour and the fortress

The Venetian or inner **harbour**, is the most attractive part of Réthimnon's waterfront, although these days its elegant sixteenth-century lighthouse looks down on a line of fish tavernas that have taken over the former quayside rather than the sailing ships and barges of bygone eras. The nearby and impressive breakwaters, which are constantly being extended, reveal some of the problems with the harbour. Soon after its completion the Venetians discovered the dock's tendency to silt up, and this has been a constant hindrance ever since: until relatively recently it was unable to handle really big ships or ferries. When the locals decided to set up their own ferry service to Pireás (the first vessel, *Arkadhi*, was bought by public subscription) the whole harbour had to be completely cleared out, and only a constant dredging operation keeps it open. Even now, the ferry is virtually the only large ship to call here and must dock in a specially constructed outer harbour alongside; the inner harbour is today given over to small fishing *kaïkia*, pleasure craft and tourist cruise boats.

If you follow the shoreline round to the west you'll emerge beneath the walls of the massive **Venetian Fortress** (Sat–Thurs 8.30am–7pm; closes 6pm Nov–Mar; €2.90). Said to be the largest Venetian castle ever built, this was a response, in the last quarter of the sixteenth century, to a series of pirate raids (by Barbarossa in 1538 and Uluch Ali in 1562 and 1571) which had devastated the town. Designed by the Italian engineer Sforza Pallavicini, the mammoth edifice took a full ten years to build at a crippling cost. Whether it was effective is another matter; in 1645 the Venetian city fell to the Turks in less than 24 hours (they simply bypassed the fort), and when the English writer Robert Pashley visited in 1834 he found the guns, some of them still the Venetian originals, to be entirely useless. The **entrance** is in the southeastern corner, opposite the Archeological Museum.

As you walk in through the walls there's a small café-bar in what must have been some sort of **guardhouse** within the bastion, and then you emerge into the vast open interior space, dotted with the remains of barracks, arsenals, officers' houses, earthworks and deep shafts. At the centre is a large domed building which was once a **church** and later a **mosque** designed to be large enough

△ Réthimnon

for the entire population to take shelter within the walls. The recently renovated church/mosque has a truly fabulous **dome** and a pretty carved *mihrab* (a niche indicating the direction of Mecca, sadly defaced by graffiti), both of which are Turkish additions. Just to the north of this are some fine arched foundations and a **stairway** leading down to a gate in the seaward defences. This was in theory for resupplying the defenders, but in reality it was through here that the Venetians fled from the Turkish attack. Among the most impressive remains are the **cisterns** where rainwater would have been collected: they are deep and cool, and dimly lit by slits through which shafts of sunlight penetrate. Although much is ruined now, the fort remains thoroughly atmospheric, with **views** from the walls over the town and harbour, or in the other direction along the coast to the west. Walk around the outside, preferably at sunset, to get an impression of its vast bulk; there are more great views along the coast, and a pleasant resting point around the far side at the *Sunset Taverna* (see p.249).

The archeological and historical museums

Réthimnon's **Archeological Museum** (Tues–Sun 8.30am–3pm; €3) lies almost directly opposite the entrance to the fortress. It occupies a building built by the Turks as an extra defence for the entry, and which later served as a prison, but it's now entirely modern inside – cool, spacious and airy. It's worth visiting, especially if you're going to miss the bigger museums in other towns: there are Minoan pottery and sarcophagi, as well as Roman coins, jewellery, pots and statues, all of them from Réthimnon province. Take a look beneath the central atrium at an unusual unfinished Roman **statue of Aphrodite**, with the sculptor's chisel marks still plainly visible, allowing you to glimpse the goddess's features – never completed – emerging from the stone.

Equally enjoyable is the **Historical and Folk Art Museum** (Mon–Sat 9am–2pm & 6–8pm; €3), located in a beautifully restored seventeenth-century Venetian mansion at M. Venardou 28, close to the Nerandzes Mosque. Inside in two rooms are gathered musical instruments (including the *lyra* of Nikos Piskopakis, one of its greatest-ever exponents), old photos, basketry, farm implements, an explanation of traditional bread-making techniques, smiths' tools, traditional costumes and jewellery, lace, weaving and embroidery, pottery, knives and old wooden chests. In a section on Cretan tapestry look out for a 1941 work depicting German parachutists landing at Máleme. There's also a quaint island visitors' map from 1965, depicting the island before it was invaded by mass tourism, and in the ceramics section there are early examples of pottery from Margarítes, still one of Réthimnon's most important pottery centres today. The displays include explanations (most of them translated) of how the items have been acquired, often as a result of a traditional craft workshop, farm or bakery closing down – although many of the museum's exhibits have just come out of someone's attic. It's a fascinating insight into fast-disappearing rural and urban lifestyles, which had often survived virtually unchanged from Venetian times to the 1960s.

Nearby is the **Centre for Contemporary Art** (Tues–Fri 9am–1pm & 7–10pm, Sat & Sun 11am–3pm; €3), at the junction of Himáras and Melissinou, which you will see signposted throughout the town. It features a programme of rather hit-and-miss temporary exhibitions, from tribal art to modern Greek painting and installations.

The rest of the city

The **city centre**, at least as far as tourists are concerned, is the area around the seventeenth-century Venetian **Loggia**, for many years the town museum; it's now home to a shop, selling high-quality (and pricey) reproductions of classical art, but still stands in the midst of shops, restaurants and bars radiating in every direction. The **Rimondi Fountain**, close by at the western end of Paleológou, is also seventeenth-century Venetian. Half-hidden under a blocked-off arcade, the fountain's lion-head spouts still splash water down to a marble bowl, and nowadays they look out over **Platía Petiháki**, one of the liveliest areas in town. Straight up from the fountain, a line of cafés and tavernas leads into Ethníkis Andistásis, the **market** street. Turn right just before this and the backstreets lead to the fine **Nerandzes Mosque**, whose minaret (currently closed for repairs), ascended by a steep spiral stair, has the best views in town. The mosque itself is not open to the public and is used as a music school and concert hall.

Up through the market area, the old city ends at the only surviving remnant of the city walls, the **Porta Guora**. Through the gate you emerge into the busy Platía Tessáron Martíron with its rather unattractive modern church. Almost directly opposite are the quiet and shady **Public Gardens**, a former Turkish cemetery now laid out with a fine variety of palms and other trees. In July, the gardens play host to the festivities of the **Réthimnon Wine Festival** (see p.250). In the newer parts of town, you'll find two more mosques: **Veli Pasha**, to the southeast of Platía Martíron, has a fine minaret, whilst **Kara Pasha** by Platía Iróon is older, but only part of the facade survives, with a small garden planted in front.

The beach

To find the **beach** you hardly need a guidebook: the broad swathe of tawny sand in the centre of town advertises itself. There are showers and cafés here, and the waters protected by the breakwaters are dead calm (and ideal for kids). Sadly, they're also crowded and often none too clean. Outside the harbour, less sheltered sands stretch for miles to the east, only marginally less crowded but with much cleaner water. Interspersed among the hotels along here is every facility you could need – travel agents, bike rental, bars and restaurants.

Shopping

Most of Réthimnon's **souvenir** stores are along Arkadhíou, Paleológou and Souliou; the market is on Andistásis, while more general stores line Arkadhíou and Koundouriótou. There's also a **market** on Thursday along Dhimitrakáki, near the Public Gardens. Atelier, attached to the pension of the same name (see p.243), sells some creative modern ceramics by a local potter, Froso Bora. **Shoe-shops** are a big feature here, especially selling leather sandals, and prices are reasonable. Souliou has the most upmarket and varied tourist stores (including one that sells nothing but herbs and herbal remedies). Réthimnon is also a centre of **lyra** production; among the workshops where you can see them being made are Yeóryios Gounakis, next to the *O Gounakis* taverna (see p.250), and Yeóryios Papalexakis, Dimakopolou 6, near the Porta Guora. Evelyn Daskalaki, Tombázi 16, near the youth hostel, has a delightful small shop selling decorative church lamps, copper coffee pots and myriad other objets d'art. For beach games and fishing or diving gear, try Spiros Spor on Petiháki.

Official shop **hours** in Réthimnon are Monday, Wednesday and Saturday 8am to 2pm, Tuesday, Thursday and Friday 8am to 1pm and 5 to 8pm.

Eating

Immediately behind the town beach are arrayed the most obvious of Réthimnon's **restaurants**, all with illustrated menus out front and most with waiters who will run off their patter in English, German, French, Swedish or whatever else seems likely to appeal. These places are sometimes reasonable value – especially if you hanker after an "English breakfast" – but they are all thoroughly touristy. Look out here and throughout town for the wonderful fresh fruit juices (especially melon) and shakes which have become a local speciality. Around the inner harbour there's a cluster of rather more expensive and intimate fish tavernas. The **kafenía** and tavernas by the Rimondi Fountain and the newer places spreading into the streets all around generally offer better value, although they lack the sea views. There are a couple of good **pizza** places here, too, and a number of old-fashioned *kafenía*, a couple of which serve great yoghurt and honey.

Takeaway food means either plumping for *souvláki* – there are numerous stalls, including a couple on Arkadhíou and Paleológou and *O Platanos* at Petiháki 52 – or buying your own. **Market** stalls are set up daily on Andistásis below the Porta Guora, and there are small general stores scattered everywhere, particularly on Paleológou and Arkadhíou; east along the beach road you'll even find a couple of mini-supermarkets and there's a fair-sized supermarket on Platía Martíron. The **bakery** *I Gaspari*, on Mesolongíou just behind the Rimondi Fountain, sells the usual *tirópita*, cakes and the like, and it also bakes excellent brown, black and rye bread. There's a good *zaharoplastío* on Petiháki, and another at Koundouriótou 49, west of Platía Martíron.

Inner harbour, Rimondi Fountain and fortress zones

Agrimia Platía Petiháki. Just one of the places touting for your custom as you walk up from the Rimondi Fountain. It's a good place to sit outside, and the food is usually reliable.

Alana Salaminas 11. A romantic, tree-filled courtyard setting for candlelit tables and (mostly) non-Greek food. High prices.

Avli Xanthoudidou 22, just west of the Rimondi Fountain ☎ 28310 26213. Upmarket place in a Venetian mansion offering carefully prepared traditional meals (the lamb is good) in one of the prettiest and most romantic garden settings in town. Prices are on the high side, though, with the cheapest bottle of wine €15; the neighbouring *To Pigadi* (see below) offers better value.

Castellvecchio Himáras 29. Inviting small family taverna next to the Fortezza, offering the usual standards and quite a few vegetarian choices. There's also a pleasant terrace with a view over the city.

Fanari Periferiakos 16. Seafront taverna with a small terrace close to Platía Plastíra, serving the usual staples and fish dishes to a high standard.

Kyria Maria Moshovitou 20. Pleasant, unassuming small restaurant tucked down an alley behind the Rimondi Fountain. After the meal everyone gets a couple of María's delicious *tiropitákia* topped with honey, on the house.

Minares Odhós Vernadou, in the centre of town, right next to the Nerandzes Mosque. A little touristy but very friendly, with reliable food served in a pleasant garden setting.

Palazzo At the inner harbour. One of the nicest places on the harbour, with tables on a rooftop terrace, but rather overpriced.

To Pigadi Xanthoudidou 31 ☎ 28310 27522. Outstanding new taverna in the old town, with an attractive garden terrace containing an old well (*pigadi*). Traditional dishes are cooked with style and reasonably priced; the service is impeccable, and there's a very good selection of wines, with wine-chiller jackets to keep your bottle at the optimal temperature.

O Pontios I. Melissinou 34. A tiny, unassuming place near the Archeological Museum and the fortress, serving surprisingly good food – a worthwhile lunchtime stop.

O Psaras Corner of Nikiforou Foka and Koronaíou. An economical and unpretentious fish taverna with tables beside a church.

Samaria Venizélou, almost opposite the tourist office. One of the few seafront places patronized by locals, serving well-prepared food at reasonable prices.

Stella's Kitchen Souliou 55. A great-value little diner, serving up six daily specials (at least two of which are vegetarian); also good for breakfast and closes at 9pm. Recommended.

Sunset Taverna On the west side of the fortress. Mostly visited for its views (spectacular sunsets) rather than the food, but the meals aren't bad value and there's usually a decent selection of fish. The terrace tables here are right by the shore

– the waiters have to cross the road from the kitchen.

Veneto Epimenidou 4 ☎ 28310 56634. Stylish upmarket restaurant in a refurbished Venetian palace which offers wider Mediterranean cuisine as well as Cretan dishes.

O Zefyros At the inner harbour. Reliable, reasonably priced fish taverna.

The rest of town

Apostolis & Zabía Taverna Junction of Periferiakos and Igoum Gavril, close to the bus station. Highly popular local taverna for meat and fish dishes with a shaded terrace.

Estiatório Laiko Moatsou 40, west of the Public Gardens. Typical town *estiatório*, off the tourist trail, where the hearty food is made daily and you choose from the heated trays behind a glass display.

O Gounakis Koronaíou 6 in the old town. Serving hearty, no-frills cooking, the family running this bar/restaurant perform *lyra* every night – when things get really lively, the dancing starts.

Kokkinos Platía Iróon. This taverna is open 24 hours a day and has decent Cretan cuisine. It's often difficult to get a seat at 4am when the bars

close and the place fills with revellers wanting a breakfast *souvláki*.

To Kombou On the edge of Atsipópolou village, 3km southwest of town (take a taxi there and back). An excellent garden taverna, popular with the locals. The Cretan specialities include *spilogáradouma* with *áfogalo* (lamb sausage with a creamy sauce). Open eves only.

Lemonokipos Andistásis 100. A charming garden restaurant concealed behind the street entrance. It serves a variety of tasty meat and fish dishes at tables under the lemon trees, with a decent selection of wines.

Mesostrati Yerakári 1, behind the church on Platía Martíron. An excellent and economical little neighbourhood taverna, serving well-prepared country dishes on a small terrace.

Drinking, nightlife and entertainment

Bars and **nightlife** are concentrated in the same general areas as the restaurants. At the west end of Venizélou, in the streets behind the inner harbour, pavements soon fill with the overflow from a small cluster of noisy **music bars** where party-goers gather before the nightly opening of the local discos. The café-cum-cocktail places around the Rimondi Fountain are great for people-watching, but the cacophony of late-evening noise from competing bars is less than relaxing. A string of more subdued **cocktail bars** can be found up Salaminos towards the fortress, and there are more of these below the *Ideon* hotel on Platía Plastíra. Larger **discos** are mostly out to the east, among the big hotels, but there are one or two in town as well.

Every August the town puts on its **Renaissance Festival** (*Anagennisiakó*). Held in the fortress, it includes folk and classical music concerts and theatrical events, as well as performances of Classical tragedies and comedies; a full programme is available from the tourist office. There's more public entertainment on offer at the annual **wine festival**, staged in the Public Gardens in the second half of July. The nominal entrance fee includes all the wine you can drink from barrels set up around the gardens, and there are also food stalls and entertainment laid on. You'll need to take your own cup or buy one of the souvenir glasses and carafes on offer outside. Although it tends to be rather touristy, the locals go too, and as the evening progresses and the barrels empty, the organized entertainments give way to spectacular displays of the local dance steps.

Cafés, bars and discos

Cul de Sac Platía Petiháki. Stylish *kafenion* overlooking Rimondi Fountain. The prices are higher than average, but it's a great place to people-watch over a coffee.

Dimman Arkadhíou 220. One of the noisiest rock

bars in this zone with a young clientele and good views from the first-floor balcony tables.

Float Club Nearchou 26, near the inner harbour. New dance venue, specializing in hip-hop and R&B. Opens 11pm–dawn.

Fortezza Inner harbour. A big, glitzy disco-bar, where the action kicks in after midnight.

Galera Platía Petiháki. Large beers, toasted sandwiches and snacks served on one of the town's most popular terraces for seeing and being seen.

Metropolis Nearchou 24. A loud rock-music bar just round the corner from the *Fortezza*, on an alley which connects with Arkadhíou.

Notes Himáras 27, near the fortress. Facing the *Atelier* pension, this relaxing music bar puts on both Cretan and internationally flavoured guitar and song most nights, especially at weekends, and also does good breakfasts. Opens 9am.

Opera Club Salaminos, west of the inner harbour. One of the town's bigger music and dance clubs, with an eclectic mix of Greek and western rock, accompanied by strobe-lighting pyrotechnics.

Punch Bowl Arabatzoglou 42. The obligatory Irish pub – pleasant and convivial, and serving draught Guinness.

Rock Café Pethaki 8, near the inner harbour. Big and brash dance club attracting large crowds in high summer.

Venetsianako Close to the old harbour pier at the west side of the inner harbour. Stylish place where the smartly dressed locals go for morning, noon or afternoon coffee and – in the evenings – candlelit tables and disco sounds.

Xtreme Nearchou. Just around the corner from the fortress, on an alley which connects with Arkadhíou. A loud international rock-music bar with plenty of other bar-discos nearby.

Listings

Airlines Olympic Airways, Koumoundourou 5 (☎28310 22257), behind the Public Gardens. For Aegean Airways flights enquire at the travel agents (see p.252). Buses bound for Haniá airport leave from the Olympic Airways office two-and-a-quarter hours before flight departures; confirm exact bus times in advance with the Olympic office.

Banks ATMs are to be found throughout the centre; the National Bank, at the foot of Dhimokratias to the west of the Public Gardens, has a 24hr ATM which takes MasterCard and Eurocard. Over the road, the Interamerican Bank has another ATM, with more along nearby Koundouriótou.

Bike rental Motorbike and scooter rental outlets around town include Stavros, Paleológou 14 (☎28310 22858), which also rents out mountain bikes; and Motor Club, S. Venizélou 2 (☎28310 54253), at the eastern end of the seafront. Hellas Sports, S. Venizélou 67 (☎28310 52764, ⓦwww.hellassports.com), organizes one-day downhill (the Scott mountain bikes go "up" on a trailer) biking excursions to the White Mountains, Arkádhi, Kournás, Margarítes, Psilorítis and elsewhere.

Boat trips The *Dolphin Express* sails four times daily to Pánormos, Balí and the Skaléta "pirate" caves; there are also trips to Yeoryioúpolis, as well as evening cruises and fishing expeditions. The *Captain Hook* and its sister ship the *Barbarossa* make similar trips in more touristy "Jolly Roger" vessels, complete with sails, which are great for kids (adults €34, kids €17, including lunch). Both are located on the inner harbour.

Car rental Ellotia Tours, Arkádhiou 155 (☎28310 51981, ⓦwww.forthnet.gr/elotia) are reliable; rates for a Fiat 600 start at €180 per week, with ten-percent discount for *Rough Guide* readers with this guide. Motor Club, S. Venizélou 2 (☎28310 54253), is a good alternative.

Cinema There are several, including the open-air Asteria on I. Melissinou beneath the south side of the fortress, and Cinema Pandelis on the main road out towards Iráklion, which shows new-release films, many in their original-language versions.

Diving Diving and snorkelling trips plus PADI courses for beginners are offered by the Paradise Dive Centre, Arkadhíou 263 (☎28310 26317, ⓔpdcr@otenet.gr). A one-day introduction to scuba diving costs €80, including tuition, equipment and transport to their south-coast dive base near Plakiás.

Ferries Since the *Préveli*, the sister ship to the *Aptera*, came into service, there are now daily sailings to Pireás at 8pm. For details and tickets for ferries to Pireás as well as Kastélli, Yíthio (Gythion), Kíthira and Kalamáta, visit the very helpful Ellotia Tours at Arkadhíou 155 (☎28310 51981, ⓦwww.forthnet.gr/elotia). The *Atlantis* and *Golden Prince* also make one-day cruises to Santoríni (Thíra), currently on Tues & Sat costing €58, which includes breakfast and evening meal. The ANEK Lines office is located at Arkadhíou 250 (☎28310 29221, ⓦwww.anek.gr).

Internet access The most central cybercafé is *Galero*, on Platía Petiháki by the Rimondi Fountain (daily 9am–midnight; €3.50 per hour, €1 for 15min; ☎28310 22657). Other possibilities with similar prices are *Café Internet*, Arkadhíou 86 near the Loggia; *Café-Bar Internet*, Platía Martíron 4 next to the Porta Guora; *User Internet*, Ethnikís Andistáseos 83.

Laundry Laundry-Mat at Tombázi 45 by the youth hostel charges €7.50 to wash, dry and fold up to 5kg (Mon–Sat 8am–2.15pm & 5–9pm; ☎28310 56196).

Left luggage The long-distance bus station has a small office (Mon–Fri 6.30am–9pm, Sat & Sun 8.30am–5pm); €1 euro per item per 24hr.

Mountain climbing and walking The local EOS is at Dhimokratías 12 (☎28310 22655); besides advice on climbing, it also organizes walking tours. Walking tours from one day to two weeks are offered by The Happy Walker, Tombázi 56 (☎28310 52920, ☒www.happywalker.com), a Dutch operation located near the youth hostel. Single-day walks cost €25 and include a taxi/minibus to and from your hotel to the walk start point.

Newspapers and books Foreign newspapers are sold at several places along the seafront. Best for these, and for a wide selection of new books in English, is International Press at the junction of Venizélou and I. Petháki (not to be confused with Platía T. Petiháki). News Stand, Platía Agnostou 31 (the western continuation of Platía Iróon), also sells foreign press and has a good selection of books in

English. Good places for secondhand English-language books are Palaiobibliopoleío, Soulíou 43 in the old town and Tripoligakis, Arabatzoglou 51, west of the Rimondi Fountain.

Pharmacies Plenty are scattered about the main shopping streets, especially Koundouriótou and Arkadhíou. Check the rota on the door for late/weekend opening. The tourist office has a list of English-speaking doctors.

Post office The main post office (Mon–Fri 7.30am–8pm, Sat 7.30am–2pm) is in a smart new building on Moátsou, opposite the *Brascos* hotel.

Taxis Ranks in Platía Tessáron Martíron and Platía Iróon, or call ☎28310 25000 for a radio taxi.

Telephones The OTE office is at Koundouriótou 28 (daily 7am–10pm).

Toilets There are clean public toilets on the beach by the tourist office, and others opposite the Loggia and in the Public Gardens.

Travel agents There are several travel agents along Paleológou, Arkhadhíou and Koundouriótou, and also around Platía Iróon and along Venizélou. The following can all arrange excursions and domestic flight and ferry tickets: Ellotia Tours, Arkadhíou 155 behind the seafront (☎28310 51981); Creta Connection, Kallergi 15 (☎28310 24977); Creta Tours, Venizélou (☎28310 22915); Creta Travel Bureau, Venizélou 3 (☎28310 24983). You'd do better to arrange international flights in Haniá or Iráklion.

The Monastery of Arkádhi

Of all the short trips which you could take from Réthimnon, the most worthwhile one is to the **Monastery of Arkádhi** (daily 8am–8pm; €2), some 25km southeast of the city in the foothills of the Psilorítis range. Arkádhi is something of a national Cretan shrine to the nineteenth-century struggle for independence – aside from its historical resonance, the monastery's striking architecture and highly scenic location are reason enough to visit.

The monastery and its history

Before its notoriety, Arkádhi was one of the richest monasteries in Crete and a well-known stopover for travellers (grouchy Edward Lear spent one of his better-tempered nights here), as well as being a centre of resistance. Pashley relates a story of events in the 1820s, when eighty Muslims, who had occupied the monastery to pacify local rebels, were captured and put to death; in retaliation, many of the buildings were burned.

During the **1866 rebellion** Arkádhi served as a Cretan stronghold in which, as the Turks took the upper hand, hundreds of Cretan guerrillas and their families took refuge. Here they were surrounded by a Turkish army until, after a siege of two days, the defences were finally breached on November 9, 1866. As the attackers poured in, the ammunition stored in the monastery exploded – deliberately fired, according to the accepted version of events, on the orders of the abbot. Hundreds were killed in the initial blast, Cretan and Turk alike, and most of the surviving defenders were put to death by the enraged assailants. The following year the British philhellene J. Hilary Skinner, fighting with the insurgents, could still describe "scores of bodies unburied, half-buried, sun-dried, and mangled, to be seen within the monastery". That he was here at all is proof of the international sympathy for the cause of **Cretan independence** which this ultimate expression of the cry of "Freedom or Death" did much to promote. Figures as disparate as Victor Hugo, Garibaldi and the poet Swinburne were moved to public declarations of support, and in Britain money was raised for a ship (the *Arkádhi*) to run the Turkish blockade. Though Crete's liberty was still some way off at that stage, today the monastery remains the most potent symbol of the struggle (there are celebrations of the anniversary of the blast on November 7–9 each year). More recently the monastery lent assistance to guerrilla fighters during **World War II**: George Psychoundákis, for example, describes handing over supplies from a parachute drop to the monks.

Nowadays you can peer into the roofless **vault** beside the cloister where the explosion took place, and wander about the rest of the well-restored grounds. Despite the carnage, the bulk of the monastery buildings, including the others around the central cloister, were relatively unscathed and Arkádhi is still a working monastery. Of the surviving buildings the **church** is much the most impressive, its rich mix of styles placing it among the finest Venetian structures left in Crete. Its highly decorative facade, dating from 1587, used to feature on the Greek 100-drachma note; it seems startlingly out-of-place, isolated here in the Cretan countryside. The rest of the monastery is mainly seventeenth-century (though it was originally founded as early as the eleventh) and more familiar in layout and style. Across the courtyard from the scene of the explosion a small **museum** (same ticket) devoted to the exploits of the defenders of the faith contains a variety of mementos and tributes, blood-stained clothing and commemorative medals.

Practicalities

Transport to Arkádhi is straightforward. In addition to all the tours, there are **buses** from Réthimnon currently running at 6.15am, 10.30am, noon and 2.30pm, returning at 7am, 11.15am, 1pm and 4pm. Going up at 10.30am and back at 1pm gives you about the right amount of time, but these are the most popular times, and consequently in high summer buses can be crowded. Alternatively, **hitching** a lift back to Réthimnon should be no problem especially during the busy high-season period. There's also a route from here south to **Thrónos** in the Amári valley (see p.276), reached via an asphalted road. To pick it up head west from the monastery grounds towards Hárkia; after a couple of hundred metres the Thrónos road is signed on the left.

With your own transport, the **old road** up to Arkádhi is an attractive trip in itself. Take the route east out of Réthimnon via Perivólia and then follow the signs at Plataniás which lead under the highway towards the monastery via Ádhele and Piyí. As you climb into the foothills, the road and the valley through which it runs gradually narrow until, at the end, it's a real ravine. This opens out quite suddenly into the small plain at the centre of which stands the monastery. You'll pass a modern monument to the martyrs of independence – with displayed human skulls – and arrive at a huge spreading tree where the bus stops and cars park. There is **food** available at a rather unattractive cafeteria, and this is also a quiet place to picnic, either on benches around the outside of the monastery or out in the meadows which surround it. There's an inviting **alternative route** back to the coast through some picturesque wooded hill country dotted with interesting villages. Directly in front of the monastery a paved road cuts away to the northeast before it reaches Eléftherna, 5km away, and ancient Eléftherna (see p.263), followed by Margarítes (see p.262).

Arméni Minoan cemetery

The road south across the island, towards Plakiás or Ayía Galíni, takes off from the very centre of Réthimnon, running along the side of the Public Gardens and then climbing rapidly above the town. Look back from the final bend and you have the city, its castle and harbour laid out like a map below you, with the sea behind. Once you've passed the large service station which marks the end of the populated north coast, the road winds scenically into the back-country of rural Crete.

A little under 10km from Réthimnon, just before the village of **Arméni**, a sign to the right points the way to a remarkable **Minoan cemetery** (Tues–Sun 8.30am–3pm; free). Important discoveries have been made here in over two hundred rock-cut tombs dating from the Late Minoan period, after the fall of the great palaces. Pleasantly sited today in a shady oak wood, most of the tombs are of the *drómos* (passage) and chamber type. One large tomb on the south side of the site which the guide will point out has a spectacular *drómos* and finely cut chamber, and may well have belonged to a royal personage. Some other tombs had only the *drómos* cut, and work on them seems for some reason to have been abandoned. Many *lárnakes* (clay coffins) and grave goods found in the tombs – including weapons, jewellery, vases and a rare helmet made from boar's tusks – are now on display in the archeological museums at Réthimnon and Iráklion. One mystery yet to be solved regarding the cemetery remains: the location of the sizeable settlement which provided this necropolis with its customers.

Some 12km further south at the Koxaré junction is a **café** and truck stop marking a turn-off west on a road through the village of Koxaré to Plakiás via the Kourtaliótiko gorge and Asómatos – the route taken by buses. This café is the best place to change buses if you are travelling between Ayía Galíni and Plakiás or vice versa (there's a timetable posted outside), and is also a good spot to get a lift with passing tourists or a local truck. With your own transport you've got the option of taking another gorge route to Plakiás by continuing from Koxaré to Áyios Ioánnis and turning south down the Kotsifoú gorge, passing through Mírthios en route. Either way, the drive through the gorges is a pretty spectacular one. Sticking to the main road south from Arméni leads after a further 8km to the charming little town of **Spíli** (see p.272) and eventually Ayía Galíni (see p.281).

West of Réthimnon

Heading **west** from Réthimnon the roads are easy and efficient, but they offer little in the way of diversion. As you leave the city, you immediately start to climb; within a couple of kilometres the **old road** to Haniá peels off to head inland with opportunities to visit some charming villages such as **Argiroúpolis** and **Asigonía**.

The main E75 **highway** carries on above the coast before dropping back to sea level at **Yeráni**, 6km from Réthimnon, with a rocky cove good for swimming. There's a sign here to the Yeráni cave, site of a Neolithic cult rediscovered when the road was built, but the cave is not actually open to the public. Beyond, after another brief flirtation with the hills, the road finally levels out beside the **Gulf of Almirós**, from where it traces the shore, flat and straight, the rest of the way to Yeoryioúpolis (see p.331). A long and windswept **sandy beach** follows it all the way, separated from the road by straggling bushes of oleander; there are frequent spaces to pull over and park if you want a swim, and just a few new developments beginning to spring up. The beach itself is virtually deserted much of the way, but there can be dangerous currents so don't venture too far out; it gets further from the road and considerably more sheltered as you approach the development at Yeoryioúpolis.

Via the old road to Argiroúpolis

The scenic **old road** which heads southwest from Réthimnon is by comparison quite populous. You'll pass through five or six prosperous little villages before arriving, after 23km, at **Episkopí**, something of a local market centre with narrow, twisting hilly streets at its heart that test the clutch control of drivers. Here you're approaching the foothills of the White Mountains, which rise with increasing majesty ahead. You probably wouldn't want **to stay** in the village itself, but 2km below it on the road heading north to the sea, *Villa Pirgos* and *Villa Avra* (☎21080 72267, mobile ☎6947074657 for both; ●), are attractive sea-view apartments sleeping up to eight with pool, on a hill above the nearby beach, which lies across the E75 highway. From Episkopí a road runs up to some of the smaller villages, a rarely travelled route where the old life continues, and where there are good opportunities for **hiking** in the surrounding hills.

Continuing west, beyond Episkopí, the old road soon divides, the main way descending steadily towards Yeoryioúpolis, a secondary route climbing through the village of Kournás (see p.334) and then dropping steeply to the lake.

A turn-off at Episkopí (or along a signed bypass which avoids the latter's narrow streets) heads **south** towards Argiroúpolis. A couple of kilometres before you arrive at the village proper, the excellent *Mikedaki Rooms* (☎28310 81225; ●) is a good place to stay. A splendid garden hides spotless rooms with bath, all of which have terrace balconies with fine views of the mountains and valley behind – you can even see the sea. Guests can also use a well-stocked kitchen to prepare breakfast to eat on their balconies.

At the back of the pension, where the land falls away beyond an orchard and an ancient stone threshing floor, tracks lead down into the Moussélas river valley. There's a fine **walk** to be had by following any of these, aiming for a small chapel directly west that is easily visible across the valley. From a little beyond the chapel, a dirt track ascends diagonally to cross the shoulder of the Káto Agori peak. Following this in a northwesterly direction will lead you to the village of **Pátima**. From here it's possible to follow more tracks in a vaguely circular route, taking in the hamlets of Kástellos, Filakí and **Arhontikí**. From the last village there's a track back along the east side of the valley which emerges near to the pension; this circular walk totals about 10km. The tracks and villages are marked on the Petrákis *Réthimno Walking and Driving* map (see p.26) as is the **Pan-European E4 footpath**, which crosses the valley nearby to track the northern bank of the Moussélas to Asigonía, another fine walk.

Argiroúpolis

ARGIROÚPOLIS, 6km south of Episkopí, is a charmingly scenic village with a split personality: the lower half is located around its famous springs, while the upper village is founded on the ruins of the prestigious ancient Greco-Roman city of Lappa. With fine views over the Mouséllas river valley and surrounded by some fine walking country in the foothills of the White Mountains, it is one of the most attractive villages in this part of Crete. **Buses** to Argiroúpolis (Mon–Fri only) leave from Réthimnon at 11.30am and 2.30pm, and travel in the opposite direction (from the upper village) at 7am, 12.30pm and 3.30pm.

The lower village

The **lower village**, reached by taking a right downhill when you come to a fork (the Asigonía road), is effectively comprised of five **tavernas** in a spectacular wooded setting where gushing springwater cascades in every direction from the hill above. Vegetation is abundant in this fertile environment and, as well as great numbers of chestnut and plane trees, there are even banana plants. The roar of water is impressive and there's so much of it here that it supplies the whole of the town of Réthimnon, as signs inform you. The tavernas have all incorporated water features into their terraces – walls of tumbling water, oriental wooden water bells, as well as the more prosaic water wheel. The whole scene is especially magical at night with lights illuminating the foliage above.

All the tavernas are good, but for added interest you might visit the *Vieux Moulin*, downhill from the others, which is owned by Argiroúpolis's ebullient ex-mayor, Stelios Manousakas, who is a voluble expert on all things to do with the village and frequently corrects visiting archeologists on their facts (see p.257). Close to the *Vieux Moulin*, and accidentally discovered in 1994 by a British team, is a remarkable seventeenth-century Venetian **fulling mill** complete with a rare wooden fulling machine. Once driven by water from the spring, it was used for shrinking, beating and preparing cloth. It is hoped eventually to restore this unique piece of Crete's industrial history and open it up to the public. To find the mill, go through the restaurant's grounds and pass through a black metal gate into a road. You will see a chapel in the field opposite fronted by a Roman pillar; turn left downhill, where you'll see a blue pole carrying electricity cables. Turn right here and opposite the next pole you'll see the ruined mill. Between the fulling mill and the springs are the scanty remains of the **Roman baths** of ancient Lappa – ask at the taverna if you have problems finding these.

The upper village

Argiroúpolis's **upper village**, reached by taking the left fork uphill (or by climbing a path which ascends steps from the springs), lies around its tranquil square overlooked by the elegant seventeenth-century Venetian church of **Áyios Ioánnis**, with an extended section to the south enjoying views over the river valley. This segment of the village is built over the celebrated ancient city of **Lappa**, parts of which have recently been revealed, and archeologists have been busy over recent years excavating and documenting the city's ancient necropolis in the valley to the north, where they have unearthed a wealth of grave goods. Originally a Dorian settlement, Lappa was an ally of Lyttos (see p.131) in the latter's wars against Knossós. When it fiercely opposed the Roman invasion in 67 BC, the city was destroyed by the conquering legions. Later, when Lappa aided Octavian-Augustus in his struggle against Antony for the control of the Roman world, the victorious emperor permitted the Lappans to rebuild their town and gifted them a **water reservoir** in 27 BC which, incredibly, still supplies the village today. The city flourished for many centuries, even outlasting Roman rule, but was razed again by the Saracens in the ninth century. It recovered during the Venetian occupation and was an important centre, as is evident from in the numerous villas left behind by Venetian landlords. Remnants of buildings from all periods of the village's history have been incorporated into most of the houses: you'll spot classical inscriptions, ancient columns and bits of Venetian stone carving in the most unlikely places.

You can begin a **tour** of the upper village in the main square, opposite the church. Pass beneath a stone arch where there is a store, Lappa Avocado, selling local wine, herbs and olive oil as well as the village's avocado beauty products including soaps and skin creams. Here they will also give you an excellent free **map** which facilitates finding the village's many sights. Beyond the arch keep ahead to pass an elegant Venetian dwelling on the left with a **fine portal** bearing the legend *"Omnia Mundi Fumus et Umbra"* (All Things in This World are Smoke and Shadow). The street eventually climbs and the houses become brilliant white. This is not a tourist village however, and discreet glances inside open doorways will reveal the everyday work of the village women – rolling *bourekákia* pastries for the evening meal, peeling corncobs, or embroidering and repairing family clothing. This route will lead you past more crumbling Venetian houses, some being refurbished, to a superb **Roman mosaic floor** beneath a canopy on a street corner. Part of a third-century bath house, its quality is not only an indication of the wealth of the ancient town, but also of how much still lies buried beneath the modern village. Following the same street around the hill leads back to the arch and the main square.

At the south end of the upper village, beyond the church (itself flanked by more excavations from ancient Lappa), the village's **folk museum** (daily 10am–7pm; free) is worth a look. Assembled by the Zografakis family who have lived in Argiroúpolis for generations, the collection includes tapestries, farm implements, photos and ephemera, much of it passed down from their ancestors.

Heading downhill from the west side of the square along narrow, stepped streets, you come to a smaller square (the old **market place**), with a couple of tiny churches en route. At the northern end of the village beyond the *Agnantema* pension (see p.258), a pleasant walk will bring you to the delightful chapel of **Áyios Nikólaos**, dating from the eleventh century with fourteenth-century frescoes by Ioánnis Pagoménos (John the Frozen). To get there, take the first track right on the right off the road beyond the pension which descends into the valley; then take the first track on the left and descend to the church (which is unlocked), some 300m further.

Around Argiroúpolis

Ancient Lappa's **necropolis** lies just over a kilometre north of the town and can be reached by a signed footpath from the upper village. Located at a site known as the Five Virgins, after a nearby chapel, here hundreds of **tombs** – currently being investigated by archeologists – have been cut into the rock cliffs, many of them with elaborate interior and exterior decoration. The chapel takes its name from five young women put to death by the Romans in the third century for secretly practising Christianity in the tombs. The village commemorates their martyrdom on the first Tuesday after Easter when local shepherds bring their lambs to the shrine to be blessed, and fresh sheep's milk is boiled on site and drunk by those attending. Nearby is a gigantic 2000-year-old **plane tree** (claimed by locals to be the oldest in Crete, with a path cut through it), alongside yet another spring.

One place worth a walk or a drive is the nearby village of **Káto Póros**, a kilometre east as the crow flies, but a bit more by road. Delightfully bucolic and relatively untouched by the outside world, the village has quite a few ancient dwellings, many sprouting the uniquely Cretan herb *díktamos* (dittany) from cracks in their walls. There's even a small **taverna**, *Sarakas*, which will rustle up rations of whatever beast happens to have been slaughtered on a chopping block in the back.

Practicalities

In the midst of such spectacular walking terrain, anywhere else in Europe you would probably not be able to move for hikers. But here there's usually no problem finding a room – in fact you're spoilt for choice. A couple of excellent tavernas overlooking the Moussélas river valley to the south both offer **rooms**. First is *Rooms Zografakis* (☎28310 81269; ❸ including breakfast) with en-suite balcony rooms, whilst further along *Agnantema* (☎28310 81172; ❷) has great-value a/c en-suite balcony rooms – rooms 1 and 2 are the ones to go for – with a fantastic view down the valley and from its taverna terrace, probably giving it the edge for location. Down near the springs, *Rooms Argiroupolis* (☎28310 81148, ⓕ & ☎28310 81149; ❸ including breakfast) is another good option with en-suite rooms backing a large garden. *Apartments Alevizakis* (☎28310 81183; ❸), almost opposite *Mikedaki Rooms* (see p.255), has apartments with TV and kitchenette and will allow stays of one night. For stays of more than one night a number of other attractive **apartments** and houses are available in the village, for which Lappa Avocado (☎28310 81070), the shop beneath the arch on the square, can provide information. For **food**, besides the tavernas mentioned above and those by the springs, there is also the village's main bar on the square which can rustle up a range of *mezhédes* and is good for breakfast.

There are any number of superb **walks** to be done, many facilitated by the Petrákis *Réthimnon* map (see p.26). Seriously adventurous hikers can make a trek along the Pan-European E4 Footpath south along the Moussélas valley to follow the Kalikratiano Gorge, which reaches the sea around 25km away at

---

The vendettas of the Lefká Óri

Crete's Lefká Óri, or **White Mountains**, breed a race of folk among the toughest in Greece – people whom, so the Cretan saying goes, neither know how to forgive nor forget. **Blood feuds** are common in these mountainous regions, and resemble those of Sicily in the tight-lipped attitude towards authority that the locals adopt when outsiders from down below come prying. Fear of retribution is so great that no one wants to talk when the police attempt to investigate the acts of brutality that these feuds inspire.

The culmination of one long-running vendetta saw **Yiannis Mouzourakis**, a shepherd from Asigonía, take to the hills with his rifle in 1994 threatening to avenge the rape and murder of his mother and the death of his brother (both had been killed in an inter-family feud over grazing rights). The brother, father and cousin of the murderers were later found shot dead. When pursued, Mouzourakis sent a message to the police saying that he would be willing to give himself up, but only when he had completed the vendetta by killing the remaining relatives on his list.

The most notorious feud of all, between the Sfakían **Satzekakis and Pendaris families**, started in the 1940s and left 150 people dead before it finally ended in 1988. In recent years riot police have been sent out from Athens to patrol the pastures here, where sheep rustling still provokes venomous disputes, and in Sfakiá some villages have been completely abandoned because of vendettas. There are few who believe that the vendettas will ever end.

Frangokástello (see p.368). A track branches east off this to the resort of Plakiás (see p.286). Information on these and other walks in the area is available from Lappa Avocado (see p.257).

Miriokéfala

The road south from Argiroúpolis (leading out of the upper village beyond the church) allows visits to more villages and interesting churches. After 7km – with possible stops en route to explore the hamlets of Maroulóu and Arolíthi just off the road to left and right – the road passes through **Miriokéfala**, whose former monastery church of the **Panayía Antifonitria** has ancient **Byzantine frescoes** which are among the earliest examples of the period on the island. The tiny drum-domed edifice – located in a courtyard at the bottom of the village – has frescoes depicting the Passion dating from the eleventh and twelfth centuries, and its icon of the Virgin is held in great veneration locally. The church should be open, but the bar a little further along will be able to advise if not.

With your own transport there's a stunningly **scenic route** (also serving as the Pan-European E4 Footpath for this stretch) heading west from here, via the outlying hamlets of Kallikrátis and Ásfendos. This eventually joins up with the main Hánia–Hora Sfakíon road, just north of the village of Imbros with its beautiful gorge and accommodation possibilities (see p.264). From Miriokéfala to Kallikrátis the way is rough but not impassable by car, beyond which the 17km to Imbros is now asphalt. Alternatively, the former track from Asigonía (see below) to Imbros has been newly asphalted and makes for a smoother ride.

Asigonía

Beyond the tavernas in the lower village at Argiroúpolis (see p.256), the road continues southwest for 6km to **Asigonía**, an isolated rustic settlement at the end of a perpetually cloudy cul-de-sac. The superbly scenic road winds through the verdant cleft of the Gipari gorge where trees thrust skywards from a riverbed flowing with water all winter, but which lies arid in the summer drought. This habitat breeds a profusion of birdlife: as well as blue rock thrushes, pipits and the ubiquitous tits, you may also spot griffon vultures and hawks hovering around the crags.

The road finally arrives in Asigonía's broad *platía* – ringed by **busts** portraying Venizélou and associated village heroes, but curiously not its most celebrated recent son, **George Psychoundákis** (see p.339), now in his eighties. Psychoundákis's story of perilous wartime treks over the mountains delivering messages to the various intelligence outposts has now become part of island legend. It has to be said, though, that his status on his home turf lags far behind his international fame and, when his name is brought up, it is often pointed out that many did equally and more dangerous work in the resistance, but received few accolades for their efforts.

From the square, the **main street** climbs uphill between simple stone dwellings, their yards piled with the firewood needed to stave off the bitterly cold winters here. Many of the men still cling to the traditional *saríki* black headdress, baggy *vraka* trousers and high boots, and almost all still dress in black. The bars overlooking the square and along the main street – usually the haunt of taciturn card-playing farmers and shepherds at the end of the working day – are welcoming, although there are no places offering food or accommodation. With an economy firmly based on stockbreeding, it's hardly surprising that the village's most important **festival** (on April 23) involves flocks of sheep being brought at dawn to the church to be milked, sheared and dedicated to Áyios Yeóryios, their patron saint and protector. Village women then boil the milk on the spot and offer steaming cups of it to villagers and visitors.

The road south from Asigonía (now asphalted all the way to Imbros) forms part of the E4 Pan-European walking route. If you want a decent **hike**, from just before the hamlet of **Kallikrátis**, 10km south of Asigonía, a track heads east for 8km to Miriokéfala (see p.259). From here it's possible to return to Asigonía by way of Maroulloú (5km) or to continue 7km north to Argiroúpolis along an asphalt road. The slightly longer 27km trek from Asigonía to Imbros along the route of the E4 has been rendered less attractive to walkers now that it is completely asphalted; in your own vehicle, of course, it's a great drive.

East of Réthimnon: the coast road

Leaving Réthimnon to the east, you can strike almost immediately onto the **coast road**, which runs fast, flat and dull along the coastal plain, or follow the old road, squeezed into the narrow gap between this and the sea. On the latter route you'll pass through a string of village suburbs, connected now by an almost continuous string of hotel development for some 10km. At **Stavroménos** the old road cuts under the highway and heads inland; the new road continues to hug a featureless coastline dotted with rocky beaches, stands of reeds and piecemeal development, plus the odd luxury hotel. A little further east along the coast, the cheerful resorts of **Pánormos** and **Balí** are both welcoming places to rest up for a while, but the latter can get a bit overcrowded in high season.

Pánormos

Pánormos, 22km east of Réthimnon, marks a distinct break in topography: to the west is a long stretch of level coastline, to the east a spectacular, swooping mountain drive on the E75 highway which continues virtually all the way to Iráklion. Here, too, are the last of the large hotels for some time, curving round a headland above a small bay and beach.

The tiny village of Pánormos is just a short detour off the road, a pretty little place with a couple of bars and tavernas perched above the harbour and a small **sandy beach**. Happily, and unlike its neighbour Balí, it does not attract big crowds even in high season and as a result holds on to its appealing tranquillity. Surprisingly, this is also an ancient settlement (a minuscule river runs through to the sea) with the ruins of what was once a large sixth-century **basilica**, probably destroyed in the ninth-century Saracen invasion, and of a later **Genoese castle**. There are also quite a few new **rooms** places as well as the large hotel, so the beach sometimes fills up in midsummer, but there's usually space to breathe. However, development is low-key and the village has managed to retain a sleepy ambience, making it a relaxing place to spend a few days. In the village proper, *Lucy's Pension* (℡28340 51328; ❹) has sea-view balcony studio rooms with kitchenette as well as some attractive apartments near the harbour sleeping up to five (❺). Also on the harbour, *Captain's House* (℡28340 51352, ⓦwww.captainshouse.gr; ❹) has en-suite balcony rooms and apartments (❺). Near the centre of the village, *Taverna Panorama* (℡28340 51209, ⓕ28340 51403; ❷) has studio rooms with kitchenette, and more apartments near the beach sleeping up to four (❹). The latter is also a decent place for **food**, with tables on a pleasant garden terrace. Nearer the harbour,

Sofoklis is perhaps the best of the resort's tavernas (their *sfakiano* casserole with lamb cooked in wine is recommended), and around the small bay, *Agkyra* is another possibility for fresh fish.

Boat trips from the harbour go for day excursions to caves along the coast as well as to nearby Balí. Tickets cost around €15 and are available from the *Captain's House Taverna* on the waterfront.

Balí and around

BALÍ is a small resort set around a series of little coves, 9km east of Pánormos. Here the road descends briefly from the heights to a desolate patch of low ground behind a bay, occupied by a large garage (where the bus will drop you). Opposite the garage, a road runs around the bay towards the village; on foot, this is further than it looks – a couple of kilometres to the village, more to the best beach. What you see first, though, is a fair-sized pebbly beach at the end of the bay which often shelters a considerable collection of camper vans and tents. Sadly, although the beaches are still spectacular, they're very much over-run, and Balí has become a package resort too popular for its own good. Only well out of season, when there are bound to be bargains given the number of rooms here, is it worth staying.

Balí proper consists of three **coves**. The first has a pebbly beach and a couple of tavernas and rooms places: here, too, is the *Bali Beach Hotel* (☎28340 94210, ⓦ www.balibeach.gr; ⑥ inc. breakfast), the first and still much the most luxurious hotel. In the second cove is the original **village**, with most of the local stores as well as more hotels, rooms and tavernas. Here you could try *Mira Mare* (☎28340 94256; ③), which has excellent value a/c, en-suite, sea-view balcony rooms with fridge. One side of this cove has been concreted to form a **harbour** (there are day-trips by boat from Réthimnon), and on the other you can swim, though rarely with much space. A couple of good **tavernas** here are worth a try: *Sarlot* and the slightly cheaper *Alexander*, which specializes in steaks.

The third cove is known as **Paradise Beach**, and though it's still much the best for swimming – with a patch of sand and, on either side, crags of rock with level places to sunbathe – it's too crowded and overlooked to deserve the name any more. Two shady **tavernas** just above the beach make reasonable lunch stops however, and there are a couple of rooms places, including the swish *Hotel Nostos* (☎ & ⓕ 28340 94310; ⑥), where a/c rooms have good sea views but no TV. If you stay overnight you could have Paradise Beach all to yourself in the early-morning sun, when you may be able to appreciate why it got its name. Slightly outside the cove, but still well sheltered within the larger bay, are a couple of rocks to dive from. It's a beautiful place to splash about, surrounded by mountains which seem to rise direct from the sea to impressive heights. Behind this beach, Elpis (☎28340 94444) hires out **mountain bikes**, cars and scooters for rentals of three days or more.

A good viewpoint to appreciate Balí's setting, and a more peaceful place to break your journey, is the tiny part-ruined, part-restored seventeenth-century **Monastery of Áyios Ioánnis** (daily 9am–noon & 4–7pm), reached by a good road to the north of the coast road, about five minutes west of the resort by car. The monastery church has some fragmentary seventeenth-century frescoes and there's a serene garden fronting the monks' cells (only one monk now remains), but its reputation among Cretans today is for an energetic role in the struggle against Turkish rule, for which it was bombarded in 1866 by the Turkish navy.

East of Balí, the next access to the coast is at Ayía Pelayía (see p.113), 25km further on. Nor is there much else to stop for: **Síses**, 12km east of Balí, has

Save the turtle

This stretch of coast is one of the main breeding areas of the **loggerhead sea turtle**, now on the list of endangered species. Until recently turtles were common throughout the Mediterranean, but the demands placed on the environment by both tourism and industry have led to many of their breeding habitats being developed or polluted. A sea-going creature for most of its life, the turtle must return to a beach – always the same one – in order to lay its eggs, and the stretch of coastline between the city of Réthimnon and Skaléta is now the second largest nesting area for loggerheads in the Mediterranean. Once these beaches are developed, the turtles, governed by powerful homing instincts, are unable to relocate to another and will die infertile. Unfortunately, nesting also occurs from early June to the end of August, coinciding with the high point of the tourist season. Once the female has buried her eighty to a hundred eggs on a nocturnal visit to the beach, the eggs must then remain undisturbed for a period of two months, before the hatchlings emerge to head for the sea. But even should they avoid being skewered by a beach umbrella or crushed by the feet of bathers – both common hazards – further dangers lie ahead for the newborn turtles. When they emerge, many of them, instead of heading for the sea, guided by the brightness of the horizon, are instead lured inland by artificial lights from hotel and tourist developments, and perish from exhaustion or dehydration. Emblematic of Crete's and Greece's problem of balancing tourist development and the needs of the environment, it remains to be seen whether the loggerhead turtle will avoid the fate of the dodo.

For **information** on programmes to protect the turtle, making donations or becoming a volunteer, contact the Sea Turtle Protection Society of Greece, PO Box 30, 74100 Réthimnon (℡28310 72288, ⊛www.archelon.gr).

wonderful views from its perch beside the highway and a few rooms, but little else. From Síses village a badly rutted track cuts up to the old road. Don't be deceived by maps which show some kind of way through above Balí – there is no other practicable route inland between Pánormos (from where there's a good road to Pérama) and Fódhele.

The foothills of the Psilorítis

Taking the old roads east from Réthimnon, inland through the **foothills of the Psilorítis** range, there are a variety of routes and a number of interesting detours. The old main road, through Dhamásta, has least to offer, though it's a pretty enough drive. Striking higher into the mountains is more rewarding. For a combination of relatively easy driving and interest, the best option is the road up through Garázo and Axós to **Anóyia**, though you can also reach Axós on the even higher, stunningly scenic road from **Pérama**. Possible detours along the way include the scenically sited archeological site of **Arhéa Eléftherna**, and the remarkable caves of **Melidhóni** and **Sendóni**, both holding spectacular natural wonders. The route concludes at the village of Anóyia, a village famed for its textiles and a gateway to the summit of Psilorítis.

Margarítes

Whichever route you follow, you'll leave the coast at Stavroménos – where a Minoan cemetery has recently been discovered behind the *Astrid Hotel* – and head up through Viranepiskopí. The first potential detour comes some 5km further on, a right turn for 4km to **Margarítes**, which has a long tradition of pottery manufacture. The village is scattered with workshops, and you can buy the results in many outlets along the steep main street. While most of the output is fairly unsophisticated, one of the best places is the workshop of Níkos Kavgalákis on the village's southern edge. Jovial Níkos not only turns out a variety of pots, but also the enormous Ali Baba jars, or *píthoi*, similar to those found in the Minoan palaces and still used throughout agricultural Crete today. Recently a new market has opened up for the *píthoi* – they're now in great demand in northern Europe as the latest thing in domestic garden ornaments.

On the village's attractive **upper platía**, the shady terrace of the main **bar** overlooks the Margeritsanos valley, and is a good place to relax. Just downhill from here, towards the lower *platía*, *Lappa* is a café/shop selling wine, olive oil, honey and spices from the region. For **places to stay**, the most pleasant option is the brand new *Taverna I Velandia* (☎28340 92520; ❷), with en-suite balcony rooms with TV above a taverna. It lies almost opposite the workshop of Níkos Kavgalákis (see above). Among the cafés near the centre of the village *Taverna Gianousakis* (☎288340 92255; ❷) offers rooms with bath. A more pleasant option is *Irini Rooms* (☎28340 92494, ✉spmik39@yahoo.com; ❸), with good-value en-suite rooms and a fully equipped apartment (for the same price) at the bottom of the village, off the lower *platía*; however, the proprietor's house (signed) is at the top of the village close to Níkos Kavgalákis's workshop.

Arhéa Eléftherna and Eléftherna

Beyond Margarítes, the road climbs for 4km to the village of **ARHÉA ELÉFTHERNA** where, opposite a fountain, a paved way on the right leads after 200m to a parking place by the *Acropolis Taverna*, a good lunch stop. The taverna is perched on the edge of an archeological site dominated by the spectacularly sited acropolis of ancient Eléftherna. The city that stood here in ancient times was one of the most important of eighth- and seventh-century BC Dorian Crete. When the Romans came in search of conquest in 67 BC it put up a stiff resistance, and later flourished as the seat of a Christian bishop. The Saracen invasions finished it off, however, and only recently has excavation of the site recommenced (by the University of Crete) after British archeologists packed up and left in 1929.

Beyond the taverna the path leads across a stretch of level rock, part of the original approach, carved in ancient times to resemble paving stones. Imposingly situated on a high promontory between two watercourses, the **acropolis** proper lies beyond a hefty *pírgos* or **tower** (which in large part still stands). Soon after this, follow a path which descends to the left to reach the remarkable **Roman cisterns** carved into the hill's west side, where enormous supporting pillars of solid rock support a vast cavernous interior. Nearby are the remains of the aqueduct which fed them. Proceeding north along a path which climbs back to the acropolis, you will find significant fragments of massive walls and ancient buildings – not always easy to make sense of – and the roofless ruined church of **Ayía Ánna**, still revered as a shrine by locals who come to light candles here. Almost certainly located on the site of an earlier church, the tiny shrine still retains some poignant fresco fragments, sadly exposed to the elements, as well as a couple of ancient altars, once witnesses to pagan sacrifices but now with a Christian function. More remains lie still further north on the acropolis's tip where, by looking east into the valley, you can see the remarkable **new excavations** of the ancient town below.

Directly beneath the northern edge of the acropolis in Eléftherna's recently excavated **necropolis** on the valley floor, archeologists made a potentially very significant discovery: traces of a **human sacrifice** made in front of the funeral pyre of some local magnate. It apparently dates from the late eighth century BC, about the same time that Homer was describing very similar sacrifices of Trojan prisoners in front of the funeral pyre of Achilles. The victim, who was bound hand and foot before ritually having his throat cut, may well have been expected to serve the dead man in the next world: also found in front of the pyre were sacrificed animals and offerings of perfume and food. Other cremations on the site (some twenty have been found, though only one human sacrifice) had offerings including gold, jewellery and fine pottery, as well as four tiny, superbly crafted **ivory heads** which are among the best work of their time (ca.600 BC) yet discovered anywhere. These and other finds from the necropolis are displayed in the archeological museum at Réthimnon.

The new excavations and the Hellenistic bridge

The new excavations below the acropolis to the east have uncovered a significant part of Hellenistic and Roman Eléftherna. Although there's a **path** down from the necropolis, the way isn't always clear and necessitates scrambling through the olive groves. For more convenient access, return to the turn-off before the *Acropolis Taverna* and backtrack slightly in the direction of Margarites in order to take a road signed "Archeological Site" on the left just before the tenth-century Byzantine chapel of **Ayía Anna & Christos Soter**. Incidentally, this beautiful little church, dominated by a massive cypress tree, is worth a look: inside there's a fine twelfth-century *Pantokrátor* in the dome, the only surviving **fresco** of what must once have been a glorious painted interior. Following the dirt road to the archeological excavations, keep ahead downhill until you come to a white cabin used by the site's guardian. You should leave any transport here; the site is a short distance ahead. Many dwellings and a number of fine **Roman villas** with well-preserved mosaics fragments are already visible. One of these has a curious "garden seat" covered with mosaic decoration, and between the houses run paved streets complete with drains and sewers, and dotted with numerous altars. The excavations will continue in the coming years and this is set to become a site of major importance. Unfortunately, plans to open the site to the public – complete with a museum to display the finds – have stalled, and at the time of writing the whole area has been securely fenced off, forcing you to peer through wire mesh to get a glimpse of the excavations.

A remarkable stone-built **Hellenistic bridge** lies in the valley below the acropolis. With your own transport you should head 2km west to Arhéa Eléftherna's twin village, **Eléftherna**, which has a delightful new **place to stay** – *Villa Antigone* (T 28340 23517; 3), at the northern end of the village, with roomy studios with kitchen and balcony spaced around a pool with great views; they'll even give reductions for stays of more than one night. A track on the right at the edge of the village as you enter (signed "Ancient Eléftherna") will bring you eventually to the bridge. Once on the track (which is drivable) keep going downhill, taking the left fork as it descends into the valley. Follow this track, soon passing a parking area which is being made ready for visitors, to a new excavation area visible behind a fence across the valley, for a good kilometre. You will eventually descend to the valley floor and the track soon climbs out of the valley on the opposite flank. It winds to another fork, where you again keep left; the bridge – about 150m beyond this – lies in the river valley (often dry in summer) to the left of the road. It is not signed and, when there is dense foliage on the trees, easy to miss. When you do reach it, however, the effort is worthwhile, for the bridge, standing five metres high and three deep and employing a **vaulted arch**, is almost perfectly intact, still capable of carrying traffic across the river. Beneath the arch is a washing and bathing place cut into the rock, and it is likely that this, too, is of a similar date. A **chapel** in the cliff above is built into a cave and may well occupy the site of an ancient shrine.

There's a practicable **walk** along a section of the E4 Pan-European footpath from Eléftherna to the monastery of **Arkádhi** (see p.252), less than 5km southwest as the crow flies; you can pick up the route on the western edge of the village and it is marked on the Harms–Verlag map (see p.26). There is also an asphalted road to the monastery from Eléftherna.

From Pérama to Axós

Pérama is a substantial agricultural centre which also has a little light industry and a businesslike main street lined with banks, stores and cafés. Its chief interest is in the rarity value of seeing a Cretan town of such size that owes nothing whatever to tourism. Even if you do no more than drive through it's a refreshing sight, and you may well find yourself passing this way more than once if you take one of the local detours available.

The Melidhóni Cave

The most obvious detour in these parts is to **Melidhóni**, 5km northeast of Pérama. The village itself is unremarkable, but a thirty-minute walk (or a short drive, signed from the village) leads to the **Melidhóni Cave** (daily 9am–7pm; €3 including free map), one of the most impressive on the island. The awesome central chamber is a geological cathedral thick with gigantic stalactites, stalagmites and bunches of mighty "organ pipes" soaring between petrified "draperies", spectacular curtain-like folds formed by the calcium deposits.

In mythology this was the legendary home of **Talos**, a bronze giant who protected the coasts of Crete by striding around the island hurling rocks at unfriendly ships; the Argonauts were greeted thus when they approached. Excavations in the cave have shown that it was inhabited during the Neolithic period and later was an important shrine for the **Minoans**, who may have worshipped their fertility goddess Eileíthyia here. The Greeks and Romans transformed it into a shrine to the god **Hermes Tallaios**, evidenced by thousands of inscriptions etched into the walls of one of the cave's inner chambers (not on view).

The Melidhóni Cave was also the setting for one of the most horrific **atrocities** in the struggle for Cretan independence. Here, in 1824, around three hundred local villagers took refuge, as they had often done before at time of war, in the face of an advancing army. This time, however, the Muslim commander demanded that they come out. When the Cretans refused, and shot two messengers sent to offer safe conduct, he tried to force them out by blocking the mouth of the cave with stones and cutting off the air supply. After several days of this, with the defenders opening new air passages every night, the troops changed their tactics, piling combustible materials in front of the cave and setting light to them; everyone inside was asphyxiated. The bodies were left where they lay for the cave to become their tomb, and ten years later Robert Pashley became one of the first to enter since the tragedy, to find in places "the bones and skulls of the poor Christians so thickly scattered, that it is almost impossible to avoid crushing them as we pick our steps along". This grisly event was far from unique: numerous other caves around the island have similar histories, although none claimed so many victims. A **shrine** near the entrance to the cave today commemorates the dead. Next to the ticket office there's also a small **café**, run with diner-style efficiency and banter by a friendly Greek family who previously lived in the United States.

Axós and around

Back through Pérama, the main road wends along the valley of the Yeropótamos all the way to the turning for the small village of **Garázo**. The simple roadside cafés here are friendly and exceptionally good value, although few people seem to stop here. Three kilometres beyond the village a signed turn-off leads 1km to the peaceful **Moní Dioskoúri**. A charming monastic retreat with neatly ordered cells circling the tiny church of Áyios Yeóryios, this is a particularly serene place in the early evening when the monks fill the place with singing, and incense from the church wafts around the small courtyard.

Four kilometres further on, **Axós** makes a surprisingly hectic contrast to Garázo – especially if you arrive at lunchtime. The main road through the village is lined with mostly rather poor weaving and embroidery for sale and with tavernas crowded with tourists. This is largely because the village serves as a lunch-stop for "Photo-Safari" day-trips from Iráklion and Réthimnon. If you catch it without the crowds, Axós is undeniably attractive; the small church of **Ayía Iríni** (if it's locked, try ringing the priest on ☏28340 61311) dates from the fourteenth century and contains significant, if damaged, frescoes. The site of a **post-Minoan settlement** (signed from the centre "Ancient Axós"), also called Axós, is barely accessible on a ridge above the village, with not much above ground to see should you reach it.

The alternative upper road from Pérama arrives in Axós by the church, first passing through **Livádhia** and **Zonianá**, two rather tumbledown, straggly but atmospheric villages, as traditional as any you'll find in Crete. Should you pass through either in the early evening at weekends, you're likely to find what seems to be the entire population out in the streets, the elders in traditional dress and the young keen for a chance to try out their English. Just beyond Zonianá, 500m up a side road on the village's eastern edge, you have the chance to visit the **Sendóni Cave** (daily: April–Oct 9am–6pm; Nov–March 10am–4pm; guided visits €3), with a magnificent display of stalactites, stalagmites and petrified waves, many over five million years old. Enthusiatic and knowledgeable guides conduct you through a vast tunnel-like cavern, fitted with a series of walkways extending some 500m or so into a spur of Mount Ida. Local legend has it that the cave was discovered by an eight-year-old girl who, lured away by fairies, was later found dead in its darkest recesses. The entrance fee is intended to finance the construction of more walkways to penetrate still deeper into the cave, which is known to extend at least another kilometre beyond what is already on view. This will also allow the somewhat spooky pleasure of viewing some miniature bats which are known to breed there.

Anóyia

The road from Pérama heads through Axós to **ANÓYIA**, a small town perched beneath the highest peaks of the Psilorítis range. It is the obvious place from which to approach the **Idean Cave** and, for the committed, the **summit of Psiloritís** itself. The weather, refreshingly cool when the summer heat lower down is becoming oppressive, is one good reason to come, but most people are drawn by the proximity of the mountains or by a reputation for some of the best woven and embroidered **handicrafts** in Crete. The last is greatly exaggerated but the town still makes a very pleasant break from the coast. The impression gleaned as you look around is of a prosperous place, a fact underlined by the many pricey bars along the main street, something not usually seen this far from the coastal strip. The source of all this wealth is stockbreeding; the sheep farmers here are some of the richest in Greece, which is why you'll find a gentlemen's club in the upper town, where the wealthiest of these barons do their wheeling and dealing in opulent surroundings.

The Town

As you drive through, it seems that Anóyia has two quite distinct halves: from what appears to be the older, **lower town**, the road takes a broad loop around, to re-emerge near the modern-looking Platía Meídani of the **upper town**. In many ways this appearance is deceptive. A series of steep, sometimes stepped alleys connect the two directly, and however traditional the buildings may look, closer inspection shows that most are actually concrete. This reflects a tragic recent history – the village was one of those destroyed in 1944 as reprisal for the abduction of General Kreipe (see p.422), and at the same time all the men who could be rounded up here were summarily executed. The local handicrafts tradition is in part a reflection of this history, both a conscious attempt to revive the town and the result of bitter necessity, with so large a proportion of the local men killed. At any rate it seems to have worked, and large numbers of these surviving elderly widows (accompanied now by their daughters) are anxious to subject any passing visitor to their terrifyingly aggressive sales techniques.

The impression of an old and a new town persists even when you know it to be false. The upper half of the village has almost all the **accommodation** options as well as the bank (no foreign exchange) and post office, police, most of the non-tourist stores and the large **Platía Meídani**, lined with bars where the younger residents hang out. Walk the lanes between the two halves of town and there's a real country atmosphere: empty houses and garages closed up with wire and used to stable livestock; goats and pigs grazing in vacant lots; and more workshop/homes where the craftswomen have set up showrooms in their front parlours.

The more antique feel of the lower town is reinforced by the elderly men, baggy trousers tucked into their black boots, moustaches bristling, who sit at the *kafenía* tables on the focal **Platía Livádhi**, and by the black-clad women sitting outside their textile stores nearby. The curious **sculptures** flanking a statue in this square – a wooden carving of Venizélos, arm in a sling with a curious bird sculpture dangling from the tree overhead – are the work of revered local sculptor Algiliadi Skoulas, who died in 1996. Yéorgos Skoulas has opened a **museum** (daily 9am–7pm; free) to his father, reached by turning right behind the Venizélos statue and continuing along the line of textile shops to turn left uphill; the museum is on the right. The exhibits are a collection of Skoulas senior's bizarre sculptures and paintings, whose naive simplicity his son will explain with enthusiasm. Skoulas junior often treats visitors to a performance on the *lyra* – on which he's a deft exponent – and he may even throw in a *mantináda* vocal. There's not a great deal else in the way of sights, although enthusiasts may wish to visit the fourteenth-century church of **Áyios Ioánnis** on the main street, which has some well-preserved wall paintings.

Anóyia is a noted centre of **lyra music** – many of the greatest performers on the instrument have come from the town. The late Níkos Xylouris was a shepherd who made his own *lyra* and taught himself to play, and whose performances and compositions turned him into a Cretan legend in the 1960s and 1970s. The house where he was born is now *Kafenion Xylouris*, on the lower square, although little is served here but *raki* and house wine. His brother, Psarantonis, is also a great talent and continues to live in the town.

Practicalities

Anóyia sees a lot of day-trippers, but most stay only an hour or so. Linger a while, or stay overnight, and it's surprisingly uncommercial. It shouldn't normally be hard to find a **room** in the upper half of town, where you'll see signs leading off all along the main street. A couple of the best places are located on Odhós Pándidoni, the road that swings left (east) from the lower square. About 500m along the road as it climbs you'll come to the flower-bedecked *Rooms Aris* (℡ 28340 31460, ℻ 28430 31058; ❷) with en-suite rooms, quickly followed by the friendly *Hotel Aristea* (℡ 28340 31459; ❸ including breakfast), which has en-suite rooms with TV and sensational balcony views. There are more rooms places along Kendriko Dhrómos, the upper town's main street, such as *Rooms Kriti* (℡ 28340 31048; ❷), but the location is not as attractive.

In recent years a number of tavernas have opened along the main street making it easier than before to find **food**. Wherever you eat, ask to sample the local **cheese**, which is excellent. One taverna on the main road where it loops out of the lower village is *Prasini Folia*; it has a large open-air space for dancing and occasionally hosts "Cretan Evening" tours. It can be depressing when it's full with rowdy coastal revellers and just as disappointing when it's cavernously empty. You're best off going to the grill places on the lower square, where the choice will most likely be limited to whatever happens to be on the spit (usually succulent lamb). In the upper village beyond the *Hotel Aristea* on the right, *Taverna Mitato* is a decent restaurant, but also very popular with the bus-tour crowds from the coast. Your best bet for some peace and a fantastic view from its terrace is *Taverna Skalomata*, on the upper edge of town on the road out to Mount Psilorítis and the Idean Cave – an easy hop by car but a bit of a hike on foot. The barbecued lamb is again the thing to go for. Incidentally, over the road from here *Café@Internet* is Anóyia's solitary **Internet** café. If you're looking for an original souvenir you might want to check out Tarrha Glass, a small **glass factory** at the top of the town (on the road out to the Nídha plateau), which has stylish but pricey glass ornaments and vases made on the premises. The proprietor's fully restored sky-blue 1968 Triumph Herald convertible usually stands outside, making it much easier to locate.

Mount Psilorítis and its caves

Heading for the mountains, a smooth road swiftly ascends the 21km from Anóyia to an altitude of 1400m, to reach the **Nídha plateau** at the base of **Mount Psilorítis**. It's a steady climb most of the way, and a road travelled little except by the shepherds who pasture their sheep up here (and who nowadays travel back and forth by pick-up). Along the way in late spring, as the snow recedes, you'll see myriad wildflowers and, at all times, quite a few birds, including vultures and magnificent golden eagles, a stirring image as they glide imperiously across their mountain domain. The *mitáta* or stone huts close to

The memorial to peace

At the northern end of the Nídha plateau, German artist Karen Raeck has constructed a **rock sculpture** entitled *Immortal Freedom Fighter of Peace*, commemorating the suffering of the town of Anóyia at the hands of the German army in 1944 (see p.267). A one-woman reconciliation mission between her homeland and Anóyia, Raeck has spent most of the last twenty years living in the town and has gained the respect and trust of its inhabitants. The monument, measuring 30m by 9m, consists of a large number of huge boulders laid out in an impressionistic image of a winged figure when viewed from the air. The shepherds of the plateau assisted Raeck in carrying and positioning the stones, and during the work's assembly she lived in one of their stone huts. The sculpture is visible from the terrace of the *Taverna Nida*, and staff there have information about it and will point it out if asked; an excursion to see it at close quarters makes for a very pleasant stroll across the plateau.

the roadside – many of them ruined – are former shepherds' dwellings where traditionally sheep's milk yoghurt and cheese would be made, although many are now used as dog kennels and even chicken coops. Somewhere near the highest point a signed road leads off left for 3km to the **Skinakas Observatory**, sitting atop the peak of the same name. This is open to the public on certain Sundays throughout the summer – the dates should be posted on a board at the start of the road. A little further along, a track to the right goes to the **ski area**: an unlikely thought in summer, although it does see plenty of snow in season. Soon after, the small plateau and its bare summer pastures fan out below you, and the road – the last section unpaved – drops to skirt around its western edge.

The Idean Cave

At what is effectively the end of the road (shortly beyond, it peters out in a network of trails across the plateau), a modern **visitors' centre** stands looking over the plain, a half-derelict shell these days due to money from the state not being provided for its completion or upkeep. In one corner of this extensive building, *Taverna Nida* (T28340 31141; April–Sept daily; rest of year Sat & Sun only) serves hearty **taverna** standards and has a couple of **rooms** (2) sharing a bathroom. Stelios Stavrakakis, the friendly proprietor, is a fount of information on the plateau and can advise (in Greek) on the viability of walking routes in the mountains, as well as likely weather conditions.

Opposite the taverna, a path (about a 15min walk) leads up to the celebrated **Idean Cave** (Idhéon Ándhron), a rival of that on Mount Dhíkti (see p.176) for the title of **Zeus's birthplace**. Although scholarly arguments rage over the exact identity of the caves in the legends of Zeus, and over the interpretation of the various versions of the legend, locals are in no doubt that the Idean Cave is the place where the god was brought up, suckled by wild animals. Certainly this hole in the mountainside, which as Cretan caves go is not especially large or impressive, was associated from the earliest of times with the cult of Zeus, and at times ranked among the most important centres of pilgrimage in the Greek world. Pythagoras visited the cave, Plato set *The Laws* as a dialogue along the pilgrimage route here, and the finds made within indicate offerings brought from all over the eastern Mediterranean. Recent excavations have revealed that the cave cult had a much longer history than this, too. First signs of occupation go back as far as 3000 BC, and though it may then have been a mere place of shelter, by the Minoan era it was already established as a shrine, maintaining this role until about 500 AD.

The cave and the area around it are something of a disappointment when you finally get there, with more the feel of a mining operation than an important historical site. A major – and prolonged – **archeological dig** has now been completed and the cave is once again open, but a number of railway tracks leading away from it which were used to carry the tons of rock and rubble from these excavations remain, giving the place a rather unattractive prospect. When you've descended the concrete steps into the depths, the cave turns out to be a fairly shallow affair, devoid of even natural wonders and certainly not a patch on the dramatic interior of the Dhiktean Cave.

To the summit of Mount Psilorítis

The *Taverna Nída* and visitors' centre also mark the start of the way (now forming a stretch of the E4 Pan-European footpath) to the summit of **Psilorítis** (Mount Ida) which, at 2456m, is the highest mountain in Crete. Though it's not for the unwary or unfit, the climb should present few problems to experienced, properly equipped hikers, and there are also **guided ascents** from Thrónos (see p.277). The route, which diverts from the path to the Idean Cave just beyond the small spring and chapel, is marked with red arrows in addition to the E4 waymarkers – a guide who knows the mountain would be useful, since it's not always obvious which is the main trail, but is by no means essential. The Petrákis *Crete Trekking and Road Map* for Réthimnon (see p.26) is the best trekker's **map** available for this area and clearly marks the routes described here. Don't attempt the ascent alone, however, as you could face a very long wait for help if you were to run into trouble. If you do make the climb, allow for a seven-to-eight-hour return trip to the chapel at the summit, though in spring thick snow may slow you down. It's wise to carry enough food, water and warm gear to be able to overnight in one of the shelters should the

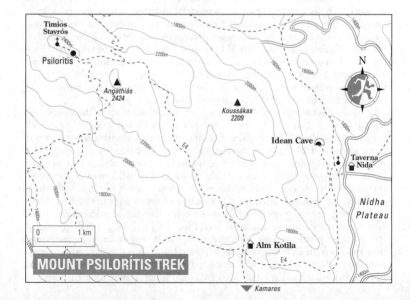

MOUNT PSILORÍTIS TREK

weather turn; in any event a night at the top, with the whole island laid out in the sunset and sunrise, is a wonderful experience.

For the first thirty minutes or so **the climb** trails south across the mountainside, a gradual ascent until you reach a gully where it starts in earnest. Head west here, away from the plain, on a rocky path up the left-hand side of the gully. After about an hour and a quarter of this you reach an open height with a stone shelter and good views back the way you came. Don't follow the most obvious trail at this point, which leads only to one of the lesser peaks, Koussákas (2209m), but instead follow the ridge downhill and south, unlikely as this may look. After barely fifteen minutes at Alm Kollita you reach a basin where several trails meet, and where there is spring water and **stone huts** for shelter. The vertiginous trail south from here leads to Kamáres, some 7km distant (see below). You, however, should turn right (northwest) and an obvious uphill trail will eventually take you to a ridge skirting the north slope of Angathiás (2424m) and on all the way to the summit (on clear days the sea can be made out to the north). However, it is only in the last twenty minutes that the peak of Psilorítis itself becomes visible and the ground starts to fall away to reveal just how high you are.

The **summit** is marked by another shelter and the chapel of **Tímios Stavrós** ("Holy Cross" – a name by which the peak is sometimes known locally), inside which Níkos Kazantzákis famously claimed to have lost his virginity. Nearby there's water in a cistern, which you should boil or purify before drinking. A picnic on the roof of the island is an unforgettable experience, and on a clear day the spectacular **panoramas** from the summit – including the Lefká Óri (White Mountains) rising in the west and the Dhíkti massif to the east – make the climb well worthwhile. Usually, though, conditions are very cold and windy, and the views are spoilt by cloud or heat haze.

Routes to and from Kamáres and Vorízia

There are any number of **alternate routes** up and down the mountain. From the west you can climb from virtually any of the Amári villages below the peak (most notably Fourfourás; see p.278), but although this is relatively straightforward in the sense that you can see the peak almost all the way, there are no real trails and you may run into difficulty with patches of thorny undergrowth or loose scree (although as this is now another stretch of the E4 Pan-European footpath it should be waymarked).

South of the mountain, Kamáres and Vorízia are possible trailheads. Descending from the summit, the trail down to Nídha divides in the basin mentioned in the account above. If you head south from the basin, a trail, that is not hard to follow but is a good deal steeper and longer than anything outlined above, takes about four hours down to **Kamáres**. About halfway, there's a junction with a trail to the huge **Kamáres Cave**, in which the first great cache of the elaborate pottery known as Kamáres ware was found (it's now in the Iráklion Archeological Museum). From the cave you either backtrack to this trail to continue to Kamáres village or carry on east to another trail, equally steep, which ends up in Vorízia, 4km west of Kamáres. Kamáres has both **rooms** and **food**: the misnamed *Hotel Psilorítis* (☏28920 43290; ❶), which is in fact a basic rooms place, has rooms in the centre sharing bath. The hotel no longer has a sign, although it *is* still open: ask in the village for directions. There are a couple of tavernas, one at each end of the village, the best of which is *Taverna Bournelis*, close to the start of the steep Psilorítis trail at the village's western end; the proprietors can advise on the testing ascent, which takes about five or six hours to the summit and back, but in Greek or German only. Kamáres has at least one **bus** a day to Míres.

The wildest cat in Crete

In Cretan myth and legend there have long been told tales of the *fourokattos* ("furious cat"), a centuries-old name which refers to a **wildcat** living in the mountains of Psilorítis. Although in 1905 two skins from such a beast were purchased at the market in Haniá by a British woman attached to a scientific mission, for most of the last century scientists regarded the existence of such a beast as impossible. They also dismissed as incredible the stories of shepherds and goatherds who claimed to have seen this wild cat.

Then, in 1996, an Italian university team studying the carnivores of the Cretan mountains were astonished when they returned to their traps one morning to find they had snared a five-and-a-half-kilo wildcat. The news created a sensation as the beast was taken to the University of Crete for study. Tawny in colour and with a snarl like a tiger, the cat does not belong to the species of cats on the mainland of Greece and the rest of Europe; its nearest relative is a species inhabiting North Africa and Cyprus. Scientists believe that it is an extremely reclusive and fully nocturnal animal, which explains why it is so rarely seen.

The cat's discovery has not only proven generations of Cretans to have been right, but has turned the zoological history of the island upside down. Scientists are now puzzling over how it got to Crete in the first place – was the cat perhaps brought over as a domesticated beast by the ancestors of the Minoans, or has it been on Crete since the island became separated from the mainland? And – the question that the Cretan media have been asking ever since the discovery – are there any more?

If you're prepared to stay at the *Taverna Nída* or camp on the plateau (there's plenty of water but conditions can be very cold), another attractive option is to tackle the peak up and down in one day, and continue south next day from the Nídha plateau on a beautiful and relatively easy hike, four hours or so down to **Vorízia**, five or six to Kamáres. For either, track around to the southern edge of the plateau, where a gully (which shortly after becomes a considerable ravine) leads off. Large red arrows direct you towards Kamáres on the trail which passes east of the Kamáres Cave. For Vorízia, follow the ravine for about an hour until a faint trail climbs out on the left (soon after this, the stream bed becomes impassable). Above the ravine there are fine views and a heady drop for another hour, when you must turn left (east) again. This is not obvious, but you should begin to see signs of life – goat trails and shepherds' huts. You cut past the top of a second, smaller ravine to a stone hut and then descend, zigzagging steeply, to a dirt road and Vorízia village, 4km east of Kamáres, where there is no food or accommodation.

Spíli and around

The pleasant country town of **SPÍLI**, tucked into the folds of the Mount Kédhros foothills 30km south of Réthimnon, is the trailhead for plenty of wild country **hikes**. The town doesn't look much as you drive through, though the mountainside which towers over the houses is impressive, but if you get off the main road, into the white-walled alleys which wind upwards towards the cliff, it can be very attractive. A sharp curve in the road marks the centre of town, by a small *platía* overlooked by lofty plane trees. Just above this there's a prodigious 25-spouted **fountain** constructed in the 1960s to replace an elegant

Venetian fountain, which was removed to a less exalted position alongside the health centre (see below). Beyond the fountain begins a steep mosaic of flowered balconies, cobbled lanes, shady archways, giant urns and whitewashed chimneypots. On occasion, Spíli can become quite crowded – many of the bus tours passing along the road make a brief stop here, usually for lunch – but between times and in the evenings it is quiet and rural. Stay overnight and you'll be woken early by the sounds of the farmyard and an agricultural community starting work.

There are numerous places offering **rooms** spread out along the main road – the flower-decked *Green Hotel* (T 28320 22225; ❷) at the north end of town is a possibility, although the rooms are rather drab. Just behind, however, is a delightful smaller pension, *Heracles* (T 28320 22411, E heraclespapadakis @hotmail.com; ❷; reductions for more than one night), with spotless en-suite balcony rooms. The genial and eponymous proprietor here also rents out **mountain bikes**, is an authority on walking in the area, will exchange money and sells his own honey, jams, *raki* and olive oil. Just along the road from these two towards the centre of the village lies *Rooms Costas* (T 28320 22040, F 28320 23040; ❷ inc. breakfast), another possibility for pleasant en-suite balcony rooms with TV.

Of the few **eating** places, *Taverna Stratidakis*, between the fountain and the *Green Hotel*, is a good bet, as is *Taverna Giannis* (50m beyond the fountain on the Ayía Galíni road). A right turn off the same road at the edge of the village leads to *Taverna Panorama*, with great balcony views and a good kitchen. The pleasant *Café Babis*, over the road from the fountain, is good for **breakfasts** (local yoghurt and honey are excellent), evening drinking and serves as one of the village's two **Internet** cafés; the other, *Milos*, is across the road opposite the multi-spouted fountain. One surprising and very attractive new bar is *Rastoni*, on a hill at the north end of the village, which has a superb **pool** that is free to use (day and night) for the price of a drink. It lies on the edge of the village just off the new road to Yerakári, up a lane on the right. Almost everything else you're likely to need is clustered around the fountain square, including most of the local stores and businesses: there's a **post office** and **bank** (with ATM) on the main road, and a metered **phone** in the souvenir/newspaper store on the corner by the fountain, as well as cardphone kiosks along the main street.

Walks around Spíli

Plenty of challenging **hikes** start in Spíli. The one across to Yerakári in the Amári valley formerly seemed something of an achievement, but these days the new road linking the two places (spectacular drive though it is) undermines it somewhat. All the routes described below are marked in detail on the Petrákis *Réthimno* map (see p.26).

One **easy walk** through the hills surrounding Spíli and which can also be done in high summer starts out from Spíli's health centre, up a side road on the left 300m along the Ayía Galíni road. A path to the right just before the health centre leads 75m to the site of the Venetian fountain which once stood in Spíli's central *platía*. The walk starts by keeping ahead beyond the health centre to a T-junction. Cross the road and go through an improvised gate (actually the base of an old bed) on the opposite side, then climb the steep rise following the red or green paint marks. You will eventually pass through a **gorge**, which opens out into a plain where there is an olive grove. Beyond the olive grove you'll meet a broad track; turn right along this, soon passing an old spring and picnic area followed by the ancient chapel of Áyios Pnefma. A kilometre or so

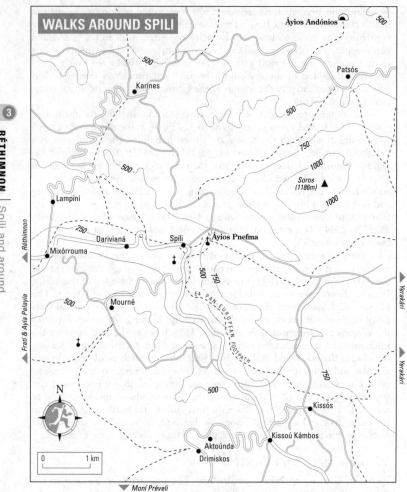

WALKS AROUND SPILI

Áyios Andónios

Patsós

Karínes

500

500

500

500

750

1000

Soros
(1186m) ▲

1000

Lampiní

250

Dariviá

Spíli

Áyios Pnefma

Réthimnon

Mixórrouma

†

500

Mourné

500

†

Frati & Ayia Pelayía

E4 PAN-EUROPEAN FOOTPATH

500

750

Yerakári

Yerakári

750

N

500

Kissós

Kissoú Kámbos

0   1 km

Aktoúnda
Drímiskos

▼ Moní Préveli

further the track crosses a river (often dry in summer) and continues for about
a kilometre to meet an asphalt road (the Spíli–Yerakári road). Turn left along
this and, beyond a bend, take a track descending on the left. This will slowly
bring you back into the upper part of Spíli and, descending along narrow lanes,
return you to the central square. The walk is about 5km in total and shouldn't
take more than two hours. In high summer, leaving the health centre around
6pm gives you ample time to complete the hike before dusk.

Another non-taxing four-kilometre hike (partly along the E4 Pan-European
footpath) follows the main road west to the village of **Mixórrouma**, where
you turn right on a road signed for Karínes. This brings you to the pretty village of **Lampiní** and its domed Byzantine **church of the Panayía**, sited
above a valley northwest of Spíli. This was the scene of a terrible massacre in
1827 (marked by a plaque) when the Turks locked the congregation inside the

church before setting fire to it. All perished, and only fragments of the fourteenth- and fifteenth-century frescoes survived the blaze.

To extend this walk, you could continue 5km beyond Lampiní to **Karínes**, another attractive village with a friendly *kafeníon* in the midst of gently terraced hills. A further 7km brings you to **Patsós**. A turn on the left 1km before Patsós leads for ten minutes to the Áyios Andónios **cave** and a beautiful gorge with trees and water which was a Minoan, and later Dorian and Roman sanctuary. Thrónos (see p.276), 9km east of Patsós and reached via the hamlets of Pandánasa, Apóstoli and Kalóyeros, is a realistic end destination with the possibility of a bed and a meal (but phone ahead in high season to book).

South from Spíli, a walk encompassing **Mourné**, **Fratí** and **Ayía Pelayía** takes in some superb scenery with views of the Psilorítis and Lefká Óri ranges besides four ancient **churches** (with fine frescoes at the last one), and offers opportunities for birdspotting. Take the road from Spíli to Mourné, beyond which a track – along which you'll see the churches – heads southwest in the direction of Fratí, approached by a stiff descent. From here there's an easy route above the Kissanos river valley to Ayía Pelayía and the main road back to Spíli. The whole circular 10km route takes about four hours in total.

Another fine trail is the 15km southwest from Spíli to **Moní Préveli** (see p.291). Take the road west to Mourné and then follow a track heading south. After about 3km and just before **Drímiskos**, follow a cross-track heading west towards the Megapótamos river. When you reach the river valley, head south to arrive at Palm Beach (see p.293). At the sea, turn right (west) to cross the river and keep ahead along a track to reach the monastery. To save yourself the return journey you could arrange to be picked up by taxi from here to take you back to Spíli; it should be arranged in advance, will cost about €15 and can be booked through the proprietor of the pension *Heracles* in Spíli, who will also answer any queries relating to any of the above hikes.

South to Triopétra

Just over 1km southeast of Spíli, the main road to Ayía Galíni passes the gorge of Ayía Fotía on the left, a favourite nesting site for **eagles** – early morning and evening are the best times to see them. The route then follows a long valley between Mount Kédhros and the lesser summit of Sidhérotas to the west. There are few diversions along the way, but a turn-off at Akoúmia on a newly asphalted road leads after 10km to the coastal hamlet of **Triopétra**, a sleepy place with a good, expansive beach. If you wanted to hole up for a couple of days in a tranquil haven for a bit of reading, lounging and swimming, this is as good a place as any. Among the handful of tavernas with **rooms**, *Alexander Rent Rooms* (mobile ☎6972834950; ③) on the way in has en-suite rooms and, nearer the sea and up a slope on the right, *Yakindus* (mobile ☎28320 71131; ③) has modern a/c studio rooms with sea-view balconies and kitchenette. Beyond a bluff at the east end of the beach, *Taverna-Pension Pavlos* (☎28310 25189, ⓦwww.triopetra.com.gr; ③) has pleasant a/c studios with kitchenette and sea view, and the taverna's fish is caught daily by the friendly and eponymous proprietor. The isolated *Studios Costas* (mobile ☎6977703043; ③), even further east, is another place with pleasant a/c studio rooms. More places for **food** include *Apothiki*, near to where the road hits the strand and, slightly further along, the equally good *To Girogiali* (mobile ☎6972302694; ③) with an attractive terrace. The latter has its own en-suite a/c rooms (③) with TV in a separate building behind.

The Amári valley

An alternative route south from Réthimnon, and a far less travelled one than the road through Spíli, is the road which turns off south at Périvolia on the eastern fringe of town towards the **Amári valley**. Amári is one of those areas, like Sfakiá, which features prominently in almost everything written about Crete – especially in tales of **wartime resistance** – yet which is hardly explored at all by modern visitors. Shadowed by the vast profile of Psilorítis, its way of life survives barely altered by the changes of the last twenty or even fifty years. Throughout the valley, isolated hamlets subsist on the ubiquitous olive, with the occasional luxury of an orchard of cherries (especially around Yerakári), pears or figs, and throughout there are a startling number of richly frescoed **churches**. It's an environment conducive to slow exploration, with a climate noticeably cooler than the coast. In midsummer the trees, flowers and general greenery here make a stunning contrast to the rest of the island.

Three **buses** a day run from Réthimnon to **Thrónos** and **Amári**, the valley's main villages; onwards from either the service is sporadic or non-existent. It's best to explore **on foot** – in which case a water bottle and the best map you can find are essential – the Petrákis *Réthimno* map (p.26) will do the job. For touring in your own vehicle, the main roads are fine and well maintained. As for staying in the valley, there are officially **rooms** only in Thrónos, Amári, Yerakári and Kouroutes, but don't let this deter you from asking in other villages: locals are often only too happy to have a paying guest for a night or two, and traditional hospitality here has not yet been extinguished by abuse.

Whenever you come, but in July or August especially, you may be lucky enough to stumble on a village **festival** in honour of the local saint, the harvest or some obscure historical event; they're worth going out of your way for, so keep an eye out for notices pasted in *kafenío* windows. Beginning in a distorted cacophony of overamplified Cretan music, *lyra* and *lauto* to the fore, the celebrations continue until the participants are sufficiently gorged on roast lamb and enlivened by wine to get down to the real business of **dancing**. Cretan dancing at an event such as this is an extraordinary display of athleticism and, as often as not, endurance – and if the party really takes off, locals will dig out their old guns and rattle off a few rounds into the sky to celebrate.

There are two roads through the Amári valley, one following the **eastern** side from the village of **Thrónos** and clinging to the flanks of the Psilorítis range, the other tracing the edge of the lesser Kédhros range on the **western** side. Both are scenically spectacular, but the eastern route probably has the edge in terms of beauty and places of interest.

Thrónos and the eastern side of the Amári valley

The first of the real Amári villages on the **eastern side** of the valley is **THRÓNOS**, situated just off the main road at the head of the valley on the site of ancient Sybritos, whose port was modern Áyia Galíni. Like so many others here, Thrónos seems lost in the past, with its beautifully frescoed **church of the Panayía** and majestic views across the valley and up to the mountains. There are more ancient remains, too. In the Byzantine era this was the seat of a bishop (hence *thrónos*, throne) and these early Christian days are recalled by the remains of a mosaic which is partly under the village church and spreads beyond its walls, with traces both inside and out. The later building, in fact, is only about a quarter of the size of the original church, whose floorplan, guarded by a low rail, can be clearly seen. The elderly keeper will usually appear with the key as soon as you start to take an interest in the church; if not, enquire at *Rooms Aravanes* (see below), who also have a key.

On the hill above the village are still-earlier remains of the **acropolis** of ancient Sybritos, easily reached by following a path signed on the left beyond the church. Founded as a settlement in the twelfth century BC in the troubled late Minoan period, the site seems to have been more a refuge (similar to those at Karfí and Présos in eastern Crete) from mainland invaders than a real town. Most of the remains visible today, however, date from the substantial Greco-Roman town that flourished from the fifth century BC into the early Byzantine period, when the modern resort of Ayía Galíni served as its port. During this period Sybritos was the seat of a diocese (possibly based on the larger basilica which preceded the church of the Panayía above) until the town was destroyed by the Saracens in the ninth century. The hill is topped by a radio mast, and besides plenty of ancient ruins when you reach the summit, there are spectacular views in all directions.

If you want **to stay** in Thrónos, simply follow the crude "Rent Rooms" signs to *Rooms Aravanes* (T 28330 22760; ②), a modern concrete structure with pink cinderblock balconies. The building is an aberration, but its balconies have the best view in the village. The rooms are pleasant, there's a **taverna** on the ground floor and the outside yard is pressed into use for periodic big *bouzoúki* get-togethers, with dozens of tables put out and fires lit for barbecuing; keep an eye out for the posters, as these are well worth attending. The only other place in the village offering **food** is a basic *kafepantopolíon* near to the church. *Rooms Aravanes* also acts as agent for a beautifully restored **stone-built house** in the village where en-suite rooms (②) come with more spectacular balcony views. *Aravanes'* owner, Lambros Papoutsakis, is a man of diverse talents: besides constructing *lyras*, he is quite a player too, and also organizes **herb-collecting rambles** in the mountains (on which he's an expert), finds fossils and distils his own *raki*; in October the **raki distilling** season begins and you can make visits to local stills to see the farmers brewing their potent firewater, as well as trying it out. In the first half of September, it's possible to take part in the village's **grape harvest**. The *Aravanes* has recently added a small school to its complex of buildings and this is used for **classes** in *lyra*, *lauto* and Cretan dance, as well as stone sculpture and Greek language classes. The classes are taught by local experts and cost around €10 per hour; details are available from the *Aravanes*.

Hikes from Thrónos

The proprietor of *Rooms Aravanes* also conducts **guided treks** to the peak of Mount Psilorítis (see p.270). Although he does guide groups up in the daytime, his preferred approach is during the full moons of June, July and August, which avoids the extreme summer temperatures. Phone in advance for details; it's not a difficult climb, but you'll need sturdy footwear and a sleeping bag. For these **night walks**, the group starts out by Landrover in the early evening to reach the start point on the mountain. After a meal cooked in the open and a short nap, the ascent begins in bright moonlight. The summit is reached at around dawn, and the sunrise is always spectacular: on clear days the mountain offers a breathtaking view of the whole island and its four seas spreading in all directions. On the route down the hike takes in a visit to a goatherd's *mitato* (stone mountain hut) where you see and sample delicious cheese made on the spot.

Other **hikes** from Thrónos include a relatively easy path leading north through the foothills in a couple of hours to the monastery of **Arkádhi** (see p.252). The first 3km are now along a newly asphalted road (the former track), and the walking route then heads off to the east of this to reach the monastery where you can pick up buses. It's worth checking directions at *Rooms Aravanes*, as more new roads are planned in this area. South from Thrónos is an extremely easy stroll on a paved road running back into the main valley via **Kalóyeros**. Fifteen minutes' walk beyond Kalóyeros, a narrow path on the left leads uphill to the small stone church of **Áyios Ioánnis Theológos**, whose fine but decayed frescoes date from 1347 – the church should be open. This walk can be extended into a two-hour trek back to Thrónos; a map detailing this is available from *Rooms Aravanes*.

Amári and around

Back on the main road, the **Moní Asomáton** is only 1km south of Thrónos. The buildings are Venetian, though the monastery itself is older; having survived centuries of resistance and revolution, it finally became an agricultural school in 1931. It's not open to the public, but no one seems to mind if you wander in and look over the lovely old buildings, with a weed-infested central courtyard containing a church, a ruined Venetian fountain and – at the rear – a prodigious plane tree.

Outside and beside a taverna, a line of fir and eucalyptus trees marks the beginning of the five-kilometre paved road to the village of **Amári**, the chief village of the valley. This is another beautiful drive or manageable walk, although the second half climbs quite steeply up the hill of Samítos, which rises right in the middle of the valley. On the way you pass through two picturesque villages, **Monastiráki** and **Opsigiás**, but Amári itself outdoes them: it looks like nothing so much as a perfect Tuscan hill village: note the steeply sloping roofs to cope with the winter snows and the chimneys for wood fires. There's really nothing to do here – even the couple of *kafenía* on the central *platía* often seem to close for a siesta in the afternoon – but there are scintillating views across to Psilorítis. For a bird's-eye view, climb the **Venetian clock tower** which dominates the narrow alleyways (the door is always open). It's not immediately obvious how to get here, but keep climbing and circling the hill until you reach the church; enter the churchyard through some wrought-iron gates and then climb a flight of steps behind to find the tower. Just outside the village, the church of **Ayía Ánna**, reached down a lane on the western edge opposite the police station, has some extremely faded **frescoes** – dating from 1225, they have a fair claim to being the oldest on Crete.

One of Amári's *kafenía*, Noukakis (☎28330 22830; ❶), on the main square, has some remarkably cheap **rooms** sharing bath and also does **meals**, making a stay here a feasible proposition. When you've eaten or taken a coffee, you could also make a brief visit to the new **museum** (9am–6pm; free) across the square, comprising a room filled with agricultural equipment and various other pots, pans, clothing and receptacles donated by the villagers. Otherwise, the village boasts an OTE and **post office**, and there's a daily **bus** to Réthimnon, currently running at 6.45am and 4pm.

Fourfourás

Continuing south, there are more lovely villages, with the peak of Psilorítis now almost directly above and the softer lines of Mount Kédhros behind the Samítos hill on the other side. **Fourfourás**, 11km south of Thrónos, is a traditional place to begin the climb of Psilorítis, although no one seems to tackle the peak from here any more (Anóyia and Kamáres are more convenient; see p.270). Fourfourás is also the trailhead of some arduous hikes to the lesser peaks. There is a friendly and excellent-value **taverna** and **rooms** place here on the way in coming from Amári: *Windy Place* (☎28330 41366; ❷) serves up hearty meals whilst its decent rooms – located in another building in the village proper – come with bath. Its proprietors will also describe a **short cut** to the Psilorítis peak which allows you to take your car a good way up the mountain along a track which ascends to the right, 5km north of Fourfourás and 2km beyond the village of Platánia. With care you can take a vehicle to the tree line (about 1hr), from where it's about a three-hour trek to the the chapel of Tímios Stavrós on the summit. The walk down takes about two hours, from when you'll have another hour's drive back to the road. The same proprietor can also advise on a 15km gorge walk along the Plátis river valley to Ayía Galíni and will collect you from there to return you to Fourfourás.

Kourites, Níthavris and around

The next village, 6km south of Fourfourás is **Kourites**, which although a fairly uneventful hamlet, does have an excellent **place to stay**, *Studios Kourites* (☎28330 41305; ❸), signed off the road through. Here new balcony rooms come with kitchenette, TV and fans in a detached house surrounded by a garden. Some larger apartments are also available sleeping up to four (❹). At **Níthavris**, 4km south of Kourites, the road divides. It's worth taking the road south towards Ayía Galíni for 3km to the village of **Apodhoúlou**, which has a number of interesting sights. On the way into the village there's a Late Minoan **passage tomb** signed on the left with its lintel still intact. Beyond here and just downhill from a bar, where a eucalyptus and an oak tree face each other across the street, lies an interesting ruined mansion known as the **House of Kalítsa Psaráki**. It gets its name from the daughter of a local official who, in the 1821 rising against Turkish rule, was abducted by Muslims and sent to the slave market at Alexandria in Egypt. By chance she was seen there by Robert Hay, an English gentleman traveller, who secured her freedom and asked her to marry him. The couple returned to Crete, where an overjoyed family built this once impressive house for them to live in. The present proprietor is trying to restore the edifice with his own meagre resources, and is usually happy to show you around.

From the centre of the village, signs indicate the church of **Áyios Yeóryios** and a **Minoan site** down a road on the right. The church, currently undergoing restoration, which lies about 1km down this lane, to the right, contains some damaged but wonderful **frescoes** from the fourteenth century by Ieréas Anastasiós, one vigorously portraying its eponymous saint slaying the dragon. Continuing a further kilometre beyond the turn-off for the church brings you to the **ancient site** (open access) beneath a number of metal canopies. These recent excavations have revealed the impressive remains of a Minoan settlement dating from the early second millenium BC, with many substantial dwellings and all the usual features of Minoan architecture including light wells, benches and narrow corridors. Back on the main road just south of Apodhoúlou, with the coast coming into view, you can head down to Ayía Galíni (see p.281) or follow the flank of the mountains east around through Kamáres (see p.271).

Turn off west at Níthavris and you can curve round to complete a circuit of the Amári valley through the villages on the lower slopes of **Kédhros** (1777m). After 4km, at the hamlet of **Áyios Ioánnis**, there is a potential detour south for 3km to **Ayía Paraskeví** and its small **church of the Panayía**, on a rise to the left behind houses and opposite a large modern church to the right. It holds fine **frescoes** dating from the sixteenth century; if locked, enquire for the house of the *papás* up a street behind who will be only too pleased to open it up, find out where you are from and probably offer you a *raki*.

The route from Áyios Ioánnis now meanders westwards, descending in a series of spectacular hairpins into the valley of the River Plátis which reaches the sea at Ayía Galíni. The road crosses a bridge over the river and toils up the west slope of the valley into a greener landscape, taking in a succession of high villages as it heads towards Yerakári, the first of which is **Hordháki** (see p.281).

The western side of the Amári valley

The villages on the **western** side of the Amári valley look little different from those on the eastern side, but they are in fact almost entirely **modern** – rebuilt after their deliberate destruction during World War II. George Psychoundákis (see p.339) watched the outrage from a cave on the slopes of Psilorítis:

I stayed there two or three days before leaving, watching the Kedros villages burning ceaselessly on the other side of the deep valley. Every now and then we heard the sound of explosions. The Germans went there in the small hours of the twenty-second of August and the burning went on for an entire week. The villages we could see from there and which were given over to the flames were: Yerakari, Kardaki, Gourgouthoi, Vrysses, Smiles, Dryes and Ano-Meros. First they emptied every single house, transporting all the loot to Retimo, then they set fire to them, and finally, to complete the ruin, they piled dynamite into every remaining corner, and blew them sky high. The village schools met the same fate, also the churches and the wells, and at Ano-Meros they even blew up the cemetery. They shot all the men they could find.

Other villages around Psilorítis, from Anóyia to Kamáres, were also burned. Officially these atrocities were in reprisal for the kidnap of General Kreipe, four months earlier. But Psychoundákis, for one, believed that it was a more general revenge, intended to destroy any effective resistance in the closing months of the German occupation. Today the villages of Méronas, Elénes, Yerakári, Kardháki and Vrísses mark the southward progress of the German troops with etched stone **memorials** dated one day apart. Áno Méros has a striking war memorial of a woman wielding a hammer and chisel as she carves the names of the dead into the monument. But even here, a number of frescoed **churches** survived the terror. Between Vrísses and Kardháki one such lies off to the right of the road, lying low in a field of grain and apparently forgotten. Push the door aside, however, and the gloom gradually reveals beautiful Byzantine paintings around the altar.

Yerakári and around

Yerakári is a bigger, more modern and prosperous-looking village than most, with several places to stop for a drink or some food, and **accommodation** at *Taverna Rooms Gerakari* (☎28330 51013; ❷) on the main street. The taverna's kitchen is a veritable pickling and bottling factory for the fruits of the region – especially cherries, for which the village is famous – which are spread out to dry on every available rooftop during the picking season. The village cheeses, *thimarísio* (thyme honey) and pickled cherries are all for sale in a couple of stores and recommended, although their cherry brandy is probably an acquired taste.

With transport, you can take the spectacular road west from Yerakári to Spíli (see p.272), which offers tremendous views along a valley between the heights of Kédhros and Sorós towards the distant and magnificent Lefká Óri. The way to the road lies up the hill at the end of Yerakári's main street. Starting out unpromisingly as a rough dirt track, almost before you know it you're bowling along a superb asphalted highway thoroughly out of sync with what has gone before.

Just to the south of Yerakári and 1km before **Kardháki**, you'll come to the unusual **Monastery of Áyios Ioánnis Theológos**, with a spreading oak tree in front providing shade for a tapped spring. There are thirteenth-century **frescoes** in an exposed side chapel, and slightly later ones as you enter the church, all very battered and open to the elements. At the time of writing major subsidence has threatened the complete collapse of the church, and the frescoed roof is currently supported by iron staves. Traces of the medieval stone road or track on which the church was originally aligned can still be made out behind it. Some 6km south of Khardháki the larger village of **Ano Méros** makes a pleasant place for a pause, and for **food** Bar O Stinos at the southern end of the main street has a fine terrace with a view across the valley. Three kilometres south from here lies **Hordháki**, with the road circuit to the eastern side of the valley completed 10km further on at Níthavris (see p.279).

Méronas

Heading north along the road from Yerakári to complete the Amári valley's western flank, beyond Mesonísia and Elénes comes **Méronas** where, to the right of the road, a soft pink Venetian-style **church of the Panayía** shelters frescoes from the fourteenth century. If the church is closed, you'll need to ask for the key across the road. Again, it takes time to adjust your eyes to take in the painstaking detail of the artwork, darkened with age: a torch would allow you to see a great deal more than the candles or nightlights which usually provide illumination. Four kilometres further on is the **Ayía Fotiní** junction, passed by buses going to and from Réthimnon.

Ayía Galíni and around

Thirty years ago, **AYÍA GALÍNI** must have been an idyllic spot: an isolated fishing community of some five hundred souls nestling in a convenient fold of the mountains which dominate this part of the **south coast**. Although this was the port of ancient Sybritos (see p.277), the modern village is barely a hundred years old, its inhabitants having moved down from the mountain villages of Mélambes and Saktoúria as the traditional threat of piracy along the coast receded.

Catch it out of season and the streets of white houses, crowded in on three sides by mountains and opening below to a small, busy **harbour**, can still appeal. But this is a face which is increasingly hard to find. Chock-full throughout the season with package tourists, and confined by the limits of its narrow situation, the village's old houses are rapidly being squeezed out by ever-larger apartment buildings and concrete hotels. Since the beach was never a major asset anyway, if you're looking for strands with space to breathe you'll need to use the resort as a base for trips to nearby beaches or opt for a shorter stay. The lack of a decent beach is a shame, as is the use of the potentially picturesque harbour area as a car park, for otherwise there's something appealing about Ayía Galíni's relatively staid and respectable brand of tourism. With a vibrant nightlife scene plus plenty of bars and tavernas, the resort is a much more inviting place than it looks, or than you'd expect from first impressions, largely because the people have stayed friendly and the atmosphere Cretan despite the development.

The **beach** at Ayía Galíni is astonishingly small for a place that bills itself as the province's major resort. Once the few patches of soft sand have been claimed you'll have to rent a chair if you hope to lounge in any comfort. It lies to the **east** of the village, reached by a narrow path that tracks around the cliff from the harbourfront, or by a very useful path that descends from the top of the town (reached via steps between the *Galini Mare* and *El Greco* hotels). You can also drive round and park by *Camping Agia Galini*. Walking round by the cliffs, you'll pass **caves** which in World War II served as gun emplacements. You can get food and drink at a number of places behind the beach; among the **tavernas**, *Kostas* is probably the best value, particularly for fish, but *Sunset*, *Acropol* and *Romantica* (across the Plátis river at the beach's eastern end) are also good.

Further afield to the **west** are some much better patches of sand. **Boats** from the harbour (get details from any travel agent, or buy tickets when boarding) make daily day-trips to the beaches of Áyios Yeóryios and Áyios Pávlos (around €10 per person) as well as to the **Paximádhia islands** 12km offshore, which have wonderful fine sand beaches but little shade, making a sun umbrella a must. **Dolphin-spotting** trips are run by the *O Faros* taverna (see p.284) and charge €25–30 for a five-hour voyage.

Arrival and information

Buses to Ayía Galíni terminate at the bus station by the church, in the village proper. It's a handy spot to get your bearings since few of the streets are named and such names as there are seem rarely used. The nucleus of the place is built around three streets which run down to the harbour. The first of these (Venizélou) is a continuation of the main road into town: along it you'll find the **post office**, bakery, doctor and a couple of car rental places. The narrow street parallel to this to the east is lined with stores, jewellery shops and travel agencies. The next street along is packed with tavernas (and known locally as "Taverna Street"). All of this falls within a very small area where nothing is more than a couple of minutes' walk away.

Many places near the post office **change money**, among them Creta Exchange, which gives bank rates. At the start of this road Ostria Rent a Car (☎28320 91554, ⓦ www.ostria-agiagalini.com) claims to have the cheapest deals for **car rental** (but don't take them at their word) and they do Internet reservations. The nearby Monza Travel (☎28320 91004), a little nearer the harbour, also rents out cars and **bikes** (with a ten-percent discount offered to *Rough Guide* readers with this guide) and is a good source of general information; they will also give money on credit cards and travel **information** and **tickets** are available here, too. **Internet access** is available at *Cosmos* (10am–2pm & 5pm–12.30am; €5/hr, €1.50/15min) on the middle of the three streets leading up from the harbour, and the slightly cheaper *Alexander* on the east side of the harbourfront. Card **phone kiosks** can be found throughout the centre. A **bookshop** with a decent selection of English fiction, books about the island and foreign **newspapers** is Le Shop Kalliopi, just in from the harbour road close to the post office; international newspapers are also available from the shops on the road in from Réthimnon. A good **laundry**, Laundry Center (☎28320 91336) is just beyond the bus station, down a street almost opposite the post office; they will wash, fold and iron 6kg of clothes on the same day for €7.

Accommodation

There are so many **rooms** in Ayía Galíni that you can usually find something – though for much of July and August all but a handful are pre-booked by tour operators. Prices are very closely linked to demand: for most of the summer both are high, but not alarmingly so, and away from peak seasons you can often get an exceptional bargain.

Probably the best place to start looking is at the top of the town where the road enters from the north. Here on the left you'll soon pass the *Hotel Minos* (☎28320 91292; ❷), an excellent-value place with sea-view rooms, all with bath and use of a kitchen, and open all year. Next door to here, *Hotel El Greco* (☎28320 91187, ⓦwww.agia-galini.com; ❺) is a pleasant upmarket possibility with a/c balcony rooms with sea view and fridge; be sure to ask for the air-conditioning remote control. Opposite the *Minos*, *Hotel Idi* (☎28320 91152, ⓕ28320 91082; ❷) is very friendly and has excellent-value en-suite balcony rooms with fridge and a/c or fans.

Heading towards town, a turn uphill on the right just after the *El Greco* leads to a number of good-value **rooms** places including – about halfway up – the *Hotel Astir* (☎ & ⓕ28320 91174; ❸ inc. breakfast) and the neighbouring *Hotel Iro* (☎28320 91160, ⓕ28320 91460; ❸), both offering en-suite rooms with balcony sea view. Along a road off to the right about halfway up the hill the modern and tranquil *Hotel Avra* (☎28320 91476, ⓕ28320 91544; ❸ including breakfast) is a delightful sparkling place with en-suite a/c rooms on a number of levels. None of these options have pools, but at the top of this hill there's an inviting **pool bar** where you can take a dip and stretch out on a sun lounger for the price of a beer.

Back on the main road, a little further towards town and on a bend, *Hotel Hariklia* (☎ & ⓕ28320 91257; ❷) is another delightful, spotless small pension with good harbour views and en-suite a/c rooms; guests also have use of a kitchen to prepare breakfasts and snacks. Further down the hill on the left, *Argiro Apartments* (☎28320 91470; ❹) offers a/c studios with kitchenette and sea-view balcony; reductions are given for longer stays. Nearby on the opposite side of the road, *Agapitos* (☎28320 91164; ❸) has attractive a/c studios with kitchenette and balcony and, at the foot of the hill, *Hotel Glaros* (☎28320 91151, ⓕ28320 91159; ❹ inc. breakfast) is a plant-bedecked upmarket place with air-conditioned rooms and a small pool. Signed up the road just behind here, *Hotel Ostria* (☎28320 91404, ⓦwww.ostria-agiagalini.com; ❸) is a leafy retreat where a/c balcony rooms come with fridge. Beyond the *Ostria*, *Neos Ikaros* (☎28320 91447, ⓦwww.neosikaros.gr; ❹) is a tempting option for a place with full-sized pool; reached over a concrete bridge but only five minutes away from the action, it's a spacious garden hotel where a/c balcony rooms come with fridge and TV. Finally, one economical possibility nearer the sea is *Akteon* (☎28320 91208; ❷), located by turning left off the end of Taverna Street; all rooms are a/c and en suite with great views over the harbour.

There's also a **campsite**, *Camping Agia Galini* (☎28320 91386), to the east near the mouth of the Plátis river, reached either by a road which takes off from the main road about 1km outside the village, or by walking out along the beach.

Eating, drinking and nightlife

One major and undeniable benefit which the crowds have brought to Ayía Galíni is a vast range of **food** and **drink**, much of it excellent and, thanks to the competition, not overpriced. The bulk of the tavernas are along Taverna Street, which in the evening is choked with pedestrian traffic. There are plenty of economical – if rather unexciting – places here with tables spilling out into the street but it's also worth hunting out some more tempting places only a few minutes away. Once you've eaten you have an opportunity to sample the town's boisterous **nightlife** scene, which lifts off around midnight in summer.

There are plenty of **bars** and **clubs** where you can carry on after you've eaten, mostly around the bottom of Taverna Street and near the harbour. Music explodes from these places after 11pm, once the diners are out of the way, and here *Zorba's*, where dancing starts after midnight, is a long-established favourite. Neighbouring *Budda* and *Juke Box* at the foot of Taverna Street are other options, whilst the nearby *Paradiso* is currently the resort's most popular venue. One place with a slightly more mature crowd is *Blue Bar* at the foot of the middle of the streets leading up from the harbour, where late-night carousing takes place to jazz and pre-1980s oldies.

Bozos On the harbourfront. One of the best places for the usual taverna standards.

Charley's Place Near the bus stop. A popular place and good for grills and *mezédhes*, besides being relatively quiet and out of the way.

O Faros On the next street west of, and running parallel to, Taverna Street. This is the resort's best and most unpretentious fish restaurant, where the friendly family who run it serve up what they catch themselves with their own boat (used also for dolphin-spotting trips; see p.282). Has a small street terrace.

Madame Hortense Set back from the east side of the harbour ☎08320 91215. Slightly pricier and more stylish than the competition and named after Zorba the Greek's floozy in the classic novel, a timber-floored dining room offers great views over the harbour. The menu is sprinkled with Greek, Mediterranean and Cretan specialities (the house *kleftiko* is recommended) and includes a few more exotic – mildly curried – dishes from Asia.

Miro To the right off Taverna Street a little way down. Almost the last traditional *kafeníon* in town stubbornly clings to its identity in the face of the surrounding mayhem; a fine place to people-watch at the outdoor tables with an ouzo and a few plates of *mezédhes*.

Restaurant Onar Taverna Street ☎08320 91121. At the bottom of this street nearest the sea, this is perhaps the best value of all for wholesome traditional food – charcoal grilled fish and meat is a speciality – and a great setting, overlooking the harbour from a rooftop terrace.

Pantheon Taverna Street. With an entrance almost opposite the *Onar*, this is another reasonably priced taverna with an attractive roof terrace.

To Petrino Fifty metres north of the bus stop up a side road. Friendly little gem of an *ouzerí* serving breakfast coffee and excellent *mezédhes* later in the day, and retains some of the flavour of the pre-tourist days.

Stelios Café On a small square slightly south of the bus stop. Famed for its breakfasts (omelettes, fruit salads and muesli all feature), it also does snack meals and freshly made *loukoumádhes* (honey puffs). At night the *Stelios* transmutes into a cocktail bar.

La Strada Close to the northern end of Taverna Street. Good pizza and decent pasta and risotto served on a street terrace; the brothers who run it are accomplished performers on the *lyra* and *laoúto* (lute) and often treat their customers to an impromptu concert.

Around Ayía Galíni

About 3km west of Ayía Galíni, the seaside hamlet of **Áyios Yeóryios** (with an asphalted road now connecting it to the Ayía Galíni–Mélambes road) is fairly easily reached on foot: take the main road up past the bus station, and at the crown of the first bend follow a left turn (signed) towards a group of apartments. Just beyond these, cross a dry river bed and head up the hillside on a well-worn path marked with splashes of red paint. The beach is almost two hours away, a shingle cove with two tavernas, one of which, *Nikos* (mobile ☎6944504859; ❸), has a/c rooms with bath. The eponymous and voluble proprietor serves whatever he's caught from the sea on the taverna's terrace; there are a couple of other, less attractive coves along the way.

Áyios Pávlos, 8km further west as the crow flies, but quite a few more along the meandering backroads, is served by **boat trips** from Ayía Galíni. It's also much more attractive than Áyios Yeóryios, with some striking rock formations around a sheltered bay, and excellent snorkelling. The main **beach** here can make for difficult bathing due to slippery rocks and, in summer, strong winds. Both of these problems can be dealt with by going a bit further west over the headland, where there's fine sand and a more sheltered beach. In addition to the people arriving by boat from Ayía Galíni, Áyios Pávlos for some years has been home to a colony of New Age **yoga** practitioners who run intensive yoga and related courses at their centre, Yoga Plus (bookable in advance only; ⓦ www.yogaplus.co.uk). Áyios Pávlos also has some apartments and two **taverna/rooms** places: the first, *Ayios Pavlos* (☎ 28320 71104, Ⓕ 28320 71105; ❷–❸), has a new hotel attached complete with en-suite a/c rooms as well as **Internet access**. The less pricey *Mama Eva* (☎ 28320 71108; ❷), also immediately above the beach, is another option for a/c rooms. The *Panorama* (☎ 28320 71106; ❸) is a taverna-rooms place set back from the sea and visible from the road on the way in: on offer are en-suite balcony rooms. Set even further back along the entry road, the *Livikon* (☎ 28320 71101; ❸) has similarly priced en-suite rooms, plus a taverna serving fresh fish caught daily with its own boat.

The boat from Ayía Galíni is perhaps the most pleasant way to get to Áyios Pávlos, but you can also drive via Áyios Yeóryios and **Saktóuria**, on a sealed road. This is now the quicker route, but another slightly longer scenic drive there (or back) is to take the old main road out of Ayía Galíni northwest through **Mélambes** towards Spíli, turning left (signed) after about 12km to go through upper and lower Saktóuria, an exhilaratingly winding route with great views. Sadly, these have been blighted due to a devastating **fire** in the spring of 2000 which swept through the valley destroying thousands of olive trees and ruining many farmers. A further fire in 2003 did little to improve matters. Mélambes is a pleasant place to break your journey and has a good **taverna**, *Aristos*, on its main *platía*.

Plakiás and around

Three routes towards Plakiás branch off from the main Réthimnon–Ayía Galíni road. The main one, signed to Plakiás, heads down towards the coast via the spectacular **Kourtalíotiko gorge**; an alternative route, signed to Selliá, comes through the only slightly less impressive **Kotsifóu gorge**. Either way, it's worth pulling over in the gorge to take time to appreciate the scenery and the wildlife, from snakes by the water to vast birds of prey soaring above. If you're coming from the south you can also turn off at Mixórrouma, from where you head to Áyia Pelayía and then join the Kourtalíotiko gorge route via the village of Fráti – a wonderfully scenic drive.

About halfway through the Kourtalíotiko gorge there are parking places and steps leading down to the chapel of **Áyios Nikólaos** near the bottom – a good place to break your journey. Further on, you have a choice of turning right for Plakiás, passing through **Asómatos** and **Lefkóyia** (see p.291), or continuing to follow the course of the stream all the way down to **Préveli** (p.291). Just before the Kotsifóu gorge there's a really excellent inexpensive taverna, *Iliomanolis*, in the village of **Kánevos**. This route eventually opens out to leave you on the main coast road west of Plakiás; turn right for **Selliá** (p.293), left for **Mírthios** (p.290) and Plakiás.

Inland from Plakiás there's plenty of country for walkers and nature-lovers to explore – especially around the gorges – as well as a number of small, relatively undeveloped villages, a couple of which have accommodation and make possible alternative bases.

Plakiás

PLAKIÁS, 35km south of Réthimnon, is these days a well-established resort, though it's still a long way from the big league. Commercialized as it is, Plakiás has a very different feel to somewhere like Ayía Galíni – the accommodation is simpler, less of it is booked up in advance, the nearby beaches are infinitely better and it attracts a younger crowd. Don't come for sophisticated nightlife or for a picturesque white Greek island village: what you will find is a lively, friendly place with a decent town beach that makes a good base for **walks** in the beautiful surrounding countryside and trips to far better **beaches** all around.

Arrival and information

The approach roads merge to **enter Plakiás** from the east, behind the beach, and then head straight into the heart of things along the **seafront**. Virtually everything in Plakiás lies along or just off this main road beside the sea, or on one of the alleys connecting it to the single street that runs inland, rapidly deteriorating into paths which wind up towards Selliá and Mírthios. Continuing through town, the coast road westwards ends after 3km or so at **Soúdha beach** (see p.288), though you can turn off to head up to Selliá and the main road west via a vertiginous series of narrow hairpin bends.

Every facility you're likely to need can be found within a few paces of the waterfront. The travel agencies here (see p.289) are the best source of local **information**; you'll also find car hire places, a post office, bike rental, ATMs and money exchange, several supermarkets and even a laundry. **Buses** arrive and depart from a stop just east of the little bridge, roughly halfway along the seafront opposite the big Forum supermarket: the timetable is usually pinned up and is also displayed at nearby Finikas Travel (whose sign reads *Moto Auto Plakias*).

The Plakiás Market supermarket, near the *Livikon Hotel* on the seafront, stocks a couple of excellent **walking** guides and a map of the area by Lance Chilton (see p.456) – try to get a recent edition, as development has altered a few of the routes (recent updates available at Ⓦwww.marengowalks.com).

Accommodation

While there are scores of new **hotels** and **rooms** in Plakiás – indeed at times it seems there's little else – you may have difficulty finding a vacancy in high season. As ever, it's a question of wandering around and asking everywhere: the places on the backstreets lack the sea views but are quieter and usually the last to fill. Many of these are found on the street parallel to the coast, heading towards the *Youth Hostel* – get there from behind the *Alianthos Garden Hotel*, or by following the street past the post office. As an alternative to staying in town there are lots of new studio/apartment complexes on the road as you approach town and, generally more attractive, along the coast towards Soúdha beach. Slightly further afield, there are also places to stay at the beaches to the west such as Dhamnóni (see p.289) or Amoúdhi (p.290).

Pension Afrodite At the back of the village near the little church ☎28320 31266, Ⓕ28230 31567. A charming pension in a gleaming white building with spotless en-suite rooms and apartments. It's set in a quiet location with lots of cascading bougainvillea. ❷

Alianthos Garden Hotel Set back at the start of the seafront road ☎28320 31280,

@www.alianthos.gr. The biggest and fanciest hotel
in town – which is to say it has a lift to connect its
three storeys and 94 rooms, as well as pool, bar,
taverna and play area. All rooms are en suite, with
TV, fridge and a/c – though even here, they charge
extra to use it. ❻

Camping Apollonia On the right as you
approach town ☎ 28320 31318, @www
.lamon-hotel.gr/apollonia.htm. Small and rather
cramped site, but the location is excellent, and
the good facilities include a minimarket and
pool. Tents and caravans available to rent. ❶

Eolos On a street running inland immediately west
of the *Alianthos Beach* hotel ☎ 28320 31022.
Tempting fate by naming their good-value accommodation after the god of the winds, the hospitable
couple here have plain but well-equipped rooms
with bath, TV and a/c. ❷

Gio-ma In a prime position overlooking the harbour at the west end of the seafront ☎ 28320
32003, @www.gioma.gr. Some fabulously sited
if small and rather basic rooms (but with bath
and a/c) above the taverna of the same name,
right on the water. Over the road there are
comfortable modern studios and apartments –
more expensive, but still good value. Rooms ❷,
studios ❸

Glaros Western edge of town, on the coast past
the harbour ☎ & ℻ 28320 31746. Above the
taverna of the same name, Glaros has a flexible
layout allowing some of its modern rooms to be
combined as apartments. Fabulous sunset views
from big balconies in their best rooms: all have
bath and fridge, some with kitchen. ❸

Ippokambos On the street parallel to the sea
☎ 28320 31525, @amoutsos@otenet.gr. Modern
rooms place with simple, well-presented rooms, all
with bath, balcony and fridge. ❷

Hotel Livikon On the seafront ☎ 28320 31216,
℻ 28320 31216. One of the oldest hotels in town,
with tired decor and sometimes grumpy management – but great, if occasionally noisy, location

right on the main street with balconies looking out
over the beach. ❷

Oasis About 1km out of town, on the main road
near the Dhamnóni turn-off ☎ 28320 31317,
@oasisnik@ret.forthnet.gr. One of the best of
the new places east of town, it makes use of
the extra space to provide gardens, a small
pool, and its own little taverna. Rooms ❷,
apartments ❸

Paligremnos Beach At the eastern end of the
town beach, about 500m from town ☎ 28320
31835, @www.paligremnos.com. Small studio
complex with its own taverna and garden with
kids' play area in a quiet location right by the
beach. Good-value en-suite studios and apartments have kitchenette and balcony overlooking
the sea. ❸

Hotel Phoenix 2km west near Soúda beach
☎ 28320 31331, ℻ 28320 31831. Tranquil hotel in
a great spot above the sea, offering well-equipped
balcony rooms; a bit pricey by local standards,
though breakfast is included. ❺

Skinos Apartments At two locations on the road
to Soúdha beach, one about 400m from town, the
other 800m ☎ 28320 31737, @www.skinos.net.
Simple rooms place, but all very quiet and en
suite, with a/c, fridge and large balconies looking
out to sea; the apartments also have kitchen.
Rooms ❷, apartments ❸

Hotel Sofia Inland from the bar *Ostraco* at the
west end of the seafront ☎ 28320 31251,
℻ 28320 31252. Pleasant, small hotel with use of
the pool at package-tour *Apollo Hotel* (immediately
behind). A few balcony sea-view rooms, though
the others can be rather dark. ❸

Youth Hostel Inland a little way behind town
(follow the signs) ☎ 28320 32118,
@www.yhplakias.com. Friendly, relaxed and well-
run independent hostel, in an attractively rural
setting, with a terrace for breakfast and evening
drinks and a busy social life. Hot showers
included. Dorms €7.

Eating

The seafront street is lined with **tavernas**, cafés and bars, but the prime position is towards the harbour right at the centre of town, where a strip of places
have tables next to the water. You'll pay a bit more here than at other places in
town – in fact food in Plakiás is generally costly by Cretan standards – but the
setting is worth it. For **breakfast**, there are a number of bakeries along here
too, and many of the cafés open early.

Candia Bakery Between the hotels *Livikon* and
Lamon on the front, a good place for breakfast,
and throughout the day for coffee, juices and takeaway snacks and pies.

Gio-Ma Along with neighbouring *Christos*, probably the best location of all, sharing a pleasant
tamarisk-shaded terrace above the harbour.
Christos is one of the longest-established in town,

famous for its fish, but standards seem to have slipped, giving its neighbour the edge.

Taverna Kastro High on the hill behind town, *Kastro*'s fine terrace with great views complements friendly service and some original and tasty dishes such as *kounéli* (rabbit with a lemon and garlic sauce). It's signed by road, or on foot you can follow the path through the olive groves beside the *Alianthos Garden Hotel*, looking out for the taverna's crenellated roofline above you.

Kri Kri Near the bridge, *Kri Kri* has good pizza from a wood-fired oven as well as all the taverna standards.

Lysseos Nice setting near the bridge, with food that's a little more ambitious than most in Plakiás.

Taverna Medousa At the eastern end of the inland street, near the back of the *Alianthos Garden* hotel, a good, traditional taverna with prices noticeably lower than those on the front.

Nikos Souvlaki Probably the cheapest place in town, by the post office on the street running inland from the front. Excellent *souvláki* or fish and chips to take away, or eat in at one of the few small tables.

On the Rocks Café-bar overlooking the western beach at the western end of town, serving good breakfasts, and later in the day ice cream and cocktails.

Secret Nest Taverna At the back of town, inland from behind the harbour, offers a change of scene as well as fish and other dishes served on a pleasant terrace.

Sofia The best of the group of tavernas right by the sea; friendly with good portions, and a slightly less tourist-influenced menu than some of its neighbours. *Sofia B*, near the *Hotel Livikon*, has no views, but does have regular performances of live Cretan music.

Psarotaverna Tassomanolis Facing west along the shore beyond the harbour, *Tassomanolis* is one of three or four good places facing this way. Specialises in fish, caught by the proprietor from his own boat.

Bars and nightlife

Nightlife in Plakiás is rather sedate, especially when compared to the excesses of the north coast or even neighbouring Ayía Galíni. The few **bars** don't take much finding, since the music will lead you there. Most are lined up on the waterfront, keeping people who stay here awake. *Smerna*, *Gialos* and *Ostraco*, right next to each other by the harbour, both offer a variety of drinks and cocktails and, as the night gets on, music. At night, the balcony upstairs at *Ostraco* is the place to be. Between these three the *Avra* crêperie offers late-night sustenance – as well as coffee, ice cream and cocktails earlier in the day, though it's more of a night spot. A few other cafés operate as bars at night, and the tavernas generally stay open until the last customer leaves, but the only more exciting spots are *Finix*, near the bridge, and the *Meltemi* club, with lasers and a light show out by the town beach near *Camping Apollonia*, where things start to get going around midnight.

Beaches

Getting to the **beach** need involve no more than a two-minute walk. The town is set at the western end of the bay, and east of the paved harbour grey sand curves around in an unbroken line to the headland 1km or more away, with an increasing amount of development behind it. Unfortunately, this beach looks better from a distance than from close up – the long open sweep of the bay means it can be exposed and windy, and the strong summer **winds** seem to affect Plakiás more than other places along this coast. There's plenty of space – especially towards the far end – but you'll find much better sands beyond the headland at Dhamnóni (see below), or to the west at Soúdha beach.

Soúdha beach is just over half-an-hour's walk west of town, past signs of encroaching development, and there are places to stop for a swim along the way. The sand is mostly grey and coarse, but there's plenty of room and the water at the far end is sheltered by rocks. Above the very end of the beach, the *Galini* **taverna** enjoys a lovely position in a miniature palm grove.

Listings

Bike rides and rental Odysseas the Cyclist, a local cycling champion, organizes excellent mountain-biking tours of the area, and offers mountain bike rental, from a place on the street leading inland directly behind the harbour (℡28320 31645). Easy Ride (℡28320 20052, ☎www.easyride.reth.gr) also rent out good modern mountain bikes as well as scooters and motorbikes. Most of the car rental places also have motorbikes.

Boat trips Numerous travel agencies can sell you tickets for boat trips to Préveli (some call at Dhamnóni en route), or simply turn up at the harbour; the *Venus* among others leaves for Préveli's Palm Beach daily at 10.30am & 1.30pm (returning at 2pm & 4pm).

Books and newspapers International press and books in English are available at most of the supermarkets on the seafront; try Forum.

Car rental There are plenty of outlets, including several on the seafront; try Moto Auto Plakiás (℡28320 31785), Alianthos (℡28320 31851) or Monza (℡28320 31433).

Diving Some of Crete's best diving is near Plakiás, and there are also easy beaches for learners. Dive2gether is a Dutch company that has a new PADI dive centre with learning pool (and accommodation) near Soúdha beach and an office on the front, west of the bridge (℡28320 32313, ✉crete@dive2gether.com); Kalypso Rocks Dive Centre (℡28320 31895) organizes dives at the nearby Kalypso Rocks resort – its office, just off the front behind the harbour, is open 5–9pm only.

Doctor A doctor's surgery and a pharmacy are in the street by the post office.

Internet The *Ostraco* and *Gialos* bars both have Internet terminals, as does the café above the Forum supermarket.

Laundry Saloon Wash, across from the *Christos Taverna* at the western end of the seafront, will get your clothes back to you washed and dried in ninety minutes.

Money There's no bank in Plakiás, but there are three ATMs along the seafront street and you can change money at most travel agents and some supermarkets.

Post office On the street running inland near the *Hotel Livikon*; Mon–Fri 7.30am–2pm.

Supermarkets The biggest are Forum, immediately east of the bridge; Plakiás Market, between the *Livikon* and *Lamon* hotels, and one on the edge of town by the *Alianthos Beach* hotel, which has a bakery on one side and an excellent fruit shop on the other.

Taxis For local tours, airport trips etc, there's a taxi office at the bottom of the street to the post office, or try ℡28320 31287 or 31922.

Tours The travel agents below can organize a wide range of local tours, or there's the Alianthos Express little train, which runs from the seafront opposite the Forum supermarket. It operates several times a day to Dhamnóni (€6 return), and four days a week it also goes back and forth to Soúdha; the other days it runs as far as Rodhákino (p.294), Préveli (p.291) and Asómatos (p.291). There are also evening trips to Dhamnóni and Mírthios.

Travel agents There are several in town, including Monza Travel on the seafront next to the *Hotel Lamon* (℡28320 31433), Alianthos Travel, next to the *Forum* supermarket (℡28320 31851) and Finikas Travel (look for Moto Auto Plakiás ℡28320 32234) nearby.

Dhamnóni and nearby beaches

Just to the east of Plakiás Bay, beyond a headland riddled with caves and wartime bunkers and gun emplacements, lie some of the most tempting **beaches** in central Crete, albeit a very poorly kept secret. Three splashes of yellow sand, divided by rocky promontories, go by the general name of **Dhamnóni**. The easiest way to get there without your own transport is with the Alianthos Express mini-train. Plenty of people walk, too: follow the main road east and turn right along a track which leads through the olive groves. After a while you'll see the beach below you and a path which runs down to it – about thirty minutes in all. **Driving**, you have to go much further round: follow the road towards Lefkóyia and turn down at the sign for Dhamnóni or, further on, for Amoúdhi.

Dhamnóni beach itself is the first you reach, and the only one that has so far really seen much development: the western half of the beach has been colonized by an ugly Swiss-owned holiday village, *Hapimag*, while the road down to the beach has an increasing number of new rooms places. The oldest of these is the charming, family-oriented *Pension Sokrates* (☎28320 31480; ❸), surrounded by a dense garden whose palms, jasmine and bougainvillea offer welcome shade; a variety of en-suite rooms are available, as well as a couple of larger apartments. The **beach** is a wonderfully long strip of yellow sand and super-clear water. Of the two **tavernas**, *Taverna Damnoni*, fronting the sand, often has grudging, slow service, though the food is good enough; *Taverna Akti*, just behind, is much more friendly.

At the far eastern end of Dhamnóni beach you're likely to find a few people who've dispensed with their clothes, at least out of season, and the little cove which shelters the middle of the three beaches (a scramble over the rocks, or a very rough track) is almost entirely **nudist**. This little enclave can get very crowded, and at times looks like an illustration from *Health and Efficiency* magazine – blow-up beach balls and all – but they're a good-humoured bunch and, exceptionally, often include quite a few Greek naturists too. Again, the water is beautiful and there are caves at the back of the beach and rocks to dive from. There's some great snorkelling to be had around these rocks with their caves and passages. Continuing over the rocks you pass another tiny pocket of sand (also nudist) before **Amoúdhi beach**, where there's a rather more sedate atmosphere and another **taverna** attached to the *Ammoudi Hotel* (☎28320 31355, ⓦwww.ammoudi.gr; ❹ including breakfast). If you want to get away from it all this is a fabulous location, with balcony en-suite rooms 100m from the shore; rooms and food are expensive for what you get, though.

Skhínaria beach is almost adjacent to Amoúdhi, but to get there you have to drive several kilometres round, via Lefkóyia. Another fine, sandy cove, it's popular with Greek families at holiday times and weekends, and occasionally hosts groups learning to scuba dive, but is otherwise delightfully quiet. There's a taverna open during the day, the *Lybian Star*.

Mírthios and inland

The village of **Mírthios** hangs high above Plakiás, with wonderful views over the bay. The youth hostel which put it on the map for generations of travellers has long gone, but several classy new **places to stay** have opened in recent years – mainly studio/apartment developments whose rooms look down over Plakiás. Among the best of them are *Apartments Anna* (☎69733 24775, ⓦwww.annaview.com; ❸–❺) and *Village Apartments* (☎28320 31835, ⓔmirthiosvillage@in.gr; ❸), both of which have a variety of different-sized, well-equipped studios and apartments. The main disadvantage of staying here is that there are few facilities beyond a couple of small shops and a post office, so you really need transport. You can, however, walk down to Plakiás, about twenty minutes steeply downhill, or to several of the nearby beaches – the walk back up is much tougher, though. Alternatively, the Plakiás **bus** usually comes up to Mírthios after it has dropped most of the passengers (it may drop you at the junction, about ten minutes' walk away) or the Alianthos Express little train makes the journey every evening.

For **places to eat**, the *Taverna Plateia* (☎28320 31560), right in the middle of the village, is the longest established restaurant, recently refurbished and taken distinctly upmarket; the excellent traditional food and decor, and stunning views are worth it though. *Plateia* can be very busy, especially at Sunday lunchtimes. *Dionysos* and *Panorama* nearby are cheaper, more straightforward tavernas with equally fine vistas.

Lefkóyia and Asómatos

If lying on the beach were your only plan, you'd have less far to walk, and you'd probably spend less, staying in the village of **Lefkóyia** rather than Plakiás. Lefkóyia is barely twenty minutes' walk from Amoúdhi or Skhínaria beaches and has a couple of minimarkets, four or five pleasant rooms places, and a couple of tavernas (try *Stelios*) by the main road. However, Lefkóyia is not especially attractive, it's not on the coast, it has no views, and it remains primarily an agricultural village where tourism is something of an afterthought.

The attractive village of **Asómatos** is a little further from Plakiás, near the bottom of the Kourtaliótiko gorge on the main route from Réthimnon, and at the junction of roads that head on towards Plakiás via Lefkóyia (the main route) or Mírthios. Built on a steep hillside, it's a bigger place than it first appears. The chief attraction is a remarkable **folk museum** (daily 10am–3pm; €2) assembled by the octogenarian, now retired, local priest Papas Michalis Georgoulákis in his elegant courtyarded family home. Besides the usual articles of everyday life, the collection includes an ancient Cretan kitchen, a section on World War II and an old office with all its antique equipment. The priest's family, who act as curators, also have some pleasant and good-value **apartments** to rent (☎28320 31158, ✆faragi@ret.forthnet.gr; ❷) in a rural spot nearby, which would serve as an ideal base for walking in the area.

Moní Préveli and Palm Beach

Between Asómatos and Lefkóyia a paved road turns off and descends into the fertile valley of the Megapótamos river, which, unusually for Crete, flows throughout the year. Where it meets the river, the road turns south to climb past the ruined **Monastery of Áyios Ioánnis** (aka Káto, or Lower, Préveli), now fenced off and with little sign of a long-promised restoration. The site of the original sixteenth-century monastery of Préveli, it was left behind during the following century by the decision to move to the greater safety of the present site further uphill. Torched by the Turks in the nineteenth century and long abandoned, only the church now stands complete amid the broken walls, cattle mangers and derelict dwellings once used by the monks.

Some 2km further on, the celebrated **Monastery of Préveli** itself (April & May daily 8am–7pm; June–Oct Mon–Sat 8am–1.30pm & 3.30–8pm, Sun 8am–8pm; in winter, knock for admission; €2.50) is perched high above the sea. The monastery is proud of its role in centuries of Cretan resistance, but is famed above all for the shelter provided to Allied troops, many of them Australian, stranded on the island after the Battle of Crete in World War II. The monks supported and fed many soldiers and helped organize them into groups to be taken off nearby beaches by submarine. There's a startling new monument to this, overlooking the sea just before the monastery, depicting a life-sized rifle-toting abbot and an Allied soldier cast in bronze. More commemorative plaques decorate the monastery interior and alongside the icons in the church are a number of offerings from grateful individuals and governments. The church also houses a cross said to contain a fragment of the True Cross; there's a small museum with other relics and religious vestments; and a fountain in the courtyard with the Greek inscription "Wash your sins, not only your face". There are also fine views out to sea towards the distant and chunky-looking Paximádhia islands, which take their name from the tooth-cracking lumps of twice-baked bread served up with *mezédhes* in the island's *kafenía*.

In summer there are four daily **buses** from Réthimnon to Préveli, and a couple from Plakiás (check current times with any tourist office). You can also

△ Feral cats, Creta Préveli monastery

get here on a weekly trip with the Alianthos Express mini-train from Plakiás, or by taking a boat to Palm Beach and climbing up from the beach – a strenuous climb of thirty minutes or so, via the car park.

Palm Beach

Further back on the Préveli road you'll have passed an ancient-looking bridge across the river (actually a nineteenth-century copy of a Venetian original), where a sign indicates a left turn to **Palm Beach**. The *Taverna Gefyra* here makes a pleasant pit stop. Almost immediately you turn right, shortly crossing another cobbled Venetian bridge, beyond which the track leads – after perhaps twenty minutes' tortuous, rough driving – to the *Amoudi* taverna (T6945704654; ❷), one of two places that offer basic **rooms**, some with a great view, on a not terribly attractive beach alongside Palm Beach. From here, Palm Beach is a five-minute climb around the cliff via a stairway carved into the rock – and your first view of it as you reach the crest is quite stunning.

An alternative, and probably easier, route is to continue towards the Préveli Monastery and follow the signs to the **car park** (€1.50). From here a well-marked, stepped path with dramatic views clambers steeply down over the rocks - a ten-minute descent to Palm Beach, fifteen to twenty sweaty minutes back up. The **boat trips** from Plakiás and Ayía Galíni will get you here with a great deal less fuss.

Sadly, **Palm Beach** is no longer really worth all this effort, except at the beginning of the season. It still looks beautiful – a sand-filled cove right at the end of the Kourtaliótiko gorge, where a freshwater estuary feeds a little oasis complete with palm grove and cluster of oleanders – but too many visitors have ruined it. The arrival of loungers and sun umbrellas have diminished the natural charm and, despite the best efforts of the authorities, there's a real problem with plastic rubbish – take everything you bring away with you. Behind the beach, you can walk up the palm-lined riverbanks or paddle through the icy water upstream. Lots of people **camp** along the banks – a lovely setting – but again they have no way of disposing of their rubbish and sewage, and the authorities are now publicizing the fact that camping here is forbidden with threats of eviction. Further upstream, before the gorge becomes too steep to follow, are a couple of deep pools nice to swim in. On the west edge of the beach, a small **bar** sells drinks and a few basic provisions, mostly tinned. A strange thought as you lie on the crowded sands is that it was from here, sixty years ago, that many of the soldiers who sought refuge at Moní Préveli were eventually evacuated by submarine.

West of Plakiás: Selliá and Rodhákino

Heading **west** from Plakiás towards Frangokástello, it's a stiff climb up towards Mírthios and then round, hugging the mountainside, to **Selliá**. You can also approach Selliá direct by an alarmingly steep, winding road climbing from the coast west of Plakiás. Looking up from Plakiás or across from Mírthios you would imagine that Selliá had the best views of all across this area, but if you drive through you see nothing: it is only the backs of the houses which face out across the sea towards Africa. If you want to stop and take a look it's easy enough to find a path through: better still, stop for a drink or bite at the *Taverna Kokkinakis*, a tiny, simple place at the bottom of the square by the "folk art museum" (actually a private gallery), with food to match the views. You can walk from the centre of the village down to Plakiás, about thirty minutes steeply below, or you could include Selliá in a long circular hike from Plakiás

Greek place names

ΑΓ ΓΑΛΗΝΗ	Αγ Γαλήνη	Ay. Galíni
ΑΝΩΓΙΕΑ	Ανώγεια	Anóyia
ΑΣΙΓΩΝΙΑ	Ασιγωνία	Asigonía
ΑΞΟΣ	Αξός	Axós
ΕΠΙΣΚΟΠΗ	Επιοκοπή	Episkopí
ΘΡΟΝΟΣ	Θρόνος	Thrónos
ΚΑΜΑΡΕΣ	Καμάρες	Kamáres
ΛΕΥΚΟΓΕΙΑ	Λευκόγεια	Lefkóyia
Μ. ΑΡΚΑΔΙΟΥ	Μ. Αρκαδίου	Arkádhi monastery
ΜΠΑΛΙ	Μπαλί	Balí
ΜΥΡΘΙΟΣ	Μύρθιος	Mírthios
ΠΕΡΑΜΑ	Πέραμα	Pérama
ΠΛΑΚΙΑΣ	Πλακιάς	Plakiás
ΠΡΕΒΕΛΙ	Πρέβελι	Préveli
ΡΕΘΥΜΝΟ	Ρεθυμνο	Réthimnon
ΣΠΗΛΙ	Σπήλι	Spíli
ΦΟΥΡΦΟΥΡΑΣ	Φουρφουράς	Fourfourás
ΨΗΛΟΡΕΙΤΗΣ	Ψηλορείτης	Psilorítis

via Mírthios – about a four-hour trek. Drivers and bikers heading west from here would be well-advised to check their fuel as there are no official supplies before Hóra Sfakíon.

Beyond Selliá the nature of the country changes and there's a real feeling of the approach of western Crete. The road runs high above a series of capes and small coves, quite a good surface all the way to Argoulés and beyond. The only village of any size is **Rodhákino**, whose two halves are set on steep streets divided by a dramatic ravine. Below is the small, grey sand and shingle beach of **Koráka**, where General Kreipe was finally taken off the island after his kidnap in 1944 (see p.422). Some development has started on the coast around here, and if you want to get away from it all there are a few good **rooms** places. *Sunrise*, a short way up the hill above the beach (☎28320 31787, ✉sunrisea@otenet.gr; ❹ including breakfast), has a small pool, rooms and apartments with sea view and a **taverna** with rooftop terrace. Down at the beach, *Arokaria* (☎28320 32161, ⓦwww.rethymno.com/arokaria; ❹) is an excellent taverna whose pleasant rooms have views as well as TV, a/c, en suite and kitchenette. The beach road continues west as far as **Políriozos** in the next bay along. Here there are more rooms places and villas above a small beach: *Panorama* (☎28320 32179; ❸), and the attached *Taverna Katerina*, are worth a try.

Beyond Rodhákino the main road west winds high above the coast. A number of beaches look incredibly tempting far below but hardly any are accessible. As you approach Frangokástello (p.368), however, there are increasing signs of development, with villas, a few isolated rooms places and even the odd taverna. There seem to be new tracks connecting these places all the time, which makes things confusing: however, if you drive towards the coast you can often find a way through, though the last bit may be on foot. Some of the best are found by following the sign from the main road to **Lákki beach** – follow the dirt road straight on (avoid being seduced by new bits of tarmac or signs to tavernas) and you'll reach a headland from which you can easily walk down to a couple of beautiful patches of sand.

Travel details

Buses

Some of these services are restricted on Sundays. For the latest timetables visit KTEL's websites Ⓦwww.bus-service-crete-ktel.com, Ⓦwww.crete-buses.gr and Ⓦwww.ktel.org.

Ayía Galíni to: Festós (6 daily; 7.45am–4.30pm; 30min); Hóra Sfakíon (1 daily; 7am; 2hr 30min); Iráklion (8 daily; 7.45am–7pm; 2hr); Plakiás (3 daily; 6.30am, 9am & 2.30pm; 1hr 30min); Réthimnon (6 daily; 6.40am–6.45pm; 1hr 30min).

Plakiás to: Ayía Galíni (3 daily; 10.30am, 11.30am & 7pm; 1hr 30min); Hóra Sfakíon (1 daily; 9am; 1hr); Moní Préveli (2 daily; 11am & 5.30pm; 20min); Réthimnon (8 daily; 7am–8.45pm; 45min).

Moní Préveli to: Plakiás (4 daily; 11.20am, 1pm, 6pm & 8.15pm; 20min); Réthimnon (4 daily; 11.30am, 1pm, 6pm & 8.15pm; 1hr).

Réthimnon to: Amári (3 daily; 1hr); Anóyia (2 daily; 5.30am & 2pm; 1hr 30min); Arkádhi (4 daily; 6.15am, 10.30am, noon & 2.30pm; 50min); Ay. Galíni (7 daily; 5.30am–7.30pm; 1hr 30min); Haniá (30 daily; 6.15am–11.15pm; 1hr 30min–3hr); Iráklion (31 daily; 6.30am–11.15pm; 1hr 30min–2hr); Moní Préveli (4 daily; 10am, noon, 4.30pm & 7.30pm; 45min); Omalós (2 daily; 6.15 & 7am; 2hr 30min); Plakiás (8 daily; 6.15am–7.30pm; 45min); Spíli (7 daily; 5.30am–7.30pm; 40min).

Ferries

For the latest information for domestic and international ferries, visit Ⓦwww.greekislands.gr or Ⓦwww.ferries.gr.

Réthimnon to: Pireás (daily at 8pm; 10hr); Thíra (seasonal day-trips Tues & Thurs). Also three-day cruises every Friday to Thíra, Kos & Bodrum (Turkey). Details from Ellotia Tours (see p.252).

4

Haniá

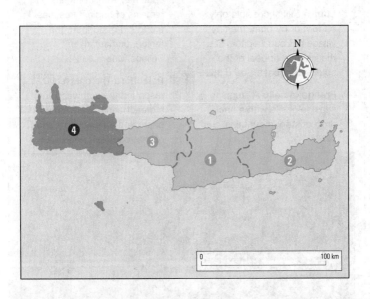

CHAPTER 4

Highlights

✳ **Haniá** A fascinating old town set around a scenic harbour, with excellent accommodation and food as well as the region's best nightlife. See p.302

✳ **The White Mountains** Crete's most impressive mountains offer a huge range of hiking opportunities – the famous Samariá Gorge is only one option. See p.343

✳ **Loutró** Still accessible only on foot or by boat, the tiny village of Loutró epitomises the isolated appeal of the southwest coast. See p.355

✳ **Frangokástello** A stunning seaside castle with a backdrop of stark mountains. See p.368

✳ **Falásarna and Elafonísi** The isolated west coast boasts two of the island's finest beaches. See p.376 & p.382

✳ **The Enneachora** Touring the "Nine Villages" offers a spectacular drive through green, wooded countryside, circling back via a spectacular clifftop corniche. See pp.378–382

✳ **Byzantine churches** Ancient churches, many of them with remains of original frescoes, are found throughout the region, particularly in Sélinos. See p.383

✳ **Paleohóra** The only real resort in the southwest, with a great beach, lively atmosphere and an enjoyably end-of-the-road feel. See p.385

△ Frangokastello harbour and fort

Haniá

aniá, Crete's westernmost province, is still its least visited, which is a significant part of its attraction. Although tourist development is spreading fast, and has already covered much of the coast around the city of Haniá, the west is likely to remain one of the emptier parts of the island, partly because there are no large sand beaches to accommodate resort hotels, and partly because the great archeological sites are a long way from here. In their place are some of the most classic elements of the island: scattered coves, unexploited rural villages, and a spectacular vista of mountains.

The city of **Haniá**, island capital until 1971, is reason in itself to explore; unequivocally the most enjoyable of Crete's larger towns, it is littered with oddments from its Venetian and Turkish past, and bustles with harbourside life. To either side, along virtually the whole **north coast** of the province, spreads a line of sandy beach – at times exposed, and increasingly developed, but still with numerous stretches where you can escape the crowds. The expanse of sand is broken by three peninsulas: **Akrotíri**, enclosing the magnificent natural harbour of the **Bay of Soúdha**; **Rodhópou**, a bare and roadless tract of mountain; and, at the western tip of the island, **Gramvoúsa**, uninhabited and entirely barren. Akrotíri is overshadowed by a NATO presence (air bases on land and naval installations in the bay), but it's still worth a day-trip, with a couple of excellent beaches – **Stavrós** above all – and two beautiful monasteries. Most of the region's tourists stay to the west, on the coast between Haniá and Rodhópou, in one of a number of villages now joined together by a string of low-key development through **Ayía Marína** and **Plataniás**, with the villas and apartments thinning out as you head further from the city.

The south is overshadowed by the peaks of the **Lefká Óri** – the White Mountains – whose grey bulk, snowcapped from January through to June, dominates every view in western Crete. Although marginally less high and considerably less famous than the Psilorítis range, they're far more rewarding for walking or climbing. Along the south coast the mountains drop straight to the Libyan Sea and the few towns here lie in their shadow, clinging to what flat land can be found around the bays. Through the heart of the massif there's no road at all, nor is there any drivable route along the south coast: unless you want to travel back and forth across the island you'll have to rely on boats here, or on walking. The hike through the National Park in the **Samariá Gorge**, Europe's longest, is a stunning experience, despite the summer hordes. With a little spirit of adventure and preparation there are scores of other, deserted, **hiking** routes to take.

The south-coast communities beneath the mountains see plenty of visitors, mostly gorge-trippers passing through, but none could really be described as a resort. **Ayía Rouméli** and **Loutró** can be reached only on foot or by boat,

Kíthira

Cape Voúxa

Bali Beach

N. Gramvoúsa

Gramvoúsa

Ayia Iríni

Gramvoúsa

Falásarna • Kaliviani

Kastélli Kissámou

Plátanos

Polyrínia

Kalathenes

Ayía Sofía Cave

Koutsamatádos

Miliá

Sfinári

Vlátos

Kámbos

Kefáli

Pervólia

Váthi

Élos

Stróvles

Dikaios (1182m)

M. Hrissoskalítissa

Sklavopoúla

Kámatera

Voutás

Elafonísi

Koundourá

Paleohóra

Diktynna

Rodhópou

Áyios Ioánnis Giónis

Afráta

Rodhopós

Áspra Nerá

M. Goniá

Kolimbári

Ravdoúha

Tavronítis • Máleme • Plataniás

German Cemetery

Yeráni

Ayía Marína

Nopríyia

Nochiá

Spiliá

Koléni

Dhrapaniás

Kaloudhianá

Episkopí

Sirili

Voukoliés

Voulgháro

Topólia

Nísi

Koutsamatádos Ravine

Roúmata

Flória

Nea Roúmata

Prasés

Omalós

Kándanos

Ayía Iríni

Plemenianá

Ayía Iríni Gorge

Gíngilos (2080m)

Máza

Kakodíki

Témenia

Moní

Koustoyérako

Azoyirés

Anídhri

Lissós • Soúyia

Ayii Theódori

Vríses

Ayiá

Alikianós

Skinés

0   10 km

Gávdhos

▲ Piréas

M. Katholikó
Stavrós
M. Gouvernetou
Horafákia
M. Ayía
Triádha
Tersanás
Akrotíri
Kalathás

HANIÁ
Kounoupidhianá
Pervolítsa
Stérnes
Allied war
Cemetery
Maráthi

Galatás
Soúdha Bay
Perivolia
Mourniés
Soúdha
Kalámi
E 75
Varípetro
Megála
Horáfia
Aptera
Kalíves
Plaka
Kókkino Horió
*Dhrapano
Peninsula*
Fournés
Stílos
Almirídha
Gavalohóri
Palelóni
Mesklá
Thériso
Neo Horió
Doulianá
Vámos
Kefalás
Kámbi
Samonás
Lákki
Kálamitsi Amigdáli
Soúrva
Tsakístra
Ramní
E 75
Vrísses
Exópolis
Yeoryioúpolis
E 75
Alíkambos
Lake Kournás
▲ *Mávri
(2069m)*
Moúri
L E F K Á   Ó R I
Kournás
Samariá
▲ *Pahnes
(2453m)*
Ammoudhári
E4
Askífou
Samariá Gorge
Ímbros
E4
Ayía Rouméli
Áyios
Ioánnis
Livanianá
Anópoli
Áyios
Pávlos
Finix
Hóra
Sfakíon
Komitádhes
Patsianós
Argoulés
*Mármara
Beach*
Loutró
Líkkos
Sweetwater Beach
Frangokástello

Réthimnon ▶
Réthimnon ▶
Plakiás ▶

although this hasn't prevented Ayía Rouméli, the end-point of the Samariá Gorge walk, from becoming crowded and somewhat overdeveloped; if you want somewhere to unwind after your exertions, the serenity of Loutró is a much better bet. **Hóra Sfakíon**, the capital of the wild region known as Sfakiá, is a pleasant enough place to stay if you can handle the influx of day-trippers; far more peace is to be found down the coast a little, at the superb beaches by the Venetian castle of **Frangokástello**.

The west end of the island, beyond Rodhópou, is very sparsely populated. The port of **Kastélli** is the only town of any size, and there's a growing resort at **Paleohóra** in the south. **Soúyia** may be the next in line, but for the moment it seems in a rather charming state of limbo. The whole of the mountainous southwestern corner, an area known as **Sélinos**, is worth exploring, with rough roads leading to untouched mountain villages and little-known ruins and churches. On the west-facing coast – hard to get to but well worth the effort – are two of Crete's finest beaches, **Falásarna** and **Elafonísi**.

The north coast

With the city of **Haniá** as a base, getting around the **north coast** is easy enough: it's a heavily populated region with excellent roads and a stream of buses along the main routes. Trying to get off the beaten track presents more of a problem if you're dependent on public transport. On the **Rodhópou** peninsula, for example, there are no regular services at all and, while most inland villages are served by at least a couple of daily buses, it can be frustrating if you want to get to several in a day.

Renting a vehicle or motorcycle is a good investment, and there are plenty of outlets in Haniá and all the resorts. Remember, though, that this is mountainous country – the smaller mopeds are (more or less) all right for one person, but with two people on board they simply won't make it up many of the hills.

Haniá

HANIÁ, as any of its residents will tell you, is the spiritual capital of Crete, even if the political title is now officially bestowed on Iráklion's urban sprawl. With its shimmering waterfront, crumbling masonry and web of alleys, it is an extraordinarily attractive city, especially if you can catch it in spring when the Lefká Óri's snowcapped peaks seem to hover above the roofs. The permanent population – fast expanding into hill and coastal suburbs – always outnumbers the tourists, although in August visitors seem to run them pretty close. Haniá has plenty to fill a good day or two's sightseeing, and highlights include the **Venetian harbours**, a quartet of **museums** dealing with archeological, naval, Byzantine and folklore themes, as well as plenty of Minoan ruins dotted throughout the old town. But the greatest pleasure of all, perhaps, is to be had wandering the narrow streets and stepped alleyways of the **old quarters** filled with Venetian and Turkish architectural gems – vestiges of a time when the city was a jewel of the Mediterranean. Include plentiful accommodation and tavernas, excellent **markets**, stores and nightlife, and it all adds up to a city worth getting to know, and – once you've been seduced by its charms – where you'll almost certainly stay longer than you intended.

Some history

Haniá's modern history, in which it featured as a hotbed of nationalist sentiment under the Turks, as well as its proximity to the scene of most of the heavy fighting in the Battle of Crete, has left it with little in the way of monuments. Yet it's one of the longest continuously inhabited city sites anywhere in the world, and remains an enticing place to wander round, with odd reminders of the past at every pace and antiquities in the most unlikely settings.

Under the name **Kydonia**, it was a **Minoan** community of obscure status: only scattered remnants have so far been brought to light, but many believe that there's a major palace still to be discovered somewhere in the vicinity, perhaps beneath modern buildings on the Kastélli hill overlooking the harbour, where Palatial-style architectural fragments and artefacts have been unearthed. After the collapse of the Minoan palace culture, it grew into one of the island's most important cities – well known enough for its citizens to warrant a mention in Homer's *Odyssey* – and remained so through the Classical Greek era. When **Rome** came in search of conquest, the city mounted a stiff resistance prior to its eventual capitulation in 69 BC, after which it flourished once more. The Kastélli hill served as the Roman city's acropolis, but dwellings spread at least as far as the extent of the walled city which can be seen today. Roman mosaics from this era have been discovered beneath the Cathedral Square and up near the present market.

In early **Christian** times Kydonia was the seat of a bishop, and under the protection of Byzantium the city flourished along with the island. As the Byzantine Empire became increasingly embattled however, so its further outposts, Kydonia (and Crete) included, suffered neglect. Not much is heard of the place again until the thirteenth century, when the **Genoese** (with local support) seized the city from the Venetians and held it from 1263 to 1285.

When the **Venetians** finally won it back they acted quickly to strengthen the defences, turning the city – renamed **La Canea** – into a formidable bulwark. The city walls were built in two stages: in the fourteenth century Kastélli alone was fortified, and within these walls stood the original cathedral and the city administration; later, in the sixteenth century, new walls were constructed as a defence against constant raids by pirate corsairs – in particular against the systematic ravages of Barbarossa. It is these defences, along with the Venetian harbour installations, that define the shape of Haniá's old town today. Within the walls, meanwhile, a flourish of public and private construction left La Canea perhaps the island's most beautiful city.

In 1645, after a two-month siege with terrible losses (mostly on the Turkish side – their commander was executed on his return home for losing as many as forty thousand men), Haniá fell to the **Turks**. It was the first major Cretan stronghold to succumb, becoming the Turkish island capital and seat of the pasha. Churches were converted to mosques, the defences more or less maintained, and there must have been at least some building: today it is barely possible to distinguish Venetian buildings maintained by the Turks from originals of Venetian or Turkish workmanship.

For the rest, it is a history of struggle – for **independence** during the nineteenth century, then in **resistance** against the Germans in World War II. In the

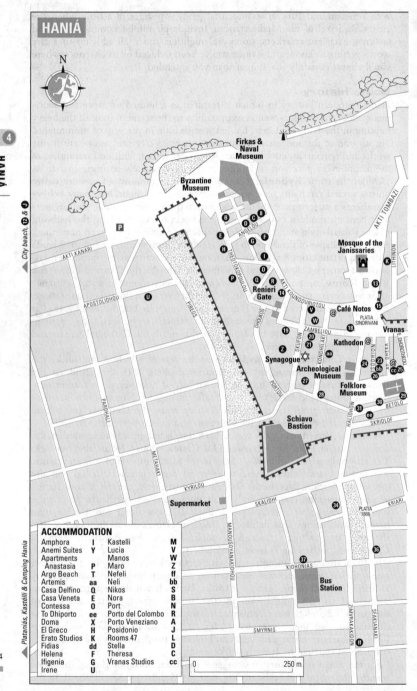

HANIÁ

N

Firkas & Naval Museum

Byzantine Museum

P

AKTI KANARI

APOSTOLIDHOU

AKTI TOMBAZI

Mosque of the Janissaries

B   **D**   **C**
E   **G**   **F**
H   **I**
ANGELOU
THEOTOKOPOULOU
O
P   **R**   **Q**
Renieri Gate
14   AKTI KOUNDOURIOTOU   @ Café Notos
PLATIA SINDRIVANI
13
K   LITHINON
15
Vranas

PIREOS

U

DHIKEOS
SKUFON
PORTOU
METAHAKI
PARDHALI

19   **20**   **V**   **W**   **18**
21
ZAMBELIOU
KONDHILAKI
Kathodon @
Z   **aa**
24   **bb**
Synagogue   **26**   @
Archeological   **cc**   **25**
Museum   Vranas
27   **28**   Folklore   **29**
Museum   **30**
31   **ee**   BETOLO
SKRIDLOF
HALIDHON

Schiavo Bastion

KYRILOU

Supermarket

SKALIDHI

34   PLATIA 1866   KRIARI

36

MANOUSOYANAKIDHOU

37   KIDHONIAS

Bus Station

SMYRNIS
ZIMVRAKAKIDHON
SFAKIANAK

ff

ACCOMMODATION

Amphora	**I**	Kastelli	**M**	
Anemi Suites	**Y**	Lucia	**V**	
Apartments		Manos	**W**	
Anastasia	**P**	Maro	**Z**	
Argo Beach	**T**	Nefeli	**ff**	
Artemis	**aa**	Neli	**bb**	
Casa Delfino	**Q**	Nikos	**S**	
Casa Veneta	**E**	Nora	**B**	
Contessa	**O**	Port	**N**	
To Dhiporto	**ee**	Porto del Colombo	**R**	
Doma	**X**	Porto Veneziano	**A**	
El Greco	**H**	Posidonio	**J**	
Erato Studios	**K**	Rooms 47	**L**	
Fidias	**dd**	Stella	**D**	
Helena	**F**	Theresa	**C**	
Ifigenia	**G**	Vranas Studios	**cc**	
Irene	**U**			

0   250 m

304

4

HANIÁ

City beach, **12** & **J**

Plataniás, Kastélli & Camping Hania

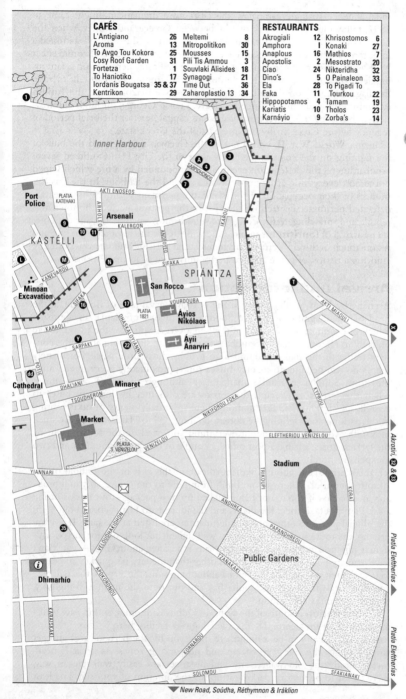

CAFÉS

L'Antigiano	26	Meltemi	8
Aroma	13	Mitropolitikon	30
To Avgo Tou Kokora	25	Mousses	15
Cosy Roof Garden	31	Pili Tis Ammou	3
Fortetza	1	Souvlaki Alisides	18
To Haniotiko	17	Synagogi	21
Iordanis Bougatsa	35 & 37	Time Out	36
Kentrikon	29	Zaharoplastio 13	34

RESTAURANTS

Akrogiali	12	Khrisostomos	6
Amphora	1	Konaki	27
Anaplous	16	Mathios	7
Apostolis	2	Mesostrato	20
Ciao	24	Nikteridha	32
Dino's	5	O Painaleon	33
Ela	28	To Pigadi To	
Faka	11	Tourkou	22
Hippopotamos	4	Tamam	19
Kariatis	10	Tholos	23
Karnáyio	9	Zorba's	14

Inner Harbour

Port Police

PLATIA KATEHAKI

Arsenali

AKTI ENOSEOS

SARPIDHONOS

KASTÉLLI

KALERGON

ARHOLEON

ANDROEO

SIFAKA

SPIÁNTZA

KANEVAROU

IKAROU

MINOS

Minoan Excavation

San Rocco

VOURDOUBA

PLATIA 1821

Áyios Nikólaos

KARAOLI

SARPAKI

DHASKALOYIANNIS

Áyii Anaryíri

AKTI MIAOULI

POTIE

Cathedral

DHALIANI

Minaret

TSOUDHERON

NIKIFOROU FOKA

KYPROU

Market

PLATIA S. VENIZELOU

VENIZELOU

ELEFTHERIOU VENIZELOU

Akrotíri, 32 & 33

YIANNARI

N. PLASTIRA

VELODHMA KALDHON

Stadium

ANDHREA

TRIKOUPI

KORAI

PAPANDHREOU

Platía Eleftherías

APOKORONOU

TZANAKAKI

Public Gardens

Dhimarhio

KARAISKAKI

KOUNAMOU

SFAKIANAKI

Platía Eleftherías

SOLOMOU

▼ New Road, Soúdha, Réthymnon & Iráklion

independence struggle campaign, the city's most dramatic moment came in 1897, following the outbreak of war between Greece and Turkey, when the Great Powers (Britain, France, Russia and Italy) imposed peace and stationed a joint force in the waters off Haniá – an event used to dramatic and comic effect by Kazantzákis in his novel *Zorba the Greek*. From here, in one famous incident, they bombarded Cretan insurgents attempting prematurely to raise the flag of Greece on the hill of Profitis Elías (see p.320). When the Turkish administrators were finally forced to leave, Prince George, the high commissioner chosen by the powers, established his capital here for the brief period of regency before Crete finally became part of the Greek state.

During **World War II**, with most of the German landings and the bulk of the fighting on the coast immediately west of the city, Haniá suffered severe bombardment, the destruction eventually compounded by a fire which wiped out almost everything apart from the area around the harbour. In the final six months of their occupation of the island, the Germans withdrew to a heavily defended perimeter centred on the city. In the postwar period, the town was rebuilt, and sprawling, traffic-congested suburbs now encircle the ancient core.

The arrival of **tourism** has inspired the will – if not the resources – to save and restore much of the city's crumbling architectural heritage, and Haniá is currently enjoying a period of peace and prosperity unrivalled in its modern history.

Arrival and information

Arriving by **boat**, you'll anchor at the port and naval base of **Soúdha**, at the head of the magnificent Bay of Soúdha, 10km east of Haniá, an approach which offers unparalleled views of the Lefká Óri as you near the island. You're unlikely to choose to stay in Soúdha – the hotels are sited right above the constant traffic of the main road and it's a grubby, dusty little place. Fortunately there's no real need to do so: **city buses** run approximately every fifteen minutes from Soúdha to Haniá's marketplace, although these can be swamped when the ferries arrive, and the ferries are also met by intercity buses to Kastélli, and Iráklion via Réthimnon. There are usually plenty of **taxis** waiting in the parking area right by the dock too (about €8 to Haniá). If you are stuck in Soúdha you'll find just about everything you need on the square right by the ferries: stores, a bank, a post office, a couple of bars and restaurants, and two inexpensive hotels.

Haniá's **airport** is about 15km northeast of the city, in the middle of the Akrotíri peninsula. There are no buses from here to the centre, so you'll probably need a taxi if you're not being picked up by a package-tour bus or hiring a car. Plentiful taxis meet the flights and the journey to Haniá costs about €15; the official prices to other popular destinations are listed at the rank. If you are driving, the route into Haniá is pretty well signed, but look out for the poorly-signed junction where you join the main road after about 3km – you don't have priority here. For all destinations other than the city, it's quicker and easier to take the left turn signed to Soúdha about 6km from the airport; this will take you down past the head of Soúdha Bay and out onto the main E75 highway, bypassing Haniá's congestion.

The **bus station** is south of the walls on Odhós Kidhonías, within easy walking distance of the centre. There's a left-luggage facility here.

Arriving by **car** can be a nightmare once you hit the harbour area and get tangled up in the one-way system and no-parking zones. As a car is near-useless inside the old walled city and distances are easily walkable anyway, there's a lot to be said for parking it up for the duration of your stay. The least stressful solution is to park outside the old town and walk in. Longer-term parking places can usually be found along Aktí Kanári to the west of the Naval Museum near the seafront, or on the sidestreets off Pireós leading down there, and to the north of the open-air theatre on the east side of the old town; there are also signposted pay car parks in the new town. Finding parking within the walls of the old town is almost impossible in high season – besides which many of the more attractive hotels simply can't be reached by car, though some of the bigger places will provide you with porter's trolleys. It's worth knowing that you are permitted to drive along the Aktí Koundouriótou waterfront **before 10am** (after which it is closed) – this is a handy way of transporting baggage to and from the many hotels in this zone. Otherwise you could opt to stay along Theotokopóulou, easily reached from the car park by the naval museum, or a little further out at a hotel with its own car park. Wherever you park make sure not to leave any valuables in the car.

Information

The very helpful **Municipal Tourist Office** is in the *Dhimarhío* (town hall) at Kidhonías 29 (Mon–Fri 9am–2.30pm; ☏28210 36155, ℻28210 36205; Town Hall open Mon–Fri 9am–8pm), four blocks east of the bus station. They have timetables for buses, sites and museums across the island, as well as details of how to get to them, local trips, gorge walks and more; much of this is pinned up on the wall, so can be checked even when the tourist office itself is closed. For details of where to buy tickets for plane, bus or ferry departures, see "Listings" on p.319.

Accommodation

There are thousands of **rooms to rent** in Haniá and, unusually, quite a few comfortable, elegant **boutique hotels**. Even so you may face a long search for a bed at the height of the season (especially in the first half of August). Perhaps the most desirable rooms – with prices to match – are those overlooking the **harbour**, west of Hálidhon, though be warned that some of those nearer the water can be noisy at night. Most are approached not direct from the harbourside itself but from the alleys leading off it, especially on the west side. The nicest of the more expensive places are here too, usually set back a little way and thus quieter, but often still with good views from upper storeys.

In the eastern half of the **old town** rooms are far more scattered, and tend to be cheaper. In the height of the season your chances of finding somewhere are much better over here. Immediately east of the harbour, reached via the alleys that lead north off Kaneváro, **Kastélli** has some lovely places with views, although they are very popular and often booked up. Another possibility is close to the **town beaches** at the east and west fringes, which are quiet and often pleasant: we've listed a couple of possibilities here. There's really not much reason to stay in the modern part of town, unless you arrive late and need to find somewhere near the bus station on your first night, or you really want a car park and business-style facilities: the hotels are, on the whole, uninspiring.

In the **addresses** below, Párodos literally means side street, so 2 Párodos Theotokopóulou, for example, is the second alley off Theotokopóulo. If you're having trouble finding somewhere, the tourist office has extensive lists and often knows where there are vacancies, or you could try the Rental Accommodations Union (Dorothéou Epískopou 20 ☏28210 43601, ⓦwww.west-crete-rooms.com), whose website has an online booking facility for over thirty rooms places in Haniá, plus dozens more across the province.

Around the harbour: west of Hálidhon

Amphora 2 Párodos Theotokopóulou 20 ☎28210 93224, ⓦwww.amphora.gr. Hotel in a fourteenth-century Venetian building, beautifully renovated with some interesting features such as spiral stair-cases and four-poster beds. The balcony rooms (such as Room 20) with harbour view are the best value; the rooms without a view are significantly cheaper. ❻–❼

Apartments Anastasia Theotokopóulou 21 ☎28210 88001 or mobile ☎6972292643, ⓔanastasia_ap@acn.gr. Rooms and fully equipped apartments in a couple of locations on this popular street. Rooms ❸, apartments ❺

Artemis Kondiláki 13 ☎ & ⓕ28210 91196. A/C rooms with bath, fridge and TV plus use of kitchen in this touristy street running inland from Zambelíu. ❺

Casa Delfino Theofánous 9 ☎28210 87400, ⓦwww.casadelfino.com. Completely over the top suites hotel offering big, deluxe suites with elegant decor, marble or polished-wood floors, satellite TV, dataports and Jacuzzis. ❾

Casa Veneta Theotokopóulou 57 ☎28210 90007, ⓕ28210 75931. Excellent-value a/c studios and apartments with kitchenette and TV, and a helpful, friendly proprietor; the large duplex apartment is particularly pleasant. ❺

Contessa Theofánous 15 ☎28210 98566, ⓕ28210 98565. One of the first of the harbour hotels to be done up, and now showing its age a bit, but bags of character and harbour views from some rooms. All rooms with fridge, TV, a/c and breakfast. ❹–❻

El Greco Theotokopóulou 49 ☎28210 90432, ⓦwww.elgreco.gr. Comfortable modern hotel that merges into its surroundings. Tastefully furnished, rather small rooms come with a/c, TV and fridge; attractive roof garden with harbour view. ❻

Helena A Párodos Theotokopóulou 14 ☎28210 95516 or mobile ☎6977007946. Charming small hotel in quiet street with pleasant, a/c balcony rooms with TV; some with views. ❺

Ifigenia A. Gamba 21 ☎28210 94357, ⓦwww.ifigeniastudios.gr. Part of a small empire of rooms, studios and apartments atvarious prices, mostly elegantly decorated and well equipped (some with Jacuzzi), in old Venetian buildings. Another branch is at Theotokopóulou 15. ❹–❻

Lucia Aktí Koundouriótou ☎28210 90302, ⓦwww.ellada.net/loukia. Harbourfront hotel with balcony rooms. Not the prettiest place, but excep-tional value for some of the best views in town, although the rooms at the back are less inviting.

All with a/c and double glazing, which should ensure peace at night. ❹

Manos Zambelíu 24 ☎28210 94156, ⓦwww.manoshotel.gr. Great location right on the harbour, though the more expensive balcony rooms on that side are inevitably noisy. All come with a/c, TV and fridge, and some have cooking facilities; there's also an Internet café downstairs. ❹–❻

Maro B Parodos Portou 5 ☎28210 54981. Probably the cheapest rooms in the old town, hidden away in a quiet, unmarked alley off Portou not far from the Schiavo Bastion. Basic but friendly and clean. ❷

Nora Theotokopóulou 60 ☎28210 72265. Charming, simple rooms in an old wooden Turkish house, some with shared bath. Pleasant breakfast café below. ❸

Porto del Colombo Theofánous and Moschón ☎28210 70945, ⓦwww.ellada.net/colombo. Hotel occupying a grand, rather dark old mansion that the management claim was once the French Embassy and later home of Eleftheríos Venizélos. All rooms with TV, a/c and minibar. ❻

Stella Angélou 10 ☎28210 73756. Creaky but charmingly eccentric old house with plain, clean a/c rooms with bath and fridge above an eclectic gift shop. ❺

Thereza Angélou 8 ☎28210 92-798. Beautiful old pension in a great position with stunning views from its roof terrace and some rooms; classy decor too. More expensive than its neighbours but deservedly so – book ahead in high season. ❻

The old city: east of Hálidhon

Anemi Suites Sarpáki 41 ☎28210 53001. Inviting apartments inside a restored Turkish wooden house; all are a/c with a kitchen and sleep 2–3 people. Prices vary, but the cheapest (No. 4) with a superb terrace is the one to go for. ❻–❼

To Dhiporto Betólo 41 ☎28210 40570. The "Two Doors" runs between Betólo and pedestrian Skridhlóf streets: the balcony rooms over the latter, especially, are quiet. Friendly and good value, with a/c, TV, fridge and coffee machine in the rooms. ❹–❻

Erato Studios Lithinón 17 ☎2310 692378. Stunning location with balconies overlooking the harbour from high on its eastern edge justifies the price of these two- and three-bed studios equipped with a/c, TV and small kitchen. ❻

Fidias Sarpáki 8 ☎28210 52494. Signposted from the cathedral. This favourite backpackers' meeting place has recently been done up to add more en-suites and better facilities, including some small kitchens. Still cheap and cheerful, though, with the real advantage of offering single rooms or arranging shares in three- or four-bed rooms, which are the cheapest beds in town (€8–10). ②–③

Kastelli Kaneváro 39 ☎ 28210 57057, ⓦ www.kastellistudios.gr. Comfortable, modern, reasonably priced pension and very quiet at the back. All en-suite rooms come with fan or a/c and anti-mosquito machines. The proprietor is exceptionally helpful and also has a few apartments and a beautiful house nearby (for up to five people) to rent. Will assist with parking. ③

Neli Isódhion 21–23 ☎ 28210 55533, ⓦ www.nelistudios.com. Larger and fancier than it appears from outside, this hotel rambles through three lovingly restored old buildings, with stylishly decorated, fully equipped rooms with balconies, a/c and cooking facilities. ⑤

Nikos Dhaskaloyiánnis 63 ☎ 28210 54783. Built directly on top of a Minoan ruin – visible through a basement window as you enter – with a beautiful and rare 3500-year-old painted pillar. Good-value, relatively modern rooms, all with shower, fridge, kitchenette; will supply fans on demand. Has a branch over the road with cheaper rooms, and there are several others nearby on this street. ③

Port Sífaka 73 ☎ 28210 59484, ⓔ lioliosk@chania .cci.gr. Pleasant rooms with bath and balcony, some overlooking a quiet garden. ④

Porto Veneziano Overlooking the Venetian harbour ☎ 28210 27100, ⓦ www.portoveneziano.gr. The plushest hotel on the east side of the old town is now part of the *Best Western* chain. Very comfortable, if bland, rooms with balcony views over the harbour. ⑧

Rooms 47 Kandanoléon 47 ☎ 28210 53243. Quiet, traditional and simple rooms place on a street leading up from Kanevaró into Kastélli. Some rooms have balconies with fantastic sea views. ④

Vranas Studios Ayíon Dhéka and Kalinákou Sarpáki, near the cathedral ☎ 28210 58618, ⓔ vranas@yahoo.com. Attractive, spacious balcony studio rooms with a/c, TV and kitchenette. ⑤

The modern city

Argo Beach Aktí Míaouli 1 ☎ 28210 40980, ⓕ 28210 86303. Truly charming and good-value old-style hotel with sea-view balcony rooms with bath, TV and ceiling fans, in a vibrant area away from the tourist maelstrom. Has its own car park. ④

Doma Venizélou 124, on the seafront 300m east off our map ☎ 08210 51772, ⓕ 08210 41578. Elegant hotel inside a late nineteenth-century edifice which once served as the Austrian Embassy and later the British consulate until it was taken over by the Germans during World War II. The house has many original features including a serene patio garden, and both breakfast room and bedrooms have fine sea views. Easy on street parking nearby. Rates include breakfast. ⑦

Irene Apostolídhou 9 ☎ 28210 89075. Big, white modern hotel with fully-equipped rooms – balconies on the upper levels have sea views. Easy parking outside and not far to walk to the harbour or the town beach. ⑥

Nefeli Zimvrakákidon 47 ☎ 28210 70007, ⓕ 28210 90855. Modern business hotel with pristine a/c balcony rooms equipped with TV and minibar. Parking nearby, and handy for the bus station. ⑥

Posidonio Moní Goniás 57, corner of Aktí Papanikóli ☎ 28210 87404. Modern hotel right at the end of the beachfront road, behind the town beach. The rooms are a bit faded, but big, with fridge and a/c (for extra charge) – all in all a good deal for seafront location and easy parking. ⑥

Campsite

Camping Hania ☎ 28210 31138, behind the beach in Áyii Apóstoli, 4km west of Haniá. A rather small site, hemmed in by new development, but it has a pool and all the facilities just a short walk from some of the better beaches. It's just about within walking distance of Haniá if you follow the coast around, but more easily reached by taking the local bus (see p.314): a large sign tells you where to get off – from here walk down towards the sea for about five minutes.

The City

Haniá's **old city** clusters around the harbour, and most tourists rightly confine themselves to this area or the fringes of the new town up towards the bus station. You may get lost wandering among the narrow alleys, but it's never far to the sea, to one of the main thoroughfares or to some other recognizable landmark. The best way to get around the city is to walk, but the terminus for most **city buses**, especially those heading west, is at Platía 1866 just south of the walls; for Soúdha and the eastern side of town you may find it easier to get on at one of the stops by the market.

Hálidhon is perhaps the most commercially touristy street in Haniá, and the major junction at the inland end of the street marks the centre of town as much as anywhere does. If you stand facing north at this junction, everything in front and below you is basically the old, walled city; behind and to either side lie the newer parts. To the east, **Odhós Yiánnari** leads past the market and, if you follow it round, either to the main coast road or out onto the Akrotíri peninsula. To the west of the junction, **Skalídhi** leads eventually out of town towards Kastélli Kissámou. Ahead of you, Hálidhon descends to the **harbour** and into the heart of the old town. Much of your **shopping** and other business will take place around the meeting of old and new represented by this main Hálidhon junction: here and down towards the market you'll find pharmacies, newspaper stores and banks. The major thoroughfares heading south off Yiánnari – Apokorónou, Tzanakáki and Papandreou – represent modern Haniá, full of clothes and furniture stores, car rental places and more banks.

Along Hálidhon

From the main Hálidhon junction, head north (and down), taking the first left to walk down beside a high stretch of wall into the vicinity of the **Schiavo Bastion**. There's not a great deal to see here, but it's strange to find yourself so suddenly out of the crowds and among the scruffy yards and inquisitive dogs of the backstreets. A little further down Hálidhon, the considerably more interesting and animated **Odhós Skridlóf** joins from the right. Here, traditionally, leathermakers plied their trade, and although many shops are now geared to tourists and given over to beach towels and souvenirs, prices for leatherware – sandals, bags and the like – remain the best in Crete.

Just below Skridlóf, the **Cathedral** is set back from the road, presiding over a small square. Given Haniá's history and importance, you might expect this to be rather impressive. In fact, it's a modest building with little architectural merit, dating only from the 1860s. The square, though, Platía Mitropóleos, has seen a revival in recent years and is now surrounded by cafés with outdoor tables – more peaceful if you head round to the back of the Cathedral. Around 1770, the rebel Dhaskaloyiánnis (see p.361) was tortured to death here. On Hálidhon immediately below the square, you can see the ramshackle domes of a former Turkish bath: this has now been converted into a fashion store, Hamam, and it's worth taking a quick look inside.

Almost opposite is Haniá's **Archeological Museum** (Tues–Sun 8.30am–3pm; €2, €3 for combined ticket with Byzantine Collection), housed in the Venetian-built church of San Francesco. Though it doesn't look like much now, with its campanile gone and a crumbling facade, this building was once one of the island's grandest. Inside, where there has been substantial restoration, you get a better sense of its former importance. The Turks converted the church into a mosque, from which a beautiful fountain and the base of a minaret have survived in the pungent, flowery garden alongside. Dominating the front part of the museum are large quantities of **Minoan pottery**, including a few of the huge Minoan storage jars or *píthoi*. In the centre is a collection of Minoan clay coffins (*lárnakes*), some wonderfully decorated, and one still containing two small skeletons. For archeologists, the most significant items are the **inscribed tablets** excavated in Kastélli: this is the only place other than Knossós where examples of Linear A and Linear B script have been found together. Towards the back of the church, the collection is arranged chronologically, progressing through a large group of Classical **sculptures**, a case full of Greco-Roman **glassware** and some third-century Roman **mosaics** reassembled on the floor. The latter are truly lovely, particularly those of Dionysos and Ariadne, and of Poseidon and Anemone. Outside in the garden courtyard are other assorted sculptures and architectural remnants, including a lovely one-legged, headless lion.

Almost next door to the Archeological Museum, signed down a narrow alley, the **Cretan House Folklore Museum** (Mon–Sat 9am–3pm & 6–9pm; €1.50) is a charming, cluttered collection of artefacts, tapestries and traditional crafts equipment set out in a replica of a "traditional" house (though few can have been quite so packed). The old traditions are continued, and embroidered cloths and tapestries made on the premises are offered for sale. On your way out, take a look at Haniá's elegant **Roman Catholic church** in the same courtyard, an interesting contrast to Orthodox churches.

Around the outer harbour

Hálidhon ends at a square by the harbour – officially called Platía Sindriváni, but known by everyone simply as **Harbour Square**. To the left, Aktí Koundouriótou circles around the outer harbour, crowded with outdoor cafés and tavernas. The **harbour** comes into its own at night, when the lights from bars and restaurants reflect in the water and the animated crowds – locals as much as tourists – parade in a ritualistic volta of apparently perpetual motion. There are stalls set up on the waterside selling everything from seashells to henna tattoos, and buskers serenading the passers-by. By day, especially in the hot, dozy mid-afternoon, it can be less appealing – deserted and with a distinct smell of decay from the rubbish washing up against the quayside.

This is the **outer harbour**, and the hefty bastion at the far end houses Crete's **Naval Museum** (daily 9am–4pm; €2). Although largely of specialist interest, the enthusiasm here is infectious, and the model ships, maquettes of the town in Venetian times, old maps and working exhibits like the old harbour light are hard to resist. One entire room is devoted to seashells and sea creatures. Upstairs a rather duller collection of marine instruments and photos of warships is enlivened by the entire bridge of a destroyer set up in its midst, and there's also an exhibition on the **Battle of Crete** of 1941. This is small and not terribly well displayed or labelled, but you still get a real sense of the sufferings of the Haniá villagers at the hands of the Nazis. Whether visiting the museum or not, it's worth going through the main gate (usually open in daylight hours) to visit the compound of the small naval garrison. Here you can climb onto the seaward fortifications of the **Fírkas**, as this part of the city defences is known. It was on this spot that the modern Greek flag was first raised on Crete – in 1913 – and there are fine sea views.

Carrying on round the outside of the Fírkas, which has been well restored, you can peer through loopholes at the great vaulted chambers within. On the far side, there's a car park (also the starting point for the "Little Train" tours of the new town), and you can follow the sea wall round towards the town beach. Turn inland, though, and you reach the **Byzantine and post–Byzantine Collection** (Tues–Sun 8.30am–3pm; €2, €3 for combined ticket with Archeological Museum), located in the small Venetian chapel of San Salvatore at the bottom of Theotokopoúlou. The beautifully displayed collection of mosaics, icons, jewellery, coins, sculpture and everyday objects is tiny, but gives a fascinating insight into an era that's largely overlooked: it covers the entire period from early Christian to the end of the Venetian occupation in the seventeenth century.

Beyond the museum, Pireós cuts inland outside the best-preserved stretch of the **city walls**. Following them around on the inside is rather trickier, but far more enjoyable. This is where you'll stumble on some of the most picturesque little alleyways and finest Venetian houses in Haniá, and also where the pace of renovation and gentrification is most rapid. Keep your eyes open for details on the houses, such as old wooden balconies or stone coats of arms. The arch of the **Renieri Gate**, at the bottom of Moschón, is particularly elegant. There are also lots of interesting art and craft stores around here, along Theotokopóulou and the many alleys that run off it down towards the harbour.

Between the Renieri Gate and Hálidhon are more such streets and alleys, though here the emphasis is more on tavernas, bars and cafés: Kóndilaki is one of the busiest. This area was the medieval Jewish ghetto, and at the end of a small alley off the west side of Kóndilaki is Haniá's fifteenth-century Etz Hayyim **synagogue** (Mon–Fri 9am–12.30pm & 6–8pm; prayers daily at 9am; free; Ⓦ www.etz-hayyim-hania.org), renovated by a fraternity of local Christians, Muslims and Jews after falling into a ruinous state. All but one of the city's Jews were rounded up by the Nazi occupation forces in 1944 and were shipped off to Auschwitz, but they met their end (along with around five hundred members of the captured Cretan resistance) when their transport ship was torpedoed by a British submarine off the island of Mílos. The synagogue is entered through the original Venetian doorway and its garden, *mikveh* (purification fountain), reconstructed interior and *bimah* (speakers' platform) have been sensitively restored with the aid of public donations. The names of the 376 Jews who perished in the transport ship are remembered on a plaque.

The inner harbour

North from Harbour Square, the curious, domed profile of the **Mosque of the Janissaries** dominates the view. Built in 1645, the year Haniá fell to the Turks, it is the oldest Ottoman building on the island, and has been well restored – apart from the jarring concrete dome. The future use of the building is uncertain, though there are plans to demolish the outbuildings at the back. Meantime, aside from occasional exhibitions, you may not be able to get in: if you do, the main feature is the **mihrab** (a niche indicating the direction of Mecca) complete with Koranic inscription.

The harbourfront Aktí Tombázi curves round to the right to the **inner harbour**, where pleasure boats, private yachts and small fishing vessels are moored, and where sixteenth-century Venetian arsenals look out towards the breakwater alongside a cluster of restaurants and bars. Many of the arched **Arsenali** are still in a ruinous state, but others have been sensitively restored: one, occupied by the Ministry of Culture, has offices, a café and a glitzy space for temporary exhibitions (times and fees vary). In another, a fifteenth century BC **Minoan ship** has been reconstructed, and should be on display from autumn 2004 as part of an exhibition of ancient navigation. Continuing round, you can follow the sea wall as far as the minaret-style **lighthouse**, where there's a bar and an excellent view back over the city. You could then take the bar's all-day (free) shuttle ferry back to the south side of the harbour. At the eastern end of the inner harbour there are more signs of regeneration and refurbishment, and this is now a fashionable part of town. Aktí Miaoúli, following the shore eastwards beyond the city walls, is packed at night with bars and cafés, mostly frequented by young locals. Behind the harbour, though, the streets are still pretty run down, and in some ways the most atmospheric in the old town.

Kastélli

The bluff that rises behind the mosque and the inner harbour, known as **Kastélli**, was the site of the earliest habitation in Haniá. Favoured from earliest times for its defensive qualities, this little hill takes its name from a fortress which originally dated from the Byzantine era. Later it was the centre of the Venetian and of the Turkish towns, but very little survived a heavy bombardment during World War II.

Walking up Kanevaro from the Harbour Square you'll pass various remains, including a couple of fenced-off sites where **Minoan Kydonia** is being excavated. Swedish archeologists have traced the outline of a substantial building engulfed by a violent fire about 1450 BC, like that which destroyed Knossós. Many believe that this is the **palace** long thought to have existed here and, if so, it would complete a pattern across the island. It was later rebuilt after the fire and, given its proximity to the mainland, may well have been the focus of Mycenaean power on Crete. Among pottery finds here were some dating back to the Neolithic era, but the greatest prize uncovered was an archive of clay tablets bearing Minoan Linear A script (see p.413), the first to be found so far west in Crete. All around this area are various **trial excavations**, usually on vacant lots between existing houses, revealing further tantalizing glimpses of the substantial Minoan conurbation which lies beneath the modern town, and there are plans for much more extensive excavations once all the relevant property has been acquired. The alleys up to the left, onto the rise, end up going nowhere, but it's worth looking up here for the traces of the old city that survive, and tantalising glimpses of the views that the old buildings afford. Lithinón, for example, has various Venetian doorways and inscriptions and, at the top, a fine old archway.

Splántzia

Inland from Kastélli, you can head through the backstreets towards the **market**. As you wander round these streets, a **minaret** keeps appearing above the rooftops, only to disappear when you head towards it: actually located on Dhaliáni, it seems to be part of a carpenter's workshop, but is fenced off and closed to visitors.

A second **minaret** (this one missing its top) adorns the church of Áyios Nikólaos in the tranquil **Platía 1821**, further over to the east. Built by the Venetians, the church was converted to a mosque under Sultan Ibrahim and reconverted after Crete's reversion to Greek authority, but has been so often refurbished that there's nothing much to see. The square itself – whose name recalls the date of one of the larger rebellions against Turkish authority, following which an Orthodox bishop was hanged here – is another pleasantly shaded space set with café chairs. Nearby are two more old churches: San Rocco, just a few metres towards the harbour, is small and old-fashioned, while Áyii Anáryiri, which retained its Orthodox status throughout the Turkish occupation, has some very ancient icons. This quarter, known as **Splántzia**, is full of unexpected architectural delights, with carved wooden balconies and houses arching across the street at first-floor level. Many of the streets between here and the inner harbour have recently been recobbled and generally refurbished, and they're among the most atmospheric and tranquil in the old town.

The new town

Modern Haniá sprawls in every direction, encircling the old town. With time on your hands, there are parts that are worth the walk. Starting from in front of the **market**, the areas to the southwest, on the way to **Platía 1866** and the bus station, have an attractively old-fashioned commercialism about them, full of general stores stocking the essentials of village life.

Heading southeast from the market, Tzanakáki leads to places of more specific interest. First of these is the **Public Gardens**, a few hundred metres up on the left. Laid out by a Turkish pasha in the nineteenth century, they include a few caged animals (not really enough to call a zoo, but there are *kri-kri*, ponies, loud monkeys and birds), a café where you can sit under the trees and a children's play area. The open-air auditorium is often used as a cinema, and is also the setting for local ceremonies and folklore displays, which can be enjoyable – look in to see what's on.

Carry on down the street, then take the second left onto Sfakianáki and you come to the **Historical Museum and Archives** (Mon–Fri 9am–1pm; free), which consists of a couple of gloomy rooms in a small and undistinguished grey building, with poorly labelled photos, a few revolutionary arms from the struggle against the Turks and relics of Venizélos, and many more rooms filled with musty papers and books.

At the end of Sfakianáki, about 500m southeast of the Public Gardens, is **Platía Eleftherías**, with a statue of Venizélos in the centre and an imposing court building along the south side. This court house was originally the government building of Prince George's short-lived administration (see p.420). From here Odhós Papandreou (the former Dhimokratías, which was renamed after Greece's recently deceased former prime minister) leads back to the centre, running past the rear of the Public Gardens and ending opposite the market again. Alternatively, you can follow **Iróon Politehníou**, which runs due north from Platía Eleftherías down to the sea. A broad avenue divided by trees and lined with large houses, interspersed with several expensive garden restaurants and a number of fashionable café-bars where you can sit outdoors, it makes for an interesting walk in a part of the city very different from that dominated by the tourist crowds of Hálidhon.

The beaches

Haniá's closest **beaches** lie in a string to the west of the city. You can walk to the city beach, or the **bus** for those further afield leaves from the east side of Platía 1866, heading west along the old coast road (#21, about every 20min 8am–10.30pm; €0.85).

The city beach at **Néa Hóra** is about a ten-minute walk from the harbour, round past the Fírkas and on by the city's open-air swimming pool and a small fishing-boat harbour. At Néa Hóra there's clean sand and sheltered water, showers, and usually crowds of people. Cafés and restaurants line the seafront, among them an outstanding fish taverna, *Akrogiali* (see p.316). Offshore is a tiny islet with a sandy beach large enough for about five people at a time, but it's an unnervingly long swim – it's better to rent a pedalo or canoe if you want to explore.

If you continue west you can walk – for some twenty minutes – over a stony, scrubby stretch of sand with plenty of signs of new development, to **Áyii Apóstoli**. Here there's a good long stretch of yellow sand, the city's campsite and a much more established, if low-key, cluster of development. The only drawback (as at most of these beaches) is the crashing breakers, which can become vicious at times. At the end of Apóstoli's beach a barbed-wire fence attempts to prevent you getting onto the next section, but if you want to continue on foot it's worth clambering over the rocks: going round to the road involves a long detour and something of a climb over a low hill. At the next section, known as **Hrissí Aktí** (Golden Beach), there's more good sand which has attracted the apartment-builders. But it's not yet overcrowded, has a good taverna and is popular with locals. If you're on the bus, it detours via these beaches: they're also signed (poorly) from the main road. There's quite a bit of new development around, mostly apartments but also a number of **restaurants**

– *Jetée*, to which you'll see signs, is good, if a little pricier than most. At the far end, as the beach curves round to a little headland, another taverna is set out on stilts over the water.

Beyond the Golden Beach headland lies a tiny sand cove, another small promontory, and then the long curve of **Oasis Beach** running on round to **Kalamáki**. This is crowded and justly so – the swimming is probably the best in the area, with a gently shelving sandy bottom and a fossil-covered (and very sharp) rocky islet/reef that fends off the bigger waves. There's also a string of cafés and tavernas, and other facilities including windsurf rental and lessons. Kalamáki is the furthest beach accessible by city bus, and it's right by the road. To walk this far would probably take a little over an hour nonstop, but it makes far more sense to dawdle and enjoy the less busy beaches along the way, arriving at Kalamáki in time to get the bus back.

Shopping

East along Yiánnari from the main Hálidhon junction – also reached from up behind the Cathedral at the end of the leather-workers' street Skridlóf – is the **market**, an imposing and rather beautiful cross-shaped structure which dates from around 1900. In full swing it's a wonderful kaleidoscope of bustle and colour, and there are some good souvenirs to be had among the stalls of meat and fish and veg. At the back is a small shaded square where locals sit outside a couple of *kafenía*. On **Saturday mornings** there's a fabulous line of market stalls along Minöos, inside the eastern city wall, where local farmers come to sell their produce.

Stores aimed at tourists are mainly found in the old town, especially **jewellery** and **souvenirs** on Hálidhon and all around the harbour. The **leather** goods on Skridlóf are excellent value. At Potié 51, Mat sells nothing but **chess** and *távli* sets in all shapes and sizes. Other interesting places to look include Saita, on Sarpáki close to the *Fidias* pension, which stocks traditional Cretan tapestries, **embroidery** and lace. The various arty-crafty stores around the harbour on Kaneváro, Zambelíu, Kondiláki and Theotokopóulou are also worth a browse: Roka Carpets at Zambelíu 61 has wonderful traditional **weaving**, and an in-store loom.

English and other foreign-language **newspapers** are sold at two places on Odhós Yiánnari, one right by the corner of Hálidhon, the other towards the market. The best selection of English-language **books**, guides and maps is in the bookstore on the west side of Platía Sindriváni, which also sells foreign newspapers. There's a more limited range at Pelekanakis, near the top of Hálidhon, and Petraki, Yiánnari 68. Paxari, an expat-run secondhand store at Dhaskaloyiánnis 46, opposite Sarpáki, has piles of English books as well as a noticeboard which often has offers of work and long-term rentals.

Eating and drinking

As far as **eating and drinking** go, evenings in Haniá for most visitors centre around the harbour, and you need not stray far from the waterfront to find a cocktail before dinner, a meal, a late-night bar and an all-night disco. Be warned, though, that these places tend to be pricey, and the quality at many leaves a lot to be desired. The most fashionable waterfront area these days, particularly with locals, is towards the far end of the inner harbour, around Sarpidónos. Away from the water, there are plenty of attractive, slightly cheaper possibilities on (among others) Kondiláki, Kanevárou and most of the streets off Halídhon, some of them in restored or partially restored ancient buildings.

Tavernas and restaurants

For eating by the waterfront, Platía Sindriváni (Harbour Square) is the obvious starting-point: fanning out from here, in a circle round the harbour, is one restaurant, taverna or café after another. Some are thoroughly touristy – employing greeters to try and lure you in – but even among these there are plenty of places serving decent food too: a very extensive menu, and lots of western food, is generally a bad sign. Places in from the water are generally a little cheaper, but striking out a little further afield can take you off the tourist trail altogether: the more local restaurants to the east and west of the centre can make a refreshing change from the brashness of the harbourfront.

Akrogiali Aktí Papanikoli 19, on the Néa Hóra seafront ☎ 28210 73110. It's worth the walk or short taxi ride to this excellent, reasonably priced seafront fish taverna. Friendly service, a pleasant seaside terrace and outstanding seafood ensure it's always packed with locals, so may be worth booking – though there are plenty of alternatives along the street.

Amphora Aktí Koundouriótou, outer harbour. The restaurant of the hotel of the same name (restaurant entrance on the harbour) is one of the best on this strip, and serves good fish and a range of Cretan specialities with no hard sell.

Anaplous Sífaka 37, east of Platía Sindriváni. Stylish restaurant inside a roofless period building. You can eat *mezédhes* by candlelight or go for their more substantial dishes, including rabbit and snails, and there's often tasteful live guitar accompaniment.

Apostolis Aktí Enóseos 6 & 10, inner harbour. The fish tavernas at the inner end of the harbour are rated much higher by locals than those further round – some locals claim *Apostolis 2*, practically the last, and just a couple of doors down from its seemingly identical sister restaurant, is the best of all. The fish is excellent, but pricey.

Ciao Hálidhon 21. Inexpensive, fast-food-style pasta and pizza restaurant with soft play area for kids. No atmosphere, but great pizza from wood-fired oven.

Dino's Inner harbour by bottom of Sarpidónos. Another good bet for a seafood meal on the inner harbour.

Ela Top of Kondiláki. Standard taverna food in an attractive roofless ruin, often with live Greek music to enliven your meal.

Faka Arholeon, back from the inner harbour. No views, but good, traditional food – ask what's recommended, as there are often seasonal dishes not on the menu.

Hippopotamos Sarpidónos 6. If you crave a change from Greek food, this Tex-Mex restaurant, bar and pizzeria has decent food and a lively, local atmosphere.

Kariatis Platía Katetháki 12. Pricey, pretentious place serving a sleek blend of Greek and Italian food on a terrace drowned in operatic arias. Also does pizzas.

Karnáyio Platía Katetháki 8, set back from the inner harbour by one of the restored *Arsenali*. Not right on the water, but one of the best harbour restaurants nonetheless. Its touristy looks belie very good food, a friendly atmosphere and prices certainly no higher than surrounding restaurants.

Khrisostomos Ikárou, by the eastern wall. Not a very attractive setting, but interesting traditional recipes served in a thoroughly untouristy environment.

Konaki Kondiláki 40. A fine old mansion near the top of Kondiláki, with attractive courtyard tables in summer. A bit of an "international" menu, but on the whole well executed.

Mathios Aktí Enóseos 3, inner harbour. Haniá's oldest fish taverna and another good choice in this area.

Mesostrato Zambelíu 31. Good service and well-prepared Greek food in the romantic, roofless remains of an old mansion.

Nikteridha 5km east of town in the village of Korakiés. Head for Akrotíri and, at the top of the hill after the Venizélos tombs, follow the signs to the village. This traditional taverna has a delightful garden setting and is especially worthwhile on Mondays and Wednesdays when there's often music and dancing. You'll pass a couple of other places with outdoor grills and views over Haniá – as well as more music and dancing – as you climb up the road out of town.

O Painaleon Venizélou 86. "The Hungry Man" is a simple place in the modern town serving large portions mainly to locals on their lunchbreaks. Closed August.

To Pigadi Tou Tourkou ("The Well of the Turk"), Sarpáki 1. Greco-Moroccan restaurant with an interesting menu combining the two cuisines. Somewhat pricey, but attractive, with a small terrace.

Tamam Zambelíu 49, just before the Renieri Gate. Excellent food from an adventurous Greek menu,

with plenty of vegetarian options. Unfortunately there are only a few cramped tables outside where you often get jostled by the passing multitude, and it can get hot inside.
Tholos Ay. Dhéka 36. A stone's throw north of the Cathedral, this is yet another recycled Venetian ruin with tables outside in a courtyard. The food is good, too: *moskhári tis yiayiás* (grandma's veal) is

a house speciality, and there are lots of seafood options.
Zorba's Aktí Koundouriótou 39. There's little outwardly to distinguish this from the other tourist traps around the outer harbour, but the cooking – especially if you stick to Greek dishes – is honest, as apparently are the claims that Anthony Quinn stayed (and ate) here during the filming of *Zorba the Greek*.

Cafés, bars and snacks

The abundant **cafés** round the harbour tend to serve cocktails and fresh juices at exorbitant prices, though breakfast (especially "English") can be good value. There are more traditional places all around town – by the Cathedral; at the market, where you also find a couple of good *zaharoplastía* (one on Tsoudherón, the other, *Kronos*, on Mousoúron, down the steps from the side entrance of the market); and along Dhaskaloyiánnis, where Platía 1821 is a delightfully tranquil oasis (*Synganaki*, on Dhaskaloyiánnis, is a good traditional bakery serving *tyrópita* and the like, with a cake shop next door). **Fast food** is also increasingly widespread, with numerous *souvláki* places and even a couple of burger joints; Platía 1866 in the new town has a number of outlets, including a branch of *Everest* for good sandwiches.

If you want to gather provisions for a **picnic**, head for the market, which offers vast quantities of fresh fruit and vegetables as well as meat and fish, bread, dairy stalls for milk, cheese and yoghurt, and general stores for cooked meats, tins and other provisions. There are minimarkets scattered through the old town, including a couple of expensive ones on Hálidhon, or a handful of larger **supermarkets** not far away: Inka on Platía 1866 and Nea Agora opposite the west side of the market have most things, but the largest is Marinopolos at the top of Pireós, just west of the Schiavo Bastion.

L'Antigiano Platía Mitropóleos, cnr Isodhíon. Authentic Italian ice cream.
Aroma Aktí Tombázi 4, next to the Mosque of the Janissaries. Pleasant café with a great harbour view to savour over lazy breakfasts or late drinks.
To Avgo Tou Kokora ("The Rooster's Egg"), corner of Ay. Dhéka and Sarpáki near the Cathedral. Pleasant modern bar with a good line in pancakes, salads and snacks.
Cosy Roof Garden Platía Mitropóleos. Pleasant roof-terrace bar overlooking the square for breakfast or cocktails and late drinks.
Fortetza Sea wall, near the lighthouse. Strange hybrid restaurant/café on the far side of the harbour near the lighthouse. A free ferry shuttle takes people across the inner harbour – a good gimmick, saving you a lengthy walk. Wonderful place to have an apéritif at sunset, but most popular late at night; there are queues for the boat at midnight.
To Haniotiko Platía 1821. Great little *kafeníon* on this quiet square. Among their *mezédhes* choices *kalitsoúnia hórta* (vegetable pie) and *ktapódi krasáto* (octopus in wine) are tasty. The bar also has a long *lyra* and *rembétika* tradition

and stages live performances during the winter months.
Iordanis Bougatsa Kidhonías 96, opposite the bus station. This place serves little except the traditional creamy *bougátsa*, a sugar-coated cheese pie to eat in or take away. Another branch is at Apokorónou 24, between the market and the tourist office.
Kentrikon Episkopí Dorothéou, cnr Betólo behind the Cathedral. Relaxed café with tables outside on the pedestrianized street.
Meltemi Angélou 2. Slow, relaxed place for breakfast with harbour view and easy chairs; later on, locals (and especially expats) sit whiling the day away or playing *távli*.
Mitropolitikon Platía Mitropóleos. Pleasant setting with tables out on the square in front of the Cathedral. Serves good juices.
Mousses Platía Sindriváni at the bottom of Kaneváro. Long-established favourite in a prime position for people-watching. Open 24 hours for drinks, breakfast and light meals.
Pili Tis Ammou Porta Sabioyera. A superb outdoor bar sited in a garden on top of the eastern harbour bastion, near the *Porto Veneziano* hotel;

it's reached through a deceptively small doorway to the left of a children's playground. Great in the evening with lights dangling from the tamarisk trees and views over the Sarpidóna district, as well as out to sea.

Souvlaki Alisides Zambelíu, corner of Platía Sindriváni. The most popular *souvláki* and fast-food place in the old town.

Synagogi Between Kondiláki and Skúfon. Taking its name from the restored old Jewish synagogue

next door, this is a peaceful café by day and later a pleasant drinks bar with good music. It occupies a Venetian mansion bombed in World War II.

Time Out Platía 1866. Fast-food Cretan style, serving everything from *yíros pítta* to lamb stews, to sandwiches and spaghetti, 24 hours a day.

Zaharoplastio 13 Platía 1866. Excellent breakfast café in the real heart of town, with an outdoor terrace to watch the action.

Nightlife and entertainment

Haniá's **nightlife** is frenetic throughout the summer, and if you want to dance until dawn there are plenty of possibilities. The local crowd tend to cruise the **bars** along Aktí Míaouli and the eastern part of the old town, before heading out around midnight to the large **discos** and **clubs** along the coast to the west: there are regular late-night police road-blocks checking for drunken drivers on this route. The big out-of-town clubs include *Privilege*, between Plataniás and Geráni, *Utopia* in Plataniás, *Mambo* on the Káto Stalós waterfront, and *Divine* in Ayía Marína. If that's too much of a long haul, there are plenty of places in town to work up a sweat. The bars around the harbour are plenty lively, though the clientele tends to be tourists and – especially when a ship is in – servicemen from the NATO bases. Aktí Míaouli, whose waterfront terrace bars are packed with young locals throughout the summer, may be less frenetic.

A few places offer more traditional entertainment, including **dancing**. *Café Kriti*, at Kalergón 22 on the corner with Andróyeo, is an old-fashioned *kafenío* where there's Greek music and dancing virtually every night. It's also worth checking for events at the open-air auditorium in the Public Gardens and for performances in restaurants outside the city, which are the ones locals go to. The hoardings in front of the market usually have details of these, together with programme information for the couple of **open-air cinemas** that show English-language films with subtitles (rather than dubbed versions): the Kipos in the Public Gardens, and the Attikon on Elefthériou Venizélou out towards Akrotíri, about 1km east of the centre. The latter has a great atmosphere, but be sure to sit near a speaker since they reduce the sound level as the evening progresses so as not to offend the neighbours.

The main annual **festival** in Haniá is the commemoration of the Battle of Crete around May 20 (when accommodation is also at a premium), with folk-lore and other events mostly in the Public Gardens. Also celebrated is June 24, the feast of Áyios Ioánnis (St John). Check with the tourist office for details of these and other celebrations in the nearby villages.

Late bars, clubs and discos

Daz Schiavo Bastion, down a narrow alley running west off Hálidhon. Hidden away beneath the bastion, this is a big new club (though no longer the newest in town) playing loud techno with a major lightshow. Things get pretty frenetic after midnight.

El Mondo Kondiláki. A survivor from the days when this street was very rowdy, and a place that is still popular with military types in from the bases.

Fagotto Angélou 16. Very pleasant laid-back jazz bar, often with live performers in high season.

Four Seasons Inner harbour. Recently refurbished music bar by the port police, where the town's youth gather to size each other up.

Pallas Aktí Tombázi 15, slightly north of the Mosque of the Janissaries. Inviting roof-garden bar on the harbours offering music and cocktails. Fine views over both harbours.

Platía Aktí Tombázi 1, by Platía Sindriváni. Quayside bar on an upper level overlooking the harbour, with live Greek music.

Point Platía Sindriváni above *Mousses* café. Another upper-floor bar overlooking the harbour; laid-back in the early evening and getting louder as the night progresses.

Prime Vision Inner harbour just off Aktí Tombázi. Occasional Greek music performances, but mostly a pretty laid-back bar.

Rudi's Bierhaus Sífaka 24, east of Platía Sindriváni. Haniá's beer shrine: Austrian Rudi Riegler stocks almost a hundred of Europe's finest beers and will explain the story behind each one if you have the time and inclination. Serves very good *mezédhes*, too.

Tessara Tetarta Aktí Kanári by the municipal swimming pool just before the town beach. Currently king of the local clubs, a fancy new venue that saves the trip out west: don't expect much action before 1am.

Listings

Airlines Olympic, with scheduled daily flights between Haniá and Athens plus frequent flights to Thessaloníki, has an office at Tzanakáki 88 (Mon–Fri 9am–4pm; ☎ 28210 57701–3) opposite the public gardens. Aegean is at Venizélou 12 (☎ 28210 51100) across from the market. For airport information call ☎ 28210 63264.

Banks The main branch of the National Bank of Greece, with two ATMs, is directly opposite the market and there's a cluster of banks with more ATMs around the top of Hálidhon, as well as free-standing ATM machines on Hálidhon itself. You'll also find plenty of out-of-hours exchange places on Hálidhon, in the travel agencies.

Bike and car rental Possibilities everywhere, especially on Hálidhon, though these are rarely the best value. For bikes, Summertime, Dhaskaloyiánnis 7, slightly northeast of the market (☎ 28210 45797, ⓦ www.strentals.gr), has a huge range, including mountain bikes. Bike Trekking, Karaoli 15 (☎ 28210 20143), offers organized mountain-biking tours. For cars, two reliable local companies are Hermes, Tzanakáki 52 (☎ 28210 54418), or Tellus Rent a Car, Hálidhon 108, opposite Platía 1866 (☎ 28210 91500). Good deals for *Rough Guide* readers are also available from El Greco Cars at the *El Greco* hotel (☎ 28210 60883, ⓦ www.elgreco.gr). Avis are at Tzanakáki 58 (☎ 28210 50510), Hertz at Venizélou 12 (☎ 28210 40366).

Boat trips A number of boats make daily trips from Haniá, mainly to the nearby islands of Áyii Theódori and Lazaretta, for swimming and *kri-kri* (ibex) spotting: you're unlikely to escape the attentions of their stalls around the harbour. The *Evagelos* glass-bottomed boat, for example, makes this trip three times daily, with an all-day alternative on Saturdays to the Rodhópou peninsula (for information call ☎ 6945874283); the *MS Irini* (☎ 28210 52001) is a more traditional vessel. If you fancy a sail in a yacht, take a look in the inner harbour where trips are sometimes offered, or try the local nautical club, based on Aktí Kanári by the swimming pool, which also has a sailing school (☎ 28210 96078, ⓦ www.nox.gr), or contact E. Barbopoulos, who has a shop at Tsoudherón 1 (☎ 28210 22244).

Diving Blue Adventures Diving, Dhaskaloyiánnis 69 (☎ 28210 40403), runs daily diving and snorkelling trips. Fundive, Aktí Papanikoli 6 behind the town beach (☎ 28210 93616), offers similar tours.

Ferry tickets The ANEK Line office is on Venizélou, right opposite the market (☎ 28210 27500, ⓦ www.anek.gr); Blue Star is at Platía 1866 14, under the *Hotel Arkadi* (☎ 28210 75444, ⓦ www.bluestarferries.gr).

Hospital For an ambulance, dial ☎ 166. The city's new central hospital is in the village of Mourniés, 1.5km south of the centre (☎ 28210 22000). Private clinics in the centre include: Therapeutiko Kentro, N. Fokás 2 (☎ 28210 56326); Medical Centre of Crete, Hatzidhákis 5 (☎ 28210 59034); and Medical Centre, Markou Botsári 76 (☎ 28210 96800).

Internet There are plenty of Internet cafés including: *Kathodon*, Isodhíon 10 at Karaoli; the more tranquil *Vranas*, Ayíon Dhéka beneath *Vranas Studios* (see p.309; minimum 1hr, though credit given); and *Café Notos*, on the outer harbour under the *Hotel Notos*.

Laundry There are plenty to choose from, including Speedy Laundry (☎ 28210 88411; 9am–9pm), junction of Koronéou and Korkidi, just west of Platía 1866, who will collect and deliver your load if you call; Afrodite, Ayíon Dhéka 22 (daily 8.30am–8.30pm) in the old town and Fidias, Sarpáki 6 (next to the pension of the same name; Mon–Sat 9am–9pm). All do service washes for around €6.

Left luggage The bus station has a left-luggage office open 6am–8.30pm; €1–2 per item per day depending on size.

Mountain climbing and walking The local EOS mountaineering club, at Tzanakáki 90 (☎ 28210 44647, ⓦ www.eoshanion.gr), provides information about climbing in the Lefká Óri and takes reservations for the mountain refuge at Kallergi, near the Samariá Gorge.

Pharmacies Several on Yiánnari between the market and Platía 1866; more up Tzanakáki.

Post office The main post office is at Tzanakáki 3 (Mon–Fri 7.30am–8pm, Sat 9am–1pm).

Taxis The main taxi ranks are in Platía 1866 and at the bottom of Karaiskáki, just off Yiánnari. For radio taxis try ☎18300, 28210 94300 or ☎28210 98700.

Telephones Cardphones are all over town; buy cards from any street *períptero* kiosk.

Tourist police Irakliou 23 (☎28210 53333 or 28210 28708), some way south of the centre in the new town.

Tours Any travel agent (see below) can sell you a day-trip to the Samariá Gorge, or Knossós, or dozens of others. A rather pointless "Little Train" tour of the new town – it's not allowed in the narrow streets of the old – sets off regularly from the waterfront car park by the Fírkas. There are lots

of other activities on offer too, such as horseriding in the country to the west (☎28240 31339).

Travel agencies El Greco Travel, Kidhonías 76 near the bus station (☎28210 86015), and Tellus Travel, Hálidhon 108, opposite Platía 1866 (☎28210 91500), are both good for inexpensive bus tickets, flights and standard excursions. For cheap tickets home try Bassias Travel, Hálidhon 69 (☎28210 44295), very helpful for regular tickets too. They also deal in standard excursions. Other travel agents for tours and day-trips are everywhere.

Waterpark Limnoupolis, a big park with some spectacular slides, play areas and several pools, as well as a number of fast-food outlets, is located close to the village of Varipetro, 6km southwest of the city. It's pricey at €15 for adults, €10 for kids aged 6–12, but it will keep children occupied for an entire day. There's a regular bus service (6 daily) from the bus station.

Akrotíri and the Bay of Soúdha

The hilly peninsula of **Akrotíri** loops round to the east of Haniá, protecting the magnificent anchorages of the Bay of Soúdha. It's a somewhat strange amalgam, with a couple of developing **resorts** along with burgeoning suburbs on the north coast, several ancient **monasteries** in the northeast, and military installations and the airport dominating the centre and south. One thing worth bearing in mind is the shortage of hotel or pension accommodation; this is very much apartment and villa country geared to families staying at least a week at a time. Outside August you should be able to find something on spec, but even then you'd be well advised to try phoning ahead, as few of the places have regular reception hours. You'll need your own transport to explore much here; there are buses to Stavrós, and occasional tours to the monasteries, but little else.

The Venizélos Graves

Following the Akrotíri signs east out of Haniá you embark on a long climb as you leave the city. At the top there's a sign to the **Venizélos Graves**, the simple stone-slab tombs of Eleftheríos Venizélos, Crete's most famous statesman, and his son Sophocles. The immaculately tended garden setting, looking back over Haniá and the coast for miles beyond, is magnificent and also historic – the scene in 1897 of an illegal raising of the Greek flag in defiance of the Turks and the European powers. The flagpole was smashed by a salvo from the European fleet, but the Cretans raised their standard by hand, keeping it flying even under fire. Two stories attach to this: one that the sailors were so impressed that they all stopped firing to applaud; the second that a shell fired from a Russian ship hit the little church of Profítis Elías, which still stands, and that divine revenge caused the offending ship itself to explode the very next day. There are several excellent **cafés** and snack places here, including *Nymphes*, *Ostria* and *KouKou Vayia*, all packed with locals at weekends, when they come to pay their respects, admire the view, and gorge on cakes and ice cream. During the week it's delightfully quiet.

Stavrós and the Akrotíri beaches

The road divides by the graves: straight ahead takes you east across the peninsula towards the **airport**. The left fork heads north to Horafákia and the beaches culminating at Stavrós, Akrotíri's most popular resort. This is pleasant country to drive around, gently rolling and dotted with villages that are clearly quite wealthy – many city workers live out here or build themselves country villas. About 5km north of the graves, past the village of **Kounoupidhianá**, the road suddenly plunges down and emerges by the **beach** at **Kalathás**, two little patches of sand divided by a rocky promontory, with a couple of tavernas including the *Estiatorio Kalathas*, right on the sand. This makes a fine place to spend a lazy day, marred only slightly by the proximity of the road: there's an offshore island to which you can swim, and good snorkelling. There are also a couple of attractive places to stay here, though both are often occupied by officers from the NATO base: *Lena Beach* (☎28210 64750, ⓦwww.lena-beach.com; ❼), the big hotel you see immediately above the beach, with attractive balcony rooms, and *Giorgi's Blue Apartments* (☎28210 64080, ⓦwww.blueapts.gr; ❼), signed from the road, with very comfortable apartments, and a pool and bar beautifully situated above a rocky coastline.

Horafákia, inland a little further on, has the bulk of the local facilities including shops and a travel agent/car hire place. From here a road leads down to the coast at **Tersanas** where there's a tiny cove beach, shallow and safe for small children, as well as a couple of tavernas: *Sunset*, near the top of the road down here, has views over the coast and a children's playground as well as decent food. Three kilometres beyond Horafákia, you finally reach **Stavrós** and its near-perfect **beach**, an almost completely enclosed circular bay. The sea is dead calm with gently shelving sand underfoot, making it ideal for kids. It's an extraordinary-looking place, too, with a sheer, bare mountainside rising just 100m away from you on the far side of the bay. This is where the cataclysmic climax of *Zorba the Greek* was filmed (the hill is known locally as Zorba's Mountain) and is also the site of a **cave**, whose entrance can just about be seen from the beach, in which there was an ancient sanctuary.

Stavrós beach is often crowded – sometimes unpleasantly so as it doesn't take many people to fill it up – but even so it's a great place to bask for a few hours, and is the one place near Haniá that's easily accessible by bus (6 daily). There's a far less visited patch of sand facing directly out to sea if you do find it oppressive. Stavrós has relatively few facilities beyond a couple of minimarkets and snack bars, while the apartments and rooms places are mostly pre-booked. There are a couple of **tavernas**, though – *Christina* behind the beach and old favourite *Zorba's* set back a little.

Practicalities

If you have your own transport, you can drive around the surrounding countryside, checking out the numerous apartment complexes; without it, you'll find it much harder to find **accommodation** in this region, though the first few of the options below are in easy walking distance of Stavrós. If you're coming from Haniá, it's worth checking at travel agents there, many of whom represent one or more of the local apartment-owners. At Stavrós, *Blue Beach Apartments* (☎28210 39404, ⓔvepe@cha.forthnet.gr; ❺) has much the best position, on the seafront at the western end of the sea beach (to get to it by road, you have to drive some way round inland), with its own tiny sand beach, small pool and a seaside terrace where meals are served. Accommodation runs from two-person studios up to three-room apartments. Immediately inland,

Zorba's Apartments (☎28210 39010; ④) are less attractive, though they also have a pool and tennis court. On the seafront next to *Blue Beach*, *Thanassis* taverna has a lovely terrace above the water, and a tiny strip of sand with free loungers for clients. In Stavrós village you could try *Sweet Dreams* rooms (☎28210 39645; ④), also with a pool, though there rarely seems to be anyone in.

Apart from these, accommodation is widely scattered in the flat plains lining the coast between Stavrós and Tersanas. Among the places to which you'll see signs as you drive around – all with pools – are *Villa Eleana* (☎28210 39480; ⑤), an apartment/studio hotel with two wheelchair-accessible studios; *Apartments Rosa* (☎28210 55970; ④); *Georgia-Vicky Apartments* (☎28210 39439; ④), an attractive complex above a rocky shore; and *Kavos Beach Studios* (☎28210 39155; ⑤), where there's no beach, but there is a poolside bar and taverna. Very near *Villa Eleana*, there's also the extraordinary new *Perle Roi Spa Hotel* (☎28210 39400; ⓦwww.perle-spa.com; ⑨), a huge complex and thalassotherapy centre with no less than five indoor and outdoor pools, plus numerous bars and restaurants, kids' club, and almost every other facility you could think of.

The monasteries

There are a number of approaches to the **monasteries** at the northern end of the Akrotíri peninsula, many of which will leave you going round in circles when the signs run out. The most straightforward are to follow the coast road as above and then turn right either in Kounoupidhianá or Horafákia, or to follow the road to the airport, just before which you'll see a sign to Ayía Triádha. On this latter route you'll see evidence of some of the other churches and monasteries that once thrived here, most notably Áyios Ioánnis, a fortress-like structure that is being restored alongside the airport road, just down from its junction with the main road.

Ayía Triádha

Ayía Triádha (daily 9am–7pm; €1.50), sometimes known as Moní Zangarólo after its founder, was established in the seventeenth century and built in Venetian style. Today, while not exactly thriving (it has only five monks), it is one of the few Cretan monasteries to preserve real monastic life to any degree. Its imposing ochre frontage is approached through carefully tended fields and olive groves – all the property of the monastery which now bottles and markets its own oil. Close up, though, some of the buildings are distinctly dilapidated and, despite an ongoing programme of renovation (one building to the west has now become the olive-oil factory), much of the premises lie redundant and empty. Some of the halls at the back of the monastery have been given over to the stabling of the monks' goats, and skinny cats wander seemingly at will.

You can walk right through the complex, though the monastic cells are locked, and sit on benches shaded by orange trees in the patio. The **church**, which appears strangely foreshortened, contains a beautiful old gilded altarpiece and, around the walls, ancient wooden stalls; like most of the monastery it is built from stone that glows orange in the afternoon sun. By the entrance is a small **museum** with silver chalices, vestments, relics and manuscripts, mostly dating from the eighteenth or nineteenth centuries, and a few icons which are considerably older. Above, you can climb up beside the campanile to look out over the monastery's fields and beyond. In the courtyard there's a water cooler, and, if you're lucky in quieter times, the traditional hospitality will extend further, to a glass of *raki* and a piece of *loukoúm* in the hall where

△ Ayía Triádha monastery

you sign the visitors' book. There's a small shop, too, selling postcards as well as the monks' olive oil, intended to raise funds for the restoration programme.

Gouvernétou and Katholikó

Outside Ayía Triádha a sign directs you north towards **Gouvernétou** (daily 7am–2pm & 4–8pm; free) – about 4km away, on a road ascending through a biblical landscape of rocks and wild olives, the final section paved but horribly rutted as it twists through a steep rocky gully. The monastery itself is a simple square block of a building, older than Ayía Triádha, with the usual refreshingly shaded patio and ancient frescoes in the church; there's a tiny museum, too. Despite its more remote location, Gouvernétou, beautifully renovated and with carefully tended flowerbeds and chapel, feels like a thriving community. Nevertheless, the stark surroundings help to give a real sense of the isolation that the remaining three monks must face for most of the year.

Immediately above Gouvernétou is a simple marble war memorial and, beyond, you can follow (on foot) a paved path which leads down towards the sea. After about ten minutes you reach a **cave** in which St John the Hermit is said to have lived and died – a large, low cavern, stark, dank and dripping, with hefty stalactites and stalagmites and a substantial bathing tank in the centre, probably for baptisms. Excavations revealed that this had been an important Minoan shrine, and in the Greek period it became a sanctuary dedicated to the goddess Artemis. Small outbuildings surround the entrance.

Thus far the walk has been easy, along an obvious path, but as you continue to descend the going gets steeper, rockier and sharper. In a further fifteen minutes you reach the amazing **ruins** of the **Monastery of Katholikó**, built into the side of, and partly carved from, a craggy ravine of spectacular desolation. This is older than its neighbours: it was abandoned over three hundred years ago when the monks, driven by repeated pirate raids, moved up to the comparative safety of Gouvernétou. The valley sides are dotted with caves which formed a centre of still-earlier Christian worship, at least one of which (just before the buildings) you can explore if you have a torch.

Spanning the ravine by the ruins is a vast **bridge** leading nowhere. Cross it and you can scramble down to the bottom of the ravine and follow the stream bed for about another fifteen minutes all the way to the sea. There's a tiny natural **harbour**, a fjord-like finger of water pushing up between the rocks, where remains of a port can still be made out. Hewn from the rock, and with part of its roof intact, is what appears to be an ancient boathouse or slipway. There's no beach, but it's easy enough, and delightfully welcome, to lower yourself from the rocks straight into the astonishingly clear green water. The walk back up takes perhaps an hour in all – and is much more strenuous than it might have seemed on the way down.

Soúdha Bay

On the **south side** of the Akrotíri peninsula there are beaches near Stérnes, pretty isolated from a visitor's point of view, but not as deserted as you might hope. Almost all of this region is a **military zone**, and the beaches are popular with the NATO personnel based here. There's an R&R base and officers' club at **Maráthi**, for example, which has sheltered, sandy beaches with views across the mouth of the bay. Boat trips from Haniá or the resorts across the bay occasionally run to the little harbour here, and there are several cafés and tavernas. The views of the bay are best on the descent towards Maráthi (watch out for unmarked junctions on this road) – above all, of a little **island** (Néa Soúdha), bristling with Venetian and Turkish fortifications which, from a distance at least, appear miraculously well-preserved. It proved as impressive a defence as it looks, holding out as a Venetian stronghold for over thirty years after the rest of Crete had fallen, before eventually being voluntarily abandoned.

For an alternative route back, you can turn left off the main road to curve around the head of the bay, on the road to Soúdha town. This again affords spectacular views of the bay (though there are signs prohibiting photography of the military secrets therein), down over the villas built into the hillside. This route is also the shortest way from Akrotíri to the E75 highway, bypassing Haniá.

The Allied war cemetery

Just before Soúdha, at the water's edge, you pass the beautifully sited **Allied war cemetery**, a melancholy and moving spot. Surrounded by eucalyptus trees, it lies 1km before the town, down a lane signed "Soúdha cemetery" close to the *Paloma* taverna (which is good and inexpensive). With its row upon row of immaculately tended headstones, many of them to unknown soldiers and very young men, the serene and dignified cemetery brings home with some force the scale of the calamity of the Battle of Crete in which most of them perished. Grave 10E on the cemetery's northern side is that of the distinguished archeologist John Pendlebury (see p.433), who took over at Knossós after Evans retired; he died fighting alongside Cretans during the German assault on Iráklion in 1941.

East to Yeoryioúpolis

Heading east out of Haniá you can either head south through the new town to pick up the main E75 road on the south side of town, or follow the buses and most of the other traffic to Soúdha and join it there. As the E75 climbs above the edge of the **Bay of Soúdha**, it follows the track of the old road; at the point of the bay stands an old fortress, originally the Turkish bastion of **Izzedin**, now pressed into service as a prison.

The new road is fast, but you'll see little through the screen of trees and flowering shrubs until you emerge on the coast just past **Yeoryioúpolis**. Once you set off down the hill past Izzedin there are a couple of turn-offs to villages but just one junction of any size, between Vrísses and Yeoryioúpolis, signed to both of them. If you're in no hurry, or you simply want an attractive circular drive, then the minor roads that head inland or out onto the Dhrápano peninsula have much more to offer.

Áptera and around

Shortly before the prison there's a junction: turn off here and you can head left to Kalámi (just a few hundred metres away, immediately below the prison) and Kalíves (which you can see on the coast way below). To the right the road climbs to **Megála Horáfia** and, turning off again, ancient **Áptera** (Tues–Sun 8.30am–3pm; free). Áptera occupies the table top of this mesa-like mountain, about 3km from – and a good climb above – the highway. You can leave your vehicle in Megála Horáfia and walk to the main part of the site, on the path described below, in about fifteen minutes; alternatively the road carries on to the hilltop, one fork heading for the fortress, the other for a parking area by the main site. The hilltop has little shade, and can be very hot.

This location appears in Linear B inscriptions, and therefore seems to have been **continuously occupied** from as early as the fourteenth century BC right up to 1964, when the monastery here was finally abandoned. Áptera's peak came from the fifth century BC into early Christian times, when it was one of the island's most important cities. Work on the very extensive remains is continuing, so new areas may be opened up, or others fenced off for excavation. The main entrance is by the **Monastery** of Áyios Ioánnis Theólogos – the most obvious building at the site. Here the biggest of the fenced areas includes the monastery, the cisterns, a bath complex and, right by the entrance, a fifth-century BC Classical Greek **temple** marked by huge stone slabs. The amazing Roman **cisterns**, brick-lined and mainly underground, must be among the largest surviving. A real highlight, they are an awesome, cavernous testament to Roman engineering genius. Below spreads a very extensive **Roman bath** complex, all of which inevitably raises the question of just how enough water to fill the vast cisterns and feed the baths was collected on what is now a barren hilltop.

Scattered around the immediate area are numerous other remains, mostly signed but not all accessible. Check the map at the site entrance (if you're lucky, there may be a leaflet) to find them. Many are reached by a well-signed path on the opposite side of the car park from the monastery. There are remains of a small **theatre** here, and of a Roman **villa** full of collapsed pillars. You also pass a World War II machine-gun post which, if it weren't signed, could easily be mistaken for another restored Roman ruin. The path continues down towards Megála Horáfia and ends, right on the edge of the village, by a substantial section of the ancient city **wall**, complete with defensive tower and gate.

Another attraction of the site is a crumbling Turkish **fort** – substantially shored up with reinforced concrete – on the lip of the hilltop. There's no access to the interior, but you can still enjoy the best of all the **views** across Soúdha to the Akrotíri peninsula. Immediately below is the Izzedin fortress, and below that the three small islands, including heavily fortified Néa Soúdha, which protect the narrow entrance to the bay. From here the islet's superb strategic qualities are plain, with the deep-water anchorages accessible only by running the gauntlet of these forts and fortified islands. According to legend the islands were formed after a musical contest between the Muses and the Sirens on the height near the ancient city: defeated, the Sirens plucked off their wings, flung themselves into the bay, and were transformed into the islands. Áptera, literally translated, can mean "featherless" or "wingless" – one derivation of the city's name.

If you're looking for **food** before or after visiting the ruins, Megála Horáfia offers a number of possibilities. The Anglo-Greek *Taverna Aptera*, right on the road, is recommended: they may also be able to steer you in the direction of one of the particularly good **villas** (some with pool) that dot this area. Most are pre-booked, of course, but if there are vacancies they can often be taken for the odd day or two.

Stílos and Samonás

From Áptera you can retrace your steps back to the main road, or continue inland to circle round via the Dhrápano peninsula, a very attractive drive. Heading south, the first place of any size is **Stílos**, which is where the Australian and New Zealand rearguard made their final stand during the Battle of Crete (this was then the main road south), enabling the majority of Allied troops to be evacuated while they themselves were mostly stranded on the island. Many found refuge in the villages in the foothills around here and were later smuggled off the island – some of these villages were destroyed in retribution. Today

Stílos is an unremarkable agricultural centre, but there are a couple of *kafenía* with shady tables beside the road where you can pull over for a drink.

Not far beyond comes the turning to **Samonás**, a narrow road winding steeply up through 180-degree hairpins, with better views at every turn. The reason to take this detour is to visit the isolated Byzantine church of **Áyios Nikólaos** at Kiriakosélia, signed beyond Samonás, which, for location and art-works, is one of the most beautiful on the island. The church, nestling in a valley, has recently been restored and contains fantastic **medieval frescoes**, as good as any on Crete. Painted in the thirteenth century, these have not been touched by the restorers – at least not recently – and are patchy and faded against their deep-blue background, but parts still seem as vivid as the day they were created. A Madonna and Child, at eye level on the left-hand side, and a dramatic Christ *Pantokrátor* in the drum dome stand out. You really need a car to see them, because the keyholders (Kostas or Roussa) live in Samonás – you pick them up there and drive on to the church, a couple of hilly kilometres further. Head for the *kafeníon* in Samonás – preferably in the afternoon – and they'll phone for someone to take you, and cheerily overcharge for a drink while you wait. By contrast Kostas or Roussa (or one of their daughters) always seem to refuse money for their time.

The Dhrápano peninsula and Vrísses

A multitude of roads crisscrosses the **Dhrápano peninsula** east of Haniá, almost all of them scenic and well-surfaced. Known as the Apókoronas region, this is rich agricultural land, a countryside of rolling green, wooded hills interrupted by immaculately whitewashed, and obviously wealthy, villages. Part of this wealth is fuelled by a real-estate boom in which foreigners and the wealthy from Haniá are buying up village houses to convert into weekend and holiday retreats; there's an enormous amount of new villa construction too. Nowhere are there individ-ual attractions to detain you long, but all these settlements have *kafenía* where you can sit awhile and wonder at the rural tranquillity away from the main-road traffic. Coming from Stílos you can either head through Néo Horío to Kalíves on the coast, or turn off later for Vámos at the centre of the peninsula. The direct approach, however, is from the E75 highway below Áptera.

Kalíves

From Kalámi, the old road drops rapidly down to the coast at **Kalíves**, an agricultural market centre of some size. As you approach, you pass a long sandy beach in the lee of Áptera's castle-topped bluff, which looks attractive but is hard to reach. The main **beach** stretches in both directions from the centre of the village, best at the eastern end where it curves round to a small harbour in the lee of a headland. The village itself is not particularly attractive at first sight, a rather straggly development lining the main road for over 2km. It's very much a package resort these days too, although the mainly low-rise apartments and studios keep it low-key. The centre of town is marked by a small square with a church, and the most attractive parts are round here, especially if you cut through to the seafront just one block away. Most facilities are just here, includ-ing a **bank** with ATM and a couple of **travel agencies** which can arrange local accommodation, as well as car hire, money exchange and excursions: *Kalives Travel* (℡28250 31473), *Flisvos Travel* (℡28250 31337; good for car hire) and *Valeria Travel* (℡28250 32392; with a good choice of apartments).

If you want somewhere **to stay**, the travel agencies listed above make a good starting point, as they tend to represent apartments slightly further out which can be very good value. There's a fair amount of choice in town too, most obviously the rather incongruous *Kalives Beach Hotel* (℗28250 31285, ℗kalbeach@otenet.gr; ❼), right in the centre of the seafront, whose facilities include indoor and outdoor pools plus a tiny gym and meeting rooms. Simpler rooms places include *Asteria* (℗28250 31330; ❹), for studios with kitchen right in the centre; *Akti Galini* (℗28250 32066; ❺), in a quieter spot just off the main road towards the beach; or *Blue Sea* (℗28250 32159; ❹), looking out over the eastern end of the beach. Places **to eat** are plentiful. On the seafront right in the centre, *Taverna Manolis* is a long-established favourite with good seafood, while at the eastern end of the beach, *Taverna Elena* is a less pricey alternative. *Zorba's*, with a large terrace at the back of the main square, opposite the church, is also good, or for snacks and drinks try the nearby *Kafenio Potamos*, with tables overlooking the river that runs through the middle of town. Another bunch of good possibilities is at the eastern end of town, including *Il Fourno*, for pizza from a wood-fired oven, and *Medusa*.

Almirídha

Almirídha, the next village along the coast, is smaller, marginally more of a resort, and considerably more attractive. A row of tavernas behind a couple of small patches of sand in a sheltered bay marks the centre. The lovely beach is a popular spot for **windsurfing**, with a fairly reliable breeze once you're slightly offshore. When the breeze blows inland, seafront dining becomes a somewhat risky experience – though on a hot day it's always a welcome refresher. Like Kalíves, Almirídha is popular with local families who drive down to swim and enjoy a leisurely lunch.

If you want to **stay**, you'll again find that accommodation is mostly in the form of widely scattered apartment blocks, and the best thing to do is to ask around in the tavernas, each of which advertises places to rent. Rooms in the centre are few and often full, but you could try *Marilena's Pension* (℗28250 32202; ❸) at the east end of the seafront for balcony en-suite rooms with kitchenette, or modern *Almira Apartments* (℗28250 31608; ❹), right in the centre. On the hill up towards Pláka, *Pension Katerina* (℗ 28250 31366; ❸) has lovely views and pleasant en-suite rooms. For **eating**, the fish tavernas are worth a try, particularly *Dimitri's*, as well as *Thalami*, which also offers standard Greek dishes. Also recommended is the attractive *Lagos* taverna, on the road at the very western edge of the village. There are also several foreign-run cafés and bars here, such as British-run *Palmers*, open all day from English breakfast time to late-night cocktails; some of them have Internet connections.

Should you want to take advantage of the breezes with a spot of **windsurfing**, French-run UCPA (℗28250 31443; 10am–6pm daily) on the seafront rents out boards for €10 an hour, as well as kayaks and catamarans. To **rent a car** or bike try *Flisvos* (℗28250 32213), with an office just behind the seafront. One sight definitely worth a look while you're here is the remains of an **early Christian basilica** dating from the fifth century, with a wonderful mosaic floor. It lies at the west end of the village, close to the *Lagos* taverna, shaded by a great plane tree.

Pláka and around the coast

Beyond Almirídha the coast becomes increasingly rocky, with cliffs almost all the way round to Yeoryioúpolis denying access to the sea. The roads and the signage also deteriorate if you go this way, but as you climb the views become increasingly worthwhile. The first place you reach is **Pláka**, a beautiful hamlet little over a kilometre to the east, with a couple of tavernas and a tempting cake shop sited on a sleepy central *platía*. Here and all around there's an extraordinary amount of villa construction, but most of it is at least reasonably sympathetic to the local environment. There are also a couple of particularly good places to **stay**: excellent balcony rooms with fans and fridges at *Studios Koukouros* (☎28250 31145; ❸), which has the bonus of a stunning garden filled with palms, cacti and bougainvillea; or the wonderfully friendly *Bicorna Family Hotel* (☎28250 32066; ❹), with another lush garden, small pool and comfy rooms.

Continuing around the coast, **Kókkino Horió,** on the steep height above Pláka, is if anything even more picturesque – both villages were used as back-drops for the film of *Zorba the Greek*. At the edge of **Palelóni**, 4km south, a narrow road drops steeply to the coast, where sits a little naval base and a rocky cove with the idyllically situated *Taverna-Café Obrogialos* – a great spot for lunch. **Kefalás**, 2km further along a road above the sea with spectacular views towards Réthimnon, is again absurdly pretty. From here you can head inland towards Vámos, or continue, a little further from the coast, in the direction of Yeoryioúpolis.

Inland to Gavalohóri and Vámos

Good roads head inland from both Kalíves and Almirídha towards the main agricultural centre of the peninsula, and regional capital, Vámos. Again, it's interesting driving, with numerous villages worth a brief stop on the way. Immediately inland from Almirídha you pass below **Aspró**, a tiny, ancient hamlet looking down over the coast. This is the old Greek village as you've always imagined it; a couple of lucky foreigners have snapped up the only empty houses. **Douliana**, a couple of kilometres southwest of Aspró as the crow flies but a few more along the back roads you're forced to take to reach it, is another delightful hamlet overflowing with plants and flowers and criss-crossed by winding lanes where time seems to stand still. There's a pleasant **taverna** here too, *Ta Douliana*, with a leafy terrace serving some great local dishes such as *arní avgolémono* (lamb with lemon and egg sauce).

Gavalohóri, 2km south of Aspró, has a particularly outstanding attraction in the shape of a small but excellent **folklore museum** (daily 9am–8pm; €2; when closed, enquire at the women's co-operative mentioned below) housed in a beautifully restored Venetian building with Turkish additions. The history and culture of the village is documented in the various rooms, with items clearly labelled in English as well as Greek. Of special interest are the examples of stone-cutting, woodcarving and **kopanéli** (silk lace made by bobbin-weaving), which is now being revived in the village. The mulberry trees planted around the village by the Turks still produce silk from the silk-worms that feed on their leaves – although the worms themselves are now imported from Japan and China. Evidence that this is an ancient settlement is scattered throughout the village's narrow, winding streets: there are Byzantine wells and Roman tombs on the outskirts, and on the corner by the museum you can see the cleverly preserved remains of a Turkish coffee-shop with inscriptions and old jars. In the central square there is a store run by the Women's Agrotourism Co-operative, an organization dedicated to reviving many of the disappearing arts and crafts of the region; the results of their work – glass, ceramics and *kopanéli* – are on sale. They also have a number of good-value country **apartments** sleeping up to four to rent for stays of two days or more, with three rooms and TV (☎28250 22038; ❹). The village **taverna**, *Aposperitis*, is also good and is sited at the beginning of the Vámos road on the right.

Vámos

Vámos itself is hard to miss – the roads converge here, and from all over the region signs direct you to the local health centre. Only size really distinguishes it from all the other villages, however, and the *kafenía* round the crossroads are as peaceful as any you'll find.

An interesting venture here is Vámos S.A., a co-operative founded with the goal of promoting eco-tourism and rebuilding and restoring houses in the village. They currently have a good **taverna** near the centre of the village, *I Sterna Tou Bloumosifi*; a little further up the main street, *Marouvas* is also good. The co-operative also has its own **café–bar** with spectacular terrace views, a grocery store selling beautifully packaged cheeses, herbs, honey, oil and wine from the region, and even a **tourist office** which changes money and offers motorcycle and mountain bike rentals, in addition to organizing **walks** to Byzantine monasteries and churches nearby. They have recently added an **art gallery** installed in another rescued ruin which sells work by a number of noted Greek sculptors and painters – much of it very expensive. If you're tempted **to stay** they have a variety of rooms, apartments and guest houses to rent, all in carefully restored traditional houses and all very comfortably equipped with bath, TV and cooking facilities plus, in some, luxuries like Jacuzzis or a steam bath (℡28250 23250, Ⓦwww.vamossa.gr; ❺–❼). While you're here, make sure to see the upper part of the village which is where most of the population lives, as it is easy to get the idea that the co-operative's half is all there is.

Heading on from Vámos towards Yeoryioúpolis, there are a couple more potential stops. Signed off the road near Litsárda is the rather bizarre **Kivotos** (8am–8pm daily; €2, children €1) – "The Ark". It describes itself as an ostrich farm, but actually it's more of a children's zoo, with some rather aggressive ostriches and rheas, plus horses (pony rides) and domestic fowl, as well as a blind dog and an orphaned monkey who form a strange, inseparable couple. At **Kálamitsi Amigdáli** nearby, another women's craft co-operative has been set up, weaving silk to sell. Watch out for signs directing you to the workshop as you drive through, or check at the local *kafeníon*, further along the road on the right.

Vrísses

Vrísses, on the south side of the E75 highway, was a major junction on the old road and is still the crossroads for the route south to Hóra Sfakíon. If you're coming from Réthimnon or anywhere else to the east, you usually have to **change buses** here. Set on the banks of the Almirós (or Trís Almíri) river, Vrísses is a wonderfully shady little town, its streets lined with huge old plane trees. On the riverside are a couple of tavernas by a bridge and a monument to the independence settlement of 1898; plenty of smaller cafés line the main street, many of them offering good local honey and yoghurt said to be the best on the island. There are also **rooms**, should you want one, though they're not desperately attractive.

Heading back towards the coast from Vrísses, the road cuts under the E75 once again, following the river valley down to Yeoryioúpolis. This is another lovely stretch, through well-watered fields and woods. About halfway you can pull over to a picnic spot shaded by cypress trees, with a whitewashed chapel by the roadside, fresh spring water and huge picnic tables.

If you're **driving** to Sfakiá, incidentally, it's a good idea to fill up here: fuel is available at a couple of villages en route and in Hóra Sfakíon, but there are only sparse, expensive supplies in other villages along the south coast. About 4km along the road to Hóra Sfakíon, and worth a look if you're passing, the village of **Alíkambos** lies just off the road. In the nave of its **church of the Panayía** there are outstanding **frescoes** by the fourteenth-century master, Ioánnis Pagomenos; they depict the Virgin and Child, Áyios Yeóryios and Áyios Dimítrios, and are remarkably well preserved, which is surprising in view of the way the locals prod them vigorously with their fingers when pointing out images or the names of the saints. The paintings around the altar are by a later artist. The church lies down a track off to the left just before the village and near a Venetian fountain. Should you miss the unsigned turn-off, the *kafeníon* in the village square, fronted by a couple of unexploded bombs from World War II, will provide directions. At **Máza**, 3km northeast of here, there's another frescoed church, although this is not quite so good nor as well preserved. The rest of the route south to Hóra Sfakíon is covered on pp.364–366.

Yeoryioúpolis

YEORYIOÚPOLIS (or Georgioupolis) lies at the base of Cape Dhrápano where the Almirós flows into the sea. It's named after the ill-starred Prince George, a son of the Greek king who was appointed High Commissioner to Crete in 1898 (see p.420). Like Vrísses it's a beautiful old place, with a tree-lined approach and ancient eucalyptuses shading the huge square in the centre. Unlike Vrísses it's now an established resort, although on a small enough scale to remain an extremely pleasant place to spend a few days.

Arrival and information

Buses drop you on the main road, just a couple of minutes' walk from the square and crossroads at the centre of town – a roadside booth here sells tickets for onward buses. Heading up towards the square from the highway, there are a couple of **banks** with ATMs, and also **travel agents** and **car rental** places: Geo Travel (☎28250 61091) is good, as is the large Ethon Tours on the square (☎28250 61269), which has everything from mountain bike hire to its own ATM. These places will also **exchange money**, and offer a range of excursions from **horse-riding** (book direct on ☎28250 61745) to the Samariá Gorge trip. **Mountain bikes** can also be hired from Petros (☎28250 61141) on the road straight down to the highway; they also do guided bike tours and offer child carriers and trailers. Next door is a combined **post office** and **bookshop** with a decent selection of maps and guides.

There are minimarkets liberally scattered around and a couple of slightly larger supermarkets, including handy Kafkalas right on the square; you can buy newspapers from a *períptero* on the square or a number of the shops. There are **cardphone** kiosks on the square and elsewhere, and **Internet** access at *Planet Internet Café* on the edge of the square towards the river. An excellent bakery, *To Pikantiko*, selling the usual *tirópita* and *spanakópita* as well as filled croissants and other temptations, is on the road from the square (by *Mythos Taverna*) down to the beach. Another good bakery is on the road heading out towards Kournás.

If you want to do some **walking** in the area, *Six Walks in the Georgioupolis Area* by Lance Chilton (see p.456) is a great little guide to getting into the local countryside; it comes with an accompanying route map and may be available from shops in the village, but you're best getting hold of it in advance (try to get the revised 2004 edition – updates also available on his website at ⓦ www.marengowalks.com). As a taster, you could try hiking up the Almirós valley towards Vrísses or tackling the steep climb to Exópolis on the road to

Vámos, where there are some wonderfully sited tavernas with magnificent views. Hikes to and around Lake Kournás (see p.334) are another possibility. Lazier tours of the area are offered by a small **land train** that transports visitors along the seafront and to various places of interest inland including the lake, and even as far as Argiroúpolis (p.255). Tickets and information can be obtained from a hut by the seafront *Taverna Edem*.

Accommodation

There are **rooms** to rent everywhere, it seems, and only at the height of season are you likely to have any trouble finding a vacancy; even then you should be all right if you arrive early in the day. The amount of competition keeps prices low. Some of the better places to stay, the first to fill up in high season, are to the right from the square, down the lanes that head towards the beach. Other rooms are to be found off the west (or inland) side of the square. Across the river are a few more secluded and tranquil alternatives. **Mosquitoes** can be a problem here, but the wildlife on the banks is some compensation and kingfishers are regular visitors. With your own transport, the hill village of nearby **Exópolis** becomes a viable alternative to staying in town.

Andy's Rooms Along the beach road from the south end of the square by the supermarket ☎ 28250 61394. Friendly place shaded by trees where good-value balcony rooms have ceiling fans, fridge and wall safe. Also has some well-equipped apartments. Rooms ❸, apartments ❺

Anna Just over the river, or info at Anna Market, between the square and the bridge, where they also have details of local villas ☎ 28250 61376, ☏ 28250 61094. Garden setting, with excellent-value balcony en-suite rooms with kitchenette. ❷

Pension Cretan Cactus Close to *Andy's*, behind the beach ☎ 28250 61449, ☏ 28250 61027. Friendly place with en-suite balcony rooms, all with kitchenette and fridge and a couple with sea views. Also has some slightly more expensive apartments. ❸

Hotel Drosia Off the west side of the main square ☎ 28250 61326, ☏ 28250 61636. Good-value a/c hotel rooms with balcony, tea- and coffee-making facilities, fridge and safe-deposit box in a leafy setting. ❸

Rooms Eleftheria Overlooking the river by the bridge ☎ 28250 61403. Pleasant new place with a variety of fan-cooled balcony rooms with kitchenette. ❸

Georgioupolis Beach Hotel On the seafront at the bottom of the road from the north corner of the square ☎ 28250 61056, ✉ geobehot@otenet.gr. Good value considering the location and facilities – a/c rooms with satellite TV, minibar, hair driers and the like, plus a pool. ❺

Rooms Irene Behind *Cretan Cactus* ☎ 28250 61278. Pleasant en-suite rooms with balcony and fridge near the sea (a few with a view) with friendly eponymous proprietor; fans provided on request. ❸

Marika Studio Apartments Above the main road in the hill village of Exópolis, 3km northwest of town ☎ 28250 61500. With your own transport, this attractive option with studio rooms around a pool and a truly spectacular view becomes a possibility. In high season you'd be advised to ring ahead (though Marika speaks no English) as it has now been discovered by tour operators. ❺

Pilot Beach Hotel On the beach 2km east of town and reached via the E75 highway ☎ 28250 61901, 🌐 www.pilot-beach.gr. Yeoryioúpolis's flagship luxury hotel is cut in two by the highway, with its own tunnel underneath: seafront location, pools, restaurants, kids' club, extensive sports facilities and well-appointed a/c rooms and bungalows, but the traffic noise is potentially a blight. ❽–❾

Rent Rooms Stelios On a cross street off the road towards *Andy's* ☎ 28250 61308. Balcony rooms with fridges and fans off a plant-packed patio, and others in nearby houses. ❸

River House Across the river near to the *Anna* ☎ 28250 61531. Studios upstairs with sea-view balcony and kitchenette or inland-facing en-suite rooms with fridge in a building surrounded by a pretty garden. ❸–❹

Rooms Voula Just off the square's southern end ☎ 28250 61359. Economical en-suite rooms above a souvenir store, which also allows use of a kitchen. ❸

Zorba's Taverna Close to the square on the road towards *Andy's* ☎ 28250 61381, ☏ 28250 61018. Larger than average a/c rooms and apartments above a taverna. The rooms come with kitchenette, the family apartments with a complete kitchen. ❹

The harbour and beaches

The main course of the river runs into the Gulf of Almirós on the northern edge of Yeoryioúpolis, by a small harbour protected by a long rocky breakwater, and there are numerous smaller streams running into the sea all around. The harbour is used by the local fishing fleet and when they return in the early morning you can often purchase a couple of *fagrí* for the pan straight from the fisherman. This area is another favoured nesting ground of the loggerhead **sea turtle** (see p.262), and "turtle trips" up the river (actually to visit colonies of their diminutive relatives, the terrapin) can be taken from a **watersports** hut on the beach at the mouth of the river, where they also hire pedalos and kayaks. For other **boat trips** – such as a day's outing to Maráthi (p.324) at the mouth of Soúdha Bay – there's a booth by the bridge, or details from the boats themselves, tied up on the river below.

The town **beach** heads off to the south, curving round to join the continuous stretch which runs alongside the Réthimnon road for miles. Close to town it shelves very gently and enjoys the protection of the breakwater, and is popular with Greek families. Showers are provided at intervals. At the far end there are new hotels and beach bars, but there are also **dangerous currents** offshore: don't venture too far out, and take heed of any warning notices on the beach. Windsurfers can be rented by the *El Dorado* hotel. Streams crossing the beach create little quicksands in places (only knee-deep), but most of these have wooden bridges to let you cross without getting your feet wet.

A second, much more sheltered, **beach** lies to the north of the river in a small bay. Swimming here is safer and there are generally fewer people, but the water can be extremely cold, owing to the rivers emptying at each end of the sand. There are a couple of simple bar/tavernas behind this beach. At the far end, beyond the smaller stream, you can follow a path over sharp rocks, past an old chapel and various caves, but in the end it leads only to more sharp rocks and eventually peters out above the cliffs.

Eating, drinking and nightlife

Restaurants and tavernas in Yeoryioúpolis are concentrated round the square, or close to it, and there are plenty to choose from; the square itself is ringed by cafés in which to sit over a long drink, watching the world go by. If you make it up to the hill village of **Exópolis** there are a number of tavernas there too, all with stunning views over the coast.

In terms of **nightlife**, Yeoryioúpolis is very quiet indeed. There are plenty of **bars** – the cafés around the square all serve cocktails and play music at night – but the discos and the open-air cinema, for which you may still see adverts around town, have all closed. For now, the highlights of local entertainment are the Tuesday-night live **Cretan music** shows at the *Georgioupolis Beach Hotel*, and the floodlit **minigolf** and children's play area at the *Café Friendly*, signed from the main square.

Anna On the square. Juices, snacks and drinks, with live TV sport.

Arkadi Towards the mouth of the river on the far bank. Not surprisingly given the location, fish is the speciality here.

Taverna Babis On the first corner of the road leading down towards the beach from the square. Good value, simple Cretan food.

Edem Taverna Right on the seafront. A somewhat bland international menu is made up for by one of the best locations in town and a free pool for clients.

O Fanis Near the bridge. Taverna that's particularly good for fish.

Café-Bar Georgioupolis On the square. A good place for breakfast or for a drink at any time of day.

Taverna Georgis Right on the edge of the village by the E75. Excellent meat and fish dishes cooked on a charcoal fire or in a wood-fired oven; it's set slightly back from the street, approached through a bower, and not to be confused with the dreary place next door.

Mythos In the northeast corner of the square. One of the town's better tavernas, if a little pricey.

Taverna Paradise Down by the river west of the square. Simple taverna food served in an attractive garden.

Taverna Platia Just off the square by *Rooms Voula*. Good, inexpensive food, though not a terribly attractive setting.

Taverna Poseidon Down an alley from the road south of the square, in a lovely riverside setting, and serving "every day fish from our own boat". Eves only.

Sirtaki Between the square and the bridge. A pleasant *ouzerí* serving excellent *mezédhes* under a vine trellis.

Lake Kournás

Crete's only freshwater lake, **Lake Kournás**, shelters in a bowl of hills 4km inland from Yeoryioúpolis. As lakes go, it's small and shallow, but it nevertheless makes for an interesting afternoon's excursion. The appearance of the lake varies greatly according to when you visit: during the day its colours change remarkably as the sun shifts around the rim of the bowl, and its size alters over the course of a year. In late summer the level drops to reveal sand (or dried mud) beaches all around, and a number of popular camping spots. Earlier in the year, the water comes right up to the tidal ring of scrubby growth and it's much harder to find anywhere to camp or to swim from. The lake and the hills around it are also a good place to seek out some of the more unusual island wildlife (see p.448). In summer it's possible to make a circuit of the lake using a path and the dried mud beaches where this runs out, about an hour's walk.

To get to the lake from Yeoryioúpolis you could take the touristy land train, hire a bike, or it's an easy walk, pleasant enough once you've crossed the E75 highway. The best route is via the hamlet of **Mathés**, where the very good *Taverna Mathes* has a fine terrace with a great view and daily specials such as braised lamb in wine. Fifty metres uphill from here the delightful *Taverna Villa Kapasa* (☎28250 61050, ⊛www.villa-kapasas.com; ➌) offers air-conditioned en-suite rooms overlooking the leafy garden of an ancient restored house. From Mathés there's a waymarked rambling route to the lake's northern edge, linking in nicely with the route around it mentioned above – ask the villagers at Mathés to direct you to the path, should you have difficulty.

On the lakeshore where you arrive there are a few simple **tavernas** – popular with the locals for outings, with lamb barbecued on spits – and a few pedaloes and canoes for rent. Most of these tavernas have en-suite **rooms** upstairs overlooking the water, including the superbly sited *Korissia* at the north end of the lake (☎28250 61653; ➋–➌), where the pricier ones come with air-conditioning and TV; very comfortable if you have insect-repellent protection. If these are full, you could try for rooms at the village of Mourí, which is straight up from the junction with the path that leads down to the lake.

The village of **Kournás** is another 4km beyond the lake, a stiff climb which reveals a charming hill settlement fanning out around its inclined main street. You may not find a room here, but one place definitely worth a lunch stop is the *Kali Kardia* **taverna** at the top of the main street. Here some of the best lamb and sausages in the area are cooked up, together with tasty *souvláki* and super salads – and don't forget to try their noted *galaktoboúreko* dessert, a lemony egg-custard pudding. After you've eaten you could take a look at the church of **Áyios Yeóryios**, downhill and signed to the right from the square. A fine old Byzantine structure with Venetian additions, it has some impressive fresco fragments. If it's locked, enquiries nearby should produce a key.

South of Haniá: Venizélos country

With a day to spare, the country behind Haniá – a small agricultural plain into which the precipitous foothills of the White Mountains intrude – deserves exploration, especially if you're prepared to embark on some serious **hiking**. For the most part oranges are grown here, which are the best in Crete and hence, as any local will tell you, the finest in the world. Many of the villages are also associated with **Eleftheríos Venizélos**, the revered Cretan statesman who, as prime minister of Greece for most of the period from 1910 to 1932, finally brought Crete into the modern Greek nation.

Being located so close to Haniá, you would think that this would be a deservedly well-trodden hiking zone, but – as is often the case on the island – the infrastructure (places to stay, waymarked routes) is lacking. For the time being it remains a picturesque, but isolated rural farming zone well off the coventional tourist trail.

Thériso

Perhaps the most attractive journey is the fourteen-kilometre drive up to **Thériso**, one of the cradles of Cretan independence and hometown of Venizélos's mother. Here in 1905 the Revolutionary Assembly was held (all baggy black shirts and drooping moustaches, as depicted in so many Cretan museums) that ousted Prince George and did much to precipitate union with Greece. The trip out to the little house, with its plaque commemorating the famous son, is an all but obligatory one for Cretans, and the village is frequently crowded with busloads of battling schoolkids. There's actually little to see apart from a traditional country village, rather sombre in atmosphere if the truth be told, but it's worth going anyway for the drive up **Thériso Gorge**. In terms of spectacle this can't, of course, compare with Samariá and, in any case, the bed of the ravine is given over to the (mostly paved) road. But it is exceedingly pretty in the lower reaches, gentle and winding with the stream crossed and recrossed on rickety bridges, and surprisingly craggy towards the top where the walls are cracked and pocked with caves. A couple of (usually empty) **tavernas** in the village cater for those visitors who decide to hang around after seeing the monuments.

Mesklá

The drive south from Thériso is a heady climb into the foothills of the mountains and over what feels like an impressively lofty ridge. This road is narrow, rocky and it's not always obvious which way to go, but it's not too bad a drive. Alternatively, the route makes a wonderful long **hike**, occasionally traversed by organized rambling groups but quite possible on your own – as long as you check the route beforehand, ask the way if in doubt, and check bus times to get you home again. There are **buses** to both Thériso and Mesklá from Haniá, and the walk between the two – with spectacular mountain views – takes less than three hours. Given the vagaries of the timetable though, the trip is liable to take all day if you do it by bus.

Right at the top lies **Soúrva**, a cluster of whitewashed houses with stupendous views over the surrounding valleys. There's nothing to do here – a lone *kafeníon* is all there is to detain you – but it is a marvellous setting. From Soúrva the way spirals slowly down to **Mesklá**, another beautiful village, set on a swift-flowing brook and surrounded by lush agricultural land and orange groves; there are several small café/tavernas here as well as a basic **pension** (❷). A particularly good place to eat is the *Taverna Manolis & Kostoula Halari*, at the top end of the village beyond the modern church, with fine home cooking and many home-grown ingredients.

Under the Venetians, Mesklá was a place of considerably more importance than it is now, as indicated by the tiny chapel of **Metamórphosis Sotírou** (Transfiguration of the Saviour), which lies at the bottom of the village, a turn up to the left if you are approaching from the Fournés end. The chapel itself is unprepossessing, but inside are preserved the remains of fourteenth-century **frescoes**: many of the paintings have been severely damaged by damp and mould, but parts remain clearly visible and are all the more remarkable for their ordinary surroundings. At the top of the village there's another chapel dedicated to the **Panayía** (next to a large modern church of the same name) which was constructed in the fourteenth century over a basilica of the fifth century which had, in its turn, been raised over a Roman temple to Aphrodite: yet another Cretan holy place which has attracted worshippers for well over two millennia to precisely the same spot. The Roman mosaic floor that had served all three shrines was recently removed to protect and preserve it. Enquiries in the village should produce a key if you wish to see the interior.

Mesklá was also the centre of one of the great legends of Cretan resistance, the **Kandanoleon revolt**. According to the story (which is certainly not historically accurate, though it probably has some basis in fact), much of western Crete rose against the Venetians early in the sixteenth century. They elected as their leader one George Kandanoleon, who established a base in Mesklá and from here ran a rebel administration, collecting taxes and effectively controlling much of the west. It was only by treachery that he was finally brought to heel. In order to legitimize his authority, Kandanoleon arranged for his son to marry the daughter of a Venetian aristocrat, Francesco Molini (see p.393). The marriage took place and the celebrations began, with Kandanoleon and several hundred of his supporters eating and drinking themselves into a stupour – at which point, by pre-arranged signal, a Venetian army arrived and captured the Cretans as they slept. Their leaders were hanged at villages around the countryside, and the revolt was over.

Fournés and Mourniés

Continuing on foot you could tackle the steep climb to Lákki (see p.345) on the main road to Omalós and the Samariá Gorge. The road, however, and the direct route to Haniá, heads down to **Fournés** and joins the Haniá–Omalós road there. Fournés is a very much larger place, with stores lining the road (good for stocking up if you're doing this circuit in reverse), heavily cultivated fields round about and a large producers' co-operative. Beyond Fournés the road to Haniá passes the Ayiá reservoir and bird sanctuary (opposite).

If you want to complete your Venizélos pilgrimage you should also visit **Mourniés**, where the great man was born in 1864. Immediately south of Haniá, this is easiest reached by heading out towards the main E75 highway. Mourniés is just a couple of kilometres southwest off this and, Venizélos's birthplace aside, has little to see, but it's another pleasant drive out of the city, along a road lined with ancient plane trees.

The coast west of Haniá

West from Haniá, the new E75 is fast and dull, speeding you towards Kastélli with little to see along the way. The **old road**, meanwhile, follows the coastline more or less consistently, through a string of small towns and growing resorts, all the way to the base of the Rodhópou peninsula. Occasionally it runs right above the water, more often 100m or so inland, but never more than an easy walking distance from the sea. The coastal route is well served by buses, running every thirty minutes between Haniá and Kolimbári from early morning to late evening. As always, though, you'll really need your own transport to explore the remoter areas **inland**.

In the early stages the various villages have merged into an almost continuous string of ribbon development – not exactly ugly, but not particularly attractive either. There are villas, hotels and sporadic pensions or rooms to rent all the way, though little in the budget range, and vacancies are scarce in season. As you leave the city behind, this development thins, giving way between towns to orange groves protected from the *meltémi* by calamus-reed windbreaks, where only the occasional path penetrates down to the sea. There is **beach** of sorts almost all the way, though much is windswept, dirty and subject to crashing breakers; for secure swimming you're better off closer to Haniá – at the city beach of Kalamáki, at **Ayía Marína** or at **Plataniás**.

This coastline was the scene of the fiercest fighting in the **Battle of Crete**, and the bridgehead from which the Germans established their domination. There are various reminders of this history along the way, although the aggressive **swooping eagle** that used to dominate the road as it left Haniá, erected by the Germans as a memorial to the paratroops who fell at Máleme, has recently been destroyed – "by lightning", according to a diplomatic tourist-office official. Along this first stretch of coast the town beaches are ranged (p.314), though the road here actually veers a little away from the sea. Frequent minor roads run either down to the beach or up into the hills, where there are some pleasant villas and small hotels looking down over the coastline, and a great deal of development going on.

Galatás and the Ayía Reservoir

Villages like Dharátsos, **Galatás** and places even less well defined, seem thoroughly unattractive as you drive along the main road, but in most cases there is a real village, up in the hills inland. Galatás actually turns out to be a fair-sized place, in whose village hall is a tiny, one-room **Battle of Crete museum**, basically a collection of rusty guns and helmets (officially Mon–Fri 9am–1pm, but not always open). Outside is a memorial to those who died here, including 145 New Zealand soldiers. *Barbayiannis*, on Platía Maíou 1941 opposite, is a good place for a snack if you're passing.

Four kilometres to the southwest of Galatás village, **Ayía Reservoir** is renowned for its **birdlife**. Despite being flanked by a couple of unsightly factories, the watery marshland is home to a rich variety of species, including crakes, avocet, marsh harrier, spotted flycatcher and squacco heron in season. The kingfishers are a particular delight and not at all put off their diving tricks, it seems, by human visitors. Terrapins too, are residents here and when not squelching around in the marshy pools they can often be spotted sunning themselves on a raised mud bank. The sanctuary is under the protection of LIFE (an environmental arm of the EU) although to date the only facility that has been provided is a large café: no sign of the promised reception centre or walking trails or hides (though there seems so much birdlife at almost any time of year that a hide is scarcely necessary). The best sightings should be in the early morning or a couple of hours before dusk; binoculars are helpful. The reservoir is clearly signed off the main Haniá to Omalós road near the centre of Ayía village. The road past the entrance (some 300m along on the right) continues to Kirtomádhos, from where you can follow an easily drivable dirt road back to the coast at Plataniás.

Ayía Marína and Plataniás

Kalamáki, where the road finally comes in sight of the beach, marks the limit of the local bus service from Haniá and also the end of this strip of sand. Beyond, low hills drop straight to the sea round a couple of bends and then you emerge at Káto Stalós, which runs into **Ayía Marína**, the first substantial village along this stretch. In fact, there's virtually no break in the development from Káto Stalós to Plataniás, creating the most built-up strip in the west of the island, with stores, restaurants, hotels, rooms for rent, travel agents, tavernas, discos and bike rental places coming one after the other. This is better than it sounds: it's all fairly low-rise, there's a decent beach almost all the way along (with facilities including jet skis, windsurfers and parascending) and, by resort standards, it's all pretty quiet.

Ayía Marína's coastal half – the older village lies a little inland – is distinguished by a small brick factory and a beautiful beach, curving round a little promontory with a fine view of the sunset and of **Áyii Theódori**. This little island not far offshore is now a sanctuary for *kri-kri* or wild goats (you're not allowed to land here). From the west of the islet a great cave gapes like the jaws of a beast; indeed, legend has Áyii Theódori as a sea-monster which, emerging from the depths to swallow Crete, was petrified by the gods. Remains found in the cave suggest that it was a place of Minoan worship in antiquity, while in more recent times the Venetians turned the whole island into a fortress against the threat of piracy and Turkish invasion. There's a wonderfully old-fashioned **rooms** place right on the beach in the centre of Ayía Marína, *Katerina Studios* (T 28210 68333; ❹): if there's a vacancy, these simple, en-suite rooms are excellent value considering their location. *Katerina* also has more modern apartments next door (❺). There's every facility and tour you could want on offer here – one of the more unusual is Hellas Bike (T 28210 60858) who, as well as regular bike hire, run easy **bike tours** around this zone and into the mountains. They do the hard work by trucking the bikes up the ascents, leaving you to freewheel down.

Plataniás

Heading west from Ayía Marína, **Plataniás** follows seamlessly, boasting a delightful old quarter perched high on an almost sheer bluff above the road. **Parking** is a pain – rather than spend time searching for a parking place or getting a ticket, it's easier to use the metered parking lot in the centre of town near the post office. There are a number of **tavernas** which attract evening and weekend trippers from Haniá, notably *O Milos*, a restaurant of repute towards the west end of the village (eves only; very expensive by Cretan standards). Specialities here, and elsewhere in the village, are *yíros* and *kokorétsi* – meat or offal cooked on huge spits over charcoal – but the *Milos* has extra attractions in the form of an old millstream which runs through a walled garden where you eat. The best locations, though, are the eagle's eyries right at the top of the village, where the *Vigli* taverna and friendly *Astrea* have spectacular, vertigo-inducing terraces with views over the coast that make the climb well worth the sweat. Another worthwhile place, in a riverside setting some 3.5km inland, is the *Taverna Drakiana* near the tiny church of Áyios Yioryíos; both are well signed and most easily reached on the dirt road that runs inland past *O Milos*.

Should you want to stay, you'll find a number of **rooms** places along the main street – try the pleasant *Anna* (T28210 68748; ④) near the *Milos* taverna at the west end of town for en-suite rooms with a garden view, or the pricier *Hotel Filoxenia* (T28210 68502; ⑥) a little further east. Other places to stay are mainly seafront apartments booked long in advance for the July–August peak by package operators or holidaymakers from Haniá. Outside these times enquire at any of the travel agents along the main street who should be able to arrange a deal. Otherwise, the main street has everything you need: as well as a **post office**, numerous **banks** (with ATMs) and **supermarkets** there's also even an open-air **cinema**, The Garden, showing films in English. Local travel agents offer all the usual tours, or there's a mini-train which sets off daily on a number of extraordinarily ambitious, two and a half hour tours of the surrounding countryside.

Whatever its other attractions, for most young people in Haniá, Plataniás means **clubs** and **discos**, and a great exodus from the city takes place in summer at around midnight when the clubs here begin to lift off (there are frequent police checks for drink-driving in the early hours of the morning). The most central, on the main road almost opposite *O Milos*, is *Utopia*, with Indiana Jones–inspired decor where inebriates are encouraged to cross a rope bridge suspended high above the ground; by day there's a beachfront music bar here with pool, and a scene all of its own. Similar places line the beach road here, including *Iguana*, and in Ayía Marína (*Divine* among others). Further out, *Privilege/Portocali* is one of the biggest clubs on the island, spilling out wild sounds and techno pyrotechnics until morning. It's just off the E75 highway beyond Plataniás on the road heading inland towards Patellári, so you'll need a taxi or car to get there.

From Yeráni to Tavronítis

Beyond Plataniás, things change little all the way to the Rodhópou peninsula, though signs of tourism get fewer the further you go, with lots of isolated villas and one or two slightly more concentrated developments in places such as **Yeráni**. These on the whole are pleasantly low-key, but the beach is rarely that great, being very open to wind and waves and with rather gravelly, grey sand. Frequent paths and tracks lead down from the road to the sea.

Máleme is perhaps the place you're most likely to stop. Just beyond lies the airfield which saw much of the early fighting in the Battle of Crete and where the German invasion began on May 20, 1941; the loss of this airfield in controversial circumstances was crucial to the German success. Although no longer a base it's still a restricted military zone, but the soldiers on guard duty don't seem to mind if you wander just inside the gate to have a peek. Slightly before the airfield, the giant *Creta Princess* luxury hotel (T28210 627023, Wwww.louishotels.com; ⑦) lies to the right of the road, dominating the only bit of sandy beach around. If you're feeling brazen you can walk through to this: the hotel also has a pool and a couple of bars in luxurious grounds.

Almost directly opposite the hotel, a narrow lane leads up to the **German war cemetery**, set on a hillside below the ridge known as Hill 107, which played a crucial role in the defence of, and the battle for, the airfield. Overlooking the battleground where so many of the four and a half thousand buried here lost their lives, the lines of flat headstones, each marking a double grave, lend a sombre aspect to an otherwise peaceful scene. In a piece of almost grotesque irony, the cemetery's keepers were for many years George Psychoundákis, author of *The Cretan Runner*, and Manóli Pateráki, who played a leading role in the capture of General Kreipe (see p.422). When offered the job, Psychoundákis was allegedly told, "You looked after the Germans while they were alive, why not look after them now they're dead?"

In a bizarre twist of fate, the discovery in 1966 of a splendid **Late Minoan tomb** nearby demonstrated that this area had already been a graveyard for over three thousand years. To reach it, follow the lane leading down from the cemetery to the first left bend, where a track (signed) on the right leads 100m along a terraced hillside to the tomb, again on the right. The *dhrómos* or entrance passage of the stone-built tomb and its heavy lintel are well preserved.

There's a final reminder of Máleme's significance in the Battle of Crete as you cross the River Tavronítis on a long modern bridge: beside it, twin pontoon bridges survive from the war. **Tavronítis** itself is still a traditional farming centre, with fruit for sale at stalls beside the road; it marks the junction with the road across the island to Paleohóra (see p.383).

Kolimbári

Continuing west, **Kolimbári**, at the base of the Rodhópou peninsula, has far more appeal than anything that has preceded it along this coast. If there were a sandy beach, it would be a perfect resort: as it is, there's a long strip of pebbles and clear water looking back along all the coast towards Haniá in the distance. It's little spoiled, and behind the narrow main street with a few tavernas, you can walk through to a concrete seafront promenade lined with more tavernas. The old harbour here is all but deserted now that a huge new concrete one has been built just beyond town: from here there are daily boat-trips in season (10am departure; ☎6972323223) up the peninsula to Diktynna (p.342).

The place is tranquil despite these stirrings of development and, should you want to stay, there are quite a few places offering simple **rooms**: try the good-value, all en-suite *Hotel Dimitra* (☎28240 22244; ❸) at the western end of the village, set slightly back from the sea. *Polichna Traditional Apartments* (☎28240 74191, ⓦwww.villa-polichna.gr; ❹) is a sympathetic modern development of an old building on the hill overlooking town, whose studios and apartments have facilities including satellite TV, a/c and kitchenettes. A good place for a drink or snack is *Mylos*, a stylish café-bar converted from an old olive-oil mill, with a pleasant seafront terrace. The best **tavernas** in the village are *Argentina* and *Diktinna*, almost opposite each other on the main street, but each with terrace tables overlooking the old harbour. More tavernas also cluster around the seafront – *Palio Arkhontiko* comes recommended – and at the top of what used to be a 500-metre-long avenue lined with magnificent plane trees, separating the village from its junction on the main road: in a breathtaking act of municipal vandalism the planes were all felled to allow the road to be widened into the soulless asphalt highway it has now become (a few new trees have been planted, but they don't amount to much yet). At the junction there's a cluster of hotels, bars and restaurants serving the passing trade, as well as a couple of grill tavernas that are favourites with the locals. *Lefka* (☎28240 22211; ❹) is reliable and also offers rooms.

The Rodhópou peninsula

The road that extends onto the **Rodhópou peninsula** goes nowhere in particular, petering out into a dirt track beyond **Afráta** and then circling back, but the first part at least is a superb drive. An excellent local website, ⓦwww.cretanvista.gr, has extensive details on the peninsula and local walks and tavernas.

The first stop, **Moní Gonía** (summer Sun–Fri 8am–12.30pm & 4–8pm, Sat 4–8pm; winter Sun–Fri 8am–12.30pm & 3.30–5.30pm, Sat 3.30–5.30pm; free; respectable dress required), is only a short walk from Kolimbári. The monastery occupies a prime site, with stupendous views and a scramble down to what appears to be a sandy cove – rumoured to be the monks' private beach. Founded at the beginning of the seventeenth century, the monastery perhaps has less to show than some, but has stirring tales to tell of resistance to the infidel Turk. Here they can point to the cannonball still lodged in the walls to prove it – a relic they seem far more proud of than any icon. Which is not to say there are no worthwhile icons: the church has a fine series of post-Byzantine examples dating from the seventeenth and eighteenth centuries (plus a few modern ones), of which Áyios Nikólaos, in a side chapel, is particularly fine. More are kept in the small **museum** (€2), along with assorted vestments and relics. Although there are only six monks left, they remain very hospitable and there's even a "tourist monk", Brother Andónios, who has been pointing things out to visitors for years, often treating them – in quieter times – to a glass of *raki* and a look at his treasured stamp collection (all contributions welcome).

Opposite the monastery and beside a fountain, a steep track climbs the cliff in five minutes to the tiny fourteenth-century church that was attached to the original monastery. The church has fragmentary frescoes, and from its terrace there's a wonderful **view** over the monastery itself and the Gulf of Haniá beyond. Just beyond the monastery is a modern Orthodox academy and from here the road follows the coast for a short way and then begins to climb, hairpinning its way to a dizzy height above the sea before turning inland. The views are magnificent – not only back along the coast you have traversed but also down into the translucent green sea.

Afráta and around

Afráta is a tiny place, little visited, with a few simple *kafenía*. Carry on down the hill past the first two of these and you'll come to *Taverna Roxani*. The charming Roxani speaks no English but, assisted by her husband Alexi, she serves good, simple food in a lovely setting with a shady terrace – try the *fagrí* (sea bream) if available, or the rabbit. Below *Roxani's*, keep right on a paved track which drops steeply, and after little more than 1km you'll reach a rocky cove at the far end of the gorge you can see from the village. The exceptionally clear water here offers great swimming, often with no one else about, though you need to watch out for sea urchins and sharp rocks.

From Afráta, an unsurfaced road is signed to **Astrátigos** and **Áspra Nerá** with a turn-off to the village of **Rodhopós**, all pleasant if unremarkable settlements with opportunities for food and drink stops. This is not too bad a drive, and on the return southward leg, shortly before Áspra Nerá, there's an interesting detour to the village of **Ravdoúha** with a church to see and a few seafront tavernas. From the village proper, 3km from Áspra Nerá, a switchback road descends to the coast. En route you'll pass the ancient church of **Ayía Marína** with some fine fresco fragments preserved within and an old – and now unused – washing place to the side of it evoking a Crete long gone. When you reach the coast a fork offers two possible directions: to the right leads shortly to three tavernas and a small seafront jetty where boats are moored close to a small patch of uninviting sand. The left fork is signed to *Braxos To Kyma* ("Wave on the Rock"; ☎28240 23133; ❷), a delightful **taverna** fronting a pebble beach shaded by tamarisks, which also has three simple rooms. This is about as far off the beaten track as you can get and, as they prize their tranquillity here, if you plan to stay it would be a good idea to give them a ring first. Returning to Áspra Nerá you can rejoin the paved Rodhopós road to head down to the base of the peninsula again.

The tip of the peninsula

Towards the tip of the peninsula you'll find no more drivable roads, though there are a couple of sites you might consider undertaking a major hike or a **boat trip** to reach. The latter is certainly the easier option – in summer the terrain is frighteningly hot, barren and shadeless for walking – especially as there are daily trips from Kolimbári (and occasionally from Haniá) to **Diktynna**, almost at the top of the peninsula above a little bay on the east side. An important Roman sanctuary to the goddess of the same name, this was probably built over more ancient centres of worship, and though it has never been properly excavated there's a surprising amount to be seen. The boats come here mainly because it's a sheltered spot to swim (when the sea is rough, fishing boats often shelter here too), but they allow plenty of time to explore.

It's a challenging hike over to the isolated **Church of Áyios Ioánnis Giónis** on the western side of the peninsula. On August 29 (the commemoration of the death of St John the Baptist), the church plays host to a major pilgrimage and a mass baptism of boys called John, marking one of the most important festivals of the Cretan religious calendar. At this time the two- to three-hour walk (each way) from Rodhopós among crowds of people is definitely worth it. Although you can approach from Afráta, the main path up the spine of the peninsula starts in Rodhopós, which you reach via the first turn off the main road after Kolimbári, and to where there is a very occasional bus (from Kolimbári).

Inland from Kolimbári

A road south from Kolimbári towards Episkopí tracks the valley of the Spiliakos river and offers an opportunity to see an impressive **cave** and a trio of superb **churches**, one of which is unique on the island.

A little over 3km south of Kolimbári is the pleasant rural village of **Spiliá**. On a hill above the village is located the **Cave of Áyios Ioánnis Xénos** (St John the Stranger), a sizeable grotto with a church – dedicated to the eleventh-century evangelist – built inside it. To reach it follow the signs from the centre of the village or consult locals; it's a popular picnicking place with villagers. On the village's southern edge lies the charming fourteenth-century frescoed church of the **Panayía**, raised on the lower slope of a hill and ringed by pines. Inside, the dark interior is decorated with fine **frescoes** from the same period – a torch is useful to inspect them properly.

Just over 2km to the south of Spiliá and beyond the village of Drakoná, a sign on the right indicates the church of "Holy Stephen". Leave any transport here and follow a wooded path for fifty metres to the **chapel of Áyios Stéfanos**, a tiny tenth-century white-walled chapel squatting beneath overhanging oak trees. It should be open, and inside you'll find the heavy stone walls decorated with exquisite **frescoes** dating from the period following the Arab conquest, when the Christian faith was being triumphantly restored.

The church of Mihaíl Arhángelos Episkopí

A further kilometre towards Episkopí the remarkable church of **Mihaíl Arhángelos Episkopí** is signed to the right. One of the oldest churches in Greece, its concentric stepped **dome** is unique in Crete and gives the structure its local name, "The Rotunda". The church was, as its official name suggests, a bishop's seat during the Venetian period, but the edifice is much older than this. The core rotunda section dates to the first Byzantine period, completed perhaps as early as the sixth century, and originally stood alone; the rest of the building was added after the end of the Arab occupation in the tenth century. Meanwhile, excavations in the graveyard are yielding evidence that the present church was built over the remains of a still earlier Christian basilica, and have revealed various layers of burials from all periods of the church's history.

Inside are **frescoes** dating back to the tenth century including a poignant fragment with the head and partial wing of Áyios Mihaíl, the church's patron. Take a look also at mosaic floor fragments (thought to date to the earliest period), and an impressive double-seated marble **font**. Father Melchizedek, the guardian monk, lives in a cell at the rear of the church and is an authority on its history and construction, which he will relate to you (in impeccable English) if you can lure him away from his plant-filled garden.

Returning to Kolimbári you may want to take a detour at Drakoná to see what has now been verified as the **oldest olive tree in Greece** and possibly even the world. Turn right at the Drakoná junction and find your way to **Ano (upper) Vouves**, a half-kilometre beyond Káto (lower) Vouves. The tree lies up a turning to the left near the centre of the village and is now the focus of an ornamental garden funded by the EU. When you reach it, the incredibly gnarled and contorted olive looks every one of the 4000-plus years attributed to it by experts from the University of Crete. A piece of living history that has seen the zenith of Minoan Crete and was seriously venerable at the time of Christ, it currently suffers the indignity of having its hollowed 3m-diameter trunk used as a dog kennel by the house nearby. Still vigorously producing foliage and fruit, the ancient tree has become a source of fame and pride for Ano Vouves, and the village now plans to build a café next to the garden to cater to visitors.

Sfakiá and the Lefká Óri

South of Haniá loom the **Lefká Óri**, or White Mountains – a formidable barrier to reaching the south of the province. Just a couple of metres short of the highest point of the Psilorítis range (trekkers are building a cairn in an attempt to overtake it), these are in every other way more impressive mountains: barer, craggier and far less tamed. There is just one road into the heart of the mountains, climbing up to the cold, enclosed plateau of **Omalós**. From here any further progress southwards must be done on foot – and the most spectacular, and spectacularly popular, is the descent through the great cleft of the **Samariá Gorge**. Famous as it is, this is just the largest of a series of ravines by which streams make their escape to the coast. Far less beaten tracks lead, for example, down the **Ímbros ravine** towards Hóra Sfakíon, or from Ayía Iríni to Soúyia. With more preparation you could also go climbing among the peaks – there's a mountaineering hut above Omalós – or undertake an expedition right across the range. Walks also thread their way along the **south coast**, although it's a great deal easier to get around by boat. Regular summer ferries link **Ayía Rouméli**, at the bottom of the Samariá Gorge, with **Loutró** and Hóra Sfakíon; in the other direction, there are slightly less frequent connections to Paleohóra and Soúyia.

Hóra Sfakíon is the capital of this region – **Sfakiá** – which for all its desolation and depopulation is perhaps the most famous, and certainly the most written about, in Crete. It is an area notorious for its fierceness: harsh living conditions, unrelenting weather and warlike people. Most men here, it is claimed, still carry a weapon of some kind concealed about their person. Historically the region was cut off and barbaric, almost a nation apart which, as occupying armies came and went, carried on with life – feuding, rustling, rearing sheep – pretty much regardless. Most of the great tales of Cretan resistance, of *pallikári* fighters and mountain guerrillas, originate in Sfakiá or in Sélinos, west of the mountains. The local version of the Creation reveals much of the Sfakiot spirit. As recounted in Adam Hopkins' book, it begins:

. . . with an account of all the gifts God had given to other parts of Crete – olives to Ierapetra, Ayios Vasilios and Selinou; wine to Malevisi and Kissamou; cherries to Mylopotamos and Amari. But when God got to Sfakia only rocks were left. So the Sfakiots appeared before Him armed to the teeth. "And us Lord, how are we going to live on these rocks?" and the Almighty, looking at them with sympathy, replied in their own dialect (naturally): "Haven't you got a scrap of brains in your head? Don't you see that the lowlanders are cultivating all these riches for you?"

Stealing was a way of life and so was feuding and revenge – with vendettas on a Sicilian scale continuing well into this century, and occasionally even now (see p.258).

The Venetians had plans to pacify the region, but their castle on the coast at **Frangokástello** was rarely more than an isolated outpost. The Turks did more, imposing taxation on Sfakiá, for example, but they also provoked more violent revenge, notably in the revolt of Dhaskaloyiánnis (see p.361) and many which succeeded it. The mountains were always a safe refuge in which bandits and rebels could conceal themselves while armies took revenge on the lowlands. In World War II Sfakiá resumed this traditional role: when the Germans invaded, King George of Greece was rushed across the island and down the Samariá Gorge to be evacuated, and it was from Hóra Sfakíon that the bulk of the Allied forces were evacuated (see p.366). Throughout the war, the mountain heights remained the realm of the resistance, and in the late 1960s two ex-civil war guerrillas were found still hiding out here, twenty years on.

Nowadays all of this seems romantically distant. There are frequent **buses** to Hóra Sfakíon and Omalós and a constant stream of people trekking between the two, but you don't have to get far off this path to realize how the reputation grew, and why it still holds such sway.

Omalós and the heart of the mountains

The little plateau around **Omalós** lies pretty much at the heart of the Lefká Óri, surrounded by the highest peaks of the range. Between several hundred and a couple of thousand people head up here daily to join the stampede down the **Samariá Gorge**, but only a handful stop to see anything on the way, and very few indeed take any of the more adventurous routes into the mountains. The gorge route is described in detail on the following pages, and while

The **Lefká Óri** take their name from the pale-coloured **limestone** of which they are formed. These rocks were laid down between 150 million and forty million years ago, when the region which is now Greece and the Aegean Sea featured a different pattern of land and water, dominated by a large landmass called Apulia.

Material eroded from Apulia was transported southwards and deposited in the sea as a series of limestones which are now seen over much of western Crete: they are known as the **Plattenkalk** or Ida limestones. The nature of the limestone varied according to the distance from the Apulian coast: those deposited close to the coast were coarse and contained quite large pebbles, while those further away were much finer and often arranged in thin layers alternating with a flint-like rock called chert.

To understand how these limestones were formed into the mountains seen today it is necessary to understand something of the theory of **"plate tectonics"**. This states that the earth's crust is composed of a number of large, very slowly moving plates, which are added to at "mid-ocean ridges" and destroyed again in ocean trenches at "subduction zones". About 35 million years ago the plate containing Africa began to move northwards relative to the plate containing Europe, forcing the Plattenkalk limestones up, and eventually causing slices of the Apulian rocks from the north to be pushed over them. This buried and deformed the Plattenkalk limestones – the results of which can now be clearly seen in the walls of the Samariá Gorge, where bands of light limestone and dark chert are intensely folded.

Eventually the movement of African plate caused some of the old sea floor to the south to be pushed under all these rocks and initiated a "subduction zone" running along the southern margin of Crete; further movement has since been taken up by subduction of the sea floor. This process has caused continued slow uplift of Crete, particularly in the south close to the subduction zone. As the Lefká Óri have been pushed up in this manner the slices of Apulian rocks on top of them have been eroded away, although old Apulian rocks can still be seen to the north of the mountains where the uplift has been less pronounced.

As the mountains move upwards only very slowly, streams flowing from the centre of Crete have been able to follow their original courses and cut through the mountains, causing the spectacular gorges now seen. This process has been going on for about the last 25 million years and is still continuing – hence gorges such as that at Samariá are getting deeper as the White Mountains continue to rise at the rate of about two metres every thousand years.

mountaineering doesn't really fall within the scope of this book, a few starter suggestions are also included. Bear in mind that this is a genuinely wild mountain zone – venture nowhere alone or without adequate equipment.

From Haniá to Omalós

The road up to Omalós turns inland from Haniá's western outskirts, heading at first across a rich but rather dull countryside of orange groves and vineyards interrupted by large modern villages. Shortly before Alikianós (see p.393), the big white building bristling with TV aerials is a prison with a fairly open regime (its inmates work in the fields). This is the building after which the Battle of Crete's "Prison Valley" was named, and at the Alikianós turn-off there's a large **memorial** to local members of the wartime resistance.

Soon after Fournés (see p.336) you begin to climb in earnest to the Lefká Óri through a series of sweeping great loops with increasingly alarming drops. **Lákki**, the only village of any size you pass, has stupendous views from its leafy churchyard, to the rear of a small *platía*. A bracingly exposed place looking back down over the plain in one direction and over the valley of the River Vrísi in the other, it makes an ideal base for walking in the surrounding hills, especially in spring when wildflowers abound. A couple of **rooms** places stand to either side of the main road, both offering more views. *Rooms Nikolas* (℡ 28210 67232; ❷) is probably the better choice, with simple, clean rooms with shared modern bathroom facilities and a **taverna** serving magnificent food (good breakfasts too), catering heartily for appetites generated by mountain air and whetted with the prospect of strenuous activity. *Kri-Kri* (℡ 28210 67316; ❷), almost opposite, is covered with an avalanche of scarlet bougainvillea in summer, and has similar rooms and another taverna. The proprietor here, Gregorios Stamatakis, is extremely friendly and despite speaking limited English will do his best to point out **walking routes** in the vicinity; some of these are marked on the Petrákis *Haniá Trekking and Road Map* (see p.26). The paths are easy to follow and none too taxing. If you encounter honey being sold around the village snap it up: it's made by local producers and is delicious.

Leaving Lákki the road climbs on, past another memorial at the spot where Kapetan Vasilios (Sergeant Major Dan Perkins) and a Cretan colleague were ambushed (a story recounted in *The Cretan Runner* – see p.453), to a **pass** at a little over 1200m, before dropping suddenly to the flat expanse of the **Omalós plain**. If you've caught the dawn bus up from Haniá, it's only now that there's enough light properly to take in the eerily deserted, enclosed little world – and to acknowledge your gratitude at being spared the details of your bus's flirtations with the void at every curve of the ascent. At over 1000m the Omalós plateau is cold, its vegetation stunted, and the enclosing ring of stone peaks is clearly visible all around.

Omalós

There's just one small village up here, **Omalós** itself, sited right at the heart of the plateau. The place is largely unaffected by the daily dawn procession in summer when up to fifty buses pass through (usually without stopping, to the local traders' annoyance) transporting walkers from all over the island to the Samariá Gorge further south. Once the hordes have gone it settles back into the tranquil rustic settlement it remains for most of the year. Walk out into the plain in almost any direction and within five minutes you'll have left all traces of modern life behind, with only the jingling of the occasional goat's bell or the deliberate piling of stones to remind you of human presence.

As is so often the case in Crete, you can't help but think that were this in northern Europe it would be a magnet for **walkers** and naturalists, for the paths into the hills surrounding the plateau (a branch of the E4 Pan-European Footpath crosses the southern edge of the village) are strewn with wildflowers in season, birdlife is profuse year round and temperatures even in high summer are refreshingly cool. But you'll usually find that most of the excellent, good-value accommodation here is empty throughout the season (the competition means prices are always low and usually identical wherever you ask) and there seems to be little interest in publicizing such a wonderful location. As a further enticement to spend the night, there are fabulous starry skies to be enjoyed up here.

A couple of new **hotels** look very out of place alongside the chapel and few crude stone houses of the original settlement. The *Hotel Exari* (℡ 28210 67180; ❷) is the biggest and most obvious of them – with comfortable, modern en-suite rooms. The nearby *Hotel Neos Omalos* (℡ 28210 67269; ❷) has pleasant balcony rooms with bath, TV and central heating. Much simpler rooms are available at the friendly *Samaria* (☎28210 67168; ❶), to the right as you enter the village. The revamped *Hotel Gingilos* (☎28210 67181; ❷) has modern en-suite rooms with bath, balcony view and TV and is run in eccentric style by an entertaining farming family. Their restaurant is good and the speciality is *thikári astó* (roasted kid); they will also drive you the 5km to the top of the gorge the next morning if you're staying at the hotel. Another friendly place for en-suite rooms with bath, TV and fine balcony views is *To Elleniko* (☎28210 67169; ❷), just beyond the village some 200m down the road from the others. Its position beyond the village lights makes it great for star-gazing. Note that all the places listed here are fully open during the April to October season; outside of this period they open weekends only. For **eating** and **drinking**, each of the accommodation places has its own bar and taverna serving up hearty mountain fare, though not all may be open at quiet times – the *Neos Omalos* does tasty *souvláki* and is usually the busiest.

Scattered about the plain are other settlements, but none has the aura of permanent habitation: in winter everything is deep in snow and deserted. In spring the land is marshy and waterlogged – almost becoming a lake if there's a sudden melt. Only in summer do people live here full-time, moving up from Lákki and other villages on the lower slopes round about (Ayía Iríni, Zóurva, Prasés) to pasture sheep and goats or to cultivate, on a small scale, cereals and potatoes.

With your own transport, if you are not planning to walk the gorge, there's a spectacular surfaced road which cuts west through the mountains to link up with the Soúyia road just north of Dimitrianá and Ayía Iríni (see p.394). This is also a possible route to Paleohóra (see p.385).

Scaling the peaks

Perched high over the Samariá Gorge at 1677m, the EOS (Greek Mountain Club) **Kallergi Hut** (May–Oct; occasional winter opening for determined skiers; ☎28210 33199 to eat here, ☎6936657954 for a bed; €12 per person) acts as the base for climbing into the peaks, and the staff here are probably the best source of information on doing so. The gorge looks exceptionally impressive from the isolation of the bare stone peaks up here, a slash of rich green in an otherwise unrelenting landscape of grey and brown. In summer the place is very popular with hikers, so if you do set out with the intention of overnighting, ring ahead first to reserve a place. Sleeping out is an option, but even in high summer the nights can be bitterly cold at this altitude. To get here from Omalós you can drive (on a rough dirt road), or it's a fairly easy hike. Follow the road towards Omalós for about thirty minutes, then turn left onto the dirt track signed to the hut, a further hour's climb; alternatively from the top of the gorge a signed path leads up in about ninety minutes.

For adventurous walkers, there's a two-day hike (partly along the E4 Pan-European Footpath) from here through the heart of the range to Anópoli and Hóra Sfakíon. This would take you right past **Páhnes**, the highest summit in the west and, at 2453m, just 3m short of Psilorítis for the title of loftiest in Crete: Haniot mountaineers regularly add stones to the cairn on the peak in an attempt to catch up. With less commitment you could follow the beginning of this trail for two or three hours for some scintillating views down into the gorge and across the seas to the south and west. A day-hike from the refuge will take you to the peak of **Melindaoú** (2133m; 16km/7hr walk) on well-marked paths off the E4 – get detailed directions locally.

You'll probably impress others more, though, if you tackle the climb to the peak of **Mount Gíngilos** (2080m), beginning from the top of the Samariá

Gorge. Its north face, the one everyone sees, is a near-vertical slope of solid rock; round the back though, you can reach the summit with only a little scrambling. It's hard work and you need confidence with heights, especially if it's windy, but no special mountaineering skills are necessary. A large yellow sign points the way from the back of the *Tourist Lodge* at the top of the gorge and the path, though not marked with the usual paint splashes, should be easy enough to follow for the two and a half hours to the top. At first you track around to the west, climbing above the plain, before cutting south, downhill slightly, towards the back of the mountain. Here, almost exactly halfway, amid bizarre rock formations which include an arch across the path, there's a spring of ice-cold water (drinkable). Beyond, you begin to climb in earnest for the final thirty minutes. The ascent is signalled with red paint – stick to the path as there are hidden hazards and even the official route needs hands as well as feet. The rewards are an all-round panorama from the summit and, with luck, the chance to spot some of the rarer animal life which crowds have driven from the gorge itself.

The Samariá Gorge

The one trip that every visitor – even those eminently unsuited to it – feels compelled to make is the hike down the **Samariá Gorge** (*Farángi Samariás*) which, at 16km in length, is claimed to be the **longest in Europe**. Protected by a national park since 1962, this natural wonder was formed by a river flowing between Mount Volakiás to the west and the towering bulk of the heart of the Lefká Óri to the east. In its descent from the plateau the stream has, over time, sliced a steep, cavernous ravine between the two. In summer the violent winter torrent reduces to a meek trickle and this is when the multitudes descend. If you're expecting a wilderness experience, an opportunity to commune peacefully with nature, think again; Friday and Saturday are the days attracting fewest visitors. On the other hand, this is not a Sunday afternoon stroll to be lightly undertaken; especially in spring when the river is roaring, or on a hot midsummer day, it can be a thoroughly gruelling test of fitness and stamina. The mules and helicopter standing by to rescue the injured are not mere show: anyone who regularly leads tours through the gorge has a stack of horror stories to regale you with – broken legs and heart attacks feature most frequently. To undertake the walk you need to be reasonably fit and/or used to lengthy walks, and you should have comfortable, sturdy shoes that will stand up to hot, sharp rocks.

Gorge practicalities

Conditions permitting, the gorge is **open** between the hours of 6am and sunset, from May 1 to October 31 inclusive; however the first three weeks after opening and the final two weeks before closure will entirely depend on weather conditions and you're advised to ring ahead to save a wasted journey. **Admission** to the national park costs €5 (under-15s free): if you enter after 3pm you're only allowed into the first couple of kilometres from each end. During winter the hike is dangerous and often impossible, and even early and late in the season flash floods are a real possibility and not to be taken lightly; in 1993 a number of walkers perished when they were washed out to sea. If in doubt, the Haniá Forest Service has a **gorge information** number (☎28210 67140) and the gorge office (☎28210 67179) at the entrance will also provide advice. Outside the official season, and at the discretion of the wardens, you may be allowed through if the weather is good, but there will be very little transport.

There are a whole series of national park rules (posted at the entrance), but the most important are **no camping**, no fires (or smoking outside the designated areas), no alcohol, no hunting and no interfering with the wildlife or

Transport to and from the gorge

The vast majority of people who walk through the gorge do so as part of a **day-trip**: a very early bus to the top, walk down by early afternoon, boat from Ayía Rouméli to Hóra Sfakíon and bus from there back home. Most go with one of the **guided tours** offered by every travel agent on the island – certainly if you're staying in a hotel anywhere in the east of Crete this is much the simplest method, and probably the only way of doing it in a single day. Most tours will include all bus and ferry connections, but not food or the entrance fee to the park itself. (If you're planning to stay on the south coast, the tour bus can save you the effort of carrying your bags; simply stow them underneath and retrieve them in Hóra Sfakíon. Do let them know your plan, though, both to guard against an unexpected switch of bus and to prevent search parties being sent out.) If, however, you are staying in Haniá, or marginally less straightforwardly in Iráklion, Réthimnon, Soúyia or Paleohóra, you can save money and avoid having to walk in a large group by taking the **public bus**, which runs a daily service during the periods when the gorge is open.

From Haniá there are four departures a day, at 6.15am, 7.30am, 8.30am and 2pm (this latter service changes to 4.30pm outside school term time), arriving at the top about ninety minutes later. You'll normally be sold a return ticket, including the return leg from Hóra Sfakíon (which needn't necessarily be used the same day), so if you don't want this you'll have to make your intentions very clear; the bus station is in total chaos when the first buses leave. There's a lot to be said for taking the **earliest bus**: more of the walk can be completed while it's still relatively cool, there's no need to force your pace, and if you're planning to stop over anywhere at the bottom you've more chance of being among the first to arrive. On the other hand, everyone now does this – there's often a procession of as many as five full buses leaving Haniá before dawn, the bus station is in turmoil, there are queues and confusion when you arrive, and you're unlikely to escape from crowds the whole way down. It may be hotter, but it's also quieter if you set out later. The first buses of the day **from Iráklion** (5.30am) **and Réthimnon** (6.15am and 7am) to Haniá continue direct to Omalós, while there are also services from **Paleohóra** (6am) and **Soúyia** (7am); the last two meet in Ayía Iríni from where one continues to the gorge and the other direct to Haniá, so you may have to change.

From the bottom of the gorge, **boats** leave Ayía Rouméli for Hóra Sfakíon, calling in at Loutró en route, at 9am (June–Sept only), 11.30am, 3.45pm and 6pm throughout the season; there's a reduced service in the second half of October, and hardly any boats from November to April when the gorge is closed. The trip takes around an hour (30 mins to Loutró). Boats also head west from Ayía Rouméli for Soúyia (45min) and Paleohóra (1hr 30min) daily at 4.45pm between May and September. **Buses** from Hóra Sfakíon back to Haniá leave at 7am, 11am, 5.30pm and 7pm; for Réthimnon there are direct ones at 5.30pm and 7pm (otherwise you change at Vrísses); for Plakiás summer only at 11am and 6pm. It's also possible to get back to Haniá via Soúyia (bus at 6pm) or Paleohóra (7pm), though this is a longer journey. There should always be enough capacity on the boats, and the buses wait for the boats to arrive.

If you want to do the gorge using **your own transport**, or while staying in Omalós, it's possible to walk down, take the boat to Soúyia, and then get a taxi back up to Omalós or the gorge parking area from there – Soúyia taxis generally charge about €30 for this.

collecting plants. There are wardens who patrol to ensure these are obeyed, that no one wanders too far from the main path (another breach of regulations unless you have a permit obtained in advance from the Haniá Forest Service) and that no stragglers are overtaken by nightfall.

As for **supplies** for the walk, you want to carry the minimum possible. On a day-trip you needn't necessarily carry anything, though a water bottle and something to munch on the way are definitely worthwhile (there are springs at regular intervals and ice-cold water in the stream, but for long periods you'll find neither – especially over the last, hottest hour) as is some means of carrying clothes you discard en route (7am at the top feels close to freezing; 1pm at the bottom may hover around 38°C/100°F). If you plan to stay a day or two at the bottom you'd do better to leave your pack at Haniá's bus station or elsewhere for collection later, taking only what's essential. For **food**, there's a café and official *Tourist Lodge* (with substantial meals and a fine terrace view) at the top, plus stalls for hot drinks, bottled water and snacks, while Ayía Rouméli is more than equipped to feed everyone arriving at the bottom.

Most walkers head **down** (rather than up) the gorge, and it would be a daunting start were it not for the well-worn trail leading clearly down below you, the buses and cars jostling for space to park, and the dozens of people hanging around ready to set off. This is a fine place for a spot of contemplation before heading down, allowing the crowds to disperse if you've arrived with a mob. There are maps showing the path and facilities en route, others with the vegetation zones marked, and lists of park regulations.

The nearby **Lefká Óri Information Centre** (May–Oct daily 8am–8pm; €1) is a great introduction to the wildlife, geology, culture and history of the gorge. One imaginative feature is a miniature gorge walk which takes you down a model of the gorge illustrating the flora and fauna to be seen at the various altitudes on the descent to the sea. Good as it is, though, the centre opens long after most of its potential visitors have passed by its gates in the early dawn, with more pressing things on their minds.

The gorge hike itself is some **18km long** (the final two kilometres to reach the sea from the mouth of the gorge) and the **walk** down takes between four and seven hours, depending on your level of fitness, and how often you stop to admire the scenery, bathe your feet and take refreshment. Be wary of the kilometre markers – these mark only distances within the park, not the full extent of the walk. At the park entrance, you'll be given a date-stamped ticket in return for your entrance fee, which should be kept and handed in at the gate by which you leave; this is partly to make sure no one tries camping in the park, partly to check that nobody is lost inside.

Accommodation

If you want to make the gorge part of a longer excursion, there are several **accommodation** options. The *Tourist Lodge* right at the top (daily 7am–9pm; ☏28210 67237) is no longer a possibility since it closed its rooms, although their **taverna** is still a great place for a meal later in the day, with spectacular mountain views from its terrace. The nearest bed you can get to the entrance is now at one of the places in Omalós (see p.346) or in the Kallergi Hut (p.347). Alternatively you could simply sleep out: there are usually quite a few people trying to find a flat space for their sleeping bags around the entrance. This has few real advantages however; you'd have to be up very early to steal a march on the first arrivals from Haniá (for much of the year this would mean setting off before daylight) and from Omalós you face an extra five-kilometre walk to reach the top of the trail (or the early buses will stop and pick you up on their way through). Nonetheless, it does make quite a change to stay up here and freeze for a night, and of course it gives you the opportunity to explore more than just the gorge.

Staying on the **south coast** for a night or more after your exertions makes more sense: there are rooms at Ayía Rouméli (see p.353), Loutró (p.355) and Hóra Sfakíon (p.366) or westwards in Soúyia (p.395) and Paleohóra (p.385).

The walk

The gorge begins, with startling suddenness, on the far side of the plateau. After the dull tranquillity of the plain you are faced with this great cleft opening beneath your feet and, across it – close enough to bounce stones off, it seems – the gaunt limestone face of Mount Gíngilos. The descent starts on the **Xilóskalon** ("wooden stairway"), a stepped path cut from the rock and augmented by log stairs and wooden handrails, which zigzags rapidly down to the base of the gorge, plunging 350m in the first 2km or so of the walk. Near the bottom the chapel of Áyios Nikólaos stands on a little terrace of coniferous trees: there are benches from which to enjoy the view, and fresh water. Beyond, the path begins gradually to level out, following the stream bed amid softer vegetation which reflects the milder climate down here. In late spring it's magnificent, but at any time of year there should be wildflowers and rare plants (no picking allowed), including the endangered large white peony, *Paeonia clusii*. The stream itself is less reliable: there are places where you can be sure of icy fresh water and pools to bathe sore feet all year round (particularly in the middle sections), but what starts in spring as a fierce, even dangerous torrent has dwindled by autumn to a trickle between hot, dry boulders, disappearing beneath the surface for long stretches.

The abandoned village of **Samariá** lies a little under midway through the walk, shortly before the 7km marker. One of the buildings here has been converted to house the wardens' office, another has been pressed into (inadequate) service as a public toilet, but for the most part the remains of the village are quietly crumbling away. Its inhabitants, until they were relocated to make way for the park in 1962, were predominantly members of the Viglis family, who claimed direct descent from one of the twelve aristocratic clans implanted from Byzantium. Certainly this settlement, as isolated as any in Crete and cut off by floodwater for much of the year, is a very ancient one: the church of **Óssia María**, from which both gorge and village take their name, was founded in the early fourteenth century.

After Samariá the path is more level, the walls of the gorge begin to close in and the path is often forced to cross from one side of the stream to the other, on **stepping stones** which at times may be submerged and slippery. Beside you, the contorted striations of the cliffs are increasingly spectacular, but the highlight comes shortly after the Christós resting point with the **Sidherespórtes** (Iron Gates) where two rock walls rise sheer to within a whisker of a thousand feet: standing at the bottom, one can almost touch both at once. For this short stretch, there's a wooden walkway raised above the stream, whose swirling waters fill the whole of the narrow passage. Almost as suddenly as you entered this mighty crack in the mountain you leave it again, the valley broadens, its sides fall away, and you're in a parched wilderness of rubble deposited here by the spring thaw.

Before long – 8km beyond Samariá – you reach the fringes of Ayía Rouméli, where there's a gate by which you leave the park and a couple of stalls selling cool drinks at crippling prices. Frustratingly, however, this is not the end of the

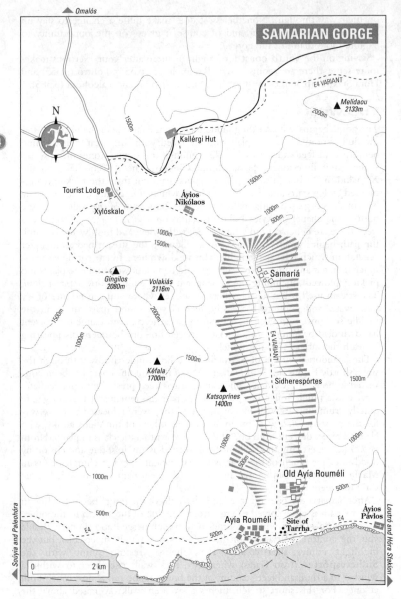

walk: old Ayía Rouméli has been all but deserted in favour of the new beachside community, a further excruciatingly hot, dull twenty minutes away. Arriving finally in **Ayía Rouméli** proper (see opposite), you face the agonizing choice between plunging into the sea or diving into one of the tavernas for an iced drink – though in the event it takes a strong will to walk past the rows of enticingly dew-dropped cans of chilled fruit juice and ice-cold beers set out to

Flora and fauna in the gorge

Gorge **wildlife** means most famously the *kri-kri* (variously the *agrimi*, *Capra aegagrus*, the Cretan wild goat or ibex), for whose protection the park was primarily created. You are most unlikely to see one of these large, nimble animals with their long backswept horns, though you may well see ordinary mountain goats defying death on the cliff faces. More likely candidates for viewing are the local birds and reptiles. Almost four hundred varieties of **birds** are claimed to have been seen here, including owls, eagles, falcons and vultures; bird-watchers after a coup should look out for the endangered lammergeier (or bearded vulture). On the ground lizards abound, there's also the odd snake and you may just spot the beech marten, spiny mouse and weasel, species of which are unique to Crete.

The multifarious **trees** – Cretan maple, pine and cypress – are remnants of ancient forests and provide the backdrop to an often dazzling array of **wildflowers**, perhaps the most rewarding finds when in season; the purple *Tulipa saxatilis* and rock plants such as aubretias, saxifrages and anemones stand out, and there are wild irises and orchids here too. **Herbs** are also to be seen in abundance; besides the intoxicatingly aromatic thyme and rosemary and common sage and oregano, there are half a dozen species which exist exclusively in the gorge and nowhere else. Also to be found here – and usually growing in the most inaccessible places – is **Cretan dittany**, a celebrated medicinal herb referred to by Aristotle and Hippocrates and taken by women in ancient times as a method of abortion; indeed modern science has shown the ancients to have been correct in believing that the herb acted as an abortifacient when taken in large quantities in early pregnancy.

Two **books** on the gorge can prove useful in identifying most of the flora and fauna and are portable enough to take along. *The Samaria Gorge Yesterday and Today* (Toubis, Athens) documents the history of the gorge from the Romans to World War II, and includes an illustrated guide to the flora and fauna along its length, whilst *The Gorge of Samaria and Its Plants* by Albertis Atonis (Albertis, Iráklion) provides a step-by-step description of the flora. Both titles are widely available from bookshops in Haniá, Réthimnon or Iráklion or can be ordered in advance (see p.450).

divert you from your course to the water. Once your senses adjust, Ayía Rouméli is a pretty unattractive place – but that drink, and the first plunge in the sea, are likely to live in the memory as the most refreshing ever.

Ascending the gorge

Starting from the bottom, the hike **up the gorge** to **Omalós** is not as hard as some imagine, though it will take rather longer – six to seven hours at a reasonable, steady pace. Few people do it all the way, which means that at the top you may well find the gorge almost empty; on the way up, however, you'll have had to pass the hordes charging down. You could also walk a short way up and come back – an outing offered as a day-trip known as "Samariá the Lazy Way". This will show you the Iron Gates, the most spectacular individual section, but it means a lot of walking in the dullest parts down by the coast and none of the almost alpine scenes nearer the top.

Ayía Rouméli

Once you've recovered from the gorge walk, drunk and eaten your fill, plunged into the sea and out again (a couple of the tavernas have showers which they'll let you use if you eat there), lain on the pebbles for a while and rested, **Ayía Rouméli**'s attractions soon begin to pall. It's a singularly unattractive example of over-rapid development, with a rash of concrete tavernas and rooms for rent

△ Trekking on the South Coast

spreading over a large shingly beach. By local standards it's expensive too, although given the difficulties of transport this is perhaps not altogether surprising. The village is, however, attempting to be environmentally conscious: the pile of huge concrete tank traps behind the beach shields an experimental solar energy plant; at night, or other times when this system can't cope, a diesel generator cuts in.

Finding anything much to do apart from laze on the beach takes some ingenuity. Although there was an ancient settlement here – **Tarra**, inhabited probably from the fifth century BC through to the fifth AD – and more or less constant later habitation, very little remains to be seen. The ruined **Turkish fort**, under which you pass as you emerge from the gorge onto the beach, doesn't really justify the scramble up to see it. Tarra straddled the stream where it ran into the sea, just to the east of the present village – the only obvious remains are the foundations of an early Christian basilica by the present **church of Panayía**, around which you may also spot a few tiny fragments of mosaic. This, supposedly, was the site of a much earlier temple of Apollo.

Practicalities

Ayía Rouméli does have its good points – mainly the sheer number of places to eat and to stay – and at night it's very peaceful. Should you be tempted **to stay**, try the tranquil *Livikon* (℡28250 91363; ❷) at the rear of the village, or the sea-view rooms attached to tavernas *Tara* (℡28250 91231; ❷) or *Zorba's* (no phone; ❷); you can also book ahead at the *Hotel Agia Roumeli* (℡28250 91240; ❸), with a few more comforts and good balcony views. Just to the east of the village (near the solar plant) is a clump of trees among which a few people are usually **camped**, and on the beach in this direction are some caves, also sometimes used to sleep out in.

The kiosk which sells **boat tickets** is plainly marked down by the beach: if you're catching the bus back to Haniá or elsewhere from Hóra Sfakíon, you could get a ticket for the last connecting boat when you emerge from the gorge, and spend the afternoon on the beach. If you plan to stay elsewhere on this coast, take the first boat available for the best chance of finding a room at your destination.

Loutró and south-coast walks

Of all the south-coast villages, **LOUTRÓ** perhaps best sums up what this coast ought to be all about. It's an incredibly soporific place, where there's absolutely nothing to do but eat, drink and laze – and where you fast lose any desire to do anything else. The big excitements of the day are the occasional arrivals and departures of the ferries. The days start bright and are soon lost in an overpowering heat shimmer; evening comes cool and darkness falls fast – by 10pm the place is virtually asleep. All this despite the fact that it has been almost entirely taken over by tourists. Little happens all summer long to interrupt this easygoing idyll, but if you're here for the great **feast of the Panayía** on August 15 the small church is the place to head for. From the early dawn, the formidable local priest conducts the service which lasts until after midday. The small churchyard then fills up with all those who had intended to come earlier – and each of whom receives a disapproving glare from the *papás* – as biblical quantities of *arní* (roast lamb), *psomí* and *krasí* are doled out and everyone enjoys a great feast.

The short waterfront arching around a beautiful little bay consists of a row of perhaps six **tavernas** and a similar number of **rooms** places plus one small **hotel**; the mountains rise immediately behind the waterfront. There's no road in – everyone here has either come on the boat or walked, which helps to keep things very low-key, prices reasonable, big groups rare and the people genuinely friendly. Although the transparent blue water here is always inviting, perhaps Loutró's main drawback is its lack of a real **beach**. There's a small stretch of pebbles in front of the eastern half of the seafront, with large signs asking bathers to remain respectable. Try lying topless here and you'll be told none too politely to cover up; those who persist risk being catcalled by the village children. But the sheltered bay is otherwise ideal for **swimming**, clear and warm, and people bask **nude** on the rocks around the point, far enough out to avoid offence. The good news is that there are other beaches in walking distance (see opposite), with small boats or rented canoes ferrying visitors to the best, at **Sweetwater** to the east, and **Mármara** to the west.

Practicalities

You can **change money** and buy supplies at the village's two minimarkets, and a second store a little further on (immediately before the beach) has a good selection of secondhand books and also changes money. There are **cardphones** behind the beach, and **canoes** can be rented from the *Porto Loutro* hotel for expeditions to the nearby coves and beaches. Any of the tavernas (try the *Blue House*) can arrange a taxi-boat to Hóra Sfakíon (about €20) and elsewhere. The *Porto Loutro* runs day **cruises** aboard its own boat to Gávdhos (see p.398), Áyios Pávlos or Palm Beach (p.293) as well as dolphin-spotting trips; details and prices should be posted outside the hotel. There's a daily **boat** at 11am to the **Sweetwater and Mármara beaches** returning at 4.30pm from each (Mármara from the jetty, Sweetwater from the eastern end of the strand). **Boat tickets** are sold from a kiosk behind the beach, but they only go on sale a few minutes before departure; try to have the right change. The smaller boats tie up at the jetty or the small dock, but the *Samaria* ferry sails straight up to the beach, lowering its bow onto the pebbles.

Accommodation

Rooms in Loutró seem uniformly basic and comfortable, though to be sure of finding one you should arrive as early as possible – an increasing number seem to be pre-booked through enterprising travel agencies and foreign holiday firms. Try for one with a balcony (the *Porto Loutro* and *Blue House* offer top-floor rooms with huge roof terraces); the quietest places are generally the furthest round to the east, but nowhere is exactly loud or stays open late. If you can't find anywhere at all to stay, you could hike or take a boat over to Fínix, Líkkos or Mármara (see p.359). You could also consider **camping** out on Sweetwater Beach (opposite), but you should be aware that freelance campers are not very popular in and around the village after years of problems.

Blue House ☎28250 91127, ⓦwww.delftmarkt.nl/thebluehouse. One of the original places here, and still one of the friendliest and best. Good-value en-suite rooms and a wonderful (more expensive) top-floor extension. ❷ Ilios ☎28250 91160. Pleasant rooms above a good taverna. ❸ Keramos ☎28250 91356. Quiet, standard rooms on the east side of the bay. ❸

Rooms Manousoudaki In the village, near the church ☎28250 91348. Simple en-suite rooms, often with vacancies after sea-front places have gone. ❷ Notos ☎28250 91501. Just along from the *Porto Loutro*, with sea-view en-suite rooms with fans. ❷ Rooms Patrudakis ☎28250 91351. Rooms with bath close to, and similar to, *Manousoudaki*. ❷

4

Hotel Porto Loutro ☏ 28250 91433, ⊛ www.hotelportoloutro.com. The only place with any pretensions at all, right in the middle of the village above the beach. It's a lovely place, whose white cubes fit in surprisingly well with the surroundings; it's not outrageously expensive, though since the rooms are pretty accurate reproductions of a simple Greek room you may question whether it's worth paying the extra. Even here you may find yourself showering in salt water if there's a shortage (as there is most summers). ❹

Eating and drinking

Because most of its visitors come from northern Europe, Loutró's tavernas tend to be busy earlier on and start to close by 9.30pm. Many of the places here have a better than usual **vegetarian** selection.

Blue House Probably the best restaurant in Loutró, recognizable from its blue-checked table-cloths (although quite a few other places are imitating this feature now); the owner is one of the village's friendliest characters.

Ilios Good fresh fish, caught from their own boat.

Kri-Kri The place to go for tasty spit-roasted lamb and chicken.

Labyrinth On top of the headland close to the castle ruins. Bar offering the closest thing to nightlife in Loutró, reached by following the lights leading up the hillside. At weekends they often have concerts with *lyra* and *bouzoúki*.

Café Bar Maistrali The westernmost building in Loutró (alongside the concrete jetty), this is where everyone heads in the evening, although they also serve breakfasts. Its cocktails and music may seem a bit slick in this setting, but it's certainly a pleasant way to wind up your day.

Notos Excellent *mezédhes* served on a pleasant small terrace.

The coast around Loutró: Sweetwater to Mármara

Anyone who spends any time at all in Loutró is eventually taken with the urge to explore – even if it's just climbing up to the ruins on the headland. There are plenty of long, tough walks available (see p.359), but there are also easier hikes to nearby beaches. Some of these can also be reached by boat.

Sweetwater Beach

East of Loutró, **Sweetwater Beach** lies in the middle of a barren coastline, approximately halfway to Hóra Sfakíon. From the sea, as you pass on one of the coastal boats, it appears as a long, extremely narrow slice of grey between sheer ochre cliffs and a dark, deep sea. Closer up, the beach seems much larger, but there's still a frightening sense of being isolated between unscalable mountains and an endless stretch of water.

The beach takes its name from the small springs which bubble up beneath the pebbles to provide fresh, cool drinking water. You can dig a hole almost anywhere to find water; there are plenty already made, but you should take care not to pollute the groundwater with soap. For years there was a little enclave of **nudist campers** here, their idyll interrupted only by the occasional intrepid cliff-walker. Over the last couple of years, though, daily boat services have started from both Loutró and Hóra Sfakíon, bringing a lot more people. So far these have not spoilt the place – the beach is easily big enough to absorb everyone – and the campers are still here, for once doing a good job of keeping the place pristine: there are signs up warning against leaving rubbish, and people regularly make an effort to pick up any junk that is left behind.

The long-term residents (including local goats) tend to monopolize the only shade, in the **caves** at the back of the beach, but you can always escape the sun at the small **bar/taverna** which sits on a lump of concrete just off the western end of the beach, reached by a rickety plank. You can get cold drinks and simple meals here and they also rent out sun umbrellas. There are no other facilities beyond the **boats**, which come once in the morning and again in the late afternoon. Walking here is also a possibility, though a very hot and shadeless one: about 45 minutes or so to Loutró, an hour to Hóra Sfakíon (p.366). On a calm day, you could even paddle a canoe over from Loutró. The path runs along behind all the houses in Loutró – to join it from there, climb up behind the beachside kiosk and church.

Fínix

Immediately to the west of Loutró, in the little bay on the other side of the promontory, stood **ancient Fínikas**, now known as **Fínix** or Phoenix. This was a major town during the Roman and Byzantine periods, and a significant port long after that: it was the harbour at Fínix, a more comfortable place to wait out the winter storms than Kalí Liménes, which St Paul's ship was hoping to reach when it was swept away. A local story has the saint actually landing here and being beaten up by the locals he tried to convert: given the attitude to Cretans revealed in Paul's epistle to Titus, it is, as Michael Llewellyn Smith points out, "safe to say that if he had landed here they would have beaten him up".

Yet again there is very little to be seen. These days the bay, with its rocky beach, has what has become quite a fashionable **taverna** and **rooms** place, the *Old Phoenix* (T 28250 91257, W www.old-phoenix.com; ❸) – somehow, despite being done up, it seems to remain exceptionally languid, the epitome of a tranquil hideaway. They also rent out sun umbrellas and loungers as well as **canoes**. It's hard to believe there could ever have been a population of any size here. Up on the headland, though, there's certainly evidence of later occupation, principally in the form of the **Venetian fortification** on the point from where – on clear days – it's possible to glimpse the island of Gávdhos, 50km out to sea. Nearby are traces of a Byzantine basilica and other scattered remains; most curiously, however, there's a building, very much in the form of a Venetian church, sunk entirely below ground level. Its arched roof is intact, the interior entirely full of water. Nowadays it is deliberately flooded and used as a storage cistern, but its original purpose remains a mystery. It could always have been a cistern, of course, but it seems too elaborate for that; an alternative theory suggests it was an underground arsenal attached to the castle.

To **walk** to Fínix by the most direct route, join the path – now part of the E4 Pan-European Footpath – that runs behind Loutró, up behind the beachside kiosk and the church. This will lead you straight up, past the castle and directly over the headland, in around fifteen minutes; if you're continuing beyond Fínix, you don't have to go down to the water as a path continues straight past the back of the bay, but it's only marginally shorter. It's also possible to get there by walking out past the last house in Loutró and simply following the rocky coast around. This is a much longer and tougher walk, but it does have the compensation of passing plenty of good rocks to swim from, and extensive remains of old buildings which you can imagine are, and may indeed be, ancient Fínikas. **Boats** to Mármara also regularly call in at Fínix, bringing supplies.

Líkkos

West of Fínix, the path continues to another, much longer bay, **Líkkos**, with three rather poorly patronized **taverna/rooms** places, making it another escapist's paradise – and there's plenty of fresh water too, which there may not be in Loutró. The name of the economical *Small Paradise* (T 28250 91125; ❷) continues the theme and is the first place you see, run by a friendly

Irish-Greek couple; they have cheaper en-suite rooms above the taverna (where the *mizithra* sheep's cheese is a speciality) or excellent new balcony sea-view rooms in their extension next door. Phone them if you want to stay and Michaelis, the boss's brother, will come and pick you up for free from Loutró or Fínix with his boat. Slightly east, *Lykos Restaurant* (T 28250 91446; ❷) has similar en-suite rooms with balcony views. Simpler rooms are on offer at *Rooms Yeoryios* (T 28250 91457; ❷), the last of the three, right in the middle of the beach, with chickens running around out front and a pleasantly eccentric (eponymous) owner. Yeóryios will also come and pick you up from Loutró or Fínix free of charge.

Unfortunately Líkkos is not a very attractive **beach**, with rocks and pebbles, and is awkward to swim from unless you wear shoes. Behind, you can look up and see the village of Livanianá, perched on the eastern flank of the Arádhena Gorge (see p.363).

Mármara Beach

The Arádhena Gorge emerges at the sea in the next bay west of Líkkos, **Mármara Beach**, which takes its name from some marble deposits visible near the jetty where you land. This is another fairly small cove, with a sandy beach surrounded by interesting rock formations full of caves and slabs to dive from or sunbathe on. Unfortunately it also sees at least three boats a day from Loutró, which in summer bring more people than can comfortably be accommodated. So although out of season it might be more attractive than Sweetwater, at peak times it is far less so – and fresh water is at a premium here, as the not always pleasant toilet block will attest. A simple **taverna/rooms place** gives the place a focus, as well as providing an outlet for renting sun umbrellas and loungers; tempting cool drinks are available from their generator-run fridge. The proprietors also try to keep the beach free of tourist litter. *Rooms Chrisostomos* (T 28250 91387 or mobile T 6932300445; open April–Oct; ❷) offers simple cabins lighted with gas lamps and the eponymous owner will pick you up with his boat from Loutró for free (providing of course, you intend to stay). He is a good source of information on the many **walking** possibilities in this zone: from Mármara you could walk up the Arádhena Gorge to Livanianá (where there's a good and friendly taverna, the *Livaniana*) about a three-hour hike, or you could do the coastal route to Áyios Pávlos (about 2hr 30min; see below) and Ayía Rouméli (one hour further).

Some people do **camp** here, but to do so you have to make a very long hike for supplies, or regularly take the boats to and from Loutró. Walking to Mármara takes a little over an hour in all, and the second half, from the far end of the beach at Líkkos, is hot and exposed, climbing high onto the cliff.

South-coast walks

Loutró lies close to the heart of the network of coastal paths linking Ayía Rouméli in the west to Hóra Sfakíon in the east. In the absence of a road, Loutró is an important junction for long, often challenging **south-coast walks**. Most real traffic nowadays goes by boat, of course, and the last inland hamlets have finally had a drivable track built to them. But the paths and tracks remain, to give a variety of possible **hikes**, even the easiest of which can be demanding in the heat of high summer. You'll need, at the very least, decent shoes to cope with rough, rocky terrain and a water bottle, which you should fill at every opportunity. You should also have a companion, since some of these paths are pretty isolated, and outside help cannot be relied upon.

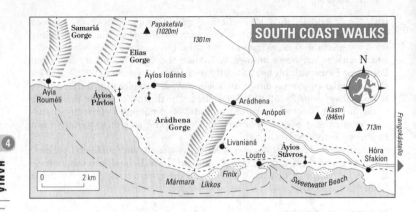

Coastal routes from Loutró

The **coastal path** – now part of the E4 Pan-European Footpath – is the most obvious, the most frequently used by tourists and, in terms of not getting lost, the simplest to follow. There's not a great deal to see en route, however, nor is it an easy walk – the path is often frighteningly narrow and uneven as it clings to the cliff face, and in summer it is very, very hot, offering no shelter at all from the sun, so headwear and protection are advised.

Heading east from **Loutró to Hóra Sfakíon** is barely a problem: it's the most heavily travelled part, the whole walk takes less than two hours (8km), and there's a rest stop at Sweetwater Beach halfway. Loutró to Sweetwater is straightforward and fairly well beaten: beyond here the path clambers over a massive rockfall and then follows the cliffs until it eventually emerges on the Hóra Sfakíon–Anópoli road about thirty minutes' walk above Hóra. This is easy to find from the other direction too, the path (to the left) leaving the road at the first hairpin bend.

Heading west, **Loutró to Ayía Rouméli** is an altogether tougher proposition. For a start you can expect to be walking for at least four hours solid, a real sweat in high summer, and for seconds, after the tavernas at Líkkos the only chance of refreshment is at Áyios Pávlos (see below). The path has already been described as far as Mármara beach (see p.359). After Mármara you climb again to track along the exposed cliff face for around an hour before reaching the first sign of civilization, a solitary cottage and a few trees. In about another hour, you'll arrive at the eleventh-century cruciform chapel of **Áyios Pávlos**, yet another site where St Paul is supposed to have landed. Here he allegedly christened locals in a spring close to the church (now only a trickle). The chapel itself is ancient and rather beautiful, set on a ledge above the water, and surrounded by dunes; inside are fresco fragments dated to the thirteenth century. You could cool off in the sea here before setting out on the final hour to Ayía Rouméli, and there is now a **taverna**, *Saint Paul* (June–Sept only), which also rents out tents for nearby camping.

Coming east from Ayía Rouméli this path is well marked, heading east out of the village. Ten to fifteen minutes after Áyios Pávlos it splits, left to climb inland to Áyios Ioánnis and Anópoli, right to continue along the coast to Mármara.

To Anópoli

If you're hiking for its own sake, or for that matter if you want to take the easiest way from Ayía Rouméli to Hóra Sfakíon without necessarily calling at

Loutró, then the **inland routes** centring on Anópoli have a great deal to be said for them.

Getting to Anópoli, which is high above the coast more or less directly above Loutró, is not easy unless you have a car. **From Hóra Sfakíon** it's 12km up a very steep, winding road with alarming hairpin bends and few barriers, making meeting a bus or truck coming in the opposite direction a pretty nerve-wracking experience if you happen to be on the outside. You probably wouldn't want to drive this at night, nor would you really want to walk it up either, but you might not have much choice, since the lone daily **bus** drives up at 4pm and down again at 6.30am. The walk up **from Loutró** also looks terrifying – you can see the path tracking back and forth across an almost vertical cliff – but is in fact not as bad as it seems: about ninety minutes, climbing steeply most of the way. This is best done very early, before the sun gets too powerful; at the top you're on the fringes of Anópoli – turn left for the centre.

Anópoli itself is a quiet country village, not much used to visitors, dominating a small upland plain with a few rare vestiges of forest. Another wonderful location to sample the simple delights of rural Crete, it has a couple of *kafenía* and a small general store on the square which lies at the end of a long road in, after the way levels following the climb. Outside of holiday periods such as the festival of Panayía on August 15, if you wanted to stay away from all the hustle of the coast you should be able to find somewhere here. The village also makes a good base for an exploration of the Arádhena Gorge (see p.363). There are several **rooms** places along the road as you approach from Hóra Sfakíon; the friendliest is the excellent-value *Panorama* (☎28250 91100; ②) for en-suite rooms where you'll get a warm Sfakiá welcome. The other good place is in the village proper, a couple of kilometres further, where *Taverna Platanias* (☎28250 91169; ③) has rooms with bath fronting the statue of Dhaskaloyiánnis (see the box below) on the main square; they also have an apartment to let for a two-night minimum stay with full kitchen and TV. The proprietor here, Eva Kopasis, speaks excellent English and can advise on walking routes in the area. Both places have good **tavernas** and any of the goat, lamb or sausage dishes here are mouthwatering. *Ta Tria Adelfia* (☎28250 91150; ②), halfway between the two, is another possibility for simpler (but not much cheaper) rooms if these are full.

From Anópoli you can walk (or even drive with care) the 4km track leading southwest to **Livianá**, a hamlet perched above the lower reaches of the Arádhena Gorge where there's a good taverna, the *Livaniana*, with spectacular views. There's also a path down into the gorge from here (see p.363).

Dhaskaloyiánnis

Anópoli was the home of the first of the great Cretan rebels against the Turks, **Dhaskaloyiánnis** – the subject of a celebrated epic ballad. To cut a very long story extremely short, Dhaskaloyiánnis, a wealthy ship-owner, was promised support by Russian agents if he raised a rebellion in Sfakiá, support which in the event never materialized. (The Russians hoped only to divert attention from their campaigns against the Ottoman Empire elsewhere.) The revolt, in 1770, was short-lived and disastrous for Sfakiá, which for the first time was brought well and truly under the Turkish heel: Dhaskaloyiánnis went to the Turks in an attempt to negotiate acceptable surrender terms. Instead the Turkish authorities seized and then tortured him in the Cathedral square at Haniá, following which he was skinned alive and executed. There's now a statue honouring him in the square at Anópoli.

To head for Ayía Rouméli from Anópoli, follow the road through to the far end of the village, where it becomes a little-used, dusty jeep track, signed to Arádhena. There may be shorter ways on the old paths than this track (ask around if you're determined), but there's so little traffic that following the road makes little difference. It takes about thirty minutes to the edge of the **Arádhena Gorge**, 3km away, on the far side of which is the virtually abandoned hamlet of Arádhena. The villagers are said to have left to escape from a series of Sfakiot vendettas, but in the light of what is happening elsewhere, such depopulation seems commonplace. With the new road, one or two people have moved back and started to restore some of the crumbling buildings.

The first thing to grab your attention when you reach the gorge is the steel **bridge** – a remarkable construction, all the more remarkable when you discover that it's a bridge to nowhere, as the road on the far side soon peters out at nearby Áyios Ioánnis. Constructed in 1986 by the local Vardinoyiannís family, controllers of an international business empire, the bridge was a gift to provide a lifeline to the outside world without which their home village of Áyios Ioánnis would probably have died. Rumble across it in a car and the terrifying crack of the wooden boards against metal thunders around the gorge below. The **views** from the bridge down into the gorge below – one of Crete's most precipitous – are vertiginously spectacular.

Across the bridge and right on the opposite rim of the gorge is the romantically picturesque Byzantine church of **Mihaíl Arhángelos**, with its curious "pepper-pot" dome standing proud against the Lefká Óri's heights. The white-walled church dates from the fourteenth or fifteenth century and was constructed on the ruins of a much earlier basilica, of which the central nave and apse may be a part. Inside, are some outstanding **frescoes** (torch useful) depicting the life and crucifixion of Christ as well as the church's patron saint. A fairly ancient iconostasis stands in the church's porch. The church is now permanently locked following a number of thefts and to obtain a key to view it you should make enquiries at Anópoli (try *Taverna Platanias* on the square). Scattered round about and beyond the nearly deserted village are a few traces of ancient Araden, a still unexcavated Greco-Roman town from whose stones the church is said to be built. Looking inland from the churchyard or the bridge you can see the old path, negotiable on foot or by pack animals only, zigzagging down to the bottom and back up the other side, which for well over two millennia was the only way across the gorge. Incidentally, this is still the path you take to follow the gorge down to the sea (see opposite).

The road from the bridge heads westwards for about an hour (5km) to end at **Áyios Ioánnis**, beneath the massed peaks of Páhnes, Troharís and Zaranokefála. A more substantial and outwardly prosperous place since the construction of the bridge, it goes so far as to have a **taverna** on the way in where you can rest up for a while or have a beer at tables beneath shady pines. Dormitory **beds** are also available at *Pension Yioryedakis* (☎28250 91480; €7), a mountain refuge-style place, which can also provide meals if required. It is located 200m from the taverna taking two left forks beyond this; should you get lost, ask any of the villagers to put you right. Close to the taverna (below the road to the left) are a couple more **Byzantine churches** with fourteenth-century frescoes; the taverna should have keys. There are also several impressively large **caves** nearby.

For the onward walk to Ayía Rouméli, ask to be put on the right track as the way isn't immediately obvious. Generally, you have to head to the left, between two chapels, after which the path becomes hard to follow for a while until it emerges on top of the cliffs. From here it loops down as a rough but obvious path to join the coast trail before the chapel of **Áyios Pávlos**. You should be able to complete the approximately seventeen-kilometre walk from Anópoli to Ayía Rouméli in about five hours, though with rest stops and wrong turnings it could well take much longer; leave plenty of leeway if you need to catch a boat back. If you are undertaking this walk in reverse, start early so as to complete the climb of the cliffs before it gets too hot.

The Arádhena Gorge

The superb hike from Loutró, up to Anópoli, through the **Arádhena Gorge** and down to Mármara beach from where you can get a boat back to Loutró (last at 4pm, or there's a taxi-boat available from the *Yeoryios* taverna at Líkkos beach, a short walk east of Mármara), has been tamed in recent years, and even become a target for bus tours. Even so, the full walk is tougher than Samariá, and you must be reasonably fit to tackle it, even if the old ladders and ropes have now been replaced with stone steps to help you over the worst parts. Parts can still be pretty scary too, not helped by the ominous presence of picked-clean skeletons of goats, which presumably have either fallen from the top or been washed away in spring floods. The sense of achievement, however, is immense, and the gorge, though far smaller than that of Samariá, is in physical terms almost as impressive. There isn't much in the way of wildlife, but the rocky river-bed is forced into an extremely narrow gap between sheer walls almost all the way down – and there'll be hardly anyone else around.

Allow **five hours** at least from Loutró to Mármara (two and a half to the top of the gorge, plus the same again down it) adding on an extra ninety minutes if you walk back to Loutró from Mármara. In the heat of summer, and even if you take a boat back, it's more likely to take eight hours once you've stopped a few times. An alternative starting-point is Anópoli: this allows you to get the gorge completed early on in the walk – although once back at Loutró you still have the ninety-minute ascent back to the village, with the possible option of a taxi (about €5) from Hóra Sfakíon if it all becomes too much.

To reach the start of the **descent** into the gorge you set off by turning right off the road and onto the old path, 600m before you reach the gorge and just before the bridge comes in to view. Heading half right across a stony stretch of ground with a small pinewood to the right, leads you to the recently repaired stepped path down to the bottom (this side should be used rather than the track on the other side, which is deteriorating fast now it's not used much). This and the first stretch, with its relatively flat bottom as you head under the bridge through an impressively deep section, conspire to lull you into a false sense of security: as it gets steeper further down, you find yourself jumping from rock to rock or taking narrow steps around dry cascades. Look out as you go for the paint marks indicating the route – these often seem to take you over unnecessarily tricky terrain, but you usually discover the reason further on when you reach an impassable portion. Fill up with water at every opportunity, as there's none towards the end of the gorge.

An **easier alternative** from Loutró (about a four-hour round trip, not allowing for pauses) is to head out past Fínix (follow the upper path, bypassing the cove) until you come to a fork in the path: the lower one goes to Líkkos, the upper to Livianá, which you can see above you. From the village a path beyond a gate just above the church (signed "Mármara") leads down into the gorge, emerging fairly near the bottom having bypassed all the hardest bits. The red markings show you the best path down the gorge and you'll reach the beach after about 45min walking. The Ímbros ravine (see p.364) is another slightly softer option, with more wildlife but less dramatic terrain.

The road south: to Hóra Sfakíon and Frangokástello

The easy way **into Sfakiá** from the north coast is by a good road which cuts south from Vrísses (p.330), almost immediately beginning to spiral up into the mountains, towards the plateau of Askífou. The climb seems straightforward from a bus or car, but the country you drive through has a history as bloody as any in Crete: you pass first through a little ravine where two Turkish armies were massacred, the first during the 1821 uprising, the second in 1866 after the heroic events at Arkádhi (see p.252); the road itself is the one along which the Allied troops retreated at such cost in the final stages of the Battle of Crete. This chaotic flight has been described in detail in just about all the books covering the battle (and also in Evelyn Waugh's *Officers and Gentlemen*) – it makes for strange reading from the comfort of a modern journey.

Askífou plateau

The **Plateau of Askífou** offers the relief of level ground for a while, now as it did then. The plain is dominated by a ruined Turkish castle on a hill to the left of the road – a hill so small and perfectly conical it looks fake, put there expressly to raise the castle above its surroundings. There are several small villages up here, chief of them **Ammoudhári**, with a couple of small tavernas and the chance of a room if you wanted to stay (one place, over the bakery, tends to be noisy in the morning; the only other disturbance to the peace here is the twice-daily convoy of buses, arriving empty and returning with sated gorge-walkers).

For keen **walkers**, a path leads from **Petrés**, immediately south of Ammoudhári to Anópoli, a long day's hike (18km) through the mountains via the hamlet of **Kalí Láki**, beyond where the path follows a rough track to reach Anópoli. Though detailed on the Petrákis *Haniá Trekking and Road Map* (see p.26), it's not a terribly easy route to follow and you should attempt to get thorough directions locally before trying this, though this may not be easy unless you speak fluent Greek. A branch of the E4 Pan-European Footpath also heads through Ammoudhári: to the west it climbs into the foothills of the Lefká Óri – initially easy walking with good opportunities for bird-spotting and then climbing seriously into the heart of the mountains to eventually reach the Kallérgi Hut (p.347), a two-day trek. In the other direction the E4 heads south across the plain to Ímbros, where one branch follows the gorge down to meet the coastal path or you can head east to Asféndou and from there to Asigonía (p.259). A shorter route leads east from Ammoudhári to the nearby village of **Goní**, from where a track leads to Asigonía, some 10km away.

In **Askífou**, right at the heart of the plateau, there are more tavernas and home-made signs to a home-made Battle of Crete museum. Gathered in the private house of an enthusiastic collector, this is an extraordinary jumble of weapons, helmets, badges and photos, much of it picked up in the immediate area. There's no charge – though donations are welcome – and you may well be offered a *raki* and a biscuit while you browse.

Ímbros and the Ímbros ravine

On the far side of the Askífou plateau lies the village of **Ímbros**, the entry point for the Ímbros ravine. For years there was little here apart from a couple of tavernas flanking the road through – *Taverna Faragi* does a great *sfakianópita* (Sfakian cheese pie with honey). But the gorge has become far more popular in recent years, with a branch of the E4 running down it and an increasing number of coach tours, and there are signs of development. There are two excellent **rooms** places, allowing a night's stay in utter rural tranquillity before attempting the gorge. The first, *Hotel Zapakis* (℡28250 95372; ➋), has en-suite balcony rooms, below the *Taverna Faragi* on the way to the gorge entrance; the other, the newly renovated and very comfortable *Hotel Zervos* (℡28250 95244; rooms ➋, apartments ➌), is located 200m further along the road south, on the left.

The **gorge walk** is clearly signed from Ímbros village, although the official **entrance** to the ravine is a few kilometres south, by the *Café-Taverna Porofarango* (if you have a vehicle, you can park it here while you do the walk). Here a well-trodden trail leading down to the stream bed leads to a booth where you will be charged an entry fee of €2 (April–Oct 7am–sunset; free outside this period). The money raised goes to support the maintenance of the gorge and village projects.

Once in the gorge, you are following a **track** which, until the completion of the new road, was the district's main thoroughfare. The hike to the end – emerging at the village of Komitádhes – is easily enough done in less than three hours, and, provided you don't coincide with a tour bus (to be sure of which, set out early), it can still be a wonderfully quiet walk, certainly in contrast to the crowds at Samariá. The only problem is that you miss the magnificent views available from the road above. In its own way the ravine is as interesting as its better-known rival, albeit on a smaller scale: narrow and stiflingly confined in places, speckled with caves in others and at one point passing under a monumental, natural stone archway. Through the ravine you simply follow the stream until, emerging at the lower end, an obvious track leads away again towards the village of Komitádhes.

Komitádhes itself is full of huge, usually empty tavernas waiting for the occasional tour party to arrive. At any of them you can get something to eat and drink while you recover from your exertions, and they'll order you a taxi if you want to be taken back up to Ímbros (about €20) or on to Hóra Sfakíon (about €10). You can also walk to Hóra Sfakíon easily enough, though this final 5km makes a hot, boring anticlimax to what has gone before. It's possible to walk the gorge as a half-day trip from Hóra Sfakíon (or Loutró, by getting the first boat from there): simply take the early bus to Haniá, and get off at Ímbros.

South to the coast

South of Ímbros, the road climbs briefly again out of the plain and then begins gradually to descend to the south coast. This stretch is lovely: an excellent, winding route which follows dramatically one side of the Ímbros ravine, tracking high through conifer-clad slopes with the cleft always dizzily below. As you approach the **coast**, still high above it, you begin to glimpse distant sparkles of water until finally the road breaks out of its confinement, way above the sea, with a broad plain to the east (and Frangokástello hazy in the distance), steeper drops to the west, and immense vistas out towards Africa ahead. Hóra Sfakíon is out of sight until you are almost upon it, an alarming plunge down through hairpin bend after hairpin bend. If you're driving, you need to watch out for buses: it can be alarming in the evening meeting the vast convoy coming the other way on these relatively narrow curves, and in the afternoon you'll pass them parked in every available spot since they can't all squeeze into Hóra Sfakíon. Should you be arriving here with your own transport and the needle is quivering around empty, a **garage** is sited just after where the road turns west along the coast towards Hóra Sfakión.

The guns of Crete

Cretans are some of the most mild-mannered and genial people on the planet, and it oftens comes as a surprise to visitors to discover that the population of Crete is one of the most heavily armed in the world – although the bullet-pockmarked road signs all over the island should have given a clue. Get to know someone well and he will soon be telling you about his stock of **weapons**, including perhaps arms handed down in the family from the wars against the Turks, and more recently against the Germans in World War II. When the German army quit the island after their defeat, they left behind a huge arsenal of guns such as Mauser pistols, which still change hands for considerable sums. The authorities are all too aware that in wilder areas such as Sfakiá every household has at least one gun and most possess veritable armouries of weapons, including machine guns and the latest status symbol, a Russian Kalashnikov. It would be pointless for the authorities to try to confiscate all these guns, as it is already illegal to keep a weapon without a permit – most people simply ignore the law.

Crete is certainly not a violent society, although in areas such as Sfakiá feuding and vendettas often do lead to arms being used to settle disputes (see p.258). It's likely that this urge to own guns has much to do with Cretan history, which has seen the island defending itself against a succession of invaders, from Dorians and Romans to Venetians, Turks and Germans. Many islanders will tell of how, at Máleme when the German parachutists invaded, their fathers and grandfathers were reduced to fighting the German infantry with axes, spades and pitchforks – "never again" is the oft-quoted reason for hanging on to their weapons. However, the only time that most of these weapons are brought out in public today is at weddings or baptisms when salvos of expensive ammunition are blasted skywards in honour of the bridegroom, bride or baptized infant – this signals that the shooter values friends and family so much that he is willing in one evening to send a whole month's wages up in smoke. Even this practice is increasingly rare – and officially illegal – following a couple of fatal accidents.

Hóra Sfakíon

Squeezed between the sea and the mountains, **HÓRA SFAKÍON** (often known simply as Hóra, meaning "chief town") couldn't grow even if it wanted to. Nevertheless it's a surprise to find the capital of Sfakiá quite so small. It is, though, a thoroughly commercial centre these days: restaurants cram the seafront promenade between the square where the **buses** stop and the pier where the **boats** dock, and every house in town seems to display a large "Rooms" sign. Although it is cheap and pleasant if you do decide to stay, and relatively quiet by the end of the day, the beach is small and pebbly (although there is a much better pebbly cove beach at the western end of town) and there is little else to distract you.

Supposedly, Hóra once had as many as a hundred churches and chapels, built for one reason or another by devout Sfakiots, but few survived the wartime bombardments. There are a couple of ancient-looking examples on the road as you curve down into Hóra, but all seem permanently locked. As for other monuments, a **plaque** on the east side of the bay commemorates the Dunkirk-style wartime evacuation, when some ten thousand Allied troops were taken off the island: almost as many were left behind to be sitting ducks as they waited to be taken prisoner or to escape as best they could. Many of the inhabitants who aided the operation were later dealt with brutally by German execution squads. A memorial opposite *Rooms Panorama* on the bend above the town commemorates their bravery; as is the custom here, the skulls of the dead are visible behind a window in the monument's base.

If you have time to spare, you're probably best off getting out to Sweetwater Beach (see p.357), an hour along the coast path west (or accessible by twice-daily boat), or to Frangokástello (see p.368), 14km east. The coast road to the east runs some way from the sea through a series of small, little-visited villages: Komitádhes has a couple of tavernas and even a few rooms, but Vraskás and Voúvas can offer no more than a *kafeníon* and a general store each. It's also possible to visit the **Cave of Dhaskaloyiánnis**, one of several large caves in the cliffs to the west of Hóra. Always a hideout in times of trouble, this was where the rebel leader (see p.361) set up a mint to produce revolutionary coinage. Sfakiá Tours or the Travellers Service Centre (see below) will provide directions on how to reach it, and also have information about local boats which can take you there if you don't fancy the hike.

Practicalities

The road into Hóra Sfakíon ends at a small square just above the water. Here the bus will drop you, and there are paid **parking** spaces (short-term immediately above the square, long-term around the bay to the east). Directly ahead the *Casa Delfini* café/restaurant is an obvious landmark: beside it are the **post office** (Mon–Fri 7.30am–2pm) and one of several small **supermarkets**, as well as a Visa-only ATM. Otherwise you can **change money** at many of the hotels, or at Sfakiá Tours (☏28250 91130), also here by the post office, or the Travellers Service Centre (☏28250 91044), on the west side of the square. Both are useful sources of **information** on everything going on locally, and for car hire and accommodation – Sfakiá Tours also sells bus tickets, while the Travellers Service Centre has a selection of secondhand books and has details of an old-fashioned country house nearby that sleeps up to ten (from about €25 per person).

There are basically just two pedestrian streets leading off the square into town, one along the waterfront with an unbroken row of **tavernas** leading round to the harbour, the other just inland, with shops and rooms as well as more places to eat. Practically the first building here is an excellent **bakery**, and there's also a supermarket with better prices than those on the front, a dairy shop for local cheese, yoghurt and honey, and several exchange places. Finding **food** is never a problem here, and all the tavernas seem to have a good array of **vegetarian** food, such as *bouréki* and vegetable-stuffed aubergines. Of the waterfront choices, the *Lefka Ori* in the corner of the harbour probably has the best seafood. Away from the water, *Tria Adelfia* (see below) is also worth trying. *Gianni's Café*, overlooking the little cove beach on the west edge of town, is a pleasant, quiet spot for a sundowner, and also has **Internet** connections.

Rooms are better and cheaper if you avoid the obvious places right on the front or the main road. Good places to try for rooms with bath are *Panorama* (☏28250 91296; ❷), on the bend as you descend into the town, where some rooms overlook the eastern harbour, or the central *Hotel Stavris* (☏28250 91220, ✉stavris@chania.cci.gr; ❸), just off the square behind the waterfront tavernas. Follow the inland street around and you'll come to *Tria Adelfia* (☏28250 91040, ⓦwww.three-brothers-sfakia-crete.com; rooms ❷, apartments ❸), with comfortable a/c, en-suite rooms. Just behind the ferry dock, the *Hotel Xenia* (☏28250 91490; ❸), a former state-owned hotel now under private ownership, has en-suite rooms with fridge in the best location in town, though a somewhat run-down atmosphere.

Boat tickets are sold from a hut at the bottom of the jetty near the tavernas: check which ferry you'll be getting, as the *Samaria* is too big for the dock and comes in instead right on the other side of town, quite a long way to run if you're waiting in the wrong place. Daily services run to Loutró and Áyia Rouméli in season (at 10.30am, 1pm & 4.55pm, also at 7pm June–Sept only); there are also departures to Gávdhos on Saturday and Sunday from May to October at 10.30am (additional service Fri June–Sept, and Thurs July–Aug), and a little boat to Sweetwater Beach at 10am daily (tickets on the boat). **Bus tickets** are sold at Sfakiá Tours on the square: for Haniá, most people already have tickets and the important thing is to get on the bus in order to secure a seat. The south-coast bus east to Plakiás leaves at 11am and 6pm in summer only, and the 6pm one is often even more crowded. A **taxi-boat** is available from the *Samaria* taverna on the waterfront.

Frangokástello

FRANGOKÁSTELLO lies 14km east of Hóra Sfakíon, about 3km south of the road heading east towards Plakiás (for a description of this route, see p.293). A series of isolated dwellings dotted across a plain between the mountains and the Libyan sea, it's a curious place to arrive in as there's no real centre or square as such, leaving you with little option but to head for the castle, the imposing silhouette of which comes into view long before anything else. Despite its lack of a focus, for peaceful lassitude the **beach** at Frangokástello is still among the best spots in Crete, with fine sand, crystal-clear water (with good snorkelling opportunities), and very little effort required either to get here or to find food and drink once you've arrived.

Once on the beach, if you want company you'll find it around the castle, where the best part of the sand is sheltered and slowly shelving. For solitude, head westwards along the shoreline, where there's less soft sand and more wind, but it's still very pleasant. There are beaches to the east too: follow the coastal path for ten to fifteen minutes and you'll arrive at the top of a low cliff overlooking perhaps a kilometre of beautiful, deserted sand and rocks. Lying in the sun here the only thing to disturb the afternoon tranquillity is the occasional muffled crump of an explosion offshore, emanating from the home-made depth charges of local fishermen going about their business in the time-honoured and highly illegal way. Watch closely, and you'll see the sudden spout of water near the boat before the noise of the explosion reaches you.

The **castle**, so impressively four-square from a distance, turns out close up to be a mere shell. Nothing but the bare walls survive, with a tower in each corner and, over the seaward entrance, an escutcheon which can just be made out as the Venetian lion of St Mark. Still, it's some shell. The fortress was originally built in 1371 to deter pirates and in an attempt to impose some order on Sfakiá: a garrison was maintained here throughout the Venetian and Turkish occupations, controlling the plain as surely as it failed to tame the mountains – even today, the orange-pink walls look puny when you see them with the grey bulk of the mountains towering behind. In 1828, Frangokástello was occupied by **Hadzimihali Daliani**, a Greek adventurer attempting to spread the War of Independence from the mainland to Crete. Instead of taking to the hills as all sensible rebels before and since have done, he and his tiny force attempted to make a stand in the castle. Predictably, they were massacred and their martyrdom became the fuel for yet more heroic legends of the *pallikári*. Locals will claim that to this day, on or around May 17, the ghosts of Daliani and his army march from the castle: they are known as *dhrossoulítes*, or dewy ones, because they appear in the mists around dawn.

Just below the castle, before the beach, there's a patch of greenery which shades a **taverna**, *Fata Morgana*, and a tiny freshwater creek with thoroughly incongruous ducks on it. Between the road and sea to the west are more little streams and marshy patches like this, home to terrapins and some type of water snake or eel.

Practicalities

Many of the places to stay and other facilities at Frangokástello lie along the road that heads in from Hóra Sfakíon: carry on past these and a turn-off immediately before the castle leads to another little group of seaside rooms places and tavernas. If you're approaching from the east, the monstrous two-storey *Taverna Kriti* ruins most views of the castle: continue past it, and the castle, to find the places listed below.

Places to stay very close to the castle include *Milos* (☎28250 92160, ⓦwww.milos-sfakia.com; ❸), with a variety of well-located en-suite rooms including the tiny mill after which the place is named, which stands right on the beach and has been refurbished as accommodation consisting of a kitchen/diner and bathroom downstairs, with a bedroom and balcony above (❹); *Maria's* (☎28250 92159, ⓦwww.marias-studios.com; studios ❸, apartments ❺), a well-equipped modern block with en-suite rooms, a/c and TV, also very close to the beach; *Corali* (☎28250 92033; ❸); and *Flisvos* (☎28250 92069; rooms ❸, apartments ❹–❺), a beachfront taverna with a/c en-suite rooms set back a little – they also have apartments and a house in the nearby village of Patsianós. The *Kali Kardia* taverna (☎28250 92123; ❷), also on the sea between these and the castle, has rather more basic rooms without a/c. On the road from Hóra, one of the first places you pass is the excellent *Studios Stavris* (☎28250 92250, ⓦwww.studios-stavris-frangokastello.com; ❹) whose beachfront rooms have a/c, bath and cooking facilities, though they can be booked up by tour groups. Soon after this a left turn leads to *Blue Sky* (☎28250 92095, ⓦwww.blue-sky-kreta.de, German only), run by a friendly Greek-German couple who rent out luxury apartments which sleep up to six (❺, but rarely available for less than a week): they also rent **cars**, **scooters** and **mountain bikes** and act as something of a local **information** centre. The *Oasis* taverna (☎28250 92244, Ⓔoasis@aias.gr; ❷, apartments ❸), between *Stavris* and *Blue Sky*, and *Babis & Popi* (☎28250 92092, ⓦwww.babis-popi.com; ❶), a little further down the road, both serve good food with sea views and have a variety of rooms, including some very basic, non-a/c ones. Wherever you stay, be warned that this can be a **mosquito zone** so make sure to come prepared if this is likely to bother you.

For **eating** and **drinking**, most of your options lie within a few minutes' walk of the castle, and most of the better choices have already been mentioned above: *Kali Kardia* started life as the village's *kafenío*, and is still the place you're most likely to see locals, as well as being good for **breakfast**, drinks and snacks. *Flisvos* has perhaps the best location and can usually offer good fresh fish; *Babis & Popi*, *Oasis* and *Corali* are all reliable. **Nightlife** mostly consists of stretching supper well into the night, or perhaps taking a bottle of *raki* down to the beach to contemplate the stars. The *Blue Sky* has a combined café, ice-cream salon and nighttime cocktail bar playing easy music, with its own **pool** (free to clients and sheltered when the wind blows); while the *Taverna Kriti*, opposite the castle, has music but is soulless and usually empty. Keep it that way and maybe they'll knock the place down. There are also a couple of **minimarkets**, selling most things you're likely to want.

In summer the daily **buses** between Hóra Sfakíon and Plakiás call at Frangokástello on their way through in both directions.

The far west

Crete's **far west** has, to date, attracted surprisingly little attention from tourists or developers, and even though that is inevitably beginning to change, such development as there is is mostly low-key: apartments and rooms rather than big hotels. The one town of any size west of Haniá is **Kastélli Kissámou**, a port with a ferry service to the Peloponnese, very regular buses to Haniá and little else to attract visitors. Beyond, Crete's west-facing coast remains remote: west of a line between Kastélli and Paleohóra there's little public transport, and despite a growing number of rooms and apartments, virtually nothing in the way of luxurious facilities. Yet here you'll find two of the finest **beaches** on the island – **Falásarna** and **Elafonísi** – both of them, sadly, beginning to suffer from overexploitation. Inland, the wooded hill country around **Élos** – with the possibility of a stay nearby at the remarkable tourist mountain village of **Miliá** – is one of the greenest parts of Crete, and for walkers there's another ravine to explore at **Koutsamatádos**. For longer stays in this part of Crete it's important to carry all the money and most of the supplies you'll need – there are some facilities at the beaches, but the villages are few and far between, and have only the most basic of shops.

On the **south coast**, good roads and several buses a day run to **Paleohóra** and **Soúyia**. The former is already a resort of some size – surprisingly large given its isolation, but far from totally despoiled – the latter is smaller and not as immediately attractive but still inexpensive and friendly. Regular boats connect the two, or you can follow the **E4 footpath** by way of the ruins of ancient **Lissós**, on the coast just west of Soúyia. Roads in this part of the island have been dramatically improved in recent years, and there are some spectacular, if roundabout, routes from Paleohóra to Soúyia and on to Omalós (for the White Mountains and the Samariá Gorge). Along the way, and on other minor roads through the mountains are isolated villages in which frescoed medieval churches are liberally scattered.

Kastélli Kissámou and the north coast

Kastélli lies some 20km beyond the crossroads at Kolimbári (see p.340). If you're in a hurry to head west, the new highway is fast and efficient, taking you right to the edge of Kastélli, where it finally ends. It has also left the **old road** – always a beautiful drive – as a delightful backwater. Going this way you wind steeply up a rocky spur thrown back by the peninsula and emerge through a cleft in the hills to a magnificent view of the Gulf of Kissámou, with Kastélli in the middle distance. Caught with the sun setting behind the craggy heights of **Cape Voúxa** at the far west of Crete, this is a memorable panorama. There's a roadside restaurant from which you can contemplate the view, and further along a number of quite large, entirely unvisited villages, such as Nochiá, Koléni or Kaloudhianá, where you could also stop for a drink or a bite to eat at a number of inviting tavernas.

As it leaves the height, the road loops back out of the hills onto the fertile plain of Kastélli. Almost as soon as you hit level ground you'll see turnings to the beach, a long stretch of grey sand which, while not the best in Crete, is at least clean and uncrowded. There are scattered rooms places here, and two attractive **campsites** on the coast about 1km from the road. Both are well-equipped and reasonably priced: the first you reach, the newer *Camping Nopigia* (☎28220 311110) near the village of Nopíyia, has a pool, while towards Dhrapaniás *Camping Mithimna* (☎28220 31444) is bigger, and also has apartments and rooms to rent nearby (from ❸). There's a regular bus service to and from Kastélli, and though the sites are popular with people arriving in Kastélli on the ferry, there should always be space (a third campsite can be found in Kastélli itself). Mithimna takes its name from the ancient town of Mithymna, thought to have been approximately where Nopíyia now stands. The village of Kaloudhianá, 4km further along, marks the turn-off for the inland route to Topólia and Elafonísi.

Kastélli Kissámou

KASTÉLLI (also known as Kíssamos, and officially Kastélli Kissámou) seems at first sight to offer little to get excited about. It's a busy little town and port with a long seafront, a rather rocky strand to the east and a small sandy beach to the west. This very ordinariness, however, has real charm once you get over your initial reaction: it's a working town full of stores used by locals and cafés not entirely geared to outsiders. **Kísamos** was the Greco-Roman city-state that stood here in ancient times – the name *Kissámou* ("of Kísamos") was appended to plain Kastélli in 1966 to avoid confusion with towns of the same name throughout Greece. Ongoing excavations in the town centre are now revealing just how important the ancient city was.

Arrival and information

On the western outskirts the old and new roads merge to head straight through town as Iróon Politehníou, south of the centre. The new road is lined with stores and supermarkets, but the heart of life is towards the sea, around **Platía Kastelliού** (aka Platía Tzanakáki). This is also where the **buses** pull in. There are a couple of banks, cafés and car hire places on Platía Venizélou on the main road, but it's more attractive, and there are more facilities, if you head down to the central square and the main street that runs through it, **Odhós Skálidi**. There's a further cluster of development along the **waterfront**, directly down from the main square, with a short promenade separating the town's **beaches** to the east and west.

All the facilities you're likely to need can be found on Platía Kastelliού or nearby, especially east along Skálidi. There are a couple of **banks** with ATMs on Skálidi, as well as a machine at the National Bank on Platía Venizélou; the **post office** (Mon–Fri 7.30am–2pm) and the **OTE** (same hours) are both east along Iróon Politehníou from here. There are phonecard **telephone kiosks** near the bus station and around the centre, and a bookshop with foreign newspapers and some English books on Skálidi east of the square. **Internet** connection is available at the *Babel Café* on the waterfront, or in the café at the campsite. For **bike rental**, try the reliable Moto Fun (☎28220 23440) on Platía Kastelliού; **car hire** from Kíssamos Travel on Platía Venizélou (☎28220 23740) or Hermes (☎28220 23678) or Horeftakis (☎28220 23250) on Skálidi. The main **taxi** rank is on Platía Venizélou, or call ☎28220 22990.

Ferry tickets for boat connections with Kíthira and Yíthio can be bought from several agents on Skálidi, including Horeftakis Tours (see above) and Halkiada (☎28220 22009); the **ferry dock** is some 3km west of town – a significant walk if you're heavily laden, or a cheap taxi-ride. At least three companies also run **daytrips** to the island of Gramvoúsa and Balos Bay from here (departures between

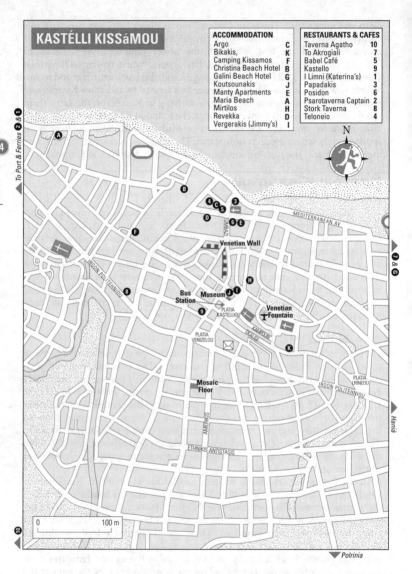

KASTÉLLI KISSáMOU

ACCOMMODATION
Argo   C
Bikakis,   K
Camping Kissamos   F
Christina Beach Hotel   B
Galini Beach Hotel   G
Koutsounakis   J
Manty Apartments   E
Maria Beach   A
Mirtilos   H
Revekka   D
Vergerakis (Jimmy's)   I

RESTAURANTS & CAFES
Taverna Agatho   10
To Akrogiali   7
Babel Café   5
Kastello   9
I Limni (Katerina's)   1
Papadakis   3
Posidon   6
Psarotaverna Captain   2
Stork Taverna   8
Teloneio   4

9.30 and 11am; €18). Try to avoid Thursday and Friday, when coach trips arrive
from the rest of the island; tickets are available from travel agents in town, on the
quayside, or call ☎ 28220 83311, 23932 or 24344. In spring and autumn **walking
tours** of the surrounding country are offered by Strata Tours (☎ 28220 23700):
more information at the *Kelari* taverna on the waterfront.

Accommodation

Kastélli has an abundance of **accommodation** that is rarely filled to capacity,
even in high season. The beachside places tend to fill before those in town.

Argo On the central seafront ☎ 28220 23563. Great location for en-suite balcony rooms with fridge. ❹

Bikakis Kampouri, east of the centre ☎ 28220 24257, ⓦ www.familybikakis.gr. The unattractive frontage on the street conceals the fact that at the back there are quiet rooms with uninterrupted sea views. Family-run, with a variety of well-equipped, a/c rooms and studios; the owner often meets the ferry, and will collect you on request. ❸

Camping Kissamos West of the centre ☎ 28220 22322. Small but well-equipped site with shade, a nice pool, and a lively café-bar, plus some very pleasant rooms. It can get busy, as it's an obvious first stop for people who bring cars and camper-vans across on the ferry from Yíthio. Rooms ❸

Christina Beach Hotel On the central seafront ☎ 28220 83333, ⓦ www.christina-beach.gr. Balcony, sea-view one- and two-room apartments around a pool with facilities such as hairdryer, room safe, TV and fridge. ❻

Galini Beach Hotel On the eastern beach, just past the football pitch ☎ 28220 23288, ⓕ 28220 23388. Friendly, good-value hotel with easy parking, sparkling en-suite, a/c balcony rooms with TV, and bounteous breakfasts (at extra cost); ask for a discount with this book. ❹

Koutsounakis Platía Kastellioú ☎ 28220 23416. Pleasant rooms place with airy balcony rooms, some with a good view, with bath and fridge. ❸

Manty Apartments On the central seafront ☎ 28220 22825. Complex built round a tiny pool: balcony rooms with a/c, TV and separate kitchen/diner are worth considering for a longer stay – those on higher floors tend to escape the late-night noise from the terrace bar downstairs. ❹

Maria Beach On the western beach ☎ 28220 22610, ⓦ www.mariabeach.gr. The best location in town, right on the sandy beach. A couple of separate buildings include some fairly plain rooms as well as new, fully-equipped sea-view apartments complete with kitchen and a/c. Rates include breakfast ❹

Mirtilos Platía Kastellioú ☎ 28220 023079, ⓦ www.mirtilos.com. Attractive new apartment complex round a large pool, right off the main square. Often block-booked in high season, but worth trying at other times – all apartments with a/c, TV and kitchen. ❻

Revekka A block back from the seafront ☎ 28220 24213. Balcony rooms with bath and fridge which are much nicer than the view from ouside suggests. ❸

Vergerakis (aka *Jimmy's*) Platía Kastellioú ☎ 28220 22663. A couple of small but pleasant doubles without bath are the cheapest rooms in town. Also some en-suite rooms and use of kitchen. Friendly and clean. ❷

The Town

Kastélli has little in the way of sights, and what it does have it seems determined not to display. The restoration of the Venetian governor's palace on Platía Kastellioú to house a new **town museum** has long been completed – however, at the time of writing it has yet to open. Designed to house finds from the ongoing excavations of ancient Kísamos, as well as items from Polyrínia (see p.374) and displays of more recent history, the museum has fallen victim to disputes over the status and ownership of its contents.

Kastélli is also home to some remarkable **archeological excavations** which have revealed remains and mosaics from the Roman city of Kísamos. Originally the port of nearby Polyrínia, Kísamos grew to become the more powerful city. The mosaics are proudly signed at two separate sites to the south of the main road, both near Platía Venizélou. One particularly fine example, apparently, filled an entire room of a rich mansion and portrays foods and fruits, various birds and a wonderful depiction of a hunter out with his fierce hound, straining at the leash. The problem is that the mosaics have now been covered in sand and gravel to protect them: if you go to the site, all you can do is stare at the dirt, and a few foundation walls, through a chain-link fence.

More worthwhile are remnants of the Venetian and Ottoman town. Immediately north of Platía Kastellioú, where the ground falls sharply away towards the coast, are substantial **defensive bastions**, and there are other bits of surviving wall nearby, particularly to the west of the square. There's also a beautiful old **Venetian fountain,** inscribed with the date 1520, about 100m east of the main square in a small courtyard to the left off Kampouri.

One **shop** worth a visit is Fotografías Anifandakis, slightly east of the main square along Skálidi, where veteran photographer Yeóryios Anifandakis has his studio. He's photographed most of the island during his long career and sells his photos here, including some excellent ones of the Roman mosaics (maybe your only chance to see them). West along Skálidi are other interesting stores: Eirini Paskali stocks musical instruments, including *lyras*, as well as a selection of tinted glass oil-burning church lamps; Níkos Lainakis sells a huge variety of products made from olive wood, from salad bowls and candle holders to toys and hair clips.

Eating and drinking

There's no shortage of **places to eat** in Kastélli, but the best of them tend to be away from the centre; many of the seafront places are disappointing. For light meals and breakfasts, though, the area around Platía Kastellioú offers plenty of choice. There are a couple of good **bakeries** here too; one in the short street between Platía Venizélou and Platía Kastellioú, another, *To Haniotis*, nearby on the corner of Platía Kastellioú. Next door to the latter is a nameless snack-bar with tables out in the square, good for breakfast. Wherever you eat, you'll probably be offered some of the local **red wine**. Made from the *roméïko* grape, which is believed to have been brought to the island by the Venetians, it is as good as any produced on Crete.

Although the central seafront area often has a listless, end-of-season air by day, it comes to life at night when the locals pile in to drink at the numerous **cafés and bars** along the central promenade. *Téloneio* and the *Babel Café* are among the most enjoyable of these.

Taverna Agatho About a kilometre inland along the road to Lousakiés ℡ 28220 22844. A little family-run village restaurant where they speak only Greek, but you're guaranteed the warmest of welcomes and a delicious spread. Eves only.

To Akrogiali On the coast east, about 1km beyond the *Galini Beach* hotel ℡ 28220 31410. A fish restaurant worth seeking out for excellent fresh seafood, served on a terrace with the waves almost lapping your table legs. It's hard to miss as it's located immediately east of a seafront soap factory whose chimney stacks are visible from some distance – but don't let the location put you off. They also have rooms here.

Psarotaverna Captain At the small-boat and fishing harbour, about halfway to the main port, a short drive or taxi-ride west of town ℡ 28220

22857. Probably the best fish in town and always busy, so booking is advisable.

Kastello Immediately west of Platía Kastellioú Skálidi. Good *souvláki* and *yíros* are served in a small garden.

I Limni (aka *Katerina's*) At the small-boat and fishing harbour (see *Captain*). Cheaper and more basic fish restaurant than *Captain*, with sometimes eccentric service.

Papadakis At the western end of the seafront promenade. The best choice down here, with decent, reasonably priced seafood.

Ouzerí Posidon Off the seafront, near *Papadakis*. Excellent *mezédhes*.

Stork Taverna On Iróon Politehníou west of Platía Venizélou ℡ 28220 22988. An excellent selection of traditional Cretan dishes.

Polyrínia

Kastélli Kissámou's name is taken from ancient Kísamos, which once stood here and served as a port for the sizeable ancient city of **Polyrínia**, located about 7km inland above the village of Paleókastro (which is confusingly also known as Polirinía). Vestiges of the ancient settlement can still be seen. There are **buses** up from Kastélli Kissámou (Mon, Wed & Fri 7am & 2pm; returning 30min later), but the walk is perfectly feasible; your best bet is to take a bus or taxi up, and walk back down. In spring, especially, it's a lovely walk, with alpine flowers and abundant water from springs.

It's something of a climb from the village to the **hilltop site**, where ruins are scattered across two horns of high ground which seem to reach out to enclose the Gulf of Kissámou. Originally an eighth-century BC Dorian colony occupied by settlers from the Peloponnese, Polyrínia – a name meaning "rich in lambs" – remained a prosperous city down to Roman times and beyond. One of its main claims to fame, however, would not endear it to most Cretans: an inscription found here and dated to 69 BC tells of how the Polyrinians created a statue in honour of the Roman conqueror of Crete, Quintus Metellus, referring to him as the "saviour and benefactor of the city". It seems that Polyrínia did not join in the resistance put up by Haniá and other cities to the Roman invasion, and as a result was spared destruction.

The most obvious feature when you reach the site is the **Acropolis** (stunning **views** of the coast from the top), which is in fact almost entirely a Venetian defensive structure, but there are all sorts of foundations and obscure remains scattered about, including the vestiges of an **aqueduct** and miscellaneous Roman and Greek masonry incorporated into the **church** that now stands on the site. The church is itself constructed on the base of what must have been an enormously impressive Hellenistic building, possibly a fourth-century BC temple. The sheer amount of work involved in cutting and dressing these stone blocks and transporting them to places as inaccessible as this makes you wonder at the phenomenal scale of manpower at the service of these towns in antiquity. The unsightly breeze blocks used for the cemetery wall of the modern church makes a starkly ironic contrast.

The *Acropolis* taverna at the foot of the hill close to the site, and the pleasant *Taverna Polyrinia* in the village of **Áno Paleókastro** – with views almost as good as those from the top – both serve good **food**.

The northwest coast

Leaving Kastélli Kissámou for the west, the road climbs back into the hills again, cutting south across the base of the Gramvoúsa peninsula. Along this first stretch there are plenty of signs of development, with new apartment blocks and small hotels. One of the most attractive of these is the *Balos Beach Hotel* (☎28220 24106, ⓦwww.balosbeach.gr; ⑦), in an isolated spot (signed from the main road) above the sea at the bottom of the peninsula, with bar, restaurant, pool, children's pool, and fabulous views back towards Kastélli and over a shipwreck on the beach. Apartment-style rooms have kitchen, a/c and bathroom. Also worth trying are the *Olive Tree Apartments* (☎28220 24376, ⑤; info at *Kelari* taverna in Kastélli) in the village of **Kalivianí** nearby, where you'll also find a couple of tavernas. A modern complex around a pool, the a/c apartments here are particularly well equipped, even including irons and hairdryers.

Gramvoúsa and its islands

Kalivianí is also the start of a track up the **Gramvoúsa peninsula** towards **Cape Voúxa** and the island of **Gramvoúsa**. This is just about drivable – plenty of locals do so anyway, though be warned that if you join them and damage the underside of a hire car, it won't be insured (four-wheel-drive recommended). The track starts at the end of the tarmac beyond Kalivianí – the *Kafenion Siponitakis* here makes a good final pit stop – heading steeply down past a church. It continues up the eastern side of the peninsula for some 9km, ending at a car park where there's a seasonal drinks stall. From here a well-marked path leads across to west-facing **Balos Bay**, ten minutes' walk or so, where there's a really spectacular white-sand **beach** (sadly with a bad tar problem) more or less opposite Gramvoúsa island. You can also walk the track from Kaliviani (in around three hours); either way, it's worth setting out early to avoid the crowds who arrive on boat trips from Kastélli (they usually arrive early afternoon). If you got a taxi to Kaliviani, you could walk up and get the boat back to Kastélli – it leaves around 4pm. **Walking** here is great – the peninsula is extraordinarily barren and quite unpopulated – but lonely, so take plenty of water and all the other provisions you're going to need, as apart from the car park stall and a spring near the chapel of Ayía Iríni, about 6km out (neither of which it's safe to rely on), there's nothing to be had beyond Kaliviani.

The easy way to do this, of course, is on an organized **boat trip** from Kastélli (p.371), which will take you to Balos Bay via the island of **Gramvoúsa**, on which the Venetians built an important castle. Along with the fortified islands of Néa Sóudha and Spinalónga, this was one of the points that held out against the Turks long after the Cretan mainland had fallen. When the Venetians left, the fort was allowed to fall into disrepair until it was taken over by Greek refugees from other Turkish-occupied islands (notably Kásos) who used it as a base for piracy. It took a major Turkish campaign to wrest the fortress back, and thereafter they maintained a garrison here. In the War of Independence it became a base for the Turkish ships attempting to maintain a blockade of the coastline. Today you can climb up to the fort, with lovely wildflowers in season, and enjoy a small beach, though this can become very crowded if the boat is full. Another slightly larger and wilder island, Agría Gramvoúsa, lies to the north just off the cape.

Falásarna

To reach the beautiful beach at **FALÁSARNA**, continue across the base of the peninsula and turn off at Plátanos: two buses a day direct from Haniá follow this route. The descent to the coast from Plátanos is via a spectacular series of hairpin bends above a narrow coastal plain, where farmers have discovered the benefits of plastic greenhouses for forcing tomatoes, melons and the like. Below, you can see two main beaches (with several smaller patches of sand between) – the southern one is much bigger, but the best sand is reached by continuing to the end of the asphalt, where there's a car park, the bus stop and a couple of taverna/rooms places above a broad crescent of yellow sand lapped by turquoise waters. Head down to the sand here, or walk a bit further north, past *Jimmy's* makeshift bar, to "Freedom". Although the beach can occasionally be afflicted by washed-up oil, tar and discarded rubbish, this doesn't detract from the overall beauty of the place. If it gets too crowded (and on Sundays in summer it will, as half of Haniá seems to head here) there are other patches of sand within easy walking distance in either direction.

Practicalities

There are an increasing number of **rooms** places scattered along the road behind Falásarna, many of them very comfortable. *Sunset* (☎28220 41204; ❸, 4-person bungalow ❺), right by the car park, has an enviable location and a good taverna, though its rooms (en-suite, with balcony) could do with modernization. The *Falasarna Beach Hotel* (☎28220 41257; ❹), immediately behind, is a definite cut above, with studios with kitchenette and balcony sea views as well as apartments. On the way here you'll have passed many others. Newest and fanciest is the Greek-German–run *Hotel Plakures* (☎28220 41581,

ⓦwww.plakures.de; ❻ including breakfast), with a pool, bar, restaurant and well-appointed rooms and apartments featuring en-suite facilities, minibar and balcony. Immediately behind, *Golden Sun* (☎28220 41485; ❸, ❹ with kitchen) has friendly proprietors, balcony rooms with bath and a shady garden. *Kalami* (☎28220 41461; ❸), nearby, has similar en-suite rooms above a seafront taverna. Finally *Hotel Panorama* (☎28220 41336; ❹) lies on the way down to the bigger, southern beach, with comfortable balcony rooms above an excellent taverna with panoramic views. Quite a few people also **camp** at the back of the beach, either in a couple of small caves or beneath makeshift shelters slung between a few stumpy trees; if you decide to join them, take your rubbish away with you.

To **eat**, the rooms places named above are as good as any – all simple, and somewhat overwhelmed on busy weekends. The *Mouraki* taverna in Plátanos, right at the top of the road before it heads down to Falásarna, with spectacular views, is highly recommended if you can face the journey. *Jimmy's* bar, signed from the car park, is an excellent spot for a sunset cocktail, and there's also a lively seasonal beach bar on the southern beach. As for other facilities, there's an excellent, if rather pricey **minimarket** – with all the necessities and more – on the road by the junction to the southern beach. A couple of slightly bigger supermarkets can be found in Plátanos, where there's also a **bank** with an ATM.

Ancient Falásarna

The **ancient city** and port of Falásarna lies just to the north of the last beach. Follow the main dirt track for 1km beyond the car park, through the olive groves, and at the edge of the archeological site you will pass the large stone "**throne**" that has puzzled experts for decades – there is still no satisfactory explanation for its function.

The westernmost of the cities of ancient Crete, and now undergoing systematic excavation, Falásarna was founded prior to the sixth century BC and remained the sworn enemy of nearby Polyrínia (see p.374). What you are now able to see are the scattered remains of a city built around a large depression – its inner **harbour** – and the bed of a canal that once joined this to the sea. The entire site is now high and dry, offering conclusive proof that Crete's western extremities have risen at least eight metres over the last 24 centuries or so. The excavators discovered large stone blocks thrown across the entrance to the old harbour; current thinking suggests that this was carried out in the first century BC by the Romans to prevent ships using the port as the base for a "pirates' nest". The harbour was defended by part of the city wall linked by a number of towers to a harbour mole, with the **South Tower**, the nearest to the sea, a formidable bastion built of huge sandstone blocks. More ruined structures are to be seen ascending the acropolis hill behind, and near to the chapel of Áyios Yeóryios a recently excavated building (beneath a canopy) revealed a number of well-preserved **terracotta baths**.

Continue on the best of the tracks past the site and you pass under Cyclopean walls to emerge above another small bay. Tempting as it is, this is too sharp and rocky for you to be able to get to the sea, but it does give you views to the north, over Cape Voúxa, which are shielded from Falásarna itself. Towards the top you can see the island of Gramvoúsa (not to be confused with the unin-habitable rock of Pontikonísi, a more distant islet which can sometimes be seen from the beach at Falásarna). It's possible to hike on from here up the **western side of the peninsula,** on an occasionally scary path above the coast, marked by blue paint and cairns. After about four and a half hours you reach a crest, the highest point on the walk, with breathtaking views over the islands. If you do try this, don't do it alone and take plenty of water.

Routes to the southwest

There are two routes **south of Kastélli Kissámou** to the southwest corner of the island. The more usual route runs inland, turning off the north-coast highway at Kaloudhianá, before Kastélli. This is a lovely rural drive up the valley of the Tiflós, and follows a reasonably good road as far as Váthi. In the sturdy farming villages of this unusually green part of Crete there are plenty of opportunities to take in the local wildlife, or to do some walking in the ole-ander- and chestnut-wooded hills and along numerous gorges. Alternatively, the **coast road** southwest of Plátanos, although lacking greenery, is spectacu-larly scenic, eventually looping round to join the inland route so that you can make this a circular drive. If you turn off the loop to continue south through Váthi, you'll end up at the romantically sited monastery of **Hrissokalítissa**, and beyond that the idyllic beaches of **Elafonísi**.

The inland route via Koutsamatádos

The area south of Kastélli between Topólia in the northeast and Váthi to the southwest includes some of the most fertile lands on the island. Here, lush **woodland** watered by tumbling streams emanating from the mountains is a haven for a rich variety of flora and fauna. Water is so plentiful around places such as Élos and Kefáli, in fact, that tourism comes a very poor second to agri-culture. Everyone it seems has a *kípos* (smallholding), with a couple of dozen olive trees or a vegetable patch. The life of these villages is dictated by the needs of the farmers, a hardworking and laconic bunch who dress in sturdy boots and lumberjack shirts and greet one another with gruff cries of *"yia!"* (abbreviated from *yia sou*) from the open windows of Japanese pick-up trucks – the ultimate status symbol around these parts, as only bona fide farmers owning above a cer-tain hectarage get a government subsidy to buy one.

Voulgháro, Topólia and Koutsamatádos

After some 4km of ascent you reach the village of **Voulgháro**, where you could stretch your legs in search of two ancient **churches**, Áyios Yeóryios and Áyios Nikólaos – the latter with fine frescoes – in the satellite villages of **Mákronas** across the valley and **Mourí** along a track 2km further south, respectively. When you reach Mourí, the church lies up a track (signed "Áyios Nikólaos" in Greek) 30m beyond the Venetian church to the right of the road as you come in from the south. Follow this for 500m up a rough track to reach another sign indicating the tiny chapel tucked away in an olive grove to the right. The impressive **fresco fragments**, especially those of Áyios Pandeleímon and the scenes from the Bible, are extremely fine. Just south of Mourí you could also descend into the ravine (see opposite), making for the village of Koutsamatádos, a **walk** of about 5km. This walk is described in reverse in *Landscapes of Western Crete* (see p.456).

By road you'll continue climbing to **Topólia**, 3km after Voulgháro, whose church of Ayía Paraskeví has more **frescoes**, this time from the late Byzantine period. You could also take in the village of **Kaláthenes**, 3km along a turn-off on the right to the south of here, where there are the remains of a fine six-teenth-century **Venetian villa** known as the Rotonda. Once you reach Kaláthenes, continue through the village until you meet a faded sign for the Rotonda. Just beyond here, opposite a house fronted by mulberry trees, go down a narrow gap between two buildings and at the end of this veer left to reach the villa, which is partly ruinous and partly still inhabited. If the occupants are around they will be pleased to show you a striking stone-vaulted room complete with fireplace now sadly appropriated by feral pigeons.

The direct route south from Topólia, however, soon enters a tunnel before skirting the edge of the dramatic **Koutsamatádos ravine**, one of the most imposing on the island. Nearing the middle of the ravine you'll come to a signed stairway cut into the rock on the right, and a muscle-taxing short climb to the **cave of Ayía Sofía**. This is one of the largest caves on Crete and remains found here date its usage back to Neolithic times; it now shelters a small chapel, along with stalactites, stalagmites and its present residents, a colony of bats.

Proceeding along the ravine, you will soon reach the hamlet of **Koutsamatádos** where the roadside *Rooms Taverna Panorama* (T 28220 51163; ❷) is a possible stopping-place for a meal (excellent *hórta* from its own *kípos*), coffee and Dutch cakes, or even en-suite **rooms** with a terrace view, should you decide to get into more detailed exploration of the area. The friendly proprietor Manolis Motakis and his Dutch wife Antonia are keen to put up walkers, and can advise on various hiking routes roundabout, including the climb of **Koproula**, the highest peak hereabouts. Less ambitiously, many of the easier local walks have been signed from the taverna: there is a ten-minute path from here to the Ayía Sofia cave, for example, as well as a path to Miliá (see below), about an hour's climb. Walking in the ravine itself, though, has been dangerous in recent years due to rock falls mainly caused by road construction: be sure to check the latest situation before attempting it.

Miliá and the eastern Enneachora

Three kilometres south of Koutsomatádos you enter an area known as the **Enneachora** – the "Nine Villages". Here – with your own transport – you can turn off (look for the sign to Miliá) to follow a beautifully scenic drive through the leafy hills and farming villages on the western flank of the Tiflós valley.

The first village you come to is **Vlátos**, where a sign on the left indicates a turning to the *Platania* **taverna**. A path through woods leads to the taverna's terrace, close to the gigantic thousand-year-old **plane tree** which gives the place its name. It's a friendly hideaway that serves up good meat and *mezédhes* to the passing trade, but makes its money from mammoth wedding feasts.

To the right, a road is signed to **Miliá**, a remarkable "eco-tourist" village. The precipitous track, only the first half of which is surfaced, climbs dizzily along the shoulder of Mount Kefáli for 5km offering magnificent **views** over the chestnut- and olive-clad valley below. You will eventually reach a car park, from where a path leads into a stunningly picturesque hamlet of stone houses, once occupied by farmers and shepherds. The isolation of the village eventually led to its abandonment around a century ago until, in the early 1980s, a relative of a former inhabitant proposed to restore the whole place as a working village, welcoming visitors. Other families who owned ruined houses joined in and they formed a co-operative, backed by EU money. Stonemasons accustomed to building traditional dwellings were brought over from the Peloponnese and helped the co-operative's members to re-create what you now see: an almost too perfect village with solid stone houses on many levels overlooking a verdant cleft brimming with chestnuts, oaks, planes and olives.

You should soon locate one house which now serves as the community centre and **bar/taverna** (open daily) offering organic food and vegetables produced on the village's land, as well as freshly baked bread. Visitors are welcome to become involved in the ongoing farming activities which include planting and sowing as well as chestnut, olive and apple harvesting (Miliá means "apple tree" in Greek); you can even help in making *raki* at the village's own still. Otherwise you can **walk** in the nearby hills – the easier paths are signed – or simply contemplate the natural surroundings; the nights up here are truly magical. The **rooms** vary from one small double with bathroom next door (❹ including breakfast) to small private houses for four (❼), but all are a delight and contain appropriate rustic furnishings and ancient fittings such as huge fireplaces and stone ovens. Most rooms are en-suite with permanent hot water, but some have hot water (heated by the fire) in the evenings only: firewood is supplied in winter, as are candles (though there is electricity). In the evening the restaurant is lit by gas lamps, and there are positively no telecommunications, save one mobile-phone link with the outside world. To stay, you can simply turn up, but it's wise to ring ahead to make a reservation (☏ 28220 51569, mobile ☏ 6945753743). This kind of imaginative enterprise is perhaps a pointer to the future for the development of tourism on the island.

Back in Vlátos, the road continues through the simple villages of Rogdiá and Límni, each with its own bar but little else, until it rejoins the direct road just before Pervólia.

Élos and Perivólia

The direct route from Koutsamatádos tracks the lower slopes of the Tiflós valley and, shortly after the turn-off to Vlátos, a turning on the left heads southwest through Aligí and Dris to meet the Paleohóra road at the village of **Plemenianá**. Three kilometres down here an alternative route, recently asphalted, forks south through some lonely, if spectacular, mountain country via Arhondikó and **Voutás** (see p.383) to approach Paleohóra from the west. Along the way scores of little streams cascade beside, under, or sometimes across, the road. You'll find hardly any traffic passes on either route, and the rare villages are ancient and rustic; their inhabitants stand and stare as you drive through, but are extremely welcoming if you stop.

The road from Koutsamatádos continues southwest past slopes covered with magnificent stands of chestnut, plane and other deciduous trees. Chestnuts, in fact, are a major local crop around here and **Élos**, 4km along, is the centre of the Enneachora **chestnut-growing** region. Élos is beautiful and, even at the height of summer, a wonderfully refreshing place. It's easy to forget just how high you are here – the mountains to the south rise to about 1200m. In the village's square, shaded by plane, eucalyptus and, of course, chestnut trees, *Rooms Kastanofolia* ("Chestnut Den"; ☏ 28220 61258; ❷) is a clean and simple place with **rooms** (some en-suite) above an excellent **taverna**. There are ducks in a pool filled by a stream running beside the taverna's terrace and, directly opposite over the road, you can stroll along a track that leads a couple of kilometres into the chestnut forests. Behind the taverna there is also an impressive old arch, claimed to be a Roman aqueduct (though perhaps more likely Turkish), and just beyond this lies a fourteenth-century **Byzantine chapel**, with fresco fragments including an impressive *Pantokrátor* in the apse; if closed, the key should be available from the taverna. Throughout the village, ancient stonework has been replaced and repaired, and old paths restored – clearly the locals take justifiable pride in their surroundings. The great event in Élos's year is the annual **chestnut festival** in late October.

Five kilometres further, a turn on the left indicates a sharp descent to the picturesque hamlet of **Perivólia**, tucked into the folds of a high gorge beneath the northern flank of Mount Áyios Díkeos Ióv (Job the Just). The village is another verdant oasis with charming narrow streets punctuated by simple white-walled dwellings and smallholdings overflowing with vigorously sprouting vegetables. Park any transport where you cross a bridge at the foot of the descent and, turning right, continue on foot to the bottom of the village and a fountain, near a recently erected bust to one of the noted local *pallikári* (guerrilla fighters) of the last century, Anagnostis Skalidis. At the house opposite you will find a small **museum** assembled by one of his descendants, Zacharia Skalidis. An amiable man who speaks only Greek, he will be delighted to show you around his collection, which includes lots of atmospheric photos from a Crete long gone, as well as old guns, letters and coins.

Kefáli and Váthi

Barely 2km beyond Pervólia, another charming Enneachora village, **Kefáli**, has a fine fourteenth-century frescoed **church**, Metamórphosis tou Sotirís (Transfiguration of Christ), down a track on the left as you enter the village; follow the path downhill turning right, then left and right again to reach the church. Inside, the fine **frescoes** depict the betrayal by Judas (whose face has been gouged) and the lowering of Christ from the cross. There is also some interesting and apparently genuine early graffiti, scratched across the paintings. An Englishman, Francis Lerfordes, has marked his contribution with the date 1553, while Turks later inscribed their blasphemous thoughts along with the crescent symbol – to the further detriment of the artworks. The main street has **rooms** with and without bath above *Taverna Polakis* (☏ 28220 61260; ❸), with a splendid balcony view over the Bay of Stomíou. The owner, Yeorgos Polakis, speaks little English, but he's a fount of local knowledge and will direct you to the church should you encounter difficulties. The aptly named *Panorama* taverna, opposite, provides meals with a view.

Váthi, 1km south of Kefáli, is another of the Enneachora villages and has two more ancient frescoed **churches** for enthusiasts: the thirteenth-century Áyios Yeóryios off the central square, and the century-older Mihaíl Arhángelos, just to the south. To reach the former take a track uphill facing the plane tree in the central *platía* to the left of a drinking fountain. Follow the track uphill for 200m, where it turns into a narrow *kalderími* (ancient footpath) which leads you to the church; it should be open. Inside, the frescoes are in good condition, with a sensitive portrayal of the Archangel Gabriel and an unusual image of the Virgin and child in the apse, in place of the conventional *Pantokrátor*. To see the church of Mihaíl Arhángelos you'll need to locate the village priest, who has the key; try at the *kafeníon* near the plane tree. He will conduct you to the south of the village, soon taking a left across fields to the church. Inside are wonderfully preserved early fourteenth-century **frescoes** depicting the Emperor Constantine and his mother Helena, the Fall of Jericho, Christ entering Jerusalem, and a moving portrayal of the betrayal by Judas. For his trouble, a contribution to church funds will be gratefully accepted by the *papás*.

The coast road

If you were to carry straight on in Kefáli, instead of turning off to Váthi, you'd be on the **coast road** running back around to Plátanos. Just out of Kefáli magnificent coastal **views** begin to unfold, with the distant beaches of Elafonísi shimmering mirage-like in a turquoise sea. Around you, olives ripen on the terraced hillsides and the villages seem to cling desperately to the high mountainsides, as if miraculously saved from some calamitous slide to the sea, glittering far below.

By **Kámbos**, 14km from Kefáli, you've descended enough for there to be a **beach** accessible below the village, albeit an hour's hike down a superb gorge inhabited by colonies of doves. The path, marked by yellow and blue dots, sets off from church by the village square: alternatively there's a steep but drivable track down, apshalted until the last 100m or so. Almost at the bottom you pass the *Hotel Agia Fisi*, with a couple of basic rooms (❸) and a couple of fancier studios with kitchen (❺) – pricey for what you get, but offering total isolation. Isolation is the main attraction of the beach too, which, close up, is rather stony. Up on the main road here there's also **accommodation** and **food** available at the rural *Rooms Hartzulakis* (☎28220 41445; ❷). On the wall here a map details walking trails around this coast, outlining a four-stage route from Kastélli to Paleohóra which avoids the roads followed by the E4.

Sfinári, a tortuous 7km north of Kámbos and slightly inland, is more developed and its quiet pebble beach is somewhat spoiled by greenhouses and derelict buildings a bit too close to the water for comfort. It is, however, a very friendly place, with plenty of rooms and places to eat both on the road and on the way down to the beach. The southern end of the strand is marginally less cluttered and here a cluster of **tavernas** gather beneath shady tamarisks: they positively encourage camping on the beach, and most provide loungers for customers. Among them, *Captain Fidias* and *Taverna Dilini* are both worth a try.

Beyond Sfinári the route climbs again and there are some terrific **views** from high above the coast as it twists and turns for 10km to cross the shoulder of Mount Manna, before dropping towards Plátanos and the turning for Falásarna (p.376). After this it's an easy descent to the coast and the Gulf of Kissámou and the main road into Kastélli Kissámou.

Hrissoskalítissa

Hrissoskalítissa lies some ten uneventful kilometres southwest of Váthi. There are a couple of tavernas and rooms places on the way down here – *Glykeria* (☎28220 61292; ❸) is good – but otherwise little beyond the weathered, white-walled **monastery** (now, in fact, a nunnery) of the Virgin of the Golden Step, beautifully sited on a rocky promontory above the sea. Today barely functioning, it has reduced from some two hundred residents to a solitary nun and one monk, whose main task seems to be keeping the place acceptable for tourists. The present church – containing a much-venerated thousand-year-old icon of the Virgin – dates only from the last century, but the monastery building is an ancient foundation: the first church was built in a cave here in the thirteenth century and recent investigations have turned up evidence of a much earlier Minoan settlement (or shrine) as well. Look out for the ninety steps that lead to the top of the crag around which the place is built: one of them appears golden (*hrissí skála*) to those who are pure in spirit – a fact which the authors are unable to verify.

Elafonísi

For **Elafonísi** you've another 5km of asphalt to traverse. This almost tropical lagoon of white sand tinged pink by shells, aquamarine waters, salt-encrusted rock pools and bright red starfish is still, despite increasing exploitation, as idyllic a spot as any in Crete. The water is incredibly warm, calm and shallow and Elafonísi – actually an island just offshore – is a short wade across the sandbar. There are more beaches on its far side (with waves), along with the odd ruined wall, seashells and a monument to Australian sailors shipwrecked here in 1907.

Not surprisingly, all this has not gone undiscovered, and there are now two **boats** a day from Paleohóra, a daily **bus** from Haniá and Réthimnon and at least one bus tour as well as scores of day-trippers who often fill an improvised car-parking space to bursting. The arrival of the crowds has brought lines of sun umbrellas and loungers to the beach, but little else in the way of infrastructure: by the entry to the car park (where buses stop) are a couple of *kantinas* and a kiosk/shop; there's a further *kantina* on the beach and there are also portable toilets and an incongruous **phone** box.

The area has also been declared a National Park, though this seems to have little practical effect other than ensuring that no permanent structures can be constructed nearer than 1km to the shore. The only **accommodation** is thus set well back, along the approach road. *Rooms Elafonísi* (☎28220 61274; ❸) is probably the best choice, with its own **taverna** and **minimarket**, and air-conditioned rooms with fridge; *Panorama*, just below, also has a good taverna with better views, but the rooms here are less good.

Walks from Elafonísi

Continuing south from Elafonísi the E4 **coastal path** to Paleohóra (about 17km away); is reasonably well marked, but it's still a tough walk, especially in the early stages (see p.390). Check the route before you set out, and don't venture this way alone, or without plentiful water.

You could also hike up a track heading inland to **Sklavopoúla** (7km away; see p.391) and its satellite hamlets. The tracks to reach Sklavoupoúla are clearly marked on the Petrákis *Haniá Trekking and Road Map* and also on the Harms-Verlag map (see p.26). By continuing east through Kalamiós, you'll reach the main surfaced road at **Voutás**, eight kilometres further, where you may be able to pick up a lift to Paleohóra, 13km on.

The south and Sélinos region

The direct route from the north coast to **Paleohóra** is a well-surfaced road that takes the line of least resistance across the mountains: consequently it feels a great deal less intimidating than the routes to either side. However, the scenery is always enjoyable with dramatic vistas, plenty of greenery and the advantage of numerous villages along the way, meaning that you're never far from a place to stop for a drink or a bite to eat. From the turning at Tavronítis, the road traces a long valley fingering its way beneath the hills as far as Voukoliés, a large village with a crowded Saturday-morning market (all over by about 10am). Hereafter you begin to climb in earnest, through several much smaller villages, towards the eparchy (province) of Sélinos, stretching roughly from the village of Flória to the south coast.

For **Soúyia**, the most direct road from the north coast leaves Haniá along the road to Omalós. Branching off at Alikianós, it follows the valleys through the western foothills of the White Mountains, passing the Ayía Iríni Gorge and a string of Sélinos villages before sweeping down the Herokténa valley into Soúyia.

Despite its isolation from the north and centre of the island, **Sélinos** has played a significant role in the island's history since ancient times. As early as the third century BC several of the communities here were important enough to form a confederation with Górtys (see p.138) and Magus, king of Cyrenaica, in Libya. Under the Romans, cities such as Lissós, Elyrós and Syia (modern Soúyia) prospered greatly. This distinguished past laid the foundations for the communal pride which created the scores of **Byzantine churches** here, perhaps the main reason to visit Sélinos today. Every village seems to offer at least one example, while some have as many as three or more.

Flória to Paleohóra

Flória, almost exactly halfway across the island, is divided into two halves: Káto (lower) Flória, straddling the road, and Apáno (upper) Flório above it. The upper village has the church of Áyii Patéres (the Holy Fathers), although here only fresco fragments remain. In the lower village, **Áyios Yeóryios** preserves thirteen panels of fine fifteenth-century frescoes. To reach it, go down a lane to the right of the second taverna you pass on the right. After about 600m you'll come to a small footbridge over a dry streambed; cross this and after 50m veer left at a fork to follow the path leading to the church. Near to the first taverna (the better of the pair), two war memorials – one German, one Greek – face each other across the road, serving as grim reminders of the terrible atrocities that happened here during World War II when, locals will tell you, they saw their parents and relatives gunned down in the self-same road.

Kándanos and Anisiráki

Kándanos, approached along a verdant valley planted with olives, is the chief village of Sélinos (though it's a great deal smaller than Paleohóra), and makes a pleasant, quiet place to stop for a coffee or even a meal. Despite an ancient name that goes back to Dorian times and the existence of as many as fifteen Byzantine **churches** in the vicinity (it was the see of the Orthodox Church in the Byzantine period and the see of the Roman Church under the Venetians), the village buildings are almost entirely new, for the place was razed to the ground by the Germans for its role in the **wartime resistance**. In 1941, after the German army had taken Máleme (see p.339), troops were dispatched urgently along this road to prevent the Allies landing reinforcements at Paleohóra. The resistance fighters of Kándanos determined to stop them, and despite a ferocious pitched battle the Germans could not break through for two crucial days; their progress was frustrated by the Cretans who also shot a number of German soldiers in the action. In retribution the Germans utterly destroyed the village and a sign was erected on the spot. The original sign is today preserved on a war memorial in the square – in German and Greek it reads: "Here stood Kándanos, destroyed in retribution for the murder of 25 German soldiers, and never to be rebuilt again."

The village that arose defiantly from the ashes is a pleasantly easy-going place today with a quartet of Byzantine **churches**. The first, Mihaíl Arhángelos, signed to the left up a lane on the northern edge of the village, has good but damaged frescoes in a restored church. The second, Áyios Mámas, has more damaged frescoes in a charming small white chapel; it's signed down a road by the petrol station on the village's main road junction, and lies 1km along here through olive groves. The third church, Ayía Ekateríni, is signed off the main street near the central *platía*, and is a beautiful old building with faded fresco fragments. The best of all though is **Áyios Ioánnis**, signed downhill off the Paleohóra road on the edge of the village. It lies 1km from the road, where another small white church contains superb fresco fragments.

Kándanos has opened up to the tourist trade in recent times and there are now a couple of **tavernas** and the odd café on the central *platía* close to the war memorial. On the outskirts is a waterworks, given to the village by the Germans after the war as an act of reconciliation, and many of the German military who served here have since returned to the village to forge friendships with their erstwhile adversaries.

A short detour from Kándanos west leads up to **Anisaráki** where you'll find more fine frescoes in the fifteenth-century churches of Ayía Ánna (signed on the left in an olive grove as you enter) with a rare stone iconostasis, Panayía and Ayía Paraskeví (both signed from the centre). Nearby, in the hamlet of **Koufalotós**, halfway between Kándanos and Anisaráki, the chapel of **Áyios Mihaíl Arhángelos** has fourteenth-century paintings by the Cretan master Ioánnis Pagoménos (see p.391). The chapel is located down a track on the right (coming from Anisaráki), and across a stream.

Plemeniuná, Kakodhíki and Kádhros

Beyond Kándanos the next few villages on or close to the main road are also worth a look and all have frescoed churches: Áyios Yeóryios in **Plemeniuná** has paintings dating from the fifteenth century, while **Kakodhíki**, known for its curative springs, has several churches nearby. These include the very ancient chapel of **Mihaíl Arhángelos**, probably early thirteenth-century, beside the modern church of Ayía Triádha, and the hilltop Áyios Isidhóros, with magnificent views and frescoes defaced by the Turks. Just off the road to the left **Kádhros**, some 9km from Kándanos, has the churches of Ioánnis Chrysóstomos and the **Panayía**, whose fine frescoes are almost complete. Many more small churches can be found throughout the area, particularly if you get off the road into the smaller villages. Few, if any, of them will be open when you arrive – but express an interest at the nearest *kafeníon* or to a local passer-by and it rarely takes long to hunt out the priest or someone else with a key.

South of Kakodhíki, the road tracks the Kakodikianós valley for 10km, before crossing to the river's west bank for the approach to Paleohóra.

Paleohóra

PALEOHÓRA was known originally as Kastél Selínou – the castle of Sélinos – and for much of its history was no more than that, a castle. Built by the Venetians in 1279, the fort was destroyed by Barbarossa in 1539 and never properly reconstructed even when the small port grew up beneath it. The ruins are still perched at the bulbous end of the headland now occupied by the settlement of Paleohóra – at its narrowest a bare four blocks across from the harbour on one side to the beach on the other.

The village is rapidly growing into a small town, and its facilities can barely cope with the increasing volume of visitors. Even so, the place has a remarkable ability to retain its enjoyably laid-back, end-of-the-line feel, helped no doubt by superb and extensive sands. Warm right through the winter, this out-of-season backwater makes an excellent place to rent an inexpensive apartment long-term.

Arrival and information

The main road from Kándanos leads you into a eucalyptus-lined avenue that becomes Paleohóra's single main street, Venizélos, lined with taverna after café after bar. The **bus** will drop you at the northern end of the street. If you come from the west, on the roads via Voutás or Sarakína, you'll emerge on the road behind the sandy western beach, by the post office. Although not particularly attractive by day, **Venizélos** is the vibrant soul of the village, and on summer evenings it is closed to traffic, brightly illuminated and filled to overflowing as the bar and restaurant tables spill across the pavement and encroach onto the road. From the main street, nothing is further than a five-minute walk away, and you have a choice of heading south towards the castle and yacht marina, east to a pebble beach ("Pebble Beach") or west to a wide sand beach (not surprisingly, "Sandy Beach").

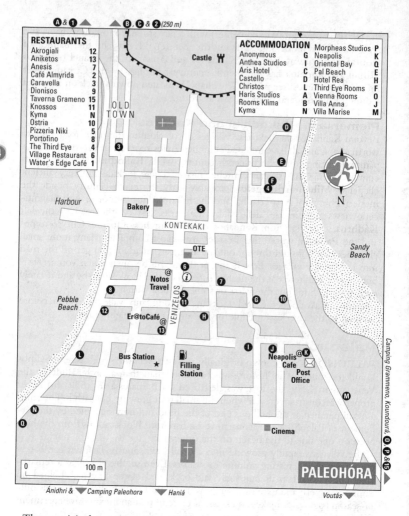

RESTAURANTS

Akrogiali	12
Aniketos	13
Anesis	7
Café Almyrida	2
Caravella	3
Dionisos	9
Taverna Grameno	15
Knossos	11
Kyma	N
Ostria	10
Pizzeria Niki	5
Portofino	8
The Third Eye	4
Village Restaurant	6
Water's Edge Café	1

ACCOMMODATION

Anonymous	G	Morpheas Studios	P
Anthea Studios	I	Neapolis	K
Aris Hotel	C	Oriental Bay	Q
Castello	D	Pal Beach	E
Christos	L	Hotel Rea	H
Haris Studios	A	Third Eye Rooms	F
Rooms Klima	B	Vienna Rooms	O
Kyma	N	Villa Anna	J
		Villa Marise	M

Castle

OLD TOWN

Harbour

Bakery

KONTEKAKI

OTE

Notos Travel

Pebble Beach

Er@toCafé

VENIZÉLOS

Bus Station

Filling Station

Neapolis Cafe

Post Office

Sandy Beach

Cinema

N

0   100 m

PALEOHÓRA

Camping Grammeno, Koundourá

Ánidhri & ▼ Camping Paleohora   ▼ Haniá   Voutás ▼

The municipal **tourist office** (May–Oct daily except Tues 10am–1pm & 6–9pm; ☎28230 41507) on Venizélos can give you a copy of their town map and advise about likely rooms places, as well as apartment lets should you be interested in a longer sojourn.

There are **travel agents** all around town: Notos Travel (☎28230 41140), on Venizélos opposite the town hall, has a finger in every pie, with a launderette and Internet access (both pricey – €9 for a full wash and dry) as well as exchange, **car and motorbike hire**, tours and more. Sabine Travel, virtually next door, also has trips, exchange, and cars, motorbikes and mountain bikes for hire (☎28230 42105). Two agencies on Kontekáki just up from the harbour – E-Motion (☎28230 41755) and Selino Travel (☎28230 42272) – are a little less frenetic, and also offer local boat-trips including **dolphin-spotting** cruises (these don't seem to have a very high success rate). Any of these can sell you tickets for the local **ferries** – in season (May to mid-Oct) the main services are to Elafonísi (daily at 10am, returning at 4pm), Gávdhos via Soúyia (Tues 8.30am) and along the coast to Soúyia and Ayía Rouméli, where you can pick up an onward service to Loutró and Hóra Sfakíon (daily at 9.45am). You can also pick up tickets at the jetty. Among the many day-trips offered by the travel agents are the **gorge walks** of **Samariá** (p.348) and **Ayía Iríni** (p.394). It's also perfectly possible to do these by public bus, with a daily service heading for Omalós via Ayía Iríni daily at 6am throughout the summer. You can then get the boat back from Ayía Rouméli or Soúyia in the late afternoon.

The **windsurf** school has now closed, so for the moment there's nowhere to hire boards or take lessons, but it's worth checking on Sandy Beach or at the *Villa Marise*; there were plans to open a new kite surf centre. There's excellent **diving and snorkelling** on this coast, and Aquacreta on Kontekáki (☎ 28230 41393, ⓦ www.aquacreta.gr) is a highly professional PADI dive school organising trips mainly to the west (they have a dive centre on a nearby beach) but also out to Gávdhos.

Internet access is available at several places including Notos Travel, Er@to Café further north on Venizélos, the *Poseidon Café* by the post office, and *Water's Edge Café* at *Haris Studios* (see accommodation). There are several **banks** (Mon–Fri 8am–2pm) with ATMs on Venizélos, just north of the town hall, and the **OTE** (Mon–Fri 7.30am–3.30pm) is immediately south – there are handy cardphones here as well as in numerous other locations. A well-stocked *períptero* on Venizélou sells **foreign newspapers**, also available at stores on Kontekáki. The **post office** (Mon–Fri 7.30am–2pm) is out on the road behind Sandy Beach. There are several **pharmacies** on Kontekáki and Venizélos. Speed Film, on Kontekáki, does fast **film processing** and the photographer/proprietor sells his own postcards taken around Sélinos. If you have a car running low on fuel, the town has three **petrol stations**; the one behind Sandy Beach has the longest hours. This is also where the biggest **supermarkets** are – Paleohóra has an extraordinary number of big supermarkets for such a small place, largely thanks to a long-running rivalry between two local family firms. There's a **taxi** office just by the harbour, or call ☎ 28320 83033.

Accommodation

Finding a **room** is unlikely to be a major problem outside August. Inexpensive places are mostly found in the backstreets away from the beach – particularly the street parallel to Pebble Beach and in the narrow streets towards the castle – but you'll see signs everywhere. We've also listed a couple of pleasant places behind the beach a few kilometres to the west, possible options with your own transport.

For **campsites**, *Camping Paleohora* (☎ 28230 41120) lies 2km northeast of the centre, reached along the road running behind the pebble beach. Attractively sited in an olive grove close to the beach with plenty of shade, its only drawback is the bonehard terrain (the neighbouring *Paleohora Club* has had its outdoor area closed, removing what was once a serious noise issue). Another pleasant site is the newer *Camping Grammeno* (☎ 28230 42125), a similar distance out along the coast to the west; however, it's increasingly beset by development, so check that it hasn't been engulfed before making the journey.

Anonymous In a backstreet behind the tourist office ☎ 28230 41509, ⓕ 28230 42333. Among the least expensive places in town, and something of a travellers' meeting place. Simple but pleasant rooms with shared bath off a charming garden courtyard. ❷

Anthea Studios Inland from Sandy Beach ☎ 28230 41594. Big, modern block with a variety of a/c rooms, studios and apartments, almost all with balcony and pleasant views inland. Rooms ❸, apartments ❺

Aris Hotel On the upper road at the south end of the peninsula, beneath the castle ☎ 28230 41502, ⓔ arishotel@cha.forthnet.gr. Charming and peaceful garden hotel. Pleasant en-suite a/c balcony rooms, most with sea view. ❻

Castello South end of Sandy Beach ☎ 28230 41143. Charming and good-value little place for rooms with bath and balcony in an elevated position overlooking the sandy beach; rooms at the back without view are less expensive (singles available too), and you can still get the views from the terrace taverna. ❸

Christos Above taverna of same name, Pebble Beach. The a/c balcony rooms right above the beachside drag can be noisy, but the cheaper rooms at the back are quieter. ❸

Haris Studios On the seafront below the east side of the castle ☎ 28230 42438, ⓦ www.paleochora-holidays.com. A friendly Cretan-Scottish–run place with a/c studios and apartments with balconies and sea views; the ones on the upper floors are better, but all are en-suite, with cooking facilities. Rooms ❸, apartments ❹

Rooms Klima Old town below the castle, above *Café Almyrida* ☎ 28230 42136. Simple rooms with fan, but a clean, well-run place and great views east along the coast. Also has a single; information in the café. ❸

Kyma Pebble Beach, by taverna of same name ☎ 28230 41550. Seafront place with attractive balcony rooms with bath, fridge and fan. ❸

Morpheas Studios 4km west of town on the road to Koundourá ☎ 28230 41697. Pleasant studios with balcony, fridge and kitchenette, in a tranquil garden setting close to the water. ❸

Neapolis Sandy Beach by post office, behind *Café Neapolis* ☎ 28230 41134. Very pleasant, simple en-suite a/c rooms and apartments set back from the road. One huge apartment at the front with two bedrooms and separate kitchen and bathroom. Rooms ❸, apartment ❼

Oriental Bay Behind taverna of same name at the northern end of Pebble Beach ☎ 28230 41076. Almost the last place on the beach, which ensures peace, and often means there's room when others are full. Plain but

pleasant en-suite balcony rooms with fridge and fan; some triples. ❸

Pal Beach Sandy Beach ☎ 28230 41512, ⓦ www.palbeach.gr. The town's priciest hotel is big and rather bland, but the a/c sea-view rooms fronting Sandy Beach are comfortable, and there are a couple of luxurious apartments. Rates include breakfast. ❻

Hotel Rea Backstreet off Venizélos, behind the tourist office ☎ 28230 41307, ⓕ 28230 41605. Friendly small hotel with a/c balcony rooms and breakfast included, the best value and most pleasant of a group of small hotels here. It also has classy new apartments, for two or four people, with satellite TV. ❺

Third Eye Rooms Behind the *Third Eye* restaurant ☎ 28230 41234. Variety of en-suite rooms at various prices: some a/c, some fan-cooled; most with kitchenette. Also a couple of larger apartments. ❷–❹

Vienna Rooms Koundourá, 5km west along the coast ☎ 28230 41478. Good-value place near the sea with tranquil en-suite rooms with fridge, plus some apartments. There's also a swimming pool and bar. ❹

Villa Anna In broad sidestreet off Sandy Beach near the post office ☎ 2810 346428 or 6944596860, ⓔ anna@her.forthnet.gr. Pricey but very pleasant apartments for two to six people – large, nicely furnished, all with kitchen and a/c, and surrounded by lush gardens. Booking recommended. ❻

Villa Marise On Sandy Beach almost opposite the post office ☎ 28230 42012, ⓔ jetee@otenet.gr. Probably the best location in town, with a variety of well-equipped, en-suite a/c balcony rooms, apartments and studios for up to six people (decent single rates too). The helpful owner has free yoga sessions for guests every evening, and can also book the slightly more expensive *Europa* and *Candia* next door – stay here and you can use their pool and tennis courts. ❹

The Town

Other than head for the beach, eat and drink, there's not a great deal to see or do in Paleohóra, which of course is a major part of its attraction. If you want to be more active, there are plenty of trips on offer, as well as attractive **walks** inland, to charming villages like Ánidhri and Azoyirés (see p.391), or along the coast in either direction. In town you can check out the **castle**, for the views back over town, or walk right around the end of the promontory to return to the beach on the other side. Neither of these options is as appealing as it might be, since the fortress itself is little more than a hillock ringed with broken walls, while a new marina dominates the point. Heading up the castle you'll see the oldest parts of town, to the south of the harbour.

Of the beaches, western **Sandy Beach** is more impressive: magnificently broad and sandy, lined with tamarisks and supplied with showers, on a bay with excellent easy windsurfing. **Pebble Beach**, facing east, is at first sight a much less attractive proposition. However, this eastern side is far livelier at night, when the beachfront promenade rivals the main street for action and choice of eating; the cafés and restaurants over here have a stunning evening view of the moon rising over the mountains. The beach is also much more sheltered when the wind is blowing, and if you venture far enough north, away from town, you'll even find some sand.

Eating, drinking and entertainment

There are plenty of **eating** places to choose from, and prices here are generally reasonable. The Pebble Beach restaurants tend to be the more touristy, though this does have the advantage that there are several places serving **breakfast**. There are plenty of **cafés** scattered around too, especially on Venizélos and around its junction with Kontekáki; a couple of lovely, tranquil spots in the old town with sea-view terraces for breakfast, coffees and drinks are the *Water's Edge Café* (see below) and *Café Almyrida*, in the street immediately behind it. There's takeaway *souvláki* and *yíros pitta* at *Aniketos*, on Venizélos half a block south of the bus station, and from a simple place near the harbour on Pebble Beach, squeezed between touristy *Captain Jim* and *Dino's Grill*. There are also a number of **bakeries** – probably the best is *Bakakis*, near the harbour behind the supermarket and opposite the *Anemos* bar.

Akrogiali Pebble Beach. Attractively old-fashioned taverna among the glossier places on Pebble Beach with good Greek standards.

Anesis Behind the tourist office. An inviting garden restaurant in a restored town house with a children's play area. Excellent food including specialities such as *kounéli stifado* (rabbit stew) – they also do seafood dishes and vegetarian options.

Caravella Old town seafront just south of the ferry jetty. Paleohóra's best seafood restaurant, with a pleasant waterfront terrace. The cooking and service are excellent, as is their chilled *hyma* (barrelled wine from the Kastélli Kissámou area).

Dionisos Venizélos, near the town hall. Attractive place which is a bit fancier than the competition here – with prices to match.

Taverna Grameno Three kilometres west towards Koundourá along the coast road, fronting Grameno beach. Highly recommended place and perhaps the area's most authentic Cretan restaurant. It's a friendly garden taverna with a play area for kids, and the cooking is excellent – take a look in the kitchen for what is seasonal and fresh.

Knossos Venizélou close to the National Bank. Good new place offering the usual taverna standards. Has a street terrace.

Kyma Pebble Beach. Big place serving decent taverna standards in a nice setting.

Oriental Bay At the northern end of Pebble Beach. With a pleasant tamarisk-shaded terrace fronting the sea, this place tends to be quiet; serves excellent juices and breakfasts.

Ostria Sandy Beach. Large and friendly taverna serving well-cooked Greek staples. On Fridays there's a "Greek night", with music and dancing.

Pizzeria Niki Off the south side of Kontekáki. A pleasant courtyard setting for excellent pizzas cooked in a wood-fired oven.

Portofino Pebble Beach. Touristy place with an international menu, but also good pizzas from a wood-fired oven.

The Third Eye Inland from Sandy Beach. Excellent vegetarian restaurant (plus a few fish dishes) run by a Greek–New Zealand couple. Worth putting up with the often brusque service for excellent food and spices rarely seen on Crete, from curries to *gado-gado* and bean salads, as well as more conventional Greek dishes. The world music background sounds go well with the cuisine, and there's a small shop selling home-made goat's yoghurt, local cheeses, thyme honey, olive oil and lots more.

Village Restaurant Venizélos between the town hall and tourist office. Young place with a modern take on traditional Greek food, and an ideal position for watching the world go by.

Water's Edge Café On the seafront below the east side of the castle ℡ 28320 42438. As well as having a lovely terrace for snacks and drinks, the *Water's Edge* serves dinner weekly on Saturday; freshly made and excellent. Booking recommended.

Drinking and entertainment

Paleohóra clings to its village origins, and has no pretensions to be anything other than a tranquil seaside resort with family appeal: if you're looking for all-night discos and raucous bars you've come to the wrong place. Most bars keep their music volume well down after dark and even the liveliest part of town, the Pebble Beach promenade, is a pretty tame affair when compared to most other resorts on the island.

After a day at the beach, entertainment in Paleohóra is confined mainly to the **bars**. Many of the most popular of these are shoehorned into the Venizélos–Kontekáki junction and down towards the harbour, where *Ayios* and *Anemos* are popular meeting spots. There are more on Venizélos itself, as well as a couple of old-fashioned café/*ouzerí* serve good-value drinks: one of the most popular is the central *Kafenion Yiannis* whose eponymous proprietor is one of the town's characters. The old town, sandwiched between the castle and the sea on the peninsula's east flank makes for a pleasant evening stroll – here the *Café Almyrida* and *Water's Edge Café* provide an opportunity for a quieter drink and the chance to watch kingfishers offshore. The bars along the Pebble Beach promenade offer more action, especially as the night wears on. Here *Skala* near the harbour, and *Sunrise* are complemented by the *Nostos Disco-Bar* where you can join locals dancing in an outside courtyard bar. There are fewer bars along Sandy Beach but those that are here, like *Jetée* right on the sand by the *Villa Marise*, offer a quiet spot to linger over a sundowner. Further out, the town's only true dance **club**, the *Paleohora Club*, lies some way out at the north end of Pebble Beach close to the campsite. Sadly its open-air dance floor is no longer allowed to open at night, and it can get hot and sweaty inside. In the other direction, at the far end of Sandy Beach about 1km out of town, the *Castaway Club* (daily 11am to early morning) is built around a pool. Here too the music has to be turned right down at night, but the cocktails are good and the atmosphere chilled: during the day the music tends to be louder, and for the price of a drink you get free use of the pool.

Nightly showings at the open-air **cinema**, *Cine Attikon*, tucked away in the northern backstreets, are also worth checking out; most of their films are in English and programmes (advertised near the harbour and outside the tourist office; tickets €5) change daily.

West from Paleohóra to Koundourá

Follow the coast either way from Paleohóra and you'll find more beaches. To the **west** it's not a terribly pretty coastline, marred by plastic greenhouses, but there are some excellent beaches and little coves along the way. The best of them are around **Grameno beach** after about 5km, where a small peninsula ensures sheltered water and there are trees for shade. On the landward side of the road here, *Taverna Grameno* (see p.389) is a superb place to eat, and there's also an excellent taverna on the small cove beach by the Dive Centre, a little before this.

Continuing along the road will quickly bring you to **Koundourá**, which also has rooms (see p.388) but is spoiled by more greenhouses. The paved road peters out 4km beyond Koundourá at **Kríos** ("cold"), another pebble beach where the water can be incredibly chilly due to underwater springs. The dirt road from here continues on to several shingly, deserted bays, where some people **camp** beside beautifully clear water. From here you can continue on foot right around the coast to Elafonísi (see p382), roughly 10km away via a section of the E4 Pan-European Footpath. This should be clearly waymarked, but it's still a comparatively tough, hot and shadeless walk, so be sure to carry plenty of water and to check conditions locally before setting out. To avoid the first rather tedious 5km of asphalt you could take a taxi as far as Koundourá.

East from Paleohóra to Soúyia

To the **east** of Paleohóra, things are simpler, although there are ominous signs of road-building and other development along the first part of the way. For now, though, the E4 Pan-European **Footpath** traces the shore for miles beyond the campsite, passing a succession of grey pebble strips with fewer people clad in fewer clothes the further you venture. This path continues to Lissós (14km/4hr; p.397) and Soúyia (18km/5–6hr; p.395), and if you time it right you can return to Paleohóra by boat from Soúyia (currently leaving at 5.30pm in summer). Again you should carefully check out both the route and the boats beforehand, as the service deteriorates rapidly out of high season. The path is waymarked, but it doesn't simply follow the coast all the way, and there are one or two steep scrambles. Since the most scenic section is through the gorge between Lissós and Soúyia, it might be easier to do it from there.

An easier alternative walk to Lissós and Soúyia descends from **Prodhrómi**, 13km inland to the northeast of Paleohóra, which you could reach by taxi, halving the total walking distance to around 9km. A track on the village's southern edge winds 3km down to the hill of Pidaraki, near the coast, where it meets the E4 footpath. Here you turn east to reach Lissós (another 3km) and Soúyia.

The village of **Ánidhri**, 6km east of Paleohóra which you pass en route to Prodhrómi, is particularly beautiful, with a fourteenth-century church, **Áyios Yeóryios**, which has an unusual double altar and fine **frescoes** depicting the lives of Christ and Áyios Yeóryios by Ioánnis Pagoménos (John the Frozen), the most prolific of several painters whose signatures appear frequently around Sélinos. The village **bar** (actually the old village school, recently converted) makes a good place to pause for a drink, and has a pleasant terrace with views.

The Pelekaniotikós valley and Sklavopoúla

With your own transport, you could follow a **spectacular drive** along the road which heads **northwest from Paleohóra** and tracks the valley of the River Pelekaniotikós, calling at a string of charming Sélinos hamlets. To join the road, head out along Sandy Beach and then turn right on the edge of town, following signs to Voutás. This area saw devastating **floods** in the spring of 2000 when heavy rain fell on the mountains for three days, turning the river into a raging torrent that swept away roads, bridges, trees, olive groves and houses on its way to the sea. The evidence of this disaster is still clearly visible, but one tangible advantage is that most of the roads have been repaved, and there's plenty of excellent, easy driving.

At **Voutás**, 12km northwest of Paleohóra, there is the possibility of a detour to the isolated village of Sklavopoúla and its wonderful frescoed churches. Take the road towards Sklavopoúla, and 1km before Kítiros the small church of **Ayía Paraskeví** is worth a stop to see some faded frescoes on its rear wall; one has a remarkable portrayal of hell with devils putting sinners into the flames whilst others are being crushed by serpents. The road then climbs among rocky heights for 5km further to reach **Sklavopoúla**, set at an altitude of 640m and one of the remotest communities in the Sélinos, as well as a place with a considerable history. The nineteenth-century English traveller Robert Pashley made it here and identified Sklavopoúla as the site of Doulópolis, a Dorian city renowned for its military prowess. The village's present name ("Village of the

Slavs") may stem from a resettlement of Slavs here by Nikiforas Fokas (see p.416) following his reconquest of Crete from the Saracens in 961, the settlers being perhaps Armenians from Bulgaria.

There are no fewer than seven churches in the vicinity of Sklavopoúla, all with wall paintings. As you come in you pass the church of **Áyios Yeóryios**, next to a school playground on the left, with some fine frescoes dating from the thirteenth century. To get the key, go behind the school to the house of Petros, the guardian. Continuing into the village, the other two notable churches – the **Panayía** and **Sotíros Christós** – are reached down a path next to the primitive *kafeníon* on the left. Continue downhill along this path (a *kalderími* – the still-used Turkish name given to ancient tracks and cobbled ways) for 400m or so until you come to the rambling house of Miháílis, the guardian. His multi-generational family are extremely welcoming, and provide a delightful insight into a rural Crete long gone from other parts of the island. You will probably be offered the traditional welcome of sweet bread and a cool drink or even a *raki* before the key emerges. Then Miháílis will lead you to see the churches nearby – the **frescoes** of the Panayía with superb gospel scenes and a portrait of the donor are the more interesting – and although he refuses money for his time, donations are welcome for the churches' upkeep.

Back on the main route north, you pass the villages of Kámatera and Arhondíko, beyond where the road winds circuitously through unpopulated but dramatic mountain scenery, to join the route that cuts across from the far west to the Paleohóra, a couple of kilometres south of **Stróvles**. From here Miliá, the Koutsamatádos ravine (p.379) and the north coast are all within easy striking distance, as is Elafonísi in the other direction. It's worth bearing in mind that **petrol stations** are non-existent in these remote regions, so you should fill up in advance.

Northeast of Paleohóra

Many other villages in the **Sélinos interior** are equally unspoilt and, if you have transport, almost any of the tracks into the hills are fascinating. More of the roads up here are paved every year, making access increasingly easy. Heading north out of Paleohóra on the main road, you'll soon reach a couple of signs to **Azoyirés**, one official, the other extolling the virtues of "Azoyirés, Paradise Village", with its museum and caves. The road up to the village is set amidst woods of cypress and pine, and is now paved all the way to Teménia, making this an excellent, if narrow and winding, short cut to Soúyia. In Azoyirés, head straight for the centre, where there are two **tavernas**, *Mikailis* and *Alpha*. The latter is exceptionally friendly and helpful, and if you so much as stop outside will ply you with maps and local information on caves and walks by the river: they also have en-suite **rooms** in a building nearby (☎28230 41620; ❸).

Armed with *Alpha*'s **map** the scattered local attractions are relatively easy to find. The **museum** (officially Sat & Sun 9am–2pm; when closed enquire at the *Alpha*), a single-room record of the Turkish occupation, full of fascinating old stuff, is in a delightful location in the valley at the bottom of the village, by the old olive-oil factory and a chapel built into a cliff. A pretty path leads down there, above a tree-filled ravine where pine, cypress, olive and maple grow. The biggest of several local **caves** is in the other direction, on an easy-to-miss road which sets off left just before the tavernas, and winds steeply upwards for nearly 2km (keep climbing and turning where there's any doubt about the way). At the top you have to park any transport and there's an obvious path leading on – look up and you'll see a cross, some 200m above, which marks your destination. Approaching the cave you may disturb quail (sometimes on the menu at the *Alpha*); the eerie sounds in the cave itself emanate from more birds, mostly pigeons, bizarrely amplified by the cave. Going down, there's a steep metal stairway and rock-cut steps descending 50m or so to a little shrine lit from above by dim, reflected light. If you have a powerful torch (the *Alpha* will lend you one if not), you can continue a fair way, although there's no proper path: frankly, it's not that impressive.

Beyond Azoyirés it's a further 10km or so to **Teménia**, where there's an interesting **church** and small archeological site. Arriving from Azoyirés, you come to a road junction on the edge of the village. Turn right downhill along the Rodováni road where soon you'll pass a rebuilt stone chapel atop a low hill to the left and, about 200m further on, a sign on the right to ancient Hyrtakína. Head down this narrow track, and on your right you will soon see the charming drum-domed church of **Sotíros Christós**, whose entrance has some curious stone steps built into the sides of a shallow porch. It should be open (enquire at the nearby monastery buildings if not) and inside are a number of fine **frescoes** including a stirring image of a mounted Áyios Yeóryios slaying the dragon. To the left, the track takes a long, steep, nerve-wracking ascent to the hilltop site of the ancient Dorian city of **Hyrtakína**. In this desolate and lonely spot it's strange to find these ruins of what was a thriving city-state two and a half thousand years ago. There are remains of fourth-century BC houses and of the Cyclopean walls of a Temple of Pan.

Haniá to Soúyia

Although you can cut through by the route outlined above, the main **road to Soúyia** is the one that runs right across the island from Haniá. This follows the route to Omalós for about 13km before turning off through Alikianós to skirt west of the highest mountains. Beside this turning there's a large **war memorial**. The Cretans commemorated here were mostly local members of the irregular forces which defended the area known as "Prison Valley" in the Battle of Crete (you've already passed the prison; see p.345). Cut off from any other Allied units – who indeed believed that resistance here collapsed on the first day of the battle – the Greeks fought on even as everyone else was in full retreat. By doing so they prevented the Germans getting around the mountains to cut the road and guaranteed that the evacuation from Hóra Sfakíon could go ahead. In much earlier history, Alikianós was also the site of the wedding massacre which ended the Kandanoleon revolt (see p.336).

Alikianós

Right in the centre of the orange-growing district known as the *Portokalahória* ("the orange villages"), **Alikianós** itself has a couple of churches worth a look. Once in the village, follow the Koufós road (signed) for a short distance to reach the small fourteenth-century church of **Áyios Yeóryios,** close to the road on the right. This used to have some fine fifteenth-century frescoes, but lost them as a result of damage in World War II. In an orange grove behind houses over the road from the church lie the ruins of the **Da Molini castle** (some locals refer to it as Da Moulin), which may have been the scene of the Kandanoleon wedding massacre. To reach it, head in along the nearest street and, when you ask the way, you'll be conducted over back-garden fences to reach the weed-festooned ruin with impressive walls. The entrance lintel (which is now overgrown) carries the inscription *Omnia Mundi Fumus et Umbra* ("All in the World is Smoke and Shadow"), a sentiment to which the Venetians were particularly attached, and which ultimately turned out to be grimly accurate regarding their Cretan possessions.

Continue along the same road for a kilometre to reach the best of Alikianós's churches, **Áyios Ioánnis**, 50m down a signed track into more orange groves on the right. A beautiful fourteenth-century building on the site of at least two previous churches dating back to the sixth century, the church employs parts of the previous basilica in the construction of its apse. Inside, surviving **frescoes** depict the Ascension as well as a number of saints.

The Ayía Iríni Gorge and Moní

Back on the route south the road soon passes **Skinés**, a large village with several tavernas and *kafenía* set among extensive orange groves, before it starts to climb out of the valley into the outriders of the Lefká Ori. Here the citrus trees give way to leafier, deciduous varieties – chestnuts and planes especially – and the villages are a great deal smaller. Just over halfway across the island, near Ayía Iríni, there's a road signed to Omalós (see p.346), an excellent road that offers an effortless and exhilarating drive over extremely high mountains, with wonderful views and plenty of vegetation.

Ayía Iríni itself, a little under 30km beyond Skinés, is another very green village, with lots of old chestnut trees, although it is still suffering the aftermath of a great fire in the summer of 1994, which devastated a vast tract of land between the **Ayía Iríni Gorge** and Soúyia, setting fire to many villages en route. The gorge can be **walked** from Ayía Iríni as far as the coast at Soúyia, roughly 12km in all, though the last five are along the road: it's about a four-hour trek. Despite the fire damage it's an attractive hike, not too taxing and usually very quiet unless you're unlucky enough to coincide with one of the occasional tours (mainly from Paleohóra). The route down into the gorge, now yet another branch of the E4 footpath and hence well marked, can be picked up on the south edge of the village and is marked on the Petrákis *Haniá Trekking and Road Map* (see p.26). The *KriKri* café at the entrance opens at 7am for breakfast (☎28230 51550, or information at *Zorba's* rooms in Soúyia) and can advise on the route. The gorge is an easy **day-trip** from Paleohóra (the 6am Omalós bus passes through Ayía Iríni, and you can get the afternoon ferry back from Soúyia) or Soúyia (any Haniá bus will drop you); you could also get a taxi to the top from either of these places.

Continuing south by road, you start gradually to descend, looping down to occasional views of the Libyan Sea and, in the last few kilometres, tracing a gorge with Soúyia framed at the far end. Beyond Rodhováni are the remains of ancient **Elyrós**, the most important city in southwest Crete in Roman times and earlier; the site is unexcavated and, although signed from the road, there's very little to see apart from odd chunks of wall. In **Moní**, the last village before the coast, the delightful fourteenth-century **church of Áyios Nikólaos** has frescoes by Ioánnis Pagaménos, including a huge and striking image of St Nicholas himself. Outside the church, take a look at the **campanile** or freestanding bell tower – it's an architectural curiosity and the only one known on the island. Before setting out for the church, ask in the first bar you pass on entering the village for the key: it's actually kept at a house a few doors along but they'll sort you out. The church lies along a track which descends from the road on the right about 50m beyond the bar.

Koustoyérako

Only about 5km short of Soúyia, a road cuts back to the ancient Sélinos villages of Livadás and **Koustoyérako**, the latter a very ancient village that is still the home of the Paterákis family, famed in the annals of resistance to

German occupation. Manóli Paterákis was one of those who took part in the capture of General Kreipe (see p.422). He died some years ago at the age of 73, when he fell while chasing a wild goat through the mountains.

The village, like so many, has a long history of resistance to foreign occupation, and was destroyed by Venetians, Turks and Germans alike. In 1943, German troops entered the village, which the men had deserted, and rounded up the women and children in the village square:

They lined them all up, and, as they refused to speak, prepared to execute the lot. But, before they could press the trigger of their heavy machine-gun, ten Germans fell dead. For some of the village men – about ten – had taken up position along the top of a sheer cliff above the village, from where they could watch every detail, and, at just the right moment, had opened fire. Not a bullet went wide. Terrified, the Germans took to their heels...

George Psychoundákis, *The Cretan Runner*

Next day the Germans returned, but by then the village was deserted; they blew up the empty houses in frustration. Cóstas Paterákis, now in his eighties, who fired the first shot and killed the machine-gunner (Patrick Leigh Fermor has described this as one of the most spectacular moments of the war), still lives here.

While the villagers have no desire to become tourist attractions, Koustoyérako is a lovely and very friendly place, set beneath the heights of the Lefká Óri looking out over the Libyan Sea. At the entrance to the village there's a striking modern **war memorial**, and a simple **taverna**, next to the school and village playground. Further along, you reach the square, with a couple of *kafenía*. The famous shot was fired from the rocky cliffs above, to your right as you face inland. At the top of the village, to your left from the square, is a tiny Byzantine chapel, **Áyios Yeóryios**. Inside are some beautiful remains of frescoes, with sixteenth-century graffiti carved into them; the chapel itself may be as early as tenth century in origin. The inscription inside the door dates from sixteenth-century restorations and records various generations of the Kandanoleon family. The last named is one María Theotokópoulos, and from this tenuous connection comes the claim that **El Greco** (Doménico Theotokópoulos) came originally from Koustoyérako. In the graveyard is the tomb of another Kandanoleon, George. One of Crete's great revolutionary leaders, he led the sixteenth-century revolt against Venetian rule (see p.336) and his body was returned to his birthplace following his execution by the Venetians. Before setting out for the church (which is kept locked) you'll need to enquire at the *kafeníon* on the square; they should be able to turn up someone to take you to the church, where the key will be retrieved from its hiding-place whilst you turn your back.

In summer French groups frequently camp by the school, and from here climb – with a guide – to Omalós and the gorge. If you ask permission, and take your meals at the taverna, you'd probably be allowed to **camp** here, too. The path to the Omalós plateau is now a branch of the E4 and so has been upgraded and waymarked; we haven't tried it, though, so if you do so be sure to get full details before setting out. Although Omalós is only some 12km away, the country in between is mountainous, remote and entirely uninhabited.

Soúyia

The south coast settlement of **Soúyia** is a small village slowly on its way to becoming a resort. However, archeological remains here have resulted in severe restrictions on building close to the sea and this means, for the moment anyway, that tourist development lags a long way behind its western neighbour, Paleohóra. There are no big hotels and no major tour operators, just lots of rooms, simple restaurants and bars, added to a couple of general stores which double as travel agents and bureaux de change. A scruffy little place – not particularly attractive at first sight – Soúyia tends to grow on you. Its best feature lies right at the end of the road: an enormous swathe of bay with sparklingly clean, clear sea and a long, pebbly beach. There's plenty of room to spread out here – even on summer weekends when it's popular with locals – and you could **camp** under the few scraggly trees if you wanted, although you'd be advised to get as far away from the central beach as possible to be left in peace. Around at the east end of the bay there's something of a nudist community – known locally as the **Bay of Pigs**.

The village **church**, down by the beach at the western end of an avenue flanked by tamarisks, is the village's only feature. The story goes – in typical Cretan fashion – that it was built after a local man slept here and dreamt that an ancient church lay beneath him and that he was being summoned to erect a new one on the site. Sure enough the ancient church was found and the new one built. Unfortunately the new building was far smaller than the old and at a different angle: as a result the sixth-century Byzantine mosaic which formed the floor of the original stuck out beyond the walls of the new one. Although much of the original mosaic has been taken away for "restoration" and seems unlikely to return, you can still see where it was. The original church was a part of ancient Syia, a port for Elyrós (see p.394) which flourished through the Roman and early Christian eras; other remains can be seen in the village and around to the east of the bay.

Practicalities

It's worth noting in advance that there is no petrol station, no bank and no ATM in Soúyia, nor any real formal tourist infrastructure – bus tickets, tours, car hire and the like are arranged through the shops, restaurants or hotels. The most useful sources of **information** on all things going on locally are the two **minimarkets** (Pelican and Polifimos) at the bottom of the main street: here you can **change money**, find out about **car hire**, check notices for local **tours**, and book **taxis** and **taxi-boats**. The latter can take you to isolated beaches along the coast, at reasonable cost split between four or five (especially if you walk one way and get the boat the other). Another supermarket, and a taxi office, are higher up the street beyond the *Raki* bar.

Bus tickets are sold at the *Roxana* snack-bar, opposite the minimarkets; the 7am departure to Haniá and Omalós offers the opportunity to walk either the Ayía Iríni or the Samariá gorge – it meets the early bus from Paleohóra in Ayía Iríni, and from there one continues to Omalós and the other to Haniá, so you may have to change. *Roxana* also sells tickets for a weekly **boat to Elafonísi** (Wed 9am). **Boat tickets** for Paleohóra, Hóra Sfakión, Gávdhos and other south-coast destinations are sold at the *períptero* on the seafront, near the bottom of the main road. There are two **cardphones** just here too.

Accommodation

There are **rooms** everywhere. The first options – and some of the best – are off the main road at the top of the hill as it enters town; others, more expensive, are right on the seafront (mostly to the right from the bottom of the main road); while another cluster of cheaper rooms can be found by turning left along the seafront and left again before the stream.

Captain George To the west off the main street, just below *Pension Galini* ☎ 28230 51133. En-suite, a/c balcony rooms, some with kitchenette, in a pleasant garden setting. ❹

Pension El Greco Down the lane past *Captain George* ☎ 28230 51186. Upper-floor rooms place, where you are welcomed with a *raki*: a choice of en-suite, a/c rooms, most with balcony and some with fridge and kitchenette. One of several down here with a very quiet, semi-rural atmosphere. ❸

Pension Galini Main road, at the top of the hill ☎ 28230 51488. Big, comfortable a/c en-suite rooms with balconies. ❸

Idomeneas Apartments Opposite *Pension Galini* ☎ 28230 51540. Modern studios and apartments with a/c, TV and balcony. ❹

Rooms Irtakina Downstairs from *Pension El Greco* ☎ 28230 51130. A beautiful garden, and choice of en-suite, a/c rooms. ❸

Paradisos On the lane by the stream, left and left again at the seafront ☎ 28230 51486. Simple en-suite rooms including some family ones with kitchenette; a couple of similar places are nearby. ❸

Hotel Santa Irene On the seafront ☎ 28230 51342, ⓔ nanadakis@cha.forthnet.gr. The fanciest place in town, with modern, a/c, en-suite balcony studios and apartments with fridge (some with sea view) around a garden. ❺

Zorba's On the seafront ☎ 28230 51353. Close to *Santa Irene*, a simpler place with a/c en-suite rooms. ❹

Eating and drinking

Places to eat are predominantly on the seafront, with a few more up the main road. At night, there are a couple of **disco-bars** which sometimes attract a crowd: the first, *Alabama*, is sited among the trees on the far side of the stream to the east of the village, whilst the other, *Fortuna*, is at the northern edge of town, on the left as you come in. Other more centrally located **bars** include elegant *Raki*, opposite *Rebetika* restaurant, and *Bla Bla Bla*, behind the *Omikron* taverna, both with music after dark.

Café Lotos On the seafront, at the corner of the main road. Coffees and juices by day, drinks in the evening, plus Internet access.

Café Santa Irene On the seafront. Top choice for breakfast, juices and snacks.

To Kyma At the western end of the seafront. Good food and great location.

Liviko At the western end of the seafront below the church. A good bet for taverna standards and fresh fish, often with live music in the evening.

Omikron On the seafront to the east of the main road. German-run restaurant with a more north European flavour, and some vegetarian choices.

Rebetiko Halfway up the main street. Well-cooked traditional dishes in a pleasant garden terrace.

Roxana At the bottom of the main street opposite the minimarkets. Cakes and savouries like *tirópita*, sandwiches and cold drinks to eat in or take away.

Lissós

The archeological site of **Lissós**, 4km west of Soúyia, is a great deal more reward-ing than anything you'll see in Soúyia itself. The **walk** there, a little over an hour, is part of the pleasure: you set out on the road which heads west, behind the beach, and at the harbour turn right onto a track leading slightly inland. The route – also the path trodden by ancient pilgrims – is part of the E4 coastal path, so it's pretty well marked with black and yellow splodges. It leads up a beautiful echo-ing gorge, which you follow for about thirty minutes, and then climb steeply out of towards the coast. After a short level stretch the sea comes into view, followed almost immediately by Lissós, below you at the back of a delightful little bay with the chapel of Áyios Kiriákos and the archeological site further inland.

An alternative way of seeing the site and saving a walk both ways is to book a **taxi-boat** (about €20 for up to five people) from Soúyia. Ideally in summer you'd either walk over early and get the boat to pick you up in the middle of the day (precarious embarkation), or have them drop you at Lissós's pebble beach late in the afternoon, leaving time for a look around the ancient site (you'll very likely have it all to yourself and it's just the place to share a chilled bottle of wine) before the walk back to Soúyia in the cool of the evening. The path back to Soúyia from the beach is fairly obvious as it climbs the steep hill on the east side of the archeological site.

The site

Originally a Dorian city, Lissós grew through the Hellenistic and Roman eras and continued to thrive, along with its neighbours Syia and Elyrós, right up to the Saracen invasion in the ninth century, when they were all abandoned. These places have little history, although it is known that they joined together around 300 BC – along with Hyrtakína in the hills behind, Pikilássos on the inaccessible coast between here and Ayía Rouméli, and Tarra, at modern Ayía Rouméli – to form the **Confederation of Oreioi**, and were later joined by Górtys and Cyrenaica (the latter in North Africa). The remains at Lissós are mostly Classical Greek and Roman.

The most important survival is an **Asklepion**, or temple of healing, built beside a curative spring against the cliffs on the east side of the site. The temple probably dates from the third century BC, although the **mosaic floor** (protected by a broken-down fence) which is its most obvious feature was added later, in the first century AD; it's a poignant ancient relic, however, depicting images of polychrome birds in its central section (including a quail) and elaborate and beautifully crafted geometric patterns on its outer borders. The excavations here revealed a hole dug through the floor which contained numerous broken statues and a headless image of Asclepius, the Greek god of healing; this was probably the work of fanatical early Christians who destroyed the temples, decapitated the statues (where they believed the spirit of the devil resided) and defaced the walls. Notice also the marble altar-base which would have supported a statue, and the "snake pit" (or hole to place sacrifices) next to it. On the gentler, western slope of the valley, opposite, are a group of tombs that look like small stone huts, with barrel-vaulted roofs – hardly the best advertisement for the healing temple. You'll also find a small ruined theatre and two thirteenth-century churches, Áyios Kiriákos – with a nearby **spring** – and Panayía, which reused older material from the site.

When you've completed your explorations, the small pebble **beach** provides solace in the form of a swim. If you're continuing the **walk west towards Paleohóra**, the path is again pretty obvious (there may be a guard in the hut at the site who can help, but don't rely on it): it's a long, hot and lonely stretch of coast though, so carry plenty of water and don't try this alone. The spring mentioned above should be a reliable place to fill any bottles, even in summer.

Gávdhos

Gávdhos, the southernmost point of Europe, is the largest of Crete's offshore islands and the only one with any significant population. Plain and somewhat barren, its attraction lies in its enduring isolation. The 50km of rough sea – over 3000m deep – separating it from the coast of Crete frequently prove too much for the small ferries, and the ports they serve have themselves only begun to see large numbers of tourists in the last few years. Consequently – and despite the fact that it's now possible to get a very basic package tour to Gávdhos – the trip to the island remains one more talked about than done.

Change, though, is approaching, and already you shouldn't expect solitude: in summer, there's a semi-permanent community of **beach-campers** who easily

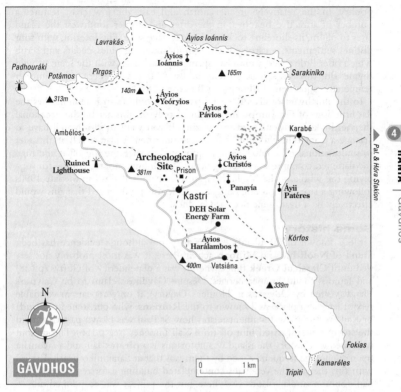

GÁVDHOS

0   1 km

N

outnumber the local population, while in **August** huge numbers of young Greek trippers add to their number – at this time the beaches, which have no real infrastructure, few toilets and no means of clearing litter, can get really unpleasant. There are also an increasing number of (mostly illegally constructed) summer houses, again mostly occupied in August. The indigenous population now comprises a mere six families (around fifty individuals), most of whom spend the summer making money from visitors and – being Cretans and Sfakians – the rest of the year feuding among themselves.

One of the reasons for the island's resurgence in popularity amongst Greeks was the publicity it received when it was discovered that several members of the November 17th terrorist group (finally broken up in 2003) had hideouts here. More obvious signs of change are the development of a huge new concrete harbour – together with a port police office and a new lighthouse – the asphalting of many island roads, and the completion of an **electricity** generating station. To date very few places have been connected to the electricity, however, because they have either been built illegally or can't prove their ownership of the land. Meanwhile, they continue to rely on diesel generators.

Kastrí serves as the island's "capital" but would hardly pass for a hamlet anywhere else, and the other villages are even more desolate clusters of bleak, stone-built dwellings surrounded by scrubland grazed by sheep, goats and poultry. In the relatively greener north and east, the low coast features a number of attractive **beaches**; in the drier and stonier southwest the island rises to 384m, its shoreline rocky and barely accessible. The interior, with four distinct settlements, is carpeted with ground-hugging pines, cedars and scrub which offer little shade, and in late spring the air is rich with the scent of wild thyme. But this can still be a pretty inhospitable environment, with summer temperatures frequently climbing well beyond 38°C.

To the northwest of Gávdhos (and passed en route from Paleohóra) lies the flat little islet of **Gavdhopoúlo**, inhabited only in summer by the occasional shepherd taking advantage of the grazing. If you want to visit, you'll have to arrange a **boat trip** with one of the local fishermen. A plan to sell off this islet to multinational oil companies who proposed to slice the top off it and turn the flattened core into a bunkering depot – with huge storage tanks – for supplying the whole of the Mediterranean was finally killed off in the late 1990s following a storm of protests, and after ecologists pronounced that this would effectively be a death sentence for Gávdhos.

Some history

Little is known of the island's early history and although evidence has been found of **Neolithic** and **Minoan** activity here, it was most probably not settled until **Classical Greek** times when it was a dependency of Górtys (p.138) and famous for its juniper berries. Despite Gávdhos's claim to be Calypso's island (visited by Odysseus in Homer's *Odyssey*), it only appears in verifiable record later as a place well known to the **Romans**, who christened it Clauda or Kaudos: the New Testament relates how St Paul was blown past Clauda in the storm which carried him off from Kalí Liménes (see p.156). Throughout its subsequent history the island was notorious as a **pirates'** lair and a favourite open anchorage frequently used by them was that at Sarakiníko beach. To deal with this menace the Venetians contemplated building a fortress here as they had done on similar islands elsewhere, but the project was abandoned due to the cost and time it would take to complete. In its more modern history the island was used by dictatorial governments as a place of **exile** for political opponents.

Since ancient times depopulation here has been acute and constant. In the Middle Ages, Gávdhos is said to have had eight thousand residents and had a bishop of its own: even in 1914 there was a population of 1400. Given the isolation and the stark severity of island life the drain is hardly surprising, but it has undoubtedly made conditions even harder for the few who remain year round.

Practicalities

Ferry connections to Gávdhos aren't bad in summer. There are ferries from Paleohóra via Soúyia (May–Sept Tues 8.30am, passing Soúyia 30min after departure; returns 3pm same day) and from Hóra Sfakíon (Sat and Sun from May–Oct at 10.30am; additional service on Fri June–Sept, and Thurs July–Aug; returns 4pm). Outside these months things are much less certain – there are occasional sailings all year round by the postboat taking essential supplies across (mostly from Paleohóra) but these are dependent on the weather, which is unpredictable even in high summer, and other circumstances. The only accurate information can be had on the spot. Whatever time of year, the **four-hour crossing** can be rough, so take precautions if your seaworthiness is in doubt. A **bus** meets the ferry and makes the short trip to Sarakiníkos, with a return trip from there about half an hour before the ferry departs.

There's a handful of rather spartan **accommodation** possibilities around the island, many of which you should be able to book from Paleohóra (to be sure of a place, this is probably the best plan). **Rooms** are most obviously available around the harbour at Karabé (see p.402) and at each of the main beaches, Sarakiníko and Kórfos (see p.402 & p.404). Accommodation can also be had inland at Kastrí (see p.403), although why anyone would want to stay here in high summer is a good question, and elsewhere if you ask around. If you're prepared to **camp** you can pick your spot just about anywhere, on the beaches or in any number of sheltered locations inland, though towards the end of the summer mountains of rubbish tend to rise close to the most popular places; be aware of local sensibilities and take your rubbish away. If you camp or stay in rooms **mosquitoes** can be a problem; the lack of electricity means the best protection are the pyrethrin coils – the minimarkets often run out and you'd be advised to bring your own with you.

The most obvious sign of the hardship of Gávdhos life is the paucity of **food** available. This is more of a problem in winter than summer, however, as during the season there is usually a decent supply of lamb and goat's meat (the island is famous for the quality of the latter) augmented with fish caught by local boats. With these exceptions and a few basic vegetables, almost everything else has to be imported from the mainland and there is little choice in any of the island's basic stores and not a lot more in the eating places (Karabé, Kórfos and Sarakiníko have the best options, with at least a chance of fresh fish). It makes sense to bring some supplies with you, especially if you plan to camp out: fresh bread and fruit would be a good idea. However, visitors who fail to spend anything at all – not surprisingly – irritate locals somewhat. The local *thimárisio* (thyme honey) is wonderful, and watch out for the island wine, which is extremely potent.

There is no bank or place to change money on the island and you would be well advised to bring sufficient **cash** with you for your stay. If you're in a fix, most of the tavernas should be able to change foreign currency but you'll be relying on their idea of what the exchange rate is (or was, perhaps months before). You can now hire **mopeds** here, which certainly facilitates island exploration, though be sure they give you a full tank, as there's little fuel to be had around the island – and running out of petrol in some of the more godforsaken regions doesn't bear thinking about. There are **cardphones** at Sarakiníko beach and the harbour at Karabé, but the minimarkets often run out of cards; again, buy these on Crete to bring with you.

Water is also in short supply; although new wells have been sunk, the water from many is not drinkable and as there is very little springwater and most fresh water has to be drawn from wells or collected in rainwater cisterns, much of the summer's drinking requirement is imported in the form of mineral water; check with locals before drinking from any source of water you're not sure of. Most rooms on the island now have showers and relatively modern plumbing, but don't join those thoughtless visitors who insist on contaminating the limited fresh-water supply with soap.

In **emergencies** there is a doctor in Kastrí (usually an intern opting out of military service) and there is now easy phone contact with Crete as well as cardphones. The best advice, however, is not to tempt fate – especially as an accident could mean being airlifted by army helicopter, incurring a hefty bill that your insurance may not cover. At least a few words of Greek would be extremely useful, though locals try their best with all visitors.

Around the island

As you approach Gávdhos, the harbour is hidden behind a headland, and the island looks totally uninhabited – only with the aid of binoculars might you pick out one or two isolated homes. The boat docks at **Karabé**, from where newly asphalted roads head north to **Sarakiníko** and south to **Kórfos**, whilst the island's main **road** heads west and inland from the harbour to **Kastrí**. The rough tracks that link the island's scattered settlements make ideal **walking** routes and following the more remote of these will lead you to some magnificent isolated **beaches** in the north or, in the opposite direction, the rock formation at **Tripití**, the southernmost tip of Europe.

Karabé

The tiny old port at **Karabé** is dwarfed by the new concrete construction, but is still the place to head. Lost in a drab expanse of rock and scrub, a *kafeníon* and a **taverna/rooms** place share the waterfront alongside a stubby concrete breakwater, whilst a few ramshackle houses and a church squat behind in silent support. The taverna and rooms belong to *Rooms Tsigonakis* (T 28230 41104; ❷), which offers rooms with and without bath. The taverna is a decent bet for meat and fish dishes. The nearby *Kalypso* (T 28230 42118, information at *Café Almyridha* in Paleohóra; ❸), on the hill above the harbour, also has rooms with showers (when the water's on) and will collect you at the harbour if you ring ahead.

If you want to get to one of the **beaches** the easy way it's normally possible to find a **boat** here (ask at the taverna); Kórfos beach to the south and Sarakiníko around the head to the north are the most popular destinations. If you do rent a boat – particularly to one of the more isolated beaches – make sure to take along sufficient drinking water and make equally sure the boatman understands when you want to be picked up. Otherwise you can take the island's **bus** which meets each boat and transports arrivals to the Korfós and Sarakiníko beach settlements. There's usually a great hubbub on the quayside when the ferry arrives (not much else happens here) and if you get offered rooms or have phoned ahead the proprietor will often transport you from the quayside to your accommodation – although the vehicle used may well be a tractor and trailer, a pick-up or, if you're very lucky, a minibus.

Sarakiníko

Forty minutes' stiff walk will take you north across the headland, past the pretty little church of Áyios Yeóryios, to **Sarakiníko**, one of the best of the island's beaches, shaded by scattered tamarisk trees. A broad strip of golden sand with nudist campers settled at each end, there are eight or nine very basic **tavernas** here too, their terraces often crowded in August with vacationing Athenian professionals yelling into mobile phones. Behind the beach and tavernas an anarchistic village of unplanned, mostly breeze-block summer dwellings is growing as people from Crete and the mainland use squatter's rights to stake their claims. The sanitary facilities are usually a deep hole in the ground beneath each house. Each evening the sun goes down behind the island of Crete on the horizon and the Lefká Óri are silhouetted against a crimson sky; at the same time a rumbling chorus of generators splutters to life and does not let up until the small hours. This is also a nesting beach used by the threatened **loggerhead sea turtle** (see p.262), and the development here does not augur well for the future of the beach as one of its breeding grounds. For **rooms** try *Gerti & Manolis* (T 28230 41103; ❸), which has en-suite rooms and is perhaps the beach's best place for **food**. Sarakiníko also has the island's **post office**, post box and a **cardphone** (all close to the taverna above) as well as a mini-market which stocks basic items and essentials.

A three-kilometre hike to the west of Sarakiníko, passing close to the church of Áyios Ioánnis brings you to a fine isolated **beach** of the same name, **Áyios Ioánnis**, with high dunes and plenty of shade under the cedars. This beach has become a favourite summer hangout for a permanent hippy occupation, despite (or because of) the fact that there are no facilities and little fresh water. In August it is often by far the most crowded place on the island. Try not to add to the litter problems if you decide to camp here.

Kastrí

Kastrí, the island "capital", is an hour's walk along a steadily climbing road from Karabé. When you get there, it turns out to be a ghostly sort of place where only a handful of dwellings, mangers, stables and barns cluster around a police station flying a tattered Greek flag. This and the diminutive *dhimarhío* ("town hall") nearby seem to be permanently closed, whilst in the surrounding parched and arid fields older dwellings gradually crumble away to become one with the weathered and fissured rock on which they stand. To the north-west of the village there is a minor (unfenced) archeological site from which some derive proof that the island was settled as far back as Neolithic times. And that's about it. The last bar here has long ago closed, there is no shop, and most of the time the only sign of life is the odd chicken running for cover or goats foraging in the scrub.

On the outskirts stands a substantial two-storey building where political prisoners were incarcerated between the wars in the 1930s; there have been attempts since to convert it to a hotel and a sanatorium, but currently it stands empty.

Ámbelos and Vatsianá

Climbing out of Kastrí the track heading west across the island reaches the ridgeline and divides. Close to this junction is the old island school, now redundant. The right branch leads to the sparse hamlet of **Ámbelos**, 3km north, from where there's a particularly fine view towards North Africa, a sealane ploughed constantly by enormous supertankers. On the way there you'll pass the substantial remains of a nineteenth-century **lighthouse** bombed by the Germans in the war. A track north from the village leads to the scenic isolated beaches of **Potamós** – behind which you can explore a couple of spectacular ravines – **Pírgos** and, further east, **Lavrakás**; you are totally on your own here, there are no facilities, and you'll need to take along plenty of drinking water.

Turning left at the junction beyond Kastrí leads, after 3km, to **Vatsianá**, another three-dwelling hamlet marooned in a rocky, almost lunar landscape. One great surprise in Vatsianá is that it not only has a **bar**, but a **museum**, too. The bar, incidentally, is the last in Europe before you reach Africa and even more curiously its proprietor is the island's priest, *Papás* Manolis Bikogiannakis. The *papás*'s wife María looks after the customers and will cheerfully overcharge you for drinks, postcards and her exquisite *kéik* (cake), which she bakes freshly each morning. The museum is also the work of her husband, who has assembled the usual collection of junk and relics that give museums a bad name. Here, though, it doesn't matter, as it is so gratifying to have something to visit and someone to talk to, breaking the monotony of this inhospitable and desiccated landscape.

Greek place names

ΑΓ ΜΑΡΙΝΑ	Αγ Μαρίνα	Ay. Marína
ΑΓ ΡΟΥΜΕΛΗ	Αγ Ρουμέλη	Ay. Rouméli
ΑΚΡΩΤΗΡΙ	Ακρωτήρι	Akrotíri
ΑΛΙΚΙΑΝΟΣ	Αλικιανός	Alikianós
ΑΠΤΕΡΑ	Ηπτερα	Áptera
ΑΛΜΥΡΙΔΑ	Αλμυρίδα	Almirídha
ΑΝΟΠΟΛΗ	Ανόπολη	Anópoli
ΒΑΜΟΣ	Βάμος	Vámos
ΒΡΥΣΕΣ	Βρύσες	Vrísses
ΓΑΥΔΟΣ	Γαύδος	Gávdhos
ΓΕΩΡΓΙΟΥΠΟΛΗ	Γεωργιούπολη	Yeoryióupolis
ΕΛΑΦΟΝΗΣΗ	Ελαφονήση	Elafonísi
ΕΛΟΣ	λος	Élos
ΘΕΡΙΣΟ	Θέρισο	Thériso
ΚΑΛΑΜΙ	Καλάμι	Kalámi
ΚΑΛΥΒΕΣ	Καλύβες	Kalíves
ΚΑΝΤΑΝΟΣ	Κάντανος	Kándanos
ΚΑΣΤΕΛΛΙ	Καστέλλι	Kastélli
ΚΟΛΥΜΒΑΡΙ	Κολυμβάρι	Kolimbári
ΚΟΥΡΝΑΣ	Κουρνάς	Kournás
ΛΑΚΚΟΙ	Λάκκοι	Lákki
ΛΟΥΤΡΟ	Λουτρό	Loutró
ΜΑΛΕΜΕ	Μάλεμε	Máleme
ΜΕΣΚΛΑ	Μεσκλά	Mesklá
ΜΟΥΡΝΙΕΣ	Μουρνιές	Mourniés
ΟΜΑΛΟΣ	Ομαλός	Omalós
ΠΑΛΑΙΟΧΩΡΑ	Παλαιοχώρα	Paleohóra
ΠΕΡΙΒΟΛΙΑ	Περιβόλια	Perivólia
ΠΛΑΤΑΝΟΣ	Πλάτανος	Plátanos
ΠΟΛΥΡΡΗΝΙΑ	Πολυρρηνία	Polirinía
ΡΟΔΩΠΟΣ	Ροδωπός	Rodhopós
ΣΑΜΑΡΙΑ	Σαμαριά	Samariá
ΣΟΥΓΙΑ	Σούγια	Soúyia
ΣΟΥΔΑ	Σούδα	Soúdha
ΣΤΑΥΡΟΣ	Σταυρός	Stavrós
ΣΦΑΚΙΑ	Σφακιά	Sfakiá
ΣΦΗΝΑΡΙΟ	Σφηνάριο	Sfinári
ΦΑΛΑΣΑΡΝΑ	Φαλάσαρνα	Falásarna
ΦΟΥΡΝΕΣ	Φουρνές	Fournés
ΦΡΑΓΚΟΚΑΣΤΕΛΛΟ	Φραγκοκάστελλο	Frangokástello
ΧΑΝΙΑ	Χανιά	Haniá
ΧΡΥΣΟΣΚΑΛΙΤΙΣΣΑΣ	Χρυσοσκαλίτισσας	Hrissoskalítissa
ΧΩΡΑ ΣΦΑΚΙΩΝ	Χώρα Σφακίων	Hóra Sfakíon
ΧΩΡΑΦΑΚΙΑ	Χωραφάκια	Horafákia

From Vatsianá you are in easy walking distance of Kórfos and its beach, to the east. Striking out more adventurously, the southernmost tip of a continent, Tripití, lies a mere 3km to the south.

Kórfos and Tripití

A twisting track east from Vatsianá leads to **Kórfos**, 2km away, where there's a good if pebbly beach – known locally as Yiorgo's beach, after the man who lives here with his family over the summer at the taverna *Korfos Beach*, on the hill behind. The beach itself is dotted with Robinson Crusoe–style shacks and in the small cedar wood behind it, *Wood Art* is the driftwood-constructed refuge of a couple of Greeks from the mainland who have opted for the simple life and live from selling wood carvings and wooden jewellery to the visitors.

The *Korfos Beach Taverna* (℡ 28230 42166; ❸) has a few **rooms** with showers to rent or you can camp nearby (but ask first). Nearby *Taverna Rooms Yiannis* (℡ 28230 42384; ❸) is a similar set-up closer to the beach, also with rooms with showers. Both tavernas own **boats** and will ferry guests to and from Karabé. The latter taverna also throws in free boat-trips to Tripití as a sweetener to get you to stay with them. Another possibility, 1km inland from here, is the isolated *Rooms Metoxi* (℡ 28230 42167; ❸) with en-suite rooms fronting a small pool, and with its own taverna; the proprietor will also rent you a moped in order to get around.

Easily reached by boat from Kórfos, or on a long, waymarked hike from Vatsianá, **Tripití** is the most southerly point of Europe. Doing it the harder way, it's a fairly easy downhill trek from Vatsianá (the way back up is more taxing) and you feel pretty elated when you reach the flat stretch of marshy ground before the **Kamaréles** strand. The beach here is pebbly with little shade but the water is brilliantly clear and a snorkeller's paradise, with lots of aquatic life to be seen. When you need a break, you can do what everyone else comes here to do: climb the famous **three-holed rock** and dangle your feet on the edge of a continent.

Travel details

Some services are restricted on Sundays. For the latest timetables visit KTEL's websites: ⓦ www .bus-service-crete-ktel.com, ⓦ www .crete-buses.gr and ⓦ www.ktel.org.

Buses

Haniá to: Almirídha (4 daily; 8.45am, 11am, 2.30pm & 6.30pm; 1hr); Ayía Marína (every 15min 8.30am–10pm, less frequently 6.30am–8.30am and 10pm–11.30pm; 20min); Elafonísi (daily at 9.30am; 3hr); Falásarna (3 daily; 8.30am, 11am & 3.30pm; 2hr); Hóra Sfakíon (3 daily; 8.30am, 11am & 2pm; 2hr); Iráklion (28 daily; 5.30am–10pm; 2hr 30min; (one via the old road at noon; 4hr); Kalives (8 daily; 7am–8pm; 45min); Kastélli (15 daily; 6.30am–11pm; 1hr); Kolimbári (every 30min 6.30am–11.30pm; 1hr); Limnopoulis water park (6 daily; 10.45am–6pm; 30min); Máleme (every 30min 6.30am–11.30pm; 45min); Mesklá (weekdays 6.45am & 2pm; 30min); Omalós for the Samariá Gorge (4 daily; 6.15am, 7.30am, 8.30am 2pm; 90min); Paleohóra (5 daily; 8.30am–6pm; 2hr); Plataniás (every 15min 8.30am–10pm, less frequently 6.30am–8.30am and 10pm–11.30pm;

30min); Réthimnon (28 daily; 5.30am–10pm; 1hr 15min; plus one via the old road at noon; 2hr); Skalóti for Frangokástello (1 daily; 2pm; 2hr 30min); Stavrós (via Horafákia; 6 daily; 7am–8pm; 30min); Soúyia (2 daily; 10am & 2pm; 2hr); Thériso (Mon, Wed & Fri 7.15am & 2.30pm); Vámos (5 daily; 7am–8pm; 30min); Yeráni (every 15min 8.30am –10pm, less frequently 6.30am–8.30am and 10pm–11.30pm; 40min).

Hóra Sfakíon to: Haniá (4 daily; 7am, 11am, 5.30pm & 7pm; 2hr); Plakiás (2 daily; 11am & 6pm; 1hr 30min).

Kastélli to: Elafonísi (daily; 10.30am; 1hr 30min); Élos (2 daily; 10.30am & 2pm; 1hr 30min); Falásarna (3 daily; 10am, 12.30 & 4.30pm; 30min); Haniá (16 daily; 6am–10.30pm; 1hr); Omalós (2 daily; 6am & 7am; 3hr); Soúdha (daily; at 6.30pm & 8.30pm to meet the ferries; 1hr 15min).

Paleohóra to: Haniá (5 daily; 7.15am–7pm; 2hr); Omalós, for Samariá Gorge (1 daily; 6am; 1hr 30min).

Soúdha to: Kastélli and Réthimnon/Iráklion (2 daily each way, connecting with the ferries; 1hr 15min; 1hr/2hr 15min).

Souyía to: Haniá (2 daily; 7am & 6pm; 2hr); Omalós (for Samariá Gorge; 1 daily; 7am; 1hr).

Yeoryioúpolis to: Omalós, for Samariá Gorge (2 daily; 6.30 & 7.20am; 2hr).

Ferries

Ayía Rouméli to: Loutró/Hóra Sfakíon (May–Oct at 11.30am, 3.45pm, 4.30pm, 5pm and 6pm, plus 9am June–Sept only; 30 min/1hr);
Soúyia/Paleohóra (May–Sept daily at 4.45pm; 45min/1hr 30min).
Gávdhos to: Hóra Sfakíon (May–Oct Sat & Sun; June–Sept also Fri; all at 4pm; 4hr); Paleohóra via Soúyia (May–Sept Tues at 3pm; 3hr 30min/4hr).
Hóra Sfakíon to: Gávdhos (May–Oct Sat & Sun; June–Sept also Fri; all at 10.30am; 4hr); Loutró/Ayía Rouméli (May–Oct daily at 10.30am,

1pm, 4.55pm, plus 7pm June–Sept only; 30 min/1hr).
Kastélli to: Kalamáta (1 weekly; 7hr 30min); Kíthira/Pireás (2 weekly; 3hr 30min/12hr); Yíthio (1 weekly; 6hr).
Paleohóra to: Soúyia/Ayía Rouméli (May–Sept daily at 9.45am; 45min/1hr 30min); Soúyia/Gávdhos (May–Sept Tues 8.30am; 30min/4hr).
Sóudha to: Pireás (ANEK Line daily at 8.30pm; 9hr; Blue Star daily at 11.30pm; 5hr 45min).

Flights

Haniá to: Athens (3–4 daily on Olympic, 3 daily on Aegean; 50min); Thessaloníki (3 weekly on Olympic; 1hr 15min).

Contexts

Contexts

History

The people of Crete unfortunately make more history than they can consume locally.

Saki

The discovery of the Minoan civilization has tended to overshadow every other aspect of Cretan history; indeed it would be hard for any other period to rival what was, in effect, the first truly European civilization. It was in Crete that the developed societies of the east met influences from the west and north, and here that "Western culture", as synthesized in Classical Greece and Rome, first developed.

Yet this was no accident or freak one-off: Crete's position as a meeting place of east and west, and its strategic setting in the middle of the Mediterranean, has thrust the island to the centre stage of world history more often than seems comfortable. Long before Arthur Evans arrived to unearth Knossós, and for some time after, the island's struggle for freedom, and the great powers' inactivity, was the subject of Europe-wide scandal. The battle for the island when the Turks arrived had similarly aroused worldwide interest, and represented at the time a significant change in the balance of power between Islam and Christianity. In fact from Minoan times to World War II, there has rarely been a sustained period when Crete didn't have some role to play in world affairs.

The Stone Age

Crete's first inhabitants, **Neolithic cave dwellers**, apparently reached the island around 7000 BC. They came, most probably, from Asia Minor, or less likely from Syria, Palestine or North Africa, bringing with them the basics of Stone Age culture – tools of wood, stone and bone, crude pottery and simple cloth. A possible clue to the origins of these peoples may lie in the importance of bull cults at certain centres in Neolithic Anatolia.

Development over the next three thousand years was almost imperceptibly slow, but gradually, whether through new migrations and influences or internal dynamics, advances were made. Elementary agriculture was practised, with domestic animals and basic crops. **Pottery** (the oldest samples of which were found beneath the palace at Knossós) became more sophisticated, with better-made domestic utensils and clay figurines of humans, animals and, especially, a fat mother goddess or fertility figure. Obsidian imported from the island of Mílos was used too. And though caves continued to be inhabited, simple rectangular huts of mud bricks were also built, with increasing skill and complexity as the era wore on. One of the most important of the Neolithic settlements was at Knossós, where two remarkable dwellings have been revealed below the Central Court, and there is abundant evidence that many other sites of later habitation were used at this time – Mália, Festós, Ayía Triádha, the Haniá area – as were most of the caves which later came to assume religious significance.

The Bronze Age: Minoan Crete

Minoan Crete has been the subject of intense and constant study since its emergence from myth to archeological reality at the beginning of the twentieth century. Yet there is still enormous controversy even over such fundamental details as who the Minoans were and what language they spoke. No written historical records from the time survive (or if they do, they have not yet been deciphered) so almost everything we know is deduced from physical remains, fleshed out somewhat by writings from Classical Greece, almost one thousand years after the destruction of Knossós. Nevertheless it is not hard to forge some kind of consensus from the theories about the Minoans, and this is what is set out below. Fresh discoveries may yet radically change this view.

One of the central arguments is over **dating**. The original system, conceived by Sir Arthur Evans, divided the period into Early, Middle and Late Minoan (see p.431), with each of these again divided into three sub-periods – a sequence that has become extremely complicated and cumbersome as it has been further qualified and subdivided. Arcane distinctions between the pottery styles of Early Minoan IIa and IIb have no place in a brief history and a simpler system is used here (following the archeologist Nikólaos Pláton) of four periods: **Pre-Palatial**, proto-palatial or **First Palace**, neo-palatial or **New Palace**, and **Post-Palatial**. This has the additional advantage of avoiding many of the niceties of exact dating and of uneven development across the island. However, as many archeological texts and guides, as well as numerous museums on the island use the Evans system, the approximate corresponding periods – Early Minoan (E.M.), Middle Minoan (M.M.) and Late Minoan (L.M.) – are given in brackets.

Pre-palatial: 3000–1900 BC (E.M.–M.M.I.)

Among the more important puzzles of Minoan society is its comparatively **sudden emergence**. During the centuries before 2600 BC, there were important changes on the island, and thereafter very rapid progress in almost every area of life. Villages and towns grew up where previously there had been only isolated settlements, and with them came craft specialists: potters, stonecutters, metalworkers, jewellers and weavers. Many of these new settlements were in the east and south of the island, and there was significant habitation on the coast and near natural harbours for the first time.

It seems safe to assume that these changes were wrought by a new **migration** of people from the east, who brought with them new technologies, methods of agriculture and styles of pottery, but most importantly perhaps, a knowledge of seafaring and trade. The olive and the vine – which need little tending and therefore help free a labour force – began to be produced alongside cereal crops. Copper tools replaced stone ones and were themselves later refined with the introduction of bronze. Art developed rapidly, with characteristic **Vasilikí ware** and other pottery styles, as well as gold jewellery, and stone jars of exceptional quality, based originally on Egyptian styles. Significantly, large quantities of seal stones have been found too, almost certainly the mark of a mercantile people. They were used to sign letters and documents, but especially to seal packets, boxes or doors as proof that they had not been opened: the designs – scorpions or poisonous spiders – were often meant as a further deterrent to robbery.

At the same time new methods of burial appear – tholos and chamber tombs in which riches were buried with the dead. These appear to have been communal, as, probably, was daily life, based perhaps on clan or kinship groupings.

The first palaces: 1900–1700 BC (M.M.I–M.M.II)

Shortly before 1900 BC, the first of the palaces were built, at **Knossós**, **Festós**, **Mália** and **Zákros**. They represent another significant and apparently abrupt change: a shift of power back to the centre of the island and the emergence of a much more hierarchical, ordered society. The sites of these palaces were also no accident: Festós and Mália both dominate fertile plains, whilst Zákros had a superbly sited harbour for trade with the east. Knossós, occupying a strategic position above another plain to the south and west of Iráklion, was perhaps originally as much a religious centre as a base of secular power. Certainly at this time religion took on a new importance, with the widespread use of mountain-top peak sanctuaries and caves as **cult centres**. At the same time much larger towns were growing up, especially around the palaces, and in the countryside substantial "villas" appeared.

The palaces themselves are proof of the island's great prosperity at this period, and the artefacts found within offer further evidence. Advances were made in almost every field of artistic and craft endeavour. From the First Palace era came the famous **Kamáres** ware pottery – actually two distinct styles, one eggshell-thin and delicate, the other sturdier with bold-coloured designs. The true potter's wheel (as against the turntable) was introduced for the first time, along with a simple form of hieroglyphic writing. Elaborate jewellery, seals and bronzework were also being produced.

Cretan bronze was used throughout the Mediterranean, and its production and distribution were dependent on a wide-ranging **maritime economy**. For though Crete may have produced some copper at this time, it never yielded tin, the nearest significant sources of which were as distant as modern Iran to the east, central Europe in the north, Italy, Spain, Brittany and even Britain in the west. While some claim that Minoan ships actually sailed as far afield as the Atlantic, it seems more likely that the more exotic goods were obtained through middlemen. Nevertheless, Crete controlled the trade routes in the Mediterranean, importing tin, copper, ivory, gold, silver and precious stones of every kind, exporting timber from its rich cypress forests, olive oil, wine, bronze goods and its fine pottery, especially to Egypt. Minoan colonies or trading posts were established on many Cycladic islands as well as the island of Kíthira off the Peloponnese, Rhodes and the coast of Asia Minor; a fleet of merchant vessels maintained regular trade links between these centres and, above all, with Egypt and the east.

Around 1700 BC, the palaces were destroyed for the first time, probably by earthquake, although raiders from the early Mycenaean Greek mainland may also have seized this opportunity to raid the island whilst it was temporarily defenceless; this may well account for the wealth of gold and other treasure – much of it obviously Cretan – found in the later royal shaft graves at Mycenae.

The New Palace Period: 1700–1450 BC (M.M.III–L.M.I)

Though the destruction must have been a setback, Minoan culture continued to flourish, and with the palaces reconstructed on a still grander scale the society entered its golden age. It is the new palaces which provide most of our picture of Minoan life and most of what is seen at the great sites – Knossós, Festós, Mália, Zákros – dates from this period.

The **architecture** of the new palaces was of an unprecedented sophistication: complex, multistorey structures in which the use of space and light was as luxurious as the construction materials. Grand stairways, colonnaded porticoes and courtyards, brightly frescoed walls, elaborate plumbing and drainage, and great magazines in which to store the society's accumulation of wealth, were all integral, as were workshops for the technicians and craftsmen, and areas set aside for ritual and worship.

Obviously it was only an elite which enjoyed these comforts, but conditions for the ordinary people who kept Minos and his attendants in such style appear to have improved too: towns around the palaces and at sites such as Gourniá and Palékastro were growing as well. (It was Arthur Evans who named Minoan society after the legendary King Minos, but there is little doubt that Minos was in fact the title of a dynasty of priest/kings, a word rather like "Pharaoh".)

Very little is known of how the society was organized, or indeed whether it was a single entity ruled from Knossós or simply several city-states with a common cultural heritage. However, in an intriguing reference to Crete in his *Politics*, Aristotle implied that a caste system had operated in the time of Minos. Clearly, though, it was a society in which **religion** played an important part. The great Corridor of the Procession fresco at Knossós depicted an annual delivery of tribute, apparently to a Mother Goddess; bull-leaping had a religious significance too; and in all the palaces substantial chambers were set aside for ritual purposes. Secular leaders were also religious leaders.

That Minoan society was a very open one is apparent too. There are virtually no **defences**, internal or external, at any Minoan site, and apparently the rulers felt no threat either from within or without, which has led scholars to emphasize a military strength based on seapower. As far as internal dissent goes, it seems safe to assume that the wealth of the island filtered down, to some extent at least, to all its inhabitants: the lot of a Minoan peasant may have been little different from that of a Cretan villager as little as fifty years ago.

Externally, **maritime supremacy** was further extended: objects of Cretan manufacture turn up all over the Mediterranean and have even been claimed as far afield as Britain and Scandinavia (amber from the Baltic certainly found its way to Crete). Behind their seapower the Minoans clearly felt safe, and the threat of attack or piracy was further reduced by the network of colonies or close allies throughout the Cycladic islands – Thíra most famously but also at Mílos, Náxos, Páros, Mikonós, Ándhros and Dílos – and in Rhodes, Cyprus, Syria and North Africa. Nevertheless, this appears to have remained a trading empire rather than a military one.

Cultural advances

If the New Palace period was a high point of Minoan power, it also marked the apogee of arts and crafts in the island: again, the bulk of the objects you'll admire in the museums dates from this era. The **frescoes** – startling in their freshness and vitality – are the most famous and obviously visible demonstration of this florescence. But they were just the highly visible tip of an artistic iceberg. It was in intricate small-scale work that the Minoans excelled above all. Naturalistic sculpted figures of humans and animals include the superb ivory bull-leaper, the leopard-head axe and the famous snake goddesses or priestesses, all of them on show in the Iráklion Archeological Museum. The carvings on seal stones of this era are of exceptional delicacy – a skill carried over into beautifully delicate gold jewellery. Examples of stone vessels include the bull's head rhyton from Knossós and the three black vases from Ayía Triádha, which are among the museum's most valuable possessions. And pottery broke out into an enormous variety of new shapes and design motifs, drawing inspiration especially from scenes of nature and marine life.

The other great advance was in writing. A new form of script, **Linear A**, had appeared at the end of the First Palace period, but in the new palaces its use became widespread. Still undeciphered, Linear A must record the original, unknown language of the Minoans: it seems to have been used in written form almost exclusively for administrative records – stock lists, records of transactions and tax payments. Even were it understood, therefore, it seems unlikely that the language would reveal much. The pieces which have survived were never intended as permanent records, and have been found intact only where the clay tablets used were baked solid in the fires which destroyed the palaces. It is possible that a more formal record, an abstract of the annual accounts, was kept on a more valuable but also more perishable material such as imported papyrus (the Minoans had strong trading links with Egypt) or even a paper produced from native date-palm leaves. There is evidence in the Iráklion museum of the use of ink which lends support to this proposition.

Destruction

Around 1600 BC the island again saw minor earthquake damage, though this was swiftly repaired. But in about 1450 BC came destruction on a calamitous scale: the palaces were smashed and (with the exception of Knossós itself) burned, and smaller settlements across the island were devastated. The cause of this disaster is still the most controversial of all Minoan riddles, but the most convincing theory links it with the explosion of the volcano of **Thíra** in about 1500 BC: a blast which may have been five times as powerful as that of Krakatoa. The explosion threw up great clouds of black ash and a huge tidal wave, or waves. Coastal settlements would have been directly smashed by the wave, and perhaps further burnt by the overturn of lamps lighted on a day made unnaturally dark by the clouds of ash. Blast, panic and accompanying earth tremors would have contributed to the wreck. And then, as the ash fell, it apparently coated the centre and east of the island in a poisonous blanket under which nothing could grow, or would grow again, for as much as fifty years.

Only at Knossós was there any real continuity of habitation, and here it was with **Mycenaean Greeks** in control, bringing with them new styles of art, a greater number of weapons and, above all, keeping records in a form of writing known as **Linear B**, an adaptation of Linear A used to write in an early Greek dialect. In about 1370 BC, Knossós was itself burnt, whether by rebellious Cretans, a new wave of Mycenaeans or perhaps as a result of another natural disaster on a smaller scale.

Such at least is the prevailing theory. But it has its problems – why, for example, should Festós have been burnt when it was safe from waves and blast on the south side of the island? And why should the eruption that vulcanologists now date to 1500 BC have had such a dramatic effect only fifty years later – indeed there are signs that away from the worst effects of the devastation many areas on Crete experienced comparative prosperity after it. As the debate continues, the best that can be said currently is that the volcano theory fits the available evidence better than most of its rivals. But many scholars still claim that the facts are more consistent with destruction by human rather than natural causes. The main counter-theory assumes an invasion by the

Mycenaeans, and points to some evidence that Linear B was in use at Knossós before 1450 BC. But if the Mycenaeans came to conquer, they would have gained nothing by destroying the society already flourishing on Crete; nor would they have subsequently left the former population centres deserted for a generation or more.

A third theory attempts to answer these inconsistencies, suggesting that an **internal revolt** by the populace against its rulers (possibly in the wake of the chaos caused by the Thíra eruption) could provide an explanation. This theory would fit the evidence from sites such as Mírtos Pírgos on the south coast, where a villa dominating the site was burned down whilst the surrounding settlement remained untouched. Needless to say this theory does not find favour with those who see Minoan civilization as a haven of tranquil splendour, but it does fit with the later Greek tradition of a tyrannical Minos oppressing not only his own people but those abroad as well. Further archeological investigation both on Crete and other islands in the Aegean may ultimately resolve this Minoan mystery.

Post-Palatial: 1450–1100 BC (L.M.II–L.M.III)

From their bridgehead at Knossós, the Mycenaeans gradually spread their influence across the island as it became habitable again. By the early fourteenth century BC they controlled much of Crete, and some of the earlier sites, including Gourniá, Ayía Triádha, Tílissos and Palékastro, were **reoccupied**. It is a period which is still little-known and which was written off by the early Minoan scholars almost entirely. However more recent excavations are revealing that the island remained productive, albeit in a role peripheral to the mainland.

In particular **western Crete** now came into its own, as the area least affected by the volcano. **Kydonia** became the chief city of the island, still with a considerable international trade and continuing, in its art and architecture, very much in the Minoan style. But Kydonia lies beneath modern Haniá and has never been (nor is ever likely to be) properly excavated – another reason that far less is known about this period than those which preceded it. In **central Crete** the main change was a retreat from the coasts, a sign of the island's decline in international affairs and trade, and perhaps of an increase in piracy. Even here, however, despite the presence of new influences, much of the art is recognizably Minoan. Most of the famous clay and stone *lárnakes* (sarcophagi) – which were a distinctly new method of burial – date from this final Minoan era.

More direct evidence of the survival of Crete comes in Homer's account of the **Trojan War**, when he talks of a Cretan contingent taking part under King Idomeneus (according to him, the grandson of Minos). The war and its aftermath – a period of widespread change – also affected Crete. In the north of Greece the Mycenaeans were being overrun by peoples moving down from the Balkans, in particular the **Dorians**. Around 1200 BC the relative peace was disrupted again: many sites were abandoned for the last time, others burnt. Briefly, Mycenaean influence became yet more widespread, as refugees arrived on the island. But by the end of the twelfth century BC, Minoan culture was in terminal decline, and Crete was entering into the period of confusion which engulfed most of the Greek world. Some of the original population of the island, later known as **Eteo-Cretans** (true Cretans), retreated at this time to mountain fastnesses at sites such as Présos and Karfi, where they survived, along with elements of Minoan culture and language, for almost another millennium.

Dorian and Classical Crete

By the end of the twelfth century, the bulk of the island had been taken over by the **Dorians**: there may have been an invasion, but it seems more probable that the process was a gradual one, by settlement. At any event, over the succeeding centuries the Dorians came to dominate the central lowlands, with substantial new cities such as Láto near modern Áyios Nikólaos.

Dorian Crete was not in any real sense a unified society: its cities warred with each other and there may, as well as the Dorians and Eteo-Cretans, have been other cultural groupings in the west, at Kydonia and sites such as Falásarna and Polyrínia. Nevertheless the island saw another minor **artistic renaissance**, with styles now mostly shared with the rest of the Greek world; in the making of tools and weapons, **iron** gradually came to replace bronze.

Much the most important survival of this period, however, is the celebrated **law code** from Górtys. The code (see p.134) was set down around 450 BC, but it reflects laws which had already been in force for hundreds of years: the society described is a strictly hierarchical one, clearly divided into a ruling class, free men, serfs and slaves. For the rulers, life followed a harsh, militaristic regime similar to that of Sparta: the original population, presumably, had been reduced to the level of serfs.

As mainland Greece approached its **Classical Age**, Crete advanced little. It remained a populous island, but one where a multitude of small city-states were constantly vying for power. Towns of this period are characterized by their heavy defences, and most reflected the Górtys laws (Górtys remained among the most powerful of them) in tough oligarchical or aristocratic regimes. At best, Crete was a minor player in Greek affairs, increasingly known as the den of pirates and as a valuable source of mercenaries unrivalled in guerrilla tactics. The island must have retained influence though, for it was still regarded by Classical Athenians as the source of much of their culture, and its strict institutions were admired by many philosophers. In addition, many Cretan shrines and caves show unbroken use from Minoan through to Roman times, and those associated with the birth and early life of Zeus (the Dhiktean and Idean caves especially) were important centres of pilgrimage.

The multitude of small, independent **city-states** is well illustrated by the Confederation of Oreoi, an accord formed around 300 BC between Élyros, Lissós, Hyrtakina, Tarra, Syia (modern Soúyia) and Pikílassos: six towns in a now barely populated area of the southwest. They were later joined in the Confederation by Górtys and Cyrenaica (in North Africa). Meanwhile Roman power was growing in the Mediterranean, and Crete's strategic position and turbulent reputation drew her inexorably into the struggle.

Rome and Byzantium

From the second century BC onwards, **Rome** was drawn into wars in mainland Greece, and the involvement of Cretan troops on one or often both sides became an increasing irritation. Hannibal was staying at Górtys at the time of one Roman attempt to pacify the island, around 188 BC. More than a century passed with only minor interventions, however, before Rome could turn its full attention to Crete – the last important part of the Greek world not under its sway.

In 71 BC Marcus Antonius (father of Mark Antony) attempted to invade but was heavily defeated by the Kydonians. A fresh attempt was made under **Quintus Metellus** (afterwards called Creticus) in 69 BC. This time a bridge-head was successfully established by exploiting divisions among the Cretans: Metellus was supported in his initial campaign against Kydonia by its rivals at Polyrínia. The tactic of setting Cretan against Cretan served him well, but even so it took almost three years of bitter and brutal warfare before the island was subdued in 67 BC. It was a campaign marked by infighting not only among the Cretans – Górtys was among those to take Metellus's side – but also between Romans, with further forces sent from Rome in an unsuccessful bid to curb Metellus's excesses and his growing power.

With the conquest complete, peace came quickly and was barely disturbed even in the turbulent years of Julius Caesar's rise and fall. Perhaps this was in part because there was little immediate change in local administration, which was simply placed under Roman supervision. At the same time, the end of the civil wars brought much greater prosperity: Crete was combined with Cyrenaica (in North Africa) as a single province whose capital was at **Górtys**, and though there was little contact between the two halves of the province, both were important sources of grain and agricultural produce for Rome.

Through the first and second centuries AD, important public works were under-taken throughout Crete: roads, aqueducts and irrigation systems, important cities at Knossós, Áptera, Lyttos and others, as well as considerable grandeur at Górtys. **Christianity** arrived with St Paul's visit around 50 AD; soon after, he appointed Titus as the island's first bishop to begin the conversion in earnest. Around 250 AD, the Holy Ten – Áyii Dhéka – were martyred at Górtys, probably during the first great persecution of the Christians initiated by the emperor Decius.

With the split of the Roman empire at the end of the fourth century, Crete found itself part of the eastern empire under **Byzantium**. The island contin-ued to prosper – as the churches which were built everywhere testify – but in international terms it was not important. Byzantine rule, here as everywhere, imposed a stiflingly ordered society, hierarchical and bureaucratic in the extreme. Of the earliest churches only traces survive, in particular of mosaic floors like those at Soúyia or Thrónos, though there are more substantial remains at Górtys, of the basilica of Áyios Títos.

Then in 824 Crete was invaded by a band of **Arabs** under Abu Hafs Omar. Essentially a piratical group who had been driven first from Spain and then Alexandria, they nevertheless managed to keep control of the island for well over a century. There was not much in the way of progress at this time – for its new masters the island was primarily a base from which to raid shipping and launch attacks on the Greek mainland and other islands – but there was a fortress founded at al-Khandak, a site which later developed into Iráklion. At the same time Górtys and other Byzantine cities were sacked and destroyed.

After several failed attempts, the Byzantine general **Nikifóras Fokás** recon-quered Crete in 961, following a siege at Khandak in which he catapulted the heads of his Arab prisoners over the walls. For a while the island revived, boosted by an influx of colonists from the mainland and from Constantinople itself, including a number of aristocratic families (the Arhontopouli) whose power survived throughout the medieval era. By now, however, the entire empire was embattled by Islam and losing out in trade to the Venetians and Genoese. Frescoed churches continued to be built, but most were small and parochial.

Ironically enough it was not Muslims who brought about the final end of Byzantine rule, but Crusaders. The **Fourth Crusade** turned on Constantinople in 1204 (at the instigation of the Venetians), sacking and burning the city. The leader of the Crusade, Prince Boniface of Montferrat, ceded Crete to the Venetians for a nominal sum.

Venetian Crete

Before Venice could claim its new territory, it had to drive out its chief commercial rivals, the **Genoese**, who had taken control in 1206 with considerable local support. By 1210 the island had been secured, though for more than a century thereafter the Genoese pursued their claim, repeatedly siding with local rebels when it looked like there was a chance of establishing a presence on the island.

The Venetians, however, were not going to surrender the prize lightly. Crete for them was a vital resource, both for the control of eastern Mediterranean trade routes which the island's ports commanded, and for the natural wealth of the agricultural land and the timber for shipbuilding. The Venetian system was rapidly and stringently imposed, with Venetian overlords, directly appointed from Venice, administering what were effectively a series of feudal fiefdoms.

It was a system designed to exploit Crete's resources as efficiently as possible, and not surprisingly it stirred up deep resentment from the beginning. There were constant **rebellions** throughout the thirteenth century, led as often as not by one or other of the aristocratic Byzantine families from an earlier wave of colonization. Certainly the wealthy had most to lose: it was their land which was confiscated to be granted to military colonists from Venice (along with the service of the people who lived on it), and their rights and privileges which were taken over by the new overlords. The rebellions were in general strictly noble affairs, ended by concessions of land or power to their Cretan leaders. But there were more fundamental resentments too. Heavy taxes and demands for feudal service were widely opposed – by the established colonists almost as much as by the natives. And the **Orthodox Church** was replaced by the Roman as the "official" religion, the senior clergy expelled and much Church property seized. Local priests and monasteries which survived helped fuel antagonism: even from this early date the monasteries were becoming known as centres of dissent.

In the mid-fourteenth century, one of the most serious revolts yet saw the Cretans and second-generation Venetian colonists fighting alongside each other, in protest at the low fixed prices for their produce, steep taxes and the continued privileges granted to "real" Venetians. Although on this occasion the revolt was suppressed particularly fiercely, the end result of this and the other rebellions was a gradual relaxation of the regime and integration of the two communities – or at least their leaders. The **Middle Ages** were perhaps the most productive years in Crete's history, with exports of corn, wine, oil and salt, the ports busy with trans-shipment business and the wooded hillsides being stripped for timber.

After 1453, and the final fall of Constantinople, Crete saw a spectacular cultural renaissance as a stream of refugees arrived from the east. **Candia** – as the island and its capital were known to the Venetians – became the centre of Byzantine art and scholarship. From this later period, and the meeting of the traditions of Byzantium and the Italian Renaissance, come the vast majority of the works of art and architecture now associated with the Venetian era. The great icon painter Dhamaskinós studied alongside El Greco in the school of Ayía Ekateríni in Iráklion; the Orthodox monasteries flourished; and in literature the island produced, among others, what is now regarded as its greatest work – the Erotókritos (see p.455).

But it was the growing **external threat** which stimulated the most enduring of the Venetian public works – the island defences. Venice's bastions in the mainland Middle East had fallen alongside Constantinople, and in 1573 Cyprus too was taken by the Turks, leaving Crete well and truly in the front line. Large-scale pirate raids had already been common: in 1538 Barbarossa had destroyed Réthimnon and almost taken Haniá, and in the 1560s there were further attacks. Across the island, cities were strengthened and the fortified islets defending the seaways were repaired and rebuilt. As the seventeenth century wore on however, Venice itself was in severe decline: Mediterranean trade was overshadowed by the New World, a business dominated by the Spanish, English and Dutch.

Finally, in 1645 an attack on an Ottoman convoy provided the excuse for an all-out **Turkish assault** on Crete. Haniá fell after a siege which cost forty thousand Turkish lives, and Réthimnon rapidly followed. By 1648 the Turks controlled the whole island except **Iráklion**, and they settled down to a long siege. For 21 years the city resisted, supplied from the sea and with moral support at least from most of Europe. The end was inevitable, though, and from the Turkish point of view there was no hurry: they controlled the island's produce, they were well supplied, and they enjoyed a fair degree of local support, having relaxed the Venetian rules – for example they allowed Orthodox bishops back into Crete. By 1669 the city was virtually reduced, and in a final effort the pope managed to persuade the French to send a small army. After a couple of fruitless sorties involving heavy losses, the French withdrew in an argument over the command. On September 5, Iráklion surrendered, leaving only the three fortified islets of Soúdha, Spinalónga and Gramvoúsa in Venetian hands, where they remained until surrendered by treaty in 1715.

Turkish Crete

It is arguable whether the **Turkish occupation** was ever as stringent or arduous as the Venetian had been, but its reputation is far worse. In part this may simply be that its memory is more recent, but Turkish rule was complicated too by the religious differences involved, and by the fact that it survived into the era of resurgent Greek nationalism and Great Power politics.

If on their arrival the Turks had been welcomed, it was not a long-lived honeymoon. Once again Crete was divided, now between powerful pashas, and once again it was regarded merely as a resource to be exploited. The Ottoman Empire was less strictly ordered than the Venetian, but it demanded no less: rather than attempt to take control of trade themselves, the Turks simply imposed crippling taxes. There were fewer colonists than in the Venetian era, and they took far less interest in their conquest so long as the money continued to come in. Very little was reinvested: outside the cities there was hardly any building at all, and roads and even defences fell into gradual disrepair. Imposition of local administration was left to local landlords and the mercenary **Janissaries** they controlled. At the local level, then, there was a further level of exploitation as these men too took their cut. Stultified by heavy taxes and tariffs, slowed by neglect, the island economy stagnated.

One way to avoid the worst of the burden was to become a Muslim and, gradually, the majority of the Christian population was converted to **Islam** – at least nominally. Conversion brought with it substantial material advantages in taxation and rights to own property, and it helped avoid the worst of the repression which inevitably followed any Christian rebellion. These Greek Muslims were not particularly religious: even among the Turks on the island, Islamic law seems to have been loosely interpreted, and many continued to worship as Christians in secret, but the mass apostasies served to further divide the island. For those who remained openly Christian the burden became increasingly heavy as there were fewer to bear it. Many took to the mountains, where Turkish authority barely reached.

As the occupation continued, the Turks strengthened their hold on the cities and the fertile plains around them, while the mountains became the strong-hold of the Christian *pallikáres*. The first major **rebellion** came in 1770, and inevitably it was centred in Sfakiá. Under **Dhaskaloyiánnis** (see p.361) the Cretans had been drawn into Great Power politics – drawn in and abandoned, for the promised aid from Russia never came. With the failure of this struggle, Sfakiá was itself brought under Turkish control for a while. But a pattern had been set, and the nineteenth century saw an almost constant struggle for independence.

At the beginning of the century the Ottoman Empire was under severe pressure on the Greek mainland, and in 1821 full-scale revolution, the **Greek War of Independence**, broke out. Part of the Turkish response was to call on the pasha of Egypt, **Mehmet Ali**, for assistance: his price was control of Crete. By 1824, in a campaign which even by Cretan standards was brutal on both sides, he had crushed the island's resistance. When in 1832 an independent Greek state was finally established with the support of Britain, France and Russia, Crete was left in the hands of the Egyptians, reverting to Turkish control within ten years.

From now on guerrilla warfare in support of union with Greece – **énosis** – was almost constant, flaring occasionally into wider revolts but mostly taking the form of incessant raids and irritations. The Cretans enjoyed widespread support, not only on the Greek mainland but throughout western Europe, and especially among expatriate Greek communities. But the Greeks alone were no match for the Ottoman armies, and the Great Powers, wary more than any-thing of each other, consistently failed to intervene. There was a major rising in 1841, bloodily suppressed, and in 1858 another which ended relatively peacefully in the recall of the Turkish governor and some minor concessions to the Christian population.

In 1866 a Cretan Assembly meeting in Sfakiá declared independence and union with Greece, and Egyptian troops were recalled to put down a further wave of revolts bolstered by Greek volunteers. Again the Egyptians proved ruthlessly effective, but this campaign ended in the explosion at **Arkádhi** (see p.252), an act of defiance which aroused Europe-wide sympathy. The Great Powers – Britain above all – still refused to involve themselves, but privately the supply of arms and volunteers to the insurgents was redoubled. From now on some kind of solution seemed inevitable, but even in 1878 the Congress of Berlin left Crete under Turkish dominion, demanding only further reforms in the government. In 1889 and 1896 there were further violent encounters, and in 1897 a Greek force landed to annexe the island. Finally, the Great Powers were forced into action, occupying Crete with an international force and dividing the island into areas controlled by the British, French, Russians and Italians.

Independence and union with Greece

The outrage which finally brought about the expulsion of Turkish troops from Crete in 1898 was a minor skirmish in Iráklion which led to the death of the British vice-consul. A **national government** was set up, still nominally under Ottoman suzerainty, with Prince George, younger son of King George of Greece, as high commissioner: under him was a joint Muslim-Christian assembly, part elected, part appointed.

Euphoria at independence was muted, however, for full union with Greece remained the goal of most Cretans. A new leader of this movement rapidly emerged – **Elefthérios Venizélos**. Born at Mourniés, outside Haniá, Venizélos had fought in the earlier independence struggles, and become a member of the Cretan Assembly and minister of justice to Prince George. Politically, however, he had little in common with his new master, and in 1905 he summoned an illegal Revolutionary Assembly at Thériso. Though the attempt to take up arms was summarily crushed, the strength of support for Venizélos was enough to force the resignation of Prince George. In 1908, the Cretan Assembly unilaterally declared *énosis* – much to the embarrassment of the Greek government. For, meantime, the "Young Turk" revolution looked set to revitalize the Ottoman Empire, and the Great Powers remained solidly opposed to anything which might upset the delicate balance of power in the Balkans.

The failure of the Greek government to act decisively in favour of Crete was one of the factors which led to the Military League of young officers forcing political reform on the mainland. With their backing, Venizélos became premier of Greece in 1910. In 1912 Greece, Serbia and Bulgaria declared war on the Ottoman Empire, making spectacular advances into Turkish territory. By the peace of 1913, Crete finally and officially became part of the Greek nation.

Though Greece was politically riven by **World War I**, and succeeding decades saw frequent, sometimes violent changes of power between Venizélist and Royalist forces, Crete was little affected. On just one further occasion did the island play a significant role in Greek affairs before the outbreak of war in 1940: in July 1938 there was a popular uprising against the dictator Metáxas and in favour of Venizélos, but it was swiftly put down.

The island was, however, hit hard by the aftermath of the disastrous Greek attempt to conquer Istanbul in pursuit of the "Great Idea" of rebuilding the Byzantine Empire. As part of the peace settlement which followed this military debacle, there was a forced **exchange of populations** in 1923: Muslims were expelled from Greece and Orthodox Christians from Turkey. In Crete many of these "Turks" were in fact Muslim Cretans, descendants of the mass apostasies of the eighteenth century. Nevertheless they left – some thirty thousand in all – and a similar number of Christian refugees from Turkey took their place.

World War II and occupation

In the winter of 1940 Italian troops invaded northern Greece, only to be thrown back across the Albanian border by the Greek army. Mussolini's humiliation, however, only served to draw the Germans into the fight, and although an Allied army was sent to Greece, the **mainland** was rapidly overrun.

The Allied campaign was marked from the start by suspicion, confusion and lack of communication between the two commands. On the Greek side Metáxas had died in January, and his successor as premier committed suicide, leaving a Cretan – **Emanuel Tsouderós** – to organize the retreat of king and government to his native island. They were rapidly followed by thousands of evacuees, including the bulk of the Allied army, a force made up in large part of Australian and New Zealand soldiers. Most of the native Cretan troops, a division of the Greek army, had been wiped out in defence of the mainland.

According to the Allied plan, Crete should by now have been an impregnable fortress. In practice, though, virtually nothing had been done to improve the island defences, there were hardly any serviceable planes or other heavy equipment, and the arriving troops found little in the way of a plan for their deployment.

On May 20, 1941 the **invasion** of the island began, as German troops poured in by glider and parachute. It was at first a horrible slaughter, with the invaders easily picked off as they drifted slowly down. Few of the first wave of parachutists reached the ground alive and many of the gliders crashed: the main German force was smashed before it ever reached the ground. In the far west, however, beyond the main battle zone, they succeeded in taking the airfield at Máleme. Whether through incompetence (as much of the literature on the Battle of Crete suggests) or breakdown of communications, no attempt to recapture the field was made until the Germans had had time to defend it and, with a secure landing site, reinforcements and equipment began to pour in. Not long before the battle, the German codes had been cracked, and the Allied commander in Crete, General Freyberg, therefore knew in detail exactly where and how the attacks would come. Whether because he didn't trust the information, however, or because of the need to keep secret the intelligence breakthrough, he did not redeploy his troops. From now on the battle, which had seemed won, was lost, and the Allied troops, already under constant air attack, found themselves outgunned on land too.

Casualties of the **Battle of Crete** were horrendous on both sides – the cemeteries are reminiscent of the burial grounds of World War I victims in northern France – and the crack German airborne division was effectively wiped out, causing a devastated Hitler to erect the monument to it which still stands outside Haniá. No one ever attempted a similar assault again. But once they were established with a secure bridgehead, the Germans advanced rapidly, and a week after the first landings the Allied army was in full retreat across the mountains towards Hóra Sfakíon, from where most were evacuated by ship to Egypt. On May 30, the battle was over, leaving behind several thousand Allied soldiers (and all the Cretans who had fought alongside them) to surrender or take to the mountains.

The resistance

One of the first tasks of **the resistance** was to get these stranded soldiers off the island, and in this they had remarkable success, organizing the fugitives into groups and arranging their collection by ship or submarine from isolated beaches on the south coast. Many were hidden and fed by monks while they waited to escape, most famously at the monastery of Préveli. In this and many other ways the German occupation closely mirrored earlier ones; opposition was constant and reprisals brutal. The north coast and the lowlands were, as in the past, easily and firmly controlled, but the mountains, and Sfakiá above all, remained the haunt of rebel and resistance groups throughout the war.

With the boats which took the battle survivors away from Crete came intelligence officers whose job it was to organize and arm the resistance; throughout the war there were a dozen or so on the island, living in mountain shelters or caves, attempting to organize parachute drops of arms and reporting on troop movements on and around the island.

How effective the sporadic efforts of the resistance were is hard to gauge: they had one spectacular success when in 1944 they kidnapped the German commander **General Kreipe** outside Iráklion, and succeeded in smuggling him across to the south coast and off the island to Egypt. Among this group were the author Patrick Leigh Fermor and Stanley Moss (whose *Ill Met by Moonlight* describes the incident in detail). The immediate result of this propaganda coup, however, was a terrible vengeance against the Cretan population, in which a string of villages around the Amári valley were destroyed and such menfolk as could be found, slaughtered. Harsh **retribution** against Cretan civilians, indeed, was the standard reaction to any success the resistance had.

At the end of 1944, the German forces withdrew to a heavily fortified perimeter around Haniá, where they held out for a final seven months before surrendering. In the rest of the island, this left a **power vacuum** which several of the resistance groups rushed to fill. Allied intelligence would no doubt claim that one of the achievements of their agents in Crete was the near-avoidance of the civil war that wracked the rest of Greece. On the mainland the organization of the resistance had been very largely the work of Greek Communists, who emerged at the end of the war as much the best organized and armed group. On Crete, groups in favour with the Allies had been the best armed and organized, and certainly in the latter stages of the war, Communist-dominated organizations had been deliberately starved of equipment. There were only a few, minor incidents of violence on the island, and these were swiftly suppressed.

Postwar and modern Crete

In avoiding the civil war, Crete was able to set about **reconstruction** some way in advance of the rest of Greece, and since 1945 it has become one of the most prosperous and productive regions of the nation. The really spectacular changes, however, date from the last thirty years, fuelled above all by a tidal wave of tourism.

Politically, postwar Crete remains deeply mistrustful of outside control, even from Athens. At the local level above all, loyalties are divided along clan and patronage lines rather than party political ones, and leaders are judged on how well they provide for their areas and their followers. This was exemplified by the Cretan **Konstantine Mitsotákis**, former head of the right-wing Néa Dhimokratía (ND) party and prime minister until his defeat by PASOK (the socialist party) in the 1993 election: many islanders respected his ability to get things done on Crete even if his party was not much liked.

Cretan politicians at the local level (there is no overall island government, only a regional **administration** controlled by appointees from Athens) continue to take an almost universal joy in standing up to central authority. In one famous incident the mayor of Iráklion organized a sit-in at the Archeological Museum to prevent artworks being taken abroad for an exhibition: fifty thousand turned out to support him, and though President Karamanlís ordered his arrest, the national government was eventually forced to back down.

Rivalries within Crete are fierce, too, most notably between Haniá, which was nominated as capital for a short period at the beginning of the century, and Iráklion, the traditional and present capital and nowadays the richer and politically more important city. This factionalism results in all sorts of anomalies and compromises: symptomatic was the rather impractical decision to spread the University of Crete across three campuses, at Iráklion, Réthimnon (which has always considered itself the most cultured town in Crete) and the autonomous polytechnic of Haniá.

In **national politics**, the island presents a more unified front as the upholder of the liberal tradition of Venizélos. After the overthrow of the Colonels in 1974, Crete voted heavily against a restoration of the monarchy and for a republican system; in the presidential election that followed, support for the right-winger Karamanlís was less than half as strong on Crete as it was in the rest of Greece. This has been an abiding pattern: PASOK has consistently polled twice as many Cretan votes as ND.

Increasingly, however, the hold of the powerful old families (Mitsotákis is a member of one such long-established clan) and traditional loyalties are crumbling as their power-broking becomes less effective. The day-to-day reality of control from Athens cannot be denied even by the most fervent Cretan nationalist. It first flexed its muscles under the Colonels, when the major tourist developments were got underway, brushing aside local qualms over planning or the desirability of mass tourism. Nowadays the EU, through directives and grants, also affects Crete in a major way – above all its farmers – through the Common Agricultural Policy. But central power – and the increasing importance of issues over personalities – perhaps manifests itself most clearly with regard to **NATO**.

Crete is home to numerous American and NATO bases, many now officially "deactivated", plus a couple of which are believed by local activists to store **nuclear weapons**. The missile base on Akrotíri is the chief suspect – its missiles (you can see them test-firing most Wednesdays) are certainly capable of carrying nuclear warheads. At Sóudha, as well as extensive naval installations, the US Marine Corps has its Mediterranean ammunition store in submarine pens. On a slightly crazier level, Crete is earmarked as a potential emergency landing site for the **space shuttle**. None of this is popular locally, and again the extent of it is a legacy of the Colonels: the Americans are singled out as the butt of most protests because of their part in the 1967 coup and their role (or lack of one) in the Cyprus affair. Crete's all-too-recent history of military occupation does nothing to make the presence of foreign troops easier.

Andreas Papandreou's PASOK, which won sixty percent of the total Cretan vote in 1985, promised that all US bases in Greece would be closed by 1988. In 1993 the base at Goúrnes shut down but there seems little prospect of all the bases closing: too much has been invested. Around a billion dollars annually in rent and military aid is hard to give up, to say nothing of the other pressures applied. Above all is the fear that if they were thrown out, both bases and aid would simply be transferred to Turkey. But at least plans for expansion seem to have been shelved: there was to have been another base on the Messará plain, possibly at Timbáki where the Germans had a big wartime base and which operates as a Greek military airport; new barracks were built but never occupied.

Into the new millennium

In the late 1980s and early 1990s Crete shared in the Greek and European economic downturn as a split developed between state employees (of which there are two-thirds more than in any other EU country) and the Mitsotákis government armed with a Thatcherite austerity programme to cut public expenditure. Strikes and mass protests ended with Néa Dhimokratía's crushing defeat in the general election of October 1993, and the return to power of a **PASOK government**, still led by the ageing and ailing Andreas Papandreou. The austerity programme of Mitsotákis was halted, but as Papandreou's health deteriorated there came no answers as to how the nation with the lowest productivity, highest inflation and largest external debt in the EU was to raise its living standards, a major election promise. The political crisis was compounded when the 76-year-old prime minister fell ill again at the end of 1995 and reluctantly resigned in January 1996 to be succeeded by **Kóstas Simitis**. Five months later, Papandreou was dead; his demise was described by the Greek press as the end of the reign of the dinosaurs – the geriatric politicians who had ruled Greece since the end of the Colonels' regime.

The rather dull technocrat Simitis (nicknamed "the book-keeper" because of his obsession with financial minutiae) surprised many by leading PASOK to another victory in the general election of 1996. Fuelled by a desire to take Greece into the EU mainstream, in the years after becoming premier Simitis attempted to overturn the "gravy train" politics of Papandreou to make another assault on the bloated public sector in order to meet the Maastricht criteria for monetary union. This goal was successfully achieved in 1999 when – after initial reluctance due to the state of the Greek economy – the European Central Bank allowed Greece to be included among the first wave of countries adopting a **single currency**, and the drachma was replaced by the **euro** in 2002. Simitis's fortunes had also been given a boost when, in late 1997, the IOC awarded the **2004 Olympic Games** to Athens and Greece. As a result, enormous funds flooded into the country and some of the EU's biggest infrastructure projects got under way, which are set to catapult much of the country's transportation system straight from the nineteenth into the twenty-first century, with new railways, roads and airports such as the one at Sitía in eastern Crete.

Riding this wave, Simitis won another **election** victory in the spring of 2000, although by an even narrower margin than his earlier victory of 1996. It was the tightest race since the restoration of democracy in 1974, with a majority of a mere 11,000 votes nationwide separating Simitis's PASOK and the conservative Néa Dhimokratía. Despite the narrow victory in an election that PASOK had been expected to lose, Simitis claimed that the poll victory was an endorsement of his pro-European modernizing policies and the drive towards a rapprochement with Turkey.

Simitis maintained the country on a relatively even keel following his election victory but angered PASOK's paymasters, the unions, with a programme to hit at restrictive practices and a reform of the pensions system. When, under pressure, he watered down these proposals he caught flak from a business lobby convinced state finances were again about to career out of control. During 2003 a general malaise on the part of the electorate fuelled by a stagnant economy and a string of corruption scandals involving the ruling party saw a rise in support for **Costas Karamanlís**, the Néa Dhimokratía leader (and nephew and namesake of the 1970s prime minister), who overtook Simitis in the opinion polls for the first time.

Smelling almost certain defeat in the spring election of 2004, PASOK's power brokers pressured Simitis into announcing that he would stand aside in favour of foreign minister **Yiorgos (George) Papandreou**, the son of the party's founder. Born in America and educated in Sweden and Britain, the open-minded, innovative and mild-mannered Papandreou was single-handedly responsible for improving relations with Turkey and impressed young voters by backing causes such as the decriminalization of cannabis. However, his obvious charisma was not enough to destabilize the Néo Dhimokratía bandwagon – in a decisive **electoral victory** ND leader Costas Karamanlís became at 47 Greece's youngest ever prime minister. The majority of poorer voters seems to have concluded that the PASOK years in power had hugely benefited fat-cat property developers, builders and professional classes who had all cashed in on the Olympics construction boom, while little of this wealth had passed down to them. Add in a grumbling discontent with low salaries, steeply rising prices (popularly attributed to the arrival of the euro) and failing public services, and the causes of PASOK's defeat become clearer. Despite a nationwide swing to the right, Crete once again stayed loyal to the PASOK cause with the socialist party polling forty percent more votes across the island than its ND rival.

The island's future

As falling prices for Crete's major agricultural products – olive oil, raisins and citrus fruits – contribute less to the island's prosperity, a greater dependence on tourism has come to the fore. But the age of mass-market **tourism** is beginning to pall as the attractions of sun, beach and cheap booze along much of the coast attract mainly younger holidaymakers, who tend to move on when prices rise. There is also a dawning realization that whilst the island has until recently been winning the "numbers war" in terms of the legions of package tourists who visit, a considerable price has been paid in terms of environmental damage as natural resources and infrastructure are stretched to breaking point in high summer.

As package tourist numbers have declined in the early years of the new millenium, efforts to build a market in **green tourism** are in their infancy, held back by an indifference to environmental concerns by politicians, farmers and a populace which has yet to realize that environmentally organized tourism – for which the island, with its extended season, picturesque landscape and rich variety of flora and fauna is an ideal location – can be enormously profitable. The creation of an autonomous Cretan tourist authority in 2000 with a brief to promote the island should also have been a force for change, but a lack of funding by Athens has left it hamstrung.

Also, for too long Cretans have adopted a part-time approach to the tourist industry – treating it as a summer sideline before returning to the farm to get in the olive and fruit harvests in the winter. This has led, barring a few commendable exceptions, to a lack of professionalism and consequent low standards in food, hotel management and tourist development, all areas where training and career possibilities are minimal or non-existent.

The island has faced up to invaders throughout its history, but the tourist invasion presents it with a new dilemma: to submerge its traditional ways in the pursuit of ever greater numbers or to try to raise the quality of its tourism and at the same time preserve Crete's unique character. In a major policy speech on this topic, the head of the EOT (Greek National Tourist Organization) encouragingly suggested that Crete should do more to cater for "the ramblers who visit the island to enjoy the paths which take them past the island's gorges, caves, mountain villages and archeological sites". More worryingly, and somewhat paradoxically, he also urged the development (with government subsidies) of marinas, conference centres with golf courses and luxury hotels with casinos. How Crete tackles these challenges in the years ahead will significantly determine the island's economic and social prosperity well into the new millennium.

Chronology

6000–2600 BC ▶ Stone Age
First inhabitants arrive from east.
Neolithic habitation of caves, and
later more settled centres at Knossós
and elsewhere.

2600–2000 BC ▶ Pre-Palatial
New migration brings more sophis-
ticated culture and settlements: first
Minoans. Settlements especially in
the larger south; Vasilikí, Móhlos and
Mírtos among the best known.

2000–1700 BC ▶ Proto-Palatial
Evidence of a more formally structured society. First palaces built at
most of the famous sites.
1700 BC Earthquake destroys the
palaces.

1700–1450 BC ▶ Neo-Palatial
Beginning of the Minoan Golden
Age. Great palaces at Knossós,
Festós, Mália and Zákros; thriving
towns at Gourniá and Palékastro.
Most of the Minoan remains date
from this era.
1450 BC Final destruction of the
palaces.

1450–1100 BC ▶ Post-Palatial
Gradual revival under Mycenaean
influence. Many earlier sites reoccupied. Kydonia the island's chief city.
Eteo-Cretans keep Minoan culture
alive at Présos and Karfí. Mycenaean
control giving way to Dorian.

1100–67 BC ▶ Dorian and Classical
Island divided between rival groups,
gradually emerging as constantly
warring city-states. Dozens of small
towns: Láto, Falásarna, along the
south coast, Knossós and Górtys.
300 BC Cities on south coast form
Confederation of Oreoi.
71 BC Failed Roman invasion.
69–67 BC Romans subjugate the
island.

67 BC–395 AD ▶ Roman
Górtys the chief Roman city. Others
include Lyttos, Áptera, Knossós.
Public works across the island.
395 AD Empire split.

395–824 ▶ Byzantine
Crete ruled from Byzantium.
Traces of early churches at Górtys,
Soúyia, Thrónos.
824 Arab invasion

824–961 ▶ Arab
Górtys sacked; al-Khandak, later
Iráklion, the Arab base.
961 Liberation by Nikifóras Fokás.

961–1204 ▶ Byzantine
Small churches built throughout
Crete.
1204 Fourth Crusade, Byzantium
sacked, Crete sold to Venice.

1204–1669 ▶ Venetian
Very extensive building. Early
remains are mostly in the form of
churches and monasteries; later
works include the shape of most
major towns and defences all over
the island: eg at Iráklion, Réthimnon
and Haniá; castles include
Frangokástello and the fortified
islets.
1453 Fall of Constantinople, renaissance of Byzantine art on Crete.
1645 Turks capture Haniá.
1669 Iráklion surrenders.

1669–1898 ▶ Turkish
Mosques and fountains in the cities,
especially Haniá and Réthimnon,
but few public works undertaken in
the rest of the island.
1770 Revolt of Dhaskaloyiánnis.
1821 Greek War of Independence.
1866 Explosion at Arkádhi.
1897 Great Powers occupy Crete.
1898 Independence under Prince
George.

1898–1913 ▶ Independence
1905 Revolutionary Assembly at Thériso, prince abdicates.
1908 Crete declares *énosis*.
1913 Union of Greece and Crete formally declared.

1913–present day ▶ Modern Crete
1941 German invasion.
1945 Liberation.
1960s Tourist boom starts.
1967–74 Dictatorship of the Colonels.

1986 Greece becomes full member of the EU.
1999 Greece joins eleven other EU states in creating the European Economic and Monetary Union (EMU) and a single currency, the euro.
2001 The drachma is replaced by the euro as Greece's official currency.
2004 Athens stages Olympic Games. Some events held in Crete.

The discovery of Bronze Age Crete

T he story of the discovery of Bronze Age Crete – dominated by two larger-than-life characters in Heinrich Schliemann and Arthur Evans – is almost as fascinating as that of the Minoans themselves. Long before the appearance of these two giants, however, others had taken soundings and laid the foundations for their discoveries.

Already ancient in antiquity, Crete had disappeared into the mists of Greek mythology and Homeric legend, and it was only during the Venetian period that curiosity about the island's illustrious past was reawoken. In 1422 a Florentine monk, **Buondelmonte**, visited Crete and reported that he had seen over two thousand columns and statues at Górtys. More monuments and inscriptions were recorded by **Honorio de Belli** in 1596. In 1675, the Dutchman **Johann Meursius**, in his book *Creta*, sifted through the Classical references relating to the island.

In 1717 a French explorer and botanist, **Joseph Tournefort**, described Crete in his *Voyage au Levant*; the English navigator **Richard Pococke** also took an interest, documenting his findings in the second volume of his *Description of the East* published in 1745. But these were largely superficial observations, and early in the nineteenth century it fell to another Dutchman, **Karl Hoeck** (who never actually visited the island), to write the first scholarly account of ancient Crete.

The nineteenth century: travellers and tradition

A more genuinely first-hand record, and the best description of Crete's monuments and sites so far, was provided by Cambridge scholar **Robert Pashley** who, in the early 1830s, travelled extensively throughout the island; it must have been a rugged journey. Pashley allied a Classical education with a keen eye, and had an uncanny knack for identifying ancient sites, written up in his entertaining *Travels in Crete* (1837). A century later, Pendlebury, the eminent British archeologist, paid Pashley fulsome tribute when he credited the traveller-scholar with identifying most of the important Cretan sites, including Knossós.

It was probably as well for those who were to come after him that it never occurred to Pashley to take up the spade. That he came near to doing so is borne out by his prophetic comments on Knossós: "The mythological celebrity and historical importance of Cnossus, demand a more careful and minute attention than can be bestowed on them in a mere book of travels."

During the years 1851–53 **Captain Spratt** (later Admiral) surveyed the Cretan coastline for the British admiralty. Taking an interest in the island's archeological remains, Spratt imperiously shipped quite a few of these back to the British Museum – often against the wishes of the local population. In an attempt to move a stone sarcophagus on board ship at Ierápetra he describes how one of his officers had to sleep in the sculptured coffin on the beach overnight "…to prevent it being injured wantonly or by local enemies (there were a party there who were opposed to our removal of the relic)… yet it did not wholly escape mischief, for some wanton hand destroyed what remained of the face of Hector."

Spratt also studied the island's natural history and geology, and it was the latter pursuit which earned him a footnote in Cretan archeology. His work for the British navy enabled him to demonstrate that, as a result of a geological convulsion in the sixth century AD, the whole island had been tilted upwards at its western end by as much as 8m, while the eastern end had sunk down. Spratt was probably wrong about the cause, but his observations remain valid, the tilting being clearly evident in the marshy swamps at the eastern site of Zákros.

The age of Schliemann

None of these early visitors to Crete, however, was concerned with pre-Classical history. The discovery of the great Bronze Age Minoan civilization was the almost single-handed achievement of Arthur Evans.

An important clue had been found as early as 1878. Digging at Knossós, a Cretan merchant, with the appropriate name of **Minos Kalokairinos**, had uncovered a number of large storage jars mixed in with Mycenaean pottery fragments – something that was to confuse later investigators. This find attracted the attention of **Heinrich Schliemann**, who had already excited world interest by his excavation of ancient **Troy** in northwest Turkey, followed by the fortresses at **Mycenae** and **Tiryns** in the Greek Peloponnese. The son of a poor German pastor who filled his head with the fabulous tales of Homeric Greece, Schliemann left school without completing his studies, to set up in business. In the course of a highly successful commercial career in which he amassed a fortune based on military contracts in the Crimean war and participation in the California gold rush, Schliemann never lost sight of the goal that he had set himself as a boy: to prove that the world of Homer was not mere myth as the majority of scholars then believed, and to discover the fabulous places mentioned in the *Iliad* and the *Odyssey*.

When he finally embarked on this quest in his late forties, Schliemann taught himself Latin and Greek which he used to dissect his Homer before setting out for Turkey and then Greece. To the chagrin of the professional classicists, he was later to claim that it was a thorough reading of Homer which had led him to his discoveries. In fact, Schliemann became so besotted with his Hellenic vision that he not only took a Greek wife, but did so after a public competition in which the celebrated archeologist offered his hand in marriage to the first Greek girl who was able to render a faultless recitation of the entire *Iliad* from memory. Given Schliemann's luck it was inevitable that the first woman to achieve this feat was also an outstanding beauty; **Sofia Schliemann** became as enthusiastic as her husband in the pursuit of Greece's Bronze Age past.

Schliemann arrived in Crete in 1887, made a visit to the site at Knossós, and became convinced that a substantial palace, equivalent to those he had discovered on the mainland, lay waiting to be unearthed. But Crete was still under the subjection of Turkey, and the authorities were often indolent and obstructive. In addition, when he attempted to negotiate the purchase of some land at Knossós, the Turkish owners proved impossible to deal with and finally, with his patience exhausted and his health declining, Schliemann departed. A chill, caught after an ear operation in Naples, led to his sudden death in 1890. It was this twist of fortune which was destined to make Arthur Evans the discoverer of Knossós and Minoan Crete.

The first excavations

Meanwhile, others had also begun to take an interest in the island's past. During the twilight period of Turkish rule there was some relaxation of the iron grip, and the sultan gave permission to a Cretan archeologist, **Joseph Hatzidhákis**, to set up the **Cretan Archeological Society**, the forerunner of the Iráklion Archeological Museum. In 1884 an Italian scholar arrived in Crete, became friends with Hatzidhákis, and the two men began to search for ancient sites.

The scholar was **Federico Halbherr**, whose name was also destined to become prominent in Cretan archeology. It was on one of their expeditions in 1885 that the first recorded discovery of Bronze Age artefacts was made at the **Psihró Cave** above the Lasíthi plateau. The following year the chance unearthing of a tomb near **Festós** gave Halbherr the idea that there was probably a settlement nearby. Preliminary excavations revealed substantial buildings as well as prehistoric pottery, but the political turmoil leading up to the end of Turkish rule postponed further progress.

Another important clue to what was to come had also been found on the volcanic island of **Thíra** in the 1860s. During quarrying operations for the enormous amounts of pumice needed to make cement for the construction of the Suez Canal, a buried settlement was revealed. Here whole rooms had been preserved intact, their walls covered with remarkable fresco paintings. Although it is now understood to be a colony or outpost of Minoan civilization, this was long before any comparable Minoan remains had been discovered on Crete itself.

Arthur Evans

In 1882 a meeting occurred at one of Athens' most elegant mansions which was to have an enormous importance for Cretan archeology. The host was the famous archeologist Heinrich Schliemann, his guest a young scholar and journalist – **Arthur Evans**. Born in 1851, the son of a wealthy and distinguished numismatist, Evans's upbringing could hardly have differed more from that of the self-made German businessman. Educated at Harrow and then Oxford, Evans was always to have the time and the financial security to pursue his interests wherever they might lead him.

Schliemann was digging again at Troy and regaled his guest with the story of his excavations both there and at Mycenae. But Evans displayed more interest in Schliemann's extensive collection of ancient artefacts, particularly some **engraved seals** bearing an octopus design which he felt must be of Aegean, possibly Cretan, origin. Schliemann then announced to Evans that his next project was to be the excavation of another Mycenaean fortress at Tiryns, following which he would dig at the site in Crete from where, as Homer put it in the *Iliad*, "came forth the men from Knossós". Little can he have realized the frustration of this goal that lay ahead, or that his attentive guest would himself be the recipient of this great archeological prize.

For the time being Evans returned to England to take up a post as keeper of the Ashmolean Museum at Oxford, although he continued to pay visits to the Balkans and Greece. Evans's studies during this period, allied to the discovery of more seal stones bearing **pre-alphabetical writing**, led him to the proposition that Crete had been an important centre of Mycenaean culture, possibly even its birthplace. When, in 1893, a great hoard of **painted pottery** was discovered by Italian archeologists at the **Kamáres Cave** on Mount Ida (Psilorítis), Evans's mind was made up: he would visit Crete to search for more seal stones and, if circumstances allowed, make a fresh attempt to carry out the excavations at Knossós which had been denied to Schliemann.

Evans arrived in Crete for the first time on March 15, 1894. Typically, in spite of an horrendously rough voyage from Pireás lasting 24 hours, no sooner had he set foot on the island than, he recorded in his diary, he toured the Candia bazaar and purchased "twenty-two early Cretan stones at about one and a half piastres apiece". Evans had started out as he meant to continue and, once the initial obstacles had been overcome, the pace was hardly to slacken over the next thirty years.

With the assistance of **Joseph Hatzidhákis**, now curator as well as president of the Cretan Archeological Society, Evans began to negotiate for the purchase of the land at Knossós with its Turkish owners. He became bogged down in the same protracted wrangles that had forced Schliemann to despair. But Evans was a man who usually got what he wanted. Even so it took five years, some valiant efforts from Hatzidhákis and a great stroke of luck in the lifting in 1898 of the Turkish yoke which had burdened Crete for 230 years. Evans, possessing a liberal political outlook, had worked with Hatzidhákis to raise funds in Britain and Crete for the victims of the insurrections during this period. Finally the major obstacle to starting excavations at Knossós had been removed.

Knossós: the early years

In 1899 the new government changed the law and most of the restrictions on foreign excavators were cleared away. Evans's purchase of the land at **Knossós** went through and work started on March 23, 1900; interestingly for the future, the team that Evans assembled for the dig included an architect, **Theodore Fyfe**, from the British School at Athens. As the excavations progressed Evans soon realized that he was dealing with a site far older than the Roman, Greek or even Mycenaean periods. Then out of the earth came **frescoes, pottery** and what came to be known as **Linear B** tablets bearing the ancient Minoan script. On April 10 the Throne Room was discovered with its elegant **gypsum throne** – named at first the "throne of Ariadne" by Evans who thought it too dainty to hold the manly posterior of Minos himself – flanked by stone benches and frescoed walls.

During the first five years of the excavations, in which most of the palace was revealed, Evans made a number of innovations. In his magisterial style he named the new civilization **Minoan** after the legendary Cretan king. He then proceeded to delineate his division of the island's Bronze Age into Early, Middle and Late Minoan based on pottery styles found at Knossós: **Early Minoan** 3000–2000 BC; **Middle Minoan I & II** 2000–1700 BC; **Middle Minoan III & Late Minoan I & II** 1700–1400 BC; and **Late Minoan III** 1400–1100 BC. In spite of problems later encountered with this system – for example, not all contemporary sites went through the same artistic developments in similar timescales – Evans's system remains the one used by archeologists and scholars, if only because no one has yet bettered it.

Restoration and controversy

Another of Evans's early decisions was to prove far more controversial: he determined that he would not only reveal the palace of Minos but that he would also **restore** large parts of it (he insisted on the word "reconstitute") to the splendour prior to its final destruction around 1400 BC. That Evans was able autocratically to decide this rested on his personal ownership of one of the major sites of antiquity – something that would be unthinkable today. "I must have sole control of what I am personally undertaking... my way may not be the best but it is the only way I can work," he wrote revealingly to his father.

What Evans had now embarked upon was one of the most expensive enterprises in the history of archeology, and in the early years funds were often stretched. But fortunately or otherwise for Knossós – depending on your viewpoint – two large legacies fell into Evans's lap eight years into the mammoth task, as a result of the deaths of both his father and his uncle (John Dickinson, the paper millionaire) within months of each other in 1908. Evans's plans for Knossós, destined to last for a further 23 years, were now financially secure.

With the assistance of architects Theodore Fyfe and later **Piet de Jong**, Evans first roofed the Throne Room and then reconstructed the **grand staircase**, replacing the **tapered columns** with his speculative concrete reconstructions (none of the wooden originals was ever found). Two Swiss artists then began to repaint the reconstructed walls with copies of the **frescoes** now in the Iráklion Archeological Museum. In 1930 the almost entirely conjectural upper storey (or **Piano Nobile** as Evans fancifully termed it) was added, using reinforced concrete. Next, the **Central Court** was extensively restored as the archeological site became a building site. Evans attempted to deflect criticism of his methods as he imposed his own grand design on the work of architects and artists by saying that he wanted to re-create the "spirit" of the palace structure and decor rather than create a literal reconstruction. This was where many scholars parted company with him. Pendlebury, who was to be Evans's successor at Knossós (see pp.101–107), put aside earlier reservations and defended Evans in a guidebook to the site, stating that "without restoration the Palace would be a meaningless heap of ruins". Others furiously disagreed, and the debate is no less heated today. One thing, however, is certain: no professional archeologist would be allowed or would expect to carry out such a work again.

In his views on Minoan scholarship Evans could be equally autocratic and blinkered. When **Alan Wace**, director of the British School at Athens, excavated a number of tombs on the site of Mycenae in the Greek Peloponnese in the early 1920s, his findings led him to conclude that Mycenae had not only been a culture independent of that of Crete – Evans stated that it had been a colony of Crete ruled by Cretan overlords – but that in the later period Mycenaeans had been in control at Knossós. For Evans this was heresy, and he used his considerable influence to attack Wace, get him sacked and stop him carrying out any further work at Mycenae. Evans went to his grave believing he was right, but in the light of the decipherment of Linear B and later investigation, it is Wace's views that are generally accepted today.

The end of an era

During the long periods that Evans spent working at Knossós, he lived in some style at the villa he had constructed for himself overlooking the palace site. The **Villa Ariadne**, as he typically named it, became the focus of scholarly life of a slightly stuffy Victorian kind. Evans revelled in the stream of distinguished visitors to Knossós, who were met at the harbour by his chauffeur-driven limousine and then plied with French champagne following a guided tour of the site. His relationship with the Greeks, not to say the native Cretans, seems to have been scratchy by comparison. A crusty, aloof man by nature, he seems never to have been able to relax with them and certainly would never be seen around a table at the *kafenío*, as later Pendlebury was. Evans's lack of fluency in modern Greek – in spite of the time he spent on the island – was also taken by many as a sign of his disdain for the degenerate latter-day occupants of such ancient lands.

In 1924 Evans donated the Knossós site and the Villa Ariadne to the British School at Athens – it was only in 1952 that the site was to become the property of the Greek government – and in the early 1930s, approaching his eightieth year, he handed over the reins at Knossós to a young English archeologist, **John Pendlebury**, and retired to his home near Oxford to complete the final volumes of his monumental work *The Palace of Minos*. It was the end of an era. Sir Arthur Evans (as he was now titled) paid his last visit to the site with which his name remains inextricably linked in 1935, when he attended the festivities surrounding the unveiling of his **bronze bust** in the palace grounds. He died six years later, in 1941.

Evans's contemporaries and successors

Although Evans stole the headlines for forty years, much important work was meanwhile being carried out elsewhere. Above all, Federico Halbherr (see p.430) was excavating **Festós** and later **Ayía Triádha**. In 1900, the same year that Evans began digging at Knossós, Halbherr started work on the beautifully situated palace at Festós. He soon acquired legendary status among the country people, thanks to his custom of riding around on a coal-black Arab mare. The bulk of the palace – including a dramatic **staircase** – was laid bare in three seasons of work. Although some restoration was done on the site, it was nothing resembling Evans's efforts at Knossós; in fact Halbherr and his colleagues pursued a far more rigorously scientific excavation, the first carried out on Crete. The Italian School continued its work at Festós, Ayía Triádha and Górtys throughout the century.

In the east **British teams** worked at **Zákros** (where Hogarth narrowly failed to uncover the palace) and the Minoan settlements at **Palékastro** and Présos. John Pendlebury also made a great impression in this period. A man with great affection both for Crete and the Cretans, he covered vast tracts of the island on foot in his search for evidence of ancient sites. He found countless numbers of these and made many friends along the way. Besides his work at Knossós he also excavated the late Minoan refuge at **Karfí** above the Lasíthi plateau. Pendlebury was killed in the early years of World War II, fighting alongside the Cretans during the German attack on Iráklion in 1941. Work by the British School has continued at Knossós as well as more remote sites such as the Minoan settlements at Mírtos Pírgos and Mírtos Foúrnou Korifí.

The **Americans** were also active in eastern Crete from the earliest days of exploration. A woman – in a field dominated by men – staked out her claim at **Gourniá** on the Gulf of Mirabéllo. **Harriet Boyd** (later Mrs Boyd-Hawes), a young classics scholar from Massachusetts, visited Athens in 1900 and was gripped by the excitement surrounding the archeological excavations then getting under way. She went to Crete, received the almost obligatory encouragement from Evans, and the following year set off by donkey for the east with her foreman, the Zorba-like Aristides, and his mother, her constant companions. After a number of false starts she alighted on Gourniá and to her own, and the world's, surprise, there uncovered the workers' village. The telegram she sent to the American Exploration Society, after three days' digging, says it all: "Discovered Gourniá Mycenaean site, streets, houses, pottery, bronzes, stone jars." It was, of course, a Minoan site, but the archeologists were still feeling their way back into a past much more ancient than anyone then realized.

Another skilled American archeologist working in the east was **Richard Seager**. In the early 1900s he excavated the important early Minoan settlement at **Vasilikí**, with its famous pottery, before moving on to the islands of Psíra and then **Móhlos**, where substantial settlements were found. Seager was a good friend of Evans, who attended the funeral following Seager's sudden death at Iráklion in 1925. "He was the most English American I have ever known" was Evans's quintessential epitaph. The North American contribution (now a joint venture with Greek scholars) continues at Móhlos, as well as at **Kómmos**, where Joseph Shaw is excavating an impressive Minoan port to the north of Mátala.

The **French** have also contributed some excellent work at **Lató**, **Ítanos** and especially **Mália**. After initial investigations by Joseph Hatzidhákis and during the years of World War I from 1915 on, the French School at Athens were awarded the site in 1922. Having excavated the **Minoan palace** they are now working on unearthing the extensive settlement which surrounded it.

Recent developments: Zákros

The discovery of ancient Crete continued steadily throughout the twentieth century – barring wartime interruptions – if not always as spectacularly as it began. The outstanding exception was **Nikólaos Pláton**'s excavation at **Zákros** which, from 1962 onwards, finally revealed the palace long suspected to have been there. Sixty years earlier Hogarth had missed the palace by a few yards, and in one of his treks around eastern Crete in 1938 the voracious Pendlebury, accompanied by his archeologist wife Hilda, had combed the area. "We must have been sitting on the very site – and we saw nothing," said Hilda Pendlebury later. Fittingly, one of Crete's greatest archeological prizes of all fell to a Cretan.

Prior to Hogarth and Pendlebury, Zákros had also been visited by Captain Spratt in 1852, as well as Halbherr, and Evans himself. **Hogarth** did expose parts of the surrounding settlement, with houses containing rich pottery, clay seals and bronze tools. The site then lay dormant until after World War II. Nikólaos Pláton became convinced that because of the submerged but excellent harbour – in a prime position for trade with the Near East – there had to be a palace here. With funds from the Greek Archeological Society and two wealthy American backers, he started work in 1962 where Hogarth had left off. The **unlooted palace**, never reoccupied after its destruction by fire around 1450 BC, was now revealed, together with a rich yield of artefacts, including over three thousand vases. Pláton continued to supervise the excavations at Zákros until his death in 1992, and work on uncovering the town surrounding the palace is still in progress.

In the recent excavations, Greek and Cretan archeologists have finally been able to play a more equal role than in the early days, when foreign archeological teams often treated them with patronizing high-handedness. Some, like Hatzidhákis and Marinátos, were there from the start but unable to compete with the wealthy foreigners in what was very much a private-enterprise affair. Now, with mainly state funding, Greek archeologists such as **Yannis** and **Efi Sakellarakis** (at Arhánes, Anemóspilia and the Idean Cave), **Davaras** (Móhlos, Psíra and many more), **Rethemiotakis** (Galatás), **Alexiou** (Leben), **Zois** (Vasilikí), **Tzedakis** (Arméni), **Karetsou** (Mount Yioúhtas), **Kanta** (Monastiráki) and **Tsipopoulou** (Petrás) are contributing greatly to the island's archeological discoveries. These continue to be added to as each season passes and, although it is unlikely that another Knossós will come to light, there are indications – such as those in the work continuing under **Andreakaki-Vlasaki** at **Haniá** – that many more sites, particularly in the west, lie awaiting the spade.

A once neglected area of Cretan archeology – the **post-Bronze Age**, Dorian and Roman – is also now being given more attention than ever before at sites across the island. These Minoan and post-Minoan sites today stand as a tribute not only to the dedicated archeologists who discovered and exposed them, but also to the work of the nameless thousands of Cretans who laboured with spade, trowel and barrow to uncover the past of their illustrious ancestors.

Crete in myth

Crete is intimately associated with much of ancient Greek mythology, and in particular with Zeus, who was not only brought up on the island, but according to some ancient Cretans was buried here as well. The Dhiktean Cave, a gash on the face of Mount Dhíkti which soars above the Lasíthi plateau, has most claims to be the birthplace of the greatest god in the Greek pantheon, and symbolizes the potent influence of Minoan Crete on the land to the north.

The birth of Zeus

According to the earliest accounts of the myth, **Zeus** was the third generation of rulers of the gods. The original ruler, Uranus, was overthrown by his youngest son Kronos. In order to prevent such a fate overtaking him, too, Kronos ate his first five children at birth. When she was bearing the sixth child, his wife, Rhea, took refuge in a Cretan cavern (a site much argued over, but most commonly assigned to the Dhiktean Cave; see p.166). Here Zeus was born, and in his place Rhea presented Kronos with a rock wrapped in blankets, which he duly devoured. Zeus was brought up secretly in the cave, his cries drowned by the **Kouretes**, who kept up a noisy dance with continuous clashing of shields and spears outside. The Kouretes, believed by Cretans to be the sons of the Earth Mother, were especially revered on the island as the inventors of beekeeping and honey as well as the hunting bow, and an inscription found at Palékastro suggests that they may well have a Minoan origin. The baby fed on milk from a mountain goat-nymph, Amalthea, one of whose horns he later made into a miraculous gift which a wish would fill with whatever was desired (hence the horn of plenty).

Having grown to manhood on Crete, Zeus declared war on Kronos and the Titans, a struggle which lasted ten years. Eventually, however, Zeus emerged as supreme ruler of the gods on **Mount Olympus**, and Kronos was banished to the Underworld. This myth has a precedent in Hittite texts of the second millennium BC which themselves had taken it over from the earlier Hurrians, a people who had settled in Syria and northern Mesopotamia. The Minoans passed it on to the Greeks.

The origin of the Cretans

The sexual prowess of Zeus led him into a bewildering number of affairs, one of which led to his best-known return to the island of his birth – with Europa – and the founding of the Cretan race. **Europa** was a princess, the daughter of King Phoenix (after whom Phoenicia was named), and Zeus lusted after her mightily. Approaching the shore of Phoenicia, Zeus saw her gathering flowers, and came to her in the guise of a **white bull**. Fascinated by the creature's docility Europa climbed onto its back, at which he leapt into the sea and carried her off across the sea to Crete. They landed at Mátala, travelled to Górtys (where one version has it Zeus ravished her beneath a plane tree which has never lost its leaves since) and were married at the Dhiktean Cave. One of the presents of Zeus to his bride was **Talos**, a bronze giant who strode round the island hurling boulders at approaching strangers. Jason and the Argonauts were greeted by a hail of stones from Talos when they approached Crete. Aided by their companion, the sorceress Medea, they brought about the giant's fall by piercing a vein on his ankle – his single vulnerable spot – thus allowing the *ichor*, a divine fluid which served as blood, to drain from his body.

Minos and the Minotaur

The Zeus of the Europa tale, taking the form of a **bull**, is almost certainly mixed up with earlier, native Cretan gods. The sun god of Crete also took the form of a bull, and the animal is a recurrent motif in the island's mythology.

In the story of **Minos**, a bull once again has a prominent role. Europa bore Zeus three sons – Minos, Rhadamanthys and Sarpedon – before eventually being abandoned. Later she married the king of Crete, Asterios, who adopted her children. Upon reaching manhood the three brothers quarrelled for the love of a beautiful boy named Miletos (a reflection of the mores and customs of the time). When Miletos chose Sarpedon, an enraged Minos drove him from the island. However, before boarding a ship to Asia Minor, Miletos killed King Asterios. Legend associates both Miletos and Sarpedon – who joined him in Asia Minor – with the founding of Miletus (see p.170), later an important city in Greek and Roman times.

With Sarpedon removed, Minos claimed the throne and settled upon Rhadamanthys a third of Asterios' dominions. Rhadamanthys became renowned as a law-maker, appears in some tales as ruler at Festós, and every ninth year visited Zeus's cave on Mount Dhíkti to bring back a new set of laws. So great was Rhadamanthys's fame as a lawgiver that Homer tells of how Zeus appointed him one of the three judges of the dead along with Minos and Aeachus.

Minos, meanwhile, was another ruler driven by lustful passions. He liaised with a succession of lovers including the Minoan goddess **Britomartis**, whom he chased relentlessly around the island for nine months until she threw herself into the sea off the end of the Rodhópou peninsula to escape his attentions. Rescued from drowning by the net of a fisherman, she became known as Diktynna ("of the net"), and a great temple to her was erected on the site (see p.342). Minos's wife and queen, **Pasiphae**, incensed by her rakish husband's infidelities, put a spell on the king: whenever he lay with another woman he discharged not seed but a swarm of poisonous serpents, scorpions and insects which devoured the woman's vitals. News of his affliction (which bears a striking resemblance to venereal disease) apparently got around, and one of his bedmates Prokris, daughter of the Athenian king Erechtheus, insisted that he should take a prophylactic draught before their tryst which apparently prevented her invasion by serpents and scorpions.

Earlier, when he had gained the throne of his father, Minos prayed to Poseidon (or perhaps his father Zeus) to send a bull from the sea which he could offer as a sacrifice, thus signifying the god's recognition of the justice of his claim to the throne. When the radiant bull emerged from the sea, Minos was so taken by its beauty that he determined to keep it, sacrificing in its place another from his herds. Punishment for such hubris was inevitable, and in this case the gods chose to inflame Minos's wife, Pasiphae (a moon goddess in her own right – again the bull symbolizes the sun), with intense desire for the animal. She had the brilliant inventor and craftsman **Daedalus** construct her an artificial cow, in which she hid and induced the bull to couple with her: the result was the **Minotaur**, a beast half man and half bull (probably human with a bull's head). To hide his shame, Minos had Daedalus construct the **labyrinth** in which to imprison the monster.

Theseus and Ariadne

Meanwhile Minos had waged war on Athens after Androgeous, one of his sons by Pasiphae, had gone off to that city and won every event in the Panathenaic games, only to be slain on the orders of the outraged Athenian king, Aegeus. Part of the settlement demanded by the victorious Minos was that an annual tribute of seven young men and women be provided as sport or sacrifice for the Minotaur. The third time the tribute was due, **Theseus**, the son of King Aegeus, resolved to end the slaughter and himself went as one of the victims. In Crete he met Minos's daughter **Ariadne**, who fell in love with him and resolved to help him in his task. At the instigation of the sympathetic Daedalus, she provided Theseus with a ball of thread which he could unwind and, if he succeeded in killing the Minotaur, follow to find his way out of the labyrinth.

At first everything went to plan, and Theseus killed the beast and escaped from the island with Ariadne and the others. On the way home though, things were less successful. Ariadne was abandoned on a beach in Náxos (where she was later found by the god Dionysos and carried off to Olympus). Approaching Athens, Theseus forgot to change his black sails for white – the pre-arranged signal that his mission had succeeded. Thinking his son dead, King Aegeus threw himself into the sea and drowned.

Back on Crete, Minos imprisoned Daedalus in his own labyrinth, furious at Ariadne's desertion and his part in it, and at the failure of the maze. Locked up with Daedalus was his son, **Ikarus**. They escaped by making wings of feathers – from birds devoured by the Minotaur – held together with wax. Daedalus finally reached Sicily and the protection of King Kokalos: Ikarus, though, flew too close to the sun, the wax melted and he plunged to his death in the sea. Still set on revenge, Minos tracked Daedalus down by setting a puzzle so fiendishly difficult that only he could have solved it: a large reward was promised to the first person who could pass a thread through a triton shell. When Minos eventually arrived in Sicily he posed the problem to Kokalos who said it would be easy. He then consulted secretly with Daedalus who drilled the shell at its point and tied a thread to the leg of an ant which was sent into the shell. When the insect emerged through the hole, Kokalos took the shell to show Minos. Now certain that Daedalus was hidden in the palace, Minos demanded that Kokalos hand him over. Kokalos appeared to agree to the request and offered Minos hospitality in the palace. There Minos met an undignified end when he was scalded to death in his bath by the daughters of the king, urged on by Daedalus.

The postscript to all this concerns **Zeus's death**. According to the Cretans, and reflecting the older Minoan idea of a fertility god who annually died and was reborn, Zeus was buried beneath Mount Yioúhtas near Knossós, in whose outline his recumbent profile can still be seen from the palace site. It was a purely local claim, however, and clashed with the northern Greek concept of Zeus as an immortal and all-powerful sky-god. The northern Greeks regarded the islanders' belief in a dying Zeus as blasphemy, and their contempt for the Cretan heresy gave rise to the saying "all Cretans are liars."

Wildlife

Although the south coast of Crete is closer to Libya than it is to Athens, the island's wildlife owes much more to mainland Greece than it does to Africa. This is because Crete lies at the end of the long range of drowned limestone mountains called the Hellenic arc which make up most of the Balkan peninsula, and you need to go a long way south into the Sahara before you again find mountains as high as the Cretan ones. Crete, then, has typically northern Mediterranean fauna and flora.

Islands tend to be short on wildlife because of their isolation from the main bulk of species on the mainland. Not so Crete – it's rich in flora and fauna, and provides the full range of Mediterranean habitats. In fact, there are over two thousand species of **plants** in Crete, of which over 180 are endemic to the island, making up nearly a third of the Greek flora, and about as many as in the whole of Britain. This profusion also resulted partly because Crete went relatively unscathed through the Ice Ages, and partly because botanical variety tends to increase the nearer you go to the equator. With the wealth of plant life come far more **insects** than you get further north. The survival of Cretan wildlife in all its richness and diversity has been facilitated by the fact that agriculture remains fairly "undeveloped". Much of the land is steep and rocky with only a thin capping of soil, and you'll see modern intensive agriculture only on the lowland plains – although the pressures are mounting, in the form of widespread use of chemicals, increased water abstraction, road construction and tourist development. You won't find many birds or wildflowers among the hectares of polytunnels around Timbáki, but you will in the mountains where such methods remain uneconomic.

The only feature really lacking, as elsewhere in Greece, is **trees**. The Minoan civilization was a seafaring one, so as early as the Bronze Age there was a high demand for timber for shipbuilding. Some of the lower hills were perhaps deforested four thousand years ago, a process completed by the Venetians. Today, native forests exist only in remote uplands and gorges.

Crete's chief drawback, at least if you hope to combine nature with the rest of the island's sights and life, is the pattern of its **climate**. Because it's so far south, the summers are long and dry, and that period equates to our northern winters, when many plants shut down or die, with a corresponding decline in activity from all other wildlife. Trying to see wildflowers or birds in lowland Crete in August is a bit like going out for a nature ramble in Britain or Massachusetts in January. For flowers, the best time to go is March: the season continues through to late June in the mountains, while around the coasts many plants keep flowering right through the winter.

Habitats

Rarely in Europe do you find such a wide range of habitats so tightly packed, or real "wilderness" areas so close to modern towns and resorts, as in Crete. Broadly speaking, you can divide the island into four major **habitats**: the coast; cultivated land; low hillsides less than 1000m; and mountains above 1000m. Crete is the only Greek island which is mountainous enough to have all four of these habitats.

Along the coast, sandy beaches and low rocky cliffs are the norm. Marshy river deltas or estuaries are rare (simply because Crete is a dry country and there aren't many rivers) but where you can find them, these wetland habitats are among the best places to look for birds.

Cultivated land is very variable in its wildlife interest. Huge wheatfields, or huge olive groves for that matter, have little to offer, but where the pattern is smaller in scale and more varied, it can be very good. This is especially true of the small market gardens – *perivólia* – often found on the edge of towns and villages, which are particularly good for small birds. Small hayfields can be a colourful mass of annual flowers and attendant insects in spring and early summer.

Low hillsides up to 1000m comprise much of Crete. Scrubby hillsides, loosely grazed by goats and sometimes sheep, are the most typical Mediterranean habitat, extremely rich in flowers, insects and reptiles. Botanically, they divide into two distinct types: the first is *phrígana*, the Greek word for the French *garigue*, and consists of scattered scrubby bushes, always on limestone, especially rich in aromatic herbs and wildflowers. You can often find *phrígana* by looking for beehives: Cretan beekeepers know where to find the thyme and rosemary that gives the local honey its wonderful flavour. The other hillside habitat is *maquis*, a dense, very prickly scrub with scattered trees. Of these two hillside habitats, *phrígana* is better for flowers, *maquis* for birds.

Mountains over 1000m are surprisingly common: three separate ranges go over 2000m, and they are responsible for much of the climate, creating rain and retaining it as snow for a large part of the year. The small upland plateaux amongst the mountains – Omalós or Lasíthi most famously – are a very special feature, with their own distinctive flora and fauna. Although the Cretan mountains don't as a rule have the exciting mammals of the mainland, they are very good for large and spectacular birds of prey.

Flowers

What you will see, obviously, depends on where and when you go. The best time is **spring**, which is heralded as early as January when the almond tree flowers, its petals falling like snow and carpeting the streets of small mountain villages. The season seriously gets under way in mid-February, however, in the southeast corner of the island, is at its peak during March over most of the lowlands (but continues well into April), and in the mountains comes later, starting in late April and going on through to June. In **early summer**, the spring anemones, orchids and rockroses are replaced by plants like broom and chrysanthemum; this ranges from mid-April in southern Crete to late July in the high mountains. These timings vary from year to year, too, exceptionally by as much as a month – in early April 1986 it was too hot to lie on the beach at Yeoryioúpolis at midday, but at the same time in 1987 there was snow on the beach at nearby Réthimnon.

Things are pretty much burnt out over all the lowlands from July through to the end of September, though there are still some flowers in the mountains. Once the hot summer is over, blooming starts all over again. Some of the **autumn-flowering** species, such as cyclamens and autumn crocus, flower from October in the mountains into December in the south. And by then you might as well stay on for the first of the spring bulbs in January.

Year-round, the best insurance policy is to be prepared to move up and down the hills until you find flowers – from the beginning of March to the end of

June you are almost guaranteed to find classic displays of flowers somewhere on the island, and you'll see the less spectacular but still worthwhile displays of autumn-flowering species from October to early December. If you have to go in July, August or September, then be prepared to see a restricted range, and also to go high up the mountains. The four habitats all have their own flowers, though some, of course, overlap.

On the **coast** you might find the spectacular **yellow horned poppy** growing on shingled banks, and **sea stocks** and **Virginia stocks** growing amongst the rocks behind the beach. A small pink **campion**, *Silene colorata*, is often colourfully present. Sand dunes are rare but sometimes there is a flat grazed area behind the beach; these are often good for **orchids**. **Tamarisk trees** often grow down to the shore, and there are frequent groves of Europe's largest grass, the **giant reed**, which can reach 4m high. In the autumn, look for the very large white flowers of the **sea daffodil**, as well as **autumn crocuses** on the banks behind the shore. The **sea squill** also blooms in autumn, with very tall spikes of white flowers rising from huge bulbs.

On **cultivated land** avoid large fields and plantations, but look for small hay meadows. These are often brilliant with annual "weeds" in late spring – various **chrysanthemum** species, **wild gladiolus**, **blue** and **purple vetches**, and in general a mass of colour such as you rarely see in northern Europe. This is partly because herbicides are used less, but mostly because the hot summers force plants into flowering at the same time.

The trees and shrubs on **low hillsides** are varied and beautiful, with colourful brooms flowering in early summer, preceded by bushy **rockroses** – *Cistaceae* – which are a mass of pink or white flowers in spring. Dotted amongst the shrubs is the occasional tree; the **non-deciduous plane tree** is an endemic variety, and the **Judas tree** flowers on bare wood in spring, making a blaze of pink against green hillsides which stands out for miles. Lower than the shrubs are the **aromatic herbs** – sage, rosemary, thyme and lavender – with perhaps some spiny species of **Euphorbia**. Particularly attractive is *Euphorbia acanthothamnos*, a rock-hugging species which forms low humps with small green leaves and delicate golden flowers. Because Crete is dry and hot for much of the year, you also get a high proportion of **xerophytes** – plants that are adapted to drought by having fleshy leaves and thick skins.

Below the herbs is the ground layer; peer around the edges and between the shrubs and you'll find a wealth of **orchids, anemones, grape hyacinths, irises**, and perhaps **fritillaries** if you're lucky. The orchids are extraordinary; some kinds – the Ophrys species – have especially fascinating and unusual flowers. Each Ophrys species is pollinated by a particular insect, which they attract by sight and smell: sight by having a flower which imitates the female insect and so deludes the male into "mating" with it; smell by imitating the particular sex pheromone which the insect uses. They're much smaller and altogether more dignified than the big blowsy tropical orchids you see in florists' stores.

The **irises** are appealing, too; one of them, a small blue species called *Iris sisyrinchium*, only flowers in the afternoon, and you can actually sit and watch them open at around midday. Once spring is over, these plants give way to the early summer flowering of the brooms and aromatic herbs, as well as a final fling from the annuals which sense the coming of the heat and their own death. When the heat of the summer is over, the autumn bulbs appear, with species of **crocus** and their relatives, the **colchicums** and the **sternbergias**, and finally the **autumn cyclamens** through into early December.

Mountains are good to visit later in the year. The rocky mountain **gorges** are considered to be the elite environments for plants, and house the greatest biodiversity; this is because most gorges are generally left ungrazed and undisturbed and it's often easy to find at least ten Cretan endemics without too much difficulty. The gorges are the home of many familiar garden rock plants, such as the **aubretias**, **saxifrages** and **alyssums**, as well as **dwarf bellflowers** and **anemones**. Look for dwarf **tulips** in fields on the upland plateaux in spring. The mountains are also the place to see the remaining Greek native pine **forests**, and in the woodland glades you will find **gentians**, **cyclamens** and **violets**. Above 1500m or so the forests begin to thin out, and in these upland meadows glorious **crocuses** flower almost before the snow has melted in spring – a very fine form of *Crocus seiberi* is a particularly early one. Autumn-flowering species of crocus and cyclamen should reward a visit later in the year.

Birds

More than 330 species of **birds** have been reported in Crete to date. There are a few endemic subspecies as well as some Mediterranean endemics that breed on the island. Greece has a good range of Mediterranean species plus a few very rare ones such as the **Eleanora's falcon** and the **Ruppell's warbler**, which have their European breeding strongholds in Greece, particularly on Crete. The great thing about bird-watching in Crete is that, if you pick your time right, you can see both resident and migratory species. Crete is on one of the main fly-past routes for species that have wintered in East Africa, but breed in eastern and northern Europe. They migrate every spring up the Nile valley, and then move across the eastern Mediterranean, often in huge numbers. This happens from mid-March to mid-May, depending on the species, the weather, and where you are. The return migration in autumn is less spectacular because it is less concentrated in time, but still worth watching out for.

One drawback is that until recently the "sport" of **shooting** songbirds was common, and although things have improved and the situation is much better here than in other areas of Greece and the eastern Mediterranean, the birds remain understandably cautious. Some are still caught for the cagebird trade, as you will realize from looking at the goldfinches and others hung in cages from the front of houses and apartments. Birds of prey get a rough deal, too, as witness the dusty cases of badly stuffed eagles in many tavernas and *kafenía*.

A general point about watching birds is that they're active at a pretty antisocial time – just after dawn is the peak activity time for most small birds. On a walk before breakfast you can see heaps of birds, yet you can walk the same area a few hours later and see almost nothing. Exceptions to this are water birds and wading birds, which are often visible all day, and big birds of prey, which frequently use the rising thermals of early evening to soar and gain height.

On the outskirts of towns and in the fields there are some colourful residents. Small predatory birds such as **woodchat shrikes**, **blackeared wheatears**, **kestrels** and migrating **red-footed falcons** can be seen perched on telegraph wires. The dramatic pink, black and white **hoopoe** and the striking yellow and black **golden oriole** are sometimes to be found in woodland and olive groves, and **Scops owls** (Europe's smallest owl) can often be heard calling around towns at night. They monotonously repeat a single "poo", sometimes in mournful vocal duets.

Look closely at the **swifts** and **swallows**, and you will find a few species not found in northern Europe: **crag martins** replace house martins in the **mountain gorges**, for example, and you may see the large **alpine swift**, which has a white belly. The **Sardinian warbler** dominates the rough scrubby **hillsides** – the male with a glossy black cap and an obvious red eye. These hillsides are also the home of the **chukar**, a species of partridge similar to the red-legged partridge found in Britain.

Wetlands and **coastal lagoons** are excellent for bird-spotting, especially at spring and autumn migration, although this habitat is hard to find. There's a wide variety of **herons** and **egrets**, as well as smaller waders such as the rare **avocet** and **marsh sandpiper** and **black-winged stilt**, which has ridiculously long pink legs. **Marsh harriers** are common too, drifting over the reedbeds on characteristic raised wings. Scrubby woodland around coastal wetlands is a good place to see migrating smaller birds such as **warblers**, **wagtails** and the like. They usually migrate up the coast, navigating by the stars; a thick mist or heavy cloud will force them to land, and you can sometimes see spectacular "falls" of migrants.

The mountains hold some of the most exciting birds in Crete. Smaller birds like the **blue rock thrush**, **cirl bunting** and **alpine chough** are common, and there is a good chance of seeing large and dramatic birds of prey. The **buzzards** and smaller eagles are confusingly similar, but there are also **golden eagles**, **Bonelli's eagles** and **vultures**. One very rare species of vulture, the **lammergeier** (or bearded vulture), is currently on the dramatically endangered list although it used to be more common in Crete than anywhere else in Europe; you may be lucky enough to spot one of the island's twenty-five remaining birds (only four breeding pairs) soaring above the Lasíthi or Omalós plateaux. It's a huge bird, with a wingspan of nearly three metres, and with narrower wings and a longer wedge-shaped tail than the other vulture you are likely to see, the **griffon vulture**.

Mammals

Cretan **mammals** are elusive, generally nocturnal, and very hard to see. Islands tend to have fewer species than the mainland, because mammals can't swim or fly to get there, and in this Crete is no exception, with about half the species that you could expect to see on mainland Greece. Even such common animals as the red squirrel and fox have never made it across the water, nor will you find large exciting mammals like wolves or lynxes in the mountains, as you might (although very rarely) on the mainland.

However, there are some compensations. Islands often have their own endemic species, and one in Crete is the **Cretan spiny mouse**, which is found nowhere else; if you happen to be on a rocky hillside at dusk you may see this largish mouse with very big ears and a spiny back fossicking around. The other compensation in Crete is the ancestral **wild goat** or *kri-kri*; a small population still exists in the White Mountains around the Samariá Gorge, and also on some offshore islands – but you'll be very lucky if you see one outside the zoos. Apart from those, Crete has quite a few bat species, as well as **weasels**, **badgers**, **hares**, **hedgehogs**, **field mice**, **shrews** and **beech martens**.

One recent addition to the zoological record was the remarkable rediscovery in 1996 of the **Cretan wildcat** (see p.272), long thought to be either extinct or a folktale. Only a single specimen has ever been captured and the population status of the animal is still unknown.

There are several marine mammals that can occasionally be seen in offshore waters. The critically endangered and extremely rare **Mediterranean monk**

seal breeds in a few sea caves around the island. The deep waters off the south coast of Haniá have recently become well known for a resident population of **sperm whales**. Up to two hundred individuals may feed here and some have even been spotted from the high cliffs of the coastal path. **Dolphins** – which so delighted the Minoans – can be seen all round the island but you'll be most likely to see them while on a boat or ferry.

Reptiles and amphibians

The hot, rocky terrain of Crete suits **reptiles** well, with plenty of sun to bask in and plenty of rocks to hide under, but the island's isolation has severely restricted the number of species occurring: fewer than a third of those that are found on the mainland. Identification is therefore rather easy. If you sit and watch a dry stone wall almost anywhere in the western half of the island you're bound to see the small local wall lizard, **Erhard's wall lizard**. A rustle in the rocks by the side of the road might be an **ocellated skink** – a bit like a lizard, but with a thicker body and a stubbier neck. In the bushes of the *maquis* and *phrígana* you may see the **Balkan green lizard**, a truly splendid bright green animal up to 50cm long, most of which is tail – usually seen as it runs frantically on its hind legs from one bush to another.

At night, **geckoes** replace the lizards. Geckoes are small (less than 10cm), have big eyes and round adhesive pads on their toes which enable them to walk upside down on the ceiling. Sometimes they come into houses – in which case welcome them, for they will keep down the mosquitoes and other biting insects. Crete has three out of four European species. The island is also one of only a handful of places where the **chameleon** occurs in Europe, although it is extremely rare, and there are only a couple of known specimens; this may (or may not) be attributed to its camouflage skills. It lives in bushes and low trees, and hunts by day; its colour is greenish but obviously variable.

Tortoises, sadly, don't occur in Crete, but the stripe-necked **terrapin** does. Look out for these in any freshwater habitat – Lake Kournás and the Ayía bird sanctuary for example, or even in the cistern at the Zákros palace. There are also **sea turtles** in the Mediterranean: you might be lucky and see one while you're swimming or on a boat, since they sometimes bask on the surface of the water. The one you're most likely to see is the **loggerhead turtle**, which can grow up to 1m long. Crete has important breeding populations on beaches to the west of Haniá, around Mátala, and the largest (over 350 nests) at Réthimnon, but tourism and the development associated with it are threatening their future. Each year, many turtles are injured by motorboats, their nests are destroyed by bikes and jeeps ridden on the beaches, and the newly hatched young die entangled in deckchairs and umbrellas left out at night on the sand. The turtles are easily frightened by noise and lights too, which makes them uneasy cohabitants with freelance campers and discos.

The Greek government has passed **laws** designed to protect the loggerheads, and the Sea Turtle Protection Society of Greece now operates an ambitious conservation programme but, in addition to the thoughtlessness of visitors, local economic interests tend to prefer a beach full of bodies to a sea full of turtles.

The final group of reptiles are the **snakes**, represented by four species, only one of which is poisonous – the **cat snake**. Even this is back-fanged and therefore extremely unlikely to be able to bite anything as big as a human. So you can relax a bit when strolling round the hillsides – and most snakes are very timid and easily frightened anyway. One species worth looking out for is the beautiful **leopard snake**, which is grey with red blotches edged in black. It's fond of basking on the sides of roads and paths.

Only three species of **amphibian** occur in Crete. The **green toad** is smaller than the common toad, with an obvious marbled green and grey back. The **marsh frog** is a large frog, greenish but variable in colour, and very noisy in spring. And **tree frogs** are small, live in trees, and call very loudly at night. They have a stripe down the flank, and vary in colour from bright green to golden brown, depending on where they are sitting – they can change colour like chameleons.

Insects

Insects are much neglected – which is a shame because many of them are beautiful, most lead fascinating lives, and they are numerous and easy to observe. You need to adjust your eyes to their scale to see them best: sit down for half an hour in the countryside by a bit of grazed turf, a patch of long grass or a shrubby bush, and think small. You'll be surprised at the variety of shapes and colours of insects that will slowly come into focus.

There are around a million different species of insects in the world, and even in Crete there are probably a few hundred which have yet to be scientifically described or labelled. About a third of all insect species are beetles, and these are very obvious wherever you go. You might see one of the dung beetles rolling a ball of dung along a path like the mythological Sisyphus. If you have time to look closely at bushes and small trees, you might be rewarded with a stick insect or a **praying mantis**, creatures that are rarely seen because of their excellent camouflage.

The **grasshopper** and **cricket** family are well represented, and most patches of grass will hold a few. Grasshoppers produce their chirping noise by rubbing a wing against a leg, but crickets do it by rubbing both wings together. **Cicadas**, which most people think of as a night-calling grasshopper, aren't actually related at all – they're more of a large leaf-hopper. Their continuous whirring call is one of the characteristic sounds of the Mediterranean night, and is produced by the rapid vibration of two membranes, called tymbals, on either side of their body.

Perhaps the most obvious insects are the **butterflies**, because they're large, brightly coloured and fly by day. Any time from spring through most of summer is good for butterflies, and there's a second flight of adults of many species in the autumn. Dramatic varieties in Crete include two species of **swallowtail**, easily identified by their large size, yellow and black colouring, and long spurs at the back of the hind wings. **Cleopatras** are large, brilliant yellow butterflies, related to the brimstone of northern Europe, but bigger and more colourful. Look out also for **Cretan Argus** – chocolate brown in colour and only found in the Psilorítis and Dhíkti mountain ranges, it is now thought to be increasingly threatened by human activity. One final species typical of Crete is the **eastern festoon**, an unusual butterfly with tropical colours, covered in yellow, red and black zig-zags. It flies in the spring, its caterpillars feeding on *Aristolochia* (birthwort) plants.

Sites

You don't need to go that far to see Cretan wildlife – even in Iráklion, patches of **wasteland** hold interesting and colourful flowers, and nearby Knossós is good for flowers, insects and reptiles. In general, though, people and wildlife don't go together too well, so it's best to get away from the towns and into the villages.

A good site is worth visiting at any time of the year, except in high summer when everything is burnt out anyway. It's also usually true that a good flower site will yield plenty of other wildlife, and vice versa: a wide variety of plants leads to a wide variety of insects, which in turn implies that birds and reptiles will be numerous. So you can often use a blaze of plants as an indicator for a spot that would be worth exploring.

One possible exception to this is birds. Birds are mobile and fickle, often choosing to congregate in unprepossessing places such as windswept estuaries or smelly sewage farms. Birds adapt well to small-scale agriculture, too, even though the native plants may have been out-competed by olives, artichokes or melons.

Lasíthi

The **eastern end** of Crete is the driest part, and also the part where **spring** comes first. So it would be good to base yourself here if you were planning a trip early in the year, say February. The extreme eastern coast is dry and rocky, although Váï boasts a much-photographed grove of the Cretan **date palm**, one of only two native European palm species. Further west, the scenery is dominated by the Dhíkti mountains and the big bay of Áyios Nikólaos: even close by the development here, some good sites for flowers and birds survive.

The nearest of these is **Lató**, overlooking plains of olives and fruit trees that run down to the sea. It's a mass of colour with flowers in the spring, and, in common with other ancient sites, its old walls and ruins are a perfect habitat for lizards. **Mália**, similarly, has good flowers in spring and early summer, and the added advantage of being close to seacliffs where you can find many of the typical Mediterranean seashore flowers. Between the ancient site and the shore are the remains of a marsh, which is likely to hold interesting birds, including herons, harriers and migrating small warblers. **Gourniá** is also worth a trip for its flowers: they're particularly good at all of these sites because goats are excluded. Look for anemones in the spring; although there's only one spring species, *Anemone coronaria*, it comes in a bewildering range of colours from white to purple and scarlet. An Asiatic buttercup species which grows round here (*Ranunculus asiaticus*, a common plant over much of Crete) is quite unlike the buttercups of northern Europe, being much larger and with colours including white, pink and yellow. Around the walls of Gourniá you'll also find a large yellow and white daisy, *Chrysanthemum coronarium*, a species which is attractive to butterflies.

Just north of Áyios Nikólaos is the island of **Spinalónga**, and nearby, the disused saltpans at **Eloúnda**. The island is good for flowers, and the saltpans are always worth checking out for birds, especially during spring and autumn migration time. Another good place for bird-spotting is **Bramiana reservoir** just a few kilometres to the northwest of Ierápetra. Created in 1986, over 150 bird species have now been seen there and the site is being developed, albeit slowly, with EU funding. A permanent hide along with nature trails are planned and even as it stands it is worth the detour if you are in the area.

Later in the year, the uplands of **Mount Dhíkti** and the **Lasíthi plateau** come into their own. The plateau is at 850m, so its spring flowers come later than those in the lowlands – April or early May would be a good time, with the summer flowers going on into June. The plateau itself is well cultivated, but the areas round the edge are rich in flowers, including many orchids. Try exploring a bit off the well-worn track from Psihró to the Dhiktean Cave. Here you may find two varieties in particular: *Ophrys tenthredenifera*, one of the largest and most dramatic of the insect-imitating orchids, with beautiful pink sepals and a brown lower lip fringed with pale yellow; and the butterfly orchid *Orchis papilionacea*, which has a compact spike of pink florets, each with a large lip spotted and streaked with darker pink. Keep your eyes on the skies, too, since you are close to the mountains: sightings of eagles and vultures, including lammergeiers, are always possible.

Mount Dhíkti goes up to over 2000m, and boasts most of the dramatic flowers of the Cretan mountains. Look for early-flowering crocus species on the edge of the melting snowfields in April and May, and maybe you'll find cyclamens and peonies under the mountain woodland as well. Rocky gullies amongst the mountains are rich in specially adapted plants called chasmophytes, including endemic Cretan species.

Iráklion

Although **Iráklion** is the only one of the four Cretan provinces that doesn't have a major mountain range, it includes the foothills of both the Dhíkti range to the east and the Psiloritis massif in the west.

The ancient Minoan site of **Festós** is an excellent start. The ruins are only average for wildlife, but the hills around are excellent for flowers, insects and reptiles, and the river running through Ayía Triádha is always worth checking out for birds. The site of Festós itself is also a good place to look for bird migration; since it's high up, you stand a good chance of seeing migrating birds of prey coming over the plain and up into the hills.

If you walk from the car park heading north, you find yourself on a lovely hillside. There are scrubby bushes of rockroses – *Cistus* species – and round these a wonderful display of anemones, irises, orchids and the whole panoply of Cretan spring flowers. *Anemone heldreichii*, a delicate blue and white variety, is one of Crete's 180 or so endemic species. Another plant with a very restricted distribution is *Ophrys cretica*, one of the insect-imitating orchids with distinctive white markings on its maroon lip. In spring, *Orchis italica* is the most obvious **orchid** – tall shaggy spikes of small pink florets, each looking like a small man with a cap ("man" is used advisedly here, as you will realize if you look closely at the plant!) One final flower to look out for is familiar as an annual garden flower, love-in-a-mist *Nigella arvensis*. With blooms varying from deep blue to pale pink, it's best known for its extraordinary inflated fruit, surrounded by a crown of deeply dissected bracts.

There are **butterflies** here too, including the scarce swallowtail, attracted by the nectar. Keep your eyes open, too, for Balkan green lizards in the bushes. Further on towards Ayía Triádha the river holds passage migrants including herons, terns and sandpipers – and the bushes are often full of migrating passerines, hotfoot from Africa. As always, a careful scrutiny of bushes and grasses will produce a horde of beetles, spiders and other invertebrates – with a chance of a praying mantis to brighten things up.

Réthimnon

The two areas selected in Réthimnon are both on the south coast. That doesn't mean that you should ignore the rest: three other extremely promising sites are the Nídha plateau above Anóyia, the foothills of Mount Kédhros above Spíli, and the Amári valley.

Ayía Galíni, for all its summer crowds, is a great spot in spring, with some excellent walks on the headlands and hills roundabout, small-scale hayfields and olive groves, and a riverbed with some marshy areas. In other words, a really good range of the typical Cretan lowland habitats, and all within easy walking distance.

The river flows into the east of the village. On the far side is a range of hills, worth exploring for spring flowers, and the caves and cliffs overlooking the river have breeding colonies of lesser kestrels and Alpine swifts. The small reedbeds and marshy areas around the river have warblers and nightingales, too, and there are hoopoes in the olive groves.

A series of tracks leads away to the north and along the cliffs to the west. Any of these go through typical *phrígana* habitat, in which are scattered small meadows with wild gladioli and tassel hyacinths. The latter species is related to the grape hyacinth which is often used in boring clumps by British gardeners, but is far more attractive growing wild. Look for Jerusalem sage *Phlomis fruticosa*, a downy shrub whose golden flowers are attractive to bees. Another plant that grows around here (and many other places in Crete) is the unmistakeable giant fennel, a huge plant over two metres tall. Its scientific name is *Ferula communis*, which implies that it was once used as a walking stick, and, seeing the size of the stems, you can see why. There are orchids growing on the hillsides, including a Cretan speciality that rejoices in the name of *Ophrys fuciflora maxima*; a large orchid, it has a "face" on its lower lip that looks rather like a Minoan bull.

Further along the coast to the west, **Moní Préveli** has a similar range of habitats and fewer people. Again, there is a river valley that repays exploration for migratory birds, open hillsides with flowers and aromatic herbs, and some rugged coastal scenery. If you see a small scrub warbler around here with a black cap and throat, a red eye and a white "moustache", then you may have seen Ruppell's warbler, probably the rarest warbler in Europe. The whole coastline from Préveli to Ayía Rouméli, some 75km to the west, is wild and rugged, punctuated by gorges, and a good place to look for large eagles and vultures.

Haniá

Haniá, at the western end of Crete, contains some of the wildest and least developed scenery in the whole of the Mediterranean. Yeoryioúpolis on the north coast and the famous Samariá Gorge are described in detail here – but there are lots of other opportunities.

Yeoryioúpolis has a wide range of habitats within easy reach – a marsh, a river with reedbeds, dry hillsides along the coast to the north, Crete's only freshwater lake – and an excellent beach as well. Between the main road and the sea are low sand dunes, often a good place for colourful flowers like Virginia stocks, sea stocks and the yellow horned poppy. Close to the east of the village is a marshy area, with birds like reed (and other) warblers, and marsh harriers floating overhead. There's a very pleasant walk along the River Almirós, branching up through olive groves and scrubby slopes to the hilltop village above. Here you'll find numerous small birds, attracted by unusually dense and lush woodland. Inland a bit is the small lake at **Kournás**, where a paddle round the lake may reveal stripe-necked terrapins poking their heads out of the water.

The **Samariá Gorge** is rightly famous for wildlife as well as scenery, but remember that you'll find very similar flora and fauna at Ímbros and the other less-known ravines. The best flowers and other wildlife all come in the higher reaches, where you have the marvellous combination of rocky cliffs coming down into upland woods.

Still better, if you have time, is to take more than a day over this trip and spend some time on the **Omalós plateau** before heading down. This is especially rewarding later in the year, when the plateau and the slopes around it will have spring and summer flowers long after everything is burnt out on the coast. The plateau is renowned for its mountain flowers, including the very variable *Tulipa saxatilis*, a small pink or purple tulip endemic to Crete. Other endemic species found here include Cretan dittany *Origanum dictamnus*, a low shrub with furry rounded leaves and pink flowers, regarded by locals as a medical panacea (you may be offered it as a tea) and *Daphne sericea*, an evergreen shrub, with very unusual two-tone flowers of pink and yellow. There are also rare birds and mammals – watch the sky for golden eagles, griffon vultures, lammergeiers and falcons, and the distant cliffs and surrounding mountains for wild goats.

The start of the gorge takes you down the wooden staircase through light woodland. There are rock thrushes on the cliffs – the male has a striking orange breast, blue head and white rump. Rock plants like *Aubretia* grow on the cliffs, along with *Linum arboreum*, a low perennial flax with brilliant yellow flowers. Two endemic cliff plants to watch for are the Cretan rock lettuce *Petromarula pinnata*, which looks nothing like a lettuce and isn't even related, with long spikes of deep blue flowers, and *Ebenus cretica*, a bushy pea with grey foliage and pink flowers.

Under the trees at the sides of the paths are orchids, including the handsome yellow *Orchis provincialis*, with a tight flowerhead of spiked yellow florets. Cyclamens and anemones grow here, and you may find a fritillary *Fritillaria messanensis*, with a drooping purple and green bell-shaped flower. Perhaps the most stunning flower is a white peony with huge, yellow-centred flowers: called *Paeoni clusii*, it grows in profusion around the ruined chapel about 3km down the gorge. There are more lovely flower meadows round the village of Samariá, about halfway down, but as you drop lower the cliffs tower above you until it is hard to see anything else, and once you are through the famous gates at the end, the walk is less interesting in every sense. Around the base of the cliffs at the bottom of the gorge are colonies of crag martins – a drab-looking bird, but a dramatic flier.

by Pete Raine and Stephen Roberts

Books

From Homer on, Crete has inspired an exceptionally wide range of literature, and in Níkos Kazantzákis the island has also produced one truly world-class author. Sadly, some of it is out of print, but many of the more popular titles below are widely available in Crete – although local editions tend to be shabby, and imported ones expensive.

The more specialist titles might be more easily found at a dedicated travel bookstore (some are included on p.27) or a Greek-interest bookshop: in the UK, try the Hellenic Book Service, 91 Fortess Rd, London NW5 1AG (☎020/7267 9499, ⊛www.hellenicbookservice.com) or Zeno's Greek Bookshop, 57a Nether St, North Finchley, London N12 7NP (☎020/8446 1985, ⊛www.thegreekbookshop.com). On Crete, Planet International Bookstore, junction Hándhakos and Kidonias, Iráklion (☎2810 289605, ⊛ritio@otenet.gr), is an excellent source who should stock any of those books below which are mainly sold on the island. If you phone, fax or email them, they will post books out to you immediately, trusting you to pay later.

Where separate editions exist in the UK and USA, publishers are detailed below in the form "UK publisher; US publisher". Where books are published in one country only, this follows the publisher's name. "UP" stands for University Press; "o/p" signifies an out-of-print – but still highly recommended – book. Titles marked ⊞ are particularly recommended.

Archeology and ancient history

There is a vast body of literature on ancient Crete, especially on the Minoans, but a lot of it is very heavy going. Below are some of the more widely available, accessible and useful books. Other names to look out for include **Nikólaos Pláton** and **Stylianós Aléxiou**, whose books you may find available in local translations. There are also local guide booklets on all the major museums and sites, often with nice pictures, but usually very poor text.

Gerald Cadogan *Palaces of Minoan Crete* (Routledge). Complete guide to all the major sites, with much more history and general information than the name implies.

Pat Cameron *The Blue Guide* (A&C Black; WW Norton). Recently updated, this is an excellent detailed guide to the churches, archeological sites and museums across the island. However, some of the directions to more remote sights often lack clarity and the newly introduced accommodation and eating recommendations are not always reliable.

John Chadwick *Linear B and related scripts* (British Museum Publications; University of California Press). A short version of *The Decipherment of Linear B* (Cambridge UP), in which the whole fascinating story is graphically told by Chadwick who collaborated with Ventris, the English architect who made the crucial breakthrough. The same author's *Mycenaean World* (Cambridge UP) vividly describes the society revealed by the tablets.

Leonard Cottrell *The Bull of Minos* (Bell & Hyman o/p;

Amereon Aeonian Press; Efstathiadis, Athens). Breathless and somewhat dated account of the discoveries of Schliemann and Evans; easy reading.

Costis Davaras *Guide to Cretan Antiquities* (Noyes Press, US; Eptalofolos, Athens). A fascinating guide by the distinguished archeologist and former director of the Áyios Nikólaos museum to the antiquities of Crete (from the ancient through to the Turkish eras). Cross-referenced in dictionary form, it has authoritative articles on all the major sites as well as subjects as diverse as Minoan razors and toilet articles, the disappearance of Cretan forests and the career of Venizélos. Widely available at museums on the island.

★ **Arthur Evans** *The Palace of Minos* (o/p). The seminal work, still worth a look if you can find it in a library.

J. Lesley Fitton *Minoans* (British Museum Publications, UK). Although part of a series aimed at general readers, this can become relentlessly academic. However, it brings together many of the more recent theories about the Minoans, debunking some familiar myths and setting their society into a wider context.

Reynold Higgins *Minoan and Mycenaean Art* (Thames & Hudson; Oxford UP o/p). Solid introduction to the subject with plenty of illustrations.

★ **J. Alexander Macgillivray** *Minotaur: Sir Arthur Evans and the Archaeology of the Minoan Myth* (Jonathan Cape; Hill & Wang). Excellent and long-overdue book which shows how Evans fitted the evidence found at Knossós to his own pre-conception of the Minoans as peaceful, literate and aesthetic

second-millenium BC Victorians. A superb read.

★ **J.D.S. Pendlebury** *The Archaeology of Crete* (Methuen o/p; Norton o/p). Still the most comprehensive handbook, detailing virtually every archeological site on the island. Pendlebury's *Handbook to the Palace of Minos* is still an excellent guide to the Knossós site by someone who – as curator after Evans's retirement – knew it inside out. A local edition has been reprinted in Crete.

Nikos Psilakis *Monasteries and Byzantine Memories of Crete* (locally published). Self-explanatory title: readable and well-illustrated.

Ian F. Sanders *Roman Crete* (Aris & Phillips; Humanities Press). Very dry, and hard to come by, but a total record of all Roman remains on Crete.

Peter Warren *The Aegean Civilizations* (Phaidon o/p; Peter Bedrick o/p). Illustrated introduction by one of the leading modern experts; it's essentially a coffee-table book, but informative and easy on the eye. Warren's other publications tend to the technical.

R.F. Willetts *The Civilization of Ancient Crete* (Barnes & Noble, US); *Cretan Cults and Festivals* (Greenwood Press); *Aristocratic Society in Ancient Crete* (RKP o/p; Greenwood Press). Rather heavy, scholarly accounts of the social structure of ancient Crete. His *Everyday Life in Ancient Crete* (Batsford o/p; John Benjamins) is a more accessible read for the layperson.

H.G. Wunderlich *The Secret of Crete* (Efstadhiadis, Athens). The secret is that the palaces were really elaborate tombs or necropoli. Sensationalist nonsense widely sold on Crete.

History and architecture

By contrast with the proliferation of ancient history, there is no book in English devoted to modern Cretan history. Good general accounts are included in Hopkins's and Smith's books on the island, but otherwise you're forced to wade through Greek or Ottoman history, selecting the relevant portions.

Richard Clogg *A Concise History of Greece* (Cambridge UP). A rigorously historical account of Greek history from its emergence from Ottoman rule to the present day, covering the wider aspects of Crete's struggle for independence and union with Greece.

Greek Traditional Architecture – Crete (Melissa Publishing, Athens). Comprehensive overview of Cretan domestic architecture focussing on Byzantine, Venetian and Turkish influences as well as the evolution of traditional village dwellings.

⭐ **Adam Hopkins** *Crete, Its Past, Present and People* (Faber & Faber, o/p). Excellent general introduction to Cretan history and society.

⭐ **John Julius Norwich** *Byzantium: the Early Centuries*, *Byzantium: the Apogee* and *Byzantium: Decline and Fall* (all Penguin; Knopf). The three volumes of Norwich's history of the Byzantine Empire are terrific narrative accounts, and much can be gleaned from them about Crete in this period.

⭐ **James Pettifer** *The Greeks: the Land and People since the War* (Penguin, UK). Excellent introduction to contemporary Greece, and its recent past. Pettifer roams the country and charts the state of the nation's politics, food, family life, religion, tourism and all points in between. Only passing reference to Crete, however.

⭐ **Oliver Rackham and Jennifer Moody** *The Making of the Cretan Landscape* (Manchester UP). An enthralling botanical and anthropological study of the Cretans in their environment, from antiquity to the present day with sections devoted to the island's geological formation, vegetation, people and settlements.

Michael Llewellyn Smith *The Great Island* (Allen Lane, UK, o/p). Covers much of the same ground as Hopkins's book, but with more emphasis on folk traditions, and a lengthy analysis of Cretan song.

World War II

Antony Beevor *Crete: The Battle and the Resistance* (Penguin; Westview Press o/p). Relatively short study of the Battle of Crete, with insights into the characters involved. Beevor looks at recent evidence to conclude that defeat was at least in part due to the need to conceal Allied intelligence successes.

⭐ **Alan Clark** *The Fall of Crete* (NEL, UK, o/p; terrible Efstadhiadis edition widely sold on Crete). Racy and sensational – but very readable – military history by the recently deceased maverick English politician. Detailed on the battles, and more critical of the command than you might expect from a former cabinet minister.

Lew Lind *Flowers of Rethymnon* ★ (Efstadhiadis, widely available on the island). A gripping personal account of his part in the Battle of Crete and subsequent escape by a (then) 19-year-old Australian soldier. The carnage of the battle is rivetingly described and shining through the grim horror of it all comes the unflinching bravery of the Cretan villagers who repeatedly and self-lessly put themselves in mortal danger of German reprisals by helping servicemen trapped on Crete – such as Lind – escape to Egypt.

W. Stanley Moss *Ill Met by Moonlight* (Buchan & Enright; Lyons). An account of the capture of General Kreipe by one of the participants, largely taken from his diaries of the time. Good *Boys' Own*–style adventure stuff. Moss also translated Baron von der Heydte's *Daedalus Returned* (o/p), which gives something of the other side of the story.

George Panayiotakis *The Battle of Crete* (local edition). Pictorial history of the battle and its aftermath using contemporary photos. Available from major bookshops on the island.

George Psychoundákis *The* ★ *Cretan Runner* (Penguin; Transatlantic Arts, US; Efstadhiadis, Athens). Account of the invasion and resistance by a Cretan participant; Psychoundákis was a guide and message-runner for all the leading English-speaking protagonists. Great, although not much appreciated by many of his compatriots who tend to dismiss him as an English lackey.

Tony Simpson *The Battle for Crete, 1941* (o/p). A very different way of looking at the subject, putting the campaign into an international context and relying heavily on oral history for details of the combat. Uncompromisingly critical of the command, and far more interesting than straight military history.

I.McD.G. Stewart *Struggle for Crete: A Story of Lost Opportunity* (Oxford UP o/p). Authoritative detail on the battle from someone who was there. Rather dry military historian's approach.

Evelyn Waugh *Officers and Gentlemen* (Penguin; Little, Brown), *Diaries* (Phoenix; Little, Brown). Both include accounts of the Battle of Crete, and particularly of the horrors of the flight and evacuation.

Travel writing

Anonymous *Greek Men Made Simple* (MUC, Athens). "Everything you ever wanted to know plus everything you never thought to ask" is the subtitle of this hilarious dissection of the Greek male and his sexual ego by a Greek-resident English woman (hence the anonymity) with plenty of experience of both. Despite clumsy editing, it's an invaluable *vade mecum* for would-be Shirley Valentines and is available at bookshops on the island.

Robin Bryant *Crete* (o/p). Thematic interweaving of the author's observations during his stay on Crete with aspects of the island's history, folklore and festivals, immediately prior to the arrival of package tourism.

Johan de Bakker (ed) *Across* ★ *Crete – From Khaniá to Heráklion* (I.B. Tauris). Fascinating anthology depicting Crete as seen through the eyes of nineteenth-century travellers including Pashley, Pockocke, Spratt and Lear. This is the first of a planned three-volume set; the later volumes are to cover travellers in eastern and western Crete.

★ **David MacNeill Doren** *Winds of Crete* (John Murray, UK, o/p; Efstathiadis, Athens). An American and his Swedish wife find enlightenment on Crete – between times, quite an amusing and well-observed travelogue documenting many of the island's customs and curiosities in addition to some hair-raising brushes with Cretan physicians. Widely available at bookshops on the island.

Edward Lear *The Cretan Journal* (Denise Harvey, Athens). Diary of Lear's trip to Crete in 1864, illustrated with his sketches and watercolours. He didn't enjoy himself much.

★ **Henry Miller** *The Colossus of Maroussi* (Minerva o/p; New Directions). Miller's idiosyncratic account of his travels in Greece on the eve of World War II includes a trip to Crete where diarrhoea, biting flies and Festós palace all get bit-parts in the epic.

★ **Robert Pashley** *Travels in Crete* (John Murray o/p). The original nineteenth-century British traveller, full of interesting anecdotes and outrageous attitudes. Try finding it at a library.

Dilys Powell *The Villa Ariadne* (Hodder & Stoughton, UK; Efstadhiadis, Athens). The story of the British in Crete, from Arthur Evans to Paddy Leigh Fermor, through the villa at Knossós which saw all of them. Good at bringing the excitement of the early archeological work to life, but rather cloying in style.

Pandelis Prevelakis *Tale of a Town* (Doric Publications, Athens). English translation of a native's description of life and times in Réthimnon during the first quarter of the twentieth century.

J.E. Hilary Skinner *Roughing It in Crete* (1868 o/p). Great title for this account of another Englishman's adventures, this time with a band of rebels. Interesting on the less glamorous side of the independence struggle, since he spent the whole time searching for food or dodging Turkish patrols.

★ **Capt. T.A.B. Spratt** *Travels and Researches in Crete* (Coronet Books, US). Another nineteenth-century Briton who caught the Cretan bug whilst surveying the island's coastline, and left behind this account of its natural history, geology and archeology.

★ **Patricia Storace** *Dinner with Persephone* (Granta Books; Pantheon). Although not specifically about Crete, this is one of the best books ever written on the Greeks by a foreign author. Storace, an American poet, learned the language and went to live with, and travel among the Hellenes for a year, delving deep into the psyche of this superficially attractive, but fiendishly complex people. Ideal holiday reading – you'll never look at the Greeks in the same light again.

Christopher Thorne *Between the Seas* (Sinclair Stevenson o/p; Trafalgar Square, UK, o/p). The account of a walk along the length of the island with observations on Cretan country life, past and present.

Jackson Webb *The Last Lemon Grove* (o/p). Published in 1977, an account of an American living in the then-remote village of Paleohóra. Wonderfully atmospheric.

Fiction

Homer *The Iliad* and *The Odyssey* (Penguin Classics and many other editions). The first concerns itself, semi-factually, with the Trojan War; the second recounts the hero Odysseus's long journey home, via Crete and seemingly every other corner of the Mediterranean. Homer's accounts were in some ways responsible for the "rediscovery" of Minoan Crete in the nineteenth century, so it seems appropriate to read them here.

★ **Níkos Kazantzákis** *Zorba the Greek*; *Freedom and Death*; *Report to Greco* (all Faber & Faber; Simon & Schuster; local editions available in Crete). Something by the great Cretan novelist and man of letters is essential reading. Forget the film: *Zorba the Greek* is a wonderful read on Crete which provides the backdrop to the adventures of one of the most irresistible characters of modern fiction. *Freedom and Death* is, if anything, even better.

Ioannis Kondylakis *Patouchas* (Efstathiadis, Athens). The story of a

Cretan shepherd on a journey of self-discovery is a wonderfully observed and humorous fictional sketch of Turkish Crete in the nineteenth century by a little-known Cretan author. Widely available on the island.

Vitzentzos Kornaros *Erotokritos* (tr. Theodore Stefanides, Merlin Press; Humanities). A beautifully produced English translation of the massive sixteenth-century Cretan epic poem.

F. Ragovin *Cretan Mantinades* (Cnossos Editions, Athens). Parallel translations of many of the best examples of the island's most popular form of vocal music dealing with subject matter as diverse as love and marriage, oaths and curses, and the war against Hitler.

★ **Mary Renault** *The King Must Die* (Sceptre o/p; Vintage); *The Bull from the Sea* (Penguin; Vintage). Stirring accounts of the Theseus legend and Minoan Crete for those who like their history in fictionalized form.

Wildlife and geology

Michael Chinerey *Collins Guide to the Insects of Britain and Western Europe* (Collins, UK). This doesn't specifically include Greece (there's no comprehensive guide to Greek insects) but it gives a good general background and identification to the main families of insects that you're likely to see.

Stephanie Coghlan *Birdwatching in Crete* (Snails Pace Publishing, UK; order direct by email:

Ⓔ coghlansm@aol.com). Slim book detailing the best bird-watching sites throughout the island and what you may see there, with checklists. No pictures for identification though, so you'll need a guide too.

Charalampos G. Fassoulas *Field Guide to the Geology of Crete* (Natural History Museum of Crete). Excellent introduction to Crete's fascinating geology, explaining the island's geological evolution, paleo-graphy and paleontology. Superb colour photos and details of where to find many of the most interesting sites. Widely available at bookshops on the island.

★ **Anthony Huxley and William Taylor** *Flowers of Greece* (Hogarth Press o/p; Trafalgar Square o/p). The best book for iden-tifying flowers in Crete.

Christopher Perrins *New Generations Guide to Birds of Britain and Europe* (HarperCollins; University of Texas Press). An alter-native look at bird ecology as well as pure identification.

Peterson, Mountfort and Hollom *Field Guide to the Birds of Britain and Europe* (HarperCollins; Houghton Mifflin). There's no com-plete guide to Cretan birds; this is probably the best general tome – ageing but excellent.

George Sfikas *Wild Flowers of Crete* (Efstathiadis, Athens). Comprehensive illustrated guide to the island's flora. Widely available at bookshops on the island.

Paul Whalley *The Mitchell Beazley Pocket Guide to Butterflies* (Mitchell Beazley; published in the US as *Butterflies* by Transatlantic Arts). A useful identification guide.

Hiking and travel guides

Bruce and Naomi Caughey *Crete off the Beaten Track* (Cicerone Press, UK). Details a large number of walks throughout the island; available in many bookstores in major towns.

Lance Chilton *Ten Walks in the Plakiás Area* and *Six Walks in the Georgioupolis Area* (both Marengo, UK, ⊛www.marengowalks.com). Well-described rambles and treks ranging from half an hour to half a day in these two scenic zones, by an experienced guide. *More Challenging Walks in the Plakiás Area* is a recent new addition. Available from book-shops in the UK or direct from the publisher: 17 Bernard Crescent, Hunstanton, Norfolk PE36 6ER (☎ & ℻01485/532710, ℮marengo@ supanet.com).

Freytag & Berndt *Crete Hiking Map* (Freytag & Berndt). Booklet and map pack in German, Greek and English describing twenty walks all over the island ranging from a couple of hours to full-day treks; the accompanying large-scale 1:50,000

map is admirably clear. Widely avail-able from bookshops on the island.

★ **Jonnie Godfrey and Elizabeth Karslake** *Landscapes of Eastern/Western Crete* (Sunflower, UK). Full of hiking and touring sug-gestions which make a useful adjunct to this guide.

Stephanos Psimenos *Unexplored Crete* (Road Editions, Athens). Bible-sized (motor)biker's guide to the island packed with loads of biker informa-tion and bonding lingo, related in an often quirky translation from the original Greek. Still, if you want to bike around the island using routes known only to goats, this is the book for you. Widely available at bookshops in all major towns in Crete.

Loraine Wilson *Crete: The White Mountains* (Cicerone, UK). Thorough guide to fifty-plus hikes in the Lefká Ori by an experienced trekker rang-ing between 3km and 20km, and enabling routes to be linked for extended treks over several days.

Food and drink

★ **Geoff Adams** *Greek Wines*
(Winemaster Publishing, UK,
Ⓦwww.greekwinebook.com). Well
researched *vade mecum* to the world
of Greek wine. Includes detail on
wine-growing regions (including
Crete), grape varieties, wine producers and individual ratings for over
450 wines.

★ **Miles Lambert-Gócs** *The
Wines of Greece* (Faber &
Faber, UK). Comprehensive survey
of the emerging wines of Greece
with plenty of fascinating historical
detail; a chapter is devoted to
Cretan wines. Now in need of an
update.

★ **María and Níkos Psilakis**
Cretan Cooking (Karmanor,
Iráklion). Long overdue and highly
recommended guide to the Cretan

kitchen – if only these dishes were
generally available in the island's tavernas. The authors have gathered
recipes from all parts of the island
and interspersed with them illustrations not only of the food but of
rural life past and present. Widely
available on the island.

George Sfikas *Fishes of Greece*
(Efstathiadis, Athens). Handy pictorial guide to all the fish you're likely
to encounter in the island's tavernas.
Widely available in Crete.

Sofia Souli *The Greek Cookery Book*
(Toubi's, Athens). Good book to
start you cooking Greek food when
you get back home. Everything
from *tzatzíki* to *kataífi*, including a
few Cretan specialities. Profusely
illustrated and widely available on
the island.

Cretan music

Your first encounter with traditional Cretan music is likely to be in a taverna or back-street *kafeníon*, where a couple of put-upon youths churn out the strains of *Zorba*, or on an organized "Cretan folk evening" offered by travel agents across the island. You can also strike lucky and witness genuinely excellent music and dance. Either way, if your interest is piqued, you'll often find the real thing by visiting local festivals or joining guests at one of the hundreds of wedding feasts taking place across the island throughout the summer where musicians are an essential feature. Alternatively, in major towns like Haniá and Réthimnon there are cafés such as *Café Kriti* (see p.318) and *O Gounakis* (see p.250), where skilled performers can deliver unforgettable performances.

The **musical tradition** of Crete is one of the most active and vibrant in Europe. Sadly, outside Greece it gets little attention or recognition, and equally frustratingly little is known about the history and origins of the music itself. In the island's early history we do know that the **Minoans** were great practioners of the vocal and musical arts, and the Ayía Triádha sarcophagus (see p.93) depicts a flute-player as well as a minstrel with a seven-stringed lyre. Evidence of cymbals, *sistrum* (a sort of maraca) and even bagpipes have all been discovered in excavations across the island, but anything demonstrably Minoan in Crete's later musical development is impossible to discern.

Subsequent **influences** would seem to be those of the Dorian Greeks who dominated the island in the early first millennium BC and the Romans, Byzantines, Venetians and Ottoman Turks who came after them. Here again, what is known is frustratingly limited although during the Greek period Crete introduced to the mainland the **paean**, a solemn hymn to the god Apollo performed to the accompaniment of lyres and flutes as well as the **nomos**, a solo hymn with lyre accompaniment to the same god first performed at Delphi by Chrysothemis the Cretan. During the same period the music of lyres and flutes accompanied Cretan armies into battle.

The problems encountered by ethnomusicologists in searching for influences on Cretan music over the centuries have not been confined to ancient music – in fact, there's virtually nothing to go on prior to the first recordings made in the twentieth century. What we now refer to as Cretan music belongs squarely in the **Eastern Mediterranean** family of modal musical traditions and has noticeable foreign traits with other traditions of the region such as Arabic, Turkish and, of course, the music of other regions of Greece. The principal instruments in use today are the **lyra**: a small three-stringed, pear-shaped fiddle held upright on the left knee and bowed horizontally with a bow (which in earlier times had bells on it) held in the right hand, and the **laoúto**: a large lute closely related to the Arabic *oud* with four courses of double strings made of steel, and movable frets made of nylon filament. One of the interesting aspects of the *lyra* has to do with the fingering technique of the left hand. Unlike the violin and most other related instruments, the strings are not pressed by the fingertips of the left hand, rather they are merely touched lightly from the side by the back of the nails. In this respect, the Cretan *lyra* resembles other *lyra* types found in the Eastern Mediterranean and Balkan regions such as the Turkish *fasil kemence*, the Bulgarian *Gadulka*, as well as the *lyras* of the Dodecanese islands, southwest Turkey, Thrace, Macedonia, certain regions of southern Italy, and much of former Yugoslavia. Interestingly, this playing technique is also common to the bowed instruments of northwest India and

Central Asia – although nowhere in the intermediate region between these distant lands is this technique encountered.

Numerous other instruments also have a place in Cretan music. In the far western as well as the far eastern regions of the island the **violin** is probably more common than the *lyra*. Indeed, in western Crete, a heated debate has arisen in recent decades concerning which instrument of the two is a more authentic vehicle for Cretan music. Unfortunately, this discrepancy is the result of a now obsolete ban imposed on violin-players by the state radio in the 1950s at the instigation of a researcher named **Simonas Karras**. Karras himself was under the sway of extreme nationalist ideologies, and regarded the violin as a European imposition which simply supplanted the "native" *lyra* in certain regions. In fact, neither instrument is truly indigenous to Crete (the oldest recorded presence of the *lyra* dates to tenth-century Thrace, and it only appeared in Crete as late as the early eighteenth century. Prior to Karras's intervention, it had never occurred to *lyra*-players and violin-players to look upon one another with animosity.

In the mountainous areas of central Crete a small bagpipe known as **askomandoura** (a possible descendent of the Minoan instrument) was at one time commonly found, and in the urban centers, a small long-necked lute similar to the **saz** called **boulgari** was prevalent. In the eastern regions around the Sitía area a small double-faced barrel-drum known as **daoulaki** was the main instrument accompanying the *lyra*. The **askomandoura**, **boulgari**, **daoulaki** and **sfyrohabiolo** (a small flute) are all very near to extinction, although in recent years some young musicians have taken them up, and a revival of interest in these instruments seems very likely.

Although it's been present on Crete even before Ottoman times, in the last couple of decades the **mandolin** has gained considerable popularity as an instrument to accompany the characteristic fifteen-syllable rhyming verses know as **mantinades** (from the Venetian *matinata* – evening love song). Often a group of people will sit together and engage in something between a dialogue and a competition of *mantinades*, to the accompaniment of a mandolin playing repetitive phrases known as **kontylies**, which allow considerable freedom for the singers.

Another instrument which has become popular as an accompaniment to the *lyra* in recent decades is the **guitar**. This is in many ways unfortunate, given that the guitar, with its chordal mentality, necessarily imposes western tempered tonality on an otherwise modal tradition in which microtonal intervals were once one of its central features. The contemporary accompaniment to the *lyra* (which is usually one *laoúto* and one guitar) has entirely negated the use of microtones by *lyra*-players who are now obliged to adapt to the tempered intervals of the guitar and *laoúto* (whose movable frets no longer move).

Most of the music of Crete, however, is **dance music** which is played at local festivals (*panigyria*), weddings, baptisms and other such festive occasions. These dances are usually quite fast and require considerable skill on the part of the dancer, but also restraint and finesse. The main dances are the **Malevyziotikos**, the **Pentozali** (slow and fast), the **Sousta**, and the **Syrtos**. Other dances do exist, but for the most part they're subcategories of those already mentioned.

The remainder of the Cretan repertoire is comprised of songs which are not intended as accompaniment to dance. Perhaps the most important of these songs are those which are referred to by the generic name **rizitika**. These songs were originally sung exclusively on western Crete, without the accompaniment of instruments, by a group of men sitting around a table. For this reason they are also known as **traghoudia tis tavlas**, literally "table songs". *Rizitika* (sing. *riz-itiko*) songs are characterized by their very serious, austere nature, their remarkable verses which reflect a very developed poetic tradition (frequently allegoric and obscure in meaning), as well as by their intricate melodies. The **rizitika** songs are also the only texts found in Cretan music which don't employ the technique of rhyming verses. Rhyming verses were introduced to Crete during the time of the Venetian occupation (1204–1669), and some researchers suggest that the unrhymed *rizitiko* lyrics perhaps reflect an older poetic form and that, potentially, some of the extant lyrics themselves could perhaps pre-date this time. There is a case for suggesting connections between the *rizitika* songs and Greek Orthodox church hymnology.

Other song-types are those found in urban centres and ports which reflect clearly influences originating from Asia Minor. Also worthy of special note are the melodies used to accompany the epic poem **Erotokritos**, which was written in the mid-seventeenth century by **Vitsentzos Kornaros**. This enormous epic poem holds a revered place in Cretan culture; until relatively recent times it was not unusual for even an illiterate person to know it in its entirety by memory.

Cretan musicians

Once you get to the beginning of the twentieth century, there's no shortage of recorded traditional music. Type "Cretan music" into any Internet search engine, and you'll be spoilt for choice. Listening to the older recordings by players of the early twentieth century, it's immediately apparent that Cretan music has undergone major changes during the ensuing decades. Some great masters of the past include:

Andreas Rodinos Legendary *lyra*-player whose renditions of Cretan music are still today *the* point of reference. He died in 1937 aged only 22.

Manolis Lagos A very "classical" *lyra*-player from Réthimnon, who was active in the early twentieth century.

Giorgos Tzimakis *Lyra*-player and excellent singer from Haniá, who today is still playing in his mid-nineties.

Nikolaos Saridakis A very sensitive violin-player from Kissámos in the far west.

Stelios Foustalierakis The greatest exponent of the rare *saz*-like instrument the *boulgari*; he's also the composer of some of the greatest classics of Cretan music.

Giannis Bernidakis or **"Baxevanis"** The foremost singer and *laoúto*-player of the early twentieth century.

Kostas Mountakis One of the greatest *lyra*-players of the twentieth century, and an extraordinary singer; he was also the teacher of Ross Daly (see the box on p.112).

Athanasios Skordalos A superb *lyra*-player from Spíli in central Crete. The friendly forty-year rivalry between Skordalos and Mountakis accounts for a large percentage of the creative work done in Cretan music during the second half of the twentieth century.

Michalis Papadakis or **"Plakianos"** The finest representative of the school of *lyra*-playing from the Apokoronas region; unfortunately, recordings are rare.

Nikos Xylouris Generally regarded as the greatest Cretan singer ever (and also a very fine *lyra*-player and composer), Xylouris was tragically struck down by cancer in 1980 while still in his forties.

Giannis Dermitzogiannis A *lyra*- and violin-player from Sitía, Dermitzogiannis was especially adept in the use of bells on the bow of the *lyra*.

Leonidas Klados A very innovative and creative *lyra*-player from the Messará region, and still active today.

Discography

Leonidas Klados & Manolis Kaklis *Pantermo Rethemnos* (Panivar). A *lyra*-player of the older generation, Klados is still very active today and is renowned for his highly refined sound and brilliant improvisations. Here he accompanies Manolis Kaklis, an outstanding singer of Cretan music.

Kostas Mountakis *Rare Recordings* (Seistron/MBI). A four-CD collection of live recordings by perhaps the greatest *lyra*-player in recorded history; this collection is absolutely essential for anyone seriously interested in Cretan music.

Stelios Petrakis *Oi dikoi mou filoi* (Seistron/MBI). An exceptional recording made by the young Sitían *lyra*-, *laouto*- and *saz*-player with Iranian percussionist Bijan Chemirani. One of the very best of the new projects coming out of Crete.

Protomastores *Kritiko mousiko Ergastiri* (Aerakis). A ten-CD anthology of recordings made between 1920 and 1955, including almost all of the great players of the period – the most important sound record of the twentieth century's greatest Cretan musicians.

Psarantonis *Anastorimata* (Seistron). Another formidable performer on the *lyra* demonstrates his talents on this CD.

Athanasios Skordalos *Kriti Patris tou Minoa* (Aerakis). Skordalos was an exceptional *lyra*-player and a prolific composer especially adept at the *syrtos* form. This instrumental CD highlights the best aspects of his playing.

Nikos Xylouris *Dimotiki Anthologia* (Columbia/EMI). Early recordings by one of Crete's legendary and much lamented singers and performers.

Most of the above recordings can be obtained from Cretashop in Iráklion (⊛www.cretashop.gr/br).

by Ross Daly

Language

Language

Language

So many Cretans have been compelled by poverty and other circumstances to work abroad, especially in the English-speaking world, that you'll find someone who speaks some English in almost every village. Add to that the thousands attending language schools or working in the tourist industry – English is the lingua franca of the north coast – and it's easy to see how so many visitors come back having learnt only half-a-dozen restaurant words between them. You can certainly get by this way, even in quite out-of-the-way places, but it isn't very satisfying.

Greek is not an easy language for English-speakers, but it is a beautiful one, and even a brief acquaintance will give you some idea of the debt western European languages owe to it. More important than that, the willingness and ability to say even a few words will transform your status from that of dumb

L

LANGUAGE

Learning Greek, phrasebooks and Greek dictionaries

Breakthrough Greek (Pan Macmillan; book and 2 cassettes). First-rate, basic teach-yourself course – completely outclasses the competition.

Get By in Greek (BBC Publications, UK; book and 2 cassettes). One of the BBC's excellent crash-course introductions which gets you to survival-level Greek (bars, tavernas, asking the way) in a couple of weeks.

Greek Language and People (BBC Publications, UK; book and cassette available). An in-depth study course which, whilst more limited than the *Breakthrough* course in scope, is good for acquiring the essentials, and gets you using the Greek alphabet from the start.

A Manual of Modern Greek (Anne Farmakides; Yale; McGill; 3 vols). If you have the discipline and motivation, this is one of the best courses for learning proper, grammatical Greek; indeed, mastery of just the first volume will get you a long way.

Teach Yourself Instant Greek (Elisabeth Smith; Hodder & Stoughton; NTC/Contemporary Publishing). Claims to be able to get you speaking Greek in six weeks if you devote 45 minutes per day to study. Quite well structured, with optional tapes, and should enable you to get results if you stick at it.

Phrasebooks
The Rough Guide to Greek (Rough Guides). Practical and easy-to-use, the Rough Guide phrasebook allows you to speak the way you would in your own language. Feature boxes fill you in on dos and don'ts and cultural know-how.

Dictionaries
The Oxford Dictionary of Modern Greek (Oxford UP). A bit bulky but generally considered the best Greek–English, English–Greek dictionary.

Collins Pocket Greek Dictionary (HarperCollins). Very nearly as complete as the Oxford and probably better value for money.

Oxford Learner's Dictionary (Oxford UP). If you're planning a prolonged stay, this pricey two-volume set is unbeatable for usage and vocabulary. There's also a more portable one-volume *Learner's Pocket Dictionary*.

tourístas to the honourable one of *kséno*, a word which can mean stranger, traveller and guest all rolled into one.

On top of the usual difficulties of learning a new language, Greek presents the added problem of an entirely separate **alphabet**. Despite initial appearances, this is in practice fairly easily mastered; a skill that will help enormously if you are going to get around independently (see the alphabet and transliteration box on p.472). In addition, certain combinations of letters have unexpected results. This book's transliteration system should help you make intelligible noises but you have to remember that the correct **stress** – marked in the book with an accent – is absolutely crucial. With the right sounds but the wrong stress people will either fail to understand you, or else understand something quite different from what you intended.

Greek **grammar** is more complicated still: nouns are divided into three genders, all with different case endings in the singular and in the plural, and all adjectives and articles have to agree with these in gender, number and case. (All adjectives are arbitrarily cited in the neuter form in the following lists.) Verbs are even worse. To begin with at least, the best thing is simply to say what you know the way you know it, and never mind the niceties. "Eat meat hungry" should get a result, however grammatically incorrect. If you worry about your mistakes, you'll never say anything.

Greek words and phrases

Essentials

yes	né	more	perisótero
certainly	málista	less	ligótero
no	óhi	a little	lígo
please	parakaló	a lot	polí
okay, agreed	endáksi	cheap	ftinó
Thank you (very much)	Efharistó (polí)	expensive	akrivó
		hot	zestó
I (don't) understand	(Dhen) katalavéno	cold	krío
Excuse me, do you speak English?	Parakaló, mípos miláte angliká?	with	mazí
		without	horís
Sorry/excuse me	Signómi	quickly	grígora
today	símera	slowly	sigá
tomorrow	ávrio	Mr/Mrs	Kírios/Kiría
big	megálo	Miss	Dhespinís
small	mikró		

Other needs

to eat/drink	trógo/píno	bank	trápeza
bakery	foúrnos, psomádhiko	money	leftá/hrímata
pharmacy	farmakío	toilet	toualéta
post office	tahidhromío	police	astinomía
stamps	gramatósima	doctor	iatrós
petrol station	venzinádhiko	hospital	nosokomío

466

Requests and questions

To ask a question, it's simplest to start with *parakaló*, then name the thing you want in an interrogative tone.

Where is the foúrnos?	Parakaló, o bakery?	how much?	póso?
		when?	póte?
Can you show me the road to...?	Parakaló, o dhrómos ya...?	why?	yatí?
		at what time...?	ti óra...?
We'd like a room	Parakaló, éna dhomátio	what is/which is...?	ti íne/pió íne..?
for two	ya dhío átoma?	how much (does it cost)?	póso káni?
May I have a oranges?	Parakaló, éna kilo of kiló portokália?	What time does it open?	Tí óra aníyi?
where?	pou?		
how?	pos?	What time does it close?	Tí óra klíni?
how many?	póssi/pósses?		

Talking to people

Greek makes the distinction between the informal (esí) and formal (esís) second person, as French does with tu and vous. Young people, older people and country people nearly always use esí even with total strangers. In any event, no one will be too bothered if you get it wrong. By far the most common greeting, on meeting and parting, is yá sou/yá sas – literally "health to you".

Hello	Hérete	Speak slower, please	Parakaló, miláte pió sigá
Good morning	Kalí méra		
Good evening	Kalí spéra	How do you say it in Greek?	Pos léyete sta Eliniká?
Goodnight	Kalí níkhta		
Goodbye	Adhío	I don't know	Dhen kséro
How are you?	Ti kánis/ti kánete?	See you tomorrow	Tha se dho ávrio
I'm fine	Kalá íme	See you soon	Kalí andhámosi
And you?	Ke esís?	Let's go	Páme
What's your name?	Pos se léne?	Please help me	Parakaló, na me voithíste
My name is...	Me léne...		

Greek's Greek

There are numerous words and phrases which you will hear constantly, even if you rarely have the chance to use them. These are a few of the most common.

Éla!	Come (literally), but also Speak to me! You don't say! etc.	Po-po-po!	Expression of dismay or concern, like French "O la la!"
Oríste?	What can I do for you?	Pedhí mou	My boy/girl, sonny, friend, etc.
Bros!	Standard phone response	Maláka(s)	Literally "wanker", but often used (don't try it!) as an informal address
Ti néa?	What's new?		
Ti yínete?	What's going on (here)?		
Étsi k'étsi	So-so	Sigá sigá	Take your time, slow down
Ópa!	Whoops! Watch it!	Kaló taxídhi	Bon voyage

Accommodation

hotel	ksenodhohío	hot water	zestó neró
a room	éna dhomátio	cold water	krío neró
for one/two/ three people	ya éna/dhío/tría átoma	Can I see it?	boró na to dho?
		Can we camp here?	Boróume na váloume ti skiní edhó?
for one/two/ three nights	ya mía/dhío/trís vradhiés	campsite	kamping/kataskínosi
with a double bed	me megálo kreváti	tent	skiní
with a shower	me doús	youth hostel	ksenodhohío neótitos

On the move

airplane	aeropláno	Where are you going?	Pou pas?
bus	leoforío	I'm going to...	Páo sto...
car	aftokínito	I want to get off at...	Thélo na katévo sto...
motorbike, moped	mihanáki, papáki		
taxi	taksí	The road to...	O dhrómos ya...
ship	plío/vapóri/karávi	near	kondá
bicycle	podhílato	far	makriá
hitching	otostóp	left	aristerá
on foot	me ta pódhia	right	dheksiá
trail	monopáti	straight ahead	katefthía
bus station	praktorío leoforíon	a ticket to...	éna isistírio ya...
bus stop	stási	a return ticket	éna isistírio me epistrofí
harbour	limáni		
What time does it leave?	Ti óra févyi?	beach	paralía
		cave	spiliá
What time does it arrive?	Ti óra ftháni?	centre (of town)	kéndro
		church	eklissía
How many kilometres?	Pósa hiliómetra?	sea	thálassa
How many hours?	Pósses óres?	village	horió

Numbers

1	énos éna/mía	13	dhekatrís
2	dhío	14	dhekatésseres
3	trís/tría	20	íkosi
4	tésseres/téssera	21	íkosi éna
5	pénde	30	riánda
6	éksi	40	saránda
7	eftá	50	penínda
8	okhtó	60	eksínda
9	enyá	70	evdhomínda
10	dhéka	80	ogdhónda
11	éndheka	90	enenínda
12	dhódheka	100	ekató

150	ekatón penínda	1,000,000	éna ekatomírio
200	dhiakóssies/ia	first	próto
500	pendakóssies/ia	second	dhéftero
1000	hílies/ia	third	tríto
2000	dhío hiliádhes		

The time and days of the week

Sunday	Kiriakí	What time is it?	Ti óra íne?
Monday	Dheftéra	One/two/three o'clock	Mía/dhío/trís óra/óres
Tuesday	Tríti	Twenty to four	Tésseres pará íkosi
Wednesday	Tetárti	Five past seven	Eftá ke pénde
Thursday	Pémpti	Half past eleven	Éndheka ke misí
Friday	Paraskeví	half-hour	misí óra
Saturday	Sávato	quarter-hour	éna tétarto

Months and seasonal terms

NB: You may see *katharévoussa*, or hybrid, forms of the months written on schedules or street signs; these are the spoken demotic forms.

January	Yennáris	August	Ávgoustos
February	Fleváris	September	Septémvris
March	Mártis	October	Októvrios
April	Aprílis	November	Noémvris
May	Maïos	December	Dhekémvris
June	Ioúnios	summer schedule	Therinó dhromolóyio
July	Ioúlios	winter schedule	himerinó dhromolóyio

A food and drink glossary

Basics

neró	water	fitofágos	vegetarian/hortofágos
psomí	bread	avgá	eggs
olikís aleseos	whole grain	tirí	cheese
siskalísio psomi	rye bread	(horís) ládhi	(without) oil
aláti	salt	katálogo/lísta	menu
yiaoúrti	yoghurt	o logariasmós	the bill
méli	honey	sto foúrno	baked
kréas	meat	psitó	roasted
psári(a)	fish	sti soúvla	spit roasted
lahaniká	vegetables	tis óras	grilled/fried to order

Soups and starters

soúpa	soup	taramósalata	fish roe paté
avgolémono	egg and lemon soup	tzatzíki	yoghurt and cucumber dip
dolmádhes	stuffed vine leaves		
fasoládha	bean soup	melitzanosaláta	aubergine/eggplant dip

Vegetables

patátes	potatoes	spanáki	spinach
hórta	greens (usually wild)	fakés	lentils
radhíkia	wild chicory	rízi/piláfi	rice (usually with sáltsa – sauce)
piperiés	peppers		
domátes	tomatoes	saláta	salad
fasolákia	string beans	horiátiki (saláta)	greek salad (with olives, feta etc)
angoúri	cucumber		
angináres	artichokes	yemistés	stuffed vegetables
yígandes	white haricot beans	papoutsákia	stuffed aubergine/eggplant
koukiá	broad beans		
melitzána	aubergine/eggplant	bouréki	courgette/zucchini, potato or cheese pie
kolokithákia	courgette/zucchini		

Meat

kotópoulo	chicken	sikóti	liver
arní	lamb	patsás	tripe soup
hirinó	pork	nefrá	kidneys
vodhinó	beef	biftéki	hamburger
moskhári	veal		

Meat-based dishes

moussaká	aubergine/eggplant, potato and mince pie	pastítsio	macaroni baked with meat
stifádho	meat stew with tomato and onion	païdhákia	lamb chops
		brizóla	pork or beef chop
kleftiko	meat, potatoes and veg cooked together in a pot or foil; a Cretan speciality traditionally carried to bandits in hiding	keftédhes	meatballs
		loukánika	spicy sausages
		kokorétsi	liver/offal kebab
		tsalingária	garden snails

Fish and seafood

garídhes	prawns	kalamária	squid
okhtapódhi	octopus	kalamarákia	baby squid
astakós	lobster	glóssa	sole

barbóuni	red mullet	soupiá	anchovy
xifías	swordfish	marídhes	whitebait
sinagrídha	cuttlefish	gávros	bogue (cheap!)
gópa	bogue	fagrí	sea bream

Sweets, fruit and cheese

karidhópita	walnut cake	fráoules	strawberries
baklavá	honey and nut pastry	kerásia	cherries
rizógalo	rice pudding	stafília	grapes
galaktobóuriko	custard pie	pobrtokália	oranges
pagotó	ice cream	pepóni	melon
pastéli	sesame and honey bar	karpoúzi	watermelon
		míla	apples
kasséri	hard cheese	síka	(dried) figs
graviéra	gruyère-type cheese	fistíkia	pistachio nuts

Drinks

neró fialoméno	mineral water	gálakakáo	chocolate milk
		portokaládha	orangeade
bíra	beer	limonádha	lemonade
krasí	wine	gabzóza	generic fizzy drink
mávro	red	boukáli	bottle
áspro	white	potíri	glass
rosé/kokkinéli	rosé	Stiniyássas!	Cheers!
tsáï	tea	Yiásou!	Cheers!
kafé	coffee		

Set out below is the Greek alphabet, the system of transliteration used in this book and a brief aid to pronunciation.

Greek	Transliteration	Pronounced
Α, α	a	a as in father
Β, β	v	b as in vet
Γ, γ	y/g	y as in yes when before an e or i; when before consonants or a, o or ou it's a breathy, throaty g as in gasp
Δ, δ	dh	th as in then
Ε, ε	e	e as in get
Ζ, ζ	z	z sound
Η, η	i	ee sound as in feet
Θ, θ	th	th as in theme
Ι, ι	i	i as in bit
Κ, κ	k	k sound
Λ, λ	l	l sound
Μ, μ	m	m sound
Ν, ν	n	n sound
Ξ, ξ	ks	ks sound
Ο, ο	o	o as in toad
Π, π	p	p sound
Ρ, ρ	r	rolled r sound
Σ, σ, ς	s	s sound
Τ, τ	t	t sound
Υ, υ	i	ee, indistinguishable from η
Φ, φ	f	f sound
Χ, χ	h	harsh h sound, like ch in loch
Ψ, ψ	ps	ps as in lips
Ω, ω	o	o as in toad, indistinguishable from o

Combinations and diphthongs

ΑΙ, αι	e	e as in get
ΑΥ, αυ	av/af	av or af depending on following consonant
ΕΙ, ει	i	ee, exactly like η
ΟΙ, οι	i	ee, identical again
ΕΥ, ευ	ev/ef	ev or ef depending on following consonant
ΟΥ, ου	ou	ou as in tourist
ΓΓ, γγ	ng	ng as in angie
ΓΚ, γκ	g/ng	g as in goat at the beginning of a word, ng in the middle
ΜΠ, μπ	b	b at the beginning of a word, mb in the middle
ΝΤ, ντ	d/nd	d at the beginning of a word, nd in the middle
ΤΣ, τσ	ts	ts as in hits
ΣΙ, σι	sh	sh as in shame
ΤΖ, τζ	ts	j as in jam

Note: An umlaut on a letter indicates that the two vowels are pronounced separately; for example Aóös is Ah-oh-s, rather than A-ooos.

Glossary

ACROPOLIS Ancient, fortified hilltop.

AGORA Market and meeting place of an ancient city.

AMPHORA Tall, narrow-necked jar for oil or wine.

ÁNO Upper, as in upper town or village; eg Áno Zákros.

APSE Curved recess at the altar end of a church.

ARCHAIC PERIOD Late Iron Age from around 750 BC to the start of the Classical period in the fifth century BC.

ARSENALI Arsenals – a term used rather loosely for many Venetian defensive and harbour works.

ASKLEPION Sanctuary dedicated to Asclepius, the Greek god of healing, where the sick sought cures for their ailments.

ATRIUM Central altar-court of a Roman house.

ÁYIOS/AYÍA/ÁYII Saint or holy (m/f/pl), common place-name prefix (abbrev. Ag. or Ay.): Áyios Nikólaos is St Nicholas; Ayía Triádha is the Holy Trinity.

BASILICA Colonnaded "hall-type" church.

BYZANTINE EMPIRE Created by the division of the Roman Empire in 395 AD, this was the eastern half, ruled from Byzantium or Constantinople (modern Istanbul). There are many Byzantine churches of the fifth to the twelfth century on Crete, and Byzantine art flourished again after the fall of Constantinople in 1453, under Venetian rule, when many artists and scholars fled to the island.

CENTRAL COURT Paved area at the heart of a Minoan palace.

CLASSICAL PERIOD Essentially from the end of the Persian Wars in the fifth century BC to the unification of Greece under Philip II of Macedon (338 BC).

DHIMARHÍO Town hall (modern usage).

DHOMÁTIA Rooms for rent in private houses.

DORIAN Civilization which overran the Mycenaeans from the north around 1100 BC, and became their successor throughout much of southern Greece, including Crete.

EPARHÍA Greek Orthodox diocese, also the smallest subdivision of a modern province.

ETEO-CRETAN Literally true Cretan, the Eteo-Cretans are believed to have been remnants of the Minoan people who kept a degree of their language and culture alive in isolated centres in eastern Crete as late as the third century BC.

GEOMETRIC PERIOD Post-Mycenaean Iron Age, named for the style of its pottery: beginnings are in the early eleventh century BC with the arrival of Dorian peoples – by the eighth, with the development of representational styles, it becomes known as the Archaic period.

HELLENISTIC PERIOD The last and most unified Greek empire, created by Philip II and Alexander the Great in the fourth century BC, finally collapsing with the fall of Corinth to the Romans in 146 BC.

HÓRA Main town of a region; literally it means "the place".

IKONOSTÁSIS Screen between the nave of a church and the altar, often covered in icons.

IPNÁKOS Greek version of the siesta, which is widely practised in Crete, especially during the hot summer months. It usually lasts from around 1.30pm to 5.30pm. Many larger stores and businesses close during these hours.

JANISSARY Member of the Turkish Imperial Guard: in Crete under the Turks a much-feared mercenary force, often forcibly recruited from the local population.

KAFENÍON Coffeehouse/café: in a small village the centre of communal life and probably the bus stop, too.

KAÏKI A caïque, or medium-sized boat, traditionally wooden. Now used for just about any coast-hopping or excursion boat.

KÁMBOS Fertile agricultural plateau, usually near the mouth of a river.

KAPETÁNIOS Widely used term of honour for a man of local power – originally for guerrilla leaders who earned the title through acts of particular bravado.

KÁSTRO Medieval castle or any fortified hill.

KÁTO Lower, as in lower town or village; eg Káto Zákros.

KERNOS Ancient cult vessel or altar with a number of receptacles for offerings.

KRATER Large, two-handled wine bowl.

LÁRNAKES Minoan clay coffins.

LUSTRAL BASIN A small sunken chamber in Minoan palaces reached by steps: perhaps actually some kind of bath but more likely for purely ritual purification.

MEGARON Principal hall of a Mycenaean palace.

MELTÉMI North wind that blows across the Aegean in summer and can be vicious in Crete. Its force is gauged by what it knocks over – "tableweather", "chairweather" etc.

MINOAN Crete's great Bronze Age civilization which dominated the Aegean from about 2500 to 1400 BC.

MONÍ Monastery or convent.

MYCENAEAN Mainland civilization centred on Mycenae ca.1700–1100 BC: some claim they were responsible for the destruction of the Minoans, and certainly Mycenaean influence pervaded Crete in the late and post-Minoan periods.

NEOLITHIC The earliest era of settlement in Crete, characterized by the use of stone tools and weapons together with basic agriculture.

NÉOS, NÉA, NÉO New.

NOMÓS Modern Greek province: Crete is divided into four.

ODEION Small amphitheatre used for performances or meetings.

PALEÓS, PALEÁ, PALEÓ Old.

PALLIKÁRI Literally "brave man": in Crete a guerrilla fighter, particularly in the struggle for independence from the Turks, also a general term for a tough young man.

PANAYÍA The Virgin Mary.

PANIYÍRI Festival or feast, the local celebration of a holy day.

PANTOKRÁTOR Literally "The Almighty", a stern figure of Christ or God the Father frescoed or in mosaic on the dome of many Byzantine churches.

PARALÍA Seafront promenade.

PEAK SANCTUARY Mountain-top shrine, often in or associated with a cave, sometimes in continuous use from Neolithic through to Roman times.

PERÍPTERO Street kiosk.

PERISTYLE Colonnade or area surrounded by colonnade, used especially of Minoan halls or courtyards.

PÍTHOS (pl. PÍTHOI) Large ceramic jar for storing oil, grain etc, very common in the Minoan palaces and used in almost identical form in modern Cretan homes.

PLATÍA Square or plaza. "Kentrikí Platía" means the main square.

PROPILEA Portico or entrance to an ancient building.

RHYTON Vessel, often horn-shaped, for pouring libations or offerings.

STELE Upright stone slab or column, usually inscribed.

STOA Colonnaded walkway in Classical-era marketplace.

THEATRAL AREA Open area found in most of the Minoan palaces with seat-like steps around. May have been a type of theatre or ritual area, but not conclusively proved.

THÓLOS Conical or beehive-shaped building, especially a Mycenaean tomb.

ACRONYMS

ANEK *Anonimí Navtikí Evería Krítis* (Shipping Company of Crete Ltd), which runs most ferries between Pireás and Crete, plus many to Italy.

ELTA The postal service.

EOS Greek Mountaineering Federation, based in Athens with branches in Haniá and Iráklion.

EOT *Ellinikós Organismós Tourismoú*, the National Tourist Organization.

KKE The Communist Party, unreconstructed.

KTEL National syndicate of bus companies. The term is also used to refer to bus stations.

ND *Néa Dhimokratía*, the Conservative and – following an election victory in 2004 – currently the government party led by Costas Karamanlis.

OSE Railway corporation.

OTE Telephone company.

PASOK Socialist party (Pan-Hellenic Socialist Movement) currently led by Yiorgos Papandreou and the governing party for all but five of the last thirty years. Lost the general election of 2004.

...music & reference

Also! More than 120 Rough Guide music CDs are available from all good book
and record stores. Listen in at www.worldmusic.net

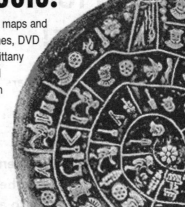
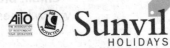

small print

and

Index

A Rough Guide to Rough Guides

In the summer of 1981, Mark Ellingham, a recent graduate from Bristol University, was travelling round Greece and couldn't find a guidebook that really met his needs. On the one hand there were the student guides, insistent on saving every last cent, and on the other the heavyweight cultural tomes whose authors seemed to have spent more time in a research library than lounging away the afternoon at a taverna or on the beach.

In a bid to avoid getting a job, Mark and a small group of writers set about creating their own guidebook. It was a guide to Greece that aimed to combine a journalistic approach to description with a thoroughly practical approach to travellers' needs – a guide that would incorporate culture, history and contemporary insights with a critical edge, together with up-to-date, value-for-money listings. Back in London, Mark and the team finished their Rough Guide, as they called it, and talked Routledge into publishing the book.

SMALL PRINT

That first *Rough Guide to Greece*, published in 1982, was a student scheme that became a publishing phenomenon. The immediate success of the book – with numerous reprints and a Thomas Cook prize shortlisting – spawned a series that rapidly covered dozens of destinations. Rough Guides had a ready market among low-budget backpackers, but soon also acquired a much broader and older readership that relished Rough Guides' wit and inquisitiveness as much as their enthusiastic, critical approach. Everyone wants value for money, but not at any price.

Rough Guides soon began supplementing the "rougher" information about hostels and low-budget listings with the kind of detail on restaurants and quality hotels that independent-minded visitors on any budget might expect, whether on business in New York or trekking in Thailand.

These days the guides – distributed worldwide by the Penguin group – offer recommendations from shoestring to luxury and cover more than 200 destinations around the globe, including almost every country in the Americas and Europe, more than half of Africa and most of Asia and Australasia. Our ever-growing team of authors and photographers is spread all over the world, particularly in Europe, the USA and Australia.

In 1994, we published the *Rough Guide to World Music* and *Rough Guide to Classical Music*; and a year later the *Rough Guide to the Internet*. All three books have become benchmark titles in their fields – which encouraged us to expand into other areas of publishing, mainly around popular culture. Rough Guides now publish:

- Travel guides to more than 200 worldwide destinations
- Dictionary phrasebooks to 22 major languages
- History guides ranging from Ireland to Islam
- Maps printed on rip-proof and waterproof Polyart™ paper
- Music guides running the gamut from Opera to Elvis
- Restaurant guides to London, New York and San Francisco
- Reference books on topics as diverse as the Weather and Shakespeare
- Sports guides from Formula 1 to Man Utd
- Pop culture books from *Lord of the Rings* to Cult TV
- World Music CDs in association with World Music Network

Visit www.roughguides.com to see our latest publications.

Rough Guide Credits

Editors: Fran Sandham, Keith Drew
Layout: Ajay Verma
Cartography: Ashutosh Bharti, Manish Chandra, Rajesh Mishra and Animesh Pathak
Picture research: Veneta Bullen
Proofreader: Diane Margolis
Editorial: London Martin Dunford, Kate Berens, Helena Smith, Claire Saunders, Geoff Howard, Ruth Blackmore, Gavin Thomas, Polly Thomas, Richard Lim, Lucy Ratcliffe, Clifton Wilkinson, Alison Murchie, Sally Schafer, Alexander Mark Rogers, Karoline Densley, Andy Turner, Ella O'Donnell, Andrew Lockett, Joe Staines, Duncan Clark, Peter Buckley, Matthew Milton; **New York** Andrew Rosenberg, Richard Koss, Yuki Takagaki, Hunter Slaton, Chris Barsanti, Steven Horak
Design & Pictures: London Simon Bracken, Dan May, Diana Jarvis, Mark Thomas, Jj Luck, Harriet Mills; **Delhi** Madhulita Mohapatra, Umesh Aggarwal, Ajay Verma, Jessica Subramanian

Production: Julia Bovis, John McKay, Sophie Hewat
Cartography: London Maxine Repath, Ed Wright, Katie Lloyd-Jones, Miles Irving; **Delhi** Manish Chandra, Rajesh Chhibber, Jai Prakash Mishra, Ashutosh Bharti, Rajesh Mishra, Animesh Pathak, Jasbir Sandhu, Karobi Gogoi
Cover art direction: Louise Boulton
Online: New York Jennifer Gold, Cree Lawson, Suzanne Welles, Benjamin Ross; **Delhi** Manik Chauhan, Narender Kumar, Shekhar Jha, Rakesh Kumar
Marketing & Publicity: London Richard Trillo, Niki Smith, David Wearn, Chloë Roberts, Demelza Dallow, Kristina Pentland; **New York** Geoff Colquitt, Megan Kennedy
Finance: Gary Singh
Manager India: Punita Singh
Series editor: Mark Ellingham
PA to Managing Director: Julie Sanderson
Managing Director: Kevin Fitzgerald

Publishing Information

This sixth edition published August 2004 by
Rough Guides Ltd,
80 Strand, London WC2R 0RL.
345 Hudson St, 4th Floor,
New York, NY 10014, USA.
Distributed by the Penguin Group
Penguin Books Ltd,
80 Strand, London WC2R 0RL
Penguin Putnam, Inc.
375 Hudson Street, NY 10014, USA
Penguin Books Australia Ltd,
487 Maroondah Highway, PO Box 257,
Ringwood, Victoria 3134, Australia
Penguin Books Canada Ltd,
10 Alcorn Avenue, Toronto, Ontario,
Canada M4V 1E4
Penguin Books (NZ) Ltd,
182–190 Wairau Road, Auckland 10,
New Zealand
Typeset in Bembo and Helvetica to an original design by Henry Iles.

Printed in Italy by LegoPrint S.p.A

496pp includes index
A catalogue record for this book is available from the British Library

ISBN 1843532921

The publishers and authors have done their best to ensure the accuracy and currency of all the information in **The Rough Guide to Crete**, however, they can accept no responsibility for any loss, injury, or inconvenience sustained by any traveller as a result of information or advice contained in the guide.

1 3 5 7 9 8 6 4 2

Help us update

We've gone to a lot of effort to ensure that the fifth edition of **The Rough Guide to Crete** is accurate and up-to-date. However, things change – places get "discovered", opening hours are notoriously fickle, restaurants and rooms raise prices or lower standards. If you feel we've got it wrong or left something out, we'd like to know, and if you can remember the address, the price, the time, the phone number, so much the better.

We'll credit all contributions, and send a copy of the next edition (or any other Rough Guide if you prefer) for the best letters. Everyone who writes to us and isn't already a subscriber will receive a copy of our full-colour thrice-yearly newsletter. Please mark letters: "**Rough Guide to Crete Update**" and send to: Rough Guides, 80 Strand, London WC2R 0RL, or Rough Guides, 4th Floor, 345 Hudson St, New York, NY 10014. Or send an email to **mail@roughguides.com**

Have your questions answered and tell others about your trip at **www.roughguides.atinfopop.com**

Acknowledgements

We are especially grateful for help on this sixth edition to Nikos Karellis, editor of *Stigmes* magazine, for sharing his encyclopedic knowledge of all things Cretan; Professor Costis Davaras, J. Alexander (Sandy) MacGillivray and Joseph and María Shaw for archeological advice and information, and to Stephen Roberts at the Natural History Museum of Crete. Also to Jackie Richardson in Sitía, Yiannis and Katerina Hatzidakis in Kserókambos, Carline Harber and Eftichios Botonakis in Paleohóra, Heracles Papadakis in Spíli, Kostas Kamaratakis in Iráklion, Manolis and Jakobus Sergentakis in Kastelli Kissámou, Vangelis Androulakakis in Loutró, Alexandros Stivanakis, Irene Michaelakis and Stavros Badoyiannis in Haniá, Froso Bora in Réthimnon, Yiorgos Tsigonakis on Gávdhos, and the indomitable Haris Kakoulakis and the staff of the Iráklion tourist office. Yet another very special *"efharistó pára polí"* must also go to Stelios Manousakas and Johanne Gaudreau in Argiroúpolis. Valuable help on the ground was also given by Yiorgos Margaritakis, Kostas Tsagkarakis, Yeorgos Yeorgamlis, Yiorgos Sergentakis, Manolis Nikoloudakis, Irene Koundouraki, Chrisostomos Orfanoudakis, Apostolis Kimalis, Lambros Papoutsakis, Chryssy Karelli, Yiorgos Saridakis, Maria Kalaïtzaki and Yiorgos Aretakis. We were also greatly assisted by Nick Pizzey at the National Bank of Greece and Calli Travlos and the staff of the Greek Tourist Office in London.

John would like to say thanks as ever to A and the two Js, for putting up with it all (especially in the holidays). Geoff's special thanks go yet again to Han for all her tireless help and support.

We'd also like to thank all at Rough Guides for another fine editorial and production job: bouquets go particularly to proofreader Diane Margolis, typesetter Umesh Aggarwal and picture researcher Veneta Bullen. A special plaudit is also due to our unflappable editor Fran Sandham, who kept the ship on course.

Readers' letters

We'd like to thank the readers of previous editions who took the time to send us their comments and suggestions. For this edition we were greatly helped by letters, faxes and emails from:

Joe Abrams, Steve Albert, David Authers, Anne Barnett, Andy Berryman, Yiannis Bikakis, John Bowman, Judy Bremson, Paul A. Bristow, Tim Brooks and Claire Etty, Monica and Michael Brothers, Jim Burke, Iain Cameron, Rob Cameron, Chris and Andrea Chadburn, Matthew Chapman, Mike Clarkson, Heather Cramp and Andrew Paterson, Michael Curran, Jan Davidson, Angie Dean, Gwyneth de Lacey, Lara de Moor, Liesbeth Deturck, Frank and Marina Donald, Dr Martin H. Evans, Jack Edwards, Peter R. Edwards, T. Egan, Dick and June Elliot, Roswitha Esslinger, Jeanette Evans, Michael and Carol Fairbairn, Tom and Julia Fiese, Tony Fennymore, Stan Fletcher, Russ Grant, James Grigg, J. and P. Gruncell, Denise Hall, Patrick Hannett, Clare Hargreaves, Liz Harris, Patricia Harrison, Karen Henchley, Caroline Henry, Marjorie and Steve Hickingbottom, Denis Hill, Mark Holmström, Paul Hughes, Robert Hutt, Peter J. Isherwood, Carole Jones, David Jones, Mary Jones, Pamela Jones, Judith Keeves, Alice Kildsgaard and Lau Mølgård, Trusha Kofflard, Robin Law, Kiriakos Loulos, Dimitrios Lolos, Julian Lord, Bo Lundin, K. McGovern, C. McNicol, Anne Magee, Malcolm Mallison, Charles Manton, Barry M. Marsden, Mark and Barbara Mascall, Harry Mawdsley, Govert-Jan Mennen, Ton Mensenkamp, Prisca Middlemass, John Middleton, Geoff and Marianne Millin, Huw Morgan, Steve Morgan, Denis and Marie Murphy, Teresa Needham, Tony Nichols and Yves Jatteau, Liz Nunan, Bernie O'Reilly, Laura Papadakis, Dan Parker, David Pearson, Sergio Pereiro, Edward Peters, Laura Phillips, Michael and Janet Pickavance, Ruth and John Pigneguy, Martin Podd, Lyn Protopsaltis, John Rayworth, Julie Reason, John Rayworth, David Redhead, Bill Reed and Sharon Nolan, David Reeves, John Rix, Jan Rhodes, Barry Rodgers and Jenny Kemp, Yair Rubin, Lucia Sanou, Jon Satow, Carol Scanlon, Barbara Schofield, Vanessa Seal, Irene Sharp, Gerry Simpson, Mary Smith, Sue Spencer, John Stephens, Carole Strachan, P.M. Straughan, Debra and Rohan Taylor, Brian Telford, Martin Thomas, Martin Thomas, Rita Thompson, Ruthie Thompson, Jan Tinsley, Andrew Todd, Richard Tofts, Eleni Tsioptsia, Sheila Turner, Joanne Turpin, Tom Vach, Toos van den Berg, Catherine and David Walker, Judith Whitworth, Margaret Wilkinson, Diana Wood and Claire Young. Special thanks to Lance Chilton and Ronald Turnbull for hiking information and advice.

Photo Credits

SMALL PRINT

Index

Map entries are in colour.

INDEX

Map symbols

maps are listed in the full index using coloured text

-------	International boundary	🅱	Fuel station
------	Chapter division boundary	🏛	Monument
=====	Major road	🌳	Gardens
=====	Minor road	⌂	Cave
....	Tracks	⌂	Refuge
———	Unpaved road	✈	Airport
:::::::::	Road under construction	🅿	Parking
------	Footpath	★	Bus/taxi stop
▥▥▥▥▥	Steps	⌁	Lighthouse
▬▬▬	Railway	ⓘ	Information office
— – —	Ferry route	⊠	Post office
=====	Waterway	♦	Point of interest
⁄⁄⁄	Hill	)(	Bridge
▲	Mountains peak	@	Internet access
⋏	Mountains range	♜	Castle
⸎	Gorge	∴	Archeological site
~~	Cliff	⬭	Stadium
▥	Mosque	▦	Building
✡	Synagogue	➕	Church
♦	Church	▨	Park
♠	Monastery or convent	▨	Forest
▪▪▪	Wall	▨	Beach

496